Alex Austin · Martina Fischer · Norbert Ropers (Eds.)

Transforming Ethnopolitical Conflict

Alex Austin · Martina Fischer
Norbert Ropers (Eds.)

Transforming Ethnopolitical Conflict

The Berghof Handbook

VS VERLAG FÜR SOZIALWISSENSCHAFTEN

VS Verlag für Sozialwissenschaften
Entstanden mit Beginn des Jahres 2004 aus den beiden Häusern
Leske+Budrich und Westdeutscher Verlag.
Die breite Basis für sozialwissenschaftliches Publizieren

Bibliografische Information Der Deutschen Bibliothek
Die Deutsche Bibliothek verzeichnet diese Publikation in der Deutschen Nationalbibliografie; detaillierte bibliografische Daten sind im Internet über <http://dnb.ddb.de> abrufbar.

1. Auflage Juni 2004

Der VS Verlag für Sozialwissenschaften ist ein Unternehmen von Springer Science+Business Media.
www.vs-verlag.de

Umschlaggestaltung: KünkelLopka Medienentwicklung, Heidelberg
Satz: COXORANGE Grafikdesign, Berlin
Druck und buchbinderische Verarbeitung: MercedesDruck, Berlin
Gedruckt auf säurefreiem und chlorfrei gebleichtem Papier
Printed in Germany

ISBN 3-8100-3940-3

Berghof
Research Center
Forschungszentrum
for Constructive
für konstruktive
Conflict Management
Konfliktbearbeitung

Content

Preface 9

Introduction 11
Martina Fischer, Norbert Ropers 11

Concepts and Cross-Cutting Challenges 23
Dieter Senghaas 25
The Civilisation of Conflict: Constructive Pacifism as a Guiding Notion for Conflict Transformation
Cordula Reimann 41
Assessing the State-of-the-Art in Conflict Transformation
Hugh Miall 67
Conflict Transformation: A Multi-Dimensional Task
Diana Francis 91
Culture, Power Asymmetries and Gender in Conflict Transformation

Analysing Conflict and Assessing Conflict Transformation 109
Dan Smith 111
Trends and Causes of Armed Conflict
Alex Austin 129
Early Warning and The Field: A Cargo Cult Science?
Thania Paffenholz 151
Designing Transformation and Intervention Processes
Mark Hoffman 171
Peace and Conflict Impact Assessment Methodology
Mary B. Anderson 193
Experiences with Impact Assessment: Can we know what Good we do?

Enhancing the Capacity for Conflict Transformation 207

Ron Kraybill 209
Facilitation Skills for Interpersonal Transformation

Friedrich Glasl, Rudi Ballreich 227
Team and Organisational Development as a Means for Conflict Prevention and Resolution

Norbert Ropers 255
From Resolution to Transformation: The Role of Dialogue Projects

Structural Reforms, Institutionbuilding and Violence Control 271

Günther Baechler 273
Conflict Transformation through State Reform

Wibke Hansen, Oliver Ramsbotham, Tom Woodhouse 295
Hawks and Doves: Peace Keeping and Conflict Resolution

Dusan Reljic 321
The News Media and the Transformation of Ethnopolitical Conflicts

Christine Bigdon, Benedikt Korf 341
The Role of Development Aid in Conflict Transformation: Facilitating Empowerment Processes and Community Building

Recovering from War: Reconstruction versus Just Peace 371

Martina Fischer 373
Recovering from Violent Conflict: Regeneration and (Re-)Integration as Elements of Peacebuilding

David Becker 403
Dealing with the Consequences of Organised Violence in Trauma Work

Gunnar Theissen 421
Supporting Justice, Co-existence and Reconciliation after Armed Conflict: Strategies for Dealing with the Past

Kevin Clements 441
Towards Conflict Transformation and a Just Peace

Glossary 463

About the Contributors 467

Preface and Introduction

Preface 9

Introduction 11
Martina Fischer, Norbert Ropers

Preface

Confronted with a wide variety of conflicts, the international community has attempted to respond through humanitarian assistance, development aid, crisis prevention and conflict resolution programmes. To date many of these activities have exacerbated conflict dynamics as much as they have enhanced the opportunities for sustainable development and peace. In an effort to understand what works, lessons learned and best practices are being collected usually in the form of evaluations of individual projects or programs. Although the number of studies undertaken has increased, few lessons have been systematised or accumulated for broader discussion in the academic field or for practitioners' use.

The Berghof Research Center for Constructive Conflict Management produced this Handbook in response to the contemporary challenges which have to be faced by those who are working in and on violent conflict. The intention is to give an overview of recent developments in the field of conflict transformation from various perspectives: from academic analysts and practitioners as well as from experts representing different areas of work inside and outside of conflict zones.

The Handbook has been presented in several steps. First, it has been launched in successive series of articles on the interactive website (www.berghof-handbook.net). This site is organised as a platform to gather feedback from users and to stimulate debate on the content and focus of the articles. This feedback, as well as additional articles and input, allow the creation of an evolving manual and reference that reflects developments in the conflict transformation field. Second, we decided to publish this hard copy version, as we observed that many scholars and practitioners still asked for the complete compilation of all contributions.

We are grateful to the very positive reaction to our initiative among the colleagues, from all over the world, whom we have asked to contribute to the Handbook. They are experienced practitioners and scholars, some of them pioneers in the field and/or working on key tasks of conflict transformation. They accepted the demanding job of adapting their style of presentation to the common standards of this Handbook. Without their knowledge, motivation and flexibility the Handbook project would not have been possible. We would like to thank all the authors who contributed to both the internet and hardcopy version of the Berghof Handbook. We hope that we can establish a continuing discourse with them as well as with our readers about cutting-edge practice and theory in our field.

This publication represents a compilation of articles that have been launched up to mid-2003 on the website. The hardcopy version is not meant as a final point, but has to be seen as an 'interim report' of findings, as the Berghof team endeavours to develop the Berghof Handbook project further. Future developments will include

1. *actualization of themes and issues* which have been focused on in the past;
2. *debates and dialogues* on issues which are considered as areas of special interest and importance;
3. *providing services and feedback fora* as part of the process of restructuring the website.

This means that friends and colleagues who are interested in results of peace practice and analysis in the field of ethnopolitical conflict are invited to visit our homepage from time to time in order to discover innovative articles which can be found and downloaded by searching 'what's new'.

In the future, debates and discussions will be developed as 'work in progress' similar to the debate on 'Peace and Conflict Impact Assessment' which was initiated in the first version of the Handbook. This debate has already been published in a print version by the Berghof Center (*see* Alex Austin, Martina Fischer, Oliver Wils (eds.): Peace and Conflict Impact Assessment. Critical Views on Theory and Practice, Berghof Handbook Dialogue Series, Berghof Research Center for Constructive Conflict Management, Berlin 2003). Therefore only the initial contribution by Mark Hoffman is included in this volume.

Many thanks have to be directed to those institutions and organisations who gave financial support to the Berghof Handbook, especially the Berghof Foundation for Conflict Research (*Berghof Stiftung für Konfliktforschung*) and the German Federal Ministry of Education and Research (*Bundesministerium für Bildung und Forschung*).

Finally we want to thank all those persons who joined the Berghof Handbook team since the beginning of the project, colleagues who helped at different stages and thus contributed to the first edition, especially our co-editor, Alexander Austin, Claus-Dieter Wild, Reiner Steinweg, Oliver Wils, Clem McCartney, Hillary Crowe, Constanze Helmchen, Eric Manton, Astrid Fischer and Ulrike Hesse.

Martina Fischer & Norbert Ropers
Berlin / Colombo, July 20, 2003

Introduction

Martina Fischer, Norbert Ropers

The scale and number of violent conflicts after the end of the Cold War have created disillusionment in the world about the possibility of moving towards a new phase of peaceful settlement of disputes at the beginning of the 21st century. It seems that even inter-state conflicts are back on the agenda in the context of the struggle for a new world order between US-led unilateralism and efforts to safeguard the achievements of multilateralism from the last decades.

Most of the current violent conflicts though are, and most likely will be, intra-state conflicts, either connected with civil wars or with the formation of states. It means that either different groups struggle over the control of the government or that governments are set against one or other group, mainly ethnopolitically defined. The issues at stake are to maintain or gain political power, civil rights, cultural identity, economic advantage or natural resources. Some wars spring from the decay and implosion of states, others are targeted at establishing new states. Many of them affect entire societies or regional economies and last over long periods.

While the inter-state conflicts are primarily dealt with and debated within the existing institutions of the international system, it was the focus on intra-state conflicts that led to new practices and institutional orientations, to new discourses and even to a new terminology in the field of responding to conflicts. It is exactly in this latter field where the *Berghof Handbook* for Conflict Transformation is located.

It is still an open question in how far this area of work, and discourse of practical and conceptual reflections, will establish itself as an area with a distinct professional identity. But there is no question that many institutions and organisations in the field of development policy and action, humanitarian assistance, human rights, diplomacy and peace work are now heavily involved in activities responding to intra-state conflicts. They have invested time, energy, human and financial resources and many of them have already institutionalised or are prepared to institutionalise their activities in this field.

Several scholars and practitioners have argued that responding to intra-state conflicts should be based on the common understanding of all like-minded actors involved that they must take the root causes of these conflicts into account. Secondly they argue that there needs to be a comprehensive framework for all activities, which is integrated with working on the legacies of the conflict in the realms of rehabilitation, reconstruction, reconciliation, development and state formation. Thirdly there is a widespread understanding that this kind of multidimensional approach, targeted at the root causes of the conflict as well at addressing the implications of many years of violence and hostility, has to be placed on various levels of interaction: the international, national, regional and local. And it has to go beyond the track 1 activities of state actors and mobilise many non-state actors for a broad spectrum of 'multi-track' endeavours.

Implementing such a comprehensive approach is obviously not easy. Furthermore, each and every conflict is different. What might have worked in one situation, is not suitable in another. We are convinced that exchanging and sharing knowledge is essential for moving towards a better understanding of how to respond to intra-state conflicts. With many colleagues, we share the belief that the time is ripe for summarising the practical, empirical and theoretical knowledge in conflict transformation. Various textbooks, field manuals, and specialised handbooks on conflict resolution, third party intervention and peacebuilding have been published during the past years.

The Berghof Handbook gives an overview of core issues in the field of conflict transformation and on recent developments from the perspectives of academia and of practice. We believe that the combination of the two can make a particular contribution to well informed, enlightened and effective practice. The Berghof Handbook is not a textbook summarising the consolidated knowledge in a well-established discipline. It is an effort to take stock and to draw attention to established practices and concepts as well as to the thorny issues and challenges. The Berghof Handbook is not a collection of recipes nor does it offer a readymade set of tools. It is meant to put the practical routines into a broader conceptual framework in order to understand their functions, strengths and weaknesses more thoroughly.

The aim of the Handbook is to give practitioners and scholars an overview of the currently available approaches, methods, techniques and theories of conflict transformation. This means to document and assess the 'state of the art' in the field as well as to offer opportunities to reflect on the strengths and weaknesses of these approaches. Moreover dilemmas which have to be faced by individuals and organisations working in and on conflict need to be addressed. Furthermore, we would like to encourage the development of more coherent and theoretically sound concepts to integrate the complexities of the field and to facilitate effective and efficient strategies of transformation.

The Handbook therefore

- describes systematically the field of conflict transformation by summarising concepts, methods, strategies and tools;
- explores the critical debates about theory, both to provide an overview and to overcome the current theory gap in the field;
- examines ways of balancing structure-oriented approaches with process-oriented initiatives of peacemaking and peacebuilding;
- analyses the roles of the various actors in peacebuilding, including international governmental organisations (IGOs), national governments, development agencies, non-governmental organisations (NGOs), and other players in civil society;
- discusses strategies of co-ordination and networking between these actors;
- reflects upon lessons learned, best practices, and the difficulties of assessing the impact of conflict transformation efforts.

The compilation of such diverse current knowledge is not an easy and straightforward task. Among the predominant challenges in the field are the weak relationships between practice, research and theory. In many areas of conflict transformation we perceive a growing interest in conceptualising and assessing systematically the available knowledge and in identifying lessons, best practices and innovative thinking. However, there are only a few endeavours to develop precise theoretical frameworks and models for contextualising specific practical micro-interventions with respect to their impact on the macro social and political levels. Apart from this general theory gap, specific strategies remain elusive in many individual areas of conflict transformation beyond the simple recommendation 'the more the better'. It is therefore our interest to contribute particularly to strengthening the link between practice, systematic reflection, research and theory.

Several terms are used to describe the field as well as activities within this field, such as conflict management, conflict resolution, conflict transformation, conflict prevention, peace building etc. We regard the term *conflict transformation* as the most comprehensive to cover all activities which influence inter-group conflicts with the aim of promoting sustainable peace and social justice. This understanding comprises structure- and process-oriented endeavours of crisis prevention, strategies for empowering groups and building communities, conflict management and resolution activities, as well as rehabilitation, reconstruction and reconciliation efforts in post-war situations.

During the last decade, the concept of conflict prevention became very fashionable in the discourses of peace research and international relations as well as within international organisations. Approaches and instruments for preventing violent conflicts have been discussed in many books and articles. Based on an ideal type notion of the dynamics of violent conflict a dynamic concept of prevention emerged according to three stages, which demand different efforts and approaches:

1. *Early prevention* in order to prevent evolving situations of violent conflict;
2. *"Last-Minute"* prevention in order to impede horizontal or vertical escalation of already existing violent conflict;
3. *Post-conflict activities* to prevent the outbreak of further violence after cease-fires and peace agreements.

The concept of conflict transformation did not gain the same attention. Nevertheless we are convinced that effective efforts for conflict prevention must include conflict transformation as a precondition: that means that individuals or groups who are involved in conflict should be enabled to deal constructively with the causes of conflict and to develop strategies in order to eliminate or overcome these causes. In our understanding, conflict transformation is a generic, comprehensive concept referring to actions that seek to alter the various characteristics and manifestations of conflict by addressing the root causes of a particular conflict over the long-term with the aim to transform negative ways of dealing with conflict into positive constructive ways. The concept of conflict transformation stresses structural, behavioural and attitudinal aspects of conflict. It refers to both the process and the structure of moving towards 'just peace'.

The concept of conflict transformation was elaborated particularly in response to one prototype of intra-state conflicts: the 'protracted social conflict'. This term was first coined by Edward Azar in the late 1970s. It is now widely used to describe long enduring ethnopolitical conflicts that share common features. According to him they have four key characteristics:

- they are conflicts between identity groups, of which at least one feels that their basic needs for equality, security and political participation are not respected;
- they are essentially about access to state related power, often in the form of an asymmetric conflict between a government and an insurgent party;
- they cannot be understood without various types of international linkages affecting the course of events (kinstates, diasporas, international interference);
- they are often based on deeply rooted antagonistic group histories.

Stressing the need for transformation with respect to protracted social conflicts means that all four constituent aspects of this understanding have to be addressed: The legitimacy of ethnic demands in multi-ethnic political systems has to be acknowledged. Comprehensive concepts of power sharing and state reform are necessary. The roles of international actors and the international community have to be assessed properly and some kind of integration of the violent and painful past will be necessary. The need for transformation is furthermore based on the experience that long enduring bloody conflicts not only take lives, destroy livelihoods and deteriorate infrastructures, but they also undermine the overall social capital of the society. Therefore, transformation comprises relief, rehabilitation, resettlement and reconstruction, as well as regaining humanity and working on reconciliation.

Because of this comprehensive understanding we choose conflict transformation as the leading concept for the *Berghof Handbook*.

The topic structure is organised according to the various dimensions of conflict transformation. The *first section* is devoted to the concept of conflict transformation in the context of other basic concepts such as conflict management and conflict resolution. Moreover this section focuses on cross cutting challenges and gives an overview of the core dimensions for intervention in conflict.

Dieter Senghaas opens this section by discussing theoretical questions concerning the civilisation of conflict. He regards 'causal' or 'constructive' pacifism as a guiding notion for conflict transformation. If civil or international war is a result of anarchy, this can only be eroded by a social order that can contribute to enduring peace. This has to be built at national, regional and international levels. The author develops a model of a complex peace architecture ('civilisational hexagon'). The six components (1. monopoly of force by the state; 2. rule of law; 3. democratic participation; 4. constructive conflict management; 5. social justice and equity; 6. interdependencies and affect control) are the very basis for civilising conflicts in a potentially violence-prone political, socio-economic and socio-cultural environment. The author argues that causal pacifism established the right framework for 'thinking about peace' and 'making peace' and should be a source of inspiration for current endeavours. A guiding principle could be the notion that the measure of peace is peace itself. This is a legacy of an idea which originated in the early years of the twentieth century and which should now be revived.

Cordula Reimann offers a general overview and a tentative interpretation of the state of the art in the field of conflict management. This includes a review of the field's research agenda and research questions on the one hand and an analysis of the role of theory and research methods on the other. The author introduces three distinct approaches: conflict settlement, conflict resolution and conflict transformation. One of the most important conclusions is that the concepts of conflict resolution and conflict settlement do not address the complexity of most protracted, intractable inter-state conflicts. Therefore it is necessary to synthesise and integrate different theoretical frameworks with actors and strategies. The author's discussion of the role of theory and research methods in the overall field makes clear why, and to what extent, theoretical complementarity must be given in ontological (the study of what is being analysed) and epistemological (the study of how it is being analysed) terms.

Hugh Miall identifies the key theorists and modes of practice of conflict transformation, and attempts to distinguish these from the theories and practices of conflict resolution and conflict management, while at the same time arguing that conflict transformation draws heavily on these earlier traditions. The author comes to the conclusion that further developments in theory and practice are underway as the nature of contemporary conflict continues to change. Local armed conflicts may have increasingly global causes and consequences and there is globalisation both of conflict and of interventions in conflict. The author argues that the subject of analysis has to shift from conflict to conflict-in-context, from the society in conflict to the global and regional environment. This creates cultural challenges for those theories and practices that are still dominated by western perspectives, but also ethical questions for practitioners who seek to uphold non-violent methods in contexts where coercion and the use of force are widely accepted.

Diana Francis highlights that conflict transformation approaches necessarily have to deal with power asymmetries, gender inequalities and cultural differences. These categories are closely linked and have to be taken carefully into account, especially by external actors who intervene in conflict. The author argues that the overarching, global culture of domination provides the framework for oppression and exploitation, including that of women by men and of Southern Hemisphere countries by the West. The asymmetry of power resulting from colonialism has injected into cultural difference an explosive charge, which makes its handling extremely difficult. Gender is a cultural construct, and the oppression of women is frequently justified by reference to culture and the positioning of women's emancipation as a Western project. Nevertheless oppressive gender relations and constructions have to be addressed and specific gender roles and images that contribute to conflict have to be analysed. The author argues that the emancipation of women, and marginalised groups in general, both stimulates and results from the fundamental culture shift which conflict transformation implies. Those who intervene in conflict with this purpose have to be transparent in relation to their values and goals, implementing them within their own organisations.

The *second section* reviews the tools for analysing and predicting conflicts and highlights the current debate on how to assess the impact of interventions in conflict.

Dan Smith gives an overview of the current findings on the causes of armed conflict at the end of the 20th and the beginning of the 21st century. Emphasis is placed upon where to look for signs of potential escalation when analysing conflicts, as well as where to seek opportunities for preventing violent escalation. The author then discusses the state of theoretical knowledge in this area, before proceeding to outline methodology, moving away from a theoretical and towards an applied approach for the study and analysis of armed conflict. Emphasis is placed upon the interplay between background and foreground causes. Injustice and mobilisation turn out to be key concepts for interpreting the causes of armed conflicts. To illustrate this the author gives an example: the significance of perceived injustice and identity as objects for political mobilisation towards conflict during the decay of the former Yugoslavia.

Alex Austin gives an introduction to early warning activities. The author critically discusses whether early warning systems can a) identify the causes of conflict, b) predict the outbreak of conflict and c) mitigate conflict. He argues that unless the early warning system has a mechanism to mitigate the conflict, there is little utility to be gained in refining the accuracy of current models. The article outlines the state of the art in the field of early warning and identifies the different areas of focus, methodologies and mechanisms employed. It ends by summarising these mechanisms into a model for early warning and outlines the major challenges facing the transition from early warning to early response.

Thania Paffenholz outlines concepts and experiences for designing and assessing intervention strategies. The article discusses the problems which result from the question of which actor can intervene with which strategies and instruments, and at what time in any particular situation of conflict. Drawing upon her field experience, the author formulates ten issues that need to be addressed in intervention design: 1. the need for vision, goals and commitment; 2. methods of analysing conflicts and actors; 3. strategies and roles of intervening actors; 4. the ongoing search for adequate partners and entry points; 5. timing and exit options of interventions; 6. thinking in processes and building structures; 7. criteria for the recruitment of field staff; 8. co-ordination and co-operation; 9. the inclusion of the goals of sustainability and 10. building learning into the process of interventions. These aspects are examined from the perspective of NGOs' reality in conflict and finally the author raises the difficulties of creating knowledge management mechanisms within organisations and programmes.

Mark Hoffman reviews the state of the art in evaluation by focusing on peace and conflict impact assessment (PCIA) methodology from three perspectives: traditional donor evaluations, methodologies of assessment in development work and evaluations that focus on conflict resolution and peacebuilding NGOs. After outlining the practical implications of PCIA, the article concludes by identifying open questions, problems and ways forward. These revolve around the use of general or specific indicators, inter-linkage between different types of evaluation, contextualisation and finally the inter-relatedness of different sectors.

Mary B. Anderson considers how international agencies that undertake programmes to provide humanitarian assistance, development aid and/or support peace processes can determine what their impacts are. The chapter deals with collaborative efforts undertaken by external agencies to learn more about their impacts on conflict within the societies where they work. Part of the chapter is dedicated to the Local Capacities for Peace Project (LCPP), while another part discusses recent findings from the Reflecting on Peace Practice Project (RPP) which had been co-ordinated by her organisation, Collaborative for Development Action (CDA) and the Swedish Life & Peace Institute. According to the author, tracing and assessing interventions to lessen conflict has to face two major challenges: first to identify criteria or indicators for assessing progress (this relates to the question of the appropriate forms and means of measurement in relation to conflict transformation), and second, to determine attribution. When so many things are happening in a complex environment, how can one know which actions bring about which outcomes? The author ends with a clear message: it is not sufficient for aid workers and peace practitioners to 'do no harm' in their programmes and they must push impact assessment as integral to their work. Using the knowledge gained over many years of work, they can increase their effectiveness and contribute to the achievement of just societies that solve differences without resort of violence.

The *third section* of the Handbook deals with activities for enhancing the capacity for handling and intervening in conflicts on the interpersonal level and inter-group level. This section is dedicated to the psychosocial dimension of conflict transformation and to individual and collective learning processes.

Ron Kraybill describes the most important skills and tools which facilitators need in order to enhance capacities at the individual and interpersonal level for transformation of inter-group-conflicts. The author explores the question of what makes these communication skills and tools transformative. Three categories of facilitation tools are then reviewed: skills used in moment-by-moment interaction with parties; techniques for facilitating sustained dialogue and principles of process design for addressing the larger institutional and structural realities of conflicts. The author concludes that the dual focus of transformation on 'empowerment of self' and 'relationship-building with others' lie at the heart of skills and techniques in all three categories.

Friedrich Glasl and Rudi Ballreich deal with conflict transformation approaches within groups and organisations. The authors identify five levels of co-operation within teams: the individual members, the content level, the interaction level, the procedural level and the level that governs external relations of the group to its environment. The authors offer approaches for addressing conflict within teams at all these levels, especially they propose the rethinking of individual roles and methods of team decision making and correct diagnosis of the team's level of development. According to the authors, teams will be able to quickly recognise conflicts at their inception and constructively approach them, if they are enabled to understand both conflict potentials and opportunities for conflict management.

Norbert Ropers is convinced that dialogues can be viewed as the classical means of dealing constructively with conflicts, following the popular formula "As long as you are talking, you can't be shooting". In the sphere of classical diplomacy, skills in negotiation and dialogue have long formed part of the basic repertoire of any prudent management of international relations, but dialoguing skills of official track diplomacy have too often been driven into the background by the constraints of power politics. Representatives of non-official, track II diplomacy, by contrast, have instead chosen to place communication, direct encounters and mutual understanding centre-stage. There are a huge number of dialogue projects underway which are designed to influence or contribute to the settlement or resolution of armed or potentially violent conflicts that take place in ethnopolitical settings, mostly within societies. Many of these projects, as third party interventions, are driven by external actors. The author gives an overview of the ideal types of dialogues and identifies the basic elements of most dialogue processes. He discusses dialogue in the context of various approaches to handling conflict in order to establish criteria for measuring success. He concludes that the most important conceptual contribution that a dialogue project can make to the creation of peace constituencies is to promote a dialogue-based dispute culture, which becomes a basic paradigm of political culture.

In the *fourth section*, the contributors focus on the necessity of structural reforms, institution-building and violence control as preconditions for conflict transformation and peace-building. The authors give an overview of the main approaches of state and civil society actors.

Günther Bächler explores the significance of state reform for transformation of war-torn areas. He points out that, especially for fragile states, state reform is a prerequisite for peaceful conflict resolution and democratic development and he argues that there is a need to involve the population in efforts to establish at least some 'islands' of security. The author presents three strategic approaches to state reform and conflict transformation. The first one consists of participatory strategies that might enhance social and political stability (democratisation, strengthening of civil society, dialogue-oriented approaches). The second encompasses all forms of institution-building and institutional reform, contributing to a stronger societal fabric (federalisation, decentralisation, the constitution and justice system). The third addresses security needs and demands (human rights, human security and absence of military threats). As the author concludes, there is widespread agreement among scholars that democracy is a necessary condition for stable peace. The debate revolves around whether it is a sufficient condition and which factors must be combined in order to prepare the ground for a constitution that will insulate society against violence. A number of open theoretical questions remain: Is there such a thing as 'democratic peace'? If so, which factors are important to it? How can a 'culture of dispute' be established or preserved in times of radical transition or rapid change in a society?

Wibke Hanson, Oliver Ramsbotham and Tom Woodhouse highlight the importance of peacekeeping both for violence control and for enhancing capacities for peacebuilding. The authors argue that peacekeeping can serve as an important instrument as long as its practice is sufficiently reformed. New thinking about peacekeeping has evolved in response to changing environments of conflict, and places emphasise primarily on the strengthening of enforcement powers while at the same time reinforcing peacebuilding capacities. The new doctrine sets for itself the dual goal of controlling violence while simultaneously maintaining consent and rebuilding co-operative relationships. According to the authors this dual goal can only be achieved if current approaches developed in the academic field are thoroughly integrated with the practice of peacekeeping. Moreover the article points out where knowledge developed in conflict resolution theory can be of relevance for peacekeepers, as well as commenting on perspectives for application and addressing the question of the future needs for peacekeeping.

Dusan Reljic analyses the role of news media in the transformation of ethnopolitical conflicts. News media often contribute to the constitution of national identities. In ethnically divided societies, exposure to the media can reinforce feelings of exclusion and thereby strengthen negative spirals of communication between ethnic groups that eventually lead to violence. The author presents proposals advanced by peace researchers and journalists on options for reporting on ethnopolitical conflicts in a manner which fosters peace. He argues that in practice journalists have little chance to influence the outcome of conflicts in a positive way, primarily as the news media often serves as an instrument of the authorities. Nevertheless he offers a basic model designed to explain the impact of media. It is grounded in the assumption that the effects of mass media on political communication in a society are largely determined by the political and economic situation, as well as by the skills and training of journalists and the prevailing political attitudes of the public. The article ends with a brief discussion of NGO-activities in this field and a proposal for efforts on the European level for the reform of news media both in established democracies and transition countries.

Christine Bigdon and Benedikt Korf highlight the role of development assistance in relation to structural aspects of peacebuilding. The article explores both the theoretical assumptions, as well as the practical experiences with empowerment approaches, in the field of development aid, paying particular attention to their potential for conflict transformation. The authors build upon the recent discourse in development policy and they review empowerment approaches within the field of community development. As they further explore the nexus between participation, empowerment and conflict transformation, the authors critically discuss the potential of common participatory approaches at the community level and their impact for conflict transformation on the local level. One of the findings is that development agencies operate within a very narrow space of action and have to face various dilemmas and ambiguities, which might impede their success. Nevertheless empowerment processes can support conflict transformation if they contribute to developing local community and to promoting inclusive citizenship.

In the *fifth section* of the Handbook, the emphasis is on conflict transformation as a challenge for reconstruction, rehabilitation and reconciliation in post-war situations and war torn societies.

Martina Fischer's article gives an overview of the problems of reconstruction, rehabilitation and (re)integration in war torn societies. In the context of post-war situations reconstruction turns out to be an ambiguous or even contradictory concept: it is considered as useful by some actors and others refuse the notion that society can and should be reconstructed. The author argues that (re)integration of refugees and displaced persons is one of the main challenges and precondition for conflict transformation. Support and intervention from external actors are all too often reduced to material reconstruction of houses and infrastructure whereas the need for rebuilding communities is forgotten. In order to move from reconstruction to constructive conflict transformation and peacebuilding, joint efforts are needed which combine development approaches, economic perspectives and empowerment of local actors for civil society issues, peace-education and social work. In order to make third party intervention effective, co-ordination of activities is needed. Positive and negative lessons can be drawn from the Balkans.

David Becker illustrates, through practical experience in Latin America and the Balkans, problems that have to be addressed in the psychological dimension in order to deal with the consequences of violence. The chapter discusses theories of trauma and argues that trauma concepts need to be continually reinvented, always relating them specifically to the political and cultural context in which traumatisation occurs. With reference to the intrapsychic dynamics of trauma, it is argued that fragmentation is a central characteristic and can only be overcome within a close relationship that recognises and accepts the destruction that has occurred and helps construct a space in which symbolisation can take place. The author suggests that trauma work should be part of an integrated approach in crisis regions and should cover the psychological, pedagogical and economic dimensions.

Gunnar Theissen's article explores the different approaches to investigating and regulating injustices in the aftermath of armed conflict. It reviews the potentials and risks of tribunals, community courts and truth commissions. Moreover the author discusses how amnesty, reparation and grassroots initiatives for reconciliation can contribute to conflict transformation. He points out that practitioners in the field must be aware of the changing power relations and limited options for action in war-torn societies. Third party intervention should encourage local actors to develop their own approaches for dealing with the past. Thus, the current enthusiasm for the emerging international criminal law system should not divert attention from local initiatives and institutions. Dealing with past injustices turns out to be a long-term process. The degree of understanding that can be reached within a single generation is thus very limited. Reconciliation might be a legitimate vision for post-conflict rehabilitation, but cannot be forced on former enemies. Victims often have good reasons for refusing to reconcile, if past atrocities are not investigated and injustices not abated.

Kevin Clements deals in greater detail with the challenges of linking theory, research and practice, and offers strategies to implement these approaches in all relevant areas of social change. The chapter illustrates some lessons learned from interventions in Africa, the Caucasus and Asia. The author argues that the structural sources of conflict – political and economic in particular – have been relatively underdeveloped in conflict analysis and in the design of intervention processes. This has meant that many track II interventions in conflict have been oriented towards attitudinal and behavioural change rather than situational or structural change. Until this situation is reversed and more attention is paid to the transformation of institutions and processes, it will be difficult to generate stable peaceful relationships.

The contributions in the *first edition* of the *Berghof Handbook* address the initial themes that the editorial team had in mind. Still this volume represents a selection of issues and topics. Many important questions must be left for further debate and more detailed exploration. Several challenges remain.

- One of the first challenges raised in the conflict related discourse was how far *Western-based approaches* of conflict transformation can be applied to *non-Western contexts*? The debate on this question is still going on, but in a much more differentiated way than initially. It became clear that the emergence of protracted social conflicts was largely linked to the globalisation of a Western concept of statehood and that its reform had to take into account its cultural genesis. But it also transpired that many traditional forms of conflict handling can enrich and enhance substantially the chances for effective transformation. The question remains, though, how to balance the respect for cultural diversity in peacebuilding efforts with other values like social and gender equality.
- More thorough analysis and reflection is needed to explore the *significance of gender roles* in conflict transformation and to achieve *gender equity*. As Diana Francis has pointed out in her chapter, the gender dimension is closely linked to cultural diversity and power imbalances. Important questions in this context include, for example, how to move towards practical steps of 'gender mainstreaming' in deeply divided and polarised societies where men have more or less a monopoly of decision making. Also how to safeguard the potential new and active roles that women often acquire during war times, when they had to guarantee the survival of families of which they became tragically the single heads? With regard to development and human rights, it is important to focus on women's legal and social equality, their participation in the political process and their self-confident involvement in civil society. But the task of enhancing gender sensitivity in peacebuilding must go beyond this aim and cannot focus exclusively on the specific situation and role of women, either as the victims of violence (and war) or as actors. It must also focus on questions of the identity of women and men, the extent to which social constructs of masculinity and femininity contribute to violence in conflicts and also what can be done in order to change these constructs and their symbolic significance so that cultures of violence can be dismantled. A real challenge for the organisations involved in post-conflict peacebuilding is to improve the range of instruments for gender impact assessment and to elaborate criteria in relation to the strengthening of identity patterns of militarised masculinity. Identifying methods to develop projects that overcome these patterns is a key issue in this context.

- The traditional concept of 'protracted social conflicts' was challenged, when Paul Collier, David Malone and others started the 'greed and grievance' debate and emphasised the economic motivations behind political violence. They argued that in many conflicts it was not more or less legitimised political grievances of marginalised groups that led to the outbreak of violence, but rather economic strategies and calculations of fragmented elites. This debate has triggered a new focus on the *political economy of civil wars* and led to many thought-provoking questions on the linkages between economic factors and the escalation and de-escalation of internal conflicts.
- Another more recent development is the revitalised interest in the *security dimension* of intra-state conflicts. For some time the analysis of arms transfers, of military aid and cooperation as well as of military and police regimes was somewhat marginalised from issues of conflict transformation and peacebuilding. That has changed substantially. Now there is an emerging consensus that confidence and security building measures (CSBMs), security sector reforms (SSR) and similar measures can be essential ingredients of supporting processes of conflict transformation.
- One of the areas where the need for conflict resolution and transformation was expressed quite early and explicitly, is in the realm of *human rights work*, based on the experience that gross human rights violations are most likely to happen in areas of violent conflict. Nevertheless, there are some clear distinctions between human rights and conflict transformation work and the promotion of either of them might not automatically lead to the promotion of the other, at least not in the short term. This dichotomy is related in some conflict regions to two different approaches dealing with asymmetric conflict transformation: the "conditionality approach", which stresses that the less legitimised party has to 'earn' its participation as an equal actor in any negotiation process and the "transformative approach", which emphasises the need for parity of status, for recognition and constructive engagement to enhance the co-ownership for the process and its impact for social change.
- A common area of research and practice within conflict transformation as well as within international relations has been the topic of the architecture and dynamic of *peace processes*. This topic becomes more interesting the longer the processes takes from a first truce initiative to the implementation of a lasting peace agreement. Most peace processes to overcome protracted social conflicts cover many years and are characterised by many hurdles and critical stages of re-escalation. This has encouraged practitioners to contribute to 'road maps' and other modelling processes according to 'multi-step', 'multi-issue' and 'multi-track' approaches.
- Finally, conflict transformation cannot be seen as independent from the trends and disputes concerning the global order. The most important caesura is obviously the 11th of September 2001, which has led the Government of the United States of America under President George Bush Jnr. to strive for a new hegemonic world order and to question the fundamental basics of multilateralism and the peaceful settlement of disputes. What does this mean for the future of conflict transformation? Will these approaches, concepts, methods and practices be integrated into the emerging hegemonic revolution or are there possibilities that they might contribute to upholding the achievements after the end of World War II in establishing ways to civilise conflicts?

These issues – among others – will be the focus of future editions of the *Berghof Handbook*. Further editions will be developed, as before, in a double track procedure: Articles will be launched *first* on the web, and *second*, be published in the *Berghof Handbook Dialogue Series*. We hope that the interest and feedback will continue and we invite our colleagues and readers to give feedback and/or join the future discussions.

Concepts and Cross-Cutting Challenges

Dieter Senghaas 25
The Civilisation of Conflict: Constructive Pacifism as a Guiding Notion for Conflict Transformation

Cordula Reimann 41
Assessing the State-of-the-Art in Conflict Transformation

Hugh Miall 67
Conflict Transformation: A Multi-Dimensional Task

Diana Francis 91
Culture, Power Asymmetries and Gender in Conflict Transformation

The Civilisation of Conflict: Constructive Pacifism as a Guiding Notion for Conflict Transformation

Dieter Senghaas

1. Introduction 26
2. A New World Order 26
3. Social and political transformation in the 20th Century 27
4. Conditions for the peaceful regulation of conflict 28
5. The reluctant development of a culture of constructive conflict management 30
6. Alternative responses to social and political transformations 31
7. Building an international culture of constructive conflict management 34
8. Peace policy 35
9. A global system for peace 35
10. Activities to promote a global system of peace 36
11. Reference and Further Reading 37

The Civilisation of Conflict: Constructive Pacifism as a Guiding Notion for Conflict Transformation

Dieter Senghaas

1. Introduction

How, and by what means, is peace constituted? In the first two decades of the twentieth century, a leading pacifist, Alfred H. Fried, set this fundamental question at the heart of the pacifist programme. *Causal pacifism* was the key term: "If we wish to eliminate an effect, we must first remove its cause. And if we wish to set a new and desirable effect in its place, we must substitute the cause with another which is capable of creating the desired effect" (Fried 1918, 10). This sounds abstract in terms of its methodology, but was posed as something quite specific: If war is the outcome of international anarchy, which still prevails in relations between states, this anarchy itself must be abolished in order to remove its effect, which is war. Moreover, in place of anarchy, a 'social order' must be established whose effect is to allow conflicts in general to be managed in a non-violent reliable manner. In other words – in the political sense of the term – peace is created.

The doctrine of causal or cause/effect pacifism is therefore rooted in an attempt to think systematically about the prerequisites and conditions for peace. In an analytical sense, then, it was comparable with the current endeavours to develop a peace theory which is appropriate for the modern age, including a programme of constructive conflict management that is compatible with this theory (Senghaas 1995; Czempiel 1998).

Irrespective of whether or not this specific term was used by individual authors, causal pacifism was a key academic and practical issue in the classical pacifism debate. It is one of the great tragedies of the twentieth century that this concept declined in popularity among pacifist movements and finally became a non-issue. In a twentieth century marked by violence, war, genocide and mutual threats of destruction within the framework of deterrence, antimilitarism – for quite understandable reasons – came to dominate the pacifist agenda and shape its thinking and action. Yet there remained what the Slovenian peace researcher Vlasta Jalusic once described as an 'empty hole': for while antimilitarism seeks to dismantle the structures and mentalities which cause aggression, violence and war, causal pacifism, by contrast, aims to create structures and mentalities that promote lasting peace. In short, causal pacifism and comparable approaches could therefore also be described as 'constructive pacifism' – a pacifism that is geared to the construction and architecture of peace.

2. A New World Order

The classical doctrine of causal pacifism was intended – as formulated explicitly by Alfred Fried in 1918 – to establish "a new world order" (Fried 1918, 42): a new form of global governance. This intention was not rooted in an eschatological goal but in manageable approaches which were "inspired by a purposeful spirit of peace" (Fried, ibid.). This new world order was defined as the outcome of the "sociation of states", a process which was already under way and which would culminate in a *"contrat social"*, or social contract, between states. This would lead not to the abolition of conflict but to what, in current terminology, is known as conflict transformation: "the reshaping of international relations in a way which will imbue conflicts with a character which frees them from violence and makes them entirely suitable for management by legal means" (Fried 1918, 12). This conflict transformation – 'transforming the nature of conflict' – is precisely what is meant by 'civilising conflict' in the current peace theory debate (Senghaas 1994b; Vogt 1996).

In the classical doctrine of causal pacifism, the civilised management of conflicts within states (internal conflicts) was assumed to have been achieved to a greater or lesser extent – successful 'sociation' having already taken place – but this premise can no longer be taken as given today. For a glance around the world reveals that at present: there are virtually no wars any more between states although the international community is still far from being a society of states. Instead, there are numerous military intrastate conflicts, primarily civil wars in many different forms (Gantzel & Schwinghammer 1995). Thus facilitating internal peace – and not only the new world order – once again becomes a key analytical and practical focus for constructive peace analysis.

3. Social and political transformation in the 20th Century

When researching the causes of peace and the conditions for internal peace, it is necessary to consider the radical changes which took place first in Western countries but, in recent decades more strikingly in non-Western countries. When the concept of causal pacifism was formulated at the end of the nineteenth and beginning of the twentieth century, the world – especially the majority of today's industrialised countries – was still largely agricultural in organisation. Although little has been written about this subject, the last hundred years (1900-2000) will go down in history as the century of the worldwide erosion of the traditional peasant economy ('depeasantisation'). Today, most people no longer live in subsistence economies but in entirely commercialised or market economies with an increasingly globalised frame of reference. The developing countries are no exception to this economic transition despite obvious differences exemplified by countries in East Asia and Central Africa.

In contrast to agricultural communities in a traditional rural framework, this new socio-economic environment has greatly expanded people's horizons and scope for action. The urbanisation associated with structural change also intensifies communications and – for the first time in history – allows people to organise themselves politically on a broad basis. At the same time, mass literacy has resulted in a broad-based and highly effective mobilisation of intelligence: in other words, it has lead to intellectual emancipation and a skills revolution. People's level of competence has been rising dramatically. Thus, a conversion is taking place: "from ignorance to self-consciousness, to an interconnectedness with the world", as a nun working with the underclasses of Indian society aptly described it some time ago (Frankfurter Allgemeine Zeitung, Jan. 6, 1999). In contrast to traditional societies, this opens up opportunities for upward mobility. Moreover, the globalised media allows expectations and lifestyles to be both globally compared and illustrated. Indeed, the globalisation of such possibilities or demonstration effects in a graphic way may well have a greater political impact nowadays than the mere globalisation of the economies.

Thus traditional societies are evolving into politicisable and, in reality, politicised societies, where traditional identities are challenged and questioned. 'Truths' can no longer be defined in absolute terms. Diverging notions of justice, and interests, proliferate. Given the plurality of projects to reshape and redefine the political order, the question of what constitutes a 'good society' becomes a fundamental problem. The *tranquillitas ordinis*, the 'tranquillity of the social order' – once the subject of writings by St Augustine and many non-European authors in traditional societies – can no longer be pinpointed. What emerge are modern forms of society which, in terms of their structure, are rife with the potential for conflict and even violence and which – unless they are restrained by dictatorship or despotism – can no longer be reduced to a common denominator. Yet under these new socio-economic and socio-cultural conditions, even dictatorship and despotism are doomed to failure in both the short or long term: for socio-cultural, socio-economic and, consequently, political plurality is unassailable, and the politicisation of identities, truths, notions of justice and interests is irreversible because it emerges from the very basis of socially mobile societies. Moreover, what results from all of this is the demand – presently heard in every corner of the world – for political participation.

Fundamental politicisation has occurred, when social, economic and cultural conflicts present themselves as political conflicts, and when political conflicts present themselves as social, economic and cultural conflicts. The key issue, which then arises in an acute form in many societies today, is coexistence despite fundamental politicisation (Senghaas 1998; 2001). The dubious alternative to peaceful coexistence – in an extreme case – is civil war, as political events around the globe demonstrate each and every day.

4. Conditions for the peaceful regulation of conflict

But how can civil war be avoided in this situation? This transformation of the world in which we live was initially the outcome of the agrarian and industrial revolutions from the mid-eighteenth century and especially in the nineteenth century in Western Europe. This, then, was where the issue outlined here – i.e. coexistence despite fundamental politicisation – first became acute; as a result, some of the conclusions drawn from the experience and debate about these issues are most readily available in Western Europe (Senghaas 1994b).

What then are the essential conditions for the civilised – i.e. the non-violent – resolution of unavoidable conflict? In the light of the European experience six cornerstones can be identified:

The first is a legitimate monopoly of force by the state, i.e. safeguarding the community based on the rule of law, which is of paramount importance for any modern peace-order. Disarming citizens is the only way to force them to conduct their conflicts over identity and interests through argument rather than violence. Only when these conditions are in place can potential conflict parties be compelled to deal with their conflicts through argument and thus through deliberative politics in the public arena. The crucial importance of this condition becomes apparent wherever the monopoly of force breaks down and citizens re-arm again, with the re-emergence of feuds and warlords – presently a common feature of military conflicts all over the world.

Secondly, such a monopoly of force also creates a need for control under the rule of law that can only be guaranteed by, and indeed, epitomises, the modern constitutional state. Without this control, the monopoly of force is simply a euphemistic way of describing the arbitrary behaviour of dictatorial rule. The rule of law provides 'the rules of the game' for the shaping of opinion and the political will, as well as for the decision-making process and the enforcement of law. Alongside the general principles that are set forth in catalogues of basic rights, these rules of the game are essential, precisely because in politicised societies serious disagreements on substantive issues prevail.

The third major condition for internal peace is affect control, which arises from the range and wealth of many inter-dependences characterising modern societies. Such societies are highly ramified, and people within them play out a variety of roles that reflect their wide span of loyalties. Conflict theory and real-life experience show that highly diverse social roles lead to a fragmentation of conflict and thus to the moderation of conflict behaviour and affect control: Without affect control, in complex environments such as modernising and modern societies, peaceful social relations would be inconceivable.

On the other hand, fourth, democratic participation is essential, precisely due to the indispensability of affect control. 'Legal unrest' – *Rechtsunruhe* in the term of Sigmund Freud – will result from situations where people are unable to become involved in public affairs, either for ethnic or other forms of discrimination, and at worst a conflict will escalate and, in politicised societies, can become a hotbed of violence. So democracy, as the basis for legal development, is not a luxury but a necessary precondition for the peaceful resolution of conflicts.

Fifth, however, in politicised societies, this approach to conflict management will only have permanence if there are continual efforts to ensure social justice. The great majority of modern capitalist societies are run on market lines, and social inequality is ever present. Unless efforts are continually made to counter this dynamic of inequality, such societies will develop deep social fissures. Therefore if the credibility of the constitutional state is not to be called into question by disadvantaged individuals or groups, on the grounds that the rules of the game are no longer fair, there must be an ongoing effort to ensure distributive justice. By contrast, genuine efforts to achieve social justice and fairness give substance to constructive conflict management, and also provide legitimacy to public institutions.

If there are fair opportunities in the public arena to articulate identities and achieve a balance between diverse interests, it may be assumed that this approach to conflict management has been reliably internalized and that conflict management competence based on compromise – including the necessary tolerance – has thus become an integral element of political action. The legitimate monopoly of force, the rule of law and democracy – in short, the modern democratic constitutional state – become anchored in political culture. The culture of constructive conflict management thus becomes the emotional basis of the community. Material measures ('social justice') emerge as an important bridge between the institutional structure and its positive resonance in people's emotions ('public sentiment'). What develops finally – to use Ralf Dahrendorf's phrase – are "ligatures", in other words, deeply rooted political and cultural bonds and socio-cultural allegiances.

5. The reluctant development of a culture of constructive conflict management

The political culture of constructive conflict management does not mark the beginning of modern coexistence. On the contrary, it is a latecomer to the historical process. While similar to the other five cornerstones identified above, in the past it had no place in Europe's traditional – i.e. pre-modern – culture. On the contrary, the emergence of each individual cornerstone can be described far more accurately as a 'reluctant process' or a process *contre cœur* (Senghaas 1998; 2001): for historically, disarmament was invariably the outcome of defeat in warfare. The strong triumphed over the weak; the superior over the inferior. The rule of law originated in historically contentious compromises which were wrung out of the conflict parties and were naturally unpopular, yet – in fragile power relationships – were viewed first and foremost as temporary concessions. As far as affect control was concerned, self-determined life in clearly defined micro-contexts was always viewed as preferable to integration into self-referential functional systems with their own dynamics. After Sigmund Freud, at the latest, it has been recognised that affect control is governed by the imperatives of the reality principle and not the pleasure principle: in other words, it cannot be achieved without a substantial measure of affective sublimation.

The struggle for greater participation, too, always took place against entrenched opposition. In a world where inequality is endemic, the same applies to the struggle for fairness and distributive justice: Political participation and fair distribution had to be forced out of the power holders in every case. Finally, a culture of constructive conflict management could only be established under a fortunate combination of circumstances, i.e. when each cornerstone of civility, defined above, became a historic and mutually reinforcing reality which was finally anchored in people's emotions. Only under these extremely favourable conditions were the civilisation of conflict and thus the fundamental principle of non-violent conflict management likely to take root in an environment dominated by fundamental politicisation.

The process itself must therefore be viewed as the historical outcome of many conflicts that, in the European context, took place progressively as described above. What emerges is a model of conflict management, to be labelled the *civilisational hexagon* (Senghaas 1994b; Calließ 1997) that has constitutional, institutional and material dimensions but is also characterised by specific mentalities and, in sum – and this must be underlined – represents an artificial product of the civilising process:

It can be plausibly argued that the conditions which characterise fundamental politicisation in emancipated mass societies, such as absolutist claims, the fixation on particular

Box 1: The Civilisational Hexagon

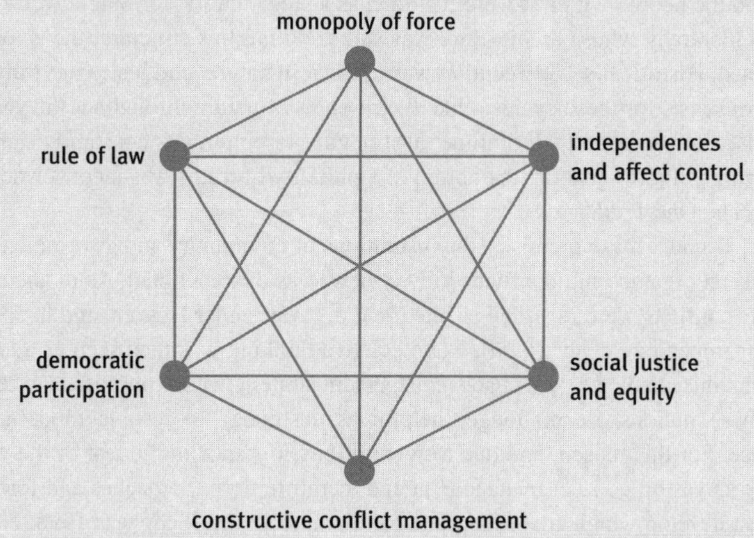

interests, the emphasis on specific identity, possessive individualism and lobbyist pressure are in some ways 'natural', whereas tolerance, an awareness of the rules of the game, moderation, the separation of powers, the willingness to compromise, and a sensitivity to more than just one's own interests tend to be 'artificial', i.e. the outcome of laborious collective learning processes. Especially in Europe, all these broad-based civilisational achievements, were hard-won in the face of – and in conflict with – the old indigenous European estates-dominated social traditions and, indeed, the modern class society which emerged in the nineteenth century. Thus today's democratic constitutional state is not the result of cultural or genetic predisposition. Rather, it is the outcome of a series of innovations and, in two and a half millennia of European history, only manifested in its most recent development within the last 150 years (Senghaas 1998; 2001).

6. Alternative responses to social and political transformations

The lesson which Europe had to learn painfully and laboriously, by trial and error, by direct as well as circuitous or even erroneous routes – namely tolerance as a solution in the face of pluralisation which was initially perceived as a threat – will be repeated, in principle if not in detail, in other parts of the world. Here, too, with the proliferation of fundamental politicisation due to the transition from traditional to socially mobile societies, as described above, mastering the problems of coexistence is a task that can no longer be postponed. Yet as with traditional Europe, there are no viable responses to these modern problems within the conventional culture of traditional non-European communities. The self-perception of these communities was generally cosmocentric: in classical mythology in particular, the cosmos, society and the people within it were regarded as a single entity, forming a well-ordered, well-organised hierarchy whose architecture was static. Within this structure, the actors' roles were pre-ordained. Historical self-perception was cyclical in nature, and hence not truly historical in the modern sense, for these cycles – like the rhythms of nature throughout the year or political life (the rise, flowering and fall of imperial structures or empires) – constantly came back to the same starting point. In general, the notion of a plurality of truths was inconceivable since there was only 'The One Truth'.

If under these premises, the institutions of community and government in particular are seen as an organic unit, conflicts will be viewed as dysfunctional. As in ancient China and elsewhere, conflicts were regarded as 'the great disorder under Heaven' and hence the onset of existing or impending chaos (*luan*). Counteractive thinking was then seen as a contribution to overcoming this chaos, i.e. as a chaos management strategy whose purpose is to restore 'cosmic order'. These notions are no longer helpful as a strategy to resolve modern problems of coexistence. For this reason, and due to force of circumstance in the rest of the world as well, new perspectives on conflict management and therefore new approaches and forms of internal peace must develop which are appropriate for the modern era (Senghaas 1998; 2001).

Unlike development in the West, the collective learning processes in the non-European world are not only determined by the radical social and cultural changes taking place locally. They are also shaped by the developments under way in the West. In this context, four distinct responses can be observed in the non-European world:

The first is a modernistic, imitative response, which accepts the West's challenge as well as its experiences and 'solutions'. The West is regarded as a model in the struggles against what is considered to be the burden of one's own tradition – including one's own traditional culture. In the first half of the twentieth century, such responses could be observed in many places, including China, but they failed to stand the test of time. Today, however, these responses are proving highly successful in two of the four East Asian newly industrialising countries (NICs), namely Korea and Taiwan. These young industrial countries are evolving into 'newly democratising countries', whose political culture – despite its entire local colour – will not differ fundamentally from those of Western countries in the foreseeable future. When the upheavals of modernisation take place and the problems of coexistence become acute, the guardians of tradition appear in various guises: as traditionalists, as reactionaries, but in general as conservatives. They seek to turn back the tide of history and, in particular, to stop the onward march of modernisation.

This second type of reaction can be observed all over the world, wherever Western modernism collides with traditional ways of living. Gandhi could be cited as an example in this context, for his philosophy of life was rural, anti-commercial and egalitarian. It favoured small units and consensus-based direct democracy within a manageable framework. Today, similar concepts can still be found in Central Africa in particular.

Third, wherever such upheavals occur, semi-modernists can be observed. They are enthusiastic about Western know-how, but seek to shield their society from all other intellectual influences. Japan has successfully pursued this course since the middle of the last century, whereas really existing socialism was unsuccessful. More recently, the 'Singapore School' has become a pre-eminent example of semi-modernism. Another example is Islamic Fundamentalism. However, the political problems of an increasingly complex and pluralising society – whether in Singapore, China, in many Islamic societies, or elsewhere – cannot be resolved, or brought closer to a solution with this type of prescriptive programme of governance, least of all in those places where there is a reliance on theocratic approaches which are rooted in Islamic Fundamentalism. These latter endeavours (as presently in Iran) have fascinating historical parallels, but also demonstrate the futility of the 'theocratic counter-revolution' against modernism, which could also be observed in Europe – and especially in France itself – during the first half of the nineteenth century in reaction to the French Revolution. In such a theocratic programme, pluralism was – and is – regarded as an immoral concept which in practice destroys the fabric of society, breaks down traditional values and culture, and represents the epitome of moral blindness (*jahiliyya*). On the other hand they regarded as entirely appropriate for the modern day the untrammelled religiously-motivated exercise of power.

Ultimately, however, whenever modernism and traditions collide and social upheavals occur in the non-European world, innovations will be required. As with Europe, these changes in the non-European regions cannot be predicted with certainty. Nonetheless, Europe's experience is likely to be repeated in some places: As soon as traditional culture is confronted with modernising tendencies and societies undergo a structural and therefore also a mental shift, these cultures – with bitter inevitability – come into conflict with themselves. This triggers the necessary collective learning processes – and may also prompt problematic and undesirable developments.

According to the theory of *The End of History* (Fukuyama 1922), all innovations of modernism have already been realised exhaustively in the Western/European countries and non-European countries have nothing more to offer in terms of dealing with the problems of coexistence. Contrary to this theory, however, four-fifths of humanity again in the coming decades will be compelled, generally against their will, to experiment with finding locally appropriate solutions to the problems of social mobility and fundamental politicisation. The solutions that ultimately prove their worth are unlikely to be invented as abstract concepts on the drawing board. What is more likely in this context is a repetition of the European experience: the arrangements for coexistence and sustainable conflict management – in other words, internal peace – which ultimately prove viable on a long-term basis will have developed as the unintended outcome of political conflicts.

Thus the non-European states will not be spared a fate similar to Europe's laborious, painful and conflict-ridden journey towards the democratic constitutional state, its institutions and ethos. The process will be similar to the European experience, although its outcome may be different, especially if genuine innovations are actually to take place. However, in this latter case, in particular, the outcome would not reflect the profound dimensions of conventional culture, but new aspects – against its own traditions.

Viewed on a global level, one of the great challenges for humanity in the twenty-first century is to find the solution to pluralisation in patterns of tolerance – a tolerance that is safeguarded at the institutional level and anchored in people's emotions. This challenge is no less weighty an issue than the burgeoning environmental problems world-wide. A glance back to the twentieth century demonstrates the urgency of this problem. During that century, many 'alternatives' to tolerance were tested in barbaric and brutal ways: exclusion, ghettoisation, apartheid, expulsion, ethnic cleansing or genocide, and civil wars in many different forms (Heinsohn 1998; Dabag and Platt 1998).

In contrast to causal pacifism at the beginning of the twentieth century, the irreversible nature of pluralisation therefore means that the quest for a legal, institutional, material and psychological system of coexistence within societies remains at the top of the agenda. The need to reach internal peace is therefore not a peripheral problem; today more than ever, it is an acute, life-threatening and global problem. In every corner of the world, acceptance of traditional and conventional structures is declining; as a result, conflicts of interests and orientation, power struggles and cultural clashes, motivated by the search for new social and political structures, are unavoidable.

7. Building an international culture of constructive conflict management

What is a difficult task even within individual societies, and what, even under the best of conditions, can only be considered a fragile achievement with no guarantee of permanency – the shaky stability of internal peace – seems all the more difficult at the international level, namely achieving and safeguarding international coexistence (Falk 1995; Ferencz 1994). States have still not disarmed, despite the fact that under international law, a fundamental ban on the use of force has existed in the United Nations (UN) Charter since 1945: The UN Security Council has in principle a 'monopoly of force' based on the UN system of collective security, though it must be conceded that it is problematic. The question of what might be implied by 'control through the rule of law at the international level' has only begun to be discussed in recent years (Bauer 1996; Gading 1996; Lailach 1998). Who, for example, is actually authorised at the international level to exercise control over the Security Council, the body entrusted under the United Nations Charter with this quasi monopoly of force? Where is the authority responsible for dealing with complaints against Security Council decisions, when such decisions are considered by those affected to constitute a breach of international law? (Bedjaoui 1995; Falk 1993; Höffe 1999; Martenczuk 1996; Zürn and Zangl 1999).

Furthermore, it is true that striking processes of internationalisation, transnationalisation or – as it has become fashionable to term it – globalisation are under way (Beisheim et al. 1999). However, these processes are taking place in what is still a deeply divided world that generates very few system-related (and globally effective) constraints on affect control (Senghaas 1994a). Only in technical/functional areas, such as international air transport, do universally accepted rules exist. Imagine if there were comparable rules for the transactions of international finance, whose function would be to domesticate the psychology of the stock markets! What might democratic participation at global level entail? Who – apart from the states, which do this already – would have to organise themselves at international level, and how would they have to do it, in order to satisfy the democratic imperative and avert violent conflict? Would interest groups be represented alongside governments – such as employers' and employees' associations, alongside the states, in the International Labour Organisation (ILO) – or, indeed, professional associations, cultural and religious communities of every kind and size, and multinational companies? And what about the often-quoted 'civil society' – the many non-government organisations (NGOs) such as Greenpeace, Amnesty International? But what are the bases of their mandate? Indeed, what form would a representative democratic constitution take at international level? What would 'participation by citizens' mean in this context? (Archibugi and Held 1995; Held 1995; Höffe 1999). Question after question arises, to which – in view of the gradually emerging "postnational constellation" (Habermas 1998; Zürn 1998) – a solution must be found in the twenty-first century.

In other respects, it can be assumed that at the international level, too, the chances of civilising conflict remain slim if no efforts are made to eliminate inequalities and at least to work towards fair distribution. Only if serious and purposeful efforts are undertaken will it be possible to prevent the kind of build-up of ultimately uncontrollable explosive political force generated by the dynamics of privilege and discrimination (Brieskorn 1997). Only then – underpinned in substantive terms – will a culture of constructive conflict management have a chance at the international level (Bobbio 1998).

8. Peace policy

If we examine the experiences with internal peace and the requirements for international peace and an appropriate order, it can be stated with regard to dependable and civilised management of conflict or lasting peace (Senghaas D. and Senghaas E. 1996) that peace, defined as the lasting and sustainable civilising of conflict, must be viewed as a non-violent political process geared to preventing the use of force. Through this process, agreements and compromises must be used to create conditions which enable peaceful relations to be established between social groups or between states and nations, without jeopardising their existence, and without violating the perceptions of justice or interests of individuals and groups so seriously that, after exhausting all peaceful remedies, they deem it necessary to resort to violence. Shaped in this way, peace policy can then be understood as an indispensable, continuous and constructive handling of political virulence which, in the modern world, results from fundamental politicisation.

9. A global system for peace

If peace policy is to be successful, even in a smaller arena, i.e. within societies and states, the conditions must be favourable; indeed, adverse conditions often lead to situations in which non-violent conflict resolution gives way to violence. Nevertheless, as the earlier questions imply, the necessary prerequisites at the global level with regard to the creation of a new world order are even broader in scope since conditions here are far less conducive (Rittberger 1994).

The pacifists of the early twentieth century, who endeavoured to formulate constructive concepts of peace, thought in international terms; they genuinely aimed to achieve a world peace-order. Nowadays, we would call it 'global governance', reflecting the many old and, indeed, very new global interdependences. Nevertheless, they were realistic enough to realise that such an order needs regional or continental building blocks in order to be truly functional.

At the regional level, too, political community-building is a difficult collective learning process. This is borne out, in particular, by the experiences with European integration. This integration process requires certain shared basic values, enhanced communications, fair exchange which benefits all parties and above all a responsiveness to the needs and concerns of weaker participants in the integration process. However, such a process of integration at the regional level must be successful, even if only in the European context at first, because this alone will provide proof that a lasting peace-order beyond the national-state is not an illusion, but can be "constituted" (*gestiftet*), to use Kant's term, on reliable foundations with the prospect of permanence through constitutional, institutional, material and emotional endeavours (Deutsch et al. 1957; Zielinski 1995; Senghaas 1992).

In the efforts to establish global governance, the aim – as clearly identified by the proponents of causal pacifism – is to create an architecture and inner life for a world peace-order: from the lower level, of the peaceful individual state (what a prerequisite!), via its integration into loose or broad-based integrated regional organisations, up to the highest level where international organisations and international rules (international regimes) create sustainable institutional and legally constituted framework conditions for the civilised resolution of unavoidable conflicts. The task is to work against violent conflict at all levels, and, indeed, overcome it in principle. This was once the idea of visionaries; today, this must become a key element of pragmatic *realpolitik*.

10. Activities to promote a global system of peace

Who can be expected to initiate this realpolitik aimed at the creation of global governance? Pacifists with constructive programmes once believed that a new world order would result from the prudent behaviour of leading statesmen; in other words, from clever diplomacy based on internationalist, cosmopolitan norms and with the backing of international organisations. They had no problems with the state per se, as they recognised the qualitative difference between states. Above all, they already understood the meaning of the term 'rogue state' (Fried in Benz 1998, 73). This denoted those actors in the international community who steadfastly refuse to accept the international order. Reflecting the prevailing attitudes and conditions of the day, this pacifist philosophy thus relied heavily on the state and state actors, although for the purposes of civilising the community of states, social movements such as civic, women's or socialist pacifist movements and their international networks were considered useful. Anarchist thought was entirely foreign to this brand of pacifism.

Admittedly, there are still states with different characters; it would be frivolous to downplay this fact, for it opens up opportunities for civilising conflict. However, the modern world's deeper and broader interdependencies mean that, at least in the Organisation for Economic Co-operation and Development (OECD) the significance of state and statehood is decreasing. Such interdependencies allow not only economic and cultural actors but also social actors in particular to play a role in international politics (Czempiel 1993).

Alongside the increasingly economic nature of foreign policy, which has been observed for some time, foreign relations today are also becoming 'socialised'. This itself has an impact on foreign policy: The media, interest groups, parties, political foundations, professional associations, NGOs and other social groups are increasingly networked across national borders, with some of them having already acquired remarkable authority (Calließ 1998).

Moreover, in the management of disasters and emergencies, but especially in responding to ethno-political conflicts, NGOs are absolutely essential in today's world. A new and diverse field of peace policy action is emerging for socially committed citizens, which makes a variety of demands in terms of staff presence and skills. Activities include assisting politically and socially disadvantaged groups ('empowerment'), escorting persons in danger, support for refugees, post-conflict peacebuilding, reporting on incipient conflicts and signs of escalation ('early warning'), observing demonstrations, organising dialogue between hostile groups, mediation and process assistance, the provision of judicial observers, a physical presence in potential and real areas of tension, the provision of electoral observers, and advising official missions such as the UN, Organisation for Security and Cooperation in Europe (OSCE) and European Union (EU) (Merkel 1998).

In the longer term, these activities cannot be organised on an ad hoc basis; besides the necessary commitment, they require appropriate training. In other words, what is needed is a problem- and situation-specific 'civilian peace service', or, indeed, a specialised peace service in which civil commitment can be matched by appropriate skills. This opens up another broad new area of activity for constructive pacifism, which also requires preparatory and accompanying research and assessment. However, this has only begun to develop since the 1990s.

The need to develop concepts for these peace activities increases with the demand for their services, which reflects real needs, and especially with initial experiences. These experiences – particularly those gained in crisis and conflict situations – demonstrate the extent to which state and civil society actors rely on each other in many instances, even though they operate on different levels and have different target groups (Lederach 1994). Even military security measures may prove indispensable on some occasions to ensure that in armed conflicts, for example, civil society actors are able to play a role at all. Dogmatic fears of inter-agency contact have proved to be counterproductive in this context, whereas shared learning processes – i.e. 'multi-track activities' – have shown themselves to be the way forward (Ropers 1997).

11. Reference and Further Reading

Archibugi, Daniele, and David Held (eds.) 1995. *Cosmopolitan Democracy: An Agenda for a New World Order*, Cambridge: Polity Press.

Bauer, Andreas F. 1996. *Effektivität und Legitimität. Die Entwicklung der Friedenssicherung durch Zwang nach Kapitel VII der Charta der Vereinten Nationen unter besonderer Berücksichtigung der neueren Praxis des Sicherheitsrates*, Berlin: Duncker and Humblot.

Bedjaoui, Mohammed 1995. *The New World Order and the Security Council: Testing the Legality of its Acts*, Dodrecht: Nijhoff.

Beisheim, Marianne et al. 1999. *Im Zeitalter der Globalisierung? Thesen und Daten zur gesellschaftlichen und politischen Denationalisierung*, Baden-Baden: Nomos.

Benz, Wolfgang (ed.) 1988. *Pazifismus in Deutschland*, Frankfurt am Main: Fischer.

Bobbio, Norberto 1998. *Das Zeitalter der Menschenrechte. Ist Toleranz durchsetzbar?*, Berlin: Wagenbach.

Boulding, Kenneth 1978. *Stable Peace*, Austin: University of Texas Press.

Brieskorn, Norbert (ed.) 1997. *Globale Solidarität*, Stuttgart: Kohlhammer.

Calließ, Jörg (ed.) 1997. *Wodurch und wie konstituiert sich Frieden? Das zivilisatorische Hexagon auf dem Prüfstand*, Loccum: Ev. Akademie.

Calließ, Jörg (ed.) 1998. *Barfuß auf diplomatischem Parkett. Die Nichtregierungsorganisationen in der Weltpolitik*, Loccum: Ev. Akademie.

Czempiel, Ernst-Otto 1993. *Weltpolitik im Umbruch*, München: Beck.

Czempiel, Ernst-Otto 1998. *Friedensstrategien*, Opladen: Westdeutscher Verlag.

Dabag, Mihran and Kristin Platt (eds.) 1998. *Genozid und Moderne*, Bd. 1., Opladen: Leske & Budrich.

Deutsch, Karl W. et al. 1957. *Political Community and the North Atlantic Area: International Organization in the Light of Historical Experience*, Princeton: Princeton University Press.

Falk, Richard et al. (eds.) 1993. *The Constitutional Foundations of World Peace*, New York: State University of New York Press.

Falk, Richard 1995. *On Humane Governance: Toward a New Global Politics*, Oxford: Polity Press.

Ferencz, Benjamin B. 1994. N*ew Legal Foundations for Global Survival: Security Through the Security Council,* New York: Oceana.

Fried, Alfred H. 1918. *Probleme der Friedenstechnik*, Leipzig: Verlag Naturwissenschaften.

Fukuyama, Francis 1992. *The End of History and the Last Man*, New York: The Free Press.

Gading, Heike 1996. *Der Schutz grundlegender Menschenrechte durch militärische Maßnahmen des Sicherheitsrates – das Ende staatlicher Souveränität?*, Berlin: Duncker & Humblot.

Gantzel, Klaus-Jürgen and Torsten Schwinghammer 1995. *Die Kriege nach dem Zweiten Weltkrieg 1945 bis 1992. Daten und Tendenzen*, Münster/Hamburg: Lit.

Habermas, Jürgen 1998. *Die postnationale Konstellation*, Frankfurt am Main: Suhrkamp.

Heinsohn, Gunnar 1998. *Lexikon der Völkermorde*, Reinbek bei Hamburg: Rowohlt.

Held, David 1995. *Democracy and the Global Order: From the Modern State to Cosmopolitan Governance*, Cambridge: Polity Press.

Höffe, Otfried 1999. *Demokratie im Zeitalter der Globalisierung*, München: Beck.

Krell, Gret and Harald Müller (eds.) 1994. *Frieden und Konflikt in den internationalen Beziehungen*, Frankfurt am Main: Campus.

Lailach, Martin 1998. *Die Wahrung des Weltfriedens und der internationalen Sicherheit als Aufgabe des Sicherheitsrates der Vereinten Nationen*, Berlin: Duncker & Humblot.

Lederach, John Paul 1994. *Building Peace: Sustainable Reconciliation in Divided Societies*, Washington: US Institute of Peace Press.

Martenczuk, Bernd 1996. *Rechtsbindung und Rechtskontrolle des Weltsicherheitsrates*, Berlin: Duncker & Humblot.

Merkel, Christine (ed.) 1998. *Friedenspolitik der Zivilgesellschaft*, Münster: Agenda.

Meyer, Berthold (ed.) 1996. *Eine Welt oder Chaos?*, Frankfurt am Main: Suhrkamp.

Rittberger, Volker 1994. *Internationale Organisationen. Politik und Geschichte*, Opladen: Leske & Budrich.

Ropers, Norbert 1997. *"Prävention und Friedenskonsolidierung als Aufgabe für gesellschaftliche Akteure"*, in Senghaas, op. cit., 219-242.

Senghaas, Dieter 1992. *Friedensprojekt Europa*, Frankfurt am Main: Suhrkamp.

Senghaas, Dieter 1994a. *"Interdependenzen im internationalen System"*, in Krell and Müller (eds.), op. cit., 190–222.

Senghaas, Dieter 1994b. *Wohin driftet die Welt? Über die Zukunft friedlicher Koexistenz*, Frankfurt am Main: Suhrkamp.

Senghaas, Dieter (ed.) 1995. *Den Frieden denken*, Frankfurt am Main: Suhrkamp.

Senghaas, Dieter (ed.) 1997. *Frieden machen*, Frankfurt am Main: Suhrkamp.

Senghaas, Dieter (ed.) 1998. *Zivilisierung wider Willen. Der Konflikt der Kulturen mit sich selbst*, Frankfurt am Main: Suhrkamp.

Senghaas, Dieter 2001. *The Clash Within Civilizations: Coming to Terms with Cultural Conflicts,* London/New York: Routledge.

Senghaas, Dieter and Eva Senghaas 1996. "Si vis pacem, para pacem – Überlegungen zu einem zeitgemäßen Friedenskonzept", *in* Berthold Meyer, op. cit. 245–275.

Vogt, Wolfgang R. (ed.) 1996. *Frieden durch Zivilisierung? Probleme – Ansätze – Perspektiven*, Münster: Agenda.

Zielinski, Michael 1995. *Friedensursachen. Genese und konstituierende Bedingungen von Friedensgemeinschaften am Beispiel der Bundesrepublik Deutschland und der Entwicklung ihrer Beziehungen zu den USA, Frankreich und den Niederlanden*, Baden-Baden: Nomos.

Zürn, Michael 1998. *Regieren jenseits des Nationalstaates*, Frankfurt am Main: Suhrkamp.

Zürn, Michael and Bernhard Zangl 1999. "Weltpolizei oder Weltinterventionsgericht? Zur Zivilisierung der Konfliktbearbeitung", *Internationale Politik,* 54:8, 17–24.

Assessing the State-of-the-Art in Conflict Transformation

Cordula Reimann

1. Introduction 42
2. Research Agenda / Research Questions 43
Sources and Nature of Conflict
Third-party Characteristics
Third-party Strategies
3. Different Approaches to Conflict Management 47
The Case of Conflict Settlement
The Case of Conflict Resolution
The Case of Conflict Transformation
4. Role of Theory and Research Methods Employed 55
5. Ongoing Questions and Challenges 61
6. Reference and Further Reading 61

Assessing the State-of-the-Art in Conflict Transformation – Reflections from a Theoretical Perspective

Cordula Reimann

1. Introduction

The following analysis aims to provide some direction through the jungle of conceptual and definitional imprecision that is prevalent in the overall field of conflict management and conflict transformation. At best, the following description suggests one possible, and hence tentative, interpretation of what may be regarded as the state-of-the-art. In any case, the author's comments remain more indicative than comprehensive.

The guiding question in this analysis is how to map out conceptually and theoretically the fields of conflict management and conflict transformation. This question will be discussed in the context of the conflict management field with reference to three possible approaches: conflict settlement, conflict resolution and conflict transformation (*see* Figure 1).

Before venturing any further in the task, it is necessary to make some introductory remarks. First, despite, or perhaps even due to, its innate multidisciplinary nature, the overall field of conflict management is fraught with conceptual and definitional imprecision. In most of the academic literature, the terms *conflict management*, *conflict resolution* and *conflict transformation* are often used loosely and interchangeably, in many cases referring to the same strategies. Similarly, one may also come across the term mediation to cover all different forms of third-party intervention. In short "non-uniform terminology" (Ropers 1997; p5) is now more the norm than the exception in the overall field: this definitional imprecision of core concepts continually increases as more actors become involved.

The term conflict management is itself rather unfortunate, as it may well include approaches such as conflict transformation that go far beyond the 'logic of management'. However, in the lack of a better alternative, I will accept the use of conflict management as an umbrella term, while cautioning against its definitional and conceptual pitfalls.

Second, most recognised scholars bring to the field of conflict management expertise drawn both from academia and from actual conflict management practice. As a consequence, most defy easy classification and their work does not fall exclusively into one category.

Third, despite the complexity of the different approaches, the research community of conflict management has done little in the last thirty years to attempt state-of-the-art reviews or even to stress the interdisciplinary nature of the field by providing usable introductory textbooks (one of the few exceptions may be Miall, Ramsbotham and Woodhouse 1999).

Fourth, the research on individual and group conflict management, like community mediation and alternative dispute resolution (ADR), has had a major impact on conflict management in international relations. Moreover, given the quality of most current violent, protracted conflicts, it becomes increasingly difficult to distinguish conflict management in internal domestic conflict and external international conflict. These conflicts are protracted to the extent that the crisis usually patterns itself around the social and political make-up of different groups, drawing its characteristics from their language, religion, clan affiliation, political and social identity and structure. Thus, to some extent the following analysis of protracted conflicts in the international arena may also hold true for inter-group conflict management carried out at other social levels.

To give the following analysis a useful framework, I will first focus on the research agenda and research questions, and then move forward to review the role of theory and research methods.

2. Research Agenda / Research Questions

The general field of conflict management as theory and practice is best understood as a thoroughly complex, multidisciplinary study area of a wide variety of disciplines including international law, psychology, philosophy, socio-biology, international relations, conflict/peace research, political science, economics and social anthropology. As in the case of international relations and peace research, there is no one predominant, legitimate subject matter. This should hardly be surprising given not only the broad scope of the field, but also its focus on conflict and its management as a generic social phenomenon from the inter-personal through to the international levels.

In the past, research has largely been devoted to the analysis of contextual and process variables concerning inter-personal, inter-group and international conflicts, such as the *sources* and *nature of the conflict*, as well as *third-party characteristics and strategies* that may be conducive to better conflict management. (*See*, for instance, Bercovitch and Rubin 1992, pp1-29). This can be illustrated by looking briefly at the principal debates that have taken place around these issues for the last thirty years.

2.1 Sources and Nature of Conflict

Until recently, research into the sources and nature of conflict has usually centred around two ontological strands: the *subjectivist* and the *objectivist* approach. The subjectivist approach to conflict focuses primarily on the perceived incompatibility of goals. The essential implications of this are, first, many goals are subjectively perceived as incompatible, whereas from an objective point of view they can be thoroughly compatible. This may be due to misinformation, cultural misunderstanding, or misperceptions such as stereotypes, mistrust and emotional stress. Second, structurally unfair or unjust relationships are often not recognised while at least one of the parties involved fails to perceive their own dependence and unequal treatment by the other. This can be exemplified by the phenomenon of the 'happy slave'.

It is exactly with the latter situation that the objectivist approach is concerned. It seeks the origins of conflict in the social and political make-up and structure of society. Here, the crucial point is that conflict can exist independently of the perceptions of the parties involved. The conflict/peace researcher, Schmid, gives the example of a class conflict which

"...is not a conflict because the classes have incompatible goals, fight each other, and hate each other. . . [but rather] a conflict because the social structure is such that one class loses what the other class wins" (Schmid 1968, p226).

Despite this, the distinction between subjectivity and objectivity, in the end, says little of analytical value. The 'objective' observer, in labelling the structure of a system as conflictual or violent contrary to the perception of the parties involved, is making a subjective interpretation. This is based on his or her own subjective values and criteria as to what constitutes a conflict in the first instance. Accordingly, the objectivist approach cannot be deemed value-free, as it only reflects "another subjective assessment of the situation [...] by some third party rather than by the participants" (Mitchell 1991, p221).

As the current realities of protracted, ethno-national conflicts are considered, it seems evident that most of these are best explained as dynamic processes involving a mixture of subjective features (such as identities, needs and interests) and – supposedly – objective, structural ones (such as unequal distribution of resources). Consequently, any exclusive reliance on either a subjectivist or objectivist framework will prove insufficient to capture the nuances of the conflict. With regard to the practice of conflict management, it appears safe to say that some conflict management approaches may, even if more implicitly than explicitly, effectively bridge the theoretical divide between subjectivity and objectivity. This is achieved through the combination of different conflict management strategies, for example, conflict settlement strategies, such as *power mediation*, and conflict resolution strategies, exemplified by facilitation or dialogue workshops. The quality and quantity of these combined methods are highly dependent on the conflict stage within which they are employed.

2.2 Third-party Characteristics

Concurrent with the recurring debate on the sources and nature of conflict, there have been extensive discussions among theoreticians and practitioners concerning the characteristics of third parties. This is especially applicable to the issue of his or her impartiality and neutrality. In the past, academics and practitioners were evenly split on the question of how far the notion of impartiality/neutrality achieves and explains an outcome of third party intervention that is considered to be successfull (*see* contribution of Ron Fisher on the website version of this Handbook).

Given the nature of most global intra-state conflicts, it seems appropriate not to treat notions of impartiality and partiality as mutually exclusive characteristics of third parties, but rather to focus on their somewhat ambivalent and complementary nature.

On the one hand, *impartiality* of third parties seems to be essential especially when those parties lack the leverage necessary to reach a successful outcome to the dispute. An illustrative example can be the informal mediation efforts of the Quakers, private individuals and of scholars-practitioners. On the other hand, partiality of the third party may prove to be key when this leverage is present (Kleiboer 1996, p372). Here, the role of the superpower, USA, as third party in most Middle East peace talks comes immediately to mind.

Having said that, the development of procedures for conflict management should not be regarded as static or rigid, but rather as dynamic features that must be easily adapted to the changing framework conditions. As this analysis will show, it is paramount to effectively contextualise the different means of conflict intervention such as facilitation or conciliation on the one hand, and power mediation on the other. This becomes even more important and challenging when considering the multiple and diverse involvement of Track I, II and III actors in most intractable and deep-rooted conflicts. The next section will draw attention to these activities.

2.3 Third-party Strategies

What exactly do we mean by the terms *Track I*, *Track II* and the more recent addition, *Track III* (*outlined in* Box 1)? In the past attention has focused primarily on the differences in substance and emphasis between Track I as conflict settlement strategies and Track II as conflict resolution strategies. While Track I was mainly reserved for the official and formal activities of diplomatic and governmental actors, Track II referred largely to more informal and unofficial efforts by other non-governmental parties.

Track I activities range from official and non-coercive measures, such as good offices, fact-finding missions, facilitation, negotiation/mediation and peacekeeping, to more coercive measures, such as power-mediation, sanctions, peace-enforcement and arbitration. (See Ron Fisher's article on the website version of this volume, for a good discussion of the changing nature of peacekeeping, as well as that of Hansen, Ramsbotham and Woodhouse in this volume).

In contrast to Track I, Track II refers to all non-official and non-coercive activities, illustrated by facilitation or consultation (occasionally, one comes across the more general term mediation in reference either to facilitation or to consultation). Generally, these are conducted in the form of problem-solving workshops or round table discussions.

This distinction between Tracks I and II further suggests that there will be striking differences in strategies employed. Although, the strategies are different in emphasis, it seems clear that in most third-party interventions Track I and II strategies go hand in hand and, in many instances, will be purposely combined. In practice, conflict settlement measures, such as mediation by Track I actors, may actually be mirrored with conflict resolution strategies, such as the facilitation/consultation by Track II actors. The crucial point is that some features of both Tracks may not only complement one another, but also overlap in both theory and practice. A good example of this is the conflict management effort in Northern Ireland during the early 1990s: David Bloomfield (1997) has illustrated just how far conflict settlement efforts on Track I, by the British Secretary of State of Northern Ireland, overlapped with the Track II conflict resolution work of the Community Relations Council.

Conflict settlement should not be understood as a necessary pre-condition for conflict resolution. Experience has shown, for example, that, if negotiations on Track I become embroiled in a deadlock, unofficial and informal fora in the form of facilitation and problem-solving workshops (Track II) may not only be initiated or continued, but also helpful in producing a breakthrough.

This can be illustrated by the back-channel, conflict resolution process in Norway that eventually led to a framework for conflict settlement and subsequently a negotiated agreement between the Israeli government and the PLO in 1993 (*see* Lederach 1997, pp32-34; Corbin 1994). In this process, a Norwegian scholar and his wife hosted and facilitated these secret talks in 1992 between Israeli and Palestinian officials, each of whom enjoyed top-level access while maintaining their independence. The attainment of a reasonably cooperative relationship between these two adversarial parties, before the actual start of the formal negotiations, proved to be not only crucial to the success of the negotiation process itself, but also clearly illustrated the rather limited potential of conflict settlement strategies such as power mediation/bargaining, when they are attempted in isolation. The underlying assumption lurking behind this analysis is that very few conflict management strategies will be fully effective by an exclusive reliance on either a Track I or Track II framework.

Since the early 1990s an appropriate analytical focus on inter-relatedness and interdependence has emerged and is now occupying the middle ground in this field. By the mid-1990s it has been possible to see a shift in the literature that stresses an integrative and complementary approach to conflict management. It emphasises further the need to combine conflict settlement strategies, such as mediation and negotiation, with conflict resolution strategies, such as facilitation/consultation (some good examples of this can be found in the work of Glasl 1982; Fisher and Keashley 1991; Prein 1994).

These complementary and integrative approaches not only shed a different light on the dichotomy between Track I and Track II strategies, but also provide orientation and new insights into the various complexities of contemporary violent conflict situations and peacebuilding activities. It is crucial to make a more conscious combination of different actors with conflict management activities and strategies. These must be properly matched with the political and social priorities, which will arise at the different stages of conflict escalation and de-escalation.

According to the most popular and widely discussed 'contingency model' put forward by Fisher and Keashley (1991), the greater the level of conflict escalation, the more directive the intervention must be in order to be effective. These models have two implications: first, that some peacebuilding activities will be more critical at some stages rather than at others; and second, that practitioners may need to return to an earlier stage of conflict management strategies as they gauge the progress of their peacebuilding activities. It is beyond the scope of this article to discuss the different contingency models in depth, or even to review the critiques of the common assumption of homogeneity between parties or of the rigid chronological phases of conflict escalation (for a more in-depth discussion, see Webb, Koutrakou and Walters 1996, pp171-189).

The key point to be raised from these complementary and integrative approaches is that the synthesis of different models and concepts, in the light of complex conflict interests and needs, can bring great value and insight to analysis. Indeed, some scholar/practitioners have taken the complementary and integrative approaches a step further by introducing the concept of further tracks, which has now been dubbed the 'multi-track approach'. The most recent conceptual development is the creation of an addition specific track – Track III. This is taken to refer to all process and structure oriented initiatives undertaken by actors involved in grassroots training, capacity building and empowerment, trauma work, human rights and development work and humanitarian assistance (Günter Baechler's article, in this volume, offers a particularly insightful discussion of structure oriented initiatives, such as state reform). In the past, the simple distinction between Tracks I and II has failed to adequately capture the richness of peacebuilding activities and efforts typical of Track III and, as a result, all that did not fall into this dichotomy was excluded.

Box 1: Track I, II and III Actors and their Strategies

	Track I	Track II	Track III
actors involved	Political and military leaders as mediators and/or representatives of conflict parties	From private individuals, academics, professionals, 'civil mediation', 'citizens diplomacy' to international and local non-governmental organisations involved in conflict resolution	From local grassroots organisations to local and international development agencies, human rights organisations and humanitarian assistance
strategies taken	Outcome-oriented: From official and coercive measures like sanctions, arbitration, power mediation to non-coercive measures like facilitation, negotiation, mediation, fact-finding missions and 'good offices'	Process-oriented: Non-official and non-coercive measures mainly facilitation, consultation in the form of problem-solving workshops and round tables	Process- and/or structure-oriented: Capacity building, trauma work, grassroots training, development and human rights work

3. Approaches to Conflict Management

In the context of the above analytical background, this section will provide an examination of the three distinctive but related approaches to conflict management: conflict settlement, conflict resolution and conflict transformation. For a proper understanding of these three approaches, it is crucial to realise that they should not be viewed as distinct, single and all-comprehensive theoretical systems. It is dubious whether such isolated systems would even be attainable given the multidisciplinary and heterogeneous underpinning of all three approaches. Rather, they are more fruitfully understood as a variation on Weber's 'ideal types'. To give the following analysis some shape, this section will concentrate on the various understandings of:

- underlying theory;
- origin of protracted violent conflict and core concepts;
- conflict;
- actors involved;
- strategies taken;
- criteria for successful outcome and the nature of peace.

The discussion of theory raises the underlying, implicit, theoretical assumptions of the three approaches. As each attempts to analyse the origins of protracted violent conflicts, they will in turn produce very different understandings of the root causes of conflict.

In order to propose an analytic approach to this issue that manages to avoid the rather problematic subjective/objective dichotomy, three distinctive but not necessarily exclusive understandings of conflict are helpful:

- as a problem of political order/status quo;
- as a catalyst for social change;
- as a non-violent struggle for social justice.

This three-fold understanding of conflict is largely inspired by the comparative in-depth study of conflict theories put forward in social theory by Weber (1948), Dahrendorf (1957 and 1994), Coser (1956) and Simmel (1955). It has been further stimulated by recent debates in social theory primarily revolving around Critical Theory (*see*, for instance; Featherstone and Parkin, 1997; Featherstone 2000) and Anthony Giddens' Structuration Theory (*see,* for instance, Jabri 1996).

As the following analysis aims to illustrate, the central question seems to be under which particular understanding of conflict do the different conflict management approaches work. The underlying assumption is that any particular understanding of conflict will necessarily have both direct and indirect repercussions on the self-understanding, including the ideology, of conflict management scholars. Understanding conflict as primarily a problem of political order remains a rather conservative, status quo oriented and, at best, a therapeutic approach to conflict management. By contrast, conflict management approaches that view conflict as a catalyst for social change or as a non-violent struggle for social justice constitute a more radical, transformation oriented approach.

This does not presume that one approach is necessarily better than the other; rather, all three understandings of conflict set worthwhile aims for conflict management efforts in their own terms. Nevertheless, I would further argue that all three understandings must be held in tension if we are to engage in any form of transformative, sustainable peacebuilding process. A conflict management approach that is, for example, oriented to the *status quo* without taking into account the ways dysfunctional relationships might be fundamentally changed will run the risk of an implicit fostering of oppressive and unequal social conditions (*see* Clements 1998, p138). An approach, on the other hand, which instead aims to foster the radical transformation of a given society without, at the same time, maintaining some sense of how to uphold social order and continuity, is likely to lead to anarchy.

It can be seen that the received analysis concerning the actors and strategies distinguishes between, not only Track I, II and III actors and their distinctive qualities, but also similar strategies. In addition, the underlying interpretations of success imply very different assumed evaluation criteria and raises the question of just when are we justified in deeming the different conflict management approaches successful?

In the end, the analysis of the three approaches turns out to be less straightforward and a rather tricky task. This results from the assumptions about these issues that are held by most scholars in the field, though more implicit than explicit, and particularly in terms of the underlying theory they employ.

3.1 The Case of Conflict Settlement

Conflict settlement shall refer to all outcome oriented strategies for achieving sustainable win-win solutions and/or putting an end to direct violence, without necessarily addressing the underlying conflict causes. Illustrative examples of research along these lines may be found, for instance, in the work of Bercovitch (1984 and 1996), I. William Zartman (1985 and 1995) and Fisher and Ury (1981) at Harvard University's Programme on Negotiation.

Based on the 'ideology of management', most research in the sense of conflict settlement defines conflict as a problem of political order and of the *status quo*: violent protracted conflict is thus deemed the result of incompatible interests and/or competition for scarce power resources, especially territory.

While such a definition indeed implies that conflict is a zero-sum game, conflict settlement need not necessarily follow this same line of thinking. Depending on the particular interests of the actors involved and the stage of escalation, conflict settlement may easily transcend the zero-sum game, and lead instead to a non zero-sum if not to a positive-sum outcome. This point is clearly illustrated in the research into realist rational actor models on which Bercovitch and Zartman base their work and game theory which has influenced the work of Ury and Fisher (*see also* Brams 1990).

As both rational choice and game theory are applied to the practice of conflict settlement, political and military leaders who function as primary actors with high visibility are viewed above all as rational actors. They will calculate their interests and will in the end work together towards a rational and mutually profitable goal. Both theories then aim to delineate an optimal strategy for use by players interacting under conditions of uncertainty.

Game theory modelling based on this rational actor assumption then shows how the mutual satisfaction or the optimal accommodation of differing, selfish interests are the natural results of egoistic (realist) power politics. In other words, conflict settlement can be conceptualised as a non-zero sum game in which a gain for one party need not necessarily be at the expense of the other. Integrative and distributive bargaining based on rational choice models of behaviour will, thus, prove to be cost-beneficial to decision makers on both sides (*see also* Bennett 1996, pp157-184). While the distributive approach is traditionally associated with zero-sum bargaining, the integrative approach considers bargaining to be a shared problem between the negotiation partners and seeks to identify and capture a non-zero sum or positive-sum result.

It is also essential, under the conflict settlement approach, that both parties adequately clarify contextual conditions, focusing especially on the difference between positions and interests: while positions define a rather superficial, short-term standpoint, interests reflect more the fundamental and long-term stakes which each party has in the negotiation.

In conflict settlement situations, positions are generally assumed as non-negotiable, while there is more possibility that the interests of each party can be accommodated to each other. The more psychological aspects of each party's point of view will be strongly influenced and determined by the degree of compatibility between their real interests.

Much of the research in the area of conflict settlement has been devoted primarily to third-party characteristics and strategies that help transform a zero-sum into a non-zero sum conflict management process and, thus, to end the violence and enable some form of political agreement.

The principal actors in this field are the military, political and religious leaders, and decision-makers at Track I level. Most strategies employed range from official and non-coercive measures such as good offices, fact-finding missions, facilitation, negotiation and mediation, to more coercive processes such as power mediation, sanctions and arbitration (*see* above). While the more coercive strategies of conflict settlement are usually evidence of a rather short-term involvement of third parties, the non-coercive measures such as facilitation, fact-finding missions and good offices are undertaken from a longer-term perspective.

The focus on direct violence and on its negative and destructive consequences is clearly outcome oriented. In one way or another, all strategies that aim to end violent conflict through a cease-fire or cessation of hostilities may hopefully, in turn, lead to a more permanent political agreement. Conflict settlement strategies, thus, work from a relatively limited concept of success and peace: success is defined as a sustained win-win solution. Moreover, peace is seen in purely negative terms, with no set objective of longer-term positive peace or social justice.

3.2 The Case of Conflict Resolution

Conflict resolution refers to all process oriented activities that aim to address the underlying causes of direct, cultural and structural violence. Structural violence defines the social, political and economic structure of a conflict situation when unequal power, domination and dependency are perpetuated, while cultural violence refers to the social and cultural legitimisation of direct and structural violence. As Burton has very much left his mark on the conflict resolution approach, both as an academic and a practitioner, his work will be taken as an illustrative example. Other scholar-practitioners working in the field of conflict resolution are Herb Kelman, Ron Fisher and Louis Kriesberg.

Conflict resolution attempts to use game theory in order to overcome the self-defeating dynamics of the zero-sum conflict management approaches and, thus, to reframe the conflict as a shared problem with mutually acceptable solutions. Burton has used models of game theory, cybernetics, and system theory, for instance, in *Systems, States, Diplomacy and Rules*, in order to make it clear that most inter-state conflicts are the result of dysfunctional decision-making (*see* Burton 1968). In contrast to the conflict settlement approach, conflict resolution begins by defining protracted conflict as a natural result of unmet human needs. Consequently, the origin of protracted conflict can be found in the underlying needs of its participants.

This interpretation of conflict has been greatly influenced by Burton's 'world society approach', and in his work on human needs theory. The latter points to the universal drive to satisfy basic and ontological needs, such as security, identity, recognition, food, shelter, safety, participation, distributive justice and development (*see* Burton 1990). Conflict resolution then aims not to eliminate the conflict as such; rather, it is held that conflict expressed in a non-violent manner is an essential catalyst for social change. The aim then becomes to eliminate the violent and destructive manifestations of conflict that can be traced back to the unmet needs and fears of the conflict parties. The key is to make the parties aware of these underlying needs for identity, security and participation, and then to use them to redefine both interests and positions.

While Burton does not spell out under what conditions all needs might be satisfied at the same time, he does urge practitioners to deepen and broaden the analysis of conflict to better clarify both needs and relations. Two consequences emerge from this kind of analysis. First, a broadened analysis of the conflict, with its emphasis on needs, will call for strategies that go far beyond the outcome oriented conflict settlement strategies with their focus on negotiable interests. This has resulted from needs and fears being – contrary to interests – non-negotiable, but on the other hand it is possible to deal with each parties needs and fears in a synergetic way. Burton, among others, has proposed more process oriented and relationship oriented strategies, approaches that are non-coercive and unofficial (Track II) activities such as facilitation or consultation in the form of controlled communication, problem-solving workshops or round-tables. Facilitation and consultation, pursued in this way, constitutes an effective third party attempt to facilitate creative problem solving through direct communication and in-depth conflict analysis.

Second, the deepening of conflict analysis and the widening of strategies will also require that a greater number of actors become involved in the process. These can be drawn from the civil society groups, from academic institutions and from all forms of civil mediation or citizen diplomacy groups, including local and international conflict resolution NGOs operating at Track II level.

While most of the strategies, such as a series of problem-solving workshops, take the form of medium-term involvement, the very process of sustaining and developing a dialogue should be best understood as short-term involvement. In fact, a deeper common interest and shared needs through increased cooperation and improved communication between parties may constitute a form of successful outcome of conflict management. Along the lines of Burton's human needs approach, any form of successful outcome must be based on the minimum requirement of the satisfaction of the needs of both parties.

3.3 The Case of Conflict Transformation

Conflict transformation refers to outcome, process and structure oriented long-term peacebuilding efforts, which aim to truly overcome revealed forms of direct, cultural and structural violence. The most significant scholar/practitioners working in this field are Lederach (1995 and 1997), Curle (1971) and the conflict/peace researcher Galtung (1996).

Conflict transformation moves beyond the aims of both the previous approaches, while at the same time taking up many of the ideas of conflict resolution, and particularly of John Burton's notion of 'conflict provention'. "Conflict provention means deducing from an adequate explanation of the phenomenon of conflict, including its human dimensions, not merely the conditions that create an environment of conflict and the structural changes required to remove it, but more importantly, the promotion of conditions that create *cooperative* relationships" (Burton and Dukes 1990, p2).

What Burton had in mind were primarily horizontal relationships, i.e. the dialogue and cooperation of actors or conflicting parties of relatively equal status in the context of, for example, Track II problem-solving workshops (*see* Lederach 1999, p29-30). The conflict resolution approach, however, missed an important opportunity to further develop and build vertical relationships that develop dialogue and cooperation between actors of unequal status, as is often the case with decision-makers on Track I and the grassroots leaders of Track III. This opportunity has now been taken up by the conflict transformation approach (ibid, pp30-31). Especially as put forward by Lederach, conflict transformation puts central emphasis on this question. This analytical and practical shift in focus is based on several assumptions.

First, building on Burton's notion of needs satisfaction, any successful conflict transformation strategy must include Track III actors in the peacebuilding process, as they deal with those most affected by the effects of violent conflict (*see* Lederach 1995 and 1997). The lack of fulfilment of their basic needs gives rise to deep-rooted violence and hatred in the first instance.

Second, the inclusion of Track III actors and strategies is a far cry from the 'logic of management' predominant in the conflict settlement approach. In fact, Track III strategies such as capacity building and empowerment workshops reflect the 'logic of (local) empowerment'. Moreover, bottom-up Track III strategies aim to support or even generate local struggles for social justice and hence for radical, structural change.

The underlying assumption is that the potential for peacebuilding already exists in the particular region or community and is rooted in its traditional culture. Conflict management techniques thus cannot, and should not, be simply transferred across cultures with little or no understanding of the cultural knowledge and resources at work in the particular conflict setting (Lederach 1995). To build on local struggles means to be aware of the pre-existing traditional ways in which that society handles conflict. A good example of this is the system of the elders in Somalia, who, as clan members, can exert their traditional authority to coerce the conflict parties into settling a conflict and accepting an agreement.

Track III activities are, in general, best situated and understood in the context of the theoretical framework of non-violent action put forward by Sharp (1973), Gandhi (1938 and 1950) and King (1963). While these three activists/scholars were influenced by very different religious convictions and ideologies, they all shared a notion of conflict as a non-violent struggle for social justice. "Non-violent action brings tensions and contradictions to the surface that already exist but are denied and covered up." (McCarthy and Sharp 1997, xvi). It is primarily through the employment of "constructive non-violent tension" (Ibid.) in the form of people's power that latent conflict becomes manifest. Thus, socially or politically deprived groups can mobilise in this way to free themselves from the constraints of exploitative and suppressive relationships. Such people's power can manifest itself in different forms of non-violent struggle, ranging from demonstrations, strikes and non-cooperation to (economic) boycotts.

Viewed this way, protracted violent conflicts turn out to be primarily the result of unequal and suppressive social and political structures. Dealing effectively with them, therefore, will call for the empowerment and recognition of marginalised groups in the form of non-violent struggle. Only in this way will it be possible to deal with issues of immediate concern at the local level, or to put the appropriate pressure on Track I (and Track II actors), to end the violence and enter into good-faith negotiations.

An illustrative example can be found again in the Somalia context during the early 1990s (Lederach 1997, pp52-53). The bottom-up approaches commenced with a series of discussions and agreements on how to end the war, conducted within local peace conferences that brought the various sub-clans together. These conferences took care to invite legitimated representatives who could properly advocate each clan's fears and concerns, and, thus, put centre-stage issues of immediate concern at local levels. As these local conferences approached agreements, a similar decision-making process was then repeated at higher levels involving an ever-wider range of clans.

Whereas Track I and Track II actors in the conflict settlement and conflict resolution approaches tended to view (and render) the civilian population and grassroots levels as passive, Track III strategies put them centre-stage. Thus, conflict transformation will not be primarily the result of third-party intervention as it was under conflict resolution or conflict settlement.

It is clear that neither Track I nor Track II approaches (nor even both together) can provide a complete and satisfactory understanding of the complex nature and dynamism of peacebuilding activities called for in the context of contemporary violent conflicts. Not only does this point to the necessity for the inclusion of Track III strategies in the peacebuilding process, but also it implies that practitioners will need to link activities on all three tracks if they are to build domestic peace constituencies or strategic alliances between the different local, national and international actors.

This in turn suggests that all three track strategies are best understood when they are integrative and complementary, and, given what was said earlier, it seems safe to say that all three of these forms of conflict intervention have their proper place in the life-cycle of a conflict. Thus, Track II and III activities may complement Track I activities, although they must not be regarded as a substitute or even a panacea for apparently failed Track I strategies. Here, one might turn again to the example of the Norwegian couple who hosted and facilitated the peace talks between Israelis and Palestinians; while their work effectively laid the ground for formal negotiations, it did not at any point obviate the need for a negotiated settlement on substantive issues (*see* Lederach 1997, p34).

By the same token, Track I activities and strategies may not be well equipped to take on the lofty goals of long-term reconciliation and social justice. While Track III activities may foster these broader objectives, they will in the end remain ineffective, if not doomed to failure, unless they are complemented by structural changes on the Track I level such as the embodiment of models of minority rights and power-sharing and autonomy models across ethnic boundaries in legal and governance structures.

The underlying assumption is that any exclusive reliance on one practical or theoretical approach to conflict management will fail to deal effectively with the complexity and contradictions of causes and consequences evident in most protracted conflicts. The logical extension of this point might be an effort to integrate and synthesise Track I, II and III activities not only on the practical, but also on the theoretical level. In the past, most conflict management scholars have been reluctant to synthesise different theoretical approaches such as game theory, human needs theory and non-violent theory (and if they did, they certainly were not explicit about it).

There are several conceivable reasons as to why this has not occurred. First, conflict settlement, with its focus on the logic of management, may be viewed as too strongly associated with the now widely discredited realist power politics paradigm. Especially in the early work conducted in the field of conflict management, scholars tended to focus more on identifying differences than discovering similarities between schools of thought, as the discussion about the competing merits of conflict settlement and conflict resolution approaches amply illustrates. In general, the field has for a long time been marked by a well-entrenched dichotomous way of thinking: the objectivist in opposition to subjectivist understanding of conflict, and conflict settlement compared to conflict resolution strategies.

As shown above, those scholars focusing on conflict resolution and working, for example, with problem-solving workshops have tended to make use of very different analytical frameworks (such as needs and fears mapping) than have conflict settlement scholars, with their focus on interests and rational choice models of behaviour (*see* Clements 1998, p136). A final and more general reason for the persistent divergence between the approaches may be that some scholars have based their work on implicit rather than explicit assumptions, thus failing to verbalise the theoretical underpinnings of their argumentation.

If one is to consider conflict transformation as a conceptual and practical extension and a useful combination of the pre-existing models, it would make good sense to have some type of synthesis of game theory, rational choice, human needs theory and non-violence action. An illustrative example can be found in the problem-solving workshops, which were inspired by different sources of non-violent action, such as those of Gandhi, King and Sharp, that all stressed the need for respect for the adversary and the search for mutually beneficial outcomes (Mitchell 1981, pp71-86). Mutually beneficial outcomes are, in turn, one of the core concepts and aims of most game theory approaches.

In short, if complementarity is the key and if it is to be taken at face value, it must be theoretical in nature and bring about an effective cross-fertilisation or strategic marriage between game theory, human needs theory and non-violent action. While synthesising the different understandings based on conflict theory, human needs and non-violent action, a conflict transformation strategy must begin from a three-fold understanding of the nature of conflict.

Not only does this school of thought view conflict first and foremost as an element of political control and a catalyst for social change, but also as a natural expression of non-violent struggle for social justice. Conflict transformation, thus, takes up a dual understanding of conflict as an agent of both social control and change (Clements 1998, p138).

Moreover, conflict transformation does not stop here. It also fundamentally redefines the dichotomy between conflict resolution and conflict settlement. By placing its primary emphasis on the question of social justice, the conflict transformation approach rejects the traditional aim of conflict management to restore the *status quo ante* and, instead, elaborates on the notion of conflict as a positive agent for social change.

Conflict transformation is an open-ended, long-term, multi-track and dynamic process, which significantly widens the scope of actors involved. It effectively combines Track I, II and III activities along the continuum of short-, middle-, and long-term involvement. It is thus likely to engage a wide variety of actors, including: official, military and political leaders (Track I); informal conflict resolution experts, INGOs and NGOs working in conflict resolution (Track II); grassroots, indigenous NGOs providing development cooperation and humanitarian assistance (Track III). An approach, which is applied so widely, can and should no longer be reduced to a label of 'peacebuilding from below'. This three-fold understanding of conflict also suggests a corresponding triple interpretation of success; it can be outcome, process, and/or change oriented.

As far as outcomes are concerned, conflict transformation aims to achieve a settlement of substantive issues raised by the needs and fears of the conflict parties. This has two elements: first, a process orientation approach emphasising the need to change mutually negative conflict attitudes and values among parties in order to increase cooperation and communication between them; second, a change oriented approach stressing the political imperative to create a new infrastructure for empowerment and recognition of underprivileged groups, thus fostering and enabling social justice. In short, the satisfaction of basic needs on the personal and relational levels will not be sufficient. Rather, practitioners must work to achieve equal access to resources and assemble the infrastructure that will make it possible to address structural inequalities with the aim of longer-term social reconstruction and reconciliation.

To define a successful outcome is more difficult under the conflict transformation approach than it was in the simpler cases of conflict settlement and resolution. For peace is now defined in positive terms. Forms of negative peace must be transcended as the diverse forms of structural and cultural violence are successively addressed. This will require, for many contemporary protracted conflicts, nothing less than a root-and-branch transformation of social relationships and social structures.

4. Role of Theory and Research Methods Employed

The field of conflict management in general and these three approaches in particular have touched only a few small 'islands' of theory. In contrast to recent debates in international relations for instance, the field of conflict management has remained largely devoid of theorising, especially about ontological and epistemological questions such as the purpose of scientific inquiry, methodologies applied and the justification of knowledge.

The following analysis shall illustrate and exemplify this rather harsh critique. It is a truism that any theorising about different approaches to conflict management must necessarily base itself on some specific theory of conflict. One must expect, therefore, any theorising about conflict management to start with a theoretical debate on the underlying understanding of violent conflict. From this, it would seem to follow that such an understanding of conflict is not merely theoretical, but that it will lead to radically different conclusions for conflict management and conflict transformation in theory and practice.

A glance through the conflict management literature unfortunately suggests that most conflict management approaches or strategies are not based on such a broad or explicit theoretical concept of conflict (*see* Scimecca 1993, pp211-221). In general, the field seems to have "significantly surpassed theory building" (Wall and Lynn 1993, p182). Thus, Scimecca stresses that there is "…no real theoretical justification for when [, who] and why to use conflict intervention techniques" (Scimecca, *op. cit.*, p217). It cannot be surprising that most research has not been systematically theory-driven. (Exceptions might be the avowedly theory-driven (comparative) case-studies of Stedman 1991 and Princen 1992.)

It is for this reason that Scimecca makes the case for the establishment of a theoretical framework drawn from the sociology of Weber (Weber 1948): He claims that Weber's conflict theory lends itself well for use as a single overarching framework within which to situate both the practice and the theory of different approaches to conflict management. While many scholars (and practitioners) might challenge his exclusive reliance on Weber's sociology, Scimecca raises important questions concerning the theoretical shortcomings of the field of conflict management and its lack of any explicit theory of conflict.

What seems to be of primary concern is that most of the assumed realities of the theory and practice of conflict management are, in fact, imposed by an implicit theoretical framework of conflict (such as the earlier discussion of objectivist and subjectivist understandings of conflict). Furthermore, they seem to work even when the understanding of the role of the theory is limited. Usually, the interpretation of theory evident in the field of conflict management is limited to some sort of explanation of observable or personal experience, viewed in terms of causal logic with ensuing policy recommendations.

The ultimate test of a theory will be found in the degree of its usefulness and technical applicability as it seeks to guide and orient policy towards given ends, such as the settlement of violent conflicts. If the focus is to be on conflict management practice (that is, 'the real world out there') one could argue that a scholar-practitioner does not need to be concerned with theory? Apart from anything else, this way of thinking only reveals a rather limited understanding of the general place of theory in the field of conflict management, as most conflict management research seems empirically to approach and work with the understanding of theory.

Theory, thus, should first offer a framework enabling scholars and practitioners to more accurately analyse and describe (and sometimes predict) the real world. This assumed real world of conflict management consists of, and is bounded by, the behaviour of the conflict parties and intervening variables, such as third-party characteristics, resources and strategies, such as coercion, expertise and reward (*see* Bercovitch 1992, pp10-21). If theory is understood in this way, one can then identify at least four different ways in which the field of conflict management can approach the "theory-research-practice loop" (Fisher 1997b, p263).

Some analysts, such as Stedman (1991), Bercovitch and Rubin (1992), Rubin (1981), Princen (1992), Zartman (1985) and Jabri (1990) have offered comparative, descriptive and empirical case study documentation of either conflict management practice which have been perceived as failed or successful (*see also* most issues of The Negotiation Journal and International Negotiation). Systematic theory-driven comparative case studies seem to be more the exception than the norm.

On other occasions scholars, such as Bercovitch and Wells (1993) and Nicholson (1992), aim to discover and develop regularities and correlation or even causal explanations about what constitutes effective conflict management. They inductively construct theories, making use of quantitative methods in order to test and frame hypotheses about, for example, the contextual variables of mediation. These might be concerned with the nature of the parties or the identity and rank of mediators. Research of this type will take the form of large-scale systematic studies on effective conflict management, such as can be found in Bercovitch, or constitute more experimental and laboratory-based approaches to third party intervention as attempted by Rubin (1980). The large-scale systematic studies are followed particularly closely for the policy-relevant findings that they can generate for political decision-makers (Bercovitch 1997).

Scholars such as Fisher and Ury (1981) and Burton, especially in his earlier work (1969), are less empirical in nature, taking instead a rather descriptive, sometimes anecdotal and prescriptive form. This approach is one of inductive theorising: most of its adherents present "...a number of processes which are dependent upon the idiosyncratic expertise of the individual practitioner" (Scimecca, *op. cit.*, p214). Most of these will turn out to rely on rather static models that are "...inductive descriptions of core components of practice, with some prescriptive guidelines for interventions" (Fisher 1997). The most predominant example may be the work of the Harvard Negotiation project.

Kleiboer points to the fine line between empirical evidence and conjecture in the field of conflict management when she stresses that most "... research is represented as evidence but turns out to be based primarily on usually un-stated conjectures, opinions and ad hoc observations" (Kleiboer 1996, p376). In fact, many of the findings of Fisher and Ury (1981), Ury (1991) and Burton (1987) come in the form of manuals, handbooks or 'cookbooks' offering rules or instructions for successful conflict management exercises (*see* Mitchell 1993).

There seems to be some confusion as to whether, for example, the exercises of problem-solving workshops, introduced by Burton and others, are meant as opportunities for inductive theorising about ideas and hypotheses on conflict and conflict resolution processes (*see, for instance*, Fisher 1997b, p256; Hill 1982) or whether they are instead the result of deductive theorising – i.e. generalising about conflict and conflict resolution and thus drawing on a more generic theory of human needs (*see, for instance*, Featherstone 1991). Perhaps this lack of clarity, or even evidence of contradiction, inherent in much of the conflict management literature, could be traced to the general ambiguity and definitional imprecision that can be found in Burton's work, or at least on generalisations resulting from selective reading of his rather elusive work.

Yet a study of different forms of problem-solving workshop exercises, as proposed by Burton (1969), (1972) and Fisher (1983), reveals a more general but equally serious problem: most research on these workshops seems to deduct and induct hypotheses simultaneously. This is not particularly surprising when one considers that the initial enthusiasm for problem-solving workshops as opportunities for theory generation among some scholars never actually led to a systematic testing of theories (*see also* Mitchell 1993, pp89-90).

Still others take a rather different route to inductive theorising in conflict management and transformation: other scholars have been heavily influenced by 'grounded theory' (*see, for instance*, Weiss 1999) and by anthropology and ethnography (*see, for example*, Wolfe and Honggang 1996). The primary focus of this kind of qualitative research is an attempt to derive research questions from data and to test these during field-work before refining and reviewing them at the end of the data collection phase.

Different as these approaches may be methodologically, it seems fair to say that they are all underpinned by some notion of research which is objective and free of value judgements, and assume that objective knowledge of the real world out there is possible, whether or not such knowledge is grounded in subjective experience. Along the way, such scientific, objective findings not only sharpen the contrast with value judgements, which are considered highly subjective, but are also usually given epistemological priority.

Only a few scholars, such as Curle and others working with grounded wider social theory, question this approach, subscribing instead to Galtung's definition of "objectivity as an inter-subjective dialogue based on explicit premises *i.e. values...*" (Galtung 1996, p16; emphasis added). They will insist that the primary analytical focus of conflict management research must be on empirical evidence, without explicitly considering that theoretical notions already inform the practice of conflict management itself. Thus, most of the past research in the field of conflict management, especially in the Anglo-American research community, has largely focused on a detached analysis of third-party strategies and behaviour and of the nature of conflicts.

Consequently, it was possible in the past to focus on the apparent reality of conflict management practice without acknowledging just how far that practice was already informed by highly normative, but as yet unquestioned, assumptions. These concerned, for example, the legitimacy, power and neutrality of the third party, the nature of universal and generic human needs, the unequal distribution of power between the parties, and the success and impartiality of the conflict management process.

When theory is viewed as an empirical tool, most theoretical or conceptual approaches to conflict management turn out to be problem-solving approaches: they work within a given dominant framework of institutions and social relations. By definition, the problem-solving approach, "...takes the world as it finds it, with the prevailing social and power relationships and the institutions into which they are organised, as the given framework for action" (Cox 1981, p129). It should be noted that this is a very different type of problem-solving approach than that implicit in Burton's problem-solving workshop mechanism.

It seems clear that the problem-solving approach fails to critically reflect upon the underlying frameworks it assumes, especially those of social order and status quo, of gender, or to question its assumptions about universality and objectivity. This may explain why most of the existing problem-solving conceptual and explanatory frameworks operate within implicit and tacit agreement about the concepts of social justice and, therefore, of negative and positive peace (*see* William Zartman et al. 1996, pp79-98). While Bush and Folger concentrate their analysis on domestic conflict resolution, and here particularly on the development of ADR in the US, they also offer some provocative questions for further discussions about the assessment of conflict management success (*see* Bush and Folger 1994). Some scholars and practitioners may deem certain conflict management efforts to be effective without properly defining what effective actually means. Is, for example, the overall reduction of hostility and of violence or the establishment of a cease-fire a form of effective conflict management?

What is notably missing from most conflict management research efforts is any type of explicit normative theoretical grounding, which would be essential for the proper understanding and evaluation of conflict management success (*see also* Kleiboer 1996, p377; Kleiboer 1998). Thus, Rasmussen, Rouhana and Rothman have stressed that most evaluation is either conducted poorly or even completely omitted, principally because "the theoretical grounds on which an intervention has been built have not been clarified" (Folger 1999). We should dare to rock the boat of conflict management. After all, just what are these sacrosanct and unspoken values which inform all analysis but which are never spelled out or questioned?

A good example of such a sacrosanct value might be found in the issue of gender. What is our largely implicit image of the individual in the field of conflict management? Do we view him/her as rational but also empathetic and cooperative, as gender-neutral? Apart from anything else, conflict management scholars may well be criticised for portraying the theory and practice of conflict management as a gender-neutral enterprise; their working assumption has always been that conflict management has no perceptible effect on the relative positions or roles of women and men in society during times of war and peace.

Especially the concerns of women and 'devalued men' (those who are coloured, non-Westernised, working-class, or gay), their social interests, ideas and experience, have been simply left behind by the analysis and management of protracted conflicts (*see* Reimann 2001). A cursory glance at the conflict management literature will quickly show that conflict management on the conceptual and especially more practical level remains a man's world; in contrast to those involved in work on domestic and local conflicts, most of the practitioners and academics involved in conflict management in the international arena are still men.

Feminists can argue that this field of conflict management actually perpetuates, and indirectly enforces, the exclusionist power structures and hierarchies found in most patriarchal societies. Clearly, most third-party interventions tend to reduce or suppress social conflicts such as those arising from gender inequality. One might well ask from this perspective: is there a wolf in sheep's clothing? Does conflict management change the symbols but at the same time continue to subscribe to the 'old' invisible principles and practices of patriarchy in the 'new' post-settlement social order? Thus, conflict management remains mired in the logic and practices of management and, as such, neglects the underlying power arrangements of conflict management initiatives such as gender inequality.

This leads directly to the larger questions: if conflict management is not gender-neutral, just what is its hidden understanding of the public and private spheres in conflict management approaches? What does it mean to be an embodied, gendered mediator or conflict management scholar; that is, how does the practice of conflict management define a man or a woman? Alternatively, what is the underlying understanding of masculinity and femininity in conflict management theory and practice?

The analysis shows that most conflict management approaches work from a fairly static and simplistic notion of identity. Despite Burton, Azar and others considering the identity group as the most relevant unit of analysis in the study of protracted or intractable social conflicts, their work falls short of and fails to account adequately for the rich and varied ways in which identities both shift and are constructed. It is paramount to understand that notions of masculinity and femininity, and their connections with violence or peace in most conflicts, are fluid, requiring continual redefining and careful handling.

These questions serve to highlight that it is largely the unspoken and hidden values of scholar/practitioners, which serve to define success in conflict management. Viewed this way, the concept of, for example, an effective outcome of conflict management comes to look more like a highly subjective value construction than an objective description. To label a conflict management effort as a success is, in itself, to make a value judgment.

It remains to be seen how far the ongoing discussion about Peace and Conflict Impact Assessment (PCIA) (*see* contribution of Mark Hoffman in this volume) can offer some remedy in the form of a conceptual framework for systematically classifying and evaluating the success of conflict management efforts. Critics may ask whether or not increasingly popular neat and tidy boxes of success criteria in evaluation forms are in the end little more than mere drops in a theory-starved ocean.

One might further question the degree to which arbitrarily isolated and, in my view, rather static conflict indicators can add insights to the overall picture of the unanticipated, highly complex and dynamic conflict interactions inherent in most inter-group conflicts. How might one, for example, squeeze the fluid, changing and complex identities and agencies of women to make them fit into a success or conflict indicator?

Most women are likely to experience intra-state conflicts in a rather ambiguous way. While some violent conflicts may indeed represent intermediate catalysts for women's empowerment, as women find they can successfully assume roles in the private and public spheres previously dominated by men. Nevertheless, for them, most conflicts remain above all devastating experiences, marked by gross atrocities and large-scale human rights violations such as sexual violence, rape and forced prostitution. Hence, while discussing the management of the process of women's agency in violent conflict, one must perpetually keep in mind the uneasy tension between vulnerability and victimhood on the one hand, and empowerment and emancipation on the other, always resisting the impulse to prioritise the one over the other (*see* Reimann 2001).

More generally, one can even imagine a scenario in which one has classified various and diverse conflict indicators and yet is still unable to find a satisfactory explanation for the dynamics of the systemic inner-society violence that characterises many contemporary conflicts. What, then, are the political and ethical implications of PCIA?

It would appear that most PCIAs offer only limited political and ethical guidance on how to deal with its results. This is hardly surprising, as most of the success or conflict indicators proposed to date are not situated in the wider theoretical framework of a peaceful and just society. While it seems clear that PCIA may foster the economic efficiency of development cooperation projects, it is so far ill equipped to venture into ethical and political waters, by seeking to label peacebuilding efforts as a success or failure.

Burton was one of the few in the field who dared to take up and discuss in some length the shortcomings of problem-solving approaches (Burton speaks instead of "puzzle-solving approaches'"). According to Burton's approach, "...the solution is not the final end-product. It is, in itself, another set of relationships that contains its own set of problems... [P]roblem-solving frequently requires a new synthesis of knowledge or techniques and a change in theoretical structure...[T]he system of interactions is an open one, i.e. the parts are subject not merely to interaction among themselves (...) but to interaction with a wider environment over which there can be no control" (Burton 1979, p5).

This approach has some *prima facie* purchase on critical theory as an attempt at theoretical-normative critique. Like Burton, critical theory focuses on challenging and dismantling traditional forms of problem-solving approaches by questioning "entrenched forms of social life that constrain freedom" (Devetak 1996, p148). The starting point here is, as it was for Burton, the problematisation of the origin of any given framework of institutions and social relations. And, like Burton's problem-solving approach, critical theory aims to then clarify possible ways to bring about social change and, thus, to transform the dominant social and political system (*see* Cox 1981, pp129-130).

Another intriguing question is how far Burton's problem-solving workshop mirrors Habermas' 'ideal speech situation'? According to Habermas' ideal speech situation, all participants have an equal opportunity to participate and raise questions. Finally, similar to Burton, Horkheimer stresses that knowledge is not simply a reflection of a concrete historical situation, but must be understood as a social force to generate social change (*see* Horkheimer 1972, p215).

Yet, Burton's anti-positivist line of argumentation somehow clashes with his wider emphasis on a positivist approach to the scientific study of conflict: most of Burton's work reflects in one way or another his search for a non-ideological model of social order in general and a value-free concept of objective human needs in particular. In others words, Burton's credo to move "from subjectivity to theory-based objectivity" (Burton 1993, p57), turns out to be "...inappropriate because any analysis of the social world will be infused with the values of the analyst. In a world of competing values, the merits of any particular model, therefore, are not self-evident. No model is free from ideology. Since John Burton wishes to change the world, he has no alternative but to make the argument for change in ideological terms. It is counter-productive to dress one's values in natural science garb. A non-ideological model of social order is a chimera which it is a mistake to claim or pursue" (Little 1984, p95).

5. Ongoing Questions and Challenges

This chapter has aimed to clarify that the still dominant Anglo-American empiricist methodology, which seeks to combine scientific methods with policy oriented judgements, as put forward by Burton or Bercovitch, borrows heavily from conventional scientific theories of causality. Thus, the split between fact and value, so prevalent in social science, is accepted as given and somehow inevitable, and most research in conflict management leaves this seemingly irrevocable separation between facts and values unchallenged.

This in turn explains why dichotomous thinking is so prevalent in most conflict management research. This brief review of the conflict management literature suggests that much research has for far too long, unfortunately, been based on flawed dichotomies such as those between objectivity and subjectivity, between conflict settlement and conflict resolution strategies, and between impartiality and partiality (*see also* Beckett 1997).

There is a very real need for the field of conflict management and conflict transformation to open itself up to the wider debates of social and political theory, seeking especially to integrate approaches which attempt to bridge dichotomous thinking and theorising by use of insights drawn from feminism, critical theory and social constructivism (*see* Reimann 2001, for a discussion of the likely success of a more gender-sensitive approach to conflict management). Further discussion, both in and outside the fields of conflict management and transformation, will make it clear how far wider debates in social and political theory have begun to make important inroads into and ground-breaking contributions to the overall field.

6. Reference and Further Reading

Azar, Edward E. 1990. *The Management of Protracted Social Conflict*, Hampshire: Dartmouth.

Banks, Michael (ed.) 1984. *Conflict in World Society: A New Perspective on International Relations*, Brighton: Wheatsheaf.

Banks, Michael and Christopher R. Mitchell 1991. *A Handbook of the Analytical Problem-solving Approach*, Fairfax, Va: Institute for Conflict Analysis and Resolution.

Beckett, Gavin 1997. "Social Theory and the Theory and Practice of Conflict Resolution.", *in* Broadhead, op.cit., 59–86.

Bennett, D. Scott 1996. "Security, Bargaining and the End of Interstate Rivalry," *International Studies Quarterly*, 40, 2: 157–184.

Bercovitch, Jacob 1992. "The Structure and Diversity of Mediation in International Relations", *in* Bercovitch and Rubin, op. cit., 10–21.

Bercovitch, Jacob 1984. *Social Conflicts and Third Parties: Strategies of Conflict Resolution*, Boulder, Co: Westview.

Bercovitch, Jacob (ed.) 1996. *Resolving International Conflicts: The Theory and Practice of Mediation*, Boulder, Co: Lynne Rienner.

Bercovitch, Jacob 1997. "Mediation in International Conflict," *in* Zartman and Rasmussen, op. cit., 133.

Bercovitch, Jacob and Jeffrey Rubin (eds.) 1992. *Mediation in International Relations. Multiple Approaches to Conflict Management*, London: St. Martin's Press.

Bercovitch, Jacob and R. Wells 1993. "Evaluating Mediation Strategies: A Theoretical and Empirical Analysis", *Peace and Change*, 18, 3–25.

Bloomfield, David 1997. *Peacemaking Strategies in Northern Ireland: Building Complementarity in Conflict Management Theory*, New York: St. Martin's Press.

Bomers, Gerald B.J. and Richard B. Peterson (eds.) 1982. *Conflict Management and Industrial Relations*, Boston, The Hague and London: Kluwer/Nijhoff Publishing.

Brams, S.J. 1990. *Negotiation Games: Applying Game Theory to Bargaining and Arbitration*, New York: Routledge.

Broadhead, Lee-Anne (ed.) 1997. *Issues in Peace Research 1997–98*, Bradford: Department of Peace Studies, University of Bradford.

Burchill, Scott and Andrew Linklater (eds.) 1996. *Theories of International Relations*, London: Macmillan Press.

Burton, John 1968. *Systems, States, Diplomacy and Rules*, Cambridge: Cambridge University Press.

Burton, John 1969. *Conflict and Communication: The Use of Controlled Communication in International Relations*, London: Macmillan.

Burton, John 1972. *World Society*, London: Macmillan.

Burton, John 1979. *Deviance, Terrorism and War: The Process of Solving Unsolved Social and Political Problems*, Oxford: Martin Robertson Press.

Burton, John 1987. *Resolving Deep-Rooted Conflicts: A Handbook*, Lanham, Md: University Press of America.

Burton, John (ed.) 1990. *Conflict: Human Needs Theory*, London: Macmillan.

Burton, John 1993. "Conflict Resolution as a Political Philosophy", *in* Sandole and van der Merwe, op. cit.

Burton, John and Frank Dukes (eds.) 1990. *Conflict: Readings in Management and Resolution*, London: Macmillan.

Bush, R. A. Baruch and Joe Folger 1994. *The Promise of Mediation: Responding to Conflict Through Empowerment and Recognition*, San Francisco: Jossey-Bass.

Charles Stewart Mott Foundation 1999. *Reaching for Peace: Lessons Learned from Mott Foundation´s Conflict Resolution Grantmaking, 1989-1998*, Evaluation conducted by CDR Associates and the Berghof Research Center for Constructive Conflict Management, Flint, Michigan: Charles Stewart Mott Foundation.

Clements, Kevin 1998. "A Field in Tension: From Alternative Dispute Resolution to Conflict Transformation," *in* Pressis and Fougere, op. cit., 129–148.

Corbin, Jane 1994. *The Norway Channel: The Secret Talks that Led to the Middle East Peace Accord*, New York: Atlantic Monthly Press.

Coser, Lewis A. 1956. *The Functions of Social Conflict*, New York: Free Press.

Cox, Robert W. 1981. "Social Forces, States and World Orders: Beyond International Relations Theory", Millennium, 10, 2, 126–155.

Cox, Robert W. 1983. "Gramsci, Hegemony, and International Relations: An Essay in Method", *Millennium*, 12, 2, 162–175.

Curle, Adam 1971. *Making Peace*, London: Tavistock Publications.

Dahrendorf, Ralf 1957. "Towards a Theory of Social Conflict", *Journal of Conflict Resolution* 2, 2, 170–183.

Dahrendorf, Ralf 1994. *Der moderne soziale Konflikt. Essays zur Politik der Freiheit*, München: DTV.

Devetak, Richard 1996. "Critical Theory," *in* Burchill et. al., op. cit., 210–251.

Diamond, Louise and John McDonald 1996. *Multi-Track Diplomacy: A Systems Approach to Peace*, Washington, DC: Kumarian Press.

European Platform for Conflict Prevention and Transformation 1998. *Prevention and Management of Violent Conflicts. An International Directory*, Utrecht: European Platform for Conflict Prevention and Transformation (in cooperation with PIOOM and the Berghof Research Center for Constructive Conflict Management).

European Centre for Conflict Prevention 1999 *People Building Peace: 35 Inspiring Stories from around the World*, Utrecht: European Centre for Conflict Prevention (in co-operation with the International Fellowship of Reconciliation (IFOR) and the Coexistence Initiative of State of the World Forum).

Featherstone, A. Betts 1991. "The Problem-Solving Workshop *in* Conflict Resolution," in Woodhouse, op. cit., 252–255.

Fetherston, A. Betts 2000. *From Conflict Resolution to Transformative Peacebuilding: Reflections from Croatia. Working Paper 4 (April)*, Bradford: University of Bradford.

Fetherston, A. Betts and A. C. Parkin 1997. "Transforming Violent Conflict: Contributions from Social Theory." *in* Broadhead, op. cit., 19–57.

Fisher, Roger and W. Ury 1981. *Getting to Yes: How to Negotiate Without Giving In*, London: Arrow Books.

Fisher, Ronald J. 1972. "Third Party Consultation: A Method for the Study and Resolution of Conflict," *Journal of Conflict Resolution* 16, 1, 67-94.

Fisher, Ronald J. 1983. "Third Party Consultation as a Method of Conflict Resolution: A Review of Studies," *Journal of Conflict Resolution* 27, 2, 301–334.

Fisher, Ronald J. 1997a. *Interactive Conflict Resolution*, Syracuse, NY: Syracuse University Press.

Fisher, Ronald J. 1997b. "Interactive Conflict Resolution," *in* I.W. Zartman & J.L. Rasmussen (eds.), op. cit., 239-272.

Fisher, Ronald J. and Loraleigh Keashly 1991. "The Potential Complementarity of Mediation and Consultation within a Contingency Model of Third Party Intervention," *Journal of Peace Research* 28, 1, 29–42.

Folger, Joseph P. 1999. "Evaluating Evaluation in Ethnic Conflict Resolution: Themes from, and Commentary on, the Haverford-Bryn Mawr Conference," *in* Ross and Rothman, op. cit., 214.

Folger, Joseph P. and Tricia S. Jones 1994. *New Directions in Mediation: Communication Research and Perspectives,* London: Sage Publications.

Galtung, Johan 1996. *Peace By Peaceful Means: Peace and Conflict, Development and Civilization*, London: Sage Publications and Oslo: PRIO.

Gandhi, M.K. 1938. *Hind Swaraj, or Indian Home Rule*, Ahmedabad: Navajivan Publishing House.

Gandhi, M.K. 1950. *Satyagraha in South Africa*, Ahmedabad: Navajivan Publishing House.

Glasl, Friedrich 1982. "The process of Conflict Escalation and Roles of Third Parties," in Bomers and Peterson, op. cit., 119–140.

Hill, Barbara 1982. "An Analysis of Conflict Resolution Techniques: From Problem-Solving Workshops to Theory," *Journal of Conflict Resolution* 26, 1, 109–138.

Horkheimer, Max 1972. *Critical Theory*, New York: Seabury Press.

Jabri, Vivienne 1990. *Mediating Conflict: Decision-Making and Western Intervention in Namibia, Manchester*: Manchester University Press.

Jabri, Vivienne 1996. *Discourses on Violence: Conflict Analysis Reconsidered*, Manchester: Manchester University Press.

King, Martin Luther 1963. *Why We Can't Wait?*, New York: New American Library.

Kleiboer, Marieke 1996. "Understanding the Success and Failure of International Mediation," *Journal of Conflict Resolution* 40, 2, 360–389.

Kleiboer, Marieke 1998. *Multiple Realities of International Mediation*, Boulder, Co. and London: Rienner.

Lederach, John Paul 1995. *Preparing for Peace: Conflict Transformation Across Cultures*, New York: Syracuse University Press.

Lederach, John Paul 1997. *Building Peace. Sustainable Reconciliation in Divided Societies*, Washington, D.C.: United States Institute of Peace Press.

Lederach, John Paul 1999. "Justpeace: The Challenges of the 21st Century," *in* European Centre for Conflict Prevention 1999, op.cit.

Lewer, Nick 1999. *International Non-Governmental Organisations and Peacebuilding - Perspectives from Peace Studies and Conflict Resolution. Working Paper 3 (October)*, Bradford: University of Bradford.

Little, Richard 1984. "The Decision Maker and Social Order: The End of Ideology or the Pursuit of a Chimera?," *in* Banks, op. cit., 78–95.

McCarthy, Ronald M. and Gene Sharp 1997. *Nonviolent Action. A Research Guide*, New York and London: Garland Publishing, Inc.

Miall, Hugh 1992. *The Peacemakers: Peaceful Settlements of Disputes since 1945*, London: Macmillan.

Miall, Hugh, Oliver Rambotham, and Tom Woodhouse 1999. *Contemporary Conflict Resolution*, Cambridge: Polity Press.

Mitchell, Chris 1981. *The Structure of International Conflict*, London: Macmillan.

Mitchell, Chris 1991. "Recognising Conflict," *in* Woodhouse, op. cit.

Mitchell, Chris 1993. "Problem-solving Exercises and Theories," *in* Sandole and van der Merwe, op. cit., 83.

Moore, Christopher W. 1986. *The Mediation Process: Practical Strategies for Resolving Conflict*, San Francisco: Jossey-Bass.

Nicholson, Michael 1992. *Formal Theories in International Relations*, Cambridge: Cambridge University Press.

Prein, Hugo 1994. "A Contingency Approach for Conflict Intervention," *Group and Organisation Studies* 9, 1, 81–102.

Pressis, Rosemary du and Geoff Fougere (eds.) 1998. *Politics, Policy and Practice: Essays in Honour of Bill Willmott*, Christchurch, New Zealand: University of Canterbury.

Princen, Thomas 1992. *Intermediaries in International Conflict*, Princeton, NJ: Princeton University Press.

Reimann, Cordula 2001. "Engendering the Field of Conflict Management: Why Gender Does Not Matter! Thoughts from a Theoretical Perspective," *Peace Studies Papers*, Working Paper 2. Fourth Series, January, Bradford: University of Bradford.

Ropers, Norbert 1997. *Roles and Functions of Third Parties in the Constructive Management of Ethnopolitical Conflicts*, Berlin: Berghof Research Center for Constructive Conflict Management.

Ropers, Norbert 1998. "Towards a Hippocratic Oath of Conflict Management? Eight Critical Statements Relating to the Contribution of NGOs in Conflict Prevention and Conflict Transformation," *in* European Platform for Conflict Prevention, op. cit., 27–33.

Ropers, Norbert and Tobias Debiel (eds.) 1995. *Friedliche Konfliktbearbeitung in der Staaten- und Gesellschaftswelt*, Bonn: Stiftung Entwicklung und Frieden.

Ross, Marc Howard and Jay Rothman (eds.) 1999. *Theory and Practice in Ethnic Conflict Management: Theorizing Success and Failure*, London: Macmillan Press.

Rubin, Jeffrey Z. 1980. "Experimental Research on Third-Party Intervention in Conflict," *Psychological Bulletin*, 87, 2, 379–391.

Rubin, Jeffrey Z., (ed.) 1981. *Dynamics of Third-Party Intervention: Kissinger in the Middle East*, New York: Praeger .

Rupensinghe, Kumar (ed.) 1995. *Conflict Transformation,* London: Macmillan.

Sandole, Dennis J.D. and Hugo van der Merwe (eds.) 1993. *Conflict Resolution Theory and Practice: Integration and Application*, Manchester and New York: Manchester University Press.

Scimecca, J. A. 1993 "Theory and Alternative Dispute Resolution. A Contradiction in Terms?" *in* Sandole and van der Merwe, op. cit., 211–221.

Schmid, Herman 1968. "Peace Research and Politics," Journal of Peace Research, 5, 3, 217–232.

Sharp, Gene 1973. *The Politics of Nonviolent Action*, Boston: Porter Sargent.

Simmel, Georg 1955. *Conflict and the Web of Group Affiliations*, New York: Free Press.

Stedman, Stephen J. 1991. *Peacemaking in Civil War: International Mediation in Zimbawe, 1974–1980*, Boulder, Co: Lynne Rienner.

Ury, William 1991. *Getting Past "No": Negotiating with Difficult People*, New York: Bantam Books.

Wall, J. and A. Lynn 1993. "Mediation: A Current Review," *Journal of Conflict Resolution* 37, 1, 160–194.

Weber, Max 1948. *The Theory of Social and Economic Organization*, Glencoe: The Free Press.

Webb, K, Koutrakou, V. N., and Walters, M. 1996. "The Yugoslavian Conflict, Europe Mediation and the Contingency Model: A Critical Perspective," *in* Bercovitch, op. cit., 171–189.

Weiss, Anja, 1999. "Rassistische Effekte unter antirassistisch engagierten MultiplikatorInnen. Zur interaktiven Reproduktion einer symbolisch vermittelten Dimension sozialer Ungleichheit." *Unpublished Doctorate Dissertation*, Humboldt Universität zu Berlin.

Wolfe, Alvin W. and Yang Honggang (eds.) 1996. A*nthropological Contributions to Conflict Resolution*, London: University of Georgia Press.

Woodhouse, Tom (ed.) 1991. *Peacemaking in a Troubled World*, Oxford: Berg Books.

Zartman, I. William 1985. *Ripe for Resolution: Conflict and Intervention in Africa*, New York: Oxford University Press.

Zartman, I. William 1987. *Positive Sum: Improving North-South Negotiations*, New York: Transaction Publishers.

Zartman, I. William (ed.) 1995. *Elusive Peace: Negotiating an End to Civil Wars*, Washington, DC: The Brookings Institution.

Zartman, I. William et. al. 1996. "Negotiation as a Search for Peace," *International Negotiation* 1, 79–98.

Zartman, I. William and Maureen Berman 1982. *The Practical Negotiator*, New Haven: Yale University Press.

Zartman, I. William and J. Lewis Rasmussen (eds.) 1997. *Peacemaking in International Conflict. Methods and Techniques*, Washington, DC: United States Institute for Peace.

Conflict Transformation: A Multi-Dimensional Task

Hugh Miall

1. **Introduction** 68
2. **Theories of Conflict Transformation** 69
   Is There a Theory of Conflict Transformation?
   Contributions to Theories of Conflict Transformation
   From a Theory of Conflict to a Theory of Conflict-in-Context
3. **Practices of Conflict Resolution** 80
   Actors of Conflict Transformation
   Coordination and Multi-Track Diplomacy
   Assessing the Impact of Practice
4. **Conclusion** 86
5. **Reference and Further Reading** 87

Conflict Transformation: A Multi-Dimensional Task

Hugh Miall

1. Introduction

What is the state-of-the-art in conflict transformation theory? Does a theory of conflict transformation already exist, and if so, what are its main foundations? Can practitioners rely on this theory to guide their practice? Can analysts make use of it to understand the dynamics of conflict and to assess the effects of interventions?

This paper aims to identify what is distinctive about conflict transformation theory and practice, as well as to identify its key dimensions. We need such a theory of conflict transformation if we are to have an adequate basis for the analysis of conflicts, as well as for devising appropriate responses to them and evaluating the effects of these responses. The paper argues that such theories need to be continually adjusted in response to the changing nature of conflicts, and that current theories must be adapted in order to take proper account of the globalisation of conflicts and conflict interventions.

The first section of the article distinguishes conflict transformation theory from theories of conflict management and conflict resolution. It explores some of the principal conflict transformation approaches in more detail, and then asks whether they add up to a coherent body of theory. Following this, it suggests a shift from *theories of conflict to theories of conflict-in-context*, arguing that in the context of globalisation our analyses of conflict must give proper consideration to the social, regional and international context. We need to consider both the factors that promote peacebuilding and those that exacerbate conflict at these different levels over an extended time period from before the outbreak of violent conflict to well after its resolution. Within this broader setting, this section thus attempts to extend Galtung's and Azar's theories of conflict formation to theories of conflict transformation. It also proposes a framework of five types of conflict transformation, which should be useful as a basis for planning and assessing interventions in conflicts.

The second section of the article discusses current developments in conflict transformation practice as they have occurred in the four principal kinds of practice – that of governmental and intergovernmental representatives, of development agencies, of non-governmental organisations (NGOs), and of local parties and groups within the conflict setting. The issues involved in coordinating initiatives between these different groups are also discussed.

The final section of the paper discusses conflict transformation as a potential seed for change, requiring change both in the peacebuilder as well as in the society in conflict.

2. Theories of Conflict Transformation

2.1 Is There a Theory of Conflict Transformation?

At the very least, the foundations of a theory of conflict transformation have now been laid. Nevertheless it is also true that a wide variety of theoretical approaches are in use among different schools of thought and practice in the field. These theories reflect both differing paradigms and different types of intervenors (state and non-state, internal and external). Different authors and practitioners use basic concepts and terms in inconsistent ways. In particular, it is not clear whether the term conflict transformation is intended to describe the field broadly, and thus be synonymous with conflict management and conflict resolution, or whether conflict transformation instead is characterised by distinct elements that can be differentiated from the other two approaches.

I will argue here for the latter: a distinctive theory of conflict transformation is indeed emerging. Nevertheless I note also that this new theory draws on many of the familiar concepts of conflict management and conflict resolution, and that it also rests on the same tradition of theorising about conflict. It is best viewed not as a wholly new approach, but rather as a re-conceptualisation of the field in order to make it more relevant to contemporary conflicts.

Certain crucial changes in the nature of conflict call for such a re-conceptualisation. First of all, most contemporary violent conflicts are asymmetric, marked by inequalities of power and status. Second (*see* contribution of Dan Smith in this volume), many contemporary conflicts are protracted, crossing repeatedly into and out of violence and thus defying cyclical or bell-shaped models of conflict phases. Thirdly, protracted conflicts warp the societies, economies and regions in which they are situated, creating complex emergencies fuelled on the one hand by local struggles and on the other by global factors such as the arms trade and support for regimes or rebels by outside states. The complexity of these situations contrasts starkly with the relative simplicity of the core theories we can find in conflict resolution, especially those advocating win-win outcomes in two-party contests.

It is helpful to distinguish three separate schools within this overall field (*see* contribution of Reimann in this volume), while at the same time recognizing the significant areas of overlap between them. All three not only articulate varying approaches to conflict intervention, but also reflect different conceptualisations of conflict.

Conflict management theorists see violent conflicts as an ineradicable consequence of differences of values and interests within and between communities. The propensity to violence arises from existing institutions and historical relationships, as well as from the established distribution of power. Resolving such conflicts is viewed as unrealistic: the best that can be done is to manage and contain them, and occasionally to reach a historic compromise in which violence may be laid aside and normal politics resumed. Conflict management is the art of appropriate intervention to achieve political settlements, particularly by those powerful actors having the power and resources to bring pressure on the conflicting parties in order to induce them to settle. It is also the art of designing appropriate institutions to guide the inevitable conflict into appropriate channels. In the words of Bloomfield and Reilly:

> *Conflict management is the positive and constructive handling of difference and divergence. Rather than advocating methods for removing conflict, [it] addresses the more realistic question of managing conflict: how to deal with it in a constructive way, how to bring opposing sides together in a cooperative process, how to design a practical, achievable, cooperative system for the constructive management of difference (Bloomfield and Reilly 1998, 18).*

Conflict resolution theorists, in contrast, reject this power political view of conflict, arguing instead that in communal and identity conflicts, people cannot compromise on their fundamental needs. However, they argue that it is possible to *transcend* conflicts if parties can be helped to explore, analyse, question and reframe their positions and interests. Conflict resolution therefore emphasises intervention by skilled but powerless third-parties working unofficially with the parties to foster new thinking and new relationships. They seek to explore what the roots of the conflict really are and to identify creative solutions that the parties may have missed in their commitment to entrenched positions. Conflict resolution is about how parties can move from zero-sum, destructive patterns of conflict to positive-sum constructive outcomes. The aim is to develop "processes of conflict resolution that appear to be acceptable to parties in dispute, and effective in resolving conflict" (Azar and Burton 1986, 1).

Conflict transformation theorists argue that contemporary conflicts require more than the reframing of positions and the identification of win-win outcomes. The very structure of parties and relationships may be embedded in a pattern of conflictual relationships that extend beyond the particular site of conflict. Conflict transformation is therefore a process of engaging with and transforming the relationships, interests, discourses and, if necessary, the very constitution of society that supports the continuation of violent conflict. Constructive conflict is seen as a vital agent or catalyst for change. People within the conflict parties, within the society or region affected, and outsiders with relevant human and material resources all have complementary roles to play in the long-term process of peacebuilding. This suggests a comprehensive and wide-ranging approach, emphasising support for groups within the society in conflict rather than for the mediation of outsiders. It also recognizes that conflicts are transformed gradually, through a series of smaller or larger changes as well as specific steps by means of which a variety of actors may play important roles. In the words of Lederach:

> *Conflict transformation must actively envision, include, respect, and promote the human and cultural resources from within a given setting. This involves a new set of lenses through which we do not primarily 'see' the setting and the people in it as the 'problem' and the outsider as the 'answer'. Rather, we understand the long-term goal of transformation as validating and building on people and resources within the setting (Lederach 1995).*

2.2 Contributions to Theories of Conflict Transformation

Theorists of conflict transformation draw on a variety of conceptual building blocks, some recent, some older and some borrowed from other schools. The idea of conflict formation was already present in the work of the European structural theorists who analysed conflict formations (e.g. Senghaas 1973; Krippendorf 1973). Perhaps the most influential work to date has been that of Galtung (brought together in Galtung 1996, 70-126), which offers a rich brew of core concepts.

Conflicts, he suggests, have both life-affirming and life-destroying aspects. They form from contradictions in the structure of society. They then become manifest in attitudes and behaviour. Once formed, conflicts undergo a variety of transformational processes: articulation or dis-articulation, conscientisation or de-conscientisation, complexification or simplification, polarisation or depolarisation, escalation or de-escalation (1996, 90). The incompatibility which arises between parties may be eliminated by transcending the contradiction, by compromise, by deepening or widening the conflict structure, and by associating or dissociating the actors (1996, 116). Galtung, Krippendorf and others also emphasise the relationship between conflicts and larger conflicts embedded in the structure of world society and the world economy.

Curle's work (1971) built on Galtung's approach. He traces how asymmetric relationships can be transformed, through a shift from unbalanced to balanced relationships achieved through a process of conscientisation, confrontation, negotiation and development. Lederach took up Curle's ideas, as did Francis who develops them in her contribution to this handbook. Contributions from theorists on non-violence have also been important (Sharp 1973; Wehr, Burgess and Burgess 1994; Clark 2000). A non-violent campaign can transform conflict by detaching the props sustaining it such as groups resisting land reform and harnessing them to support social alternatives (International Alert 1996, 22, 31-33).

Azar's work (1990) on protracted social conflicts has also had an important influence on conflict transformation theory, by offering an explanation for the protracted quality of contemporary conflicts. He suggests an approach that is more appropriately suited to the characteristics of contemporary conflicts in fragile states. His work concentrates on the genesis and maintenance of protracted conflicts. By developing his theory, it can also be used as a theory of conflict transformation.

Figure 1 is drawn from Azar's model of protracted social conflict. It is extended here to demonstrate that, with some modification, Azar's model can be used to capture both the formation and the transformation (or deformation) of this type of conflict.

Reading the diagram from left to right, as in Azar's book, one can trace the formation of a protracted conflict. It arises from the historical context, and from the denial of basic human needs of access, identity and security, as well as through the roles played by the state, international political and economic linkages and the military in politics. If the state and communal groups choose suppression and violent rebellion as their strategies, a conflict may then become destructive. Reading from right back to left, destructive conflict then results in a more dependent and exploitative pattern of development, a distorted pattern of governance and a militarised form of politics. This leads to the further denial of basic needs. The result is a protracted cycle of institutional deformation and destructive conflict.

On the other hand, if there is sufficient capacity in governance and society, if politics are not too militarised, and if the international environment is supportive, states may instead choose accommodation, and communal groups may choose political forms of confrontation. This can lead to a pattern of constructive conflict that in turn promotes legitimate decision-making capacity, strengthens autonomous development and sustains civil rather than military politics. All these are conducive to the meeting of basic needs. The model goes beyond simple

Figure 1: Transformation of Protracted Social Conflicts (adapted from Azar 1990)

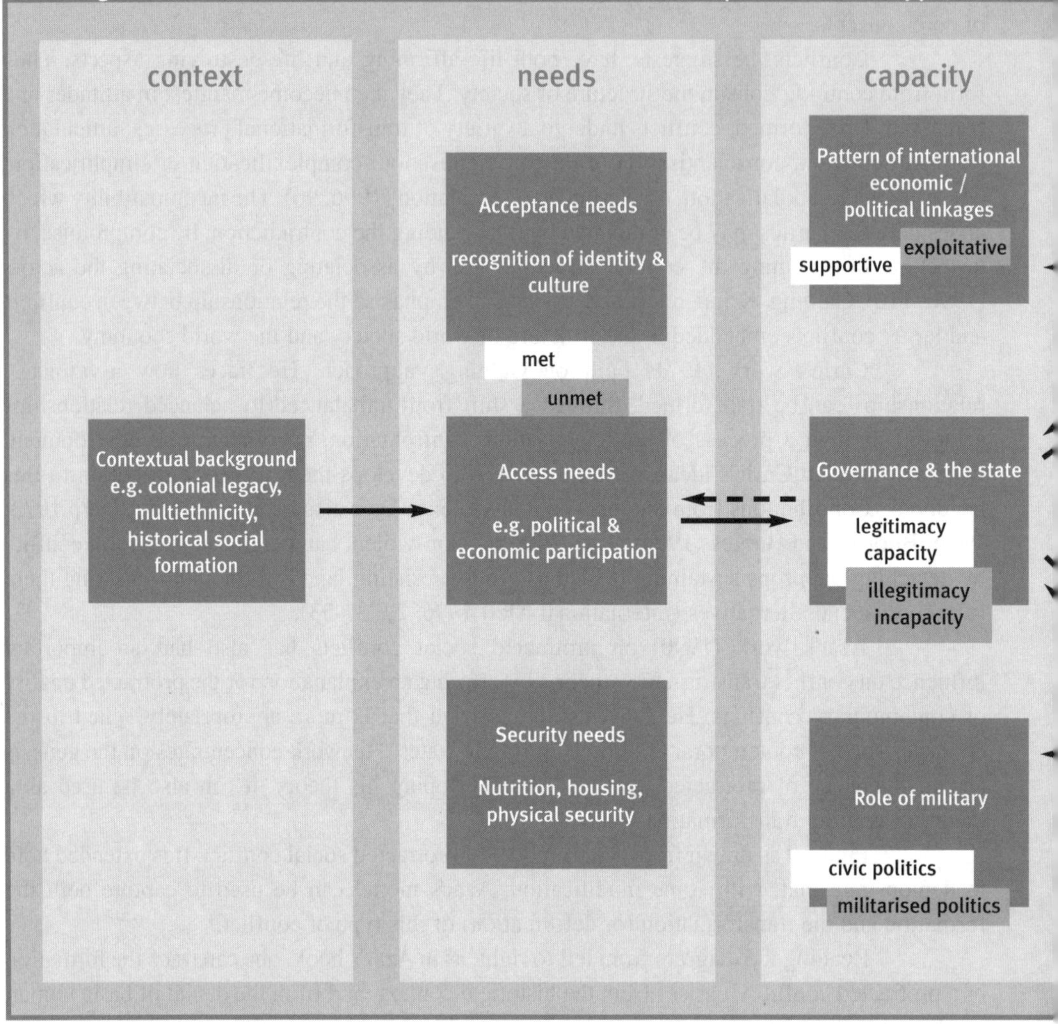

structural or behavioural explanations and suggests how patterns of conflict interact with the satisfaction of human needs, the adequacy of political and economic institutions and the choices made by political actors. It also suggests how different options can lead to benign or malignant spirals of conflict.

Vayrynen argues for a conflict theory based on the idea of transformation rather than settlement, stressing that it is important to understand how conflicts are transformed in dynamic terms:

> *The bulk of conflict theory regards the issues, actors and interests as given and on that basis makes efforts to find a solution to mitigate or eliminate contradictions between them. Yet the issues, actors and interests change over time as a consequence of the social, economic and political dynamics of societies (Vayrynen 1991, 4).*

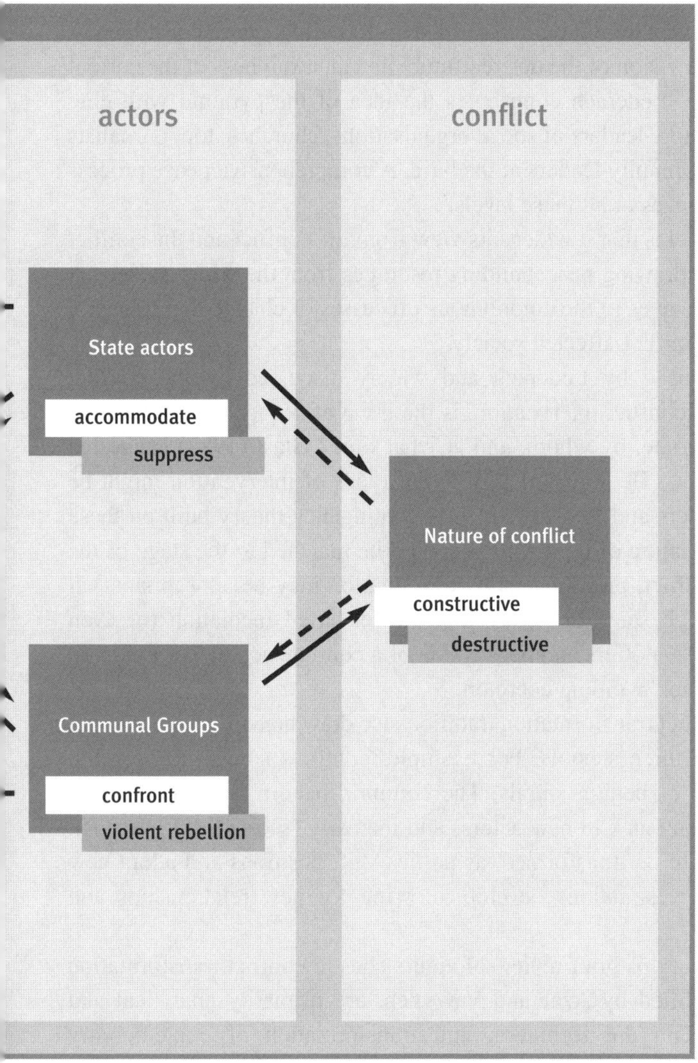

His approach is primarily analytical and theoretical, but is also suggestive of the types of intervention that peacebuilders should be considering (*see* Vayrynen 1991):

- actor transformations – internal changes in parties, or the appearance of new parties;
- issue transformations – altering the agenda of conflict issues;
- rule transformations – changes in the norms or rules governing a conflict;
- structural transformations – the entire structure of relationships and power distribution in the conflict is transformed.

Rupesinghe (1995, 1998) argues for a comprehensive, eclectic approach to conflict transformation that embraces multitrack interventions. He proposes building peace constituencies at the grassroots level and across the parties at the civil society level (where it exists), and also creating peace alliances with any groups able to bring about change, such as business groups, the media and the military. He sees conflict transformation as a broad approach incorporating conflict resolution training and Track I interventions including diplomatic interventions and peacekeeping.

Lederach's work (1997) serves as one of the most comprehensive statements to date of conflict transformation thinking for practitioners. He sees peacebuilding as a long-term transformation of a war system into a peace system, inspired by a quest for the values of peace and justice, truth and mercy. The key dimensions of this process are changes in the personal, structural, relational and cultural aspects of conflict, brought about over different time-periods (short-, mid- and long-term) and affecting different system levels at different times.

Peacebuilding is thus seen as a structure-process. An appropriate strategy (such as networking between mid-level leaders with links to parties across the conflict) is linked to an appropriate time-frame (such as concentrating on mid-term steps to build a peace constituency, while at the same time embracing a vision of the desired future and an awareness of the current crisis). In thinking about structure, Lederach contributes the idea of the pyramid with elite leaders and decision-makers at the top, leaders of social organisations, churches, top journalists in the mid-level and grassroots community leaders at the base. A comprehensive peace process should address complementary changes at all these levels.

One strength of his model is that it widens its view from the conflict and the conflict parties and indicates the scope for drawing peacebuilding resources from the wider society. A weakness is the limited attention it gives to the autonomous processes of change that transpire within the political system of the conflict-affected society.

An important issue, raised by Lederach and widely discussed by the conflict resolution school in the context of conflict intervention, is the issue of sequencing. What type of action or intervention is appropriate, by whom, and at what time? Glasl (1982) suggested nine stages of escalation in conflicts. He argues that different types of intervention might be appropriate at different times. Fishers and Keashly's (1991) contingency theory built on these foundations. Their idea is that the nature of intervention should be matched to the stage of the conflict. At the early stages of conflict, they suggest that facilitation may be appropriate; but when a conflict has reached a high stage of polarisation power-based mediation (or even coercion) is required. Lederach (1997) offers another version of a contingency model based on Curle's (1971) progression of conflict, avoiding coercion.

Authors within the conflict transformation tradition also draw heavily on ideas about conflict dynamics common to all three schools. For example, conflicts sometimes develop strong tendencies towards vicious or benign spirals. The common pattern is for conflict to broaden (suck in new issues), widen (suck in new actors) and intensify (suck in new victims). But it is also possible for conflict to be transformed, as parties shift positions and adopt new goals, new actors emerge and new situations develop allowing for new relationships and changed structures.

It should be evident from this brief review of approaches to conflict transformation theory that some theories, exemplified by Azar and Vayrynen, are primarily analytical and interpretative, attempting to explain the formation and transformation of contemporary conflicts. Others, such as Curle and Lederach, are prescriptive, offering peacebuilders a means to conceptualise the path from conflict towards desired outcomes. Perhaps Galtung's approach comes closest to a synthesis.

2.3 From a Theory of Conflict to a Theory of Conflict-in-Context

As the practice of peacemaking has extended from prevention to post-conflict peacebuilding, and as globalisation exerts an increasing impact on internal conflicts, the scope of conflict transformation theories must correspondingly be extended. On the one hand, they need to be concerned with the factors exacerbating conflict and restraining conflict over a number of different phases (*see* Box 1):

On the other hand, however, these theories must also deal adequately with the interplay of causes and preventors at all the different levels of the international system. One can

Box 1: Factors Exacerbating or Restraining Conflict at Different Phases					
phase / factors	pre-violence	crisis	escalation	protracted	post-settlement
exacerbating	underlying causes	triggers	escalators	deformers	triggers
restraining	deep preventors	light preventors	de- escalators	transformers	peacebuilders

identify five different levels at which contemporary conflicts are caused: the global, regional, societal, conflict party and individual/elite (Miall, Ramsbotham and Woodhouse 1999). Box 2 provides specific examples of causes and preventors of violent conflicts at these levels, using examples from Rwanda.

Box 2: Causes and Preventors of Violent Conflicts at Different Levels		
level	examples of causes	examples of preventors
global	post-colonial legacy	international minority rights
regional	conflict spillover in great lakes	conflict prevention by OSCE
state/society	state capture by ethnic groups	cross-ethnic party voting
conflict party	Hutu hostility towards Tutsi	pragmatic approach of minority
elite/international	Hutu leaders launch genocide	president accepts OSCE advice

Conflict theories, if viewed too narrowly, will be seen to concentrate overly on the conflict party level, focusing on parties, issues, goals and so on to the exclusion of the context within which the conflict is situated as well as of the factors which characterize the self-fuelling of conflicts, e.g. markets and cultures of violence. It is possible, however, to add more representation of the background, for example building on Galtung's simple triangular formulation of conflict. On to 'contradiction', we can build 'context'; on to 'attitudes', 'memory' and on to 'behaviour', 'relations' (*see* Figure 2). This recognizes that the meaning of a conflict depends largely on the context out of which it arises. The attitudes the parties have towards one another are shaped by previous relationships. The behaviour they adopt is not purely reactive but is based on their memory of what has happened in the past, and expectations of what may happen in the future.

The *context* of conflict includes the society in conflict and the wider international and regional level. Within the society, crucial background aspects are culture, governance arrangements, institutions, social roles, norms, the rules and codes in place in a society, and its path of development. For example, in conflicts involving ethnicity, minorities or challenges to state structures, it is the very structure of the state that is at issue. As globalisation proceeds, local conflicts are inevitably influenced by wider economic and political forces. These have tended to strengthen trade investment and technological networks in some areas of the world, but also to marginalise other areas such as Africa and the former Soviet Union. The result is a weakening of states and economies in these areas and, in some cases, the creation of a real crisis of the state. Internal conflicts are increasingly associated with fragile states and mal-adaptive reactions to the impact of globalisation.

Relationships involve the whole fabric of interaction within the society in which the conflict takes place as well as beyond to other societies. As Lederach (1997) argues, these relational aspects of conflict are crucial. Poor relationships between groups are all too often a trigger for conflict, and remain a critical hindrance to peacebuilding efforts after the violence is over.

Figure 2: Expanding the Conflict Triangle: Transformers and Triggers of Conflict at Different System Levels

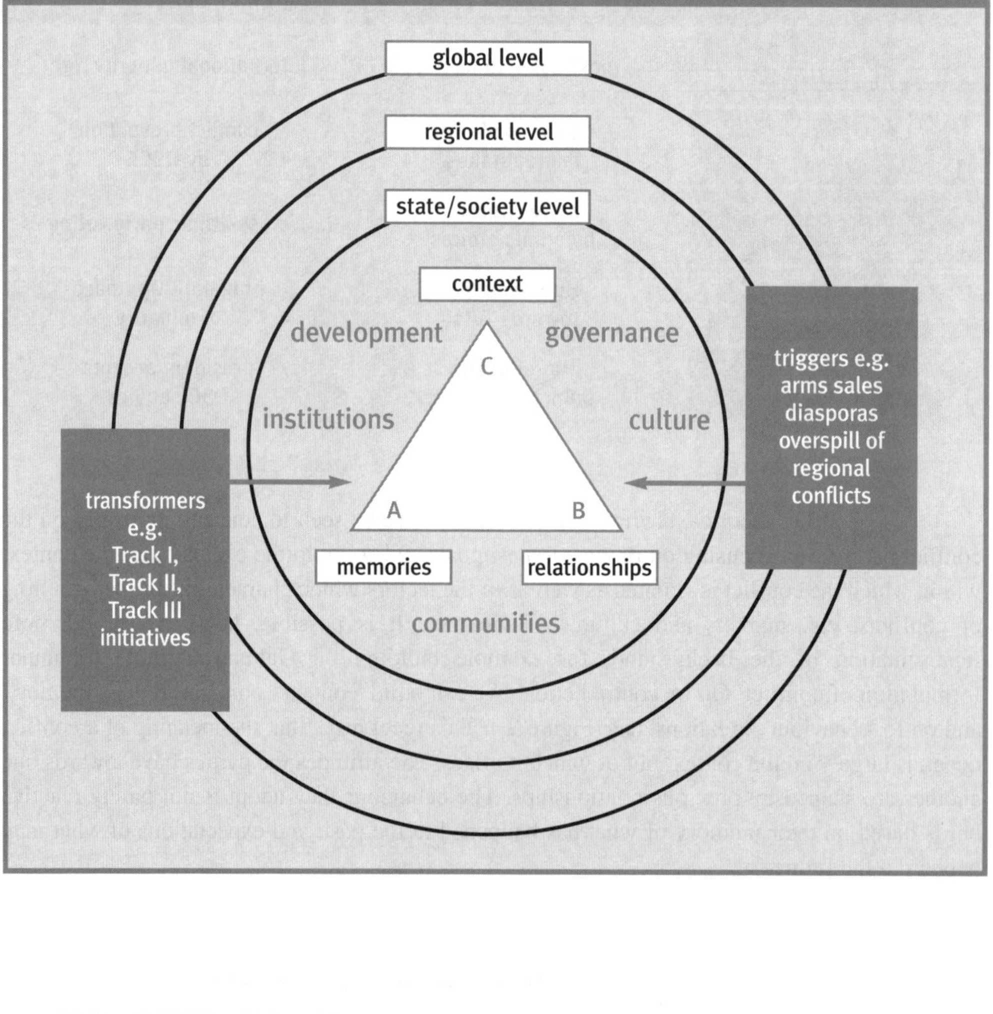

Memories are part of each party's socially constructed understanding of the situation, shaped by culture and learning, and discourse and belief. The way groups remember and construct their past is often central to the mobilization for conflict, and thus a crucial matter to address in reconciliation and cultural traditions work.

Context, relationships and memories are all part of the tissue connecting the contradictions, attitudes and behaviours in the conflict formations, within the wider background in space and time.

This template enables a better understanding of the types of transformation that take place. Building on Vayrynen's approach, Box 3 illustrates five types of transformation, or transformers.

Context transformations refer to changes in the context of conflict that may radically alter each party's perception of the conflict situation, as well as their motives. The impact of the end of the Cold War on regional conflicts is a dramatic example. A somewhat less far-reaching instance might be the proposed change in the rules of the diamond trade to outlaw 'conflict diamonds', that could well have a significant impact on the conflicts in Sierra Leone and Angola. The establishment of the World Diamond Council (www.worlddiamondcouncil.com) is a promising start but it is, as yet, too early to see if it will have a significant impact.

Structural transformations refer to changes in the basic structure of the conflict, that is to the set of actors, their issues, incompatible goals and relationships, or to the society, economy or state within which the conflict is embedded. Asymmetric conflicts cannot be transformed, for instance, without changing the unbalanced and contested relationships that lie at their roots. While such changes will take place only gradually, internal and external actors can support them along the way. For example Steve Biko's 'Black Consciousness' movement raised awareness of the power of the poor people in the townships in South Africa, and the Anti-Apartheid Movement helped to press the case for dis-investment by foreign-owned businesses well before the end of the apartheid regime. Many recent conflicts in West Africa have demonstrated the futility in attempting conflict transformation without addressing the economic interests that fuel wars.

Actor transformations include decisions on the part of actors to change their goals or alter their general approach to conflict. This would include decisions to seek peace or to initiate a peace process. They also include changes of leadership, often crucial to the securing of transformation in conflicts. Also included are changes in the situation of the public constituencies and supporters of the respective political leaders. This opens a number of lines for specific conflict transformation work, as those who work within a party to bring about change in that party's position often prove to be crucial actors in the peace process, and may have more influence than external Track I and Track II actors.

Issue transformations concern the reformulations of positions that parties take on key issues at the heart of the conflict as well as the way in which parties redefine or reframe those positions in order to reach compromises or resolutions. A good example of an issue transformation was the decision by the Unionist Party in Northern Ireland to accept a de-linking of the decommissioning issue from the question of the convocation of the Northern Ireland Assembly. Making 'progress' on issues in conflict is often tortuously slow and painfully subject to reversals, and of course what counts as progress is itself contentious.

Box 3: Transformers of Conflict	
type	examples
1. context transformations	change in the international or regional environment
2. structure transformations	change from asymmetric to symmetric relations change in power structures changes of markets of violence
3. actor transformations	changes of leadership changes of goals intra-party change change in party's constituencies changing actors
4. issue transformations	transcendence of contested issues constructive compromise changing issues de-linking or re-linking issues
5. personal/elite transformations	changes of perspective changes of heart changes of will gestures of conciliation

Personal changes of heart or mind within individual leaders or small groups with decision-making power at critical moments may be crucial. Some external intervenors try to reach these leaders and bring about this personal change directly (Curle 1987; Mitchell 2000). Conciliatory gestures by leaders, which express personal changes, would play an important role in this context.

These five types of transformation can be readily related to the levels of conflict causation or prevention identified above. Context transformations usually occur within the global or regional setting. Structural transformations usually happen at the state/society level. Actor and issue transformations take place at the conflict party and elite levels. Personal transformations demand competencies on the individual level.

The transformation types can also be connected to the different parts of conflict formation, whether this is seen in Azar's terms (*see* Figure 1) or in Galtung's (*see* Figure 2). Context, structural and issue transformations all affect the context and contradictions at the heart of the conflict. Actor and personal transformations particularly affect attitudes and memory, behaviour and relationships. These in turn, of course, are interrelated.

Finally, these different types of transformation further relate to the phases of conflicts and the timing of intervention. Context and structural changes tend to take place over a longer time-scale, and affect the setting of the conflict; the other types of transformations occur more rapidly and sequentially, as part of the dynamics of the conflict. The sequencing of changes varies with each peace process depending on the logic of the situation (*see* Box 4 for the Northern

Ireland case). Only in the very simplest conflicts is conflict transformation likely to be a rapid or immediate process. More typically, it is slow and tortuous with turning points usually followed by sticking points. This makes the evaluation of individual measures extremely difficult.

Box 4: Transformers of the Northern Ireland Conflict

As one of the most intensively managed conflicts, as well as one of the more intractable conflicts of the twentieth century, Northern Ireland offers many lessons for conflict transformation. We can find evidence of all five levels of transformation at different points. The *context* of the conflict was altered by long-term changes in the British and Irish societies, the development of the EU and the end of the Cold War. The conflict *structure* changed as the pan-Nationalist coalition developed sufficient alliances and confidence to balance the hitherto asymmetric relationships between the parties. *Actor transformations* included changes of government in Britain, the fundamental shift in thinking within the Sinn Féin leadership, and division and change among the Unionists. *Issue transformations* included the mutual agreements reached in the Good Friday agreement to reconcile the legitimacy of the two cultural traditions and establish institutions which reinforce both the Irish and British dimensions of governance. All this could not have taken place without significant changes of mind at the *individual and elite level*. Even so, conflict remains and continues, as each marching season reinvokes the old atmosphere of division and fear. Northern Ireland offers a striking example of the complementarity of approaches on different tracks and of the interrelationship between 'structural' and 'cultural' approaches (Bloomfield 1997). For example, the patient work of the Community Relations Council on the ground built sufficient credibility to enable the Council to facilitate quiet dialogue with young politicians (Fitzduff 1999). We have not yet gained a clear understanding of the role that 'civil society' played in this peace process and in the longer term process of healing the divisions between the communities. Cochrane and Dunn (2002) provides an in-depth assessment.

The dynamics of conflict and conflict transformation are also related to the social and international capacity for handling conflicts. In general, this capacity is likely to be higher in societies with a past tradition of handling change peacefully, in which institutions are legitimate and rules and norms are accepted. Correspondingly, it may be threatened and undermined in times of extreme conflict and war. The modified version of Azar's theory, presented in Figure 1, suggests the relationship between conflict dynamics and conflict handling capacity in divided societies.

Constructive conflict handling reinforces the society's confidence in its civic institutions, culture and capacity to manage conflict peacefully. Further it not only transforms relationships in conflict, it also strengthens the society's system of governance and capacity for conflict handling and peaceful change.

Destructive conflict, on the other hand, results in an intensification of damage to the participants in conflicts and the bystanders. It further destroys their cooperative capacities, including the system of governance, the economic order and the social relationships of the society, in some cases even the state. In protracted conflicts, all the institutions of society become thoroughly deformed.

These rather broad theoretical considerations suggest a framework through which we can analyse and evaluate conflict transformation practices, and consider the gaps and weaknesses in the international capacity for handling conflict.

3. Practices of Conflict Resolution

3.1 Actors of Conflict Transformation

Conflict transformation usually involves a broad range of actors, who make use of a wide repertoire of practices. These can, however, be categorised into four main groups of actors, who shape the development of contemporary practice:

- states and inter-governmental organisations;
- development and humanitarian organisations;
- international NGOs concerned with conflict prevention and transformation;
- parties to the conflict and other relevant groups within the affected societies.

I will briefly discuss some of the characteristic practices of each group, before considering the issues that arise when they come together.

Track I practitioners, states and international organisations, are among the most influential of all the actors as their practice impinges most directly and powerfully on the conflict parties, and the positive and negative consequences of their interventions are fully in the public eye. The 1990s began with a hopeful phase in which the UN set out to implement the expanded conception of peacemaking envisioned in Boutros Boutros-Ghali's *Agenda for Peace*, with notable peacebuilding operations in areas with recent peace settlements, including Cambodia, Namibia, Angola, Mozambique and El Salvador.

A general model for UN peacebuilding has emerged from these cases. It calls for military measures to secure the demobilization, disarmament and cantonment of opposing forces; constitutional measures to implement elections and establish a transitional government; governance measures to support civilian government and infrastructure, including the training and, if necessary, supervision of local police; human rights measures; return of refugees; and restoration of the war-damaged infrastructure. At first, this model appeared to have striking successes, and in some cases such as Namibia and Mozambique a peaceful transformation from war was indeed achieved. In others, however, such as Angola and Cambodia, violent conflict resumed. The UN and the major states continue to learn from these operations and are extending their peacebuilding operations, for example in Bosnia and Kosovo. While international interventions have in these cases seem to have halted ethnic wars, the extent of transformation of the underlying conflict remains limited. Ethno-nationalist leaderships remain and settlements based on the realities of ethnic divisions in the war have preserved these divisions in the peace.

These high-profile cases, of course, involved imposed settlements, achieved after considerable vacillation on the part of a divided international community. More impressive have been the cases in which conflicts were prevented even before they became violent, and where deep or structural and light or operational conflict prevention have worked together. Here, real changes in the context of the conflict and in the structure of the societies have resulted in some impressive transformations.

In the case of Estonia, for example, a potential ethnic conflict was averted in part through the well-known interventions of the OSCE High Commissioner on National Minorities, supported by the EU and Scandinavian governments. In part, the transformed economic context served to change the incentives for the Russian-speaking community. Moreover an additional key factor was the introduction of an electoral system that created incentives for cross-ethnic voting, thus resulting in a transition from ethnic politics to a politics of economic and regional interest groups. Non-Estonian politicians were included in the party lists of Estonian parties, and the Estonian Centre Party won wide support from Russian-speakers as a vehicle for promoting their interests. This is a particularly striking success for the conflict management and ethnic accommodation approaches, made possible by the transformation of the Estonian context after 1991.

The second type of actors are development and humanitarian agencies. In the 1980s and 1990s, these agencies were increasingly drawn into the costly business of rebuilding war-torn societies, and were responding to the acute damage to development, which had resulted from armed conflicts, by targeting development programmes specifically towards peacebuilding. In some cases, their activities supported UN peacebuilding operations, for example in Mozambique where donors helped to keep the elections on schedule and supported the transformation of RENAMO into a political party. In other cases, development aid can be channelled to directly mitigate conflict, as when donors supported refugees in neglected parts of Somalia with the intention of reducing discontent in a politically unstable area. Programmes to support the re-integration of child soldiers or the rehabilitation of agricultural land are further examples of development tasks that can readily have a peacebuilding component. Capacity-building and support for indigenous conflict handling capacity are also crucial. A notable example of such work is Oxfam's conflict transformation work in Northern Kenya (*see* Box 5).

Development aid can, of course, have unintended as well as intended consequences; in some circumstances, aid is captured by the parties to conflict and then sustains the fighting. Current work on establishing a framework of indicators for assessing the impact of development projects on conflicts goes some way towards meeting the need for a framework for better evaluation (*see* contributions of Mark Hoffman and Mary Anderson in this volume). Such a framework of indicators should in turn be linked to a framework for understanding the overall transformation of the conflict, such as the one offered above.

Although development agencies are increasingly important and influential in this field, they generally see their role as principally to support and encourage the work of others, rather than to take prime responsibility for transforming particular conflicts (this role is still seen as a new and untested function). Most of the conflict transformation work has therefore been left to NGOs.

Box 5: Conflict Transformation Work in Northern Kenya

In Northern Kenya, the growing pressure on arid land and the introduction of a Kalashnikov culture into traditional cattle-raiding has led to an increase in both the extent and intensity of conflicts between nomadic pastoral communities, as well as between pastoralists and agriculturalists. Not only historical rivals such as the Turkana and Pokot or Somali and Borana, but also communities which coexisted peacefully in the 1980s are now engulfed in war. The militarisation of these pastoralist communities is severely affecting the security of Kenya and the neighbouring territories, and damaging the affected communities. In response, Oxfam facilitated peace talks relying on local elders in the Baragoi Pastoral Project of 1997. A crucial aspect of Oxfam's ongoing work in the area is an effort to appreciate the codes of honour and conduct of these peoples and their understanding of conflict, through lexical and ethnographic analysis (Kona 1999). In this vein, a local committee of women from the affected communities set up the Wajir Peace and Development Committee, a network of 27 governmental organisations and NGOs in north-eastern Kenya. This group conducts training and capacity-building, and contributed to a cease-fire in 1993 and continuing efforts to prevent and resolve local conflicts in the region.

(European Platform for Conflict Prevention 1999a, 152; 1999b, 243-47)

Of all the groups of practitioners discussed here, it is probably the NGOs who have paid most attention to theories of conflict transformation. Following Lederach, NGO practitioners advocate a sustained level of engagement over a longer time-period. They seek an in-depth understanding of the roots of conflict, working closely with people both within and outside the conflict parties. They seek to open a space for dialogue, sustain local or national conferences and workshops on paths towards peace, identify opportunities for development and engage in peacebuilding, relationship-building and institution-building over the longer term.

The methods and tools employed by Track II actors include supporting and sustaining local groups and social movements, building peace constituencies, strengthening capacity, empowering key actors, organisational development and networking and training. A notable example of this kind of work is the programme of the London-based NGO Conciliation Resources (CR) in Fiji, undertaken in coalition with local actors. CR supported the Citizens' Constitutional Forum in Fiji, an organisation which made a significant contribution to the new constitutional settlement in 1996 with the introduction of the alternative-vote system and power-sharing (Conciliation Resources 2000). Unfortunately, the coup in Fiji in May 2000 and the return to a narrowly-based government indicates only too clearly the setbacks confronted by this kind of work.

One key requirement for this work is good conflict analysis (*see* Box 6), which is best developed in conjunction with groups in conflict. Tracking the changing dynamics of a conflict over time is clearly one of the areas in which practice must draw on appropriately developed theory.

Box 6: Conflict Analysis

The original conflict mapping guide of Wehr (1979) is still of value. More recent guides can be found in Miall, Ramsbotham and Woodhouse (1999, 92-3), Bloomfield and Reilly (1998, 41-43) and Leonhardt (2000). The basic technique is to take a snapshot of the conflict, identifying key actors, stakeholders, issues and relationships, and then identify the actors, third-parties or potential peace alliances capable of bringing about change. More sophisticated conflict tracking relies on indicators of conflict which are also used for early warning purposes and impact assessment (Schmid 1997; Jongmaan 2000; *see* contribution of Paffenholz in this volume).

Finally, and most importantly, the local actors themselves have the greatest responsibility, and the greatest opportunity, for transforming their own conflicts. There are cases of 'embedded third-parties' who emerge out of conflict parties and play a significant role in opening channels of dialogue and opening political space – such as John Hume in Northern Ireland; cases of groups within political parties who can bring about an actor transformation such as the shift towards political forms of struggle in Sinn Féin; and civil society actors and local NGOs who often have an enormous influence on bridge-building between political parties and local communities exemplified by the Clonard monastery in Northern Ireland, and the Corrymeela Community working on respect for cultural traditions thereby addressing the problems of historical memories and reconciliation. The impact of this peacebuilding on the macro level of the conflict is hard to evaluate; but on a small scale, the personal and group transformations that it can achieve are keenly felt.

3.2 Coordination and Multi-Track Diplomacy

A particular challenge for conflict transformation work is the question of how best to work effectively with interventions occurring at other tracks. At times, very effective collaboration takes place, for example in the case of Macedonia (*see* Box 7).

All too often, however, internal and external actors in the various tracks are at cross-purposes. This is not surprising, given the clash between paradigms. Actions on one track can sometimes wreck efforts on another. For example, it may be difficult for an organisation that strives for non-violent resolution of conflicts to cooperate with a government that relies on coercive methods to pressure the local protagonists to accept a settlement. Conversely, foreign ministries are not usually enthusiastic about the intrusion of NGOs into diplomacy.

Practitioners of conflict transformation activities at the non-state level must pursue their aims with sensitivity to both the culture of the conflict area and the goals and constraints of other actors. They must always remember that they may not be able to influence other actors whose actions will in turn affect their own work. Moreover, their task may broaden when conflict transformation involves changing the policies of Track I bodies outside the conflict area. For example, it is increasingly recognized that bodies like the World Bank can have a significant impact on conflicts. Campaigns to influence their policies have thus become a regular part of the wider task of conflict transformation.

Box 7: Cooperative Multi-Track Diplomacy in Macedonia

Macedonia offers a case in which the various initiatives of different tracks appear to have been genuinely complementary. For example, the OSCE High Commissioner on National Minorities (external Track I) together with the Open Society Institute in Skopje (internal Track III) proposed several compromise solutions on the university issue. The International Conference on the Former Yugoslavia (Track I) brokered a compromise between Macedonia and the ethnic Serbs, while Mr. Holbrooke and the US government (Track I) clinched the agreement between Greece and Macedonia which ended the blockade. The NGO Search for Common Ground (external Track III) developed a long-term programme aiming to meet the common needs of both communities at the grassroots level, particularly by promoting 'inclusive journalism', respect for the common cultural legacy and the monuments of both communities, and also bicommunal efforts to protect the environment (Ackermann 2000). Tensions between the two communities remain sharp and have been further exacerbated by the effects of the war in Kosovo. Indeed the fighting in May/June 2000 threatened to expand into civil war. Underlying disagreements over the acceptance of the identity and status of the groups have not been resolved. Nevertheless, an inter-ethnic coalition is still intact in Parliament (Track 1) – this is probably the most vital factor in restraining violent conflict. Although at the time of writing these tensions could still overwhelm Macedonia, internal and external actors have so far worked together effectively to create a significant capacity, at least at the top-level, for accommodating differences.

3.3 Assessing the Impact of Practice

What is the overall impact of these kinds of practice on conflict? It is still difficult to say. There are reports of significant achievements in building peace constituencies for example in Lederach's work (1997). Compilations of recent work include some impressive stories of apparent successes (European Platform for Conflict Prevention 1999a,b). Only recently, however, some comparative research studies have started to identify key variables of impact assessment more systematically such as *Reflecting on Peace Practice (RPP)* and *Lessons Learned in Conflict Interventions* by the European Platform for Conflict Prevention and Transformation. Bercovitch's research (1996) suggests that conflict management approaches, including the use of power resources, are the most effective at delivering settlements. On the other hand, these settlements often fail to genuinely transform the conflict, and the long-term work necessary to build relationships and capacity may be more important than reaching fragile short-term political settlements.

The overall evidence of the ending of ethnic conflicts is particularly sobering. In a study of peacefully settled conflicts in Europe, the Middle East and Africa since 1945 (Pfetsch and Roloff 2000) the authors found only 13 out of 121 cases of conflicts over ethnicity, religion or regional autonomy that were resolved through peaceful negotiation (these include the Aland Islands, Northern Epirus, the Saar and South Tyrol). 51 remain undecided, 8 were resolved by the threat of force or other forms of coercion, and 49 by violence. The great majority of the peaceful cases were republics of the former Soviet Union which peacefully broke away in 1991. Indeed, despite the violent conflicts in Chechnya, Tajikistan, Nagorno-Karabakh and elsewhere, the number of ethnic conflicts which appear to have been transformed without violence in the former Soviet Union is startling.

A useful line of work is to identify these peaceful cases and ascertain the reasons why violence has been avoided, and how ethnic and other internal conflicts have been managed or addressed. But conflict ending measured by the end of violence is too final and crude an indicator on which to base the planning and assessment of conflict transformation initiatives. For this, a more finely-grained, differentiated approach is needed and indicators such as those developed in work on Peace and Conflict Impact Assessment (PCIA) systems offer one such approach (*see* contribution of Hoffman in this volume). If conflict transformation can be broken down into a sequence of changes in the conflict structure, the parties' goals and into issues over time, as suggested in the first part of this paper, it may become more feasible to relate interventions to particular transformations in the conflict.

The impact of endeavours for conflict transformation should not only be seen as an issue which affects the parties in conflict. It is also of direct relevance for all the individuals involved. The challenges, difficulties, hardships, setbacks and tenacity inherent in all conflict transformation mean that we must also 'transform the transformers'. We must include this group as we focus on activities designed to enhance peace education, to improve training programmes and to create opportunities for self-reflection and spirituality (*see* Box 8).

Box 8: Transforming the Transformers – Smiling as a Method

One of the world's most notable transformers of conflict uses a method that does not usually appear in books about conflict and is completely absent from conflict theories. It is, however, a method that works. The method is to smile. "Breathing in, I calm my mind and body. Breathing out, I smile. This is the present moment. This is the only moment." Thich Nhat Hanh is a Vietnamese Buddhist monk, poet and peace activist. He is not the only exponent of the smiling approach to conflict transformation. The Dalai Lama, Adam Curle and Nelson Mandela are all instinctive smilers. Thich Nhat Hanh not only smiles wonderfully, he also offers a comprehensive guide to the theory and practice of smiling, rooted in traditional wisdom and experience (Nhat Hanh 1987). "If we are peaceful, if we are happy we can smile and blossom like a flower and everyone in our family in our entire society will benefit from our peace." The idea of smiling as an approach to conflict transformation is based on the theory of interdependent co-origination. The practice of smiling is part of the practice of engaged mindfulness and reminds us that the conflict transformer must also take responsibility for transforming him- or herself in the process. The theory of interdependent co-origination states that everything has an influence on everything else. Everything inter-is with everything else. A flower is partly a flower, but it also has the sun and the rain and the earth inside it. The flower is made up of non-flower elements. Similarly, our self is made up of non-self elements. We can touch that of ourselves in the other and be touched by that of the other in ourselves. According to Buddhist psychology, we have a mental consciousness and a storehouse consciousness. Seeds develop in the storehouse consciousness and when they come to occupy our mental consciousness, we water them and they grow. In conflict we water the seed of anger until the anger within our storehouse consciousness grows very strong. It can then govern our thoughts and behaviour. But this is not inevitable. The practice of engaged mindfulness can transform anger, pain, and hate into compassion, joy and love. Conflict transformation, like mindfulness, tends and waters seeds, without knowing exactly how they will grow. Memory, relationships and conflicts are seeds in the collective storehouse consciousness. Transforming collective conflicts requires a deep awareness of ourselves and our interbeing with others.

4. Conclusion

This paper has argued that a distinctive school of conflict transformation theory and practice has developed over the past decade. This new approach can be differentiated from conflict management and conflict resolution, although all three schools rely on a shared tradition of thinking about conflict and intervention.

Conflict transformation is a comprehensive approach, addressing a range of dimensions (micro- to macro- issues, local to global levels, grassroots to elite actors, short-term to long-term timescales). It aims to develop capacity and to support structural change, rather than to facilitate outcomes or deliver settlements. It seeks to engage with conflict at the pre-violence and post-violence phases, and with the causes and consequences of violent conflict, which usually extend beyond the site of fighting.

This paper has argued that the ambitious prescriptive theories need to be better integrated with the incremental analytical approach. At the same time, the analytical theories must be extended in time-scale and scope. The paper proposed expanding conflict theory to include conflict-in-context, and suggested a theoretically informed framework for evaluation.

A number of questions and gaps in the theory remain. We still lack sufficiently precise dynamic theories to adequately capture the emergent properties of conflict, including the formation of new actors and new issues. Most theories concentrate either on the causes and development of conflict or on the creation and sustenance of a peacebuilding capacity, and fail to sufficiently integrate an understanding of how the preventors and causes of conflict interact. There has been a somewhat uncritical willingness to embrace multi-track diplomacy, without an adequate conceptualisation of how activity in the various tracks can fit together. We still have an incomplete understanding of the impact of conflict transformation activities on conflict, which makes them difficult to evaluate.

As the task of conflict transformation broadens, it may seem even more daunting. Any one practitioner or theorist can tackle only a part of this enormous field. All we can to is, to undertake a piece of work in good faith and do it well is all we can do. We plant seeds, and trust that interdependent co-origination will take care of the rest.

5. Reference and Further Reading

Ackermann, A. 2000. *Making Peace Prevail: Preventing Violent Conflict in Macedonia*, Syracuse: Syracuse University Press.

Anderson, M. 1999. *Do No Harm: How Aid Can Support Peace – or War*, Boulder: Lynne Rienner.

Axelrod, R. 1984. *The Evolution of Cooperation*, New York: Basic Books.

Azar, E. 1990. *The Management of Protracted Social Conflict*, Aldershot: Dartmouth.

Azar, E. and John W. Burton, 1986. *International Conflict Resolution: Theory and Practice*, Boulder: Lynne Rienner and Wheatsheaf.

Bailey, S. 1993. *Peace is a Process*, Quaker Home Service and Woodbrooke College for the Swarthmore Lecture Committee.

Bercovitch, J. (ed.) 1996. *Resolving International Conflicts: The Theory and Practice of Mediation*, Boulder: Lynne Rienner.

Bloomfield, D. 1997. *Peacemaking strategies in Northern Ireland: Building Complementarity in Conflict Management Theory*, Basingstoke: Macmillan.

Bloomfield, D. and Ben Reilly 1998. "The Changing Nature of Conflict and Conflict Management," *in* Peter Harris and Ben Reilly (eds.), op. cit.

Burton, J. 1987. *Resolving deep-rooted conflict: a handbook,* Lanham, Maryland: University Press of America.

Burton, J. and F. Dukes (eds.) 1990. *Conflict: Practices in Management, Settlement and Resolution,* vol 4 of the Conflict Series, London: Macmillan.

Carnegie Commission on Preventing Deadly Conflict 1997. *Preventing Deadly Conflict,* Washington DC: Carnegie Corporation of New York.

Clark, H. 2000. *Civil Resistance in Kosovo*, London: Pluto.

Cochrane, F. and Seamus Dunn 2002. *People Power: The Role of the Voluntary and Community Sector in the Northern Ireland Conflict*, Cork: Cork University Press.

Conciliation Resources 2000. *Annual Report 1999*, London: Conciliation Resources (see http://www.c-r.org)

Coogan, T. 1995. *The Troubles: Ireland's Ordeal 1966-1995 and the search for peace*, London: Hutchinson.

Corbin, J. 1994. *Gaza First: the Secret Norway Channel to Peace between Israel and the PLO*, London: Bloomsbury.

Curle, A. 1971. *Making Peace*, London: Tavistock.

Curle, A. 1987. *In the middle: non-official mediation in violent situations*, New York: Berg.

Curle, A. 1996. *Another Way: Positive Responses to Violence*. Oxford: John Carpenter.

De Reuck, A. 1984. "The logic of conflict: its origin, development and resolution," in *Conflict in World Society*, ed. M. Banks, Brighton: Harvester.

Duffield, M. 1997. "Evaluating conflict resolution," in Serbe G, Macrae J. and L Wohlgemuth, *NGOs in Conflict – An Evaluation of International Alert*, Fantoft-Bergen, Norway: Christian Michelsen Institute, 79-112.

European Platform for Conflict Prevention 1999a. *Searching for Peace in Africa: An Overview of Conflict Prevention and Management Activities*. Utrecht: European Centre for Conflict Prevention.

European Platform for Conflict Prevention 1999b. *People Building Peace*, Utrecht: European Centre for Conflict Prevention.

Fisher, R. and Loreleigh Keashly 1991. "The potential complementarity of mediation and consultation within a contingency model of third-party intervention," *Journal of Peace Research*, Vol 28, No. 1, 29-42.

Fitzduff, M. 1999. "Changing History - Peacebuilding in Northern Ireland," in European Centre for Conflict Prevention, *People Building Peace*, Utrecht: European Centre for Conflict Prevention.

Galtung, J. 1969. "Conflict as a way of life," *in* H. Freeman, Progress in Mental Health, London: J. & A. Churchill.

Galtung, J. 1996. *Peace by Peaceful Means*, London: Sage.

Galtung, J. and Carl G. Jacobsen 2000. *Searching for Peace*, London: Pluto.

Glasl, F. 1982. "The Process of Conflict Escalation and Roles of Third-parties," in G.B.Bomers and R.B. Peterson (eds.), *Conflict Management and Industrial Relations*, Boston, The Hague, London: Kluwer Nijhoff.

Harris P. and Ben Reilly (eds.) 1998. *Democracy and Deep-rooted conflict*, Stockholm: Institute for Democracy and Electoral Assistance (IDEA).

Hume, C. 1994. *Ending Mozambique's War*, Washington: United States Institute of Peace.

International Alert 1996. *Resource Pack for Conflict Transformation*, London: International Alert.

Jabri, V. 1996. *Discourses on Violence: Conflict Analysis Reconsidered*, Manchester: Manchester University Press.

Joongman, A. 2000. "Mapping Dimensions of Contemporary Conflicts and Human Rights Violations," *World Conflicts and Human Rights MAP 2000*. PIOOM, Leiden: Leiden University.

Kona, Epokhorr S.1999. *A framework for cross-cultural conflict resolution theory: Prospects for Cultural Contributions from Africa*, Richardson Institute, Lancaster University: Unpublished thesis.

Kriesberg, L. 1998. *Constructive Conflicts: From Escalation to Resolution*. Lanham: Rowman and Littlefield.

Krippendorf, E. 1973. "Peace Research and the Industrial Revolution", *Journal of Peace Research*, Vol 10, 185-201.

Lederach, J.P. 1995. *Preparing for Peace: Conflict Transformation Across Cultures*, New York: Syracuse University Press.

Lederach, J. P. 1997. *Building Peace: Sustainable Reconciliation in Divided Societies*, Washington, D.C.: United States Institute of Peace Press.

Leonhardt, M. 2000. *Conflict Impact Assessment of EU Development Cooperation with ACP Countries: A review of literature and practice*, London: International Alert/Saferworld.

Miall, H., Oliver Ramsbotham, and Tom Wodhouse 1999. *Contemporary Conflict Resolution*, Cambridge: Polity.

Mitchell, C. R. 1981. *The structure of international conflict*. London, Macmillan.

Mitchell, C. R. 2000. *Gestures of Conciliation: Factors Contributing to Successful Olive-Branches*, Basingstoke: Macmillan.

Nhat Hanh, T. 1967. *Lotus in A Sea of Fire*, New York: Fellowship of Reconciliation.

Nhat Hanh, T. 1987. *Being Peace*, Berkeley, CA: Parallax Press.

Pfetsch, F. and Christoph Rohloff 2000. *National and International Conflicts 1945-1995*, London: Routledge.

Phuong, C. N. 1991. "Compassionate Action in the Midst of War," *Karuna*, 11 (Spring).

Ramsbotham, O. and Woodhouse, Tom 1996. *Humanitarian Intervention in Contemporary Conflict*, Cambridge: Polity.

Rapoport, A. 1989. *The Origins of Violence*, New York: Paragon House.

Reychler, L. and Thania Paffenholz 2001. *Peacebuilding: A field guide*, London and Boulder: Lynne Rienner.

Ruane, J and J. Todd, 1996, *The Dynamics of Conflict in Northern Ireland*, Cambridge: Cambridge University Press.

Rupesinghe, K. (ed.) 1995. *Conflict Transformation*, London: Macmillan.

Rupesinghe, K. 1998. *Civil Wars, Civil Peace*, London: Pluto.

Schmid, A. 1997. "Early Warning of Violent Conflicts" in A.Schmid (ed.), *Violent Crime and Conflicts*, Milan: ISPAC (International Scientific and Professional Advisory Council of the UN Crime Prevention and Criminal Justice Programme).

Senghaas, D. 1973. "Conflict Formations in Contemporary International Society," *Journal of Peace Research*, vol.10, 163-184.

Sharp, G. 1973. *The politics of nonviolent action*, (3 vols), Boston: Porter Sargent.

Ury, W. 1999. *Getting to Peace: Transforming Conflict at Home, at Work, and in the World*, New York: Viking.

Vayrynen, R. (ed.) 1991. "To Settle or to Transform? Perspectives on the Resolution of National and International Conflicts," *New Directions in Conflict Theory: Conflict Resolution and Conflict Transformation*. London: Sage, 1-25.

Wehr, P. 1979. *Conflict Regulation,* Boulder, Colorado: Westview.

Wehr, P., Heidi Burgess & Guy Burgess (eds.) 1994. *Justice Without Violence*, Boulder: Lynne Rienner.

Weller, M. et al 2000. *Missed Opportunities of Conflict Prevention in Kosovo: A transatlantic evaluation*, Ebenhausen: Conflict Prevention Network/SWP.

Culture, Power Asymmetries and Gender in Conflict Transformation

Diana Francis

1. Introduction 92
2. Culture, Gender and Power: The relationship 92
The culture of domination
The impact of dominatory patterns on conflict and its conduct
3. Implications for Conflict Transformation 96
Culture transformation: responding to charges of neo-colonialism
Addressing power asymmetries and injustice
Dilemmas in terms of supporting equality
4. Good Practice 104
Cultural sensitivity, gender equality and the respectful exercise of power in organizations
Cultural sensitivity, gender equality and the respectful exercise of power in intervention
5. Ongoing Questions and Perspectives 106
6. Reference and Further Reading 107

Culture, Power Asymmetries and Gender in Conflict Transformation

Diana Francis

1. Introduction

To try and address these three issues in one chapter is quite a challenge. It also makes sense, since they are intimately related. I shall argue that the overarching culture of domination, which has prevailed for thousands of years, provides the framework and cultural sanction for oppression and exploitation, and is characterized by oppressive male/female relationships. I shall relate the need to challenge this culture – and its manifestation in asymmetrical gender constructions and relationships – to the need to address another global power asymmetry created by the last five hundred years of colonization, the asymmetry between 'the West and the rest'. This history and the resulting structural relationships have made respectful and honest dialogue about culture-related issues extremely difficult. It also explains the suspicion with which conflict transformation is regarded outside the West. Unless it gives due emphasis to questions of power, to the need for justice in global relationships and to the right to equality of women and other marginalized groups, it will not be taken seriously by most of the world's people, or enriched by their experiences and insights. It will also fail to address the question of domination, and arguably help to perpetuate it, acting as a tool for pacification, rather than for the achievement of genuinely peaceful (i.e., just) relationships.

In the first part, I shall discuss the relationship between culture, attitudes to power and power asymmetry, constructions of gender and gender relations and the impact of all three (and of their mutual influence) on conflict and its conduct. In the second part, I shall examine the implications of this for conflict transformation, some of the tensions between the values and ideals it embodies and the realities of the situations it seeks to transform. In the third part of the chapter, I shall consider how the needs of equality, cultural sensitivity and constructive approaches to power can be incorporated into organizations that seek to contribute to conflict transformation, and suggest some elements of good practice in conflict intervention itself. I shall conclude by reflecting on the immensity of the challenges that face us, suggesting that we need to add to rigour and analysis a more fluid and tentative approach.

2. Culture, Gender and Power: The relationship

2.1 The culture of domination

Cultures are not fixed or monolithic, but fluid, complex and changing. Culture is indeed quite hard to define. The best my very large dictionary can do (for the sense we need here) is "[a] particular form of intellectual development". What I mean by culture is the patterning of assumptions about life, its realities and requirements, and intrinsic or accompanying values and norms. One could argue that the very notion of culture is itself a cultural construct – and in this sense, a relatively recent one. It could also be argued that it is a concept so nebulous and problematic as to be near meaningless; yet its difficulties do not disprove its importance. Since it provides a way of talking about the foundations of human thought, activity and relationships, and bears such a close relationship to the equally difficult and important concept of identity, it is far too important to ignore or dismiss.

While it is essential to the very notion of culture that it is variable and particular not only to societies but to individuals within them, Riane Eisler (1990) argues convincingly that a thread running through almost every generalized, mainstream culture in recent millennia is the central value placed on domination: of one species over others; of one group over others; of one person over others and of one sex over the other. She describes this as a "dominatory culture." Eisler's contention is that, despite assumptions to the contrary, egalitarian, cooperative relationships have, in the past, in some societies at least, been the norm – and could be again. In the meantime, the culture of domination overshadows our view of both past and present, and that perspective reaches out, depressingly, into the future.

Domination has power asymmetry as its goal and is dependent on it. It represents the kind of relationship that most people, in most cultures, most readily associate with the word power, i.e., meaning power over people and things, as against the capacity to do something or the responsibility to act on behalf of others (Boulding 1978). There are many different vehicles for the exercise of power over others: wealth; control of resources and terms of trading; language; education; fashion; political structures and practices; laws (their enactment and application); imprisonment and physical violence, or the threat of it, on whatever scale, including military systems and wars. Violence, the harmful and destructive exercise of power over others, is both the means and the outcome of domination. A culture of domination is a culture of violence. In the words of Johan Galtung, "cultural violence makes direct and structural violence look, even feel, right – or at least not wrong." (Galtung 1990, p291)

The oppression of women is often explained, and indeed justified, in terms of culture. Gender can be defined as the social construction of sex difference, expressed in constructions of masculinity and femininity (Francis 2000). As traditionally constructed, gender differences are integral to the culture of domination, having power asymmetry at their heart. Masculinity is constructed as powerful, aggressive, controlling; femininity as inferior, weak, submissive, serving or (more positively) nurturing. In the more extreme versions of this construction, women are regarded as a subspecies, to be treated by men as their chattels. Since women are those who also spend the most time with children and are their chief educators, it is clear that they participate in the perpetuation of this cultural viewpoint. The domination of men over women is the most fundamental and widespread form of power asymmetry in human society and societies. In some parts of the world, the oppression of women by men is lessening; in others it continues unabated. However, in most (if not all) societies, domestic violence against women is common and in many it is tacitly, if not explicitly, sanctioned. In some countries, women's movements and activities are restricted and their treatment under the law is harsh and discriminatory. Women are also oppressed economically. The work that they do, overall, far exceeds that which is done by men, yet they 'earn' on average far less than men, control a small fraction of the world's wealth and are often debarred from inheritance. In global terms, then, there is a clear power asymmetry between men and women.

The colonial activities of the last few centuries have brought about another global skewing of power: the domination of a few nations over the others (what Alexander, 1996, calls "global apartheid"). Broadly speaking, this can be seen in terms of the North and West on the one hand and the South and East on the other, though in reality the picture is far more complex. The domination takes different forms: military; economic and cultural. The cultural imperialism of the West, combined with its military and economic power, colours interactions between those who are associated with its domination and those who are on the receiving end. It engenders patronizing and dismissive attitudes – and underlying fear and hatred (*see* Said 1978) – on the one side and suspicion and resentment on the other. It means that expressions of difference, particularly in relation to culture, are liable to be seen as either unwarranted and disturbing or disrespectful and autocratic. Since culture and identity are closely related, cultural differences in dominatory relationships are seen as a threat.

Since identity, like culture, is complex, so are experiences of domination. Western women, for instance, and men in other parts of the world, belong in global terms to the categories of both dominators and dominated; and within any country there will be different social or ethnic groups that are in unequal relationships. In all rich and powerful countries there are poor and marginalized people – the so called 'fourth world'. Sometimes identity groups that constitute a numerical minority within a given society are, overall, more powerful politically or economically than the majority. At times, victimized groups use their victimhood as a source of power, both as moral leverage and in building support.

Individuals within all groups and in any sphere of life compete for power, and most individuals in some areas of their lives are likely to be relatively powerful and in others relatively powerless. Furthermore, all human beings are likely to display, in different contexts, both dominatory and cooperative approaches to power. I do not wish to suggest that men are born more aggressive and controlling than women, or that those born in the West are by nature more aggressive and controlling than those born elsewhere. There are many powerful and exploitative women and men, North and South. I am arguing that within an overall culture of domination, it is the 'power over' or dominatory power model that is favoured, as against the cooperative, 'power with' and 'power for' model. Within that overarching cultural context, the gender roles assigned to women and to men result in gross power asymmetry between them, which is expressed both structurally and in terms of behaviour. In addition, the acts and processes of colonialism, supported by the culture of domination, have resulted in structural power asymmetry between different parts of the globe. This occasions structural injustice and cultural imperialism, and renders dialogue about anything – particularly about things attributable to culture – sensitive and difficult. In the context of existing geopolitical power asymmetries, since the emancipation of women is seen as a Western project, it is liable to be associated with cultural imperialism.

Although the broad, overall, power asymmetries between men and women and between the West and the rest, constitute the main focus of this chapter, the relationship between culture and oppressive power structures and behaviours is one which applies in a multitude of spheres (for instance, in employer/employee relations, within organizations, in political systems and between ethnic groups).

2.2 The impact of dominatory patterns on conflict and its conduct

Conflict is likely to be experienced whenever ideas, activities, structures and people change in relation to each other. Since change is not only inevitable but also often desirable, conflict is unavoidable as well. Broadly speaking, it may be handled either cooperatively or competitively. In a dominatory culture, as we have seen, it is the competitive model which is chosen, associated with violence in different forms. The hostility associated with conflict in such a cultural context is typically exacerbated by cultural differences: dominatory motives are imputed to others, and 'otherness' is seen as a threat. When difference is associated with power asymmetries, fear and mistrust will be further increased, with those in power expecting insurrection and those underneath feeling threatened and abused. Cultural difference is then a source not of enrichment, but of alienation, misunderstanding and misinterpretation. It is associated with disapproval or non-respect on the one hand and feelings of victimhood, resentment and affront on the other.

The desire to dominate or escape from domination is a constant motivation for organized violence, whether for control within existing territory or for territorial expansion (territory here being both literal and metaphorical). The hidden conflict of injustice is perpetuated and opposition suppressed by organized violence and the threat of it. Organized violence is also often seen as the only effective recourse for those who suffer injustice. When those with little power act to become more powerful, they are accused of causing conflict (*see* King 1963) and, in all too many circumstances, those who have benefited from their powerlessness use violent or controlling means to keep them in their place. Women are beaten, slaves are punished, revolutionaries are attacked by government forces, and small nations are attacked or threatened by the superior armies and nuclear arsenals of big ones. The culture of domination and violence makes all of this seem 'normal'.

In war – the archetypal dominatory exercise – the male dominatory gender role is played out in particularly crude and brutal ways. The culture of domination gives glory, approval and status to men for their participation in violent conflict, especially when it is associated with collective identity. The world's towns and cities are disfigured by symbols of martial domination – typically, men on horses brandishing swords. From this cultural viewpoint, women are regarded as mothers and supporters of fighters, but also as victims and peacemakers. Rape, of both women and men, is part of the pattern of war behaviours – a horrible emblem of domination and the brutalisation of human beings. The wholesale rape of women because they are seen as belonging to a particular group is not uncommon, signifying not only male/female domination but also the triumph of one group of men over another.

The victimization and suffering of women in war does not mean that they play no part in hostilities. Although there are impressive stories of women's peacemaking, women are also involved in the social polarization that lays the ground for war, and there are other stories that recount their role in encouraging and goading their men to fight and sometimes fighting themselves. At the same time, war can give women greater domestic, economic and social power than they enjoy in times of peace. When their husbands are away at war, women often become the sole breadwinners and heads of household. When families are displaced, it is often the women who manage to earn enough for them to survive, by making and selling things, for example. (Their men folk may resent this and feel marginalized, but the needs of children exert an undeniable pressure.) In industrialized societies, women may be drafted into jobs that have previously been closed to them, and in others forced into domestic service (Reimann 1999). At the same time, there are countless examples of women's involvement in challenging those who are waging war and in efforts to bring war to an end, as well as in caring for those displaced or otherwise affected by hostilities. (Men also may choose to take a role that deviates from their gender stereotype: opting for draft avoidance or resistance; joining the peace movement or aiding those who are victimized.) However, since wars are fought not for the rights of women but for other goals, once they are over, those who have traditionally assigned women their place in society will expect to do so once again, and it will be hard for women to hold the ground they have gained. It is even difficult for them to get redress for gender related crimes against them (particularly rape). In the aftermath of war, levels of domestic violence against women are high, and the objectification through the sex trade is common (with the male staff of UN, OSCE and other international organizations sometimes among the main users).

3. Implications for Conflict Transformation

3.1 Culture transformation: responding to charges of neo-colonialism

It is widely acknowledged within the field that a key to the constructive management of conflict is to understand and address the basic human needs of those involved (Burton 1990). The way in which these are experienced and can be met will be culturally influenced. Max-Neef (1985) argues, for instance, that in Western cultures material considerations play a more central role in meeting identity needs than they do in other cultures where dignity suggests other priorities (*see* also Salem 1993). The challenges that such differences imply for the cross-cultural development of conflict transformation are not, in themselves, insurmountable. Indeed, to address them is a potentially enriching process, likely to sharpen our overall understanding of the nature of conflict and of the range of human responses to it. If women begin to have more voice, that may also have an impact on the cultural range and insights of conflict transformation.

It is clear that war, as a method of dealing with conflict, does not address the needs of women, children and other socially marginalized or oppressed groups caught up in it. It is also clear that it is widely sanctioned culturally. However, particular cultures not only shape, but are also shaped by, values and those who hold them. Their variations and manifestations in time and place are infinite, and they are changed by those they have helped to form. There are endless variations within any culture, and some of these can be described as counter-cultures. In addition to this, conflict transformation too can be seen as counter-cultural by seeking to address the immediate manifestations of violent conflict, as well as its structural and attitudinal causes, and to bring about long term change. The term not only refers to action for change and a body of theory informing and informed by action; it also implies certain goals, based on particular values. It is not domination by one party over another, but the transformation of dominatory and violent relationships and structures and manifestations of violence. Conflict transformation instead aims towards relationships of respect, cooperation and consent and constructive means and norms for dealing with conflict.

Many people outside the West – academics, politicians and socially active people among the vast majority of the world's population – are suspicious of a field which they see as emanating largely from North America and Europe, most often referred to as conflict resolution and frequently in association with the term conflict prevention. Their arguments can be summarized like this: "Of course they want to stop conflicts – not theirs, ours. Conflicts disturb the status quo, which is to their benefit. They don't want opposition. They don't want their power contested. They march around telling others what to do, bombing and threatening, but they want us to stay in our place and keep the peace. There is no peace without justice. We have to be prepared to fight, when our honour and our dignity are at stake. We won't be pushed around forever. This is the latest insult. They, who are the biggest militarists, tell us how we should deal with conflict. They're too ignorant to understand us anyway. Their theory is based on cultural assumptions that just don't apply for us. We may have to pretend to go along with it all sometimes, because they have the money and call the shots; but it would be better if they'd stay at home and put their own house in order. Most of the world's ills come from there anyway."

This is, of course, a crude simplification of the argument (for a more measured and refined expressions, *see* Salem 1993), but I believe it is a reasonable generalization of what is a just case, which I have heard voiced in one way or another on many occasions. If conflict transformation is to be found useful and relevant outside the West, it will need to be clear that its goal is not conflict prevention, but rather the prevention or diminution of violence in all its forms, direct, cultural and structural. It will need to communicate more strongly the message that resolution cannot happen when peace is bought at the expense of perpetuating gross injustice. It is a process in which the needs and identities of all are understood and respected. I believe also that the proponents of conflict transformation will need to acknowledge that the current mainstream conduct of affairs between the West and the rest is not in line with its principles and aspirations, and that they are in solidarity with those who seek a more just world order. If these things are done, maybe the space will be created for the further development of conflict transformation in cultures beyond the West, so that it finds different forms and expressions, and is enriched by the knowledge and experience of others and a truly international exchange.

The need for constructive engagement in conflict is indicated by global injustices and also in relation to many other forms of oppressive power relationships, including gender issues and the place and treatment of women in society. As I have already suggested, since the notion of human rights and its application to women are seen as originating in the West, to query their place in society means to question the culture of that society; hence feminist agendas are easily dismissed as imperialist. In countries where discrimination against women is justified by dominant local traditions, many men and some women defend that discrimination in the name of culture, accusing those who question it of cultural infidelity and collusion with this imperialism. However, while cultural influences and power asymmetries may help to explain attitudes and behavioural patterns, they do not justify them. Cultures, like structures and actions, are open to evaluation, critique and change. Counter-cultures can become mainstream. Wherever I have travelled, I have met women who are outraged when violence against them is justified in the name of culture, and who are working with courage and determination to confront it – whether it takes the form of female circumcision, restriction of movement, debarment from inheritance, or discrimination and harassment at work. They are also aware of the need to challenge the cultural basis for this oppression. Unfortunately, there are some societies which are at present so oppressive that to speak out is to court terrible punishment. In such cases, international pressure seems not only justifiable, but also necessary. Solidarity and imperialism may be open to confusion; they are nonetheless distinguishable and the distinction needs to be made. The same applies to other culturally sanctioned forms of oppression, whether related to caste, ethnic identity, sexuality or ability.

3.2 Addressing power asymmetries and injustice

Oppression can be considered as a hidden or latent conflict: one waiting to happen or to be brought into the open (*see* King 1963 and Curle 1971). When groups organize themselves to increase their power and confront their oppression, they are acting within the framework of domination, in order to break out of it. They are in a position to act cooperatively with each other and with those who support them, and they need not seek domination over their oppressors. They cannot, however, cooperate with them, since the existing relationship will not allow for cooperation. Within the model of conflict transformation, they will seek to increase their power in relation to those who oppress them through nonviolent[1] means. Only when they have done this will the cooperative processes of conflict resolution become a realistic option.

If addressing power asymmetries and consequent injustices is a major component of conflict transformation, the emphasis so often given to preventing and ending conflict, and to facilitative mediation (which can be effective only when there is relative power parity), can be seen as disproportionate. The notion of conflict prevention has to give way to that of constructive, nonviolent engagement in and with conflict. Impartiality, from this viewpoint, is not the automatic and only good. Partisan roles can be seen as potentially constructive, and support for constructive action by those in conflict (whether that support is partisan or non-partisan) as the primary form of intervention.

Figure 1 (developed with Guus Meijer) depicts stages and processes by which a situation of oppression, or latent conflict, characterized by major power asymmetry, can be transformed. The words contained in oval shapes describe conflict stages, while those in rectangular boxes describe actions or processes by which those stages are reached. The arrows go in different directions because these processes are mutually reinforcing. Power relations begin to change when those who are oppressed bring their oppression into awareness (a process which Paulo Freire (1972) termed 'conscientization'); then to mobilize themselves and others for action. Mobilization involves the formation of groups and networks, the articulation of common values and goals, the development of a common strategy (within the framework of conflict transformation, this will be a nonviolent one) and building support of all kinds. Only when they have increased their own relative power, and acquired sufficient leverage to make a difference to their oppressors, will they be able to confront them effectively – whether that confrontation takes the form of private dialogue, public action or (most likely) both.

Once that stage has been reached, it becomes realistic to think in terms of the conflict's resolution, and the processes indicated within the dotted lines can begin. However, it

1 There is an important distinction between "non-violent" meaning the use of methods which are not violent and "nonviolent" which goes farther and indicates the espousal of the philosophy which holds the rejection of violence as a principle and not simply a tactic. The latter is the way the term is mainly used in this chapter.

should be noted that at no stage is progress likely to be smooth. Nor is conflict simple or monolithic, and the stages are never really separate from one another. The diagram represents not the messy reality of conflict but a set of objectives that are roughly sequential. Reconciliation, which can be seen as the fruit or culmination of conflict resolution, is often, in practice, reached only after generations – if ever. It is nonetheless a valid aspiration, and it will be achieved/consolidated largely through long term cooperation in rebuilding society. The maintenance will require mechanisms and a culture for constructive conflict management; and conflict management will include the management of power asymmetries within society.

Most people who find themselves caught up in a conflict, whether in its hidden form of oppression or in open confrontation, have not chosen to be involved. In complex political situations, deliberate political decisions and actions are taken by a relatively small number within the wider group, while the rest are in a position of powerlessness. One aspect of conflict

Figure 1: Stages and Processes in Conflict Transformation

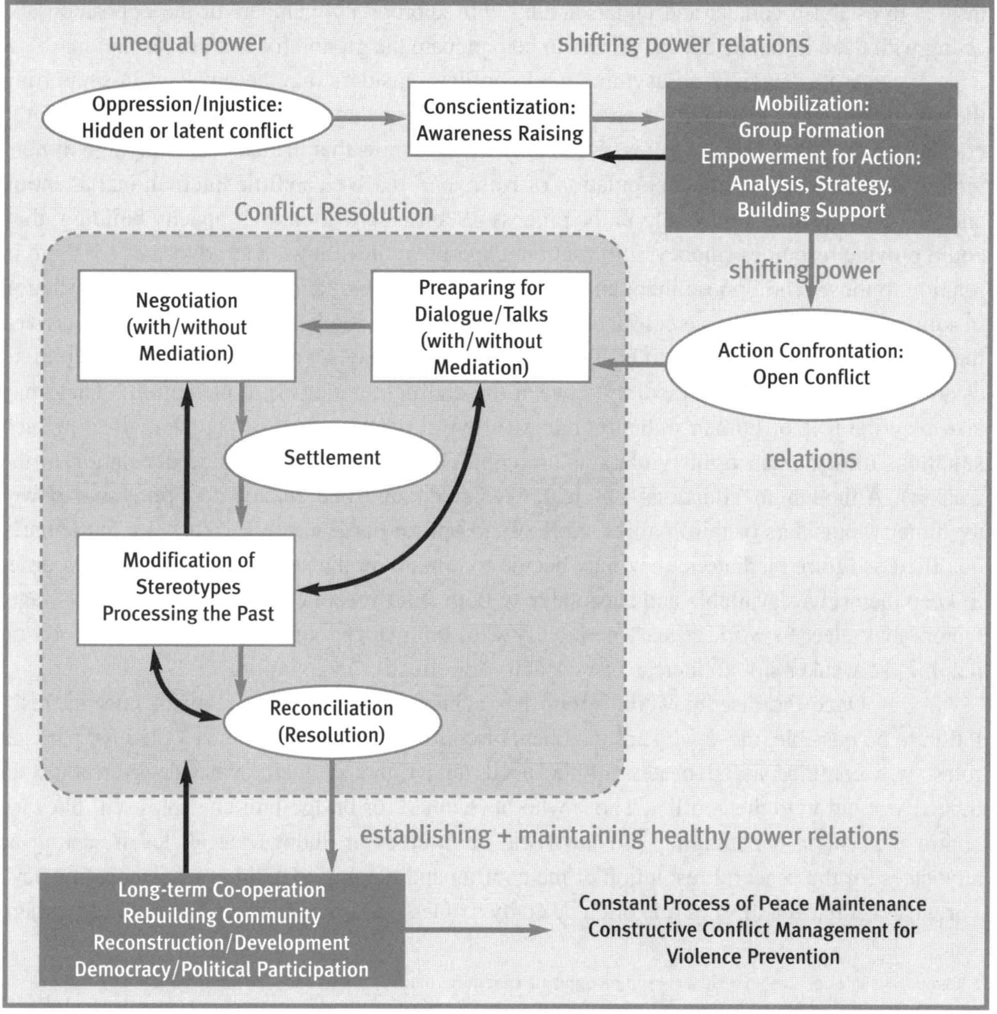

transformation is the conscientization or awakening of those who currently take no power, so that they become active for constructive change. If they are to act effectively, they will need to consider their own possibilities in relation to the conflict: their understanding of what needs to be changed; their existing involvement, if any; their standing in relation to different groups and individuals; their personal gifts and capacities; and the forms of support they can enlist. If they see their own group as disempowered, needing to strengthen its position before conflict resolution can become a possibility; they may well choose a partisan role, working as educators within their own group and preparing them for non-violent action; they may undertake the function as advocates for it in relation to other power-holders (including the wider public and political opponents); they may work as movement organizers, public activists and support-builders, reaching out to and involving others and building coalitions.

Those insiders who, despite their identification with one or other of the conflicting parties by birth and by ascription by others, wish to play a bridge-building rather than a deliberately partisan role, may choose to leave the addressing of power asymmetries to others. They may work instead to establish contact and understanding with appropriate members of the opposition and acting with them as public educators, and to help prepare the ground for conflict resolution.

At this stage in an asymmetrical conflict, outsiders may be involved in supporting the nonviolent empowerment of an oppressed group, so that the inclusive resolution of the conflict becomes a possibility. (It is all too easy to regret now that the ten year campaign of non-violent action by the Albanian population of Kosovo/a[2] received so little international attention and support.) Outsiders may help in the process of conscientization and capacity building; they could provide resources (money, information, expertise); they may act as advocates for them in relation to those who oppose them and to potential supporters; and they can take public action in solidarity with them. Since conflict resolution is not yet a realistic option, mediation between the different sides is not likely to be useful, but outsiders may act as bridge builders, helping to establish contact and understanding between the conflicting sides (pre-mediation). They may also play the role of human rights monitors (often in practice seen as partisan, since in such situations most human rights violations are committed by the stronger side in relation to the weaker). Although in situations of clear, one sided injustice related to oppressive power asymmetry, outsiders or third parties are likely to opt for partisan roles, if they are particularly qualified as future mediators, they may decide to remain on the sidelines at this stage in order to keep themselves available and acceptable to both sides for a facilitative role at a later stage. Others may elect to work at least nominally with both sides, but concentrate their efforts on helping the weaker side to increase its capacity for effective negotiation.

Once the disempowered group has achieved sufficient leverage for conflict resolution to be possible, those who are members of conflicting parties and have opted for partisan roles, will continue as advocates for the needs and rights of their own side in seeking an inclusive solution to the conflict. Those who have opted for bridge-building roles will likewise continue in them, encouraging and involving themselves in dialogue at all levels, acting as advocates for the peaceful resolution of the conflict and helping to build a 'peace constituency'. For whatever reason, this is a role often taken by women – as for instance in Sierra Leone, where

2 Kosovo/a is intended as an inclusive term recognising that in Serbian it is spelt "Kosovo" and in Albanian "Kosova".

the Women's Movement for Peace (formed in partnership with the pre-existing Women's Forum) has been both active and influential, and in Russia, where the mothers of conscripts ran a high profile campaign for an end to hostilities against Chechnya.

Having reached this stage, third parties will, ideally, leave the work of advocacy to the parties themselves, confining their efforts to support for peace constituencies and for the resolution process itself. They may now act as facilitative mediators of unofficial political processes such as problem-solving workshops and other forms of pre-negotiation (even of official negotiations), and corresponding dialogue at the grassroots and local level. (Power mediation, in which a third party imposes a process of 'negotiation', and even its outcome – even though it may be part of the way things currently often happen – is not part of the concept of conflict transformation.) Once a settlement has been reached, efforts to address continuing tensions at the local level, and to deal with the traumas and crimes of the past, may well benefit from third party facilitation. There may also be a role for outside monitors to check, for instance, human rights violations or ceasefire infringements.

In societies which have suffered from violent conflict, the (re)establishment of participatory, democratic politics (though not necessarily on a Western model), and the development of a culture, structures and skills for the positive handling of conflict will be vital for the maintenance of peace. Since conflict is integral to everyday life, and power asymmetries will constantly need to be managed and exclusions and injustices addressed, the development of these capacities is vital for the prevention of future violence, whether cultural, structural or direct.

At this peacebuilding stage, as at all stages of conflict, support from outside may have an important role to play in the form of the provision of training and consultancy, whether for constructive partisan groups, bridge-builders, human rights monitors, workers for democracy or others, at whatever level. It should, however, be offered tentatively and given sensitively, with close attention to local culture, perceptions, wisdom and realities. This means that a flexible, context specific and broadly elicitive approach is needed (Lederach 1995), rather than off the shelf, didactic packages.

3.3 Dilemmas in terms of supporting equality

Women are commonly very active in processes of conflict transformation, whether in women-only groups, like the international Women in Black, or as the backbone of gender inclusive organizations: resisting war and calling for peace; fostering dialogue between different groups; working for human rights; supporting refugees and others affected by the war; or developing peace education for all ages. Supporting women's work is therefore productive both in terms of helping them to play a full role in social and political life, and in terms of the transformation of the political conflict they are helping to address. However, as already noted, since wars are not fought for women's rights and they are not often involved in military and political decisions to end them, once war is over the contribution and rights of women are all too often overlooked.

Sometimes the supposed solution to a conflict is to give greater autonomy to minority groups and the freedom to organize civil life in line with their own culture and traditions – that is, according to the dominant culture within that group, which is often oppressive towards women (*see* Saghal and Yuval-Davies 1992). So, in many circumstances, after the emancipation of their ethnic or cultural group, to which they have contributed, the need for women's emancipation has been overlooked or denied by the male leadership, so that the lot of women is not improved or is even worsened. More generally in post-war situations, those who have played an important role in the search for a peaceful solution to conflict or who have stepped into new roles during a war are returned to the margins once an apparent peace has been secured.

Marginalized ethno-political groups remain peripheral throughout, are co-opted or caught in the crossfire and their needs are often excluded from the provision and/or implementation of any settlement.

When levels of violence and suffering are high, there is strong moral pressure to focus actions and interventions on immediate and urgent needs and solutions. This tends to translate into working within existing cultural constraints and power realities. Not only women, but also cultural minorities outside the main axis of the conflict (Roma, for instance, in South East Europe), are excluded from the top level and, at the same time, they themselves often avoid explicit political involvement and are unwilling to be seen as players, so that each tendency reinforces the other. Those who wish to intervene in favour of rapid progress towards the settlement of violent political conflict are therefore likely to devote their attention to the key players, so confirming the marginalization of women and weak minority groups. In other words, there is a tension between the long term goals and values of conflict transformation, which include societal change, and the short term goal of ending immediate political violence.

Box 1: International Campaign "Women Building Peace"

In order to strengthen women's role in peacebuilding the British NGO International Alert (IA) has launched an international campaign named "Women Building Peace: From the Village Council to the Negotiating Table". IA addressed an open letter to UN Secretary General Kofi Annan and the International Community, with calls to sign and circulate the following appeal[3]:

"Dear Secretary-General Kofi Annan,

Women everywhere applaud the efforts made for peace by the United Nations. Women recognise the progress made in including women in peace making and peace building efforts within the UN itself and the pledges made to women during the UN Fourth World Conference on Women in 1995. However, we believe that five years later not enough has been done to make these pledges a reality. They must be implemented, as sustainable peace can only be achieved with the full participation of women from all levels of society. We ask the governments of the international community and the United Nations to stand by the commitments they have made to women. These are to:

- Include women in peace negotiations as decision-makers;
- Put women at the heart of reconstruction and reconciliation;
- Strengthen the protection and representation of refugee and displaced women;
- End impunity for crimes committed against women and ensure redress;

3 For more information, contact gendercampaign@international-alert.org or visit the website of International Alert: www.international-alert.org

• Give women and women's organisations the support and resources they need to build peace.

"The organizers aim to collect a minimum of 250.000 signatures. The campaign is supported by more than 100 NGOs worldwide and works to achieve global policy changes to strengthen women's participation on all levels of peace processes – locally, nationally and internationally.

The exclusive nature of peace processes will also have implications for the choice of personnel in interventions. For instance, I know of one organization which has reluctantly chosen to use all male teams in unofficial political mediation in Sri Lanka, since their first concern is to gain access to, and credibility with, political leadership there. This tension between long term goals of conflict transformation and the short term expediency of using existing power structures is felt also when internal democracy is sacrificed to the perceived need for decisive action by the main political players in a given context. For instance, leaders who have a sense of urgency about reaching a settlement do not consult adequately with their constituencies during the negotiation process. The secrecy that negotiations often entail militates against accountability and the building of internal democracy. Those who hold the power to sign a cease-fire or endorse a settlement are, moreover, often those who have abused their power and will continue to do so. The problem is the same: in order to reach a situation of long term peacebuilding, it seems necessary to work through existing power relations, which are in themselves contrary to what a just peace requires. The result is that the long term needs and rights of marginalized groups are never adequately addressed. Their continuing oppression represents a deeper, hidden layer of ongoing latent conflict.

The use of armed 'peacekeepers' or 'peace enforcers' presents the same dilemma in another form. By the exertion of dominatory or coercive power, they constitute a continuation of the mechanisms and relationships which erupt in wars; yet often they seem to offer the only practicable route out of them. They also represent a shift in the use of coercive power. Ideally, instead of being an instrument of selfish domination, it is used to provide space for the establishment of more equal, cooperative relationships; but the contradiction remains. The development of peace and human rights monitoring is arguably less problematic, and the idea of unarmed peacekeeping is being developed and pioneered by many groups around the world. In any case, it is important that the composition of such forces or teams is mixed in terms of gender, ethnicity and other identities – both because of the message that this will convey and because of the capacities it will bring. It will also be a matter of equal opportunities at the point of recruitment.

The values of equality and inclusion which, in conjunction with the current realities of war, underlie the dilemmas alluded to above, are the values of a particular identity group: that which is formed by the adherents to conflict transformation and the wider value group from which they come (culturally liberal, philosophically egalitarian, politically democratic, concerned with socio-economic justice and unhappy about war). These values are confined to no particular culture and are universal in none, but they constitute a culture in themselves. They are in clear opposition to the universally prevalent culture of domination, which has its own long term as well as short term agenda. They are also in clear opposition to sexism, racism and discrimination of all kinds. This needs to be honestly acknowledged. It also challenges those who work for conflict transformation to do their work in respectful, non-dominatory ways – in line with their own theory and values.

In my next section I will consider ways of doing the work of conflict transformation respectfully and responsibly; in other words, good practice.

4. Good Practice

4.1 Cultural sensitivity, gender equality and the respectful exercise of power in organizations

The first challenge for those who wish to promote the theory and practice of conflict transformation is to develop non-dominatory, respectful culture, structures and processes and live them in their own organizations. The example set by such organizations may have a multiplying effect; but in any case integrity requires it:

- **Embodying respect in the organizational culture**: this is fundamental and, within the parameters of transparent organizational values, should include respect for different cultural, gender and other identities and the needs and rights of minorities. This culture will be expressed in the organization's collective vision, its articulation of its mission and goals, its policies, publicity and ethos.
- **Creating and implementing equal opportunities policy** for the recruitment and selection of paid and volunteer staff, and for appointments to the board; also for chances of development and promotion (and, of course, pay) within the organization, and the opportunity to contribute to the body's vision and culture. When it comes to field work, the dilemma may have to be faced of choosing to challenge local stereotypes by appointing, for instance, women to positions that, in the local context, would be unusual or even unacceptable for them to hold, as against bowing to local custom for the sake of minimizing obstacles to immediate goals. If the latter choice is made, it and the reasons behind it should be made explicit, in consultation with those thereby excluded. When the organization in question works on behalf of one particular identity group, it may be appropriate for members of that group to hold key positions within it; but this should be clearly and honestly reasoned and communicated. The question of approaches to power, and other aspects of culture and identity (including gender, if it is not a women's organization) will still be relevant.
- **Creating organizational structures and practices that embody the 'power with and for' approach**, being designed in terms of responsibility and function rather than hierarchy and involving cooperative processes for learning and the preparation of decisions. Participatory processes and power sharing will require transparency and clarity about the goals and realities of procedure and structure, with codes of practice to set standards and provide a reference point.

4.2 Cultural sensitivity, gender equality and the respectful exercise of power in intervention

The term conflict intervention can tend to suggest that the actors in question come from outside the area of conflict. This is the first question to be addressed, in terms of conflict transformation and the respectful exercise of power. Who are the primary actors in transforming conflict? I would argue that, both morally and practically, it is those who are most directly affected by it. The following suggestions for good practice are framed in terms that allow them to apply either to inside actors or to those who intervene from outside, or to both. Some, however, are clearly directed mainly at outsiders:

- **Paying explicit attention to questions of culture** in preparatory research and project/program design; identifying cultural differences within and between conflicting groups and seeking to understand how those relate to power.
- **Identifying cultural differences** between any who are intervening from outside and those who are involved in the conflict, and exploring the implications of those differences, both in terms of what is respectful to the human beings involved and of what will be needed in addressing the conflict.
- **Paying explicit attention to the ways in which women are affected by and can have an impact on the conflict**; considering the potential for contributing to the empowerment of women – both short term and long term – in any intervention; seeking to include work with marginalized groups where this is feasible.
- **Paying explicit attention to the role of power asymmetries in conflict** – to the ways in which these are being exploited and experienced by the parties – in order to make well informed decisions about effective action in support of conflict transformation.
- **Assessing the likely impact of proposed action on changing power dynamics** and being aware of the extent and limits of one's own power and responsibility; being sensitive to culture/power perceptions and language capacities; not using (even inadvertently) language to dominate; making clear agreements with partners and being open about values and goals.
- **Considering the full range of constructive roles** which are possible and for whom they are appropriate – partisan, semi-partisan/bridge-building, non-partisan (facilitative/supportive of processes and capacities) – and making a clear and open choice; remembering that third parties are less important (or should be) than the parties to a conflict; acting on the 'power for and with' principle, rather than seeking to impose.
- **Being wary of motivation by one's own personal/organizational need or desire for power;** asking whether the proposed action is something that will be really useful and who is best equipped to do it; providing training for staff to strengthen personal and organizational self-awareness and to create willingness to confront and wrestle with dilemmas and contradictions; building in processes for feedback, monitoring, reflection, evaluation and adjustment in relation to all aspects of practice.

5. Ongoing Questions and Perspectives

Those who work for conflict transformation are constantly confronted with the fact that current realities conform only exceptionally to the theories and values they espouse. The present global culture of power, the broad realities of power relations and the destructive approaches to contemporary conflict make the project of conflict transformation seem more than a little quixotic. Yet if there were nothing that needed to be transformed, the notion of transformation would have no meaning. The heart of the challenge is that it is necessary, in a largely hostile (though changing) climate, to advance on so many fronts at once, trying at the same time to hold together both short term and long term objectives, and balance competing benefits. Fortunately, those individuals and organizations committed to contributing to the project of conflict transformation are as many and various as the problems to be confronted, have different priorities and expertise and work at different levels of the socio-political pyramid (Lederach 1995). Given the size of the overall task, however, and at a time when devastating wars are taking place in so many parts of the globe, it is easy to be discouraged. At a time of rapid change, culture has become, for many people, a desperately needed garment for identity; at the same time it is used to cloak injustice and cruelty and to justify violence. Moreover, our theories have to be dragged through the hedges of situations which they did not envisage. In practice, conflict transformation has to find ways of operating in the midst of conflict as usual (or even worse).

One thing that may help us to deal with the size and complexity of what we are trying to do is to turn away from the illusion that we can control outcomes and accept that we can only participate in processes, recognizing that means and ends are, in the last analysis, inseparable. Insistence on hard approaches to planning and evaluation, the reification of outcomes, and unwillingness to acknowledge that they can never be fully predicted or assessed, are part of a culture of control which, according to currently prevalent constructions of gender, is male (Belenky et al. 1986). It is also very Western. While clarity of purpose, thorough analysis and strategic planning are important, they need to be complemented by flexibility, responsiveness and even (dare I say it?) intuition. Assessment will need to include the evaluation of changes made to what was originally planned and outcomes that do not correspond neatly to those that were envisaged. It will have to evaluate work in terms of its own quality and reasonableness, even when outcomes are disappointing or surprising, and it will need to accept that longer term impact may never be known. This may be difficult, in the light of the demands of funding agencies that the resources they provide should be used to good effect and of the criteria by which they propose to judge such effectiveness. (Power relations between conflict transformation organizations and funding agencies would make an interesting area for study and reflection.) I believe, however, that if we allow ourselves to be dominated by demands for hard evidence and instant rather than long term, diffuse results, we are in danger of being led into dishonesty, illusion and disillusion.

Conflict transformation, wide scale and long term, will involve the transformation of culture and of structural relationships. If we are to replace the methods of domination with those of equality and cooperation, we shall need the equal involvement of all kinds of people in that change: women and men and those from all cultural backgrounds. Not only does justice require it, but, without the involvement and contributions of all, there can be no adequate and inclusive process. We have to work within current realities and at the same time be open and steadfast in holding to the values of justice and respect which conflict transformation implies. This will involve us too in conflict, as we struggle to confront our own internal differences and divisions, and to find ways of being in dialogue with different world views; – but conflict is our business.

6. Reference and Further Reading

Alexander, Titus 1996. *Unraveling Global Apartheid: An Overview of World Politics*, Cambridge: Polity Press.

Belenky, Mary Field, et al 1986. *Women's Ways of Knowing: The Development of Self, Voice and Mind*, New York, NY: Basic Books.

Boulding, Kenneth 1978. *Ecodynamics*, London: Sage.

Burton, John (ed.) 1990. *Conflict: Human Needs Theory*, London: Macmillan.

Curle, Adam 1971. *Making Peace*, London: Tavistock Publications.

Dworkin, Andrea 2000. *Scapegoat: The Jews, Israel And Women's Liberation*, London: Virago.

Eisler, Riane 1990. *The Chalice and the Blade: Our History, Our Future*, London: Unwin Paperbacks.

Francis, Becky 2000. *Boys, Girls and Achievement*, London: Routledge.

Freire, Paulo 1972. *Pedagogy of the Oppressed*, London: Penguin.

Galtung, Johan 1990. "Cultural Violence," *Journal of Peace Research* 27, 3, 291-305.

Gutmann, Amy (ed.) 1994. *Multiculturalism*, Princeton, NJ: Princeton University Press.

King, Martin Luther 1963. *Why We Can't Wait*, New York, NY: New American Library.

Lederach, John Paul 1995. *Preparing for Peace: Conflict Transformation Across Cultures*, New York, NY: Syracuse University Press.

Max-Neef, Manfred 1985. "Reflections on a Paradigm Shift in Economics," in *The New Economic Agenda*, Inverness: Findhorn Press.

Reimann, Cordula 1999 (unpublished). *Towards Gender Mainstreaming in Crisis Prevention and Conflict Management: Guiding points for the German Development Cooperation Agency.*

Saghal, Gita and Nira Yuval-Davis (eds.) 1992. *Refusing Holy Orders: Women and Fudamentalism in Britain*, London: Virago Press.

Said, Edward 1978. *Orientalism*, London: Routledge and Keyan Paul.

Salem, Paul 1993. "In Theory: a Critique of Conflict Resolution from a Non-Western Perspective," *Negotiation Journal IX*, 4, 361 - 369.

Taylor, Charles 1994. "The Politics of Recognition," *in* Gutmann, op. cit., 25-74.

Analysing Conflict and Assessing Conflict Transformation

Dan Smith 111
Trends and Causes of Armed Conflict

Alex Austin 129
Early Warning and The Field: A Cargo Cult Science?

Thania Paffenholz 151
Designing Transformation and Intervention Processes

Mark Hoffman 171
Peace and Conflict Impact Assessment Methodology

Mary B. Anderson 193
Experiences with Impact Assessment: Can we know what Good we do?

Trends and Causes of Armed Conflict

Dan Smith

1. Introduction 112
2. Armed Conflict in the 1990s 113
3. Theories of Conflict Causes 115
4. Background Causes and Foreground Factors 117
5. Methodology and Typology 119
6. Injustice and Mobilisation 119
7. Ethnicity and Conflict 120
8. Conclusion 124
9. Reference and Further Reading 125

Trends and Causes of Armed Conflict[1]

Dan Smith

1. Introduction

From the start of 1990 to the end of 1999 there were 118 armed conflicts world wide, involving 80 states and two para-state regions and resulting in the death of approximately six million people. If we seek to prevent conflict from escalating into armed warfare, or, failing that, to at least achieve an end to fighting as soon as possible, and if we want to maximise the opportunity for avoiding the return of the war after apparent settlement, we must first be sure that we properly understand armed conflicts and their causes.

This chapter attempts to provide a brief overview of what is known and understood about the causes of armed conflict. The theoretical basis of that knowledge is both limited and important. It is limited, in that it does not offer much by way of general explanation of the phenomenon of armed conflict; this is, perhaps, hardly surprising, given its complexity and diversity. It is also important because it provides valuable guidance as to where to look when analysing individual conflicts for signs of potential escalation and when seeking opportunities for preventing violent escalation. Given the limitations of current theoretical knowledge and the objectives of this volume to assist in the development and dissemination of practical knowledge, the theoretical discussion in this article is relatively brief. The emphasis, however, will not be on theory but rather on an applied methodology for studying and analysing armed conflict.

The chapter begins by discussing the incidence and nature of armed conflicts during the 1990s. It then reviews the current state of theoretical knowledge with the aim of providing not only an overview but also a source of further reference, before proceeding to methodology. A key issue is that there are not just a variety of causes of armed conflicts but different types of causes. This in turn calls for different types and levels of theory and analysis. For that reason, the methodological issues are in part typological; they concern the organisation of theory and data. The article then identifies the paired concepts of justice and mobilisation as the best way to link different types and levels of causes, to connect the short-term with the long-term and to relate the socio-economic background with the political foreground. It illustrates this by looking more closely at the category referred to as ethnic conflict.

1 Data on armed conflicts in this chapter update the information, and use the same definition and data rules, as in the atlas, The State of War and Peace (Smith 1997). Compared to the data produced at the Department of Peace and Conflict Research, Uppsala University, and published annually in Journal of Peace Research (see Wallensteen and Sollenberg 1996, 1997, 1998, 1999, and 2000) these data are similar in broad outline but significantly different in detail. Both data-sets use 25 war-deaths per year as a threshold for inclusion, but I place the annual total in a context of a total of several hundred war-deaths, rejecting a more precise total figure as too demanding for the available data. I do not follow the Uppsala team in including as part of the definition the involvement of a recognised state on at least one side.

2. Armed Conflict in the 1990s

Armed conflicts are defined as open, armed clashes between two or more centrally organised parties, with continuity between the clashes, in disputes about power over government and territory. Of the 118 armed conflicts which ensued from 1990 to 1999, ten can be strictly defined as inter-state conflicts. Although it is often these conflicts that dominate the headlines and shape the popular view of how contemporary wars are fought, today they account for only a relatively small proportion of overall war. Five can be strictly defined as wars of independence, although the insurgents in many more wars would themselves define their conflicts in those terms. One hundred wars were largely, primarily or even exclusively internal conflicts. The fact that such loose terminology must be used is an indication of the extent to which many wars defy neat categorisation. For instance, two wars that are not included in 1999 and 2000 in that total of 100, were entirely internal Ethiopian affairs in every respect except that the site of most of the fighting took place in neighbouring Somalia. The war that went on in the Democratic

Table 1: Armed Conflicts 1990-1999

Region	1990	1991	1992	1993	1994	1995	1996	1997	1998	1999
Asia & Pacific	21	21	25	24	23	21	22	24	19	20
Central & South America	7	6	5	3	4	5	4	3	3	2
North Africa & Middle East	7	8	8	9	9	9	8	8	6	4
Sub-Saharan Africa	17	22	18	18	23	21	18	19	18	16
Europe	4	10	12	8	6	4	2	3	3	5
Total	56	67	68	62	65	60	54	57	49	47

Republic of Congo (former Zaire) from 1998 into 2000 is in a category by itself that is perhaps best regarded as trans-national. It was, in part, a civil war, fought to determine whether President Laurent Kabila should remain in power, and in part an international war for regional power and influence. Angola, Chad, Namibia, Sudan and Zimbabwe were allied with President Kabila's forces, while Rwanda and Uganda fought against them and, in 2000, against each other as well.

As Table 1 indicates, the global, annual number of armed conflicts rose sharply in the early 1990s, from 56 in 1990 (and 47 in 1989) to 68 in 1992. In those years the initial optimism about the end of the Cold War was quickly supplanted by a new pessimism, in reaction to the apparent wave of new conflicts in the post-Cold War era. As it turns out, however, the number of armed conflicts each year has since stabilised and then even declined (the total of 118 wars 1990-1999, therefore, is made up of 100 primarily civil wars, 2 essentially civil wars, 5 wars of independence, 10 inter-state wars and 1 trans-national war).

New violent conflicts in Europe (including Russia, Turkey and the Caucasus) account for two-thirds of the increase in the annual incidence of wars in the early 1990s. At that time, the region quickly became one of the most violent in the world. The decline in the annual number of armed conflicts after 1992 is likewise largely due to changes in Europe, until the particularly sharp fall between 1997 and 1998. The upsurge in violent conflict in Europe was itself highly concentrated in the Balkans and the Caucasus, in the context of the processes of disintegration in Yugoslavia and the USSR. The fact that that upsurge has now abated suggests that the proliferation of war in Europe in the early 1990s did not herald a new era of violent conflict on the continent, as many commentators feared at the time. Those conflicts were, rather, the violent and tragic symptoms of social, economic and political readjustment following the collapse of the systems of power in Yugoslavia and the USSR. As the effects of those complex readjustments are assimilated at both the national and international levels, their consequences have fortunately become less dramatic and less violent.

Nevertheless, any optimism generated by this conclusion should be tempered by two further considerations. First, on the global level, the old conflicts are very much present. Of the armed conflicts active in 1999, 66 per cent were more than five years old, and 30 per cent had lasted for longer than 20 years. These protracted armed conflicts have proven to be extremely difficult to bring to an end. The world, therefore, is not necessarily entering a new and more peaceful era. Second, in Europe, most of the armed conflicts that began in the late 1980s or early 1990s, and that are now inactive, have not really been brought to an end. Rather, they have been suspended.

This difference between 'ended' and 'suspended' is crucial to understanding the problem of armed conflict today. The international political landscape is disfigured by wars that resume after not only the signing of cease-fires, but even after the conclusion of peace agreements. In the past decade alone, among the wars that have resumed after the conclusion of cease-fires or apparent peace agreements, it is possible to count those in Angola, Burundi, Cambodia, Chechnya, Croatia, Democratic Republic of Congo, Eritrea and Ethiopia, Kosovo, Liberia, the Philippines, Rwanda, Sierra Leone and Sri Lanka. Often the wars return with even greater ferocity and destructiveness, and almost always at particularly high cost for the civilian population.

There are many different reasons for the resumption of war: these can be grouped under four headings. The first is simple insincerity by one or both parties (the Revolutionary United Front (RUF) in Sierra Leone is a case in point; it cannot be trusted to keep any agreement). The second reason is disappointment on the part of one or both of the parties. This may often seem, from the outside, to be the same thing as insincerity. There are many cases in which one side's acceptance of a peace agreement is only conditional, although the condition is neither publicly stated nor part of the peace agreement. In some cases, one side strongly expects to win the post-war election and only for that reason agrees to sign the peace agreement. If that expectation is not realised, they go back to war. UNITA in Angola is an example.

The third reason is internal disagreement and even fragmentation on one or both sides. This, too, may seem to be insincerity. Peace agreements often bring the tensions and conflicts within each party to the surface; the unity that was maintained for the sake of the war can quickly disintegrate if and when peace comes.

Indeed, the imminence of peace can often appear to be a threat to one part of the coalition on one side of the conflict, frustrating their capacity to fulfil long-term aims. Consider the splinter groups from the IRA in Northern Ireland in this context, or the rejection of the peace process in Israel and the West Bank by militants both in Israel and among the Palestinians.

The fourth reason for the resumption of war is that the underlying causes of armed conflict remain. Failure to address the long-term causes of the conflict will mean that all efforts at reconstruction are doomed to be, at best, cosmetic. Five years after the Dayton Agreement to end the war in Bosnia-Herzegovina, most observers continue to see a high risk that the war will resume if the international armed peacekeeping force were to withdraw.

The fundamental instability of peace agreements is one primary explanation for the fact protracted conflict is common – a major feature of contemporary war, as noted briefly above. Taber (1970, p45) explains a second reason for contemporary wars lasting for many years in terms of the relative weakness of the insurgent forces. The guerrillas can control the pace and intensity of combat by deciding where and how to strike; unless government forces are able and willing to locate major targets and strike pre-emptively the result will be a long, limited war, a rumbling conflict that erupts intermittently.

This is why combat zones are very often confined to one part of the country. It is perfectly possible for reporters, politicians, researchers, businessmen, diplomats, World Bank experts and other outsiders to visit the capital of a war-torn country and yet not to know that a war is going on. Because many armed conflicts are localised and remain relatively low-level for several years on end, they do not make good stories for the international news media. These conflicts rarely produce clear-cut events such as victories, triumphs and disasters; they simply linger on as a slow torture for the participants. However, this should not create the illusion of their capacity to escalate suddenly and viciously. When that escalation occurs, it often seems to international observers to have come out of a clear blue sky. Such was the initial reaction to the massacres in Rwanda in 1994. Regardless of this, not only did those massacres take place against a historical background of repetitive cycles of mass killings, but also it is now known that there were many signs of imminent tragedy that were ignored until after it was too late (Adelman and Suhrke 1996).

3. Theories of Conflict Causes

The decision to take up arms is a complex process involving many actors in a wide range of conditions and circumstances. Thus the history of a war's outbreak is usually complex, and the historian must make carefully nuanced choices as to which factors to stress and what evidence to trust. Attempting to develop theoretical explanations for the causes of armed conflict as a general phenomenon involves the analysis of multiple, interactive variables. This is true even when looking at a limited period of time such as the post-1945 era, or even the years since the end of the Cold War. The task is complicated because, as Welch (1993, p8) points out, there are very few necessary conditions for war and very many sufficient conditions, of which only a few of these may apply in any single conflict. War is possible as soon as weapons are available with which to fight it and as long as there is a dispute between two or more parties. What makes war probable, however, is a far more complicated question.

Despite the work of scholars such as Gurr (1970), Horowitz (1985), and Rapoport (1989), most research conducted before 1990 on the causes of armed conflict focused on international conflict. This is remarkable, because, since at least 1945, civil or internal conflicts have been more common than international or inter-state conflicts (Singer 1996, p35). However, the relative importance of internal or civil conflicts from a global perspective has only been generally recognised since the end of the Cold War. Even as recently as that, the conclusions of a major analytical review of the University of Michigan's Correlates of War database concentrated almost exclusively on inter-state wars (Vasquez 1987). Since 1990, however, there has been an impressive growth in the scope of scholarly research and literature on the causes of armed conflicts that are not between two or more established states. Current research on internal conflicts focuses particularly on ethnic, environmental, political and economic factors.

Relative deprivation theory (Gurr 1970) offers an explanation that is based on the contrast between groups' expected and actual access to prosperity and power. This approach is closely related to *group entitlement theory* (Horowitz 1985), which places more explicit emphasis on ethnic factors which accompany the economic and political (*see* also Gurr 1995). However, ethnic diversity does not in itself seem to be a cause of war. If it were, the most war-prone states would be the most ethnically diverse, which is in fact not the case (Smith 1997, p30). Indeed, it may well be that ethnic and religious factionalization even reduces the risk of violent conflict (Collier 1999), perhaps because it encourages divergent groups to learn the skills of living together despite diversity. When this learning process fails, however, ethnic diversity may turn out to exacerbate conflict and increase the likelihood of serious escalation, precisely because it offers fertile material for political mobilisation. A prime example here is the disintegration of Yugoslavia during the 1990s, which is discussed below.

Research on the links between environmental degradation and conflict explores the varying (sometimes catastrophically low) capacity of states and societies to adapt to changing environmental conditions without resorting to violence (Homer-Dixon 1994). Those research approaches that have identified significant, simple and direct connections leading from environmental degradation to violent conflict, have, however, been strongly challenged (Gleditsch 1998, Lipschutz 1997). The most recent exposition of the argument downplays its theoretical claims considerably (Homer-Dixon 1999). The contention now is simply that there are some armed conflicts, such as those in Haiti and the Philippines, whose causes cannot be understood without reference to environmental degradation.

Research on the relationship between political systems and peace starts with the observation that democratic states almost never go to war with each other (Russett 1993). Levy (1989, p270) describes this finding as being "as close as anything we have to an empirical law in international relations." This claim has generated controversy (reviewed by Chan 1997), both as to its empirical robustness and as to its theoretical soundness. MacMillan (1996) contends that such a conclusion is based on a misguided research focus. The empirical assertion, however, is widely accepted, even if further theoretical and conceptual clarification is still necessary (Starr 1997).

The hot topic today in this aspect of research on the causes of armed conflict is the question of whether democracies are in general as peaceable with themselves as they are with each other. The argument that they are in fact more peaceable is set out by Rummel (1995), and disputed by Risse-Kappen (1995). Hegre, Gates, and Gleditsch (1999) introduce an essential nuance to the discussion by identifying the different propensities to internal conflict of different kinds of democracies. They conclude that it is the not quite democratic, yet also not quite autocratic regimes that are the most war-prone. Transition towards democracy is particularly dangerous (Jaggers and Gurr 1995, pp477-8). This argument throws considerable light on the violent conflicts in former Yugoslavia and the ex-USSR as societies in the midst of systemic change and the disintegration of a federal state, and likewise on the upsurge in violence in Indonesia since the end of the Suharto regime in 1998.

Overall, however, economic conditions emerge as the most important explanatory factors. The key issue here is a low level of economic development (Hauge and Ellingsen 1998). This may be indicated by a low average Gross National Product per capita, by a disporportionately large agricultural sector, or by a country's economic vulnerability to shifts in world markets in commodities and capital (Avery and Rapkin 1986). Like Hauge and Ellingsen (1998), Auvinen (1997) identifies lack of democratic openings as an important secondary factor in addition to poor economic conditions. These findings are qualified by the arguments and evidence put forward by Collier (1999; *see* also Collier and Hoeffler 1999) that, even in poor societies, leaders are usually competing with one another for control of the available economic surplus, small as that may be. When the available surplus is small, as in poor societies or where there has been catastrophic slump, competition for it may be particularly intense, and a violent escalation will very likely result. The terrible violence in Liberia from 1989 to 1997, the war in Sierra Leone since 1991, decades of warfare in Angola and the cycles of massacre and brutality in Burundi and Rwanda are among the many examples highlighted by this approach.

A very general conclusion from all this could be drawn as follows:

- Poor economic conditions are the most important long-term causes of intra-state armed conflicts today;
- Repressive political systems are also war-prone, especially in periods of transition;
- Degradation of renewable resources (specifically soil erosion, deforestation and water scarcity) can also contribute significantly to the likelihood of violent conflict, but are in general not as central to the problem as political and economic determinants;
- Ethnic diversity alone is not a cause of armed conflict, but parties to a conflict are often defined by their ethnic identities.

4. Background Causes and Foreground Factors

Social science theories of the causes of armed conflict concentrate on background conditions and long-range causes in order to develop general explanatory power. However, these theories should not be regarded with much greater respect than we might give to any other reasonable generalisation. They are based on statistical generalisations, to which there are almost always exceptions. Poor, undemocratic countries, for instance, are especially prone to armed conflict, but there are many armed conflicts in countries that are not among the poorest and most repressive of the world. Likewise, there are countries that are both extremely poor and repressed, yet in which there is no war.

One problem in the academic literature is that it usually focuses attention on the question of which is the most important cause of armed conflict. In most cases, however, this is a misleading way to look at the issue. The question is not which cause is more important than any other, but rather how do the different causes interact? In particular, the attempt to force a choice between economic and political explanations of armed conflict is misguided. Explanations that highlight economic deficiencies and environmental degradation deal with how the problems of securing the basics of life can lead people into conflict. Violent conflict can easily develop if large numbers of people become convinced that taking up arms is not only legitimate but may perhaps be the only way to secure the necessities of life. In other words, they feel that they are in an unjust situation and must therefore decide to rectify it. However, large numbers of people do not make such decisions spontaneously. They mobilise politically, as leaders win their hearts and minds, as well as their loyalty and commitment, and as they are persuaded and exhorted into war. No meaningful analysis of violent conflict and of its escalation and diminishment can therefore afford to ignore the political dimension.

One of the analytical problems in this connection lies in the incompatibilities between political theory and political practice. Theory tends to focus on long term conditions and general explanations, and loses precision by aiming for universality (Levy 1989, p297). In the big picture, the details of political behaviour are likely to be lost. By contrast, although political leaders are often prone to emphasise grand strategic visions, ultimately their survival depends on their capacity to deal with the details. Social science theories take the long view, but in politics the short term predominates. Thus any attempt to understand armed conflict as a global phenomenon must deal with the big socio-economic picture, while efforts to analyse a particular armed conflict will need to focus instead on politics and on the actions of specific organisations and individuals.

Rather than allowing these different levels – broad theoretical generalisations on the one hand and detailed analyses on the other – to exist in complete isolation, it is more productive to seek ways to combine them. Only then can the broad generalisations give the analyst useful guidance as to which cases to prioritise, and where to look for the greatest dangers.

If such an approach is taken, causal explanations will not only need to reflect the social, cultural, economic and environmental background, but also consider the political foreground. Put differently, in addition to longer-term structural explanations, we need to also consider politics. The great Prussian military philosopher Clausewitz (1832/1976) defined war as "an act of force to compel our enemy to do our will" and "the continuation of policy by other means." Keegan (1994, pp3-12) argues that such a definition of war is misleading because it ignores the way that culture shapes both why and how people go to war. To allow Clausewitz to dominate the exploration of causes would be a clear error; yet background factors influence events in the direction of armed conflict only via politics. Wars are conscious and consciously decided affairs. Explanation of their causes must embrace the background as well as the foreground, both the structural causes and the factors that lie within the decision-making power of political actors. A comprehensive explanation of the causes of armed conflicts, in short, must be based on a combination of both levels and types of analysis.

5. Methodology and Typology

Dessler (1994) offers a good point of reference for such a multi-level analysis. In the multiplicity of potential causes of armed conflicts, he sees not just different causes but different types of causes, and presents a four-part typology in which to organise them. With just a few changes in terminology and one of content, the analytical framework derived from his arguments can be summarised as follows:

- **Background causes** (channels in Dessler, 1994) are fundamental lines of "political, social, economic, or national cleavage ... found at the level of the group, rather than the individual." These may be constituted by the exclusion of some groups from power, by the systematic favouring of others, or by regional economic differences. What is seen here, in short, are the basic elements of social and political structure. To explore them is to explore the background causes and underlying conditions of conflict.
- **Mobilisation strategy** (targets in Dessler, 1994) consists of both the objectives of key political actors and (this is my variation on Dessler's theme) the way in which they go about trying to fulfil their objectives. In other words, when we analyse mobilisation strategy, we are considering the full range of political behaviour – both how issues are conceptualised, and how they are presented. Therefore, we are looking at the causes for which people fight and considering how they understand their cause.
- **Triggers** are the factors that affect the timing of the onset of armed conflict; referring to these can help explain not why a conflict started at all, but why it started then. They are often events or actions undertaken by significant actors, which narrow the choices of the players, making peaceful approaches less, and violent options more, attractive.
- **Catalysts** are factors that affect the intensity and duration of the conflict; they may be internal, such as the military balance between the opposing sides, or external, such as UN intervention. These may include tactics (whether insurgents avoid attacking civilian areas, for example), or natural phenomena such as the terrain, the seasons and the weather. They may be material factors, such as the availability of arms, or even less concrete but no less important factors like cultural views on how war should be fought.

This typology switches the focus from background conditions to actors and back again. It does not provide a theory of causation, but is rather a way of organising theory. It also indicates the angles we should explore, and suggests ways of organising the analysis of individual cases of conflict escalation. It is particularly the first two categories – the background causes and the mobilisation strategies – that must be addressed in any attempt to prevent violent conflict escalation. The last category – catalysts – may be equally important when considering how to bring violence to an end.

6. Injustice and Mobilisation

There are two concepts that together depict the point at which the long-term and short-term causes intersect, where political actors address structural, background issues. Those concepts are justice and mobilisation.

The combination of poor economic conditions and a lack of political openings functions as a double injustice. Political mobilisation occurs around the theme of injustice: people commit themselves to a cause because they believe it to be just, or because they at least think that it will redress the injustice they see in their own lives. An exploitable sense of injustice, arising out of the underlying divisions of power and prosperity in a society or between different countries, is thus the basic material for political mobilisation.

Some careful distinctions need to be made at this point in the discussion. The argument here is not that, for example, Yugoslav leader Slobodan Milosevic has acted as he has out of a burning sense of injustice about the plight of the Serbs. The evidence is rather that he has been primarily interested in perpetuating his own power and that of a narrow group united around his leadership (Little and Silber 1995; Judah 1997; 1999). But Milosevic's rhetoric is replete with complaints about the injustice suffered by Serbs. Since 1987 he spoke regularly and repeatedly of Serb grievances. Regardless of whether he felt injustice himself, he knew how to utilise the concept. In this aspect of his political career, he is an archetype. He played effectively upon an exploitable sense of injustice.

This idea of justice as a motivating factor in armed conflict has been challenged by emphasising "not the loud discourse of grievance, but the silent force of greed" (Collier 1999). In part, the argument revolves around just how much emphasis should be placed on language and discourse. The key methodological point is the contention that, for research purposes, "[t]he demand for justice can be reformulated as the circumstances which generate grievance" (Collier and Hoeffler 1999, p5). However, to reformulate a subjective demand as objective circumstances is misleading, for it is precisely in the demand that mobilisation and perception lie. In part, however, the argument about greed versus grievance can be summed up and put into a proper perspective by asking whose greed, whose grievance? That Milosevic is greedy for power, for example, does not in itself mean that ordinary Serbs feel no grievance. In other words, it may not be necessary to choose between greed and grievance as explanatory variables. These may rather be complementary and mutually reinforcing elements of political mobilisation.

7. Ethnicity and Conflict

To illustrate the themes above and to explore their implications for analysis, it might be helpful to look more closely at the category referred to in both the scholarly literature and more popular commentaries as 'ethnic' conflicts. This is usually understood to mean not only that the parties involved are ethnically different, but also that that ethnic difference is central to the conflict. It implies not only a description of at least one of the parties, but also an ascription of at least one cause (if not the cause) of conflict as ethnic difference.

The definition of ethnic difference is much contested and notoriously difficult to pin down. Generalisations are particularly difficult and misleading because ethnic identity is recognised on a wide variety of different bases. In different cases, groups identify themselves as an ethnically united community by means of some combination of markers such as language, skin colour, religion, location, or history. What is decisive in constituting a particular ethnic identity is not shared historical experiences, myths and religious beliefs, or other features per se; these only become decisive when there is a shared perception that they distinguish members of that group from those who belong to other groups in some significant way. Two factors that can foster this kind of shared perception are experiences of discrimination compared with other groups and deliberate political mobilisation in defence of the group's perceived interests.

In the Balkan conflicts of the 1990s, diplomats and politicians of the external powers began by regarding the problem as easily amenable to treatment by stern diplomacy – just a matter of banging a few heads together (Little and Silber 1995, p159). It was as if there were no underlying causes more profound than simple irresponsibility. When that view proved to be clearly wrong, deeper causes were sought, but no more accurately. US Secretary of State Warren Christopher stated that war in Bosnia-Hercegovina was caused by "ancient ethnic hatreds" (Calhoun 1997, p61). The International Commission on the Balkans (1996, pp13-14) noted and at the same time criticised a common view which blamed the problem on the hot-blooded nature of the Balkan people. It is implicit in such arguments (though not always in the use of the term ethnic conflict) that not much can be done to resolve such conflicts or to help such people.

This form of argument uses the same terms and sometimes arrives at the same conclusions as those reached by protagonists in what are called ethnic conflicts. Kaufman (1996), for example, concludes that ethnic civil wars can only be ended through forced separation of the populations. This is otherwise known as ethnic cleansing and appears to assume, as the ethnic cleansers themselves do, that everybody is either in one group (e.g., Serb) or another (e.g., Bosniak), with no possibility that anybody is the off-spring of a mixed marriage.

Leaving aside the moral problem, the intellectual shortcomings of this way of depicting the causes of conflicts are best exposed when analysts make use of the abstract categories of the typology outlined above. The ancient hatreds and hot blood explanations of wars in the Balkans make three errors about the present (and usually many more about the past): they understand ethnicity exclusively as a background cause; they understand it to be the only background cause and they fail to consider the role of any other type of cause. Especially significant is the fact that they entirely ignore mobilisation strategy.

The error lies not in regarding ethnic difference as one of the underlying social divisions and therefore as a background cause. Rather, it is to neglect the question of how that underlying division can create the conditions for war. Numerous case studies have made it clear that ethnic difference is often embroiled in conflicts and that the individuals affected frequently believe that the fundamental issue over which they are fighting is in fact ethnic difference. This is important, but it is not sufficient, for, as we have already noted, it is not the most ethnically diverse countries in the world that are the most prone to violent conflict. This suggests that, even in cases of armed conflicts involving parties divided by ethnicity, we cannot analyse the situation adequately by looking at ethnicity alone. The results of the quantitative research cited above indicate the importance of economic conditions and of the political system. It would therefore make sense to examine other background causes beyond ethnicity.

The second change of focus is to look at political mobilisation. Ethnicity is very often a central component of group identity and therefore also a powerful component of common prejudice. As such, it can easily be manipulated by political leaders seeking to mobilise a population, especially when a society is undergoing major socio-economic change. It is at such times that nationalist politics come to the fore.

Nationalism is a political ideology claiming that nations and states should be territorially congruent (Gellner 1983, p1), but it is also more. It can be regarded as a complex social, cultural, intellectual and emotional reaction to socio-economic and political destabilisation (Plamenatz 1976). Such destabilisation can come in the shape of the impact of modernity (Smith 1983), the imposition of colonial rule (Anderson 1991; Seton-Watson 1977) or the collapse of state socialism (Smith and Østerud 1995). It can be argued that the creation of a single world market, the driving force behind the process known as globalisation, has a similar destabilising impact. The effect of globalisation on ethnocentrism and nationalism is ambivalent. On the one hand, it is a force that homogenises cultures and life styles and promotes a more cosmopolitan awareness. On the other hand, the fast relocation of investment capital and the integration of markets world wide create new winners and losers, which can lead to fragmentation and marginalisation of some ethnic and national groups and a reaction against cultural homogenisation.

The social destabilisation that these large and blind historical processes can unleash not only creates the conditions for intense power rivalries between different factions of a country's social and political elite. It can also throw large numbers of ordinary people into a situation of deep insecurity and uncertainty. The impact of such historical changes on individuals' lives is arbitrary, often devastating, and difficult to understand. The assertion of group identity at such a time is attractive to many ordinary people; it may be the only thing that helps them make any kind of sense out of what is happening to them. Thus, whatever the issues at stake in a conflict that itself arises out of such large-scale change and destabilisation, political leaders are most likely to mobilise their constituency successfully if they can present their stance as a battle for national identity, pride and justice.

We could summarise these arguments as follows: it is not ethnic diversity as such that is a cause of armed conflict, but rather ethnic politics. It is the injection of ethnic difference into political loyalties, and the politicisation of ethnic identities, that is so dangerous.

In explaining the break-up of former Yugoslavia, it is important to note not only that Yugoslavia was a multi-ethnic state, but also that that state looked back on a history of ethnonationalism for more than 100 years. Ethnicity had long been politicised, and the period of Tito's rule from 1945 to 1980 was no exception. While Tito repressed the kind of nationalist politics that could have threatened the unity of the Socialist Federal Republic of Yugoslavia, he at the same time distributed constitutional and political power on an ethno-national basis. This shaped the organs of both state and party. When Tito died, his rule was replaced by a Presidency that rotated, year to year, between the six republics and two provinces that made up the Federation. Thus, when in 1987, nationalism started to become the strongest political currency in Yugoslavia, it did not come out of the blue; neither was it a product of hot blood. It was the direct product of the political system.

The renewed salience of nationalism began in Serbia where Slobodan Milosevic was the first post-Tito communist leader to play the nationalist card in 1987. Within two years, nationalist politics in Serbia had brought forth responses, first from Slovenia, then from Croatia.

As soon as nationalist rivalries started to be expressed by the leaderships of the different republics, momentum towards break-up was created, bolstered by the system of the rotating presidency.

Milosevic's motive, howcvcr, was not to destroy the Federation. His initial aim was to mobilise popular support in order to gain control of the Serbian party (Little and Silber 1996). The first instance of the systematic sense of grievance on which he was to play effectively came in a 50-page memorandum issued by the Serbian Academy of Arts and Sciences in 1986. In this now famous document, sixteen academics complained at length about the unfair treatment of the Serb people under the 1974 Yugoslav constitution, and in particular about 'genocide' against Serbs in Kosovo (Vetlesen 2000).

Whether or not Milosevic truly believed in and felt the sense of resentment and injustice that he exploited in political mobilisation is irrelevant to the argument here. In former Yugoslavia, neither Milosevic, who played the nationalist card first, nor Slovenia's leader Milan Kucan, who played it second, had any record of previous nationalist views. On the other hand, Croatia's Franjo Tudjman, Bosniak leader Alia Izetbegovic, and several of the rivals for leadership of the Kosovar Albanians can all be regarded as principled nationalists. In the case of all these individuals, whatever their personal differences, they rose to power in essentially the same way: by mobilising popular support around the theme of national injustice. These competing perceptions of injustice made an explosive mix that blew Yugoslavia apart.

Equally, it does not really matter whether an outside observer would share the sense of injustice in any one (or more than one) of the component populations of former Yugoslavia. Nor is it important whether that observer would agree, as a matter of impartial judgement, that one (or more) of the leaders had a political programme that would redress the injustice to which his followers had been subjected. What is essential is only whether the people feel it, and whether a leader can and will exploit it.

What are commonly called ethnic conflicts, then, are in the end conflicts over power or for access to economic resources (including environmental resources in cases not discussed here), which come to wear an ethnic mask. Ethnic difference is of central importance not as a sole cause of armed conflict, but rather as an instrument of mobilisation for political leaders. Thus, ethnic difference has an important place in the explanation but should not dominate it.

Use of this metaphor of an ethnic mask to focus attention on this particular strategy of political mobilisation should not be misinterpreted as any attempt to downplay the reality or importance of a sense of identity, either in or out of violent conflict. There is little doubt, for example, that the Russo-Chechen wars of the 1990s are characterised by a deep, clear and bitter sense of ethnic identity on the Chechen side, as well as by an all too widespread Russian racism against the Chechens. For over 200 years, Chechen movements have resisted Russian control. Even so, the conflict between Russia and Chechnya cannot be properly understood if it is analysed as simply being about ethnicity.

There are interesting parallels between this conflict and the break-up of Yugoslavia. The struggle for power between new and old political elites was a significant part of the explanation of the build-up to the war between Chechnya and Russia in 1994. It was a crucial factor in the seizure of power in Chechnya by General Dzhokhar Dudayev and his allies in August and September 1991 (Tishkov 1997, pp200-206). The leaders of both Chechnya and Russia seemed unable to avoid escalation of their disputes into full-scale war during the second half of 1994, partly because of government deficiencies on both sides (Lieven 1998, pp80-84, 94-96), and partly due to rivals manoeuvring for power in both Chechnya (Tishkov 1997, pp216-218) and Moscow (Shapiro 1995).

The tragedy is that, once the ethnic mask has been donned, it is very difficult to remove. When a revived sense of group identity coheres around resentment and grievance, especially in time of crisis and war, it can produce apparently irreconcilable hatred in protracted and often cyclical conflicts.

The prime contemporary example of this can be seen in the Hutu/Tutsi rivalries of Burundi and Rwanda. These do not date from time immemorial. It was colonial administrators who defined the two groups as different and then proceeded to favour one at the expense of the other. This engendered resentment. From the moment of independence, political leaders systematically exploited this group grievance in order to maintain (or challenge) power, thereby bringing about forty years of wars and massacres (Copson 1994). The Singhalese/Tamil conflict in Sri Lanka unfolded in a similar way in the years after independence, as comparable feelings of grievance led to prolonged civil war (Uyangoda 1996).

In the processes of mobilisation that led up to these conflicts, one of the elements that can be observed over and over again is the fervent, popular support that is expressed for the cause on one side or on both. This belief in the cause is a belief in its rightness, in its justice. Both the Serbs and the Albanians in Kosovo before the war in 1998 and 1999, strongly resented the injustices they felt that they faced. Both Hutus and Tutsis in both Burundi and Rwanda can speak stirringly of the injustices meted out to them by the other. Both Singhalese and Tamils in Sri Lanka can recount the injustices they have suffered at the hands of the other. In many armed conflicts today, the tactics and strategy of one party or both involve direct attack on civilians – ethnic cleansing, massacre and systematic rape in Bosnia-Hercegovina and Rwanda, bombing civilian areas in Chechnya. The memory of these horrors perpetuates a bitter sense of group identity, serving as fertile ground for mobilisation for the next time around.

8. Conclusion

There is now a significant, useful and growing body of literature on the causes of armed conflicts. While the theoretical conclusions in this literature so far are necessarily limited, they are also important, because they direct our attention towards the key issues of poor economic conditions, lack of political openings, and environmental damage, while at the same time warning us not to regard ethnic diversity as such as a cause of armed conflict.

This research has so far been primarily concerned with the long-term socio-economic and political conditions that generally lie behind armed conflict today. In order to use it as a contribution for the analysis of specific cases of armed conflict, we must also find a way to relate these long-term underlying conditions to the short-term considerations that any case study will also highlight.

In this article, we have looked at two related means of achieving such a link. The first is a methodology that helps organise both theoretical and empirical material, and can therefore guide the analysis. The second is a conceptual pairing that links long-term and short-term issues – the concepts of justice and of mobilisation. For as long as the world and the countries within it are socially and economically structured in unjust ways, there will always be people who feel that injustice, and leaders who can cement their power by exploiting it. Justice is thus the keynote for conflict analysis – and for peace.

9. Reference and Further Reading

Adelman, Howard and Astri Suhrke 1996. "Early Warning and Conflict Management," in Joint Evaluation of Emergency Assistance to Rwanda, *The International Response to Conflict and Genocide: Lessons from the Rwanda Experience*, Copenhagen: DANIDA.

Anderson, Benedict 1991. *Imagined Communities*, London: Verso.

Auvinen, Juha 1997. "Political Conflict in Less Developed Countries 198–89," *Journal of Peace Research*, 34, 2, 177–195.

Avery, William P, and David P. Rapkin 1986. "World Markets and Political Instability within Less Developed Countries," *Cooperation and Conflict*, 21, 2, 99–117.

Calhoun, Craig 1997. *Nationalism*, Buckingham: Open University Press.

Chan, Steve 1997. "In Search of Democratic Peace: Problems and Promise," *Mershon International Studies Review*, 41 (Supplement 1), 59–91.

Clausewitz, Carl von 1832/1976. *On War* (Translated by Howard, Michael and Peter Paret), Princeton, NJ: Princeton University Press.

Collier, Paul 1999. "Doing Well out of War," Paper prepared for Conference on Economic Agendas in Civil Wars, London, April 26–27, 1999.

Collier, Paul, and Anke Hoeffler 1999. *Justice-Seeking and Loot-Seeking in Civil War*, Washington, DC: The World Bank/CSAE.

Copson, Raymond W. 1994. *Africa's Wars and Prospects for Peace*, New York: M.E. Sharpe.

Dessler, David 1994. "How to Sort Causes in the Study of Environmental Change and Violent Conflict," *in* Græger and Smith, op. cit.

Gellner, Ernest 1983. *Nations and Nationalism*, Oxford: Blackwell.

Gleditsch, Nils Petter (ed.) 1997. *Conflict and the Environment*, Dordrecht: Kluwer Academic.

Gleditsch, Nils Petter 1998. "Armed Conflict and the Environment: A Critique of the Literature," *Journal of Peace Research*, 35, 3, 381–400.

v. d. Goor, L., K. Rupesinghe and P. Sciarone (eds.) 1996. *Between Development and Destruction: An Enquiry into the Causes of Conflict in Post-Colonial States*, The Hague: Netherlands Ministry of Foreign Affairs/The Netherlands Insititute of International Relations.

Græger, N and D. Smith (eds.) 1994. *Environment, Poverty, Conflict*, Oslo: International Peace Research Institute.

Gurr, Ted Robert 1970. *Why Men Rebel*, Princeton, NJ: Princeton University Press.

Gurr, Ted Robert 1995. *Minorities at risk: a global view of ethnopolitical conflicts*, Washington, D.C.: United States Institute of Peace Press.

Hauge, Wenche, and Tanja Ellingsen 1998. "Beyond Environmental Scarcity: Causal Pathways to Conflict," *Journal of Peace Research*, 35, 3, 299–317.

Hegre, Håvard, Scott Gates and Nils Petter Gleditsch 1999. *Estimating the Relative Risk of Civil War* (unpublished paper, International Peace Research Institute, Oslo).

Homer-Dixon, Thomas 1994. "Environmental Scarcities and Violent Conflict: Evidence from Cases," *International Security*, 19, 1, 5–40.

Homer-Dixon, Thomas 1999. *Environment, scarcity and violence*, Princeton, NJ: Princeton University Press.

Horowitz, David 1985. *Ethnic Groups in Conflict*, Berkeley, Ca: University of California Press.

International Commission on the Balkans 1996. *Unfinished Peace*, Washington, DC: Carnegie Endowment for Peace.

Jaggers, Keith, and Ted Robert Gurr 1995. "Tracking Democracy's Third Wave with the Polity III Data," *Journal of Peace Research*, 32, 4, 469–482.

Judah, Tim 1997. *The Serbs: History, Myth and the Destruction of Yugoslavia*, New Haven, Conn: Yale University Press.

Judah, Tim 1999. "Kosovo's Road to War," *Survival*, 41, 2, 5–18.

Kamenka, E. (ed.) 1976. *Nationalism: The Nature and Evolution of an Idea*, London: Edward Arnold.

Kaufman, Chaim 1996. "Possible and Impossible Solutions to Ethnic Civil Wars," *International Security*, 20, 4, 136–175.

Keegan, John 1994. *A History of Warfare,* New York, NY: Random House/Vintage.

Levy, Jack S. 1989. "The Causes Of War: A Review Of Theories And Evidence," in Philip E. Tetlock et al. (eds.) *Behavior, Society, and Nuclear War. Vol. 1*, New York: Oxford University Press, 209-333.

Lieven, Anatol 1998. *Chechnya, Tombstone of Russian Power,* London, New Haven, Conn: Yale University Press.

Lipschutz, Ronnie D. 1997. "Environmental Conflict and Environmental Determinism: The Relative Importance of Social and Natural Factors," *in* Gleditsch, op. cit.

Little, Alan and Laura Silber 1995. *Yugoslavia: Death of a Nation*, New York, NY: Penguin Books.

MacMillan, John 1996. "Democracies don't fight: a case of the wrong research agenda?" *Review of International Studies*, 22, 3, 275–299.

Plamenatz, John 1976. "Two Types of Nationalism," *in* Kamenka, op. cit.

Rapoport, Anatol 1989. *The Origins of Violence: Approaches to the Study of Conflict*, New York, NY: Paragon House.

Risse-Kappen, Thomas 1995. "Democratic Peace – Warlike Democracies? A Social Constructivist Interpretation of the Liberal Argument," *European Journal of International Relations*, 1, 4, 491–517.

Rummel, R.J. 1995. "Democracies ARE Less Warlike Than Other Regimes," *European Journal of International Relations*, 1, 4, 457–479.

Rupesinghe, K. and K. Mumtaz (eds.) 1996. *Internal Conflicts in South Asia*, London: Sage.

Russett, Bruce 1993. *Grasping the Democratic Peace*, Princeton, NJ: Princeton University Press.

Seton-Watson, Hugh 1977. *Nations and States. An inquiry into the origins of nations and the politics of nationalism*, London: Methuen.

Shapiro, Margaret 1995. "Return of the Apparatchiks," *International Herald Tribune*, 16 January.

Singer, David 1996. "Armed Conflict in the Former Colonial Regions: From Classification to Explanation," *in* v. d. Goor et. al., op. cit.

Smith, Anthony D. 1983. *Theories of Nationalism*, 2nd ed., London: Duckworth.

Smith, Dan 1997. *The State of War and Peace Atlas*, London & New York, NY: Penguin Books.

Smith, Dan and Øyvind Østerud 1995. *Nation-State, Nationalism and Political Identity*, Oslo: University of Oslo.

Starr, Harvey 1997. "Democracy and Integration: Why Democracies Don't Fight Each Other," *Journal of Peace Research*, 34, 2, 153–162.

Taber, Robert 1970. *The War of the Flea: A Study of Guerrilla Warfare Theory and Practice*, St. Albans: Paladin.

Tishkov, Valery 1997. *Ethnicity, Nationalism and Conflict in and after the Soviet Union*, London: Sage.

Uyangoda, Jayadeva 1996. "Militarization, Violent State, Violent Society: Sri Lanka," *in* Rupesinghe, op. cit.

Vasquez, John A. 1987. "The Steps to War: Toward a Scientific Explanation of Correlates of War Findings," *World Politics*, XL (October), 108–145.

Vetlesen, Arne Johan 2000. "Genocide: A Case for the Responsibility of the Bystander," *Journal of Peace Research*, 37, 4, 519–532.

Wallensteen, Peter and Margareta Sollenberg 1996. "The End of International War? Armed Conflict 1989-95," *Journal of Peace Research*, 33, 3, 353–370.

Wallensteen, Peter and Margareta Sollenberg 1997. "Armed Conflicts, Conflict Termination and Peace Agreements, 1989-96," *Journal of Peace Research*, 34, 3, 339–358.

Wallensteen, Peter and Margareta Sollenberg 1998. "Armed Conflict and Regional Conflict Complexes, 1989-97," *Journal of Peace Research*, 35, 5, 621–634.

Wallensteen, Peter and Margareta Sollenberg 1999. "Armed Conflict, 1989-98," *Journal of Peace Research*, 36, 5, 593–606.

Wallenstein, Peter and Margareta Sollenberg 2000. "Armed Conflict, 1989-1999," *Journal of Peace Research*, 37, 5, 635–649.

Welch, David 1993. *Justice and the Genesis of War*, Cambridge: Cambridge University Press.

Early Warning and The Field: A Cargo Cult Science?

Alexander Austin

1. Introduction 130
2. Mapping Out the Field of Early Warning 132
Qualitative early warning
Quantitative early warning
Qualitative and quantitative early warning
Networks
Concluding remarks
3. Conflict Mitigation and Crisis Prevention 142
Factors inhibiting the move from early warning to early response
Some tentative recommendations
4. Identifying the Causes and Predicting Conflict 144
Quantitative empirical evidence – the search for unicorns
5. Conclusion 148
6. Reference and Further Reading 148

Early Warning and The Field: A Cargo Cult Science?

Alexander Austin

1. Introduction

Early warning is a large field with many different methodologies operating on different levels and with a wide range of issues. There are a broad variety of actors involved in these systems from grassroots projects to academics working on computer simulations. Few people would disagree with the concept of early warning: to obtain knowledge and, what is more, to use that knowledge to assist in the mitigation of conflict. In this sense, early warning is an irrefutable necessity. There is a need to actively engage in crisis prevention where the first step is the prognosis of when, why and where conflict will erupt. This is the same process as any troubleshooting: what is the problem and cause, how imminent and what can we do about it? The options that can be taken are necessarily tied to the understanding of the cause. It is, in this sense, that crisis prevention is coupled to early warning.

Although related, it is different to ask whether early warning systems are essential or whether they can be successful. They are related to each other because the concepts of early warning behind their importance are in turn the criteria of success. This chapter will critically review whether early warning systems can effectively: (a) identify the causes of conflict, (b) predict the outbreak of conflict, and, what is more, (c) mitigate that conflict.

It is argued that unless the early warning system has a mechanism to mitigate the conflict, there is little utility to be gained in refining the accuracy of current models. Therefore, after outlining the field of early warning, I will discuss the challenges and problems facing these systems in relation to conflict mitigation before addressing the accuracy in identifying the causes and predicting the outbreak of violence.

Section II will outline the state-of-the-art in the field of early warning and identify the different areas of focus, methodologies and mechanisms employed. It will end by summarising these mechanisms into an archetypical model for early warning. Section III will assess the third goal of early warning and outline the major challenges facing the transition from early warning to early response. Contained within this section, I will propose some tentative recommendations on bridging the gap. Section IV will assess quantitative early warning systems against the first two goals of early warning by drawing on the work of Peter Winch (1995) in *The Idea of a Social Science and its Relation to Philosophy.*

The term *early warning system* (EWS) will be used generically to mean any initiative that focuses on systematic data collection, analysis and/or formulation of recommendations, including risk assessment and information sharing, regardless of topic, whether they are quantitative, qualitative or a blend of both. "*Risk assessments* are based on the systematic analysis of remote and intermediate conditions. Early warning requires near real-time assessment of events that, in a high risk environment, are likely to accelerate or trigger the rapid escalation of conflict." (Gurr 1996, 137) Leading on, *early response* will refer to any initiative that occurs in the latent stages of a perceived potential armed conflict with the aim at reduction, resolution or transformation. The term mechanism will refer to the individual units of an EWS such as data collection, data formatting, data analysis with the understanding that there is a relationship and process between these units for the system to operate. Although a term from the natural sciences, nothing more is implied than a sub-unit that interacts with other units to form a system. The term *model* will refer to the systems that are theoretically constructed such as *Minorities at Risk*[1] has developed, which is dependent upon predefined indicators.

Table 1: Overview of Acronyms of EWS	
AKUF	Working Group on Causes of War (Arbeitsgemeinschaft Kriegsursachenforschung)
BCOW	Behavioural Correlates of War
CASCON	Computer Aided System for Analysis of Conflicts
CEWS	Conflict Early Warning System
CEWP	Conflict Early Warning Project
CHE	Complex Humanitarian Emergencies
COPDAB	Conflict and Peace Data Bank
EAWARN	Network for Ethnological Monitoring and Early Warning
EEWS	Epidemiological Early Warning System
EWNET	Early Warning Network
EWS	Early Warning System
FAST	Early Recognition of Tensions and Fact Finding
FEWER	Forum on Early Warning and Early Response
FEWS	Famine Early Warning System
FUGI	Future of Global Interdependence
GEDS	Global Event Data System
GIEWS	Global Information Early Warning System
HEWS	United Nations Humanitarian Early Warning System
HURIDOCS	Human Rights Information and Documentation System
ICB	International Crisis Behaviour
ICG	International Crisis Group
ICOW	Issue Correlates of War
IDEA	Integrated Data for Event Analysis
KEDS	Kansas Event Data System
KOSIMO	Conflict Simulation Model (Konflikt-Simulations-Modell)

1 See http://www.cidcm.umd.edu/inscr/mar/home.htm

LIVA	Life Integrity Violations Approach
MAR	Minorities at Risk
PANDA	Protocol for the Analysis of Nonviolent Direct Action
PCIA	Peace and Conflict Impact Assessment
PIOOM	Interdisciplinary Research Programme on Root Causes of Human Rights Violations (Programma Interdisciplinair Onderzoek Oorzaken Mensenrechtenschendingen)
QnEWS	Quantitative Early Warning System
SIPRI	Stockholm International Peace Research Institute
TABARI	Textual Analysis by Augmented Replacement Instruction
TWEED	Terrorism in West Europe: Event Data Project
UNDHA	United Nations Department of Humanitarian Affairs
USAID	United States Agency for International Development
WEIS	World Events Interaction Survey (event data set)

2. Mapping Out the Field of Early Warning

EWS are not new mechanisms. They have been in existence since the 1950s, since when different focal issues have been addressed using different methodologies. The origins of the modern EWS can be found in two stems: first, the military strategic intelligence gathering to predict an attack. Second, those used to forecast humanitarian and natural disasters such as drought and famine exemplified by the United Nations Humanitarian Early Warning System (HEWS). This article will focus on current developments of the latter strand and its broadened application to include the analysis of ethnopolitical conflict.

The litany of contemporary EWS have analysed and warned on many different issues and areas. This spectrum has included: genocide, minorities, Complex Humanitarian Emergencies (CHEs), terrorism & human rights violations (*see* Table 2).

Early warning is a term that is often used to describe a variety of activities that are not all strictly early warning, including conflict analysis and monitoring, data analysis, risk assessment and advocacy. While some systems belong to one sector alone such as AKUF

Table 2: Early Warning about What?	
refugee / interdependencies / development / human rights violations	Future of Global Interdependence (FUGI)
	Amnesty International
	Human Rights Watch
	Interdisciplinary Research Programme on Root Causes of Human Rights Violations (PIOOM)
ethnopolitical conflict	Early Recognition of Tensions and Fact-finding (FAST)
	Forum on Early Warning and Early Response (FEWER)
	International Crisis Group (ICG)

Genocides and politicides	Accelerators of Genocide
	Genocides and Politicides Project
	Life Integrity Violations Approach (LIVA)
armed conflict / military expenditure / arms production	Global Event Data System (GEDS)
	State Failure Project
famine and food supplies	Famine Early Warning System (FEWS)
	Global Information Early Warning System (GIEWS)
successes and failures in preventing violent inter-group conflict	Conflict Early Warning System (CEWS)
militarised disputes	Correlates of War
crisis development and effectiveness of attempts at management	International Crisis Behaviour (ICB)
telecommunications and its relation to conflict	Leland Initiative: African Telemetric Project
Minorities	Minorities at Risk (MAR)
direct political action	Protocol for the Analysis of Nonviolent Direct Action (PANDA)
CHEs	ReliefWeb (UNDHA)
terrorism	Terrorism in Western Europe: Event Data Project (TWEED)

(conflict analysis) others often straddle sectors such as FAST (conflict analysis and monitoring, data analysis, risk assessment and advocacy).

Table 3: Sectors of Early Warning

Monitoring / Conflict Analysis	Model Data Analysis	Risk Assessment / Early Warning	Lobbying recommend	Networks
AKUF	KEDS	MAR (Minorities at Risk)	ICG (International Crisis Group)	FEWER (Forum on Early Warning and Early Response)
KOSIMO	PANDA	FAST	Human Rights Watch	Network on Ethnological Monitoring and Early Warning of Conflicts
SIPRI	Accelerator of Genocide	USAID		HURIDOCS (Human Rights Information and Documentation System)

Monitoring / Conflict Analysis	Model Data Analysis	Risk Assessment / Early Warning	Lobbying recommend	Networks
ICOW (Issue Correlates of War)	WEIS	FEWS		HEWS (Humanitarian Early Warning System)
UPSALLA	State Failure Project	GIEWS		EWNET
PIOOM	Accelerator Project	EEWS		Conflict Watch Inter Press Service
ICG (International Crisis Group)	GEDS	FUGI		
Human Rights Watch	KEDS	ICG		
	PANDA			

All the systems can be further divided into four methodological categories: quantitative, qualitative, a dual process of quantitative and qualitative, and finally networks (*see* Table 4). Table 2 provides a simplification of the main activities of the early warning systems.

2.1 Qualitative early warning

These systems are characterised by the '*watch*' group (Adelman et al. 1996, 47), exemplified by Human Rights Watch, Amnesty International and the International Crisis Group (ICG). They employ field-based analysts or special envoys, often posted within the region in question, to monitor and conduct specific research. The resulting recommendations are then lobbied with key decision makers and policymakers.

Case Study 1: The International Crisis Group (ICG)

The strength of ICG comes from the decision-makers being part of the internal structure of the organisation in its hourglass shape. It comprises field analysts who stay long term in a specific region such as Central Asia, Africa, South America, especially Columbia and the Balkans. The analysts generate up-to-date, on-the-ground reports about the latest changes in the situation which are then processed at the offices in Brussels, Paris and Washington from where they are distributed to the 40 board members, comprised of former prime ministers, foreign ministers and advisors, who then lobby the recommendations with key policy makers. The reports move simply beyond the abstract "something must be done" to concrete tailored policy recommendations with further speculation about future scenarios and their consequences. By the transmission of on-the-ground information to the toplevel leadership, it is one of the few organisations that successfully breaches the micro-macro divide. It is an attractive forum for local actors to be heard and moreover to be given the channel to communicate this information. Policy meetings at the regional and head offices further support the work with key policy makers, where the field analysts are often present. The organisation also uses the media to gain maximum visibility, while also targeting the media in general when partial reporting has aggravated the situation. ICG is a system that has managed to successfully bridge the gap between early warning and early action.

2.2 Quantitative early warning

Quantitative early warning systems (QnEWS) celebrated their heydays during the 1960s and 1970s in the form of event data-coding. Granted large budgets by governments, they aimed to construct theoretical models for understanding political behaviour. Two examples are the *World Events Interaction Survey (WEIS)* established by McClelland in 1976 and Azar's *Conflict and Peace Data Bank (COPDAB)* in 1982. However, due to the consuming human and financial resources required to code the data, they had lost favour by the mid 1980s. Their second boom came in the 1990s due to the collapse of the Iron Curtain coupled to the significant advances in computer technology as well as new information sources such as the internet.

The methodology employed is based on the systematic collection and processing of empirical information according to a given set of criteria. The main objective of quantitative analysis is to "... isolate factors that contribute to the outbreak of war or make warfare more likely...[and] one tries to reveal a direct link between them and the outbreak of war." (Conrad & Schlichte 2000, 4) From empirical evidence, they try to ascertain the antecedent contextual structures, events and processes that caused the outbreak of violence. I will use the analogy of a glass shattering to illustrate the different objects of analysis.

To develop upon Gurr's typology (1998), systems based upon quantitative methodologies can be classified into five main models: structural models, accelerator models, threshold models, conjunctural models and response models.

Structural models

These models, also referred to as causal models or risk assessments, aim to identify the conditions and structural contexts under which violent conflict will erupt. From a predefined list of indicators, the models review causal relationships between these indicators and their magnitude in relation to the objective whether this is state failure or minority risk. The base data, which is data of previous conflicts, is used to identify the indicator magnitude. The results are then tested retrospectively on different conflict data to verify the indicator constellations. Through analogy, in trying to discover why the glass shattered, they look for elements such as brittleness and the degree of brittleness.

Case Study 2: Minorities at Risk

The underlying assumption of the project is that future violent rebellion will be instigated by groups who are most at risk. To date, there have been four project phases spanning from 1993 to the present. Originally identifying 227 groups, the current phase is now working with 275. A minority is defined as "...a group in which (the country of residence) has a population greater than 500,000 in 1995, the group itself has a population larger than 100,000 or one per cent of the country's population." The conditions under which a group will instigate violent rebellion are: collective incentive, capacity for joint action and external opposition.

Collective incentives are equated with the perception of disadvantage or grievance felt by the group. This can be broken into (a) history of lost political autonomy and (b) active political, economic, cultural discrimination in the 1990s.

The group capacity for collective action is based on the feeling of shared identity and this in turn is directly related to the extent of the difference with the host group. This theme further examines whether the group is politically organised.

The group opportunities for collective action arise from a variety of factors; the two most important being (a) the time since the last dramatic change in the political structure and (b) the amount of external support provided, either materially or symbolically.

The project divides the world into six geo-political regions: the Western Democracies and Japan (region 1), Eastern Europe and the former Soviet Union (region 2), Asia and the Pacific (region 3), North Africa and the Middle East (region 4), Sub-Saharan Africa (region 5) and Latin America and the Caribbean (region 6).

The rules of inclusion for groups have already been discussed, but as with most rules, there are grey areas and caveats to note. Group discrimination and bias are only relevant to this project as they exist in relation to other groups within the country. Thus, denial of the right to vote is only relevant if some groups in the country do have the right to vote. The focus of these indicators is the relative status and condition of the group, not its absolute condition. Also, the identity of the group must be relevant in some way to its discrimination or disadvantage. Likewise, if the group is mobilized, the mobilization must centre on group issues vis-á-vis other groups or the state. Mobilisation as part of some non-ethnic campaign (e.g., ideological) does not qualify as group mobilisation in the context of this project.

Source: Minorities at Risk at http://www.bsos.umd.edu/cidcm/mar/projdesc.html

Accelerator models

The aim of these systems, also referred to as sequential or processural models, is to identify the triggers and antecedent processes that spark and lead to conflict. Barbara Harff points out that "...certain events cluster prior to an outbreak of geno/politicide" (Harff 1998, 71). These events can then be traced backward as a process prior to the specific outbreak. Developing upon risk assessment by adding a timeframe, accelerator models identify sequences that lead from high-risk situations to conflict. To use the analogy, with the knowledge that glass is brittle, it infers that when a stone's trajectory crosses the glass that the glass will shatter. An example of such a model is the *Global Event Data Survey (GEDS).*

Threshold models

These models are based on event data analysis and, although they do not try to identify the causes or processes of conflict, attempt to abstract the information from other conflicts and to identify similarities in the patterns formed by the event data.

Case Study 3: Event Data and Event Data Coding

An event is simply an action such as "July 23, 1990: Iraqi newspapers denounce Kuwait's foreign minister as a US agent". This data is acquired from services such as LEXIS / NEXIS which holds news wires from press agencies through specifically written programs such as the NEXIS SPIDER. Using Boolean statements (linking terms by using AND, OR or NOT), the spider can isolate the relevant data, for example in the study of the Levant 1979 – 1995 by Schrodt, the search was limited to Israel, Jordan, Egypt, Lebanon, Syria, PLO, Palestine, Kuwait and Iraq. Any wire with these words in the headline is downloaded. For these criteria, there were approximately 100,000 events of which fifty per cent were relevant.

Once downloaded, the reports are converted into machine-readable text such as "900723 IRQ KUW 122" i.e. date (1990 July 23rd) Iraq Kuwait denounce (code 122). There are several coding mechanisms such as the Behavioural Correlates of War (BCOW), Conflict and Peace Databank (COPDAB), Integrated Data for Event Analysis (IDEA), and World Event Interaction Survey (WEIS). The WEIS system assesses 22 cue codes which are subdivided into 223 secondary codes i.e. there are 22 clusters each forming a certain range of actions such as ACCUSE (cue code 12) which contain variations such as DENOUNCE (secondary code 122). Each of these codes is given a value such as those identified in the Goldstein scale. For example the above secondary code 122 (denounce) has a negative scale of -3.4 while the secondary code 071 (external economic aid (as gift and/or loan)) within cue code 7 (reward) has a positive scale of 7.4.

Concerning speed and accuracy, due to recent developments KEDS can code up to 45 events per second. A second system Textual Analysis by Augmented Replacement Instruction (TABARI) has reached speeds of 3,000 events per second, depending upon the computer. The advantage of such systems can be seen when placed next to the 40 events per individual per day of human coding. KEDS has managed to accurately code 91 per cent of Reuters newswires.

This event data can then be used in several ways for the analysis: deductively or inductively through factor analysis, discriminant analysis, use of event count rather than scaled data, clustering using time as a variable and clustering using alternative matrices

(Schrodt & Gerner 1998)

Almost all of the event data coding is now automated. Schrodt et al. (2001) identifies five main advantages: cost, sharing software, lack of bias and, finally, the possibility to experiment with coding rules. As it is no longer necessary to input the code manually, the only cost is the purchase of the information source. Concerning bias, although both human as well as machine coding result in bias: "…that even expert [human] coders in the military tend to overestimate the military capability of China during the 1980s because they know China to be a large communist country" (ibid; citing Laurance 1990), the bias in machine coding is consistently incorrect in contrast to human coding where there are as many bias positions as there are coders. The machine bias holds the advantage that the program can be continually re-adjusted to compensate for the bias. The dataset would then require to be re-run, which for the Levant dataset would take approximately three hours.

What is the advantage of using event-data in analysis and how can it be used in early warning? Again Schrodt argues that coding brings data to a "...theory rich but data poor field...", and addresses the "...need to be able to systematically study alternative theoretical explanations for the behaviour" (ibid). Event data is now being applied to early warning. The assumption is that the event data will form a cluster before there is a shift in conflict phase. These phases or stages in conflict are defined within the respective systems such as those identified by Computer Aided System for Analysis of Conflicts (CASCON) and SHERFACE that divide conflict into six phases: dispute, conflict, hostilities, post-hostilities, post-hostilities conflict, post-hostilities dispute, and settlement. In the simplified analogy, the model does not search for the cause of the glass shattering or even the process leading to the shattering but rather after a review of many instances of shattering identify the patterns just before the glass will shatter.

Conjunctural models

These models, such as those speculated by Peter Brecke (2000), are still in their infancy and have not reached any practical application. Similar to causal models, they operate using predefined indicators but differ insofar as they do not examine the magnitude but rather the relationship between, and combination of, indicators. By identifying the constellations present in the pre-conflict phase, they hope to build an early warning. In the analogy, it moves beyond the throwing of a stone and the brittleness of glass to identifying that the stone was thrown 'at' the 'stationary' glass.

Response models

Similar to threshold models, the response model does not attempt to identify the cause of conflict but rather the impact of various interventions and their appropriateness to the conflict. The main product is to produce various hypothetical scenarios in response to different combinations of intervention.

Case Study 4: Life Integrity Violations Analysis (LIVA) – A Good Enough model

The aim is to detect signs and portents of escalation of violence towards genocide/politicide: to relate the levels of violation to underlying and intervening causes and to relate life integrity violations to other kinds of rights violations. With regard to preventive action, LIVA aims at tracing the impact of government intervention and aid on the level of violation: considering the efficacy of different response strategies at different levels of violation and tracing the impact of NGO campaigns against various classes of violators.

While there is much agreement between Fein and Harff on the precipitating events leading to genocide/politicide, Fein proceeds to focus on the responses at the pressure points. The indicators derived from the theoretical model are to recognize, not to explain (a Good Enough Model instead of Causal Explanatory Model). The testing of models should thus not be the testing of indicators (as Harff does), but the testing of the effect of intervention/response.

Source: van de Goor, L & S. Verstegen 1999 Conflict Prognostication: Part 1 Bridging the Gap from Early Warning to Early Response, Netherlands Institute of Internal Relations, Appendix V.

2.3 Qualitative and quantitative early warning

In a few cases, some projects employ both methodologies running parallel to each other such as the Early Recognition of Tensions and Fact Finding (*Frühanalyse von Spannungen und Tatsachenermittlung* – FAST) of the Swiss Peace Foundation. This system utilises four information sources: constant monitoring (qualitative analysis), event data analysis (quantitative analysis), expert network (external expertise), and fact finding missions (field investigations). These sources feed into the core outputs which are (a) Country Risk Profile: baseline studies, risk assessment, policy options and supportive data (b) Up-Dates (regular, executive summary, risk assessment and supportive data).

Case Study 5: Early Recognition of Tensions and Fact Finding (FAST)

(1) FAST Country Risk Profiles

- The annual FAST Country Risk Profile presents an in-depth base-line assessment of the situation in the target countries. It discusses root, proximate and intervening factors that may lead to armed conflict, hamper conflict resolution or provide a window of opportunity for de-escalation and peace-building efforts.
- The core indicators derived from this analysis are depicted in the Analytical Monitoring Roster used for daily monitoring and continuous updates.
- A crucial feature of the annual assessment is the formulation of case scenarios and detailed policy options identifying an overall strategy, steps toward implementation (including obstacles to be overcome) and specific tools/programs.
- In addition, key actors are profiled and a set of background information is provided (e.g. chronology of events, tension barometers, strategic information on political, economic/ecological, socio-demographic and military aspects of a country).

(2) FAST Updates

- In order to keep clients in touch with the developments in the countries monitored, FAST provides quarterly updates of the situation on the ground. FAST Updates utilise the Analytical Monitoring Roster as basis and mainly focus on the factors that either increase or decrease the likelihood of armed conflict. Intentionally kept short, FAST Updates do not exceed more than three pages of text and provide only the essential supportive information in the form of a short chronology of main events and tension barometers.

Source: FAST – Early Recognition of Tension and Fact Finding, Swiss Peace Foundation, 2001

2.4 Networks

Although in a strict definition a network is not a formal system, nevertheless networks provide a contributive role in the warning about conflicts. These networks cooperate with one another to share field reports and information both from NGOs as well as inter-governmental agencies. There are various forms of networks ranging from the United Nations Office for the Coordination of Humanitarian Affairs (OCHA) to Humanitarian Early Warning System (HEWS). These networks require some type of central coordination and have the advantage of being more cost effective than conducting repetitive field studies. They continue to offer the greatest chances for bridging the divide between the private and public sectors. Further examples of these networks are the Forum on Early Warning and Early Response (FEWER) based in London, the Human Rights Information and Documentation System (HURIDOCS), and the Network for Ethnological Monitoring and Early Warning (EAWARN).

Case Study 6: Network for Ethnological Monitoring and Early Warning (EAWARN)

Main activities

- interaction by means of electronic communication between leading specialists for the dissemination and exchange of analytical information
- regular analysis of ethnopolitical situations through reports and analytic papers based on local and national expertise
- work on the model of ethnological monitoring and early warning
- publication of bulletins, reports and methodological materials
- the use of global experiences and updating conflict analysis in annual seminars and other international contacts
- consultation with specialists for the purpose of developing a system of management with procedural negotiations of issues in regions experiencing conflict as well as the preparation and implementation of programmes in the area of nationalities policy

Source: Network for Ethnological Monitoring and Early Warning, http://www.eawarn.ras.ru/centr/eawarn_engl/index.htm

2.5 Concluding remarks

Early warning systems can be categorised by the methodology that they use.(*see* Table 4). Despite these different methodologies, a number of general remarks can be made about the mechanisms within an early warning system. To achieve the three main goals: (a) identify the causes of conflict, (b) predict the outbreak of conflict and, what is more, (c) mitigate that conflict, an early warning system should contain six core mechanisms. To address the first objective, the archetypical system should have a systematic process of: (i) data collection (quantitative and/or qualitative) and (ii) data analysis. In order to predict conflict, it is necessary to have (iii) an assessment for warning or identification of different scenarios. To move towards the mitigation of conflict and bridging the gap between early warning and

Table 4: Early Warning Methodologies			
Qualitative	Quantitative	Qualitative & Quantitative	Networks
LIVA	MAR	FAST	HEWS
ICG	State Failure Project	Interdisciplinary Research Programme on Root Causes of Human Rights Violations (PIOOM)	FEWER
Fund for Peace	Accelerators of Genocide		EAWARN
Canada Peacekeeping Initiative	Conflict Early Warning Project (CEWP)		HURIDOCS
Human Rights Watch	Cluster Analysis		Early Warning Network (EWNET)
Amnesty International	Protocol for the Analysis of Non-violent Conflict (PANDA)		Conflict Watch Inter Press Service
	Global Event Data Survey (GEDS)		
	Kansas Event Data Survey (KEDS)		
	Future of Global Interdependence (FUGI)		
	World Events Interaction Survey (WEIS)		
	Conflict & Peace Data Bank (COPDAB)		

response, the model should in a continual circle: (iv) formulate an action proposal, (v) transmit recommendations and (vi) assess the early response, which in turn feeds back into the formulation of action. The need for this continual circle is that warning must not stop with intervention. The intervention itself will have an impact on the specific context and that context will change. EWS must then review this impact and then if necessary revise the first set of recommendations. It is unclear exactly where the demarcation line lies between early warning and assessment methodologies such as the Peace and Conflict Impact Assessment (PCIA) (*see* Austin, Fischer and Wils 2003). One area that has received no attention is this relationship and it would be of considerable advantage to review and consider the potential merging of the two areas: reducing early warning to simply analysing the conflict setting while expanding PCIA to link directly into the recommendation phase of early warning as well as maintaining its planning mechanism.

3. Conflict Mitigation and Crisis Prevention

This section will aim to review the challenges facing early warning systems in the mitigation of conflict. It is one of the core arguments of this paper that it is insufficient to assume that early response will follow from making sure that the right information is given at the right time to the right department or person. Man is not a rational animal. This can be seen in the case of Zaire, where despite clear warnings, little or no action was taken at an early stage (*see* Adelman forthcoming). In fact the difficulties are even larger than warnings not being heeded. As illustrated by Rwanda, even when the conflict is at a violent stage, response was either slow in coming or non-existent. If there is no response, even when there are signs more clear than the potential outbreak of violence, what chances are there for responses to early warning? The inverse is also true, early response has occurred where there has been no explicit warning such as in some countries belonging to the former Soviet Union – for example in Estonia (*see* Birckenbach 1999) or Moldovia.

Until there is a better understanding of the conditions, motivations and reasons for response, as well as the relationship between early warning and early response, there will be little utility in focusing on improving the accuracy and methodology of the specific early warning system. Until there is an improved design cohesion between the systems and the intervenors, there can be little hope of bridging the gap between response and warning.

The remaining part of this section will be devoted to those challenges and issues that force this breach wider apart beginning with the underlying assumptions of early warning and crisis prevention. This will include factors outside of the structural design of the system. The second part of this section will make some tentative recommendations concerning ways in which the breach can be bridged.

3.1 Factors inhibiting the move from early warning to early response

Early warning is faced by substantial, possibly unobtainable, evaluation criteria. In few other fields, is there such a success criteria as high and ideal as peace or the prevention of conflict. Whether systems can mitigate conflict is based on two lurking assumptions: (a) that conflict can be mitigated in the first instance, and (b) that one knows how to mitigate it – both are highly contentious. Concerning the latter, the field of conflict management is moving from a young age to a more reflective state. For the past two years, there has been an ever-increasing speculation about what is working and what is failing through the various lessons learned and best practices projects. This has occurred both on the conceptual as well as the practical level.

The conceptual level can be characterized by the *Handbook* group of initiatives such as Paffenholz and Reychler's *Peacebuilding: A Field Guide* (2000) as well as this volume. These publications aim to collect the state of the art throughout the field and to raise critical challenges and open questions. A second conceptual trend should also be alluded to here – namely the precursors of the best practices movement. From the 1950s onwards, a small section of academics have continually attempted to isolate, from the broad spectrum of activities, the most appropriate options for each stage or phase of conflict. These have resulted in various frameworks under the title of *contingency models* and can be exemplified by Fischer & Keashley (1996) and Blénesi (1999). The practical arm of lessons learned and best practices has developed through initiatives such as the *Local Capacities for Peace Project* and the large conference *Towards better Peacebuilding Practice* held in Soesterberg (2001) organized by the European Platform for Conflict Prevention and Transformation. This conference aimed to collect examples of successes and failures; it remains to be seen whether the results can be transposed beyond the site-specific context to broader surroundings.

In short, even if conflict can be mitigated, the broader field of conflict management is at the moment trying to isolate ways to engage successfully. As Lund points out "[t]here is a lack of understanding and knowledge, particularly at the high and middle policymaking levels of the US government and other key entities, of the range of potential risks posed by post-Cold War trends and of their real costs, of the various policy method and entities that can in fact be used to reduce them, of the particular strategies that appear to work the best and of how to implement those strategies." (Lund 1996, 28) Until there is more concrete information resulting from best practices and lessons learned initiatives, early warning will continue to be faced with major challenges on recommending what, when and by whom initiatives should be taken.

Lund (1996) and Adelman et al. (1996) have outlined several difficulties with moving from early warning to early response. These have revolved around the role and motivation of the intervenor and have included: the press of daily commitments, altruism versus egoism, confusion of the intervention and noise. The latter refers to more pressing matters, such as actual violent rather than potentially violent conflicts, that tend to override the prevention of conflict with the management of conflict.

One significant factor is the by-stander syndrome. The review of this syndrome is currently being undertaken within the socio-psychological field by academics such as Levine (1999). Although Levine asks the same questions as those posed by early warning experts, namely why was there no responsive action, there has been, as yet, little or no application to the conflict setting. As Staub asserts "[t]he by-stander plays a central part in the establishment and maintenance of human rights abuses. By turning away or remaining passive in the face of threats to human life, the conditions for genocide are maximised" (Staub 1999).

In 1964, a woman by the name of Kitty Genovese was raped and murdered. In an attempt to explain why 38 witnesses failed to provide help to her, socio-psychologists have devoted considerable attention to why people fail to intervene. Although the results cannot be directly applied to the ethnopolitical context, they are worth mentioning here as potential areas for further research.

In reviewing when assistance was given, the findings are as follows. First, it was more common to assist people from the in-group, i.e. people belonging to a similar group as the intervener. Second, intervention is more likely to out-groups closer to home rather than out-groups at some distance. Third, the number of witnesses usually had an inverse relationship to whether intervention occurred: the more witnesses there were the less likely that intervention would follow. This was attributed to audience inhibition, social influence and diffusion of responsibility. Finally, whether a group or individual intervened was found to equate to a cost against reward relationship.

It is unclear whether the results would be of any utility to understand the complex reasons that form a lack of intervention in ethno-political conflicts. Nevertheless, it is an area that remains underdeveloped and requires work.

3.2 Some tentative recommendations

There are two possible ways to address the gap between early warning and early response. New early warning systems must be:

- built back-to-front. To increase the likelihood that the recommendations would be followed, the early warning systems must directly engage the support and, what is more, the capacity of the decision makers. Unless, this is achieved at, then it will make little difference how much is invested in the accuracy of the system.
- built as a satellite around specific conflict prevention mechanisms thereby directly linking warning with actual response initiatives. The system should not be built in isolation.

In addition, van de Goor & Verstegen (1999) have identified ways in which the outcome of the analysis can be dealt with more effectively. They stated:

1. The standardised analysis needs to be applied for the purpose of:

- helping to identify and prioritise options for operational response;
- finding the right mix of short-term, medium-term and long-term projects;
- committing to sustained efforts instead of ad hoc operations and betting on instant successes;
- identifying shortcomings in existing policies and instruments, adapting these, or developing new ones.

2. Catalogue and assess the situation in relation to the policy and response capacity available. It is imperative to focus analysis of conflict situations in such a way as to derive guidelines for policy interventions. Analysis should be directed towards understanding, anticipation and intervention:

- Understanding requires analysis directed towards conflict processes in general as well as the particular contextual conditions (country profile);
- Anticipation asks for the monitoring and analysis of dynamic processes and risk evaluation criteria (trend analysis);
- Intervention refers to an inventory of the institution's toolbox, an analysis of the applicability of the policy tools to the goals and the conflict's various needs, and identification of potential moments and field for intervention.

4. Identifying the Causes and Predicting Conflict

This section will critically review the ability of quantitative early warning systems against the first two goals: (a) identification of the causes of conflict, (b) prediction of the outbreak of conflict. The main argument will follow that of Peter Winch as outlined in *The Idea of a Social Science* (1958) as I believe that many of the problems that arose in the 1950s with the social sciences are still present in quantitative early warning systems (QnEWS). The similarities between QnEWS and the social sciences of that time are: (a) complexity of empirical evidence, (b) causal relationships, (c) generalisations from empirical evidence.

4.1 Quantitative empirical evidence – the search for unicorns

The following questions cannot be equated through a degree of empirical complexity: how much does it take to raise the temperature of a bucket to make the water boil? and how much grievance must be endured before a conflict will erupt? To equate them would be a misconception of the words grievance and endurance. In the former question, the evidence can be collected empirically and the facts would press themselves upon the researcher in an unmistakable fashion; in the latter, the threshold line is one that we must chose as researchers and one that the individual must chose before taking to arms.

This can be illustrated through the present crisis in datasets. Chojnacki and Eberwein (2001), in a presentation at the Uppsala Conference on Data Collection, clearly outline this dilemma with various comparisons between different conflict datasets. One of these comparisons concerned four datasets and the logged occurrences of interstate conflicts between 1950 and 1999. The results were startling: KOSIMO identified 19 instances against 39 instances identified by AKUF. Chojnacki and Eberwein argue that it is necessary to run the empirical evidence of one dataset through the parameters of the other and thereby use the methodology to resolve the dilemma.

However the problem is not due to insufficient or inaccurate parameters and consequently it cannot be resolved by re-using empirical evidence with different parameters; it is a problem of different concepts. David Hume has alluded to this in his statement "In vain do you pretend to have learned the nature of bodies from past experience, their secret nature, and consequently all their effects and influence may change, without any change in their sensible qualities. This may happen sometimes, and with regard to some objects: Why may it not happen always and with regard to all objects? What logic, what processes or argument secures you against this supposition?"

The way through this dilemma is to examine the relationship between early warners and their specific focus on the concepts and assumptions that they are using about conflict. Decisions are made not on the environment but on the individual's perception of that environment; warnings are not given about the outbreak of conflict but the perceived outbreak of conflict. In order to understand why KOSIMO logs 19 instances while AKUF 39, it is necessary to review their assumptions about interstate conflict.

The same argument must also apply to the subjects of the analysis and it is here where there is a misconception of the concept of grievance. If early warners reach different conclusions based on their understanding of conflict, why then must an individual who takes arms have the same quota of grievance tolerance as the next person, and, what is more, why then must it remain static for each individual? To do so would be to reject the idea that grievance can be manipulated.

In the case of Kosovo, as well as many other conflicts, one argument is that the sense of grievance was manipulated to mobilise groups into violence for the greed of the elite. Whether this is through hate messages transmitted through the radio or through appealing to a selective view of the past, the grievance that can be tolerated by an individual before taking arms continues to be a dynamic ever-changing force, an ever-changing quantity with no fixed starting point. As a result, it is not important whether the minority has a history of lost political autonomy or cultural discrimination (as identified in the Minorities at Risk project); it is whether it is perceived as such.

To conclude, grievance is not an empirical state and the search for the causes of conflict outside of perception will remain similar to a search for unicorns. This latter search could be conducted through an empirical methodology – the idea of a unicorn is generally accepted – an animal akin to a Welsh pony with a horn in the centre of its forehead. All that would be required is to empirically search the globe and prove the existence or non-existence of unicorns. However, levels of grievance tolerance vary considerably from person to person, and cannot be known empirically – only conceptually. As a result, QnEWS will remain to be a quest for a mythical beast.

4.2 Causes of conflict – cargo cult early warning systems

The residents of Papua, Yaliwan, Vanuatu and other places noticed that when the colonial occupiers built wharves and airstrips, the wharves and airstrips were soon visited by ships and airplanes that delivered cargos of goods. They concluded that the ships and airplanes arrived as a consequence of the building of the wharves and airstrips, so they built their own wharves and airstrips in the expectation of receiving their own cargoes (FitzGerald 1999).

QnEWS, in trying to find the causes of conflict, examine data for causal relationships: when A is present how often is it followed by B. John Steward Mill defined a causal relationship as follows: "The temporal succession of A and B is an instance of a generalisation to the effect that events like A are always to be found in our experience to be followed by events like B" (cited by Winch 1958, 67).

These systems operate in the same manner – to look for causal relationships from which generalizations can be made. To repeat Conrad & Schlichte, the main objective of quantitative analysis is to "... isolate factors that contribute to the outbreak of war or make warfare more likely...[and] one tries to reveal a direct link between them and the outbreak of war" (Conrad & Schlichte 2000, 4). In response to why there are many mispredictions as well as non-predictions, it can be easily argued, similar to Mill, that the answer lies in the complexity of the subject matter. In defence, Mill argued that although hard and fast rules have not yet been found, it does not mean that they do not exist. He made a comparison to the movement of the tides where although it is not possible to give a precise prediction for any given circumstances it (a) does not deny that there are rules and generalisations that apply, and (b) that "...an approximate generalisation is, in social inquiries, for most practical purposes equivalent to an exact one; that which is only probable when asserted of individual human beings indiscriminately selected..."

Following Winch suggests that the origins of conflict, as with human behaviour, lie along a different framework. QnEWS have an inverted sequence of events. For example, suppose that the LTTE (Liberation Tigers of Tamil Eelam) continues the peace dialogue with the Government of Sri Lanka because they intend to achieve a homeland. It would be wrong to say that the LTTE infers their intention of achieving their homeland in the same way as the imminent shattering of a glass might be inferred from the throwing of a stone or from its brittleness, or even the landing of planes can be inferred from the building of landing strips. Applying the way in which Winch summarises this distinction, the action of the LTTE "...is not of the form 'Such and such causal factors are present, therefore this will result', nor yet of the form '[we] have such and such a disposition, which will result in my doing this'; it is of the form: 'In view of such and such considerations, this will be the reasonable thing to do" (Winch 1958, 81).

In short, it is not B that follows A, but rather B presupposes, or is the preceding reason for, A. It was unfortunately to the Pacific Islanders detriment, that they had the sequence of events inverted: planes did not land because landing strips were built, but rather, landing strips were built because there was a preceding intention to land planes.

To summarise the argument so far in relation to the first aim – identify the causes of conflict – QnEWS cannot identify the origins of conflict because they are based on empirical causal relationships. Empirical evidence is insufficient because the issue remains conceptual in contrast to the boiling of water where facts will press themselves upon us. Conflict analysis is where the researcher must draw the line himself and the consequences of this can be seen in the vividly different datasets. Second, the origins of conflict do not lie in causal relationships outside of the individual but rather within the perception of the individual or group. These reasons cannot be ascertained through empirical evidence unless they are to fall into an inversion of events.

4.3 Prediction and understanding

Regardless of this, can QnEWS still provide some insights into the second aim: predicting conflict? Both human behaviour and conflict contain regularities. These regularities can be monitored and various predictions may be possible. These conflict predictions may be similar to the prediction of a word in a foreign language. Winch raises the proposition that, although it is not possible to understand what is spoken nor the grammatical rules, statistical predictions can be made as to whether a word will appear.

This argument would lend support event data analysis that searches for these statistical predictions and not causal relationships. However, "...statistics, though...are not the decisive and ultimate court of appeal...[Nevertheless,] someone who interprets a tribe's magical rites as a form of misplaced scientific activity will not be corrected by statistics about what members of that tribe are likely to do on various occasions" (Winch 1958, 113).

Again there is an inherent problem, empirical evidence will not correct a false hypothesis. One of the linguistic philosophers pointed out the hypothesis that the globe was at the centre of the universe (because that is the way that it looked), now we know different – how has the empirical evidence changed?

To summarise, there are regularities in conflict behaviour from which predictions can be made about future scenarios. Nevertheless, as empirical evidence will not correct a false hypothesis, quantitative EWS are left in a perpetual purgatory where they may be right or wrong but without any proof either way.

5. Conclusion

The aim of this article has been to illustrate the breadth and scope of the field of early warning by categorising the systems by their focus, methodology, and mechanism. From this, EWS were reviewed against their three aims (a) identify the causes of conflict, (b) predict the outbreak of conflict and, what is more, (c) mitigate that conflict. By first examining the challenges that face the transition from early warning, the third section argued that unless these issues are addressed, there is little utility in concentrating on the refinement of the accuracy of EWS. In short, the accuracy of a system does not ensure that recommendations will be listened to. To analyse the first two goals, section four critically reviewed quantitative early warning systems and proposed that, due to the nature of conflict and grievance, it was not possible to empirically quantify data. This was a result of two core positions, first, grievance is not a static quota given equally to all people but rather an ever-changing force where there are as many grievance tolerance levels as there are people. The second position concerned the sequence of events and the difference between cause and reason, and drew upon an analogy to cargo cults. This aimed to illustrate that a search for preceding events to a conflict were insufficient, not due to the empirical complexity of conflict, but due to the nature of intention that, as mentioned above, cannot be attained empirically.

This article has left many areas un-addressed, not least an assessment of qualitative early warning systems as well as networks. A further area only mentioned is the role of continual assessment after the intervention has occurred and this may be possible to link directly to Peace and Conflict Impact Assessment. It may also be worthwhile to consider situations where intervention is not taken and to draw upon the current work in the social-psychology field.

6. Reference and Further Reading

Adelman, H. forthcoming. *Early Warning and Conflict Management in Zaire: March 1996 – March 1997.*

Adelman, Howard and Astri Suhrke 1996. "Early Warning and Conflict Management," in *Joint Evaluation of Emergency Assistance to Rwanda*, op.cit.

Alker, Hayward R., Ted Robert Gurr and Kumar Rupesinghe (eds.) 2001. *Journeys through Conflict: Narratives and Lessons*, Lanham, Maryland: Rowman & Littlefield Publishers.

Austin, Alex, Martina Fischer and Oliver Wils (eds.) 2003. *Peace and Conflict Impact Assessment. Critical Views on Theory and Practice*, Berlin: Berghof Research Center for Constructive Conflict Management.

Azar, E. 1982. *The Codebook of The Conflict and Peace Data Bank*, College Park: Center for International Development, University of Maryland.

Birckenbach, H. M. 1999. "Warum kein Krieg? Ein Beitrag zur Kriegsursachenanalyse," in Thomas Greven and Oliver Jarasch (eds.), *Für eine lebendige Wissenschaft des Politischen. Umweg als Methode* (Festschrift für Ekkehart Krippendorff), Frankfurt/M: Suhrkamp, 151-165.

Blénesi, É. 1998. *Ethnic Early Warning Systems and Conflict Prevention*, Global Security Fellows Initiative, Occasional Paper No. 11.

Brecke, P. 2000. *Risk Assessment Models and Early Warning Systems*, Arbeitsgruppe: Internationale Politik (at http://skylla.wz-berlin.de/pdf/2000/p00-302.pdf).

Carment, D. and Garner, K. 1999. "Conflict Prevention and Early Warning: Problems, Pitfalls and Avenues for Success in Canadian Foreign Policy," *Principal Investigator*, Winter 1999, 103-118.

Chojnacki, S. and W.-D. Eberwein 2001. *Scientific necessity and political utility. A comparison of data on violent conflicts*, Paper for the Uppsala Conference on Data Collection June 8-9, 2001, Uppsala (revised update: http://skylla.wz-berlin.de/pdf/2001/p01-304.pdf).

Collier, P and A. Hoeffler 2000. *Greed or Grievance in Civil Wars* (Draft paper).

Conrad, B. and K. Schlichte 2000. *Quantitative Research: Four Limits and One Alternative,* paper presented at the Uppsala Conflict Data Conference 8-9 June 2000.

Davis, J. and T. Gurr (eds) 1998. *Preventive Measures*, New York, NY: Rowman & Littlefield.

Fisher, R J. and L. Keashly, 1991. "The Potential Complementarity of Mediation and Consultation within a Contingency Model of Third Party Intervention," *Journal of Peace Research (special Issue on International Mediation)*, Vol. 28.

FitzGerald J. 1999. *Contemporary Cargo Cults*, on http://www.coolth.com/cargo.htm.

Gurr, T. 1996. "Victims of the State: Genocides, Politicides and Group Repression from 1945 to 1995," in A. J. Jongman (ed.), *Contemporary Genocides: Causes, Cases, Consequences*, Leiden: PIOOM/University of Leiden.

Harff 1998. "Early Warning of Humanitarian Crises: Sequential Models and the Role of Accelerators," in Davis & Gurr (eds.), op. cit.

Joint Evaluation of Emergency Assistance to Rwanda 1996. *The International Response to Conflict and Genocide: Lessons from the Rwanda Experience*, Copenhagen: DANIDA.

Laurance, E. 1990. "Event Data and Policy Analysis," *Policy Sciences*, 23, 111-132.

Levine, R.M. 1999. "Rethinking bystander non-intervention: social categorisation and the evidence of witnesses at the James Bulger murder trial," *Human Relations*, 52, 1133-1155.

Lund, M. 1996. *Preventing Violent Conflict: A Strategy for Preventive Diplomacy*, Washington, DC: United States Institute of Peace Press.

Machado, Lourenco & Silva 2000. "Facts, Concepts, and Theories: The Shape of Pschology's Epistemic Triangle," *Behaviour and Philosophy*, 28, 1-40.

Mill J.S. 1986. *A System of Logic*, Classworks.

Paffenholz, T. & L. Reychler (eds.) 2000. *Peacebuilding. A Field Guide*, Boulder Co: Lynne Rienner Publishers.

Schrodt, P. A., E. Simpson and D. Gerner 2001. *Monitoring conflict using automated coding of newswire reports: a comparison of five geographical regions*, Paper presented at Uppsala Conference on Identifying Wars, 8-9th June 2001.

Schrodt, P. A. and D. J. Gerner 1998. "Cluster Analysis as an Early Warning Technique for the Middle East, 1979-1996," in John Davies and Ted R. Gurr (eds.), *Risk Assessment and Crisis Early Warning Systems*, New York: Rowman and Littlefield, 95-107.

Staub, E. 1999. "The origins and prevention of genocide, mass killing, peace and conflict," *Journal of Peace Psychology*, 5, 303-336.

Swiss Peace Foundation (ed.) 2001. FAST – *Early Recognition of Tension and Fact Finding*, Bern: Swiss Peace Foundation.

van de Goor, L & S. Verstegen 1999. *Conflict Prognostication: Part 1 Bridging the Gap from Early Warning to Early Response*, The Hague: Netherlands Institute of Internal Relations.

van Tongeren, P. & A. Galama 2002. *Towards Better Peacebuilding Practice: On Lessons Learned, Evaluation Practices and Aid and Conflict*, Utrecht: European Center for Conflict Prevention.

Walraven, K. van (ed.) 1998. *Early Warning and Conflict Prevention. Limitations and Possibilities*, The Hague: Kluwer Law International.

Winch, Peter. 1958. *The Idea of a Social Science and its relation to philosophy*, London: Routledge.

Designing Transformation and Intervention Processes

Thania Paffenholz

1. Introduction 152
2. Conditions and Parameters for Good Intervention Design 153
   Visions, goals and commitment
   Analysing conflicts and actors
   Strategies and roles
   Finding the right partners and entry points
   Timing: the need for long-term engagement and windows of opportunity
   Thinking in processes and building structures
   Getting the right people: qualification versus commitment
   Cooperation and coordination: identifying strategic alliances for peacebuilding
   Making the process sustainable
   Building in learning mechanisms
3. Open Questions and Challenges Ahead 166
4. Reference and Further Reading 167

Designing Transformation and Intervention Processes

Thania Paffenholz

1. Introduction

Most of the problems commonly encountered in designing intervention processes centre, in principle, around one question, "Which actor can intervene with which strategies and instruments, and at what time in any particular situation of conflict?" Scholars and practitioners have sought to answer this question by employing a single page graphic matrix depicting an intervention framework.

Reality is different. Similar to other interventions in crisis areas, peace interventions are not planned from an overall matrix by multiple actors, but usually by a single actor through intuition and rule of thumb. Possibilities of how to intervene are, therefore, directly related to the options and limits of the intervening actors in relation to a particular conflict situation.

Issues such as intervention strategies, entry points or coordination are, in reality, practised in different ways. Actors seldom even ask what are the right strategies or instruments; rather, they have developed their own ready-made intervention design. For example, scholars tend to propose instruments such as problem-solving workshops or mediation training; development agencies initiate projects to deal with the root causes of conflict; journalists support media programmes and governmental Track I actors provide good offices, facilitation or mediation. It is more accurate to talk about a market situation, with the intervening actors on the supply side, and each offering their own particular 'product'. This supply of instruments is sometimes so rich that it far outstrips the demand.

Entry points are, in practice, less often matters for discussion than given facts. Conflict actors come from a variety of constituencies and will naturally tend to support 'their' constituency in the crisis regions: peace actors support local peace groups; church organisations assist their local churches. Entry points can also occur by chance as in the case of the Norwegian mediation in the Middle East, in which the participants of a Norwegian research project had access to the leadership level on both sides and where one of the researcher happened to be the wife of the Norwegian Foreign Minister, who then initiated negotiations on the Track I level.

Coordination tends, in general, to be a theoretical issue. Every intervening actor wants coordination but nobody wants to be coordinated! This is especially applicable to peace intervenors, who are particularly sensitive about sharing information with other actors and often have vested interests that are sometimes not even compatible with the overall objective of conflict transformation and peacebuilding.

However – scepticism aside – within the last ten years, both scholars and practitioners have learned much from many different peace interventions. In this chapter, the author focuses on a set of lessons that form conditions for intervention in the field of conflict transformation. Since intervention strategies vary between actors, it should be noted that the parameters and conditions introduced and analysed in this article are primarily addressed to non-governmental actors such as conflict resolution non-governmental organisations (NGOs) or action-oriented research institutes. Nevertheless, many of the parameters will also be of general interest to other intervening actors.

The chapter presents a variety of approaches and instruments used in the external planning of civilian peace interventions, taking into consideration that outside intervening actors' role is to support actors from within the conflict region. On three different levels of intervention: *macro (top-level), meso (mid-level)* and *micro (grassroots)*, the author discusses ten critical issues: the need for vision, goals and commitment; methods of analysing conflicts and actors; strategies and roles of intervening actors; the ongoing search for right partners and entry points; timing interventions; thinking in processes and building structures; criteria for the recruitment of field staff; coordination and cooperation; the inclusion of the goals of sustainability and building learning into the process of interventions.

The set of conditions for interventions developed in this article synthesise insights found in the literature with the author's own practical field experience, as we well as lessons from the handbook *Peacebuilding: A Field Guide* (Paffenholz and Reychler 2000) and from the study on the Life and Peace Institute's (LPI) peacebuilding involvement in Somalia (Paffenholz 2001).

2. Conditions and Parameters for Good Intervention Design

2.1 Visions, goals and commitment

Before practitioners attempt to develop conflict transformation/intervention strategies, they would be well advised to take a closer look at the underlying vision supporting the stated wishes and needs to intervene. When intervening actors lack a clear vision of a peaceful outcome, they usually run the risk that their intervention will be determined by the market of suppliers, rather than by the demand side or real needs of the region in conflict. Operating from a genuine commitment for peace and conflict transformation increases the chance that the intervention will minimise harm and eventually facilitate effective processes that will lead to constructive conflict transformation.

However, vision alone is insufficient: intervening actors must also turn their visions into operational and achievable goals that can then form the basis for the development of effective intervention strategies. Goals are best clarified through analysing an intervening actor's/institution's capacities and limits, values and interests, as applied to the relevant problems and needs for conflict transformation. While goals must be clear, the strategies employed to reach these goals can vary and will most likely be adapted or modified during the process of conflict transformation.

The roles of the different actors within the Somali peace process, for example, clearly demonstrate the value of clear vision and commitment for any effort in peacebuilding and conflict transformation. While the United Nations (UN) and, later, other bilateral governmental actors (Track I) tried unsuccessfully to mediate various peace agreements among the warlords, the parallel work of the Swedish church-based NGO, LPI, had a far greater impact on peace-building in Somalia. During the course of the last eight years, LPI has effectively empowered many different Somali civil society groups and grassroots communities (Paffenholz 2001).

The strength of LPI`s involvement in Somalia lay in the vision which was the driving force behind all strategies employed. The evident commitment of the entire LPI staff, and the strongly held belief in the bottom-up, community-based peacebuilding approach, eventually helped to overcome all the difficulties encountered in the process. For example, LPI had initially supported the establishment of District Councils, which had been quite successful in southern Somalia. These collapsed, however, as soon as the warring faction of Aideed intervened militarily in the area. While the UN withdrew from the region, LPI continued its efforts. LPI had further supported local reconciliation in the northwest of Somalia: Somaliland. Even when war broke out in 1994, LPI continued to believe in the ability of Somaliland society to achieve reconciliation and was among the first to support the peace process when it continued, while all other external actors stayed away.

Box 1: LPI's Vision

The basic philosophy of LPI`s approach to peacebuilding can be characterised as follows:

- Sustainable peacebuilding is a long-term process that can only be achieved from within the society in conflict;
- Sustainable peacebuilding is a process that involves the entire society and not only the elite;
- Sustainable peacebuilding will lead to a process of conflict transformation: the transformation of a culture of violence into a culture of peace;
- Sustainable peacebuilding must start at the local community level.

In order to make a meaningful contribution to sustainable peacebuilding, LPI has developed a two-fold approach, terming it "bottom-up peacebuilding" or "community-based peacebuilding". Within this approach, LPI defines its own role as that of an external facilitator with the aims to:

- strengthen the role of civil society actors during peace processes in a way that they are able to make a meaningful contribution to peacebuilding in their region;
- inculcate the philosophy of people-based sustainable peacebuilding throughout all levels of society.

2.2 Analysing conflicts and actors

Like all social phenomena, conflicts tend to be extremely complicated. In addition to the already complex parameters inherent in any interpersonal conflict, the many actors and issues that characterise armed conflict are even more difficult to understand (Wehr 1979). It is therefore crucial that intervening actors work to understand the particular conflict setting.

There are different approaches for analysing conflicts. These strategies and tools can be distinguished between academic and practical, quantitative and qualitative, and participatory and non-participatory methodologies, as seen at all three levels of analysis (macro, meso and micro).

(i) Macro level: This level is dominated by the more academic approaches to the analysis of conflicts and actors. Here, a more general approach is taken to the definition of crisis indicators that has been developed within early warning systems and was then taken up by the aid community. These crisis indicators categorise countries into "high", "low" and "no risk", so that aid agencies can then better adapt their instruments and information needs to the particular conflict situation (*see* Spelten 1999).

Other general analytical approaches recently developed within the aid community have combined the established instruments of development cooperation, such as participatory rapid appraisals, with classical conflict analysis (Mehler and Ribeaux 1999). A good example of an approach that links general causes of conflict with intervening activities is the European Union (EU) Guide *Peace-Building and Conflict Prevention: A Practical Guide* (Lund and Mehler 1999).

A more academic approach to conflict analysis is the "conflict mapping" guide originally developed by Paul Wehr (1979). This guide emphasises five aspects that should be properly considered in any effective conflict analysis: conflict history, conflict context, conflict parties, conflict issues, conflict dynamics. A shorthand version of conflict mapping produces a visualised qualitative analysis of the actors and their relationships with each other.

For such a visualised qualitative analysis, mappers gather information about the conflict context, parties and causes. Such a mapping exercise can be performed both from an academic and also a participatory perspective on all the different levels of conflict, from a general review of the overall situation to a deeper analysis of the values, interests or needs of the conflicting parties (*see* Wehr 1978). This technique is particularly helpful as practitioners seek to simplify and understand the complex nature of group conflicts.

John Paul Lederach has developed a similar approach, more focused on understanding the actors involved in armed conflict. He provides an actor analysis that distinguishing between levels of leadership in conflict areas, differentiating top- from mid-range from grassroots leaders. He suggests analysing possible or existing peace actors within the same matrix, and then presents corresponding intervention strategies (Lederach 1997). This type of mapping is particular useful for external intervening actors as it opens their view for internal peace actors.

The most elaborate approaches to conflict analysis are found in the field of 'early warning'. Scholars differentiate between qualitative and quantitative approaches to conflict analysis. Classically qualitative analysis looks into the root and proximate causes of a particular conflict, also analysing positive and negative intervening factors. The crucial issue for this kind of analysis concerns information gathering. Information can be obtained from international and local experts, the media and the Internet, news agencies or from scientific publications that provide the basis for qualitative analysis. Participatory analysis may also be employed: either researchers present their analysis to an audience of experts from both outside and within the conflict area or the analysis takes a joint identification of causes of conflict as a starting point. The selection of participants is crucial for participatory analysis. This methodology can be used on all levels of analysis.

Quantitative approaches to conflict analysis, such as 'event data analysis, work instead with the coding of world-wide news wire reports, employing a data lens that is sensitive to both non-violent and violent struggle, and general information that can be used for early warning. The coding is performed manually or automatically by specially developed software. This can be exemplified through the work of the American firm Virtual Research Associates (VRA) who have developed 'Automated Event Data Development Tools' that are used by different early warning mechanisms.

The *Frühanalyse von Spannungen und Tatsachenermittlung* (FAST) early warning project of the Swiss Peace Foundation, for example, combines both qualitative and quantitative as well as participatory approaches for conflict analysis (*see* Krummenacher and Schmeidl, 1999). FAST follows a traditional qualitative analysis but further monitors and analyses early action intervening factors using an analytical framework that has been specially developed for each country monitored. This entire system is then further enriched by manual and automatic coding to produce an event data analysis, as well as by the views of local and international expert networks consulted to verify the results of both the qualitative and quantitative analyses.

(ii) Meso level: Most of the approaches illustrated above can also be employed at the meso level. Especially qualitative and/or participatory conflict mappings and quantitative methods, such as used by VRA, are appropriate here. However, VRA techniques have, to date, not been used at the regional and local level. As a response, it is envisaged within the FAST project to use these methods at both of these levels within specific countries.

A number of specific approaches to conflict analysis have been developed at this level of intervention. Two of the most notable are the action-oriented research methodology of the War-torn Societies Project (WSP) and the community development approach expanded by the NGO *Aktion Afrika Hilfe e.V.* (AAH) (*see* Erasmus 2000). Under the WSP approach, relevant information is gathered by means of research and participatory workshops, thereby combining academic and practical methodologies. AAH represents a more practical approach and combines participatory approaches drawn from development cooperation with process-oriented methodologies developed by social scientists in order to produce a joint (external actors together with local partners) participatory analysis of conflict.

(iii) Micro level: Conflict and actor mappings are also extremely useful on the local/project level of intervention, especially when implemented in a participatory manner. Many of the analytical tools developed within the AAH approach will also find effective application at this local level of project intervention. Moreover, it is of less importance to know which exact approaches and methodologies are being used, as long as they are process-oriented and participatory. Sometimes, even a combination of methodologies developed in different fields can serve as an effective tool for the analysis of conflicts and actors.

A good example of this is Project Cycle Management (PCM), which combines several different process-oriented and participatory approaches. PCM is a modified and enlarged logical framework approach based on the German *Zielgruppen-orientierte Projektplanung* (ZOPP), which was originally developed as a guide for the gathering of information for the planning of aid interventions on both the programme and project levels (*see* Information, Training and Development Ltd 1999). Both PCM and ZOPP start with a participatory problem analysis using paper cards (one for each problem), followed by a clustering of the problems. In a second step, the problems are then turned into objectives and further clustered before project intervention strategies are developed. The elaborate tools of PCM and

ZOPP can be put to effective use for conflict analysis. Actor analysis is best conducted with an enlarged stakeholder analysis as part of a properly implemented PCM exercise.

The main shortcoming of integrated PCM/ZOPP conflict analysis is the lack of developed tools that can be implemented in practice. However, aid agencies are beginning a process of research to address this need.

2.3 Strategies and roles

By itself, vision will not guarantee success. Intervening actors must succeed in turning their visions into effective operational intervention strategies. While their goals need to remain clear, strategies developed in the pursuit of these goals can vary and be adapted or modified during the process of conflict transformation.

From the very beginning of an intervention, actors should clearly understand their role in the process. External actors must recognise that their role as outsiders is limited, and that their effectiveness will depend on the degree to which they manage to support internal actors.

Strategies to strengthen internal actors need to be developed. Experience shows the need for a combination of a set of strategies with a flexible adaptation to the situation. Practitioners must judge whether it is best to engage in facilitation or mediation, to offer training or capacity building, to organise problem-solving workshops or just to fund local peace efforts. This will depend not only on an organisation's capacity, but also on the needs of the particular peace process and which local actors are involved. While the LPI, for example, implemented a set of strategies in Somalia such as grassroots training, capacity building for local administrative structures as well as advocacy and support to local reconciliation conferences, the Italian NGO, Community San Egidio's engagement in the Mozambique peace process concentrated instead on mediation and facilitation between the main conflict parties (*see* Paffenholz 2000a).

Furthermore, it is necessary for external organisations to avoid conflicting strategies. For example, while long-term democratisation projects can often be in discord with short-term crisis prevention measures, the support of a direct peace project such as a peace radio can be well positioned along side support of a local human rights centre.

Practitioners should also clarify the limits of their organisation prior to engaging in new strategies. A critical analysis of LPI's strategies employed in Somalia show that LPI was sometimes driven too much by external developments than guided by an adequate reflection of its own capacities. At other times, LPI focused excessively on the implementation of specific strategies such as training, thus neglecting the pursuit of other important tasks. Consequently, it is crucial to always remain aware of the entire set of strategies that an organisation requires and with which it can cope in order to then implement the most appropriate approach.

There are several essential elements: clear vision; the development of appropriate strategies and the transparent and cohesive definition of an organisation's role in the process. Nevertheless, this should never compromise the concurrent need for flexibility: practitioners must constantly adapt strategies and roles to meet new developments. The challenge is to find the optimal combination of clear strategies and instruments and a flexible way to implement and adapt them to the process.

2.4 Finding the right partners and entry points

Finding the right partners and entry points are two issues that are closely intertwined. Often partners determine entry points and even strategies. Some partners are 'natural, some are selected and some are a combination of both. Governmental Track I actors and large donors usually enjoy easier access to a wide variety of actors in the conflict arena, whereas non-governmental Track II actors often only have access to their particular constituency or to the host that invited them (Paffenholz 2000a). Obviously, third parties working on the macro level must work directly with representatives of the main parties to the conflict, while actors working on the meso level and micro level will have a much broader spectrum of partners from which to choose. The following two considerations apply mainly to this latter group of actors.

First, the strengths and weaknesses of all potential partners need to be analysed. While some partners have few resources, others may lack capacity or strategic options. Others differ in their perceived legitimacy in the eyes of the conflict parties. These assets and liabilities must be carefully considered when assessing candidates partner for partnership (CIAA 2000).

Second, a good relationship between the external and the internal partners is absolutely essential to the success of any intervention. Usually, the local partner will accept the intervention strategy of outside partners simply because they are in need of the resources. In all cases, both sides need to be clear about their respective interests and values (Mott Foundation 1999).

(i) Donors: Often, donors do not support local peace actors directly, but rather provide assistance through international organisations such as UN agencies, NGOs, church-based or action-oriented-research organisations. These external UN agencies or NGOs function as gatekeepers or facilitators between the external donor and the internal actors; often, the external NGO is the only party personally visible to the internal actors. External donors can, of course, also directly support internal actors; many Western embassies, for instance, directly fund smaller local project in conflict areas. The norm, however, is for larger projects to be supported through international NGOs or UN agencies.

For international NGOs, it is crucial to work with the right donor. These NGOs or research institutes usually function most efficiently when they receive basic funding for the organisation's headquarters and core operations, supplemented by unconnected flexible funding for conflict transformation and peacebuilding projects.

The EU as a donor, for example, provides funds for European NGOs working in crisis areas. The complicated funding procedures and payment delays, which are inherent in the ungainly bureaucratic apparatus of the EU, make it extremely difficult for EU-funded peace NGOs to address the needs of local peace constituencies in a flexible and timely manner. Often, individual governmental donors are better able to adapt their funding to the needs of the situation. This is even more efficient, when there is sufficient trust between the donor and the international NGO, as well as a shared vision.

(ii) External actors: External Track I actors, are usually UN agencies, UN missions, and regional organisations such as the Organisation for Security and Cooperation in Europe (OSCE) or individual states. External Track II or III actors, are usually international peace organisations as well as development NGOs, action-oriented research institutes or church-based organisations. These actors usually work as gatekeepers, facilitating communication between external donors and local peace actors. While they are helpful in selecting and supporting local partners, they can also bar the way, effectively preventing the local partner from direct interaction with the donor. However, the facilitation role of international NGOs is often necessary, as direct communication with external donors is frequently problematic for local partners due to the complicated procedures and differing project cultures.

Moreover, external intervening actors who operate with a process-oriented conflict transformation approach can only be reliable partners for internal actors if they also practise what they preach. Thus, they must also demonstrate the philosophy of their peacebuilding approach within their own organisation. If this is not the case, civil society representatives working with them will soon realise this and cease to take them seriously.

(iii) local partners: The difficult question for most external intervenors seeking to support internal peace actors is whom would it be best to support. Most international NGOs or research institutes tend to link up with the people and organisations within the conflict region that belong to their own constituency. Thus, church-based organisations will support local churches while research institutes tend to work with the academic elite.

Often other criteria also play a role. Local people are chosen, for instance, simply because they can communicate in the language of the intervenor and are able to cope with a Western way of thinking. This is definitely dangerous, as it is often precisely these people who prevent intervenors from accessing many important local constituencies. The educated, smart urban elite frequently function as gatekeepers determining who will talk to whom. Special attentions should therefore be given to reducing the influence of these local gatekeepers.

How, then, should local partners be selected? Experience of the last years has shown that certain groups are particularly well suited for effectively negotiating the challenges of conflict transformation and peacebuilding. On the Track I level, one can work with actors who either maintain close links to the main conflict parties or even from within the conflict parties, engaging them in facilitation efforts, dialogue projects or conflict resolution workshops. On the Track II and III levels, the most interesting actors are local peace and human rights groups, women's peace and advocacy groups, traditional authorities, churches, the media, professional organisations and often the local business community or particularly well-known or well-connected individuals.

Different instruments can be useful in the intervenors' efforts to identify such groups. For instance, an external analysis of existing and potential groups can deliver useful information. Such a study can be then combined with a participatory peace actor inventory compiled on the ground.

Usually, the best way to select people and organisations is to leave the selection to them. One method of selection is simply to make inquiries of those involved in a particular intervention area, asking them who are the relevant actors and which would they recommend inviting for a planning exercise. This questioning is often the beginning of a process that has intrinsic value and that maximises ownership for all involved. Ron Kraybill has suggested a useful set of questions and methodologies for such a process design on the micro level of intervention (*see* contribution of Ron Kraybill in this volume).

As soon as groups have been identified, the following selection criteria should be applied with priority given to local groups. Groups should:

- support peaceful conflict transformation;
- operate within the country;
- demonstrate self-initiative;
- express a willingness to make a substantive contribution to project work;
- represent the entire spectrum of society (multi-ethnic and gender-balanced);
- maintain independence from governments;
- adhere to fundamental democratic rules.

Criteria for the selection of local partners should also be consistent with an institution's own principles. Experience shows that working with like-minded organisations proves to be effective.

However, what can be done if there are no relevant internal actors in place who could be supported? Usually, the concept of empowering civil society assumes that it is pre-existing and partially organised. Nevertheless, the Somalia situation once again shows that support to civil society is possible even without organised groups in place.

When the LPI began its Somali engagement in 1992, there were no existing local groups that fulfilled the above criteria. As a result, LPI chose to implement its programme by training their own trainers, while at the same time supporting individual activists and larger groups, belonging to categories such as teachers or artists, although not yet well organised. This had several beneficial effects: non-clan and group based individuals could come together. The mere bringing together of all these different people proved to be a reconciliation exercise in itself. LPI further discovered that the formation of groups could sometimes be facilitated through workshops. The largest success of this approach was the effective empowerment of many of these actors as seen, for instance, in the fact that more than fifty per cent of the delegates who gathered in Djibouti and formed a Somali 'government' in 1999 were trained by LPI.

2.5 Timing: the need for long-term engagement and windows of opportunity

Discussions about the effective timing of interventions take up a major portion of the literature on conflict transformation and peacebuilding. For many years, individuals have debated the issue of the 'ripeness' of conflicts for resolution, and discussed the corresponding need to time peace interventions according to this ripeness. Zartman and others argued that a peace intervention could only contribute to solving a conflict, if that conflict was ripe for resolution (Zartman 1989; Stedman 1991).

This concept of ripeness, and the debate it has provoked, has led most researchers to agree that, while the idea is helpful as it makes actors more aware of this need, its practical use is limited. This is because ripeness can usually only be analysed *ex post facto*, and is empirically very difficult to distinguish from the question of the success of outcomes. In the end, it becomes a tautology: if the conflict was not ripe, there was no chance for successful peace intervention; if peace intervention succeeded, then the conflict must have been ripe! (Kleiboer 1994). Moreover, by focusing overly on this concept of ripeness, external actors further run a risk that they will always remain inactive as they continue to wait for a ripe moment (Paffenholz 1998).

With the evolution of transformation and process-oriented approaches to peacebuilding, the concept of ripeness has lost importance for most scholars and practitioners. The focus has shifted towards long-term engagement in order to establish sustainable structures for peacebuilding and conflict transformation through the existence of many different local and international interventions. As a consequence, long-term timeframes have now come to be thought of as the sum total of many different interventions at various times within an overall process. It is only through this shift that we can approach successful conflict transformation (Fitzduff 2000).

What does this mean for the concept of ripeness? The consensus is that, while ripeness is still a valid concept, it needs to be modified and adapted to the reality of modern peace interventions. First of all, the term 'ripe moments' (Zartman 1989) should be replaced by the term 'windows of opportunity'. For while the term moment implies a very short time frame and thereby limited opportunity for intervention, windows can be opened and closed and consequently reflect the reality that the chances for intervention come and go and must be continually monitored and analysed.

Furthermore, the concept of ripeness must be further adapted to the realities of modern, transformation-oriented approaches of peacebuilding. These have illustrated that peace intervenors dare not wait until a window is fully opened, as it may well then close before the actor is ready to intervene. Actors need to combine both a long-term engagement with an ongoing analysis of potential windows of opportunity. Only long-term involvement will enable actors to properly identify these windows of opportunity, and utilise them for peace interventions in a timely manner (Paffenholz 1998).

Practitioners have also found that there is often any number of windows of opportunity which might open and close before a conflict is transformed in a peaceful manner and before an official peace agreement is signed. In the end, windows of opportunity need to be seen as bricks in the wall of the house of peace. For example, the Norwegian mediation in the Middle East, now known as the Oslo Process, made effective use of such a window of opportunity that was identified by a Norwegian NGO and then supported by the Norwegian Foreign Ministry. The latest developments in the region show that the Oslo Process utilised an important window, although much more is required if there is to be successful conflict transformation in this difficult part of the world.

2.6 Thinking in processes and building structures

The example of the Oslo Process also demonstrates the need to think in terms of long-term processes and to build structures that will establish the dynamics necessary for peaceful conflict transformation. The contribution of the Oslo Process was not so much linked to the peace agreement itself, but rather to the structures for peacebuilding that were established when the process was initiated.

Another example of processes and structures facilitating conflict transformation is the successful mediation with a wide variety of conflict actors in the process that led to the peacebuilding effort in Mozambique. A number of different Track I and II actors working together, both from outside and inside Mozambique, managed to establish mediation structures and a peace process on different levels of intervention that proved to be invaluable, especially at stages of the process that were marked by setbacks. The Mozambique process was also notable in that these structures continued to exist even after the agreement was signed in 1992 (Paffenholz 2000a). Since 1992, although there have been numerous violent threats on the local level, the conflict transformation structure established during the mediation process continues to ensure that none of the key parties seriously consider a return to war in Mozambique (Paffenholz 2000b).

These examples illustrate that effective conflict transformation requires the building of flexible but sustainable structures. This must be done on both the level of sustaining peace processes through the establishment of these structures, as well as the macro level. Concerning the latter, Luc Reychler (2000, p13) has proposed a set of four peace-enhancing structures that should be built around interventions:

> *The first is of a political nature: it is the establishment of a consolidated democracy. Such a democracy consists of ten building blocks and internal and external support systems. The second structure necessary for the establishment of a sustainable peace is an effective, legitimate, and restorative justice system. The creation of a restorative justice system has been strongly promoted by Howard Zehr. The third structure that needs to be built is a social, free market system. The chances of establishing a sustainable peace are greater in a social, free market system than in a centralised or pure free market economic environment. Of greater importance are the privatisation process and the creation of a vibrant economic society. The fourth structure that needs attention is the education, information, and communication system. Here we look at the degree of schooling, the level of discrimination, the relevance of the subjects and the attitudes held, the control of the media, the professional level of the journalist, the extent to which the media play a positive role in the transformation of the conflicts, and the control of destructive rumours. Finally, structures are needed to cope with refugee problems in a satisfactory way.*

2.7 Getting the right people: qualification versus commitment

All of the levels of intervention will require personnel who are both qualified and committed: these two qualities, above all others, are essential for building peace (Mott Foundation 1999). Qualification alone will be insufficient to effectively master the difficult personal and professional challenges endemic to crisis regions; commitment, openness, flexibility and self-confidence by themselves will not be enough for an actor to make a meaningful contribution to the peacebuilding effort. The combination of these two qualities must be sought through rigorous training.

To find such people, a good field staff recruitment process is essential. This should include the provision of a comprehensive application form on which candidates can write about themselves, their motivation, commitment, experience, education and training, skills and qualifications. It should also insist upon feedback from relevant reference persons. A proper recruitment should further include individual interviews as well as a recruitment seminar (Kruhonja 2000).

Box 2: OSCE Mission Members – General Minimum Requirements

OSCE applicants are required to possess the following minimum requirements in order to qualify for any OSCE field mission:

- Ability to work in English;
- Excellent physical condition;
- Possession of a valid driving licence and ability to drive using a manual transmission;
- Ability to operate Windows applications, including word processing and email;
- Demonstrated ability and willingness to work as a member of a team, with people of different cultural and religious backgrounds, different gender, and diverse political views, while maintaining impartiality and objectivity;
- Cultural sensitivity and judgement;
- Flexibility and ability to work under pressure and with limited time frames;
- Ability to cope with physical hardship and willingness to work extra hours and in an environment with limited infrastructure.

Desirable:

- Previous international work experience and/or experience in field missions;
- Knowledge of other languages;
- Management and supervisory experience;
- Negotiation/mediation experiences.

Source: (OSCE 2000)

Nevertheless, it seems to be extremely difficult to find candidates who fulfil all the relevant criteria. Therefore, it is all the more necessary to recruit good teams, as, within a team, individual weaknesses can be compensated. Finding the dream-team rather than looking for the superwoman or superman seems to be the right approach. Far too often, the recruitment focuses excessively on professional qualifications; the importance of motivations is underestimated in many organisations. But experience shows, at least when working in crisis areas, that personality matters as individual limitations become, in effect, the limitations of what organisations can contribute to conflict transformation (Kramer 2001).

2.8 Cooperation and coordination: identifying strategic alliances for peacebuilding

The literature offers many insights around the themes of cooperation and coordination. On coordination, most practitioners and actors on all levels of intervention believe in its usefulness; however, in practice, coordination hardly ever works. Everybody wants to coordinate, but nobody wants to be coordinated!

Research findings confirm that only the existence of many different and multi-focused interventions will, over time, lead to a truly sustainable conflict transformation (Fitzduff 2000; Paffenholz 2000a). Nevertheless, these findings do not mention that coordination among all these different actors will give added value to the process. Moreover, this coordination will only be effective if certain preconditions are met. Most importantly, the objective of coordination must be clear and valued by every actor involved.

In most areas of violent conflict, there is either a peacekeeping mission already in place, or at least a number of external actors working to implement peace or relief aid projects. If there is a peacekeeping mission, it has usually established a coordination office. In these cases, it is crucial for NGOs to organise themselves into some type of strategic alliance in order to develop strategies for the best way to link up with the mission.

This is often not an easy task, as NGOs tend to have cultures of rivalry rather than cooperation. Here, the commitment to support peace and stability in a war zone must become the binding force overcoming confrontational behaviour on all sides. Usually NGOs have access to more in-depth information concerning the situation on the ground in different areas of a country compared to governmental organisations. Missions will usually seek to make use of this information for their own purposes. If Track I, II and III actors are to cooperate effectively, a clear definition of appropriate roles and behaviours is an essential precondition.

Well-organised NGOs will find that they can maximise their contribution to peaceful conflict transformation by taking certain basic steps. To promote effective coordination the first step might be the nomination of a leading actor. Second, organisations must enhance their internal coordination systems prior to engaging in external coordination efforts. Finally, organisations may find that it is better not to establish formal coordination mechanisms, but rather to rely on ad hoc task forces designed for specific purposes.

In cases where there is no international mission in place, there are two different scenarios. Either the very few NGOs on site will engage in cooperation with each other out of recognition that this is the only way to establish some sort of working structure to support their operations, or the conflict area will have become so 'popular' that a continually increasing number of NGOs will have been attracted to work there. This usually hinders good cooperation. Nevertheless, actors should engage in some form of coordination, even if it is only for the purpose of sharing information and security arrangements.

The best way to coordinate is through the creation of strategic alliances involving all relevant actors on all levels in order to establish a structure for the support of peace and conflict transformation. Due to the confrontational behaviour of many NGOs, to which reference has already been made, this is not an easy endeavour. In all too many conflict regions, coordination mechanisms will concentrate excessively on the security and humanitarian aspects of the conflict, leaving the peacebuilding considerations unaddressed.

The establishment of a structure in support of the peace process is therefore a very valid instrument. Ideally within such a structure, different tasks should be performed:

- registration of all involved external actors on the ground;
- dialogue between Track I, II and III actors;
- information sharing;
- dialogue on the potential for conflict transformation;
- division of labour;
- linking up with relevant internal actors;
- sidelining 'the wrong guys' (both internal and external);
- support peacebuilding structures within the conflict situation.

Once again, the experience of the LPI in Somalia demonstrates the difficulty of coordination and cooperation. In the beginning of the process, LPI and the United Nations Operation in Somalia (UNOSOM) were engaged in a strategic partnership that contained all the difficult challenges of partnerships on all the different levels of intervention. This strategic alliance held the advantage for LPI that it could crucially influence the decision-making of the UN in Somalia, thereby contributing significantly to the overall peacebuilding effort. Nevertheless, the effort would have been even better served had LPI also found a way to form a similar strategic alliance with a set of NGO actors on the ground.

For LPI, this experience had two consequences. On the one hand, LPI became increasingly critical of any further effort to coordinate and cooperate with the growing circle of interventing actors. On the other hand, this scepticism had the positive effect that LPI, as an agent for the civil society, never grew tired of sending out warning signals geared to sideline the wrong guys as effective partners.

2.9 Making the process sustainable

The goal of sustainability needs to be incorporated into intervention design from the very beginning. Different strategies are required for different levels of intervention. On the macro-level, we can distinguish between short- and long-term interventions – for example concerning funding commitments. Short-term interventions, such as good offices, facilitation and mediation efforts, should build in sustainability as a criteria to be discussed (Paffenholz 1998). Moreover, actors on the macro level of intervention should develop an exit strategy prior to their engagement (CAII 2000). This means, for instance, that external intervening actors must be prepared to leave the continuation of the intervention to local actors or to other external actors at the appropriate time. The process and not the involvement of the external actor must be sustainable!

It is also critical for donor agencies, on all levels of intervention, to ensure that the intervention can be sustained. There are two simple mechanisms that can help them to accomplish this. First, they should develop a joint activity plan, complete with built-in follow-up mechanisms, including the assignment of specific tasks to particular individuals who have assumed responsibility for implementation. Second, they should develop a built-in monitoring system that provides continual feedback to the constituency concerned. In order for trust to develop and for relationship building to succeed, the report-back mechanism will be essential. This further ensures ongoing ownership of the process by all parties, which is the best guarantee for sustainability.

For example, training programmes to empower civil societies in conflict areas are not sufficiently focusing on sustainability. This notion of empowering people is fundamentally right and powerful, but it must also include some sort of methodology aimed specifically at achieving sustainability. It is necessary to both believe in the long-term trickle-down effects of empowerment and, at the same time, to develop effective medium-term strategies for sustainability. Empowering people is the right approach, but if these processes are to be sustained, these people will also need sustainable structures. In the short- to mid-term, training can help. This can be achieved through the building of appropriate follow-up mechanisms that will guarantee a flexible response to the needs of local groups and that will eventually lead to the establishment of sustainable local structures for peaceful conflict transformation.

Another approach to make processes more sustainable is to support them by identifying suitable networking and collaboration partners. Nevertheless, there is no utility in cooperating for the sake of cooperation. On the contrary, coordination or collaboration should only be established if there is an added value for all partners involved. However, it is always necessary to elaborate the usefulness of strategic alliances in order to sustain programmes through supportive structures.

2.10 Building in learning mechanisms

Work in the field of conflict transformation or peacebuilding generates a great deal of knowledge. These lessons, however, are usually learned by individuals and not by organisations and institutions. As a result, when people leave an organisation, the lessons they have learned all too often disappear with them and must then be learned afresh by their successor. Evaluation units of large organisations have also a huge accumulation of knowledge but usually only learn from the individual case that they have evaluated. To date, little emphasis has been placed on the collective learning of organisations.

The new key-phrase is knowledge management. Despite similar methodologies for both, there is a difference between the management of learning and the wider concept of the management of knowledge.

It is essential to build in a learning process on all levels of intervention. While evaluations have long been a common tool for learning within the aid community, learning on the macro level has so far not been an integral part of the process of intervention. Instead, interventions on the macro level are often studied *ex post facto* by researchers, usually without a personal connection to the process. Despite the fact that learning is often part of programmes and projects, the lessons are usually not learned because they are not integrated into the ongoing process.

It is therefore advisable on all levels to combine intervention with research and expert capacity, conducting permanent self-evaluations (*see* Smillie and Helmich 1999), or at least designing some type of built-in reflection and discussion process. Another option would be to engage in a strategic alliance with partners who could manage the documentation and learning. It is not important how learning is accomplished; what matters is for the results to be permanently updated in writing and for all involved to gain a mutual understanding that learning is not just for the archives, but rather an integrated part of the process of intervention (*see* Paffenholz 2000b).

3. Open Questions and Challenges Ahead

In the last ten years, both the academic and the practitioner communities within the field of peacebuilding and conflict transformation have learned much about the parameters and conditions for working more effectively in their field (*see* the contribution of Kevin Clements in this volume). In my observation, there are several open issues preventing actors from making sufficient use of this knowledge in their daily work.

First, there is still a significant information gap in regard to learning from lessons in other situations. The research community has analysed many different peace processes and thereby gained tremendous experience. Indeed, there is hardly an armed conflict that has not been studied. Many books have been written, offering a variety of conceptual approaches to peacebuilding and conflict transformation. What is still lacking, however, is systematic comprehensive research to bring all this knowledge together. It is high time for donors to fund such a large, comprehensive academic exercise.

Peace researchers have often articulated the need for greater information about positive examples in peacebuilding. Indeed, when working in different crisis areas, it is astonishing how many interesting, good examples we can find among local organisations. Unfortunately, hardly any of this knowledge is documented, which in turn prevents practitioners learning from these experiences. This is not only a challenge for research but also for the international donors and agencies funding such initiatives. It is time to think about new ways to properly integrate learning into all such projects.

Another reason why so many actors fail to sufficiently implement the findings of these lessons is the high degree to which they are interest driven. Unfortunately, these interests are often not compatible with the goal of peacebuilding. For example, NGOs sometimes realise that they are the wrong actor for the particular process in which they are engaged, but nevertheless stay on because they need to spend the money that has been allocated. Similarly, Track I actors are sometimes consumed by a desire to win the Nobel Peace Prize! Such actors have usually lost track of their original goal of making a constructive contribution to peacebuilding and conflict transformation.

Even if all the above-mentioned issues could be dealt with in a constructive manner, there would still be no guarantee that violent conflicts would be transformed more successfully and rapidly into peaceful settings. We must always bear in mind not only the complexity of conflicts but also the personal limitations that we all face, especially as external actors. This does not mean that we should not work hard on improving our practice. Rather, we should never forget that the internal actors from within the conflict areas are the ones who will finally determine the effective rules of conflict transformation. They are the only actors who can build a sustainable peace.

4. Reference and Further Reading

Bercovitch, J. 1992. *Mediation in International Relations*, London: MacMillan.

CAII 2000. *Conflict Prevention, A Guide*, online: http://www.caii-dc.com (accessed 9.10.2000).

Commission of the European Community 1993. *Manual: Project Cycle Management, An Integrated Approach and Logical Framework*, Brussels: European Community.

Erasmus, V. 2000. "Community Mobilisation as a Tool for Peacebuilding," *in* Paffenholz and Reychler, op. cit., 246–257.

Fisher, R. and L. Keashly 1991. "The Potential Complementarity of Mediation and Consultation within a Contingency Model of Third-Party Intervention," *Journal of Peace Research*, Vol. 28, No. 1, 29–42.

Fitzduff, M. 2000. "First and Second Track Diplomacy in Northern Ireland," *in* Paffenholz and Reychler, op. cit., 110–120.

Information, Training and Development (ITAD) Ltd 1999. *Project Cycle Management Training Handbook*, Sussex: ITAD.

Kelman, H. 2000. "Intractable Conflict Resolution in the Middle East," *in* Paffenholz and Reychler, op. cit. , 97–109.

Kleiboer, M. 1994. "Ripeness of Conflict: A Fruitful Notion?" *Journal of Peace Research*, Vol. 31, No.1, 109-116.

Kramer, G. 2001. "Zur Vermittlung und Entsendung ziviler Fachkräfte," *in* Zivile Konfliktbearbeitung. Eine internationale Herausforderung (Band 8 der Schriftenreihe des Österreichischen Studienzentrums für Frieden und Konfliktlösung), Münster: agenda Verlag.

Kruhonja, K. 2000. "Motivation and Qualifications," *in* Paffenholz and Reychler, op. cit., 21–28.

Krummenacher, H. and S. Schmeidl 1999. "FAST: An Integrated and Interactive Early Warning," *The Soviet and Post-Soviet Review*, Vol. 24, No.3, 147–159.

Lederach, J. P. 1997. *Building Peace: Sustainable Reconciliation in Divided Societies,* Washington, DC: United States Institute of Peace.

Lund, M. S. 1996. *Preventing Violent Conflict*, Washington, DC: United States Institute of Peace.

Lund, M. S. and A. Mehler 1999. *Peace-Building and Conflict Prevention in Development Countries. A Practical Guide*, Ebenhausen: CPN.

Mehler, A. and C. Ribeaux 1999. *Krisenprävention und Konfliktbearbeitung in der Technischen Zusammenarbeit* (Schriftenreihe der GTZ No. 269), Wiesbaden: Universum Verlagsanstalt.

Miall, H., O. Ramsbotham and T. Woodhouse 1999. *Contemporary Conflict Resolution: The Prevention, Management and Transformation of Deadly Conflicts*, Cambridge: Polity Press.

Mott Foundation 1999. *Reaching for Peace: Lessons Learned from the Mott Foundation*, Flint, MI: Charles Steward Mott Foundation.

OSCE, 2000. *Field of Expertise: General Minimum Requirements (Semi-final version)*, Vienna: OSCE Secretariat.

Paffenholz, T. 1998. *Konflikttransformation durch Vermittlung*, Mainz: M. Grünewald.

Paffenholz, T. 2000a. "Thirteen Characteristics of Successful Mediation in Mozambique," *in* Paffenholz and Reychler, op. cit., 121–127.

Paffenholz, T. 2000b. "Conclusions: Peacebuilding: A Comprehensive Learning Process," *in* Paffenholz and Reychler, op. cit., 535–545.

Paffenholz, T. 2001 (forthcoming). "Community-based Bottom-up Peacebuilding," *Horn of Africa Series*, Uppsala: Life and Peace Institute.

Paffenholz, T. and L. Reychler 2000. *Peacebuilding: A Field Guide*, Boulder, Co: Lynne Rienner Publishers.

Responding to Conflict 1999. *Working with Conflicts. Skills and Strategies for Action*, London: Zed Books.

Reychler, L. 2000. "Conceptual Framework," *in* Paffenholz and Reychler, op. cit., 3–16.

Smillie, I. and H. Helmich 1999. *Stakeholders. Government-NGO Partnerships for International Development*, London: Earthscan.

Spelten, A. 1999. *Instrumente zur Erfassung von Konflikt- und Krisenpotentialen in Partnerländern der Entwicklungspolitik* (Forschungsberichte des BMZ, No. 126), Bonn: Weltforum Verlag.

Stedman, S. J. 1991. *Peacemaking in Civil War: International Mediation in Zimbabwe, 1974–1980*, Boulder, Co: Lynne Rienner Publishers.

Svensson, J. 2000. "Designing Training Programmes," *in* Paffenholz and Reychler, op. cit., 291–300.

Truger, A. 2000. "Training Peacebuilders and Peacekeepers,"*in* Paffenholz and Reychler, op. cit., 35–42.

Wehr, P. 1978. "Citizen Values and Forest Policymaking," *Western Sociological Review*, Vol. 9, No. 1, 39–48.

Wehr, P. 1979. *Conflict Regulation*, Boulder, Co: Westview Press.

Wouters, J. 2000. "Training Humanitarian Aid Workers," *in* Paffenholz and Reychler, op. cit., 43–49.

Zartman, W. I. 1989. *Ripe for Resolution, Conflict and Intervenbtion in Africa*, New York, NY: Oxford University Press.

Peace and Conflict Impact Assessment Methodology

Mark Hoffman

1. Introduction 172
2. Traditional Donor Evaluation 174
3. Development Projects, Conflict and PCIA 177
4. Linking PCIA Frameworks 183
5. PCIA: A Peace Practitioner Perspective 185
6. PCIA: Issues, Problems, Dilemmas and Ways Forward 188
7. Reference and Further Reading 190

Peace and Conflict Impact Assessment Methodology

Mark Hoffman

1. Introduction

Since the end of the Cold War, the international community has been confronted with a number of ongoing conflict situations. These have included: a series of protracted conflicts that pre-date the demise of the Cold War international system (Sri Lanka, Kashmir, Northern Ireland, Cyprus, the Middle East); post-Soviet transitional conflicts (Nagorno Kharabakh, Georgia/Abkhazia, Moldova/Transdniestria); violent conflicts entailing horrendous acts of ethnic cleansing (the Balkans) or genocide (Rwanda); complex emergencies (Sudan, Rwanda); and, finally, situations in which clear political objectives have been supplanted by a political economy of violence (Liberia, Sierra Leone, Angola). In addition, there are a number of situations that are characterized as conflict prone or where the potential for violent conflict lies just beneath the surface.

These conflict situations, and the need to be seen to be responding to them, now occupy a central place on the international agenda (Carnegie 1997). The responses have ranged from short term humanitarian assistance to long term and more traditional development programming and to projects aimed at promoting good governance and enhancing the various capacities of the civil society. Over the last five years, a significant and increasing amount of bilateral and multilateral funding in support of such initiatives has been channelled through non-governmental organisations (NGOs). The bulk of these funds go to development and humanitarian NGOs, but there has also been an increase in the level of funding going to projects and/or NGOs with a specific conflict resolution and peacebuilding mandate.

This has been in recognition of the need to develop 'joined-up' integrated responses based on the complex interrelationships between conflict dynamics, development and humanitarian provision, and the prospects for a sustainable peace. Increasingly, development and humanitarian agencies have accepted the need to think and act beyond narrow, technical mandates. At a minimum, many have now adopted a 'do no harm' orientation (Anderson 1999).

A number of donor countries (notably Sweden, Canada, Norway and the UK) and NGOs (CARE, Oxfam, and Save the Children Fund) have started to move beyond this minimalist way of thinking, instead developing a more holistic approach. These efforts are geared more towards mainstream peacebuilding within the more traditional mandates of humanitarian assistance, poverty alleviation and sustainable development. Increasingly, concepts, ideas and practices are migrating across the once clear demarcations between the traditional fields of development, humanitarian assistance, conflict resolution and peacebuilding.

The content of these responses, however, has not been unproblematic. As Anderson (1999), Smillie (1998) and others have shown, the nature of these programmes and projects, as well as the manner of their implementation, have all too often exacerbated conflict dynamics as much as they have enhanced the opportunities for sustainable development and peace. It is thus not surprising, given the number and range of projects funded, as well as the levels of funding involved, that there has been a growing critical interest in assessing the impact of such projects. These efforts at identifying lessons learned and developing best practices have taken the form of individual programmes or project evaluations undertaken by the donors (*see* Danish International Development Assistance (DANIDA) and Swedish International Development Cooperation Agency (SIDA)) and, more rarely, through multi-donor evaluations of a broad range of responses to a single situation or crisis (Borton et al. 1996; Lautze et al. 1998).

While the number of such evaluations has been increasing, their quality, scope, depth and methodology continue to vary significantly. Niels Dabelstein has characterized the situation as one of "methodological anarchy" (Organisation for Economic Cooperation and Development 1999). He notes that "historically, humanitarian assistance has been subjected to less rigorous and extensive monitoring evaluations procedures than development aid" (OECD 1999, 2). One might well add that evaluations of conflict resolution and peacebuilding practices are even further behind. It is only relatively recently that practitioners or organisations involved in peacebuilding have even bothered with them. Those that did often regarded such evaluations as an irrelevance or a necessary burden, performed only to satisfy their donors, or even as a positively dangerous set of practices in which ignorant outside consultants are encouraged to engage in unqualified pejorative judgments.

Box 1: Current PCIA Projects

Among those contributing to developments in this area are:

- Active Learning Network for Accountability and Performance in Humanitarian Action (ALNAP); based at Overseas Development Institute (UK);
- The Clingendael Institute (Netherlands);
- International Alert (UK);
- Department for International Development (DFID) / INTRAC (UK);
- Mary Anderson's Collaborative Development Action (Cambridge, USA) 'Reflecting on Peace Practice' – a follow up to 'Local Capacities for Peace' project;
- International Development Research Centre (IDRC) (Canada);
- European Platform for Conflict Prevention and Transformation (Netherlands);
- Organisation for Economic Co-operation and Development (OECD) / Development Assistance Committee.

Nevertheless, as the number of conflict resolution and peacebuilding oriented interventions and NGOs engaging in such practices increase, the interest in knowing whether or not they are producing beneficial results is likely to increase. While there is considerable anecdotal evidence concerning such practices, we are only just beginning to see the development and consolidation of systematic knowledge regarding the impact of these activities (*see* Box 1).

It is in the interests of donors, practitioners and end users that appropriate evaluation methodologies be developed, techniques that are able to accommodate the complex, multi-actor and highly interconnected nature of most conflict resolution and peacebuilding activities. In developing such methodologies, we must ask the following questions:

What were the intended outcomes of these interventions? Were they successful? Under what conditions or circumstances? If they failed or produced unintended negative consequences, why was that? What are the criteria, standards and indicators that might profitably be applied in such an evaluation? Given the frequently intangible nature of intended outcomes, how is evaluation possible at all?

The purpose of this chapter is to provide a snap shot of some of the current initiatives or approaches to developing 'peace and conflict impact assessment' (PCIA) methodologies. It will provide an overview of three approaches to PCIA: those that deploy standard donor evaluation criteria; those that develop methodologies for assessing the peace and conflict impact of development and humanitarian programming by multi-mandate organisations; and those that focus explicitly on interventions by NGOs with specific conflict resolution and peacebuilding aims. The article will conclude with some comments on the problems and prospects for the consolidation of these into an integrated, operational methodology.

2. Traditional Donor Evaluation

The dominant donor approach to evaluations locates them within the 'project cycle management' (PCM). While the details and nuances of this terminology will vary from donor agency to donor agency, PCM will always include the same basic components: project identification and design, project implementation and project evaluation. These are often represented as being in a dynamic, interactive relationship with a built in feedback loop (*see* Diagram 1).

Diagram 1: Project Cycle

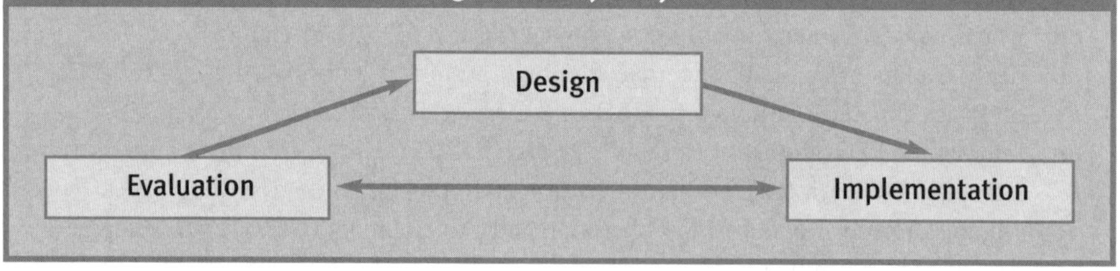

The nature and purpose of such an evaluation is: "Analysis of results and impact of the project during or after implementation with a view to possible remedial action and/or framing of recommendations for the guidance of similar project in the future" (European Commission 1993, 12).

The reality, however, is much more linear. Evaluations often take place only at the end of the project cycle. In the more thoughtful implementing and donor agencies, the summative nature of these evaluations may then lead to ongoing monitoring or feed into overall programming guidelines. More often than not, however, institutional practices inhibit the transfer of lessons learned and rarely are the insights from the evaluation of one project transferred to the design stage of similar or related projects. An interesting effort at institutionalising the follow up to evaluations was the Joint Evaluation Follow up Monitoring and Facilitation Network (JEFF). This was established after the Rwanda joint evaluation with the intention of ensuring that the report's recommendations were taken seriously and acted upon. Another example is the quarterly monitoring by the Operation Lifeline Sudan consortium (*see* OECD 1999, 27).

While many donor agencies maintain their own internal evaluation units, it is often the case that they commission outside consultants to carry out this work. Indeed, a small cottage industry of professional evaluators has now sprung up in response to this donor led demand. Over time, the best practices of these professional evaluators have started to coalesce into something approaching a standardised methodology and set of criteria. On the basis of a number of DANIDA and SIDA evaluations, as well as the guidelines of the Development Assistance Committee of OECD (OECD/DAC), the criteria most frequently invoked are:

1 Impact and coverage

Measures the lasting changes which are a consequence of the project activities. It addresses the question: what real difference has the activity made and to whom? Impacts can be positive or negative; intended or unintended; immediate or long term; and take place at the micro, meso or macro levels. Coverage refers to the differential nature of the impacts which can be seen across particular sectors (e.g. social, economic, political, and environmental) and/or target groups (e.g. individuals, particular social groups such as the elderly, children, women, or communities and institutions).

2 Relevance and appropriateness

The former criterion assesses the extent to which the overall goal and purpose of a project is in line with policy needs and priorities; the latter focuses more on the activities and inputs level, assessing whether the project activities are properly tailored to local needs. This distinction allows an evaluation to conclude that, while the overall programme or project aim may have been relevant, the particular activities or projects pursued were not the most appropriate, and that better alternatives could or should have been identified.

3 Effectiveness and efficiency

Measures the degree to which the intended results are actually what was achieved, and whether maximum results were reached within the given level of resources. This allows for a judgment as to whether the same or better outcomes might have been achieved through the use of different inputs.

4 Timeliness

Were the activities pursued at the most opportune or appropriate moment?

5 Sustainability

This measures the extent to which the impact of a project is likely to continue after donor funding has been withdrawn. It brings the longer term focus to bear on the project, highlights the possible impact on local power structures, dynamics and social capital and emphasises the need to be cautious about creating situations of dependency between the outside actors and the internal structures, processes or organisations (either in terms of funds, resources, ideas or processes) (Ebata 1999).

6 Coherence, coordination and complementarity

Here, the evaluation assesses the degree to which programmes, projects or activities were designed and implemented in a manner that is likely to ensure that their objectives and outcomes are mutually reinforcing rather than at cross purposes or even undermining one another.

In developing their evaluations in each of these areas, evaluators are likely to turn to the 'logframe' for the project. This will provide them with the overall rationale for the programme and the intended outcomes for the particular project, the activities that will achieve these outcomes, the human and material inputs to these activities and the 'observable verifiable indicators' (OVIs) that indicate progress towards achieving desired outcomes. The logframe also identifies the risks posed to the project from externalities beyond the control of the project. There are obvious connections to the criteria above.

Of particular importance in the assessment of impacts are the OVIs. In the myriad of logframe training manuals (EC; DANIDA; DFID) the relevant OVIs are often characterized as quantity, quality, target group(s), time and place. In other words, they are meant to indicate the quantity and quality of the product being delivered, to whom it is being delivered, when and where, and with what intended impact.

In contrast to this, almost anyone who has ever attempted to construct a logframe or who has ever been involved in an evaluation will have first hand experience of just how difficult the identification of appropriate indicators can be – particularly those that are qualitative rather than quantitative. Within the humanitarian field, there has been considerable effort at standardising the relevant indicators through the SPHERE project. It involved a coalition of over 225 European and North American NGOs in developing minimum standards in five key sectors of humanitarian response: water and sanitation; food security; nutrition; health services; and shelter and site selection. These are now widely used in drawing up logframes in emergency situations and are also likely to be used in subsequent evaluations. However, even in the SPHERE project, the overwhelming majority of indicators are quantitative in nature. This partly reflects the nature of humanitarian responses (such as the delivery of tents, medical supplies, safe water and sanitation infrastructure), but it also makes evident what many feel are fundamental weaknesses in both the logframe methodology and the standard donor evaluation processes.

The use of logframes undoubtedly offers certain benefits. It helps to clarify and to set the project objectives and the assumptions underpinning specific interventions. It highlights the need to consciously link planned activities with desired outcomes, and to clearly identify the type, range and amount of inputs required for each. Most importantly, it can highlight the need for and the prospects of project sustainability.

However, logframes also have limitations. Many view them as overly restrictive, forcing the implementing agencies to think mechanistically rather than being innovative. This results from their tendency to reinforce linear causal relationships between inputs, activities and outcomes. It is this tendency that also leads to an emphasis on the quantifiable when it comes to measurable indicators. It further produces a focus on the project level rather than on the overall policy goals or purposes.

The result can be a rather static analysis that does not fully engage with the risks or assumptions identified in a logframe. Nor is it a methodology that does much to highlight opportunities which exist. Thus, the problematic nature and structure of the logframe methodology almost invariably leads to conflict being located as a risk – often as a 'killer assumption' that poses a serious potential threat to a project – rather than being viewed as something the project might seek to address directly through its activities. Its defenders might well argue that this not inherent in the methodology itself, only in the manner in which it has been deployed.

A recent OECD/DAC overview of humanitarian evaluation methodology recognised some of these limitations and argues that evaluations must move beyond a narrow 'project only' focus and develop a wider, policy oriented approach (OECD/DAC 1999). This expanded orientation would focus not just on the rationale and objectives of individual projects but on the mandates, underlying beliefs, assumptions and ideologies that have led evaluators to deem them worthwhile in the first place. It would also allow for a more pointed assessment of the tensions that can well exist between these and the successful implementation of particular projects. It is argued that such an approach would better capture the fluidity, complexity and interconnectedness of a situation and the range of responses to it.

In shifting away from a narrow, linear focus on cause/effect relationships to one that puts forward textured narrative accounts of events, processes and structure, an evaluation would aim at validation rather than verification. While this shift in orientation to the wider policy level would provide the basis for a more strategic assessment of the impact of policy on conflict dynamics and peacebuilding opportunities, it would still leave a gap in project level assessments. Moreover, although there is much that is relevant and helpful for PCIA in the standardised criteria being devised for the development and humanitarian fields, these cannot, in themselves provide an adequate foundation for the creation of an operational methodology unique to PCIA.

3. Development Projects, Conflict and PCIA

One of the most significant attempts to develop a workable PCIA methodology was Ken Bush's "A Measure of Peace" (1998), produced for the Canadian International Development Research Centre's (IDRC) Peacebuilding and Reconstruction programme. In his thoughtful and provocative paper, Bush asserts that efforts at developing PCIA methodologies entailed a fundamental misconception. The difficulty he identifies is that most approaches tend to view peacebuilding as a specific type of *activity* rather than thinking of it as an *impact*.

Bush (1998,7) defines PCIA as:

> *A means of evaluating (ex post facto) and anticipating (ex ante, as far as possible) the impacts of proposed and completed development projects on: 1) those structures and processes which strengthen the prospects for peaceful coexistence and decrease the likelihood of the outbreak, reoccurrence, or continuation of violent conflict, and; 2) those structure and processes that increase the likelihood that conflict will be dealt with through violent means.*

Bush argues that, unless we manage to develop the analytical tools to answer such questions, "we can only hope to list, assert or guess at the positive or negative impacts of our actions" (Bush 1998, 4).

Bush's repositioning of peacebuilding as impact and his characterization of the nature and purposes of PCIA produces a number of interesting implications. First, the emphasis is placed on location: we have to know where to look for conflict and peacebuilding impacts, i.e. at which societal sites, sectors and levels.

Second, and following from the first, is the implication that, while developing appropriate indicators is an important task, developing an understanding of the *conditions* under which these impacts might occur is equally important. This means that a PCIA must always be sensitive to context (for example, the nature, type and stages of conflict dynamics, and also to the question of whether programming is taking place within a situation of directly militarised violence, protracted but stalemated conflict, or latent conflict).

A third implication is the undermining of the sharp demarcation between development and peacebuilding projects. For Bush, *all* development projects, not just the overtly political ones in areas of good governance, have a potential or actual peacebuilding impact.

Fourth, Bush stresses the need to differentiate between pre-project assessments that aim to anticipate likely impacts and post-project evaluations that assess actual impact but do not do so in narrow developmental terms and rather look at wider peacebuilding impacts. This is important, Bush argues, because "...a project may fail according to limited developmental criteria but succeed according to broader peacebuilding criteria... (and conversely) a project may succeed according to pre-determined developmental criteria but fail in terms of a beneficial impact on peace" (Bush 1998, 6).

Bush gives the example of an education project that fails to achieve its targets in terms of numbers of students passing exams, yet succeeds in reducing inter-group/communal tensions. In narrow terms, such a program would be deemed a failure; but in wider peacebuilding terms, it would be a success. Bush also points out that the opposite case might well apply: while most of the students might pass their exams, inter-communal tensions might in the process have been exacerbated, especially if they were all from a particular group, or section of society reinforcing the perceptions of a group that they were being marginalised. The positive developmental outcomes thus might produce negative peacebuilding consequences.

Bush characterizes the pre-project assessment as a screening exercise that examines the dynamics of the conflict environment and its likely impact on the proposed project (Bush 1998, 12-19). He identifies four broad areas of concern for such a pre-assessment: location, timing, political context and other salient factors. These provide the basis for a general characterization of the conflict, its dynamics, its legacies in the proposed project area, including its impact on political structures, processes, and relationships, its impact on the economic and physical infrastructure, and its impact on human and social capital. Once such a broad assessment of the conflict dynamics has been carried out, evaluators should then focus their attention on three specific categories of questions:

1 Environmental / contextual considerations

- Are minimally predictable and stable political, legal and security structures in place? This assesses the damage that a conflict may have caused to the functional competencies of these structures, and whether the level of damage and non-functioning poses an acceptable risk to the project.
- What are the infrastructural conditions? This assesses how a project will work within existing damaged and/or decaying infrastructure and how will it contribute to its development/ reconstruction.

- Is the window of opportunity opening or closing? This assesses the ebb and flow of the political, economic and social dynamics and whether they will facilitate or hinder a project. Drawing on experiences in post-apartheid South Africa, for instance, Bush notes that an open situation does not necessarily ensure a successful peacebuilding impact.

2 Project specific considerations

- Does the project have the right mix of resources?
- Does the lead organisation have the requisite experience or comparative advantage in the region? This assesses the track record of the implementing organisation, its network of partners; and the extent to which it brings to bear unique skills, capacity, or expertise to the project.
- What are the project's 'tolerance levels'? This assesses the capacity to respond to uncertainty, indeterminacy, risks, losses and change.
- Are suitable personnel available? This assesses both narrow technical capacity as well as the capacity to find, create and optimise political space within which to manoeuvre.

3 Project – environment correspondence

- What is the level of political support for the project? This gauges the support from local, regional and national political actors, as well as from other interested parties (donors, IGOs, other NGOs). Further measured is the support within one's own organisation.
- Does the project have the trust, support and participation of the relevant authorities and the community? This assesses the degree and character of the participatory dimensions of the project.
- Is the project sustainable? This assesses the ability to continually generate the resources (institutional, human and financial) necessary for the continuation of the project.

Once an assessment is made based on the above criteria, questions and concerns, it may then be necessary to alter the timing, structure or objectives of a project. A decision can then be made either to proceed with a project as planned, replace it with a revised, different or complementary project, or do nothing until the situation becomes more opportune to the project's specific objectives. Most importantly, this also provides a baseline from which to assess actual peacebuilding impacts.

In pursuing post-project evaluations, Bush identifies four broad areas in which to explore the wider peacebuilding impacts of a project (Bush 1998, 22-24):

1 Did the project produce substantial or politically significant changes in access to individual or collective material and non-material resources

For example, did it facilitate access to water, land, food, political institutions and processes, economic resources, social and/or cultural status, information, legitimacy, authority?

2 Did the project create, exacerbate or mitigate socio-economic tensions

Did it serve to reinforce privileged access by one group over others in economic, educational, agricultural, industrial sectors or did it serve to reduce hierarchies and dependencies in these areas?

3 Did the project produce substantial changes in the material basis of economic sustenance or food security

For example, did it provide new techniques/technology that directly affect livelihoods? Did it affect the logics of the political economy that minimise opportunities for or the impact of warlordism? Did it create local economies that opt out of the political economy of civil conflict (Anderson 1999)?

4 Did the project produce challenges to or changes in content of or control over existing political, economic and/or social systems

Did the project serve to empower individuals/groups to assert control over the political, economic, social aspects of their lives; to challenge existing systems of control and develop alternative systems of governance?

In the final part of his paper, Bush identifies five concrete points of reference as an example of a PCIA framework that might lead us to look in the right *locations* and ask the right *questions* (*see* Box 2). These would provide the basis for assessing past or potential impact on peace and conflict conditions (Bush 1998, 25-31). Bush notes that his lists of question are suggestive rather than comprehensive. The specific questions employed in a particular evaluation would of course need to be determined on a project by project basis, as would the assessment of the specific impacts.

This is also true of the indicators that might provide a basis for measuring such impacts. According to Bush, these should be "user driven". Donors will have different questions and indicators from those that an implementing agency might identify. These in turn would be different from those that the recipients or participants in a project might identify. Bush argues that a *priori* indicators often obscure as much as they reveal, often saying more about the evaluation system employed than they do about the project being evaluated. He calls instead for a "kaleidoscopic" set of indicators that can better accommodate all the varied needs of the different project stakeholders and participants in an assessment process.

There are several points worth noting regarding Bush's efforts at articulating a viable PCIA framework. First, what Bush offers is a multi-layered, almost cascading series of interpretive PCIA frameworks that move from the broad and general to the ever more specific. The precise nature of the linkages between the different frameworks, however, is not particularly clear. Although Bush suggests that his pre-project assessment would provide a baseline for post-project evaluations, there does not appear to be a ready correspondence or correlation between the factors identified in the pre-project phase and the PCI areas identified towards the end (cf. Leonhardt 1999).

Even Bush's more specific framework is still rather broad and general, offering a very limited amount of detail. Bush regards this as one of the strengths of his approach. While he is correct in arguing that fixed, *a priori* indicators may say more about the evaluation system than about the project to be evaluated, it is also true that the lack of clarity on indicators can also

Box 2: Areas of Potential Peace and Conflict Impact	
PCI Areas	**Examples**
Institutional Capacity to Manage/Resolve Violent Conflict & to Promote Tolerance and Build Peace	Impact on the capacity to identify and respond to peace and conflict challenges and opportunities; organisational responsiveness; bureaucratic flexibility; efficiency and effectiveness; ability to modify institutional roles and expectations to suit changing environment and needs; financial management.
Military and Human Security	Direct and indirect impact on: the level, intensity, dynamics of violence; violent behaviour; security and insecurity (broadly defined); defence/security policy; repatriation, demobilisation and reintegration; reform and retraining of police and security forces/structures; disarmament; banditry; organised crime.
Political Structures and Processes	Impact on formal and informal political structures and processes, such as: government capabilities from the level of the state government down to the municipality; policy content and efficacy; decentralisation/concentration of power; political ethnicisation; representation; transparency; accountability; democratic culture; dialogue; conflict mediation and reconciliation; strengthening/weakening of civil society actors; political mobilisation. Impact on rule of law; independence/politicisation of legal system; human rights conditions; labour standards.
Economic Structures and Processes	Impact on strengthening or weakening equitable socio-economic structures/processes; distortion/conversion of war economies; economic infrastructure; supply of basic goods; availability of investment capital; banking system; employment impact; productivity; training; income generation; production of commercial products or services; food insecurity. Impacts on the exploitation, generation, or distribution of resources, especially non-renewable resources and the material basis of economic sustenance or food security.
Social Reconstruction and Empowerment	Impact on: quality of life; constructive social communication (e.g. those promoting tolerance, inclusiveness and participatory principles); displaced people; adequacy of health care and social services; incompatibility of interests; trust/distrust; inter-group hostility/dialogue; communications; transport; resettlement/displacement; housing; education; nurturing a culture of peace.

(source Bush 1998, 25)

speak volumes about an assessment system. In particular, it may well hinder the ability of donors, implementing agencies, stakeholder, participants or external evaluators to effectively operationalise such a PCIA framework.

There needs to be a balance struck between the loose approach of letting the evaluation criteria be generated on a case by case basis and the pre-determined, pre-judging set of indicators. What is needed is the development of broad typologies of indicators, with suggestive detailing of indicators within sectors, levels, types of projects, and conflict situations – which interestingly Bush starts to do in his discussion of indicators relevant to good governance and human rights projects (Bush 1998, 21-22).

Second, Bush's identification of five PCI areas or sectors does push PCIA methodologies in the right direction. Differences might arise over the precise characterization of these areas and, clearly, work is needed in identifying and agreeing these categories and refining their content. It is interesting to note, however, that efforts in this area seem to be converging on what might be characterized as a "revised human security approach to peacebuilding" (Cockell 1998; Leonhardt 1999). The UN Staff College training programme on early warning and preventive measures uses a revised human security approach. It identifies six sectors: human rights and personal security; governance and political processes; societal and communal stability; socio-economic; military and external. These are used as the basis for engaging in dynamic sectoral conflict analysis, scenario building and the identification or risks and opportunities for preventive action, including peacebuilding (*www.itcilo.it/UNSCP/programmefocus/earlywarning*).

Leonhardt, in her overview for International Alert, identifies four thematic areas – governance, economics, socio-cultural factors and security – that she deploys in developing indicators for conflict analysis, project risk assessment and project monitoring and evaluation.

The real limitation of Bush's framework as it stands at the moment is that it offers no way to examine the dynamic interaction between sectors. It is not only what is unfolding within a particular PCI area but also what are the implications of the interaction of these different areas with one another. How does social empowerment inter-relate with, reinforce or undermine military and human security? What is the relative weight that we should give to each sector at any particular juncture?

Third, although Bush does note the need to distinguish between development projects that have a peacebuilding potential and those projects that are explicitly concerned with peacebuilding, his framework is still biased towards the former. While Bush might well argue that much if not all of what he has outlined would also be relevant to explicit peacebuilding activities, we still need to explore much more thoroughly whether the particularities of such programmes or projects require a distinctive PCIA approach.

4. Linking PCIA Frameworks

One current endeavour at developing and deploying a working PCIA methodology is that being developed by INTRAC for the UK Department for International Development (DFID). Noting that none of the various efforts at developing PCIAs to date have had much success in translating these into "frameworks and tools that can be integrated into donor policy", the INTRAC project sets out to develop a "smart planning and management tool that can assist policy makers and practitioner to mitigate conflict and promote peace in a more systematic manner" (INTRAC 1999, 6). Drawing on an earlier DFID discussion paper (Warner 1999), it identifies three different components of an overall "conflict assessment methodology": strategic conflict assessment (SCA), conflict impact assessment (CIA), and a peacebuilding framework.

The first component, the strategic conflict assessment, is designed to offer an analysis of the conflict environment and would be conducted at a regional or country level. Similar to Bush's pre-project assessment and the OECD/DAC proposal for 'narrative analysis baselines', it offers a contextual analysis of the conflict dynamics within a particular situation, an assessment of the risks associated with pursuing development and humanitarian programming in such an environment, and an assessment of the peacebuilding opportunities.

The second component, the conflict impact assessment, is intended to be a tool for desk officers in the screening, appraisal, monitoring and evaluation of projects. This second tier focuses especially on the project level, and establishes a basis for better assessing their capability to mitigate conflict related risks and to support peacebuilding opportunities. Such a tool also enables the conflict proofing of projects (minimising the impact of the conflict on the project), minimisation of harm (the impact of the project on the conflict) and maximisation of benefits (enhancing opportunities for conflict prevention and peacebuilding). Thus, evaluators could carry out the initial project assessment based on the information generated in the SCA and, if risks or opportunities were deemed to be high, a more detailed CIA could then be undertaken.

The third component is the peacebuilding framework. This would be used to assess, monitor and evaluate projects with an explicit and dedicated focus on peacebuilding. It would build upon the detailed project CIA, but also examine stakeholders' perceptions as the basis for developing indicators that could be used to assess impacts. The distinction between the second and third tiers is that the former focuses on 'risk mitigation' while the latter on 'exploiting opportunities'.

Interestingly, rather than attempting to pre-determine the specific content, categories or indicators that the three different methodologies would be likely to deploy, the INTRAC project sought to develop these in the course of the work, as undertaken by specialist consultants engaging in four pilot case studies. In order to better explore the question of context specific as opposed to general frameworks, four different conflict situations were chosen for analysis: post-Soviet stalemate/transition; open and escalating conflict; escalating but not yet widespread open conflict; and latent or pre-escalatory conflict.

To date, only three of the four case studies have been completed, so that any insights and conclusions must still be regarded as preliminary. Yet, it is certainly possible to point to some interesting features of the results produced so far.

The first of these is the realisation that the most important contribution of these evaluations is likely to come in the form of the *SCA*. This would make donor country policy more sensitive to political dynamics and, carried out on an ongoing basis, allow programming to be adjusted accordingly.

Second, while it is of course important to be able to properly identify and analyse the dynamics within the different sectors of a conflict situation, it is equally important to analyse the *interplay between them*. As Woodward notes in her report on Moldova, "the interactive effects of the different sectoral areas are the most difficult to analyse, but the greatest contribution that a conflict impact assessment methodology can make" (Woodward 2000, 25). Linked to this is the need to be alert to the cumulative impact of different interventions.

Third, the SCA needs to make explicit the various *assumptions* underpinning the aid programming: what approach does it take towards conflict and conflict resolution and what outcomes are expected. This resonates with the OECD/DAC proposals for policy wide evaluations as noted above, and would effectively expose the potential contradictions between underlying assumptions, actual programming, expected outcomes and actual outcomes.

Fourth is the importance of *context*. Universal tools might be easier to apply, but will have only limited validity, as they will almost certainly fail to capture the complexity of a given situation. As Goodhand notes, "The challenge is to find the right balance between 'off the peg' tools that are too general and 'customised' tools that are too specific and make comparisons difficult" (Goodhand 2000, 9).

Fifth, conflict impact assessments must always be the product of a *dialogue* between the assessment team, the local stakeholders, the implementing agencies and the donors. Effective assessments will adopt a process oriented, learning approach. Only through such participatory methods can evaluators hope to overcome the formalism of standard assessment and evaluation methodologies.

Sixth, is the need to be cautious about the possibilities of assessing specific impacts. At best, PCIAs deal in *probabilities*, identifying the general direction and overall pattern of change.

Nevertheless, it is also clear that there are limitations to the INTRAC approach. First, it has so far been unable to identify or even clearly articulate a policy tool or set of criteria for the evaluation of programmes or projects. Like the Bush model, its usefulness has been limited to the suggestion of some types of questions that might be worth asking or some issues which should be explored, and this with even less specificity than Bush provides. This shortcoming is likely to significantly inhibit the institutional internalisation of the methodology, leaving it in the hands of a pool of expert external consultants.

Second, its emphasis on the strategic level of analysis has unfortunately left the second two tiers of the initial methodology underdeveloped. Indeed, as the project has progressed, it would seem that efforts at pursuing the peacebuilding framework have been more or less abandoned. There are several attendant dangers in this almost total reliance on strategic level analysis.

At the broader level, it may well leave the PCIA producing nothing further than 'conflict mindfulness' on the part of donors. Given the still serious lack of conflict awareness amongst many donors, this would not be an insignificant outcome, but it does unnecessarily limit the potential of PCIA methodologies. At the project level, the reliance on strategic assessments may easily degenerate into seemingly *ad hominem* evaluations of individual projects or, at the very least, create a greater weight of expectations regarding impacts on wider socio-economic or political dynamics that few individual peacebuilding projects could easily bear. An over reliance on strategic assessment may stymie support for innovative, small scale peacebuilding projects.

Third, there is the danger of 'over-contextualisation'. While the INTRAC project, along with Bush and others, is certainly correct to stress the importance of context, this merely serves to highlight a further set of important questions that PCIA methodologies need to address: namely, what is it about different contexts that produces different outcomes? What works (or doesn't), where and why? It is here that the possibilities of developing generalisations across cases may be the most productive and enlightening.

Finally, there is the potential difficulty that with its emphasis on the strategic level, the INTRAC approach could become donor dominated so that it becomes a tool that will only meet the needs of donors, but not those of implementing agencies and NGOs or stakeholders on the ground.

5. PCIA: A Peace Practitioner Perspective

One of the most interesting and innovative efforts at developing evaluation methodology and criteria is the Action Research Initiative (ARIA) project under the direction of Jay Rothman and Marc Ross (Ross & Rothman 1999). What is especially interesting about this project is its focus on small scale conflict resolution and peacebuilding initiatives. This differentiates ARIA markedly from most other PCIA efforts, as the latter usually tend to focus on the conflict and peace impacts of development or humanitarian programming, and often do so from a donor rather than from a practitioner perspective. What is also innovative about ARIA is its explicit use of 'action evaluation methodology'.

The purpose of the ARIA project is to develop "contextually appropriate means for the evaluation of conflict resolution activities" (Rothman 1998, 119). Rothman argues that these approaches require new methodologies that are consistent with and even constitutive of the normative values and goals of conflict resolution itself. The project seeks to create a seamless connection between evaluation processes and conflict resolution practices such that the former is no longer viewed as an external imposition on the latter. Instead, it becomes an integral part of any intervention, helping third parties to clarify their goals, activities and outcomes (Ross & Rothman 1999). Far from being a burden or imposition, evaluation should instead be seen as a source of innovation and creativity (Ross & Rothman 1999).

The impetus for the ARIA project came from the growing sense of frustration both with existing approaches to evaluations and with the inability of many conflict resolution projects to articulate explicit project goals linked to a set of concrete activities. Often, project goals were formulated in such vague and grandiose terms (such as promoting peace) that it made them meaningless as far as evaluation was concerned. In addition, projects would end up pursuing activities that were not clearly directed at the project's goals, further muddying any attempt to discern what types of conflict resolution activities and projects were successful under what circumstances. Rothman argues that the better interveners and stakeholders explicitly articulate, individually and interactively, the goals that drive their involvement in conflict resolution activities, the more readily will they define and realise success.

The ARIA process consists of three phases: establishing a baseline; negotiating interventions; and articulating evolved criteria. These are not discrete and sequential, but are rather overlapping, iterative and ongoing throughout the project.

The first layer – establishing a baseline – addresses the following questions:

- What are the project goals?
- To whom do they matter and why?
- How will they be achieved?

The intention is to make as explicit as possible the processes of goal articulation. This will make apparent the diverse range of goals and objectives that inform any particular intervention. The questions help to elucidate the different agendas and motivations that a donor may have compared with the implementing organisation as compared with the stakeholder recipients.

The second layer – negotiating the intervention – involves a presentation of the various project goals back to the different aggregations of stakeholders. This allows the points of convergence, differences and tensions to be captured, articulated, fully communicated and understood by the different project stakeholders. The intention is to make participants reflective and fully aware of the stated aims of the project, as well as to provide a baseline of objectives, so that any changes to them over time can be mapped and recorded for discussion.

The third layer – articulating evolved criteria – is a tracking and monitoring process designed to produce contextualised criteria for success. These can then be employed internally in order to modify the project as it unfolds, or applied externally to assess whether the goals are relevant and if they are being achieved. For Ross and Rothman, the most successful projects are those that adapt and evolve over time, in flexible response to the changing dynamics of the context within which the project is taking place. These changes, however, need to occur in a systematic and clear fashion, and to banish any impression of a purely ad hoc approach to the intervention.

Drawing on Banks and Mitchell (1997), the ARIA project identifies three areas in which impact or change can be assessed:

- those that occur in the workshop participants themselves;
- those which result from the workshop directly; and
- those that can be observed in the behaviour and relationships of the parties involved.

These three are then linked to a further distinction between internal and external criteria. Internal criteria relate to the direct impact the project has on the people or groups involved with it. External criteria link these specific, direct effects to the wider conflict dynamics. Rothman and Ross concur that no single conflict resolution initiative (these are often only small scale in nature) is likely, by itself, to fully resolve a conflict. Nevertheless, they argue that any project can be investigated for the impact it has on its own or on a cumulative basis, in combination with other initiatives.

The difficulty, as is often the case with developing PCIAs, is finding the appropriate criteria or standards for evaluation. As Ross and Rothman point out, no project on which ARIA has been working has yet progressed to the point at which "clear standards have been produced for evaluating a project's success" (Ross and Rothman 1999). Yet, it would not be difficult to discern the nature of possible criteria linked to the specific nature of particular types of interventions, exemplified by facilitated problem solving workshops (*see* Box 3).

Box 3: Possible Evaluative Criteria for Facilitated Problem Solving Workshops

The extent to which the workshop:

1. fosters interactive conflict analysis;
2. fosters relationships between parties;
3. encourages improved communication between parties;
4. performs an educational role/transference of ideas, concepts, processes;
5. plays a pre-negotiation role;
6. enhances the willingness to compromise;
7. assists in the negotiation process;
8. supports implementation of negotiated agreements.

(source Hoffman 1995, 16-17)

However, as is the case with the methodologies developed by Bush and INTRAC, the ARIA project is cautious about invoking generic or prescriptive criteria. Instead, it argues that these need to be specific to the intervention and are best elicited from and with the participants in the project. Such an approach, they argue, will produce more detailed, nuanced and realistic criteria, as well as generating commitment from all those involved in a project.

The criteria also need to be adjusted depending on the type of intervention taking place: those for training or skill building workshops will be different from those for a facilitated problem-solving workshop. Nevertheless, working with insights gleaned from their collaborative research efforts and ongoing case studies, Ross and Rothman have identified "illustrative standards for international or ethnic conflict resolution" (*see* Box 4). In addition, they are optimistic about the prospect of developing a contingency based model of the types of goals sought in specific types of conflicts and interventions (Ross & Rothman 1999, 250).

Box 4: ARIA Illustrative Standards for Conflict Resolution Projects

Long term outcome goals:

1. Institutionalisation: develop local capacity, establish structures that will perpetuate and deepen the work;
2. Reverberation: influence specific micro-level interventions so that they reverberate to the society at large;
3. Demonstration: establish credible and replicable models for addressing ethnic tension.

Methods to accomplish such goals:

1. Needs assessments: identification of issues;
2. Dialogue: meaningful, regular, sustainable;
3. Confidence building: mutual trust and understanding;
4. Empowering: recognition of the power to achieve creative and peaceful change;

5. Partnering: cooperation with other programmes;
6. Engaging: engaging disputants to engage in creative conflict management;
7. Localising: identifying leaders of local conflict management;
8. Catalysing: initiating concrete collaborative project between disputing parties;
9. Training: local leaders/activists in contextually appropriate concepts and skills of CR;
10. Evaluation: development of credible and useful methods for evaluating CR interventions.

(source Ross & Rothman 1999, 251)

While there is much about the ARIA project to be positive – including its focus on projects that have a direct conflict resolution/peacebuilding remit, its innovative methodology, its effort to explicitly link theories of conflict and conflict resolution with project design, implementation and evaluation – there are potential problems with the approach.

The first of these is the obverse of those confronting the various approaches discussed above. Whereas these alternative approaches fail to provide an adequate explanation of how analysis should move from the broad and strategic to the project level, the ARIA approach has yet to develop a clear account of the linkage in the opposite direction.

Second, however commendable its inclusive approach to goal articulation may be, ARIA carries with it the danger that the agreed goals will remain those of the lowest common denominator. Thus, the nature of this evaluative process might actually serve to stifle the very creativity it seeks to foster.

Third, despite its emphasis on contextual and cultural sensitivity, it is arguable that the ARIA approach is in effect a consequence of the prominence it gives to problem-solving methodologies and their associated emphasis on goal articulation, rationality and dialogue. These are deeply imbued with Western conceptions of the individual, of rationality and the nature of communication and dialogue that may be at odds with non-Western societies.

6. PCIA: Issues, Problems, Dilemmas and Ways Forward

Where does all this leave endeavours to develop PCIA methodologies? There are a number of possibilities.

One is the view that all of the experience reviewed above only indicates that current efforts at developing PCIA methodologies are slowly grinding themselves into the ground. The multiplicity of efforts, the various difficulties they have encountered, and the promises that remain unredeemed are strikingly similar to the fate that befell the high hopes for various conflict early warning systems that have since fallen out of favour.

As was the case with the efforts at early warning, it is also clear with PCIA that this indeed should be an important and useful tool for any practitioner in the international community that must respond effectively to conflict situations. At the conceptual level, there may even be general agreement about what such an approach should try to accomplish, at least in broad terms. Nevertheless, as with early warning, the translation of these worthy aims into a practical, usable tool has so far failed to materialise. The gap between theory and practice has not yet been closed; the various efforts at PCIAs are, so far, a practical dead end.

A more hopeful reading of the above would point instead to the inroads that are slowly being made in efforts to articulate the details of a workable PCIA approach. It would emphasise the growing number of cases in which the nascent approaches are actually being applied to real situations – whether it be Bush's ongoing work on Sri Lanka, the four pilot studies underway at INTRAC, or the range of rich empirical action research that is included under the ARIA project.

However, in the process of developing and refining a truly workable PCIA approach, there are a whole range of issues that will need to be addressed. Some of these are finding better ways to differentiate between interventions by multi-mandate as opposed to niche peace-building actors; resolving questions of accountability (who are PCIAs for?); setting proper time frames for evaluating impacts; and establishing to whom projects should be held accountable (donors? recipients?). But several further issues are perhaps even more important.

The first of these is the issues of indicators. While the reluctance to produce a set of indicators cast in stone is understandable, and correct, the limited success so far in detailing any sort of even illustrative, suggestive indicators for use in PCIAs is regrettable. If the desire is to move away from inappropriate evaluation methodologies and criteria, and transcend the constraints of logframe methodology and similar approaches, then part of making a convincing case for alternative approaches is the articulation of usable criteria and indicators.

These can be based on the theories that lie behind particular types of interventions as well as drawn from practical experience and case studies. This is not to argue in favour of 'magic bullets', but rather to suggest that broad, contingently related patterns and categories need to be identified. It is simply not good not enough to invoke the contexts and the particularities of particular situations, important as those are, as a defence against the failure to name such indicators.

One possible way forward in dealing with this lacuna in PCIAs might be to set up an initiative similar to the SPHERE project in the humanitarian field. A similar array of agencies, NGOs, practitioners, stakeholders and recipients could be involved in generating such a document.

Second, practitioners pursuing PCIAs must develop a far more sophisticated sense of the linkages and interconnections that properly exist between the different types and levels of evaluations: those at the broad policy level, those at the strategic country level and those at the project level. As should be evident from the above survey of approaches, currently the various efforts at developing a working PCIA tend to focus on one at the expense of the others. The danger in this is that the pressures of time and scarce resources will eventually lead to an over-reliance on the broader, more general strategic level analysis, thus effectively inhibiting a more sophisticated understanding of what particular types of projects can or can't do in particular circumstances.

Third is the need to further develop an understanding of contexts, conditions and circumstances and of the effect that these can have on the likelihood of positive impacts. Again, this points to the need to move beyond the mantra of the importance of contexts, and the implication that nothing more general can be drawn from a particular set of experiences in a particular set of circumstances. We must come to understand how and why contexts matter, not simply that they do.

Fourth is the need to develop an agreed and well-differentiated account of both the different sectors of PCIA and the dynamic interaction between them. A deeper exploration of the interrelationships between the different sectors will not only provide a more robust means for evaluating the positive or negative impact of particular interventions, but also to better evaluate the cumulative and spill over effects of projects.

Finally, in pursuing all of this, it is important to recognise Goodhand's injunction about the need for proportionality and humility with regard to peacebuilding endeavours, and especially about the claims we make as to their measurable impact and to our capacity for their effective evaluation (Goodhand 2000).

7. Reference and Further Reading

Anderson, M. 1999. *Do No Harm: How Aid Can Support Peace – or War*, Boulder, Co: Lynne Reinner Publishers.

Banks, M. and C.R. Mitchell 1997. *Handbook of Conflict Resolution: The Analytic Problem-Solving Approach*, London: Pinter.

Borton, J. et. al 1996. *The International Response to Conflict and Genocide: Lessons from the Rwanda Experience*, 5 vols, Copenhagen: Danish Ministry for Foreign Affairs.

Bush, K. 1998. *A Measure of Peace: Peace and Conflict Impact Assessment of Development Projects in Conflict Zones*, Ottawa: International Development Research Centre, (IDRC) Peacebuilding and Reconstruction Programme Initiative and The Evaluation Unit (Working Paper No.1).

Carnegie Commission on Preventing Deadly Conflict 1997. *Preventing Deadly Conflict*, New York, NY: Carnegie.

Cockell, J. 1998. "Peacebuilding and Human Security: Frameworks for International Responses to Internal Conflict," *in* P. Wallensteen, op. cit.

Danish International Development Assistance (DANIDA), *Evaluation Reports* (various), at www.evaluation.dk.

Danish International Development Assistance (DANIDA) 1996. *Logical Framework Approach: A Flexible Tool for Participatory Development*, Copenhagen: DANIDA.

Department for International Development (DFID) / Overseas Development Agency (ODA) 1997. *Office Instructions – Project Cycle Management.*

Ebata, M. 1999. *The Transition from War to Peace: Politics, Political Space and the Peace Process Industry in Mozambique, 1992-1995*, (unpublished PhD work, University of London).

European Commission 1993. *Project Cycle Management: Integrated Approach and Logical Framework*, Brussels: European Commission.

Goodhand, J. 2000. *Conflict Assessment Project: Approach and Methodology*, INTRAC for DFID.

Hoffman, M. 1995. "Defining and Evaluating Success: Facilitative Problem-Solving Workshops in an Interconnected Context," in *Paradigms: The Kent Journal of International Relations*, Vol. 9, No. 2.

INTRAC 1999. *Project Proposal for a Conflict Assessment Pilot Project,* Manchester: University of Manchester.

Lautze, S., B.D. Jones and M. Duffield 1998. *Strategic Humanitarian Coordination in the Great Lakes Region, 1996-97*, New York, NY: Office for the Coordination of Humanitarian Affairs (OCHA).

Leonhardt, M. 1999. *Conflict Impact Assessment of EU Development Cooperation with ACP Countries: A Review of Literature and Practices*, London: International Alert.

Development Assistance Committee of Organisation for Economic Cooperation and Development (OECD)/DAC 1999. *Guidance for Evaluating Humanitarian Assistance in Complex Emergencies,* Paris: OECD Publications.

PIOOM 1999. *Armed Conflicts*, Leiden: PIOOM.

Ross, M.H. 2001. "Action Evaluation in the Theory and Practice of Conflict Resolution," *in Peace and Conflict*, Vol.8, No.1, also available at www.gmu.edu/academic/pcs and at www.aepro.org/inprint.

Ross, M.H. and J. Rothman (eds.) 1999. *Theory and Practice in Ethnic Conflict Management: Theorizing Success and Failure*, London: Macmillan.

Rothman, J. 1998. "Action-Evaluation and Conflict Resolution in Theory and Practice," *Mediation Journal*, Vol.15, No.1, 119-131, also available at www.ariagroup.com.

Smilie, I. 1998. *Relief and Development: The Struggle for Synergy*, Occasional Paper No 33, Providence, RI: Watson Institute.

Wallensteen, P. (ed.) 1998. *Preventing Violent Conflicts: Past Record and Future Challenges*, Uppsala: Dept of Peace and Conflict Research, Uppsala University Report No. 48.

Warner, R. 1999. *Strategic Conflict Analysis and Conflict Impact Assessment: A DFID/ CHAD Discussion Paper*, London: DFID.

Woodward, S. 2000. *Strategic Conflict Analysis for Moldova*, INTRAC for DFID.

Experiences with Impact Assessment: Can we know what Good we do?

Mary B. Anderson

1. Introduction 194
2. The Local Capacities for Peace Project 195
3. The Reflecting on Peace Practice Project 197
4. LCPP Experience in Assessing and Evaluating Impacts 200
5. RPP Experience with Assessing Impacts of Peace Practice 202
6. Commonalities and Differences between LCPP and RPP 203
7. Final Comments 205
8. Further Reading 206

Experiences with Impact Assessment: Can we know what Good we do?

Mary B. Anderson

1. Introduction

Discussions of current conflicts often highlight their complexity. These conflicts involve many people, civilian and military, in both direct and indirect ways; they relate to internal, inter-group histories and to external, international interests; they are driven by multiple and competing motivations, some of which are lofty and grand while others are selfish and narrow. Furthermore, these 'complex humanitarian emergencies' (CHEs) prompt many types of international responses that range from humanitarian efforts to reduce suffering to grass roots and high level efforts to end fighting.

But, under circumstances of such layered complexity, how can international agencies that undertake programmes to promote survival and/or peace determine what their impacts are? How can they trace and assess the outcomes of their work as these affect inter-group conflict?

The difficulty of tracing and assessing humanitarian or political attempts to lessen conflict has two dimensions. The first has to do with the criteria or indicators for assessing progress. What are the appropriate forms and means of measurement of progress in relation to conflict reduction?

The second dimension involves attribution. When so many things are happening in a complex environment, how can one know which actions bring about which outcomes? If positive steps are overwhelmed by destructive violence, does this mean no progress occurred? If violence abates, can this honestly be traced to programmatic efforts to reduce violence or are other factors responsible for change?

In the pages that follow, we shall address these questions regarding the impacts of agencies that work in or on conflict. We shall begin, in Sections II and III, by describing two collaborative efforts undertaken by agencies to learn more about their impacts on conflict within the societies where they work. The first, the Local Capacities for Peace Project (LCCP), involves a number of humanitarian and development assistance agencies seeking to understand how their efforts to save lives, alleviate suffering and support indigenous development interact with, and in some cases reinforce, inter-group conflicts in areas where they provide aid. The second project, Reflecting on Peace Practice (RPP), involves a number of agencies that specifically work on conflict; that is, those agencies that undertake inter-group mediation, reconciliation, peace education, conflict management, conflict transformation and other approaches to reducing the dangers of conflict. In these sections we describe the background, approaches and outcomes of these two projects.

In Section IV, we turn to a review of what has been learned through LCCP about how to assess the impacts of humanitarian and development programmes on conflict and, in Section V, we present the findings about how to assess outcomes of efforts intended to reduce conflict and build peace. Finally, in Section VI, we discuss the similarities and differences in assessment techniques required, depending on whether one is working in conflict or on conflict.

2. The Local Capacities for Peace Project

In 1994, five years after the end of the Cold War, many international humanitarian and development assistance NGOs found themselves working in areas where serious, often violent, inter-group conflict had erupted. Many of these became areas of extreme civilian-based civil wars, fought between subgroups of what had previously been functionally cohesive societies.

Many NGO staff, both local and expatriate, were concerned by the evidence in front of them that the assistance they provided was regularly compromised. They were aware that the aid they provided very often ended up in the hands or under the control of local warlords, militias or partisan politicians, though they intended it to be targeted only to civilians in need and to be impartial with regard to the sides at war.

Sometimes goods were stolen and used to feed armies or buy weapons; sometimes authorities controlled the locations and timing of aid deliveries as a means of controlling population movements for the purposes of warfare. The misuses and abuses of humanitarian aid were endemic and prevalent. Although some aid workers believed these to be inevitable in the context of localised, inter-group warfare, others began to look for ways to avoid such negative aid-produced impacts.

Under these circumstances, the Local Capacities for Peace Project was organised as a collaborative effort of many operational NGOs working in conflict zones. The project was intended to pool the broad and varied experiences of these agencies and, through comparing and analysing them, to find out whether the conflict-worsening impacts of aid were, though regrettable, an inevitable aspect of 'doing business' in warfare or whether there were options for providing aid that would limit, or eliminate, such negative effects. LCPP set out to consider how can international aid agencies (working in both humanitarian and development assistance) do the good they mean to do in conflict areas without, at the same time, having their aid feed into, exacerbate or prolong the conflicts. Further, how might such assistance be given so that, rather than having negative, conflict-worsening effects, it instead helps local people disengage from conflict and begin to establish the systems they need for dealing with the issues that underlie the conflict?

During the next years, LCPP involved hundreds of individuals working with dozens of NGOs and other assistance agencies in examining their work and analysing it to understand how they might ensure better outcomes. In the first eighteen months of the project, fifteen case studies were written about aid programmes in fourteen conflict zones.

In the next year, over twenty feedback workshops were held, most also in conflict areas and some with NGO headquarters staffs in donor countries. In these workshops, participants were invited to test the learning from the case studies against their own experience. They were urged to add to, alter, amend, improve and rethink these lessons to make them more valid and truer to the realities faced across the spectrum of conflict areas where agencies worked.

The cumulative learning from these workshops provided the basis for the publication of the book, *Do No Harm: How Aid Supports Peace – or War* (Anderson 1999). Then, the usefulness and effectiveness of the LCPP lessons were put to the test in real time and real space by the field staff of a range of operational NGOs working in twelve active conflict areas around the world. These staff people experimented with using the 'do no harm' approaches in the ongoing design and implementation of aid projects and, from this, learned more about how to trace the impacts of international assistance on inter-group conflicts. When this phase of LCPP ended in September 2000, a number of agencies launched what they called mainstreaming efforts, taking the field-based lessons back into their headquarters to ensure that people throughout their agencies were working in the same way and with the same understanding.

What was learned through the LCPP? Three lessons have pertinence to the impact and assessment issues discussed here.

First, by looking across many settings and including many types of assistance programmes, the LCPP was able to identify clear and repeated patterns in the interaction between humanitarian and development assistance and conflict. Specifically, we now know exactly how aid can exacerbate conflict through the transfer of aid's resources and through "implicit ethical messages" (Anderson 1999). It is important to note that these patterns were identified by many aid workers reflecting on their own experiences in many different types of aid programmes in many different types of conflicts. They embody solid, field-based learning rather than hypotheses about how things might occur.

Second, the broad overview of conflict settings also provided insights into the characteristics of conflicts that have important implications for how aid and conflict interact. LCPP found that all conflicts are characterised by two types of forces. On the one hand, people within conflict areas are divided from each other along the lines of subgroup identities. On the other hand and at the same time, people within conflicts also remain connected to each other across divisional lines. The latter is especially true where conflicts occur within nations where people have previously lived as neighbours and friends; it also pertains in cross-border wars such as that between Ethiopia and Eritrea.

That wars are characterised by divisions between groups is self-evident. However, if aid workers are to understand how their aid affects conflict, they must also understand the bases and dimensions of these divisions. For example, aid personnel need to understand which subgroups are in conflict and why. They need to identify the sources of tension between groups to determine if they arise from systemic root causes or from manipulation, opportunism or other proximate causes. They need to know which issues, practices, institutions or experiences divide people. Without such clarity about 'dividers' between conflicting subgroups, aid workers are unable to understand whether the aid they give feeds into and worsens (or helps to relieve and reduce) them.

Similarly, aid workers need to understand how people remain connected to each other in spite of warfare. LCPP found a number of types of 'connectors' that served to link people on different sides of conflicts. These included: shared systems and institutions (such as infrastructural or market systems); attitudes and actions (such as when families 'adopt' children from the other side who have been separated from their families in the confusion of warfare); past or present common experiences (such as a common history of colonialism or the current reality of warfare); shared values and interests (such as a shared religion, or the value placed on children) and shared symbols and occasions (such as monuments or national holidays). Again, without awareness of these linkages between people, aid workers are not able to know whether, or how, their work either ignores and, thus, undermines connections or positively recognises and, thus, reinforces them.

People involved in LCPP have found that international assistance can worsen war when it reinforces inter-group divisions and tensions and when it undermines and weakens inter-group connections; it can promote peace when it reduces inter-group divisions and when it supports and strengthens inter-group connections.

Third, the experience collected through LCPP shows that it is in the details of an aid programme that its impacts either reinforce divisions or connectors. Programme decisions about whether to provide aid, where to work, when and for how long, who to hire locally, whom to target, the roles of international staff, how to deliver goods – these and other basic management decisions – all have effects on inter-group relationships in the areas where aid is provided.

In all situations encountered by the range of humanitarian and development assistance workers involved in LCPP, it has been possible to find ways of providing assistance that lessen, rather than worsen, inter-group divisions. It has also been possible to find programming options that acknowledge and build on existing linkages rather than undermining them. Aid workers have also been consistently creative about finding options and alternatives ways of working to avoid the negative implicit ethical messages.

Through all of the stages of the LCPP – the case studies, the feedback workshops, the application of do no harm approaches in actual project settings and the mainstreaming of do no harm into agency-wide structures and modes – the focus has been on tracing and assessing aid's impacts on conflict.

3. The Reflecting on Peace Practice Project

In September 1999, following the model of LCPP, a number of international agencies engaged in working on conflict joined together in the Reflecting on Peace Practice (RPP) project. The purpose of this effort was to look systematically at the collective and comparative experiences of these agencies in order to learn more about which of the activities they undertake are effective and which are not, and under what circumstances their actions do or do not work. Again, a broad range of experience was gathered through multiple case studies of different types of peace-promotion activities undertaken by different agencies in various stages of conflicts across a broad geographical spread of locations. Twenty-six case studies were completed and, through several consultations to read, discuss and analyse these cases, involving peace practitioners both from within and outside conflict zones, eleven issues were identified as being central across all settings to the effectiveness, or lack of it, of peace work.

Over the next months a series of feedback workshops was again held, this time with peace practitioners in many regions of the world (and in many conflict areas) to probe these issues and to learn what experience could teach about them. As more and more workshops were held, the discussions became increasingly focused on effectiveness. The central questions were

a) the knowledge about a conflict that a peace agency needs in order to plan and execute effective programmes, b) the kinds of work that are effective where and when and c) the ways to assess effectiveness in the complicated arena of peace work.

Somewhat to the surprise of all who were engaged in this project and who work daily in the complex world of peace practice, clear lessons emerged that have proved helpful for tracing and assessing effectiveness. These are gathered in a publication entitled *Confronting War: Critical Lessons for Peace Practitioners* (Anderson and Olson 2003). In September 2003, RPP will continue as groups of peace agencies working in specific areas of the world will take up RPP lessons and apply them to their ongoing programming efforts to test their usefulness and impacts over a two-year period.

For the purposes of our focus here on assessing impacts, three lessons learned through RPP are relevant.

First, a wide range of peace practitioners agree that a thorough knowledge of the context of conflict is essential for effective work. However, there is little agreement about how much knowledge is enough, which knowledge is most important and how knowledge translates into useful analysis. Nonetheless, the evidence of RPP experience did point to four essential aspects of context analysis that, if not understood, seriously undermine the likelihood of effectiveness. These four aspects of context analysis are:

1. What and who needs to be stopped? Many peace activists concentrate on how to build positive alternatives to violence or conflict, believing that if they can build a strong enough alternative, conflict will end. Experience shows, however, that many if not most conflicts are driven by the interests of people who gain politically or economically from the conflict. Unless these are understood, analysed and some explicit programmatic approach is taken to address these interests, attempts to establish peace will be consistently undermined by spoiling acts.
2. What and who needs to be supported? Too often, peace activists develop peace programmes without first identifying and analysing the areas where people do not fight and the issues about which there is agreement rather than disagreement. Without this knowledge, peace programmes miss opportunities for supporting existing mechanisms for peace.
3. What are the external, as well as the internal, factors in the conflict? Most wars have international and/or interregional, as well as local dimensions. To be effective, peace practice strategies must take account of the factors outside the actual fighting area that influence, and sometimes perpetuate, violence.
4. Has the proposed activity been tried before and, if so, with what results? Too often, peace practitioners repeat programmes that others have tried without effect. For example, many people organise dialogues, implicitly assuming that more is better. But, unless analysis of the context shows that this is true, or that a particular dialogue will succeed when others have failed, then people will be working at something that has little chance of making a difference.

Second, peace practitioners seem to agree on two major long-range goals of their work – namely the ending of violent conflict and the building of a just, sustainable peace. Some agencies concentrate on one of these goals; others focus on both simultaneously. However, experience shows that although some peace practice is explicitly directed toward reducing violence (as for example, inter-positioning and accompaniment efforts), the ultimate goal of a just, sustainable peace is more often assumed to be linked to project activities rather than directly factored into project choices and strategies. Many people do many things 'for peace' assuming that, someday, 'they will all add up.' The evidence gathered through RPP suggests that this assumption is not true. Many good actions do not simply add up to peace.

Third, although participants in RPP were at first staggered by the range of activities undertaken for peace and covered by the case studies, over time it became clear that all peace practice can be depicted in a simple chart (Figure 1 below). What this matrix shows is that strategies for peace range from those that are based on the belief that peace is built through the engagement of many people to those based on the belief that peace is possible only if certain people, holding key positions, are engaged. This range is shown in the columns under the heading 'More People' and 'Key People'. Further, peace programmers work at two basic levels, some concentrating on individual, personal change (as in programmes focused on changing attitudes or teaching peace values) and others concentrating on socio-political change (such as programmes directed toward reform or development of the institutions of justice, political inclusion, etc.). These are shown in the matrix in the rows labelled 'Personal/Individual' and 'Socio-Political' levels.

Figure 1

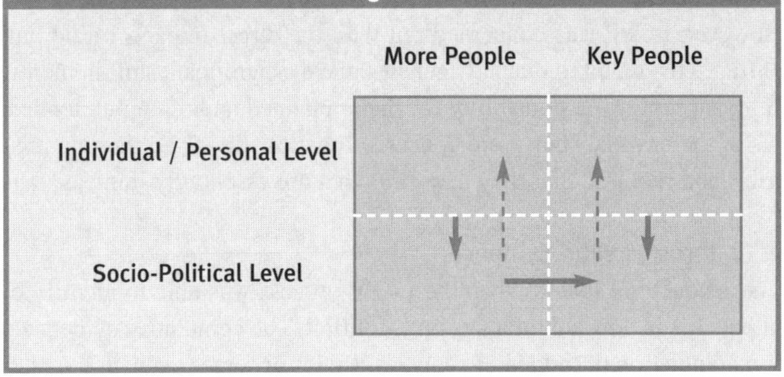

This simple charting of different strategies and different levels of work enabled the people involved in RPP to trace which types of work are, or are not, effective under which circumstances. Here the findings were remarkable.

RPP found that work that stays only at the individual/personal level, without translation into institutional impacts at the socio-political level, has no discernable impact on peace. It may be good and useful work (participants may gain from it individually) but its effectiveness in either reducing conflict, or in contributing to a sustainable peace, is not traceable. A change in people's attitudes has no effect on peace unless they also act differently in the public sphere. Such work becomes effective only if it is linked to, and engaged with, work also at the socio-political level.

In addition, RPP found that work that focuses on more people cannot, by itself, achieve sufficient momentum to end conflict or build peace; nor can work concentrated only on key people. For effectiveness, efforts to engage more people in peace practice must also link to efforts involving key people and vice versa. If leaders make treaties, for which people are not ready, these agreements will not hold; if many people want peace but they cannot affect the decisions of their leaders or the perpetuators of war, peace will not come.

These two findings – that individual/personal level work must be linked to socio-political developments and that more people and key people strategies must be linked – are shown in figure 1 by the arrows that go downward and across the bottom of the matrix.

4. LCPP Experience in Assessing and Evaluating Impacts

1. Aid agencies work with tangibles

Over the years, aid agencies have become adept at assessing the direct impacts of their work. They regularly document how many people have been fed, how many houses have been repaired, how many children have been inoculated and so on, as a result of aid. Many go further to report accurately on some of the indirect impacts of their work such as the reduction in disease that results from improved water and sanitation systems. Most aid agencies accept responsibility for tracing the impacts of the resources they provide in the spheres where these resources are intended to benefit recipients.

However, LCPP was concerned not with the direct impacts of aid but with its side effects on conflict. This required that aid agencies make a significant shift in their understanding of accountability, accepting responsibility for the unplanned and often unintended political and social impacts of their work. They were concerned that this involved them in areas where they had no expertise and required that they measure what are essentially immeasurable outcomes.

2. Patterns as Valid Evidence

These concerns abated when the LCPP process was able to identify clear, repeated and prevalent patterns in how aid interacts with conflict. The cumulative evidence regarding (for example) the manipulation of food aid to support armies or force population movements, drawn from specific, grounded experiences in multiple settings, became as compelling as any measure of the impact of food aid on nutritional status. The specificity and precision of this cumulative experience provided evidence that was seen by aid workers to be accurate and valid.

3. Differences in Assessing Negative and Positive Impacts

LCPP found that it is easier to trace the elimination of aid's negative impacts than to know precisely its positive impacts on conflict. When an NGO identifies some way that its aid is feeding into conflict, it can then take steps to end this. Identifying a specific problem makes it possible also to know when that problem is solved. For example, one agency working in a West African country found that it had inadvertently hired all of its local staff from only one of the ethnic groups in the conflict area. The result was a one-sided programme which favoured villages and individuals also from that ethnic group and, thus, fed into inter-group tensions. Once the agency staff had identified the problem of single-ethnicity, and once they had analysed how their hiring procedures led to this outcome, they were able to broaden their recruiting to other groups and reinforce inter-group connections rather than feeding into inter-group tensions. In another area, an aid agency found that every time it trained mechanics to maintain its fleet of delivery trucks, these individuals were conscripted by the local militias to maintain the military vehicles at the front lines of the war. Having recognised how their training was supporting the military, this agency decided to recruit and train women as mechanics. Women were not subject to the draft.

These two examples illustrate how the specificity of problem identification, whether concerned with the hiring of several hundred staff engaged in programmes across an entire region of a country or with the more limited impact of only a few hired mechanics, enables corresponding specificity of a solution to the problem. If we know exactly how we are making conflict worse, we can find alternatives and assess their effectiveness in eliminating the original negative effects.

4. Using Dividers and Connectors as Indicators

LCPP also found that dividers and connectors provide specific indicators of aid's impacts on conflict. The advantage of understanding conflict in terms of dividers and connectors is that these embody observable aspects of inter-group relationships.

When aid staff have identified and analysed inter-group divisions, they can observe whether these are worsening or abating. For example, if inequality in access to housing has divided groups, changes in access (opening access or further reinforcing its restrictions) can be assessed. Further, divisions between people can be seen in the rise and fall of inter-group tension, also observable in people's behaviours. Are roads considered safe and in use or dangerous and to be avoided? Do people move freely across boundaries or stay within the confines of their own groups?

Similarly, when aid agency staff have identified and analysed connectors, they can observe whether people are increasing or decreasing their use of these. For example, if trade has been a connector, are people still (or again) meeting in markets or do they avoid them? Do they send their children to schools together, do they build new separate schools or do they keep children at home?

Dividers and connectors provide a focus for immediate, observable facets of life which reflect inter-group relationships.

5. Dynamic Assessment

Through LCPP, it became clear that because conflicts are dynamic, impact assessment must also be a dynamic process. A positive impact in one period may have negative implications under other circumstances. As aid agencies analyse dividers and connectors to ensure that their impacts support the reduction of conflict, they need to keep re-doing their analysis. Under the changing circumstances of inter-group conflict, a divider in one period can become a connector (for example, war divides people but, under some circumstances, the experience of warfare actually creates a link among civilian groups) and vice versa.

6. Attribution

In some cases it is very clear that an aid programme caused a specific outcome. Our stories about hiring staff illustrate such cases. However, in most situations so many things are occurring that it is difficult to be sure how one programmatic effort has affected broad outcomes.

Nonetheless, in LCPP's work it became clear that very often people in conflict situations do attribute outcomes to specific actions. They 'know' whether an aid agency's programmes fuel the fires of suspicion and competition or are seen as fair, even-handed and inclusive. They can provide clear indications of why they know what they know. They cite evidence of cause and effect. They have opinions on impacts.

These opinions provide a very good source of attribution available to aid agencies. Knowing what people are saying about a programme's impacts is an exceedingly important measure of real impacts. Further, if people report a change of opinion and this change is observable in changed behaviour, the evidence is even better.

5. RPP Experience with Assessing Impacts of Peace Practice

Peace practitioners work largely with intangibles. They focus on attitudes, beliefs, trust, perceptions of security and other factors that contribute to inter-group tensions or to growing peace. RPP found that many peace practitioners were dubious about efforts to identify criteria by which to assess the effectiveness of their work.

There were four basic arguments against assessing effectiveness that arose repeatedly in RPP discussions. First, some noted that peace 'takes a long time to achieve' and thus, 'it is too soon' to know the outcomes of particular peace efforts. Second, some said that because peace is complicated, it is impossible to know which activities make which contributions to progress. Third, many claim that it is 'impossible' to assess what is essentially so intangible as progress toward peace is. And, fourth, some feel that they are 'called to be faithful' and 'to do what is right' rather than to 'be effective.' Many peace practitioners are motivated by their moral commitment to living and acting according to certain standards; they are less concerned with achievements and success.

At the same time, the vast majority of people involved in the RPP also noted their deep dissatisfaction and unease with the limited results they *see* from their intense, and often brave and sacrificial, efforts to make peace. Most wanted to find some way to improve outcomes, and to know when they were (and were not) making the difference they intended.

It soon became clear that specific indicators of peace progress are impossible to generalise across contexts. For example, in an area where no one has yet taken any explicit action to end a conflict, a public initiative undertaken by two people may represent a major step forward whereas in an area where anti-war demonstrations of hundreds of people are routine, another such event may represent no progress. Thus, to establish an indicator that counts, numbers of people engaged in explicit anti-war work would not capture the reality of each of these situations. The context, and what has been done, need to be understood to assess the real impacts.

However, through the broad RPP consultations, it was possible to identify generalisable criteria (not localised indicators) by which to assess the contribution of different activities to the two long-range goals of peace practice (ending violence and building just, sustainable peace.) Four criteria of effectiveness were identified as having universal usefulness for impact assessment.

Criteria of Effectiveness

The evidence collected through RPP found that a peace practice effort is effective (makes a significant contribution to the long-range goals of peace – 'Peace Writ Large' – if:

- it causes participants to take up initiatives for peace work on their own;
- it contributes to the reform or building of institutions that address grievances that underlie the conflict;
- it enables people increasingly to resist violence or manipulation to violence;
- it increases the security of people and their perception of security.

Experience also shows that an effort that does all four of these is more effective than an effort that contributes to only one of these criteria.

The project also found that three additional questions should be asked of any peace practice to assess effectiveness relative to other programmes:

- is it 'fast enough?' That is, is the approach we are taking making a positive difference in real time or is there some other approach that could produce results more rapidly?
- is it 'big enough?' That is, is our approach related to the scale of the conflict or are we being content with a small, marginal activity when there are other options that would have greater impact?
- is it going to endure? That is, will our effectiveness be fleeting or have we chosen a strategy that, above others, will have a lasting, sustainable impact?

The four criteria of effectiveness have been found to apply across contexts. Each represents a factor in increasing momentum away from conflict and toward peace. The three additional questions establish another benchmark by which to compare options and approaches. Using these criteria and questions, peace practice agencies can, having analysed the context where they are working, select the programming approach(es) that offer the greatest possibility of effectiveness in relation to the large goals of peace. Further, during and after programmes, judgments can be made as to their impacts in the four realms identified by the criteria categories.

6. Commonalities and Differences between LCPP and RPP

RPP and LCPP were both organised to involve many people active in the fields with which the projects were concerned. They were organised for inductive, rather that deductive, learning. They began with the collection of broad experience and, through analysis and comparison of findings, sought common themes, issues, lessons and patterns. They both had built-in feedback processes to engage thinkers and actors in testing and re-testing the lessons that were extracting.

There was, however, one major difference between the two projects. Whereas LCPP focused on learning about side-effects of international assistance (namely, how such aid, even as it alleviates suffering or promotes development, influences conflicts), RPP was focused on learning about how agencies working on conflict achieve, or do not achieve, their primary purpose (reducing conflict and promoting peace). In spite of this essential difference, many findings about assessing impacts were common to the two projects.

Five of these are:

1. Impacts are not abstract

Impacts are observable. One of the problems encountered in attempts to create generalisable impact indicators is the problem of distance. Both the LCPP and the RPP experience showed that, on site, it was often very easy to know, without ambiguity, the immediate impact of some programme activity. For example, one could *see* that male mechanics were being drafted but women mechanics were not. The specific identification of a problem facilitated the specific identification of the solution. Dividers/connectors analysis provided this specificity for LCPP because programmatic impacts on peace and conflict are observable in these elements of inter-group relationships. For RPP it was clear when, for example, participants in some activity took initiatives of their own, beyond those of the project planners (effectiveness criterion 1), or when communities that under specific circumstances had a history of violence faced those same circumstances and did not take up conflict (effectiveness criterion 3). For example, peace practitioners in Kenya report that, historically, when elections occur many communities experience (sometimes severe) inter-group violence. However, after concerted work by peace agencies, in the election of 2003 many communities avoided all violent conflict, recognising that they had previously been manipulated to actions that undermined their own welfare and served the interests of others.

2. Numbers Matter

In both LCPP and RPP, the accumulation of patterns, representing the experience of many people in many settings, provided convincing evidence about programmatic impacts on conflict. If a particular outcome is observable again and again and if many actors close to the situations under review agree with the interpretation of causation, the sheer numbers of examples and breadth of agreement support the credibility of findings.

3. Disaggregation of Goals Helps

Through LCPP, it became clear that assessing how a programme eliminates a harmful effect is easier than knowing with certainty how a programme promotes a positive effect on conflict. Similarly, in RPP, it is easier to trace the reduction of violence than it is to assess progress toward the ultimate goal of reconciliation and peace. The more immediate and specific the goal, the easier it is to know effectiveness in reaching it. Disaggregation of large goals (such as peace) into smaller, clear steps along the way provides a useful way of assessing progress. (However, setting small and limited goals may also be a way of avoiding accountability for more significant effectiveness. We return to this below).

4. People 'Know'

LCPP and RPP both found that people in the situation where programmes are carried out have opinions (and, often, valid opinions) about impacts and causation. They attribute outcomes to particular events. They provide a critical source of information about, and confirmation of, impacts.

5. Impacts are as Dynamic and Changing as the Surrounding Events.

Because in the contexts of conflict things change rapidly and constantly, any attempt to trace the programme impacts in these contexts must recognise that they also are dynamic. In particular, it is important to follow impacts over time to determine whether (how) they are changing. (For example, in LCPP it could have been possible that the decision to train women as mechanics resulted in a shift in conscription policies so that women were drafted).

Interestingly, the RPP lessons about assessing impacts differed from those learned through LCPP in two ways. Whereas for LCPP, context analysis focused on dividers and connectors appears to be sufficient for tracing impacts of humanitarian and development assistance on conflicts, RPP evidence showed that the more comprehensive the understanding and analysis of the history, dynamics and current interplay of conflict, the more likely an agency is to be effective. The four specific elements of context analysis, cited in the RPP findings above, were observed as necessary for assessing effectiveness. Beyond those, far more can be, and should be, known by peace workers who want to do effective work. Because peace practitioners intend to have a direct and lasting impact on the achievement of peace, they must engage more deeply and more broadly in the society where they are working. The specifics of what must be known in any given area are, however, particular to each area according to RPP. Generalisation about these was not, in RPP experience, possible.

The second important difference relates to the finding, for RPP, about the importance of linking work undertaken with different strategies and at different levels (depicted by the four quadrants in the matrix in figure 1). For LCPP, collaboration of multiple aid agencies in analysing dividers and connectors and coordination of their approaches to aid was important in ensuring that, overall, aid programmes did not feed divisions and did support connectors. However, the RPP found it central and necessary for effectiveness to link personal/individual work to socio-political activities and to link the more people strategies and the key people strategies.

A single aid agency can avoid doing harm and can support local capacities, but an agency taking one approach to peace that does not connect with work in the other quadrants will miss the mark in peace work. For peace agencies wanting to be effective, there is no option of working in isolation.

7. Final Comments

The lessons learned through LCPP and RPP about tracing and evaluating outcomes have gone some way toward demystifying impact assessment. On site, with specific goals in mind, attentive to the opinions and behaviours of local people, it is possible to know what has happened as a result of a programme effort and to evaluate the impact of this work on the immediate manifestations of conflict. Both also show that, as the goals of an effort become more lofty and far-reaching, the difficulties in tracing and evaluating impacts increase.

Earlier we noted that disaggregating a large goal into immediate and specific steps helps in the tracing of impacts. However, a danger of such disaggregation emerged in the RPP Project that is worth reporting here. Because peace is large, intangible and complicated, some peace practitioners identified a tendency toward 'feel good, do nothing' programming. In the face of such complexity, programming in small steps may simply not deal with what is required to end war and promote peace. Peace practitioners cannot be content with small progress or be patient with continued suffering. There is an urgency to be more effective and have broader impacts.

Increasingly, aid workers also are recognising that they can, and must, do more than do no harm in their programmes.

Aid workers and peace practitioners must increasingly embrace and push impact assessment as integral to their work because they have seen, through experience, that, using the knowledge gained over many years of broad work, they can in fact increase their effectiveness and contribute significantly and lastingly to the achievement of just societies that solve differences without resort to violence. Of all professions in the world, those involving the delivery of aid and the promotion of peace should constantly strive to work themselves out of a job.

8. Further Reading

Anderson, Mary B. 1999. *Do No Harm: How Aid Can Support Peace – or War,* London: Lynne Rienner Publishers, Inc.

Anderson, Mary B. and Lara Olson (with assistance from Kristin Doughty) 2003. *Confronting War: Critical Lessons for Peace Practitioners,* Cambridge, Mass: Collaborative for Development Action, Inc.

Enhancing the Capacity for Conflict Transformation

Ron Kraybill 209
Facilitation Skills for Interpersonal Transformation

Friedrich Glasl, Rudi Ballreich 227
Team and Organisational Development as a Means for Conflict Prevention and Resolution

Norbert Ropers 255
From Resolution to Transformation: The Role of Dialogue Projects

Facilitation Skills for Interpersonal Transformation

Ron Kraybill

1. **Introduction** 210
2. **Transformative Skills for Moment-by-Moment Interaction** 210
   Paraphrasing
   Summarising
   Listening for and Summarising Commonalities
   Reframing Conflict
   What Makes Facilitator Responses Transformative?
3. **Transformative Techniques for Sustained Dialogue** 215
   Samoan Circle
   Conflict Spectrum
   Interviews
   Interviews with Listening Chair
4. **Transformative Process Design** 219
   Decision-making as a Key Focus in Facilitation
   The Concept of Process Design
   Principles of Good Process Design
   The Link between Process Design and Transformation
5. **Summary** 225
6. **Reference and Further Reading** 225
7. **Web Recources** 226

Facilitation Skills for Interpersonal Transformation

Ron Kraybill

1. Introduction

The idea of "transformation" implies that facilitators bring an agenda to situations of conflict. What is that agenda and how is it promoted? I believe the aim should be to use conflict as a moment, or more precisely, a series of moments of rich opportunity to contribute to human development. Facilitators, a term I use to refer to peacemakers working in group and inter-group settings, meet this agenda with responses that fall into two broad categories:

- by assisting empowerment, that is, supporting the persons involved in conflict to more fully achieve their own potential as human beings; and
- by fostering "right relationships", that is, relationships characterized by recognition of the other, fairness, respect, mutuality and accountability.

In very simple terms, they encourage parties to pay attention to the needs of both the self and the other. As Baruch Bush and Folger (1994), I believe that transformation takes place when people are able both to empower the self and build right relationships with others.

2. Transformative Skills for Moment-by-Moment Interaction

What makes facilitator responses transformative? In exploring this question, I shall apply to commonly used facilitation skills the dual requirement of empowerment of self and recognition of the other.

In training workshops I repeatedly observe facilitators in training experiment with the challenge of getting to the negotiation table. How should they approach parties in conflict to draw them into a process of discussion with each other? Many facilitators begin their first contact with parties by outlining high-minded processes for peace and urging parties to enter them. Parties on the receiving end of these presentations often shock facilitators by responding with anger. "Don't come and try to tell us what to do!" they bristle. When we debrief these role-plays later, parties point facilitators towards a simpler agenda: "Don't begin by trying to sell us on a process. Just tell us you are concerned about what is happening and that you want to understand our views on the situation."

At stake in these conversations is a critical skill for facilitation: the ability to relate to others in empowering ways. Unless parties experience facilitators as empowering, they rarely give more than superficial access to their views, their networks, and decision-making processes. To 'empower' here does not mean to 'make powerful', rather it means:

- to strengthen people's sense of self;
- to increase their confidence that they are taken seriously by others as beings with a history, an identity worthy of respect and needs that must be addressed;

- to treat them in ways that honor and support their own resources for making decisions and pursuing solutions to their problems.

In order to empower parties in this way, facilitators need not agree with parties or approve of their actions. We need only make it clear through our eyes, body posture, and tone of voice that we are eager to understand the situation as they understand it, that we will not reject them for their views, and that we recognise in them significant resources of their own for responding to the conflict at hand. Listening well is an important skill to communicate this understanding and attitude. Three particular listening skills are widely used by facilitators: paraphrasing, summarizing and reframing.

2.1 Paraphrasing

Paraphrasing, a form of intense listening, is demonstrated by the following conversation, the setting of which is a facilitated negotiation session between two colleagues in a community organization:

Example 1: Paraphrasing

John:	She's impossible to work with in a group setting. She dominates conversations and she gets very upset if she doesn't get her way. I just don't feel that I can work with her any more!
Facilitator:	So you're very frustrated with her response in group discussions, and at this point you've given up on working with her.
John:	Look, I'm not saying I can't do anything with her. We can still do the community service work together, and I'm open to cooperating in the research project. But I can't work on the Executive Committee with her. I just can't stand the constant battles.
Facilitator:	You're prepared to work with her in most areas, but it's on the Executive Committee where you've become really discouraged about working together.
John:	Yes, I just don't think I can take it anymore.
Facilitator:	Um-hmm. Well, that gives us clarity about where you stand on this. Mary, let's hear from you. How do you see this?

Paraphrasing is a powerful tool in facilitation work for a number of reasons:

- it communicates understanding to others;
- a good paraphrase often brings further, more reflective responses from others, as in the example above – it moves the conversation to deeper levels;
- it slows down the conversation between the parties and creates a buffer between their statements;
- it can be used to 'launder' vicious or insulting statements so they are less inflammatory to the other party, if present, while retaining the essential points that were made.

Guidelines for paraphrasing include:

(i) to paraphrase is to repeat back in your own words what you understand someone else to be saying: this means keeping the focus of the paraphrase on the speaker and not on you, the listener. For example, a facilitator can say:

- *"You feel that..."*
- *"The way you see it is..."*
- *"If I understand you correctly, you're saying that..."*

Do not say:

- *"I know exactly how you feel. I've been in situations like that myself."*
- *"You know, my sister had something like that happen to her a couple weeks ago. She..."*

(ii) a paraphrase should be shorter than the speaker's own statement.

(iii) a paraphrase mirrors the meaning of the speaker's words, but does not merely parrot or repeat the exact words of the speaker: for example, the speaker might say: *"I resented it deeply when I found out that they had gone behind my back to the director. Why didn't they just come and talk with me, and give me a chance to sort things out with them?"* An effective paraphrase would be: *"You were quite hurt that they didn't come directly to you to resolve things."*

(iv) a paraphrase does not judge or evaluate; it only describes empathetically. Use, for example, phrases such as:

- *"So your understanding is that..."*
- *"The way you see it then..."*
- *"You were very unhappy when he..."*

- *"So when he walked out of the meeting you thought he was merely trying to manipulate you."*
- *"If I understand you correctly, your perspective is that..."*

Don't say:

- *"That doesn't sound like a very constructive attitude to me."*

(v) a small percentage of people seem to prefer not to be paraphrased: observe carefully the reaction of those you are paraphrasing and adjust your use accordingly.

2.2 Summarising

Paraphrasing is a moment-by-moment skill that restates what the listener has just understood an individual to say. A summary is similar to a paraphrase, but it condenses the content of several comments that may have been made over the course of many minutes. Facilitators can use it to review all the key points that have been made by one party about their views, thus communicating the sense that they understand the entire situation being presented by that person. Facilitators can also summarise comments of all speakers every few minutes as a way of keeping the discussion focused.

Example 2: Summarising

In a discussion between police and community representatives about difficult relationships, a facilitator made the following summary of issues: *"It seems that several concerns are being raised here regarding police and community relations. The community representatives are saying that they feel that police protection is completely inadequate and that the attitude of police towards community members is not constructive. The police say that they have substantially increased the number of patrols in the community and are trying hard to improve their relationships with the community, but they feel that they lack the support of community leaders needed to earn the trust of community members."* The facilitator watched the faces of the parties carefully as she spoke to make sure that people felt comfortable with her summary. Observing several nods of approval, she proceeded. *"It sounds as if one of the things that both sides agree on is that there is a need for improved relationships between the police and the community,"* she said. When heads nodded again, she continued, *"Would you find it useful to talk about this and get some ideas from both groups about what could be done to address this problem?"* In this way the facilitator used summary to focus the group's attention on a particular issue, and moved skilfully from her summary to invite the group to offer ideas for resolving the problem.

2.3 Listening for and Summarising Commonalities

In fact, the facilitator above accomplished more than summarising in her final moves. She heard and highlighted areas of commonality, a skill that can be particularly transformative in its impact. In the above example, the commonality lay in agreeing on a common problem. In other situations, the commonalities may be small concessions that are mentioned in the midst of a heated argument. Facilitators should be alert for these and retrieve them as a way of improving the atmosphere.

Example 3: Commonalities

Two organisations, A and B, providing similar services to a community had been experiencing conflict between their staff members in the field. In a facilitation session members of each organisation had made accusations, including the charge that the other was spreading rumours in the community. The following exchange then took place:

Director of A: The only way we're going to prevent this kind of thing from taking place is if field workers of the two organizations meet on a regular basis and try to co-ordinate activities between them.

Director of B: Well, that's been a problem from the very beginning. I agree with you there, but as I was saying earlier, unless you and your senior staff make a shift in attitude, we'll never solve this problem.

Facilitator: It seems that both organissations came to this meeting today because you want to try and solve this problem. From what you have both just said, it sounds like you agree that it would be a good idea to establish a regular forum for field workers from the two organisations to meet and coordinate their work. What would it take to make something like that successful?

Had the facilitator not become involved in this way, a significant point of consensus probably would have passed unnoticed, because the director of Organisation B was shifting the discussion back towards previous criticisms he had made about the management of Organisation A. Fortunately, the facilitator was alert and utilised this point of agreement well. Half an hour later, after the directors had finished working out the details for a monthly meeting of field workers from both organisations, the atmosphere had improved, and it was easier to tackle the more complicated issues separating the organisations.

2.4 Reframing Conflict

A critical question is how parties understand or frame the conflict, the other party, and the issues separating them. If, for example, one or both parties understand opponents as unprincipled killers determined to destroy them, they will frame the conflict as a battle for survival requiring warlike responses. If they view the conflict as a battle for disputed land, they will haggle over every square centimetre of territory. If the parties frame the conflict differently, the possibilities for fresh and cooperative responses increase. Thus, facilitators commonly seek to reframe the conflict in ways that assist a resolution.

Example 4: Reframing Conflict

A facilitator might seek to help the parties recognise that, in fact, the violence is the tragic result of a complex but understandable struggle to maintain cultural traditions and a sense of identity by two groups occupying the same region. Thus the facilitator might say:

"It appears that a great many people have died on both sides because they believed the future of their own communities was at stake in this struggle. It would be useful to hear from each side your aspirations and concerns for the future of your own people."

Also in the previous illustration about organisational conflict the facilitator listened carefully to comments by the opposing sides, and reframed part of the discussion in terms of a specific goal shared by both parties.

In both examples, it should be apparent that reframing does not mean a facilitator instructs the parties as to what the real issues are. Rather, the facilitator works with things identified by the parties, and asks questions that direct their attention to dimensions not previously noticed or explored. By inviting a fresh look at the needs or goals of all parties, their underlying interests and intentions, reframing seeks to assist parties in seeing problems in perspectives that suggest new possibilities for joint resolution.

2.5 What Makes Facilitator Responses Transformative?

The skills described above are ordinary communication skills that are not normally described as transformative. When and how do they become transformative? Applying the definition of transformation introduced at the beginning of this chapter, they are transformative to the extent that they both empower the respective parties and encourage them to build right relationships with others. Hence, although good listening skills are an important tool in empowering the parties, they become fully transformative only to the extent that they assist both in empowerment and relationship-building. Listening well to each party in separate sessions takes a step towards transformation because it is empowering. It develops its full transformative potential when each party is also assisted in hearing and taking seriously the perspectives of the other party. This might be accomplished, for example, by listening to both in joint sessions, or by thoughtfully presenting the concerns of the other party to each side. The technique of pointing out commonalities can be understood as particularly transformative because in one move it simultaneously empowers each side (by hearing and taking seriously its concerns) and strengthens the relationship (by pointing out linkages, common problems, or common goals). Reframing seeks to cast the perceptions of each side in a way that also takes into account the perceptions and needs of the other side as well.

The aim of this section was not to illustrate the full repertoire of responses available to facilitators (*see* further reading). Rather, it was to propose a simple theoretical framework for assessing the many tools available. By defining key components of transformation, we can more easily recognise what is required and which of the many tools we should choose to achieve transformation.

3. Transformative Techniques for Sustained Dialogue

So far we have considered individual interaction skills that facilitators often use throughout their conversations with individuals in group conflicts. However, facilitators need more than this. We also need a repertoire of tools to assist numerous people in conversations and negotiation in group settings. This section describes several techniques I have found particularly effective for these purposes, drawing on the concept of transformation to explain why these techniques are effective in enabling transformative dialogue.

3.1 Samoan Circle

Perhaps my favourite technique for group work involving large numbers of people in the same room is the "Samoan Circle". Essentially an "open fishbowl" with an added rule of no communication except among those sitting in the fishbowl, it is effective in enabling a large number of people to discuss a controversial issue without unleashing severe polarisation.

Technique 1: Samoan Circle

One or two representatives for each of the views present constitute the core of the Samoan Circle. Surrounded by 2-4 "open chairs", they sit in a semi-circle for the entire discussion. The representatives discuss the issues with each other as the larger group listens. Before they begin the discussion the facilitator announces the rules. Anyone from the larger group who wishes to join the conversation may do so by coming forward at any time and taking one of the open chairs on either end of the semicircle. If all chairs are filled, those who come forward may stand behind an open chair until it becomes available. All are welcome to participate, but there is one ground rule: No communication is allowed except within the semi-circle; no talking, booing, hissing, or clapping except for those in the semi-circle. The facilitator secures agreement to observe this ground rule from the group, via the raising of hands or nodding of heads. The discussion then begins with a brief statement by each representative in the semi-circle and proceeds as a conversation among the representatives, with others joining whenever they wish. The facilitator may withdraw and watch as a silent observer or sit in the circle and actively facilitate the conversation using techniques like those described in the preceding section.

As a rule the situation most hazardous to constructive group talk is one with large numbers of people shouting opinions from all corners of a room. Speakers in such circumstances will rise, lob inflammatory insults at others, and then sit down, withdrawing into a sea of anonymity and safety among their fellow supporters. Rhetoric and anger often escalate rapidly in such settings. The Samoan Circle blocks these dynamics. Each speaker must come forward and sit in a place of engagement that is guided by the facilitator. If provocative statements are made, the facilitator can follow up with techniques that defuse them, asking clarifying questions, using paraphrasing skills, drawing out underlying concerns, and so on. Whereas unfettered group discussion seems to bring out the worst in speakers, the Samoan Circle seems to bring out the best.

Reflecting now on this technique that I found effective long before I sought to view it from a transformative perspective, I recognise that it contains strong elements of both requirements. Empowerment is a central component, not only for each group represented, but also for each individual present. All groups are encouraged to fully express their respective views through their representatives, while individuals can also express their personal views by joining the semicircle. Furthermore, recognition of the other, and the relationship-building that comes with it, are also central to the Samoan Circle. Because this method tends to bring out the best in participants, the quality of engagement is usually high; participants often seem to hear each other in new ways and thus gain important new insights about their opponents' views.

However, even when new insights are few, a deeper form of recognition and relationship-building takes place implicitly. Participating in a structured engagement such as this is, in effect, participating in a joint ritual, a social engagement governed by a commonly accepted set of procedures with multiple layers of meaning. The procedures are minimal, of course, and the layers of meaning may be superficial and short-lived. But the result is potentially transformative: for a set period of time opponents engage each other face to face on shared terrain, jointly created by their choice to restrain their most destructive impulses and communicate with each other.

3.2 Conflict Spectrum

The conflict spectrum is a tool for initially opening the discussion in organisational or community conflicts. It gives people a chance to get a sense of where others stand on the issues, and enables participants to gather information about other views and how many people hold them. Because it requires every individual to openly indicate their views, it should only be used where there is sufficient safety for people to let their opinions be known.

Technique 2: Conflict Spectrum

Identify one end of the room for people strongly convinced about one view, the other end for those strongly convinced of the opposite. Point out that there are an infinite variety of additional places between these two locations. Ask everyone to take a position somewhere on this spectrum. Then invite individuals to briefly state why they have chosen the spot on which they stand. This can (but need not) be taken a step further by dividing the spectrum into three groups – the two ends plus a middle group, if there is one. Give each group twenty minutes to prepare a list of strengths and weaknesses of their position and then report the list to the entire group. You can go yet another step further by then inviting people to place themselves on the spectrum again; if anyone now chooses a new location, invite them to explain why.

Even people who in previous discussions have spoken in aggressive and insulting ways are often able to speak in constructive tones to one another when positioned within a conflict spectrum. Explaining "why I am standing on this spot within the spectrum", individuals seem to express themselves more positively than when they explain "why my opponent is wrong".

From the perspective of transformation, both empowerment and recognition of the other are strongly present here: the spectrum empowers by offering physical space as an aid to speakers, giving them a concrete, spatial frame of reference within which to locate themselves. It also creates an implicit sense of connection to the other: even those who stand at the opposite end of the spectrum stand in a continuum with the self. Also, like the Samoan Circle, cooperation with one's opponent in a joint activity dedicated to elucidating the views of all in a positive and constructive way, creates a temporary ritual of common purpose.

3.3 Interviews

Interviewing people in the presence of their opponents is another simple tool that can have transformative impact in settings of group conflict. The tone should be that of a friendly, informal conversation with an attentive facilitator using a lot of paraphrasing.

Technique 3: Interviews

Establishing a personal connection to each speaker at the beginning of the interview is important. Sometimes it is good to begin on a personal note:

- *"Tell me a little about yourself"* for someone new to the facilitator.
- *"How's your family?"*
- *"What do you like about this community?"*
- *"What's new in your life?"* for those with whom the facilitator is already acquainted.

Then move to the issues at hand:

- *"How do you personally view these issues?"*

- *"Tell me what's been happening here from your own perspective."*
- *"What are your major concerns here?"* The key to productive interviews is the interviewer's ability to draw out speakers beyond their inclination to merely state biases or make simplistic analyses. That is, the facilitator must follow up statements by the interviewee with responses such as:
- *"Explain that a little further..."*
- *"Help me understand why that was so upsetting for you..."*
- *"Tell me what your thoughts and feelings were as this was happening..."*
- *"Give me some background to understand why this event means so much to you..."*

The interview as a facilitation tool creates an atmosphere of deep engagement without the tension that often accompanies direct exchanges between the parties. If supported with the listening skills described above, an interview nurtures trust between the facilitator and the parties, and enables parties to express nuances they rarely voice in antagonistic exchanges. Instead of a hostile opponent, those interviewed face a supportive facilitator who actively seeks to draw them out, thereby empowering them.

The interview can be used in separate sessions with the parties to lay the foundation for an engagement with other parties later. It can also be used with the Samoan Circle as a way of assisting each speaker to go deeper, or in the context of ongoing negotiations to gain insights into the perspectives of those involved in an impasse. Only when conducted in joint sessions with opposing parties does the interview become immediately transformative, for here it simultaneously fosters both empowerment of the self and recognition of the other. The support of a skilled facilitator empowers parties to express themselves with a coherency and depth not achieved when they merely restate old demands to opponents. Furthermore, addressing a supportive listener reduces bombast so that opponents are sometimes more able to truly hear and recognise the needs of the other than in direct exchanges.

3.4 Interviews with Listening Chair

Adding a "listening chair" to interviews can have a powerful impact.

Technique 4: Listening Chair

Each person to be interviewed is invited to pick someone from the group (preferably someone with different views) to be his "listener", who then comes forward and sits in a designated listener's chair. The facilitator asks questions, the interviewee responds, and the listener paraphrases everything that the interviewee says. This requires the speaker to pause every few minutes to give the listener a chance to paraphrase. The facilitator may need to demonstrate this by serving as the listener for the first round.

This technique requires selective usage. At first it may seem clumsy and artificial, and it demands a lot of the listener. It works only when trust is high between the facilitator and the parties, when the parties are deeply motivated to address their differences, and when the individuals involved have the flexibility to engage opponents in ways they have never experienced before. However, in the occasional circumstances when all these criteria are met, the listening chair is more powerful than any other technique I know for transforming the quality of interaction between parties. This is so because it incorporates an intensive form of empowerment – supportive interviewing – with an intensive form of recognition – paraphrasing of an opponent.

4. Transformative Process Design

We have examined two categories of facilitation skills: micro skills for moment-by-moment interaction and tools for facilitating an in-depth conversation over a period of many minutes. Facilitation would be relatively easy if it were merely a matter of employing these skills to aid parties in conflict to communicate. Unfortunately, things are not that simple. Group conflicts take place in a context of larger forces and patterns. These usually contribute to the conflict arising in the first place and they impact powerfully on the possibilities of its transformation.

Example 5: Personal Gestures and Structural Transformation

At a South African conference of church delegates in 1992, a white professor of theology publicly apologised for his role in the white system of apartheid. I thought the apology was sincere and expected that the many black participants in the conference would welcome it. Instead they were angry. *"They've taken everything from us"*, said a community leader in discussions later. *"Now they think that all they need to do is say they're sorry, and we'll say 'you're forgiven' and then they can go their merry way, released of all obligations."* Another said, *"I don't want nice apologies so white people can feel good. What I want is for whites to join us in the struggle to dismantle apartheid and create justice."* The black delegates recognised that the healing of this conflict required more than transformative gestures between individuals; and they were certainly not about to participate in what they saw as an effort to limit attention to these micro-exchanges.

One cannot separate personal transformation from structural transformation, nor can we rely on skilfully facilitated dialogue alone to accomplish transformation. The final section of this article proposes the concept of process design as one useful tool in extending the concept of transformation to the larger issues at stake in many conflicts.

4.1 Decision-making as a Key Focus in Facilitation

An inescapable reality of group conflict is the competition for power and resources. How can facilitators work towards transformation in the face of these realities? To answer, we must recognise that, to a substantial extent, facilitation in group conflicts involves decision-making: that is, assisting parties to make decisions about the allocation of power and resources.

Of course, other crucial dynamics, such as the need for identity, are also at stake in these conflicts. But it is decision-making that requires answers to key questions of process and thus provides opportunity for influence on matters of long-lasting importance. Who makes decisions, i.e., who is involved and in what ways? What mechanisms are used for deciding? What information and criteria are considered? Few parties devote conscious attention to these questions; they just do it, unthinkingly, in the way they learned from predecessors and role models. Part of the task of transformative facilitators is to make these choices explicit: by enabling parties to recognise the necessary choices and their implications, facilitators increase the likelihood that parties will select decision-making processes that foster human development.

People in conflict quarrel about issues, such as land, access to resources, and power. On the surface, facilitators' work appears to be assisting parties in discussing these issues and finding solutions. But the most important contribution lies at a deeper level. The way in which people go about discussing these issues – the process – has far-reaching implications for the parties, for their long-term relationships, and the structures of society around them. As facilitators, we should aim at a transformative impact in conflict by actively and openly seeking to influence the process in which parties in conflict engage each other in decision-making. We are impartial in our commitment to the well-being of all, but this does not mean we are 'neutral'. Commitment to human development calls us to consciously advocate processes that empower participants and foster right relationships.

4.2 The Concept of Process Design

To thus support human development requires a finely developed sense of process design. This begins with understanding that there is a difference between process and content, between how and what. In particular, process design recognises that often there is more at stake in how a decision is reached than in what that decision is: i.e., people are usually more sensitive to the process than to the actual content of a decision. Consider an everyday example:

Example 6: Differing Process Design

It is time for a coffee break at a meeting of professional colleagues. The chair suggests a thirty-minute break, calls out the names of three women, and asks them to go and set up the refreshments.

The selected women are all from the same racial group, a minority in the community and the professional group. During the break, others from this ethnic group gather in a corner and angrily discuss the double burden of sexism and racism. After the break, they confront the chair and the entire group with their outrage.

In another organisation, it is also time for a coffee break. Here, too, the leader announces the names of three minority women chosen to serve tea. However, here the women laugh good-naturedly as they rise to undertake their duties. Why? Their names were chosen randomly by pulling straws.

The content was the same in both groups: individuals were chosen to prepare refreshments against their preferences. In the second group, however, the content was accepted because the process was fair.

Why are people so sensitive to process? Why do they often care more about the way in which a decision is made than about the actual content of the decision? Intuitively, people sense that process makes profound statements about human worth, about who counts. As long as they perceive the process as fair and respectful, most people can accept considerable disappointment and frustration about not attaining their desired outcomes – be they political, financial, organisational, or technical. But those same people will often rise up in bitter, defiant outrage if they feel that the way in which decisions were reached was unfair or demeaning.

Example 7: Bad Process

"They act as though we don't even exist!" muttered an outraged community leader after city officials announced plans to sell several acres of an abandoned educational institution to developers, without consulting local residents. This leader may not have reflected explicitly that assessments of human worth are implicit in the way all decisions are made. However, like most people, he was exquisitely sensitive to bad process when it was used on him. He saw that more was at stake than a mere decision about land use. He saw that failure to consult with local residents about a decision that would permanently alter the character of their neighbourhood represented a fundamental attack on the ability of residents to have a voice in their own future. Along with dozens of other outraged neighbours, he mounted a campaign that unseated an entire group of officials in the next election.

A great deal of group conflict is simply the consequence of bad process, for people commonly reject even the best ideas and proposals, if they result from processes that they find objectionable. Even thoughtful and well-intentioned leaders in non-governmental organisations, faith communities, schools and universities, governmental and public institutions regularly violate principles of good process design and are baffled by the reactions of those around them. Focused on outcomes that are often laudable, these leaders do not realise the damage they inflict on relationships when they use processes that imply that others do not deserve to be consulted or involved in decision-making. Often they find it difficult to understand why process is so important or to recognise the difference between good and bad process.

Most people find it easier to identify bad process than good process. For many years we have asked people in workshops to tell stories of times when they were on the receiving end of bad process: *"Tell us about an instance when you were upset, not so much about a decision, but about the way in which a decision was made. Explain why you were upset."* Stories pour forth in response to this invitation. As groups reflect on bad experiences, principles for good decision-making processes emerge that carry important insights for responding transformatively to group conflicts. Facilitators can use these principles to guide their work with conflicted parties.

4.3 Principles of Good Process Design

(i) Good process begins by asking, *"who should be involved?"* not *"what are we going to do?"* The answer communicates much about "who counts". Beginning with "what are we going to do?" overlooks the extremely sensitive "who" question about participation, and alienates people whose support is essential to long-term success. A commitment to the transformative value of empowerment suggests that the first step in decision-making is to determine who will be affected so as to involve them appropriately. Questions to guide this assessment include:

- Who will view themselves as deeply affected by this negotiation, project, or decision? (Usually this group should be at the heart of the decision-making process).
- Who is in a position to block implementation if they are unhappy with decisions? (These parties should always be consulted and often need to take an active part in the decision-making process).
- Whose advice or assistance will be valuable? (This question calls for broad consultation).
- Whose approval will be required to enable this project to proceed?
- What are the interests, concerns, or motivations of each of the above groups?

(ii) *Good process is conducted under auspices acceptable to all.* Parties tend to link sponsorship with whoever announces an event or invites people to participate in it, who finances it, who facilitates, who gets credit if the event is successful. When mistrust is high, it is imperative that all perceive sponsorship as impartial, for parties recognise that power and influence accrue to sponsors. Impartiality can either be achieved by securing truly impartial sponsor(s) or by using several less-than-partial sponsors who in their totality are seen as impartial.

Co-sponsorship is a further example for good process design. Take, for example, a community that is complaining about police brutality. Here, a forum for dialogue between police and community is unlikely to earn community trust, if it is sponsored solely by the police. Good process design would call for such a forum to be sponsored by an independent organisation or jointly by the police and a trusted community organisation.

(iii) *good process involves essential parties or their representatives, not only in negotiation and decision-making, but also in the design of the process itself:* it is important to consult with key parties early in planning a decision-making or negotiation process, while process plans are still tentative and flexible. Often the opposite happens: a small group of well-intentioned people plans a negotiation or decision-making process and then goes to the parties and tries to sell it to them, soliciting their participation. This approach makes it difficult to recover from even small mistakes in strategy planning and fails in the transformative goal of empowering the parties.

To earn trust and participation of primary parties, facilitators should consult with them in the early stages of planning peace efforts, so they feel that they have helped design the negotiation forum. Facilitators can approach the parties in this manner: *"We are wondering about creating a forum in which people can talk. Would you be interested? What should it look like? Who should be there? When and where should we meet? Who should convene it? Should it be on the record or off the record?"* Transformative facilitators do not build and then try to sell a process to the parties. Rather, they create one with them in tentative, low-key private discussions before announcing plans to talk. One useful way to do this is to create a Process

Committee. Composed of thoughtful people from all key parties, this group has the task of planning, announcing, and coordinating the process of negotiation or decision-making.

(iv) *good process is clear about purpose and expectations of each step:* a common cause of conflict is confusion about pivotal events, as example 8 illustrate:

Example 8: Three Cases of Unclear Processes

1. A government agency appoints a committee to study the location of proposed new housing in an area of inter-group tension. The committee makes recommendations, which the government agency then chooses to ignore. The community is polarised by this response. The director of the agency, however, says that the committee was purely advisory and that he never promised to accept its findings.
2. A vote is held in a community organisation. Afterwards, a number of people say that they didn't attend that meeting because they thought the session was merely to exchange views. The vote, they thought, would be held a month later during annual business meeting. This group agitates for a re-vote; others dismiss them as troublemakers.
3. A newly formed committee agrees to put a critical issue to 'majority vote'. Sixty percent vote "yes"; these members claim they clearly won. Others say the measure lost in voting, insisting that 67% is required for a majority. Both sides accuse the other of trying to manipulate the rules and the results.

Much misunderstanding can be avoided if each step in the decision-making process is worked out in advance. As much of the overall process as possible should be mapped out early in planning. Parties should share common information on

- the purpose of the process and of each event within it;
- what will happen and when (a timeline is helpful here);
- who will make the final decision; and
- what decision-rule applies (i.e., 51% majority, 67% majority, consensus, etc.).

These matters cannot usually all be decided at the very beginning for every step of the process, but they should be clarified as early as possible. Moreover, they should be decided in close consultation with the persons most deeply involved in the process (*see* above), and communicated clearly to all. If a Process Committee is used as suggested, the first task of such a committee could be to develop a written proposal with recommendations for these issues.

(v) *good process offers more than one kind of forum* to consider options and express opinions, so as to ensure that all can contribute in a forum in which they feel comfortable: in institutional settings, use a mix of large group discussion, small group discussion, polls or questionnaires, study circles and personal interviews. In community or political settings, in addition to the above, use conferences, community forums, publications, and study materials.

(vi) *good process provides report-backs to those participating or affected:* during the negotiation or discussion process, use open discussions, surveys, non-binding votes, questionnaires, interim reports, and so forth, to keep people informed about the trend of the discussion *before* the decision is final. If people are shocked at the outcome of a decision-making process, it is usually a sign that designers of that process failed to build adequate interim report-back mechanisms into the process. Disappointment is normal in decision-making and need not be a cause for worry. Shocked surprise is a different matter. Often it brings charges of an unfair process and reduces acceptance of outcomes.

Report-backs should:

- provide summaries of ideas, opinions, suggestions, etc., gathered thus far in the process in interviews, meetings, and written submissions: gathering such data about people's views without reporting it back often leads to charges of manipulation;
- communicate decisions made by sub-groups;
- give frequent opportunities for people to comment on how they feel about the process: i.e., whether it is fair, whether they understand the next steps, and so forth.

(vii) *good process cannot happen without careful thought, consultation, and planning:* haste is a major enemy of good process, and usually leads to great waste of time and energy in the end.

4.4 The Link between Process Design and Transformation

No matter how caring the exchange between individuals, there is little possibility for transformation if the institutions to which those individuals are connected, or the customs and structures governing their interaction, continue to inflict injuries. Therefore, facilitators should pay close attention to matters of power and structure. However, we must be careful not to lose the parties' trust by taking sides or advocating our own solutions.

But this does not mean relinquishing all values. The principles of good process described above clearly reflect transformative values. In a variety of ways they point towards strategies that *empower* those affected by conflict: by involving them in planning and decision-making; by soliciting and respecting their concerns in ways that are suitable to them and by providing them with full information. These principles also point towards helping parties interact in ways that foster *recognition* of the needs and perceptions of others: planners are encouraged to consult widely with various parties, and this in itself often causes parties to take opponents more seriously; parties are encouraged to work together in planning decision-making processes; discussion forums are created that enable participants to hear opposing perceptions; information about the trend of thinking is reported back not only at the end of decision-making, but during the course of discussion.

To the extent that principles of good process are followed in designing interaction between the parties, I believe that possibilities of structural transformation are considerably enhanced. Clearly, F.W. de Klerk would not have accepted this assertion in 1989 when he released Nelson Mandela from prison, for the signs are many that de Klerk thought he could negotiate minor concessions and retain the fundamentally unjust system of apartheid. However, de Klerk underestimated the ultimately liberating power of negotiation processes that reflect principles of good process design. Too late to turn back, he realised that he could not control the forces he had unleashed. South Africa today remains, of course, far from transformed, but there is no denying that it has taken a big step forward on a journey that will require many more.

5. Summary

The possibility of transformation at personal and interpersonal levels in group conflicts requires facilitators to work in transformative ways with multiple approaches. We must use transformative communication skills in our moment-by-moment interaction with individuals. We must draw on a repertoire of methods for engaging individuals in transformative dialogue with each other. We must also assist parties in designing overall processes of negotiation and decision-making that bring transformative influences to bear on the structural dimensions of their relationship. The twin concepts of empowerment and fostering right relationships can be applied within all three categories in guiding our choice of facilitation tools and strategies.

6. Reference and Further Reading

Baruch Bush, Robert A. and Joseph P. Folger 1994. *The Promise of Mediation: Responding to Conflict Through Empowerment and Recognition,* San Francisco, Ca: Jossey-Bass Publishers.

Kayser, Thomas 1995. *Mining Group Gold: How to Cash in on the Collaborative Brain Power of a Group,* New York, N.Y.: McGraw-Hill.

Kelsey, Dee and Pam Plumb 1997. *Great Meetings! How to Facilitate Like a Pro,* Portland, Me: Hanson Park Press.

Mindell, Arnold 1995. *Sitting in the Fire: Large Group Transformation Using Conflict and Diversity,* Portland, Or: Lao Tze Press.

Schulz von Thun, Friedemann 1981. *Miteinander Reden 1: Störungen und Klärungen – Allgemeine Psychologie der Kommunikation,* Hamburg: Rowohlt Taschenbuch Verlag.

Schulz von Thun, Friedemann 1989. *Miteinander Reden 2: Stile, Werte und Persönlichkeitsentwicklung – Differentielle Psychologie der Kommunikation,* Hamburg: Rowohlt Taschenbuch Verlag.

Schulz von Thun, Friedemann 1998. *Miteinander Reden* 3: Das *"innere Team" und situationsgerechte Kommunikation – Kommunikation – Person – Situation,* Hamburg: Rowohlt Taschenbuch Verlag.

Thompson, Charles 1992. *What a Great Idea: Key Steps Creative People Take,* New York, NY: Harper Perennial.

Morrow, Duncan and Derick Wilson 1996. *Ways Out of Conflict: Resources for Community Relations Work,* Belfast: Understanding Conflict Trust.

Mennonite Conciliation Service 2000. *Mediation and Facilitation Training Manual: Foundations and Skills for Constructive Conflict Transformation, Fourth Edition,* Akron, Ohio: Mennonite Central Committee.

Winer, Michael and Karen Ray 1994. *Collaboration Handbook: Creating, Sustaining and Enjoying the Journey,* St. Paul, Minn: Amherst H. Wilder Foundation.

Lederach, John Paul 1995. *Building Peace: Sustainable Reconciliation in Divided Societies,* Tokyo: The United Nations University.

Rothman, Jay 1982. *From Cooperation to Confrontation: Resolving Ethnic and Regional Conflict,* London, New Delhi, and Newbury Park, Ca.: Sage Publications.

7. Web Resources

Group Facilitation Listserv. Any seeking to do conflict transformation in group settings needs excellent group facilitation skills. This is a free email listserv on the general topic of group facilitation with participants from dozens of countries (albeit dominated by people in the North) and sure to inspire anyone interested in group facilitation. To subscribe, send a message to this address: LISTSERV@ALBANY.EDU (You may leave the SUBJECT field blank.) In the body of the message type: SUBSCRIBE GRP-FACL Your Real Name

- Steve Vincent, Southampton. England: essay on "Empathic Understanding", at http://users.powernet.co.uk/bapca/Training/Empathy.htm
- Jere Moorman/Center for Studies of the Person. California. USA: essay on "The Person Centered Approach to Conflict Transformation", at http://users.powernet.co.uk/pctmk/papers/conflict.htm
- Several essays on the concept of conflict transformation can be found at http://www.colorado.edu/conflict/transform/tmall.htm

Team and Organisational Development as a Means for Conflict Prevention and Resolution

Friedrich Glasl and Rudi Ballreich

1. Introduction 228
2. Teams as potential for conflict 229
3. Potential for Conflict at the Five Levels of Team Work 229
   - The individual group member as potential for conflict
   - The content or the issue level as potential for conflict
   - The interaction or psychosocial level as potential for conflict
   - The procedure/method level and its potential for conflict
   - External relations as potential for conflict
4. Development Phases of Teams 239
   - Forming and Storming – finding and coming together
   - Norming – creating one's own rules
   - Performing and performance capability
   - Reforming – self-structuring and the ability to change
5. Team Development and Conflict Resolution 246
   - At the level of the individual group member
   - At the content-specific level/issue level
   - The interaction level – psychosocial level
   - At the procedure – method level
   - At the external relations level
   - Continuous overview
6. Conclusions and Open Questions 251
7. Reference and Further Reading 252

Team and Organisational Development as a Means for Conflict Prevention and Resolution

Friedrich Glasl and Rudi Ballreich

1. Introduction

Most professional third parties working in the fields of conflict resolution, peace building and conflict settlement are themselves operating in some form of organisational context and function as members of a team in a large-scale organisation. Consequently, they are often subject to tensions and conflicts, which can impair their activity in the field.

In a representative survey conducted in the Netherlands during 1984 (Glasl 1984), social workers throughout the country were questioned about conflicts in their organisational environment. The results show that the very individuals who regularly and successfully help their clients to solve 'hot' conflicts (carried out openly and with great emotion) themselves suffer from many 'cold' conflicts (expressed covertly) in their own organisations, and generally fail to deal with these in a professional manner. Instead, such conflicts are deflected or allowed to drag on, and have destructive ramifications on the client-related work in the field of conflict. In some cases, the stress of this situation can even lead to burn-out problems and retreat from this field of occupation. Protagonists in conflicts are also faced with similar stresses.

It is for this reason that a proper understanding of conflict potential within teams and organisations is imperative. In this chapter, we will outline the most frequently observed potential sources of conflict, and then suggest some possible ways to utilise conflict transformation and resolution. After all, at least during the first three stages of escalation (Glasl 1999, 83ff), the affected parties can usually themselves undertake the work of conflict resolution with a good chance of success. It is only later that it becomes necessary for organisations to call in professional external assistance from conflict experts in order to deal with their own internal problems of conflict (Glasl 1999, 118ff).

Fig. 1: The five levels of teamwork

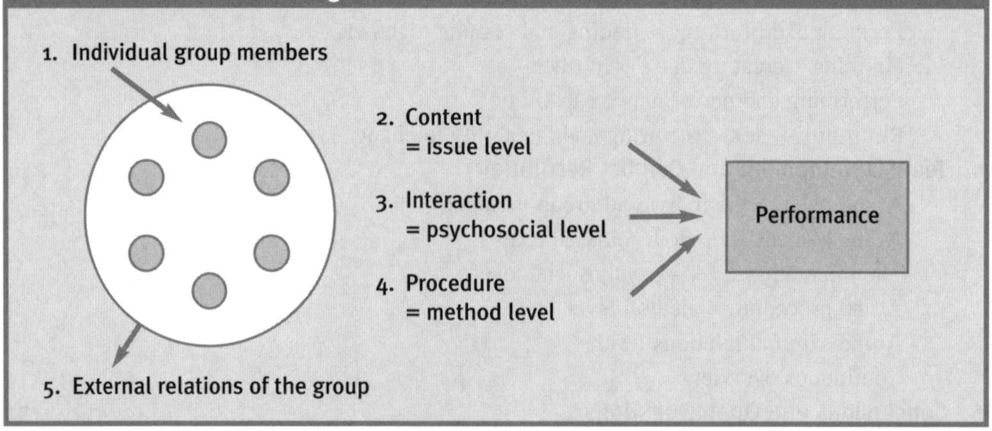

2. Teams as potential for conflict

Teams are defined as work groups that are charged with the fulfilment of a performance task that requires joint cooperation. This distinguishes them clearly from other groups, which might instead seek to attain individual learning results that are acquired in groups, or merely cultivate social and other forms of contacts.

In order to achieve this desired performance, good conditions must either exist or be created at all five levels within the team (Fig. 1).

The five levels of teamwork are defined as follows:

1. **Individual group members:** this is a function of the individual personalities, as well as of their perceptions, concepts and ideas, emotions, intentions and behaviours.
2. **Content, issue level:** the focus here is on the issue topic and on the task to be performed.
3. **Interaction, psychosocial level:** the mutual attitudes of the group members are important, as well as the state of relations between them and the observed climate, roles and behaviour patterns.
4. **Procedure, method level:** techniques of problem-solving in a team, such as analysis methods, decision methods, creativity techniques, formal internal rules for the team and use of auxiliary means.
5. **External group relations:** the way in which information and contacts are cultivated with the rest of the organisation including rules regarding deputising.

Each of these five levels can spawn potential for conflict and can therefore also be a good starting point for conflict resolution. As the levels are also mutually networked, they can also influence each other and thus create further indirect potential for conflict. The dynamics of a group are, consequently, complicated and difficult to analyse. Often a problem will arise at one level, for instance on level 4, if a complex decision is to be taken with unsuitable methods, but be manifested for example at level 3 (interaction/psychosocial level), as team relations become burdened by mutual irritation. Finally, this could conceivably lead to further consequences at level 1 (the individual group member), if one person chooses to leave the group, depriving the team of his or her knowledge and skills.

3. Potential for Conflict at the Five Levels of Team Work

3.1 The individual group member as potential for conflict

A group member can struggle with *intrapsychological* tensions and conflicts, and express these externally as he seeks to cooperate with other team members. The known conflict mechanisms in this context (Rubin, Pruitt and Kim 1994, 11ff; Glasl 1997, 34ff; Glasl 1999, 19ff) usually appear within individuals (Fig. 2) and corrupt their perceptions, thinking, feeling, volition and external behaviour.

These intra-psychological mechanisms can only be generally sketched out at this point. Nevertheless, understanding them is critical if conflicts are to be successfully processed in teams or organisations.

Fig. 2: Intrapsychological factors

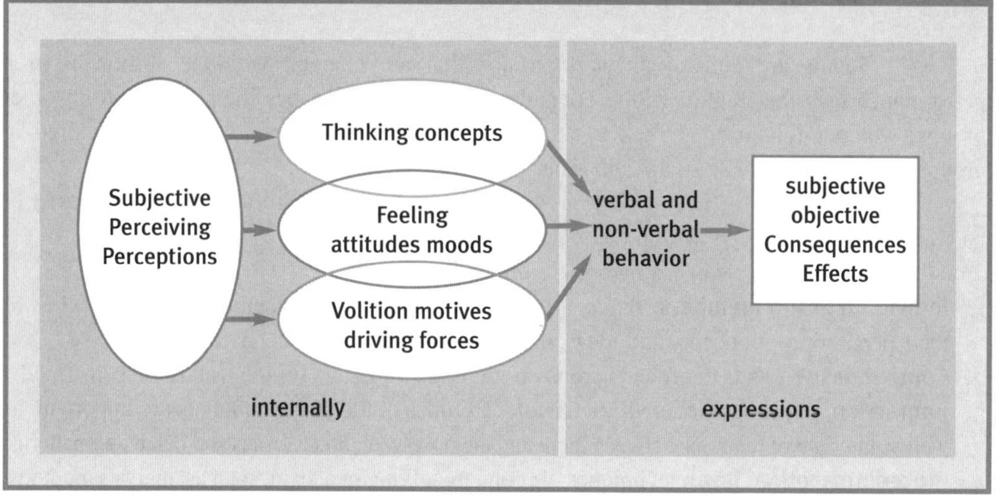

The *perception capability* of the individual can be strongly impaired through the effects of stress, tension and pressure. The result can lead to selective or distorted perception, 'cognitive short-sightedness', or even the fading out of perceptions that do not conform to the preconceived picture. This is how prejudices occur and become fixed, since all evidence which
 might contradict previous perceptions is suppressed and disregarded.

The *concepts* and *ideas* which people form on the basis of such distorted perceptions are likely to become hardened into one-sided, black-and-white pictures, which can no longer easily be corrected by further evidence or perceptions. Only information that confirms the prejudice is acknowledged.

In the *emotional sector*, empathy dries up. People become encapsulated one from another, prisoners of their own feelings. Sympathy and antipathy serve to create a polarised emotional picture. If the conflict escalates, this can take on autistic dimensions, as all point of reference to the outside world is lost.

In the *volitional sector*, unconscious and semiconscious driving forces and motives become dominant. There can even be a trend towards fanaticism, as volition hardens into an 'all or nothing' approach characterised by demands expressed in the form of ultimatums.

Perceiving, thinking, feeling and willing all mutually reinforce one another in a vicious spiral and the tensions can be even more difficult when they contradict each other. As escalation gyrates outwards, it can lead to regression in all areas dealing with values. People no longer behave in line with the maturity commensurate with their age level. Instead, in encounters with their opponents in the conflict, their thinking, feeling and volition develop patterns which would be more appropriate to earlier development phases, but now no longer conform to the degree of maturity one should reasonably expect from them.

In the *external behaviour* of these individuals, a notable impoverishment appears. A wealth of variants is lost, as behaviour becomes stereotyped and can even deteriorate to the point of compulsiveness, as the actor loses effective control of his actions.

Inevitably, this will lead to *consequences* in the conflict behaviour, which corresponds to an increasing loss of self-awareness. The undesired and subconscious side effects thus gain the upper hand over the desired and conscious consequences of willed behaviour.

Conflict resolution techniques can and should be applied to any one or more of these domains. Thus, the multi-track-approach, working at different levels, has for some time already been practised in both the micro- and meso-social sectors. Practitioners have worked at unravelling false perceptions (Blake and Mouton 1964; Burton 1969; Walton 1969), allowing distorted perception mechanisms to be cleared and hardened concepts to be dissolved. In addition to this, they have had some success in healing polarised emotions, so that empathy can be revived. Fixation on ultimatums can be properly addressed by examining alternative modes of action, as well as by reviewing one's own patterns of volition. Some of the behaviours they are referring to here can be purposeful and controlled.

3.2 The content or the issue level as potential for conflict

Officially, issues are the very substance of negotiations. Rational individuals often assume that conflicts cannot arise as long as everybody remains objective. However, as a conflict escalates, issue-related and psychosocial issues become increasingly mixed. It may be necessary to collect and unravel the various themes in a dispute and look at them more precisely. Potential for conflict can easily arise at this level if practitioners fail to recognise that any issue can be perceived and assessed differently from the different perspectives of varying subject disciplines. Unfortunately, concepts can only rarely be clarified to everyone's satisfaction: the result is misunderstandings and misinterpretations. There may be a failure to identify the real issues.

3.3 The interaction or psychosocial level as potential for conflict

Groups too must learn to deal with their differences openly. Such openness can only be possible if the necessary measures of esteem and confidence have developed among the participants – "confidence that my team mates respect me and that I will not be excluded from the group, even if I say something critical". This confidence is the 'topsoil' in which open communication and the constructive processing of conflicts flourish.

Each group will need to organise itself around certain roles if it is to both achieve its goals and also maintain cohesion as a team. Certain influences are extended onto the group both from the outside world and from interactions at the social level, which may well lead to the forming of group-specific interaction patterns from which individuals will find that they can only withdraw with difficulty.

In order for groups to be able to work productively, certain core tasks must be performed. The responsibility for these, and the corresponding actions, are frequently assigned to the same individuals. Belbin (1992) investigated a number of these role types in groups, and organised them into a model. Some group members, for instance, regularly assume responsibility for creative ideas; others are particularly active when it comes to assessing, while others in turn work mostly in the field of monitoring and control.

Fig.3: Factors influencing the crystallizing of roles in group

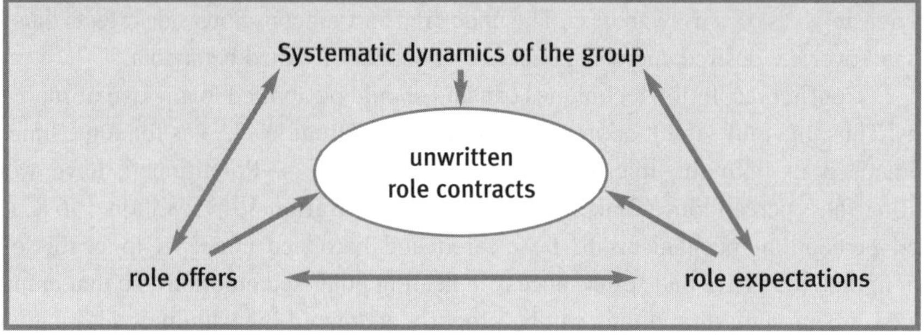

Conflicts tend to occur when a group member:

- feels pressure from the group to assume a role which they do not want and to which he or she objects;
- experiences the allocated roles as constraining and inhibiting development;
- feels that the sanctions imposed, in order to induce him or her to maintain a role, are incommensurate;
- cannot develop acquired capabilities in the assigned role;
- wishes to go beyond an extrinsic definition of his or her role to self-definition.

In every group there are hierarchy roles. Each group member will ask themselves more or less consciously: "What is my value to this organisation? Do the others acknowledge that value? Am I superfluous or can I sometimes play 'top dog?'" Aware team members will also ask themselves whether the role expectations connected with their own self-image can be fulfilled in this group and above all whether the situation in which they find themselves might one day pose a threat to their own self-confidence.

The following questions are of particular importance in this context:

- What position does the formal leader of the group occupy in terms of these hierarchies?
- Is there an informal leader who is held in higher regard by the group than the formal one?

It is essential, if good cooperation is to develop in teams, for all participants to be flexible and to assume various roles according to the requirements of the situation. For example, team members must be prepared to proceed with the objective task, or instead to work to promote the climate within the group. Sometimes they will assume leadership, while at other times, they will perform supporting tasks. Individuals who are too strongly fixated on their own roles – for example the shy person, the dominant person, the one who talks all the time, or the clown – can inhibit the process of cooperation. Group members must rather learn to recognise their own distinct behaviour patterns and role expectations, to review these and to adapt them to the given situation. Thus, a high degree of role flexibility is the critical hallmark of properly developed teams.

3.4 The procedure/method level and its potential for conflict

Conflicts are often initially experienced as relation-specific, even though the problems can actually be traced to a poor selection of work methods. If, for example, a decision is reached by means of an unsuitable method, it can lead to tensions between the group members. It is simply not possible to plane wood with a screwdriver, nor is it feasible to fasten screws with a plane. Teams must learn and familiarise themselves with a variety of working procedures and methods, and must become good at reaching right decisions as to which procedure is most suitable for which purpose.

In practice, many different methods have been developed for a wide variety of purposes. In her study of methods, Anna Grandori (1984) has distinguishes between various rules (prescriptive principles) which govern the various methods:

(i) Search rules, search methods: how can we identify alternative solutions?

(ii) Selection rules, selection methods: how can we then select the preferred alternative for this problem?

(iii) Learning rules, learning methods: how can we efficiently obtain information about a particular alternative?

These rules or methods will vary, depending on

- *the degree of uncertainty* (available information or lack of knowledge); and
- *the degree of conflicting interest* (compatibility or non-compatibility).

If all relevant facts and data are known, so that the team enjoys a fairly high degree of security, a decision will be reached differently than in situations with substantial uncertainty, for instance about future economic or political developments. Furthermore, if the persons or groups involved in the decision insist on asserting particular interests from the very start, the team will behave differently than it would if the team members were less fixated on pre-existing standpoints.

At present many training and coaching sessions teach different techniques to the extent that an adequate survey of the field has become virtually impossible. Many trainers seek to position their specific approach to decision-making as their own branded product for reasons of competition. As a result, the same methods – often only with slight changes – can be found bearing a wide variety of names, without any credit given to the original method and its creator or author. This inevitably leads to a dispute on method if practitioners make the claim that their own approach is the best and is universally applicable. If group members have thus attended different training sessions, they may subsequently find themselves in conflict with one another as to which method is best for them. It is only when they manage to recognise and clearly define which method best serves a specific purpose that such a dispute can be effectively resolved.

Alexander Bos (1974), in his model of "dynamic judgement formation" (*see* Ballreich 2000) distinguishes between two kinds of process:

(i) thinking and cognitive path, i.e. processes for analysing or diagnosing a problem in order to gain better knowledge; and

(ii) volition and decision path, i.e. processes for identifying and selecting goals and alternative courses of action.

Both cases involve a process of judgement formation in which feeling plays a central role. In the case of the *cognitive path*, the team must seek to bring about a synthesis of feeling, between perceiving and reflecting. In the case of the *decision path*, it is mainly a matter of forming a bridge, by means of feeling, between the goals and the advance thinking of possibilities for realisation of those goals by means of concrete actions and behaviours.

In conjunction with the model shown above in Fig. 2, this can be illustrated as in Fig. 4:

Fig. 4: The elements of the cognitive path and of the decision path

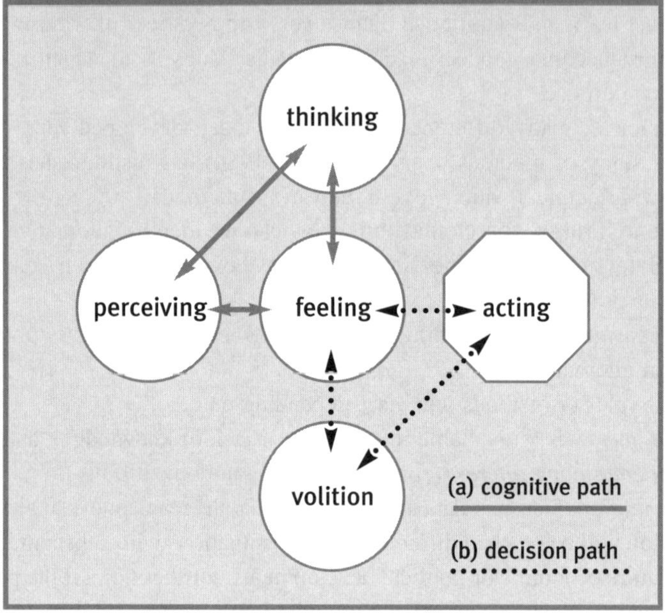

Bos also notes that some processes pursue this path in a *linear-sequential* fashion (*see* Glasl 1999, 127ff). Here, the teams gather all available facts in the cognitive path, in order that they can consider and reflect on these, then interpret and classify them. In the decision path, on the other hand, according to the linear sequential school, team goals are first set and discussed; only then can the possible implementation paths be examined and selected.

According to Bos (1974, 52ff), these approaches are to be contrasted with the "dynamic judgement forming" model, which argues instead for regular *rhythmic alternation* between the given poles of perceiving-thinking and volition-acting. In a cyclical procedure, team perceptions are continuously revisited in the cognitive path while formed concepts are repeatedly reviewed on the basis of what is perceived. Feelings of amazement or evidence-experience, of apprehension or release, of consistency or inconsistency also play a major role in this connection. In short, feeling is at the heart of judgement forming, as is illustrated below in the schematic representation. The situation is similar in the decision path, as goals are examined and tested for feasibility and desirability. Only when feelings are perceived to be congruent with what is wanted and thought out in advance, is it possible to take a firm and binding decision.

It is further possible to distinguish between different phases within this process of dynamic judgement forming. First, teams must make sure that they collect sufficient empirical material: the facts must be clearly established before interpretation and assessment can begin. Thus, qualitative phases will develop, within which a rhythmic searching motion, in the spirit of Bos, can take place. Fig. 5 shows four such qualitative phases on both the cognitive and the decision paths, from a bird's eye perspective. Although the specific features of the cognitive and decision paths are of importance, we will focus solely upon the principle features of the model.

The findings of Grandori and Bos concerning the potentials for conflict can be summarised as follows:

In the *preparation (planning and group formation)* phase, according to Grandori's model, learning methods are particularly important, since they will govern advance thinking in an initially unmanageable period. Building on this, both feeling and volition will play a crucial role; otherwise, the group activity can quickly lose energy due to a 'cold start'. If teamwork is undertaken without adequate enthusiasm, no team member will subsequently identify with the

Fig. 5: Qualitative phases of the cognitive and decision paths

1. Preparation (planning and group formation)

Define task scope, the problem and the objective. Define the framework conditions and specifications for solving the problem. Determine procedures and decision-making methods, assign roles, undertake preparatory work, provide motivation for the process!

2. Image forming

Collect perceptions, opinions, presuppositions, alternatives, creative ideas. Expand the range of attitudes, allow for spreading! No discussion yet, only intuitive classification!

3. Judgment forming

Compare and consider the identified alternatives, discuss backgrounds and connections, clarify criteria and determine priorities, discuss consequences openly and without reservations. Any hidden contradictions and conflicts of interest etc. must be stated explicitly and frankly. Controversial discussion is critical in this phase!

4. Conclusion

Test hypotheses critically, select final preferences, specify consequent activities. Clarity and commitment!

results. Here, the group may experience a struggle between flows, as some members prefer to work spontaneously and intuitively (dominance of the volition pole), while others insist on detailed planning (dominance of the thinking pole). Furthermore, if the scope of tasks, problem complexity and objectives and the decision-making methods are not clarified sufficiently from the start, the team will experience difficulties in terms of a damaging loss of orientation.

In the *image-forming phase*, according to Grandori, the searching and learning methods become the most important. As explained by Bos, the polarity between perceiving and thinking, most of all, affects an exhaustive review of perception.

Potential for conflict can arise whenever a team lacks the necessary range of perspectives and thus cannot sufficiently expand its range of approaches. Accordingly, if the team commences discussion (the judgement-forming phase) prematurely, it will risk reinforcing any existing preconceived opinions by selective perception. If gathered material is classified too early on the basis of purely rational criteria, this can also lead to tensions, as already formed and unreflective thinking patterns can hinder the discovery of new elements.

In the *judgment-forming phase*, the searching and selection methods will be the most critical. Bos emphasises the importance of feeling along with the poles of perceiving-thinking, in order by controversial discussion to derive the full benefit from existing differences and ensure that the group does not fall prey to "group-think" (Janis 1972). Janis studied group behaviour in various crisis situations and showed how group pressure can exert negative sanctions on diverging opinions. This can be exemplified by group members, who, for fear of being excluded, are forced to join the dominant group against their better principles and conscience. The constructive confrontation that would be required, here, must approach differences and contradictions not as threats, but instead as a source of enrichment for the group. The more forcefully the differences are articulated at the issue level, the more important it will be to express acknowledgement and regard for the person of the opponent or dissident at this level of interaction.

In the *conclusion phase*, Grandori says that the searching methods will dominate, as the team seeks to reach agreement on the most plausible finding. According to Bos, thinking and feeling now play the greatest roles. Potential for conflict will arise, however, as soon as doubts concerning the validity of the conclusions reached in the process arise, and the group begins to energetically contest any team member who questions the group findings. The more mature groups will make sure that they include fundamental questioning in the final phase of their work as a form of self-performed quality control. Nevertheless, it can lead to irritations if one group member brings in new information at 'five minutes to midnight', data that should have been gathered much earlier, in the concept-forming phase.

Particular attention should be drawn in this phase towards an orientation of feelings and pragmatic action, as supported by appropriate selection methods. The question as to whether the leader's vote alone is sufficient for a decision, or whether a majority decision or general consensus are necessary, cannot primarily be answered ideologically. Rather, it is better for a team to specify its preferred decision-making method earlier, in the preparatory phase, so that the rules will not need to be changed while the game is in process, which generally gives rise to conflicts.

The question of whether or not a consensus decision is advisable for a particular team situation will depend primarily on the culture of the organisation. The more important consideration is whether ownership and commitment to the decision by the group is important. If the official philosophy is that of an enterprise valuing equality, then nearly everything will have to be decided in consensus, even if this results in major delays and drains the team's energies. As soon as the group has proceeded through a maturation process, as described in Section 4 below, it will be more able to deal with issuing mandates and delegating in such a way that consensus will only be required for strategic and fundamental decisions. This will leave operative decisions to be taken by majority vote or through delegation of authority to individual team members.

The decisive tests for the quality of decisions are the questions of acceptance. To what extent do the group members stand by the decision taken? Are they willing to defend it against any attacks by others? After all, in addition to the actual problem to be resolved, the issue of acceptance is the most important facet of overall teamwork quality; and, according to Vroom and Yetton (1973), this will depend on the degree and the style of participation encountered during the decision-making process.

3.5 External relations as potential for conflict

The relations between a team and its organisational setting can also contain many seeds of conflict. One important aspect is to specify the degree of participation of the team in defining itself against higher-ranking levels or other teams within the organisation. It is therefore worth considering degrees of participation by analogy with Tannenbaum and Schmidt (1958).

A supervisor is behaving in an authoritative or directive manner if he or she will only allow the team members to participate in a decision to a small extent. If the team's opinions are considered more seriously, the management style is termed consultative. A participative management style allows for not only the voicing of opinions, but also a limited influence in the outcome of the decision. Finally, the cooperative management style grants the team overriding influence, or even complete autonomy.

Linking this graduated, mutual influence by the management and the team with phases 2 to 4 of the decision-making process set out in Fig. 7, results in a variety of forms. This is often described as 'co-knowledge' or 'co-decisions' in co-determination policy issues.

The team can ensure that its work will be harmonious and constructive to the extent that it succeeds in formally clarifying and defining tasks, areas of competence and responsibilities. This is especially relevant to higher- or equal-ranking teams within the same organisation. It is probably advisable to allow more time for this exercise at the start of the team effort, rather than risking the subsequent disappointment and disruption resulting from a lack of clarity. 'Mopping up' invariably requires more time and effort on the part of all involved than would have been expended on prevention in the first place.

When a team seeks to communicate its interim or final results, it should do this in a manner consistent with the phased model for cognitive and decision processes. It should reflect accurately just how far the team has advanced in its efforts to identify a solution, especially in relation to the rest of the organisation. If, for instance, a project team has come to a conclusion before the rest of the organisation has even become aware of the problem, the presentation of

Fig. 6: Degrees of participation in the decision-making process according to Tannenbaum / Schmidt (1958)

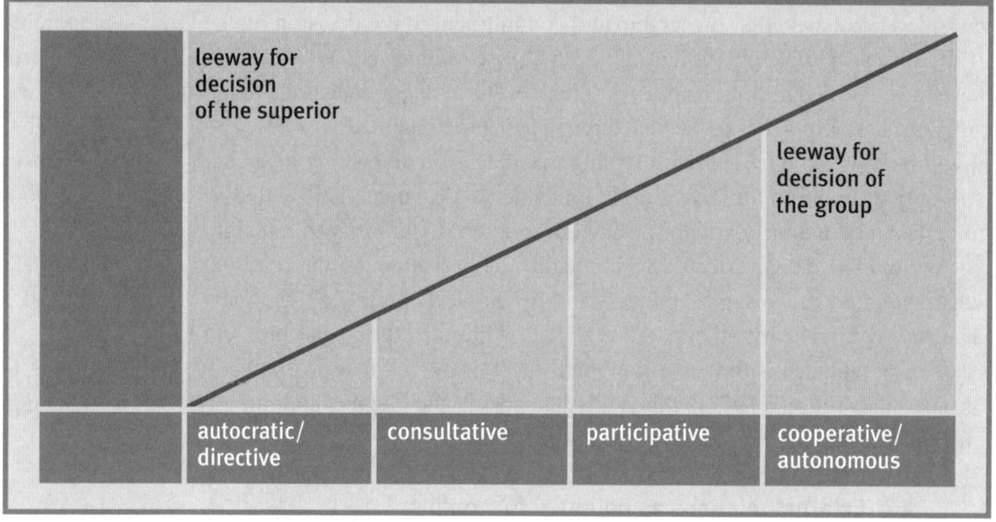

the team's findings is likely to meet with incomprehension and rejection: who needs a solution to a problem not yet perceived. Project teams would, therefore, be well advised to present step-by-step information as they progress, explaining the path that they are taking. This will assist in avoiding any 'phase misfit' in the organisation.

Any problems that may be encountered at the psychosocial level between the team and its environment are unlikely to be solved so easily by the application of formal rules. As a result, competition and overt rivalry can easily ensue. Sometimes, the team itself may have contributed to the development of 'hostile concepts' and to the eruption of open or covert struggles to form coalitions. In such cases, teams should seek to apply the methods of conflict resolution proposed by Blake et al. (1964) to break down stereotypes.

In short, even a difference in culture between the development status of a team (Section 4) and the development phase of the rest of the organisation (Glasl 1994) can generate a strong potential for conflict. In this case, the team's development is an integral part of more comprehensive development in the organisation at large. For this reason, it might be fruitful to look briefly at the general dynamics of organisational development.

4. Development Phases of Teams

The phase model of group development described below is a variation on the Tuckman model (1965), expanded by Glasl (1996). Its distinguishing characteristic is the insight that describes the stage of development of a group as it moves through development phases, forms that can develop repeatedly as the dynamics of cooperation change in response to either external or internal factors (*see* Götz 1998).

Fig. 7: Degrees of participation and phases in a decision-making process (Glasl / Lievegoed 1993, 142)

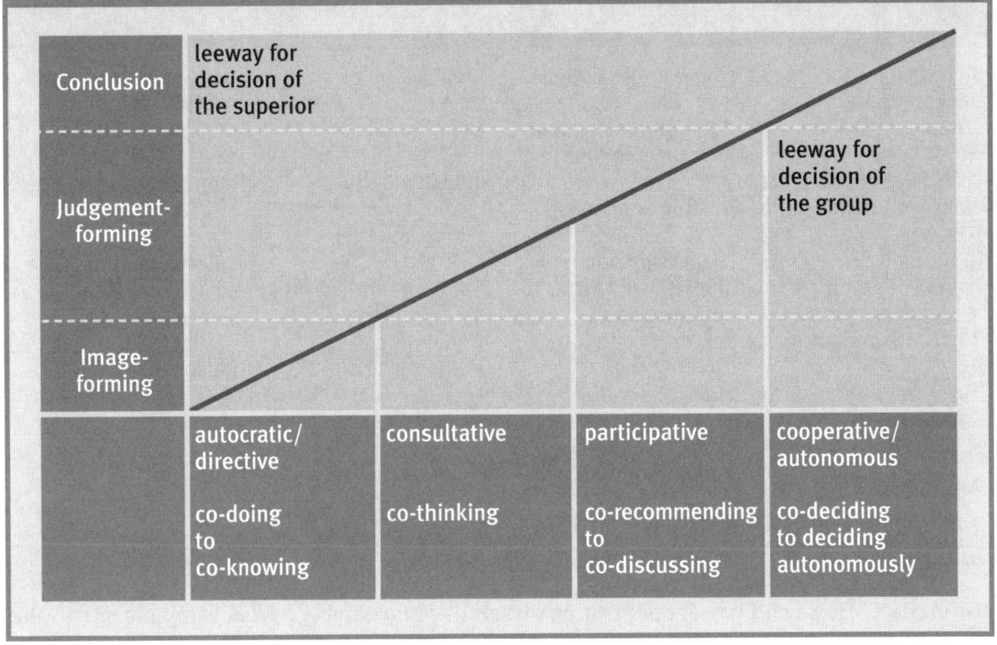

The overview in Fig. 8 illustrates the four phases of a maturation and development process through which a team is likely to pass. Nevertheless, at any stage a team can unconsciously or deliberately decide not to proceed, choosing instead to revert to the preceding phase. Alternatively, the team may remain at a certain stage of development for a longer period, as changes in membership, turbulence in its environment or other circumstances inhibit further development of the group.

Awareness of these four development phases and of their various cultures and structures will enable a more systematic consideration of the team's social development status and thus allow it to take conscious decisions regarding its next steps. The model does not seek to describe any law of nature; neither should it be regarded as a prescriptive or normative set of rules. What it does instead is to point out risks and opportunities. It is of course always up to the relevant individuals within each group to decide how to take advantage of those opportunities or whether to move towards mitigating the risks.

4.1 Forming and Storming – finding and coming together

When a group comes together for the first time, there will always be uncertainties between the team members regarding both the work objective and the group situation. It is likely that a strong desire for security and clear orientation will dominate. Contacts are first established on an 'ad hoc' basis and are characterised by a wait and see attitude. The group is explored and scanned. How should I see myself in comparison to the others? With whom can I best estab-

Fig. 8: The four development phases of teams according to Glasl			
1. Forming / Storming	2. Norming	3. Performing	4. Reforming
A: Forming Seeking contacts, scanning: What am I worth here? Orientation to external standards and symbols B: Storming Pairing off, struggle for leadership, "fight and flight" conquest games trying out role arrangements	Group draws up its own rules for success, decision-making, performance, influence Binding sanctions Leadership duo = "father" role for authority and "mother" role for securing the atmosphere Tension between rational top current and emotional undertow	Breaking up of stereotype roles/styles and clichés Role flexibility, leadership changes acc. to situation Learning partnerships Thinking-feeling-volition become explicit – geared to work objectives Balancing of performance-person-team	Self-structuring / self-renewal of the team: objectives, values, roles, structures are identified acc. to situation External relations are structured openly Ability to form and loosen relations creative constitution and dissolution of teams

lish contact? How can I present or position myself most favourably? What is my potential value to the group? In answering these questions, the team members will orient themselves in terms of the external values and status symbols that they bring to the group from the external environment.

In this initial situation, comfortable, safe behaviour will prevail, although behaviour is likely to be strongly influenced by preconceived expectations of the group and its associated positive or negative images. These are a few of the most salient features of the group finding during the forming process.

Some team members, however, may instead choose to 'grasp the bull by the horns'. They will go on the offensive in order to overcome their uncertainty. The resulting situation is likely to be unstable for everyone and can alternate repeatedly between phases of harmony and periods of friction and tension.

As group members gain their initial bearings and are no longer strangers to one another, they will begin to reveal a bit more of their real self. They will act and react in a more personal manner. Their pleasure and displeasure, their wishes and desires will come to the fore. It will be increasingly important to them to assert their own interests and maintain their position. The result is likely to be a struggle for power and influence in the group: a 'fight or flight'. The authority of the formal group leader may also be questioned in the process, as the group passes through a period of 'fermentation.' This storming is an integral component of the group-forming process.

The issue-related work of the team may be further affected by such disputes. In this phase, more energy is available for application to content-specific objectives. Just how the work is to be divided and organised, the manner in which decisions are to be taken, who is to check what, and to assume which tasks – all these questions are now discussed frankly and animatedly within the team.

It is also true that, although objective issues are discussed, there lies under the surface a struggle within the team concerning self-presentation and positions, as members seek to test or combat various forms of influence. In this process, they manage to establish who is to receive certain recognition, as well as to determine who is to fulfil specific roles or allocate them to others.

These various disputes tend in turn to produce renewed uncertainty, and to engender a feeling of mistrust among the different group members. This will lead to yet more security needs, needs that often find their satisfaction in the support offered by other team members sharing the same opinion (pairing off). Who thinks like I do? To whom do I feel linked? As a result, subgroups and cliques may develop.

These group disputes are conducted on a very personal level. As a by-product of these emotional encounters, the group develops its own sense of intimacy, thus creating its own history with shared emotional experiences.

Forming and storming, together, form the fundamentally unstable process of approximation, rebuff and re-formation, processes within which team members experiment with rank, roles and mutual relations.

4.2 Norming – creating one's own rules

In order to overcome the state of confrontation and friction, which inevitably develops from Phase 1, teams will make a number of minor and major decisions, especially as they attempt to clarify work procedures. The establishment of robust 'rules of the game' is essential if productive work is to be enabled. In this phase, a group will often fall back on norms and rules with which it has already experienced success in other group contexts.

At the level of issue-related work, the group finds that it is able to handle its terms of reference independently. It will devote considerable attention to the elaboration of proper procedures and work methods, and to securing them by means of sanctions. As a result, it will bring about internal peace and security.

At the psychosocial level, group members will now want to bring about good, rationally steered cooperation: consequently, they will refrain from engaging in competitive behaviour. The goal is to feel good in the group and to generate energy for the provision of inputs. Esteem, helpfulness, consideration and humour will now all take their places in the group. A we-feeling develops, reinforced by shared performance and experiences of success. The values, norms and rules of cooperation adapted from the external environment will form the core of an agreement culture with which all group members can identify.

Roles will be rationally clarified so that reasonable work processes can be drawn up for future tasks. Each team member will then be assigned appropriate roles in relation to the task to be accomplished. The focus moves towards issue-specific requirements; feelings of dissatisfaction will be regarded as a disturbance and consequently suppressed.

In any case these processes do not inevitably happen. They are tendencies and threats to look out for. Although this process will engender a certain short-lived stability, it is unlikely to develop further into the long-term. Thus, both motivation and work input levels of the individual members will decline. Performance will be adequate, but hardly outstanding. Although the group will work productively together at a certain level, it will be difficult to motivate it to achieve special inputs. This superficially congenial social behaviour will soon be established as an unshakable norm and will thus tend to conceal disagreements that have already formed beneath the surface. If such negative feelings are suppressed, the further development of the group will be severely inhibited.

In the long-term, the one-sided nature of this phase may well prove to be an impediment to the team's further development. As the objective comes to dominate, impersonal rules and mechanisms can make the team seem like a system in which the non-rational is afforded no place. This emphasis on objectivity may lead to both coolness and hardness in the team and force the more sentient aspects underground. A certain uneasiness can emerge. Some team members will demand more space for 'human elements' and thus risk triggering violent disputes about the meaning and limits of general rules. Others will ask for more freedom and individual responsibility. Still others will plead for even stricter rules and sanctions, fearing that as the emotional is revealed and addressed team task performance will suffer.

These tensions frequently lead to the emergence of a dual management system (Hofstätter 1957, 133ff). On the one hand, the team will recognise an issue-related and performance-driven 'father' figure who then takes on the responsibility for managing the performance tasks of the team. On the other hand, a 'mother' role is likely to develop: a team member who looks after the group's cohesion, working to foster a positive atmosphere and good interpersonal relations within the group. This second person is thus taking on a kind of counter-leadership. The proper functioning of these two roles will help to stabilise the performing phase of the team for a relatively long period.

As the second phase runs its course, the group members will have developed stereotypical images of one another based on behaviour routines, caricatures which can all too often get in the way of the development of actual personalities. Thus, team members see themselves as prisoners of role allocations imposed by the group. Tensions will increase between the rational 'surface current' and the suppressed emotional 'undertow'. New conflicts and new storming are now on the agenda.

In this phase, the external relations of the team are also likely to be highly rigid and even marked by hostility. As it seeks to reinforce its own sense of self-worth, the group will erect boundaries around itself, effectively excluding any outsiders.

4.3 Performing and performance capability

As teams move into a third phase of development, their roles are clarified and brought further into line with their personal needs. In this process, they must work to render the stereotype images of Phase 2 explicit and then to break them down.

Between them, group members must work for clarification at the levels of thinking, feeling and volition. Here, they will express and approximate to varying concepts of satisfactory teamwork, share and coordinate their personal goals and intentions, and attempt to articulate a binding vision and shared value orientation. In addition, they will examine sources of sympathy and antipathy in their mutual relations, making behavioural agreements in order to defuse negative features. This will enable the group members to integrate the various facets of their personality with their work, rather than splitting them off. If a group succeeds in forming in this way, and in making its psychosocial level compatible, it will find that its work goals are met as well.

In this third phase, the group will also improve its procedural capabilities: it will work to find appropriate methods and techniques to accomplish its assigned tasks. Rather than relying on inviolable general agreements, the team will instead learn to combine flexibility with self-discipline. In this way, a more productive and humane atmosphere can develop, based on recognition and the constructive use of differences, conducive to an agreed learning partnership. The team will now radiate strength and find that it is able to work together at a higher level of performance.

Nevertheless, this phase also harbours a risk. Newly formed behaviour modes and newly established procedures may easily become rooted and inflexible in the long-term. To guard against this, teams must work concertedly to achieve role flexibility. They must strive to constantly adjust the roles and leadership contributions of the members, in order to react as situations change.

Leadership should therefore not be centred on any one person; instead, the team members will learn to carry out their work on the basis of individual responsibility and commitment, always recognising just where new initiatives and support are called for. Following the maxim of leadership changing according to the situation, they will themselves provide the necessary steering impulses. They will duly recognise that while it is of course essential that certain impulses are given, it is less important from whom they originate.

For this to succeed, the group must become proficient in 'metacommunication': communication above and about the events taking place in the group and regarding perceived steps necessary to improve climate and performance. It must also practice 'metalearning': the group must learn how it learns best and implement this insight by means of actions which will contribute to group development and performance enhancement.

At this point, team members will identify with the team and with its scope of tasks to the extent that they will apply their entire potential into the joint task. Work results will be optimised. The team will further structure its relations with outsiders, openly and with respect, even if it still devotes its primary sympathy to the members of the group and continues to experience and intensively cultivate its we-feeling.

It is at this point that the team has matured to a level of authentic value-setting. The previous struggle between dependency and counter-dependency (according to Bennis and Shepard 1956) has become constructive "interdependency". As they learn to judiciously apply various forms of external controls, the group members will have discovered ways and means to achieve the right balance between self-determination and external determination.

4.4 Reforming – self-structuring and the ability to change

In the course of the previous three phases, the work group has learned how to harness the potential of its members to both optimise performance and enable its members to realise and develop their personal potential. These two objectives are not necessarily in themselves incompatible, rather the assignment of task capabilities and the personal development of the team members are inter-dependent team goals.

What is new in the reforming phase is that the group must learn to adapt and renew itself, a skill that will be practiced constantly and independently. In this process, it will come to understand the power of "dying and becoming", as Goethe put it. They will recognise that both the work environment and the internal/personal life of the group are constantly changing as the team continues to take on both new tasks and members.

Many modern organisations have come to expect their staff to work in several project teams at once, without becoming hindered by role or loyalty conflicts. This requires not only continuous changes in, and of, the group, but also a developed ability to change. The fact that individual team members have become a part of a number of concurrent project teams should not be regarded as treason but rather taken as an essential part of the working environment.

If they are to react flexibly to situations, i.e. to truly become a team that learns from, and can effectively organise, its own development, team members must develop a capability to accurately perceive changes both within the team and in its external environment, and then to deal effectively with these. In practice, this will mean that the team will pass through several phases of uncertainty, as it constantly seeks to redefine the roles, rules and work goals that it has acquired in the individual phases of its previous group development. The group will learn to reconstitute itself in order to take on new tasks and will run through the phases of its development with this target in mind. In addition to this, it will come to accept the need to dissolve itself again after the task is achieved, letting go of old bonds, interest constellations or feelings.

Groups that prove capable of restructuring themselves and flexibly changing in this way will learn to handle this process autonomously. They will be able to renew themselves, always taking full account of the individual interests of the team members, the processes in the group and the requirements of the environment (especially the organisation and the customers). Only by mastering these skills can teams hope to work effectively within the many internal and external networks of modern organisations.

In summary, these four development phases will show certain characteristics during the progression:

- from superficiality and lack of commitment to depth and commitment;
- from unconscious external drivers to a conscious balance between external and self-steering;
- from struggles around unilateral dependency to a constructive handling of interdependency.

In his theory of group development, Bion (1961) primarily concentrated on the first steps of forming and storming; his work with short-term training groups focused on exploring this initial situation. From this, he came to see the constantly recurring risk of teams falling into regression. However, further research into task-related work groups has shown that, beyond this, teams can expect further stages of maturation. These will not necessarily develop automatically, rather they must be deliberately willed and the group must embark on the path towards them, thus participating actively in the learning and development process.

The description shows that there are various potentials for conflict in the individual development stages.

In phase 1 of forming and storming:

- team instability;
- a struggle for profiles and positions, as well as the formation of supportive coalitions: the team will show whether it is likely to revert regularly to these initial patterns, or whether it will instead venture to the next development phase. This will lead to significant differences in attitude about conflict.

In phase 2 of norming:

- too quick and inappropriate norming and rigidity;
- tension between the superficially rational 'surface current' and the emotional undertow; leading to:
- conflicts between the roles of the dual leadership and their respective followers; or to
- efforts to do justice to the emotional dimension in group activities, while at the same time not compromising the rational, possibly preventing violently intervention by others: this is primarily achieved through even more norming;
- attempts to break out of tacitly accepted role assignments, and instead develop new role definitions: this is, however, likely to be resisted by other team members, who will instead seek to reinforce existing role arrangements through the application of sanctions;
- team friction, as the stereotypical images are increasingly regarded as restrictive and fixating, and therefore rejected.

In phase 3 of performing:

- whenever the team members come to identify the need for and thus propose different kinds of leadership and structuring initiatives; one member might wish to accelerate, for instance, while others will seek to slow down the process;
- whenever opinions differ as to the need for, and the effectiveness of, metacommunication: one team member might find 'talking about talking' ineffective, while this process may for others be the beginning of some valuable in-depth communication;
- whenever team members exert moral and psychological pressure on others, imposing excessively high expectations and demands for social competence and thus triggering tension: the problem here is that these team members fail to recognise that it is unrealistic to expect the same contributions from the different group members since each of them will never be equal in strength;
- if, as a result of this, the initial enthusiasm for the group and for teamwork and the regard that individual members have for each other, turn, first, into effusive and excessive esteem and unreasonable demands, and then plunges the team into 'negative hyperbole' after it experiences disappointments, ending in a vicious circle of self- and external denigration;
- work at the level of the 3rd development phase will regularly demand a high degree of mental activity, creativity and willingness to accept responsibility: some team members may express a desire to make life easier by returning to the simple rules of norming, while other group members may resist this.

In phase 4 of reforming:

- the group members can exhibit differing degrees of patience for the essential group finding processes, and can apply pressure to make forming, storming and norming all lead to performing at less well developed stages;
- as team processes are constantly repeated, some team members can engage in routine apparent participation, behaviour which is experienced by the others as insincere and unsupportive, and thus irritating;
- the fundamental openness of the team towards its environment can become mentally tiring for individual group members, especially if it is accompanied by a general 'desire for confluence': in other words, the individuality of the single group members becomes subsumed by the collective.

The most frequent source of tension in this phase lies in transition crises (*see* Wheelan 1990). Conflicts can arise simply because perceptions and wishes differ. 'What phase are we in now – and in which direction do we want to develop in the near future? Which actions are necessary now, and which are perhaps premature? Must a certain phase be perfected and completed before we can move on to the next phase?

5. Team Development and Conflict Resolution

Our description of the potential for conflict that can arise at the five levels of teamwork and during the four development phases of a team has shown a wide variety of potential conflict sources. If appropriate methods of team development are properly applied at each of these individual points of conflict, team problems can be dealt with effectively both before and when they arise. Methods of team development can serve, at the same time, as methods of conflict prevention and conflict resolution.

For each specific situation, practitioners must initially reflect on the development status of the team:

- Who, if anyone, is having difficulties in the group?
- What issues in a dispute are perceived by which members?
- In what phase does the team appear to find itself at the present moment?
- Are the apparent tensions indicative of a development crisis in the team?
- Or are the problems of an individual group member exported into the group? Moreover, if that is the case, what responsibility does the team then have to tackle these problems?

Effective practitioners should also survey and analyse the desires and goals of the individual team members:

- How much energy is each member prepared to invest in team development?
- What are each person's ideas as to how the team should further develop?
- Are these individual ideas and objectives mutually compatible? Are they contradictory? Do they perhaps reveal divergent assessments of the development status of the team?

Team development should not be regarded simply as an 'off-the-job' activity, which takes place only at special times and in special places, as an interruption of routine work. Rather, both 'near-the-job' and 'on-the-job' measures are conceivable, as work is linked to reflection and 'learning moments'. Impulses for team development may even be produced 'on-the-job' if teamwork processes are regularly reviewed in the light of the five different levels of team activities. As a support to this kind of analysis, moderator and/or observer roles may be allocated on a rotating basis. This will allow each team member to serve as both observer and actor at various times during the life of the team. It is clear that a team can only become a learning system once it succeeds in closely linking work and learning.

Such team development can commence at any of the levels mentioned.

5.1 At the level of the individual group member

Practitioners can work to address each of the intra-psychological factors:

- freeing distorted individual perceptions by collecting individual pictures of the team, of its organisational surroundings, etc.;
- surveying existing thought patterns by means of questionnaires and then analysing these in the group or in partnerships, with the aim of breaking them down;
- raising feelings and attitudes to the conscious level by means of imaginative and artistic interventions;
- raising the sphere of volition from the sub- and semi-conscious to the reflectively conscious level, paying special attention to personal ideal and value concepts, and above all probing to see to what extent these are compatible with the team's overall objectives;
- using feedback methods to expose and reflect on individual behaviour patterns.

Usually, practitioners will find that they can conduct these experiments in conjunction with group interventions, whether that is within the complete group, in sub-groups or in learning partnerships. After all, an overall development of the team will only be possible to the extent that the team members themselves show development as well. Ideally, team development should lead to an overall enhancement of individual perception and diagnosis skill, conflict resolution capability and social competence. Active listening, the ability to empathise with others and to accept the validity of their opinions, is just as important as is the ability to express one's own feelings, intentions and opinions.

Effective conflict capability will also be conducive to cooperative behaviour and promote a willingness to enter into compromises. This is critical, as the performance capability of a team will in the end depend on the (overall) qualifications of its individual members. This must include not only technical skills, but also social capabilities and a competency for autonomy. Team members must develop the ability to consciously review their own thinking, feeling and volition, accepting responsibility for their experience of this, as well as for providing appropriate inputs into the group in line with particular situation requirements ("be your own chairperson!"). This will require realistic self-assessment, accurate reflection on one's own capabilities, circumspection in conflict situations and a high level of frustration tolerance.

All this will in turn further team development. As we have shown, this development will move from one-sided dependence to interdependence, from externally controlled behaviour to effective self-determination and autonomy, from self-assertion in simple environments to the ability to master highly complex situations.

Depending on the particular team situation, the polarity between the individual and the team can be handled differently. If there are indications that various forms of group pressure have constrained individual scope for development, appropriate responses will require more activities that promote individual self-determination and self-definition. This will certainly be the case if the rational surface current in the group has dominated in the norming phase, to the point of oppression of the individual team members.

5.2 At the content-specific level/issue level

Here, practitioners are only likely to have success with methods that recognise the need for a multi-faceted and thorough discussion of the various points in dispute, in order to process issue topics constructively. As others have done, Eiseman (1978) has developed highly effective techniques for this context. By 'dimensionalising points in dispute', practitioners can break down major themes into smaller sub-topics, revealing elements that can be discussed better and more concretely than could the large-scale generalisations. The Harvard School (Fisher et al. 1991) offers some tried and tested methods for achieving this in a negotiation setting.

Individual team members should further work to complement one another's technical skills and expertise, continually learning from each other. Ideally, each member of the team will occupy several spheres of expertise. Finally, team members will find that consulting experts and specialists can be a good way of resolving issue-related differences.

5.3 The interaction level – psychosocial level

This is the typical point of leverage for most team development interventions. It is likely to include one or all of the following possible lines of approach:

- survey, reflect and deliberate on the *general group climate*, using, for instance, card surveys, questionnaires, painting and movement exercises: All these methods depend on the proper practice of giving feedback;
- survey the development status of the group, as described above: Temporary retraction of the authority of the leader and effective clarification of team decision-making processes can bring problems and conflicts to the surface more quickly, so that the group can begin to gain a greater understanding. These conflicts must, however, not be allowed to drag on to a point of escalation at which constructive conflict processing becomes very difficult. It can be helpful to apply the rule: 'any disturbance of personal work capability must take precedence over continuation of issue-related work!' If the group culture properly respects this rule, blockages and disturbances will be the driving force for eliminating any difficulties in work performance, or with the methods and procedures applied, or in dealings with one another. In this way, conflicts become constructive helpmates and actually assist in bringing about the necessary improvements;
- make explicit and consciously structure the development of the *group culture*: Help groups to critically review their values and norms, to identify any inhibiting behavioural patterns and to implement specific measures designed to overcome these. If the group succeeds in jointly elaborating upon rules that are helpful for achieving the work goal and for coope-

ration within the group, this will represent an important step. It must be possible to express these new guiding principles in meaningful terms. They will not materialise automatically, but rather only take hold when behavioural habits change, including accustomed roles and natural privileges. Some ways to accomplish this have been suggested by the 'U-Procedure' developed in 1970 by Glasl and Lemson (Glasl 1999, 155f), upon which are based the more recent methods of Scott-Morgan and Little (1994) for explaining the "secret rules of the game";

- depict the *group relations and roles* within the team through, for example, the application of 'systemic lists', and the processing of problematic relation patterns using methods such as psychodrama: In order that groups may succeed in developing internal cohesion between the team members, unwritten role contracts which have developed subconsciously will need to be clarified, and relations reviewed. Many tensions and conflicts will need to be overcome, as a healthy group dynamic can only develop from frank and respectful interchanges. Initially, these more emotional processes will be of greater importance for the group's development than the issue-related themes. Furthermore, mastering this part of the picture is an essential precondition for effective issue-related work;
- the "role-negotiation" put forward by Roger Harrison (1971) has proved particularly helpful in this regard, and is also relatively easy to apply (see also Glasl 1999, 139ff): This approach encourages team members to openly voice wishes about how they would like to see changes in their team colleagues' behaviour. These requests are then presented mutually, explained and negotiated in a fair process of give and take. Later, the resulting agreements are reviewed in detail and amended.

We have already drawn attention to the various ways of describing the potentials for conflict, focusing especially on the need to clarify and overcome mutual stereotypical images. The methods of "perception clarification" of Blake *et al.* (1964) are particularly useful in this regard (*see* Glasl 1999, 146ff). The concept is to ask the conflicting parties (individuals or sub-groups) to first record just how they have perceived the other party subjectively. They are then asked to present these views to one another. If they then find that their self-image deviates significantly from the picture presented to them by the other side, they must subsequently ask: 'What can we have done to contribute to such a perception from the others? And what might we do ourselves to avoid causing such a negative image in future?' Explanations offered and conclusions drawn from this are then exchanged and discussed between the parties.

These descriptions of methodology can only serve as a very general indication of what can be done. Their proper application presupposes commensurate knowledge and experience and in most cases should be left to practitioners with adequate experience in team and organisational development.

5.4 At the procedure – method level

Here many different kinds of intervention can be applied, as outlined in Section III (4). In general, it is advisable to link the work at the psychosocial level with method training for the procedural level.

5.5 At the external relations level

Clarifying the tasks, areas of competence and scope of responsibility of the team vis-à-vis the rest of the organisation are recommended methods of conflict management at this level. Project management techniques have proven to be the best way of conducting this:

- developing methods for interactive design to facilitate the exchange of information within the team, and between the team and the rest of the organisation;
- drawing 'pictures' of oneself and comparing these to the pictures offered by others, especially if relations between the teams are marked by antagonism: A good approach is the perception clarification method of Blake et al. (1964) discussed above.

5.6 Continuous overview

Teams should also regularly review their work together and find ways of improvement, in an ongoing effort to raise the quality of both cooperation and work results. This can be done after each team meeting, as well as after the completion of projects. Closed team sessions can be effective for purposes of diagnosis and basic reflection.

If this type of review process is conducted systematically, team members will enter into the habit of observing the impact of their work even as they do it: they will observe these factors while at the same time working actively on their projects. Moreover, once team members have formed this habit of observing and self-reflection, they will also develop a different feeling of responsibility concerning issue-oriented work, method-related and psycho-process dynamics. All of which is an essential precondition for the self-development of teams.

Since the teamwork we have been discussing usually takes place in the context of a larger organisation, the success of team development can only be sustained if it is embedded in a more comprehensive process of organisational development.

If change is undertaken in this way, team development processes will be seen as a fundamental and effective prerequisite for autonomous development of organisations. In addition, this will not only serve to prevent conflict in teams and organisations, but also enable practitioners to make an important contribution to the effort of conflict resolution in the wider working world.

6. Conclusions and Open Questions

Work in teams can be significantly enhanced if teams and their leaders will participate actively in the process of recognising and naming team dynamics. To help them do this, practitioners (and team leaders) have put forward a number of basic tools that allow for rapid diagnosis of the strengths and weaknesses of each of the five key levels of team functioning, as well as of their influences on each other. These are the individual team member, the content or issues, interaction, methodologies and external relations.

Unfortunately, most training sessions and experiments in this domain neglect levels 1 (the individual team member) and level 4 (methodologies). Teams are then faced with and attempt to deal with conflicts at the level of interaction; problems that would have been better addressed at levels 1, 4 or 5. The result is an illegitimate 'interactionisation' or 'personification' of the conflict.

Recognising and dealing effectively with this is a primary challenge for practitioners, and they must be provided with user-friendly and reliable tools to accomplish the task. On the other hand, complicated, time and cost intensive instruments that can only realistically be employed by expertly trained psychologists will be of little use.

It is also critical that team members learn to use these user-friendly tools to properly assess the development status of their teams, as well as to make recommendations for future development. Unfortunately, many experts in varying schools of thought within this field of group dynamics continue to persist in performing this diagnostic work in an unstructured manner, relying mainly on specific experiences of the participants to anchor their recommendations. This may be conducive to the development of good empirical perceptions, but is, once again, of little use to everyday practitioners faced with conflict problems in teams. The result is a mystification effect, as the analysis of team development becomes a secret and inaccessible science for active team members and is therefore never even undertaken.

To help, we must now work to further develop systematically existing self-diagnostic tools such as that of Goetz (1998). Especially the interdependencies between teams and their related organisations must be examined and, in some cases, restructured. For this, analysts must come to understand not only the psychosocial dynamics of teams and organisations (the primary focus of most of the received systematic approaches), but also the mutually interdependent effects of the social subsystems of an organisation with its related cultural and techno-instrumental networks. Failing this, we will be left with a reductionistic and, at best, an ineffective psychosocial approach.

The work to be done is by nature interdisciplinary, and must effectively integrate psychological, sociological, organisational and technical methods and insights.

7. Reference and Further Reading

Antons, K. 1992. *Praxis der Gruppendynamik,* Göttingen: Hogrefe.

Ballreich, R. 2000. *Problemlösen im Dialog,* Graz: Seminarunterlage Trigon.

Bennis, W. G. and H. A. Shepard 1956. "A theory of group development," *Human Relations*, No. 9, 415-437.

Besemer, Ch. 1995. *Mediation: Vermittlung in Konflikten,* Baden: Stiftung gewaltfreies Leben.

Bion, W. R. 1961. *Experiences in Groups and Other Papers,* London: Tavistock.

Blake, R., H. Shepard and J. Mouton 1964. *Managing intergroup Conflict in Industry,* Houston, Tx: Gulf.

Bomers, G. and R. Peterson (eds.) 1984. *Conflict management and Industrial Relations,* Boston: Kluwer-Nijhoff.

Bos, A. H. 1974. *Oordeelsvorming in Groepen,* Wageningen: H.Veenman & Zonen.

Brown, L. D. 1983. *Managing Conflict at Organizational Interfaces,* Reading: Addison-Wesley Longman.

Burke, W and H. Hornstein (eds.) 1972. *The Social Technology of Organization Development,* Washington, DC: NTL Learning Resources Corporation.

Burton, J. 1969. *Conflict and Communication,* London: Macmillan.

Cohn, R. 1992. *Von der Psychoanalyse zur Themenzentrierten Interaktion,* Stuttgart: Klett-Cotta.

Eiseman, J. 1978. "Reconciling 'incompatible positions'," *Journal of Applied Behavioral Science,* 14, 133-150.

Fisher, R., W. Ury and B. Patton 1991. *Getting to Yes,* Boston, Mass.: Penguin Putnam.

Gal, T. and H. Gehring 1981. *Betriebswirtschaftliche Planungs- und Entscheidungstechniken,* Berlin/New York, NY: Gruyter Verlag.

Glasl, F. 1982. "The process of conflict escalation and roles of third parties," *in* Bomers and Peterson, op. cit, 119-140.

Glasl, F. 1984. *Conflicten in organisaties voor sociaal werk.* Unpublished survey of NPI. Zeist (NL).

Glasl, F. 1994. *The enterprise of the future: How companies develop,* Stroud: Hawthorne Press.

Glasl, F. 1996. *Entwicklung und Reife von Arbeitsgruppen,* Graz: Trigon Basiskonzept.

Glasl, F. 1997. *Konfliktmanagement,* 5. Aufl., Bern/Stuttgart: Haupt.

Glasl, F. 1999. *Confronting Conflict: A First-Aid Kit for Handling Conflict,* Stroud: Hawthorne Press.

Glasl, F. and B. Lievegoed 1993. *Dynamische Unternehmensentwicklung,* Bern/Stuttgart: Haupt.

Götz, J. 1998. *Entwicklung eines Instruments zur Eigenevaluation der Gruppenreife und des Autonomiegrades von Teilautonomen Arbeitsgruppen,* Salzburg: Universität Salzburg, Unveröffentlichte Diplomarbeit.

Grandori, A. 1984. "A prescriptive contingency view of organizational decision making," *Administrative Science Quarterly,* vol. 29, 2: 192-209.

Grandori, A. 1987. *Perspective in Organization Theory,* Cambridge, Mass: Harper & Row.

Harrison, R. 1972. "Role-negotiation: a tough minded approach to team development," *in* Burke and Hornstein, op. cit.

Hax, H. 1974. *Entscheidungsmodelle in der Unternehmung,* Reinbek bei Hamburg: Rowohlt.

Hofstätter, R. 1957. *Gruppendynamik,* Reinbek bei Hamburg: Rowohlt.

Janis, I. L. 1972. *Victims of Groupthink,* Atlanta, Ga: Houghton Mifflin.

Katzenbach, J. and D. Smith 1993. *The Wisdom of Teams,* Boston, Mass: Harvard Business School.

Langmaack, B. and M. Braune-Krickau 1995. *Wie die Gruppe laufen lernt. Anregungen zum Planen und Leiten von Gruppen,* Weinheim: Beltz.

Redlich, A. 1997. *Konflikt-Moderation,* Hamburg: Windmühle.

Rosenberg, M. B. 1999. *Noviolent Communication,* Del Mar: PuddleDancer Press.

Rosenstiel, L. von 1992. *Grundlagen der Organisationspsychologie,* Stuttgart: Schäffer-Poeschel.

Rubin, J., D. Pruitt and S.H. Kim 1994. *Social Conflict. Escalation, Stalemate, and Settlement,* New York, NY: McGraw-Hill.

Scott-Morgan, P. and A. D. Little 1994. *Die heimlichen Spielregeln. Die Macht der ungeschriebenen Gesetze in Unternehmen,* Frankfurt/Main: Campus.

Simon, H. 1975. *Administrative Behavior: A Study of Decision-making Processes in Administrative Organization,* New York, N.Y.: The Free Press.

Tannenbaum, R. and W. H. Schmidt 1958. "How to choose a leadership pattern," *Harvard Business Review,* March/April, 95-101.

Tuckman, B. W. 1965. "Developmental sequences in small groups," *Psychological Bulletin* No. 63, 384-399.

Tuckman, B. W. and M. A. C. Jensen 1977. "Stages of small group development revisited," *Group and Organization Studies*, No. 2, 419-427.

Vopel, K. 1994. *Themenzentriertes Teamtraining,* Salzhausen: ISKO.

Vroom, V. H. and A. G. Jago 1978. "On the validity of the Vroom-Yetton model," *Journal of Applied Psychology*, No. 63, 151-162.

Vroom, V. H. and P. W. Yetton 1973. *Leadership and Decision-making,* Pittsburgh: University of Pittsburgh Press.

Wahren, H.-K. 1994. *Gruppen- und Teamarbeit in Unternehmen* Berlin: Walter deGruyter.

Walton, R. 1969. *Interpersonal Peacemaking: Confrontation and Third Party Consultation,* Reading: Addison Werley.

Weeks, D. 1994. *The Eight Essential Steps to Conflict Resolution,* New York, NY: Putnam Books.

Wheelan, S. A. 1990. *Group Processes: A Developmental Perspective,* Boston, Mass: Allyn & Bacon.

From Resolution to Transformation: The Role of Dialogue Projects

Norbert Ropers

1. Introduction 256
2. Approaches to the Systematization of Dialogues 257
3. Dialogue Projects in Practice 259
   Dialogue projects as grassroots peacebuilding and interpersonal reconciliation efforts
   Dialogue projects combined with individual capacity-building
   Dialogue projects combined with institution building, networking, and practical projects
   Dialogue projects as pre-negotiation
4 Dialogue Projects in the Context of Theories of Conflict Management 261
5. Lessons Learned 265
6. References 268

From Resolution to Transformation: The Role of Dialogue Projects[1]

Norbert Ropers

1. Introduction

Dialogues can be viewed as one means – if not the classical one – of dealing constructively with conflicts. As one popular formula puts it: "As long as you're talking, you can't be shooting". "What better method is there of resolving a contentious issue", so runs another down-to-earth, commonsense observation, "than through an honest exchange of views?" "And", says discourse ethics, "what other way is there of finding lasting solutions to the numerous political-cum-moral conflicts in an interdependent and pluralistic world, than through "practical discourse between the affected parties" (Apel 1990).

In the sphere of classical diplomacy, skills in negotiation and dialogue have long formed part of the basic repertoire of any prudent management of international relations, although at least in the public perception, the dialoguing skills of official 'Track 1' diplomacy have all too often been driven into the background by the constraints of power politics and *realpolitik*. Representatives of non-official 'Track 2' diplomacy, by contrast, have instead chosen to place communication, direct encounters and mutual understanding centre-stage. Interest in non-official dialogue initiatives of this kind has been further fostered by the continuing rise in the number of acute or potentially violent disputes, particularly of the ethno-political and protracted variety, increasingly taking place *within* society.

There are now a huge number of dialogue projects underway – from the grassroots right up to leadership level – all designed to settle, resolve or influence conflicts. But the trend is not without its critics. What good does it really do if it is only, as a rule, the moderate representatives of parties to a conflict that gather around a table? Even if comprehension and understanding are achieved between influential persons within the framework of a workshop or series of workshops, does the success of the whole enterprise not rather depend on how the follow-up is managed?

And lastly: do adherents of the dialogue method not run the danger of fundamentally overestimating the importance of communication in dealing with conflicts? The ultimate concerns of most disputes, after all, are not stereotypical perceptions, differences of opinion and varying cultural standards, but rather tangible conflicts of interest, structural factors and the struggle for power and influence. It would seem, then, that dialogues must be put in the context of the overall dynamics of conflict and conflict transformation.

Most scholars and practitioners will agree that protracted conflicts can only be effectively transformed through efforts which also address the structural causes and power political aspects of the conflict, in addition to the psychosocial dimensions, grievances and

1 A first version of this article is published in Wimmer et al. 2003.

relationship issues. Clearly, due to their emphasis on communication and personal interaction, dialogues are primarily used as an instrument within the psychosocial conflict transformation paradigm. It is therefore within that more narrowly defined conceptual context that I will evaluate their usefulness.

In the following, I propose to examine some of the core features of dialogue projects, looking at their variations and implications in greater detail. First I will give an overview of several different 'ideal types' of dialogues, as well as identifying the basic elements of most dialogue processes. Second, I will distinguish between four concepts of dialogue work, a taxonomy which serves primarily to illustrate the practical nature of such projects. Third, dialogue projects will be set in the context of various approaches to handling conflict, in order to better establish criteria for measuring success. Fourth, I will present a number of lessons learned in the course of recent evaluation studies. The questions raised above will be discussed at the end, on the basis of the underlying empirical experience on which this chapter is based.

2. Approaches to the Systematization of Dialogues

The recent literature gives particular attention to two ways of classifying dialogues: First, the identification of ideal types of dialogue and, second, the differentiation of phases according to the typical steps of interaction and communication which constitute a constructive process of dialogue.

Jay Rothman (1998) has proposed classifying approaches to dialogue in inter-group conflicts into three or four ideal types:

- Whether the commonest form of interchange actually merits the name dialogue is doubtful: in a *positional dialogue* the parties articulate their respective views – which may range from differing to diametrically opposed – as positions and attitudes that merely require acknowledgement. As in a parliamentary debate, communication serves primarily to score points, as one argument is set against the other.
- In the case of *human-relations dialogue* the differences of opinion on the substantive issues are relegated to a secondary place and work is instead done at the relational level, focusing on the causes of misunderstandings and the stereotypes which typically arise between the parties. These kinds of dialogues are often preceded by preparatory training sessions on basic mechanisms of perception and interaction in groups. The objectives are mutual acknowledgement of the person and increased respect by each party for the other. What impact this might have in terms of the substance of the conflict is an open question.
- *Activist dialogue* goes one step further. The subjects at issue are sorted and analysed in order to identify common ground, and/or to explore how the parties might contain their dispute through joint action.
- The most ambitious approach is the *problem-solving dialogue*, in which the disputants organize their communication in such a way that they are able to systematically work through the substance of their differences. Where conflicts are highly escalated, this kind of dialogue will generally require the presence of a third party as a co-actor – or indeed as an initiator.

These approaches are more than just a useful way of classifying dialogues according to their prevailing forms of interaction. Taken together, they also emphasize different yet complementary elements of dealing constructively with conflicts through dialogue. In a modified form, one can also conceptualise the different types of dialogues as steps in a process of enhancing the quality of communication and interaction between the dialogue partners (*see* Figure 1). Adherents of the Alternative Dispute Resolution (ADR) Movement have put forward a template of four phases for responding to conflicts through communication:

- The first phase is concerned with formulating the *differing points of view* of the various parties as clearly as possible, securing mutual acknowledgement of these, as well as identifying the substance of the conflict.
- The focus in the second phase is on reflection on the underlying needs and fears of the participating actors, their values, their experiences of conflict and their hopes. Ideally, it should also be possible, in this phase, to develop approaches for securing personal acknowledgement of and insight into the conflicting biographies of the other side.
- The third phase is devoted to the identification of shared *interests* and similar *needs and fears*. It can also be aimed at the initiation of practical cooperation on less controversial issues.
- In most cases the fourth phase requires a lengthy period of preparation, and also personal confidence-building. It involves discussing approaches and ideas for *addressing the substantive issues in dispute*, reflecting on how these approaches and ideas might be implemented and then *initiating practical measures for their resolution*.

Figure 1: Levels of Cooperation in Dialogue Processes

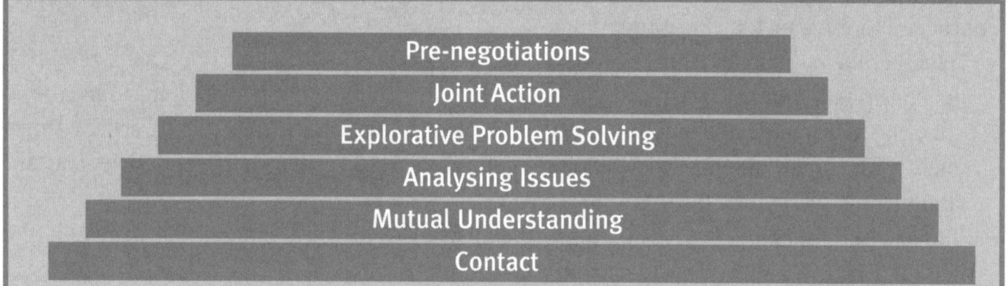

Source: McCartney 1986

In the case of protracted conflicts, dialogues between disputing groups will often be structured as a series of dialogue events, sometimes extending over a period of many months or even years. Several models help to conceptualise constructive developments for such a series of events. One of these focuses especially on the character of the relationship between the parties and the success of the joint efforts as the key characteristics, thus interpreting progress as a process of relationship building, problem solving and collaborative action (McCartney 1986):

- Contact and confidence building;
- Empathy for the other side;
- Joint analysis of conflict issues;

- Explorative problem solving;
- Joint activities in the possibility that the dialogue might feed into official negotiations or pre-negotiations.

Most dialogues take the form of *organized group encounters* of a size that allows face-to-face communication. They are usually conducted with persons below top leadership-level. They are therefore not so much official negotiations as a form of political preliminaries. As a rule, responsibility for the initiation, organization, and direction of the meetings is assumed by a third party. This third party need not come from outside the country; it can also consist of moderate individuals from inside the conflict region.

In the case of highly escalated disputes, or in divided societies, organizing a peaceful coming-together will be difficult, with intervenors often finding themselves unable to successfully get through even the first phase. In the case of protracted conflicts, several meetings will likely be necessary, and intervenors must always allow for the possibility of slipping back to an earlier phase. The need for time, as well as the general fragility of the process, demand from the organizers of dialogue projects a great deal of persistence, as well as a compelling long-term vision and the necessary resources.

The basic idea behind dialogue-based meetings is not new. It was given its initiation in post-1945 Europe, in the context of the paradigm of international intercultural understanding. Then, the prime target group was young people. What drove the endeavour was the conviction that increased contact and interaction between individuals from different backgrounds could help eliminate prejudices and enemy images and create trans-frontier loyalties. Since then, this fairly naïve 'contact hypothesis' has been supplanted by more sophisticated concepts of 'intercultural learning' (Otten/Treuheit 1994).

Dialogue-based meetings intended expressly to deal with ethno-political conflicts are a more recent phenomenon, but they draw on similar beliefs. Probably the most influential school of instruction in these methods is the 'interactive conflict-resolution' or 'interactive problem-solving' movement (Mitchell and Banks 1996; Kelman 1992; Ronald Fisher 1997). The roots of this approach go back to the 1960s, when various scholar/practitioners began to invite influential representatives of conflicting parties to workshops, in order either to then guide them through the above-mentioned four phases of constructive dialogue in a quasi-academic exercise, or to facilitate this process. Experience with the use of this approach has now been gathered in a number of different crisis regions.

Despite this, there has still been little movement to employ this interactive conflict resolution instrument on a systematic, broad-scale basis. The focus has, instead, been on selective combinations of this approach with other methods of influencing conflicts, as laid out in the following sections.

3. Dialogue Projects in Practice

To my knowledge, no representative or comprehensive overview of practical dialogue projects in conflict regions has so far been undertaken, even at a superficial level. Debates about the usefulness of this set of instruments have so far mostly been confined –

depending on the milieu concerned – to specific forms of dialogue. The result has been an academic discussion concerned primarily with interactive conflict resolution, in which the scholar/practitioners set the tone as third parties.

The NGO world, on the other hand, shows a strong preference for combinations of dialogue projects with other practical schemes designed to address the common concerns of particular groups (e.g. women, youth), advocacy events (e.g. peace rallies) or training events. Such documentation as does exist on the conduct and results of dialogue projects initially related mainly to the more academic approaches. Subsequently, the interests of the financial sponsors has led to more extensive documentation of other projects as well.

Once again, from the perspective of ideal types, four practical forms of dialogue projects can be distinguished, with particular reference to the objectives they pursue over and above the communicative purposes discussed above.

3.1 Dialogue projects as grassroots peacebuilding and interpersonal reconciliation efforts

These projects generally relate to the local or neighbourhood level, bringing together people in similar situations and with similar interests (young people, women, trade unionists, the religiously active) or persons who share a similar or interdependent fate because of a violent past (widows and orphans of war, children of victims and perpetrators etc.). The central elements are personal encounters and the elimination of barriers to communication. The governing idea is human-relations dialogue and the long-term objective is the replication of encounters of this kind, in order to better promote peace from below.

A particularly interesting example of this approach is that of the 'To Reflect and Trust' (TRT) movement, which brings together children of victims and perpetrators for sharing and exploring ways of integrating the violent past (Bar-On 2000). The effectiveness of projects like this largely depends on the extent to which it proves possible to move beyond single encounters, building up longer-term personal relations and creating more permanent shared structures.

3.2 Dialogue projects combined with individual capacity-building

Given the explicit aim of dialogue-initiatives to achieve understanding, it seems obvious that one should also make use of such occasions to enhance participants' skills in interacting constructively with one another. Another factor that speaks for this combination of training and conflict management is the fact that real encounters provide an ideal setting to try out dialogue skills. Such a combination of techniques is, however, not without its risks and disadvantages. For one thing, the target groups for conflictive encounter and for training are not necessarily the same; and secondly, participants can simply become confused if, in the course of a series of encounters, the facilitators fail to fully explain the purpose of the different exercises.

3.3 Dialogue projects combined with institution building, networking, and practical projects

Combinations such as these are usually only possible after the successful conclusion of a fairly long process of confidence-building and work on the phases of dialogue as described above. The task in many cases is either to institutionalise the dialogue in the form of inter-ethnic advisory bodies, reconciliation commissions, or NGO networks, or to set up or build the capacity of individual NGOs. In other cases, dialogue projects provide the starting-point for practical endeavours such as income-generating schemes for groups of the population particularly hard hit by the conflict – unemployed young people, for example.

It is generally agreed that these are all good ways of enhancing the effectiveness of dialogues, as well as of fully realizing their potential to bring about structural change. What is often overlooked, one has to admit, is that these kinds of follow-up measures place different demands on the practitioners involved. Thus, although many initiatives do succeed in containing macro-conflicts through dialogue, they subsequently founder on the internal meso- and micro-rivalries that surface during institution building.

3.4 Dialogue projects as pre-negotiation

The most ambitious dialogue-based undertakings are those that are designed to exert influence on the management of the conflict at the political leadership level. This is precisely what interactive conflict resolution and problem-solving approaches aim to do by holding confidential workshops at which a third party shows influential members of the conflicting parties how to develop insights and ideas, in the hope that this will later facilitate and give new life to the official negotiations. For this latter reason, this approach is sometimes also described as a part of the pre-negotiation phase. In evaluations of the practical results of these kinds of endeavours, effects were initially only classified as either internal or external – i.e. affecting either those directly involved or the broader context of the conflict. Today, however, discussions on this are significantly more nuanced.

4. Dialogue Projects in the Context of Theories of Conflict Management

How is the success of dialogue projects to be assessed? Chris Mitchell has proposed that the success of pre-negotiation dialogue projects can be assessed at three levels (1993, 82ff.):

- impact on the persons involved (changes in attitude, new patterns of behaviour);
- output, particularly in terms of ideas, proposals, practical measures, etc., that are then incorporated into the process of political goal formation;
- long-term impact on the overall conflict.

Commenting on the first level is relatively straightforward, given that there is by now an established research area of social psychology and group dynamics from which to draw. In practice, however, most evaluation consists of inviting participants to comment at the end of the events, which normally gives a preponderance of undifferentiated communication of positive opinions. Assessments of the second and third levels have so far been based entirely on the case studies conducted by the organizers, as well as on their contacts in the respective conflict regions. For example, Ronald Fisher evaluated 76 reports relating to workshops held between 1965 and 1995 and arrived at a reported success rate of 84 per cent (1997, 187ff.). However understandable this sort of positive self-assessment is, it does tell us regrettably little about just what sort of dialogue will promote what kind of impact and long-term effects, and with what sort of people (including what third party!), at what juncture, and on what scale in order to achieve success.

It seems clear that these questions cannot be answered solely from within the framework of an explicit theory and practice of dialogue, of whatever nature. This points to the broader context of macro-political conflict management (Hoffman 1995).

In general, theoretical investigation of inter-group conflict management is still rather poorly developed. Many concrete questions that have naturally emerged from practical experience in regard to appropriate strategies to be used in actual situations of conflict remain unanswered; there are to date very few useful recommendations based on detailed theoretical discussions and their empirical verification. The most high-profile approaches documented in this context are normative concepts of 'interest-led dispute resolution' (Fisher and Ury 1981), comparative case studies (Zartman 1985) and an empirical-cum-quantitative investigation of the characteristics of conflicts that appear to have been settled peacefully (Bercovitch and Houston 1996). Explicit references to theories of social change or of conflict remain the exception.

This theory gap is especially apparent when it comes to stipulating the yardsticks by which the success of individual activities or programmes of intervention are to be measured. Because of the social complexities, it is extraordinarily difficult to establish a causal link between micro-measures and macro-effects. It is therefore all the more necessary that we find a way to explicitly address the gap and to isolate and examine the unspoken assumptions underlying a large part of conflict management practice and research (Kleiboer 1996; Ross and Rothman 1999). If we fail to do this, there is a very real danger that peacemaking will be equated either with the stabilization of relationships of dominance (Francis 2003) or with the mere smoothing over of social relations.

Recently, however, we have begun to observe somewhat of a *rapprochement* between theory and practice. Indicators of this are evident in various state-of-the-art reviews and in conflict impact assessment studies (Lund and Rasamoelina 2000) which aim to formulate criteria for the effective use of conflict management measures in established fields of activity such as development cooperation.

Cordula Reimann (*see* her contribution in this volume) has proposed classifying both theoretical and practical approaches to conflict management into three ideal/typical categories. Her taxonomy permits a more precise conceptual classification of dialogue projects and the yardsticks for measuring their success (*see* Box 1). The division that she suggests also makes it clear that successes within one category cannot simply be assumed to apply to others.

The conflict settlement approach aims to secure or adjust the political order in the face of acute or potentially violent conflict, as well as to achieve a viable balance between the interests of the various leadership groups that hold power. Within this framework, dialogue projects can usefully fulfil the function of gauging the scope for official negotiations at the level of advisers and persons of influence. If it then proves possible to move initiatives for dialogue on to a broader footing, and to elicit a positive response to them in at least a section of the media, they can also create an atmosphere conducive to negotiation at this level.

The relatively small number of case studies which examine the general set-up surrounding official negotiations indicates that the results of civil society dialogue projects have so far only rarely been directly translated into official measures. Official policymakers continue to harbour significant psychological and procedural reservations about this form of citizen participation. Appointing persons of trust, on the other hand, – such as elder statesman Jimmy Carter – to carry out semi-official exploratory missions seems to present fewer problems. The influence exerted by dialogue projects must therefore generally be regarded as indirect and relatively long-term. It involves the socialization of potential future leaders, the creation of networks of personal relationships, and the airing of new ideas in safe forums – as demonstrated by Kelman's use of the preparatory measures that preceded the Israeli-Palestine accord of 1993 (Kelman 1995).

This gap between official and unofficial diplomacy is not just an expression of the differing legitimacy and power-political options that exist between states and the realm of civil society. Many protagonists of dialogue-based approaches have observed that it also reflects a fundamentally different understanding of conflict. In their view, protracted conflicts are a clear sign of the failure to satisfy basic needs in regard to security, recognition, and participation, as well as the desire for social change (Burton 1990; Burton and Dukes 1990). It is then the task of conflict resolution to deal not only with the more obvious conflicts over matters of substance, but also with the troubled relations between the parties, in order to set the substantive conflicts themselves in a new context and begin to tackle them as a shared problem.

Dialogue projects are indeed an important instrument of the conflict resolution approach, primarily because its key objectives are the mutual clarification of perceptions and relations and improvements in communication. That said, most dialogue projects turn out to be relatively brief affairs, difficult to sustain over a longer period. Where this is successfully managed, however, it usually significantly increases the likelihood that the process will indeed lead to the creation of a group of people that possess the valuable experience of dialoguing and have come to value close links with the other side. None the less the challenges with which these projects are eventually confronted all stem usually from the question of how the dialogue about the clarification of relations and the analysis of the conflict can then be moved beyond joint (exploratory) problem-solving to encompass practical implementation measures.

The third approach to conflict management builds on the notions of conflict settlement and conflict resolution, but lays additional stress on the need for structural change. From the point of view of conflict transformation, lasting peacemaking in divided societies and societies traumatized by war requires a broad range of measures aimed, on the one hand, at eliminating socio-economic inequalities and, on the other, at building up political and social capacities that will enable those involved to cope with (ethnic) plurality. Within this framework, dialogue projects can perform a valuable bridge-building function. The main criterion by which they must be measured, however, is the degree to which they help strengthen disadvantaged groups and create a changed dispute settlement culture at the grassroots level. This, in turn, raises the question as to just how and to what extent bridge-building activities and joint activities across conflict divides can have an added empowering impact on those involved.

It is clear from this classification that we are going to have to apply different measures of the success of dialogue projects, depending on the goals and context involved. As is generally the case in conflict management, success is very much a multi-faceted phenomenon. If we accept the conflict transformation assumption that conflicts are transformed through

Box 1: The Role of Dialogue Projects in the Context of Different Approaches to Conflict Management

Approach to Conflict Management	Notion of Conflict	Preferred Practical Approach	Measures of Success	Role of Dialogue Projects
Conflict Settlement	Conflict as a problem of the status quo and political order	Track 1: Diplomacy and power politics at official leadership level	Results-oriented: political settlements with stabilizing effect	Organizing pre-negotiations Promoting a political climate of understanding
Conflict Resolution	Conflict as a catalyst of social change	Track 2: Direct civil society conflict management, esp. at the middle-ranking leadership level	Process-oriented: improved communication, interaction, and relations between parties; respect for different collective identities	Creating a leadership class with experience of dialoguing Workshops on communication, problem-solving, etc.
Conflict Transformation	Conflict as non-violent struggle for social justice	Track 3: Strengthening capacities of disadvantaged groups to act/deal with conflict, and capacity of divided/war-traumatized societies to integrate	Structure-oriented: elimination of socio-economic inequalities between identity groups; good governance; power sharing; creation of cross-cutting civil society structure; building conflict management capacities at the grassroots level	Practising communication and interaction skills Providing opportunities for encounter and learning between polarized groups Empowering groups

(based on figure by Reimann in this volume)

simultaneous result-oriented, process-oriented, and structure-oriented approaches, it becomes clear that projects of this kind will need to be undertaken in parallel at several levels. The model most frequently cited for this in recent years is that of 'peace constituencies' or 'peace alliances' (Lederach 1997). The question of just what contribution dialogue projects in particular could or should make to the creation of peace constituencies has, however, not so far been much discussed. One possible route to the answer to this question is provided by the lessons learned and best practice studies that have examined individual dialogue projects in greater detail.

5. Lessons Learned

The following list of nine 'lessons' is derived from a number of published and unpublished studies (Spencer 1998; Charles Stewart Mott Foundation 1999; Haumersen/Rademacher/Ropers 2002; Wolleh 2002), as well as on the author's own experiences with problem-solving workshops on conflicts in the Caucasus. For purposes of brevity, attention is focused on those aspects that are of relevance to projects aimed at exerting influence on the political macro-conflict.

- The ambitious goal of a problem-solving dialogue between parties to protracted conflicts can only be achieved within the framework of a *long-term process of work and learning*. Personal confidence-building, clarification of positions and perceptions and reflection on background facts are important prerequisites to any substantive discussion of the material issues.
  A key role is played here by the joint handling of crises – e.g. escalatory processes within the group, as well as threats and other influences from outside – and by the realization that all the participants have similar problems of acceptance vis-à-vis their home constituency. Also important is that all participants have the positive experience of arrangements that are adhered to – e.g. agreements about the confidentiality of the talks or regarding the solution of practical problems. The initiating third party must therefore consider whether it is able to indeed ensure such a long-term process (in practice, this can extend over several years). In a worst-case scenario, one must reckon with the possibility that if there are only a few meetings, or even only one, many problems will be stirred up, but the mistrust of the participants will ultimately be even greater than before.
- If the dialogue process is to get off to a good start, the *choice of the initial protagonists* is also crucial. For one thing, these participants must prove themselves capable of getting some kind of meaningful exchange off the ground – a fact that speaks strongly for the involvement of more moderately inclined spokespersons. For another, this first choice of participants also acts as a signal that will help to determine whether the enterprise is taken seriously or merely dismissed as an outsider's or traitor's venture. There is therefore much to be said for having a mixture of moderate and well networked mainstream people involved in the initial phase. At the same time, thought should also be given to the appropriate ways in which hardliners could, in the medium term, be brought in to the process. 'Bringing in' does not automatically imply participation in meetings; it might initially consist solely of efforts to engage the hardliners in a conversation about their concerns and resistance. Those that unequivocally

advocate violence would not, in any case, be suitable for involvement in a dialoguing enterprise. It is important, however, to accurately appraise their potential for disruption and resistance.

- Contrary to popular belief, the real challenge of dialogue projects lies less in the effective mastery of facilitation methods and communication techniques during actual encounters than in the *organizational input* required simply to finance, prepare, and conduct these sessions. In the context of divided societies and communities riven by factions, the mere announcement of the intention to stage such a dialogue project will often be met with mistrust and rejection, if not downright obstruction by the responsible authorities or holders of power.
  Because of this, meetings may well need to be conducted outside the country concerned, necessitating high logistical and financial inputs. In order to prepare for these meetings, third party representatives may need to conduct various exploratory talks on both sides and, through shuttle diplomacy, achieve a consensus at least as to the proposed list of participants and programme. These activities are themselves part of the broader dialogue process, although they all too often take a back seat in discussions about the relevance of these approaches.
- Any intervention, however well-meaning, has both intentional and unintentional consequences. Initiators of dialogue projects therefore bear an *ethical responsibility* to carefully consider the consequences of their actions – especially those consequences which, though unintended or unforeseen, will nevertheless range from the conceivable to the probable. First among these is the task of working out and minimizing the security risks imposed on the meeting invitees. In highly asymmetrical conflicts, for example, participation in the dialogue will often lead to the weaker party adopting a more radical stance. Finally, any third party intervening in an acute conflict will have to consider the problem of maintaining its 'multi-partiality' especially when confronted with massive human rights violations by one or the other side.
- In general, the interactive conflict resolution movement has been dominated by a specific type of problem-solving workshop with a facilitation style which is strongly influenced by the academic-analytical, and sometimes dogmatic, world of the initiators (Fisher 1997). Given the wider practical experience that we have now been able to gather, however, there is much to be said for setting the *intervention methodology* in dialogue projects on a much broader and more flexible basis. It would, in particular, be a good idea for the wealth of experience gained in adult education, intercultural learning, group dynamics, counselling, supervision, and mediation in the narrower sense to be put to use in producing an active form of dialoguing.
  This process begins with the question of the appropriate composition of the team, as well as an examination of the normative messages that necessarily emanate from the behaviour of the team when the team itself is faced with conflicts. It continues with uncovering the different currents within the group dynamic. This is important because resistance to *rapprochement* in dialogues often expresses itself subliminally, as an apparently sudden hardening, or by the raising of unexpected new topics of discussion. Finally, the process also touches on the question of how much or how little the dialogue should be geared towards the identification of concrete problem-solving strategies.

- One method that is now quite frequently employed to encourage changes of perspective amongst participants in dialogues is the incitement to *reflect* on a *similar ethno-political conflict* and on the insights that can be drawn from this. The underlying idea is that it is often easier to understand the point of view of all the parties involved, as well as to come to a less prejudiced appraisal of the overall situation, when considering a conflict other than one's own. It is then often possible, as in a mirror, to identify new aspects of one's own conflict situation. Ideally, the analogous case will be one in which work is at a more advanced stage, so that one can then ask which settlement aspects might well also be suitable for one's own conflict. In practice, however, the process is usually not as smooth as this. Participants stress the uniqueness of their conflict, feeling that any attempt at comparison might rob them of an essential part of what gives their own case its meaning. None the less, in retrospect, participants often cite these thought experiments as amongst the most important for any breakthroughs achieved during the dialogues.
- As explained above, the macro-political effects of dialogue projects are notoriously difficult to assess. It is therefore all the more important to take a closer look at the possible impact of this work on the *meso-social level*. One of the key measures of success here is undoubtedly the degree to which intervenors succeed in increasing ownership of the dialogue process by the participants and their respective affinity groups or organizations. Do they manage to integrate the dialogue events systematically in their endeavours to clarify perceptions, positions and events, to analyse options and to explore common ground?
  Such an objective cannot be met simply by increasing the participants' level of involvement in the design of the seminars. It also requires that the dialogue sessions be fleshed out and complemented with additional opportunities for preliminary and follow-up activities, for more in-depth treatment of individual topics, and for skill-building by the participants. Possible mechanisms through which this could be enabled are local back-up forums, working groups, and training sessions. Another possible measure of success is the expansion of the circle of participants, both in terms of the numbers taking part or the subsequent replication of similar approaches, especially in terms of movement closer to the Track 1 level. In practice, the goal is to strike an appropriate balance between achieving a solid nucleus of people who will provide new impetus for conflict resolution, and at the same time continually extending this circle (outreach).
- In divided societies and communities traumatized by war, dialogue projects will sooner or later be confronted with the question of how their work and the impetus they have provided for practical measures can be *institutionally anchored*, in bodies that will replace the temporary forums set up by the third parties in the initial phase. Without this kind of institutional anchoring, there is always a real danger that the initially positive effects of the dialogue will eventually fizzle out. Institutionalisation of the dialogue can of course take very different forms, ranging from semi-governmental inter-ethnic commissions, through joint task-forces to multi-ethnic NGOs.
- But probably the most important conceptual contribution which the dialogue-project approach can make to the creation of peace constituencies or peace alliances is that of generally *promoting a dialogue-based dispute culture*. This means that the characteristic elements of interest-led constructive dialogue described at the outset should not just be used

to positive effect in a handful of inter-group projects, but should become a basic paradigm of political culture. It has become a hallmark of many ethno-political conflicts – the Middle East is a case in point – that real transformation will only be possible to the extent that a constructive dialogue takes place among the parties to the conflict.

6. References

Apel, Karl-Otto 1990. *Diskurs und Verantwortung,* Frankfurt: Suhrkamp.

Bar-On, Dan 2000. *Den Abgrund überbrücken: Mit persönlicher Geschichte politischen Feindschaften begegnen,* Hamburg: Edition Koerber.

Bercovitch, Jacob (ed.) 1996. *Resolving International Conflicts. The Theory and Practice of Mediation,* Boulder: Lynne Rienner.

Bercovitch, Jacob & Allison Houston 1996. "The Study of International Mediation: Theoretical Issues and Empirical Evidence," *in* Bercovitch, op. cit.,11-35.

Bercovitch, Jacob & Jeffrey Z. Rubin (eds.) 1992. *Mediation in International Relations,* London: Macmillan.

Burton, John 1990. *Conflict: Resolution and Provention,* London: Macmillan.

Burton, John & Frank Dukes (eds.) 1990. *Conflict: Readings in Management & Resolution,* London: Macmillan

Charles Stewart Mott Foundation 1999 *Reaching for Peace: Lessons Learned from Mott Foundation´s Conflict Resolution Grantmaking,* 1989-1998, Evaluation conducted by CDR Associates and the Berghof Research Center for Constructive Conflict Management, Flint, Michigan: Charles Stewart Mott Foundation.

Fisher, Roger and William Ury 1981. *Getting to Yes,* Boston, Ms: Houghton Mifflin.

Fisher, Ronald J. 1997. *Interactive Conflict Resolution,* Syracuse, NY: Syracuse University Press.

Haumersen, Petra, Helmut Rademacher and Norbert Ropers 2002. *Konfliktbearbeitung in der Zivilgesellschaft. Die Workshop-Methode im rumänisch-ungarischen Konflikt,* Münster: LIT.

Hoffman, Mark 1995. "Defining and Evaluating Success: Facilitative Problem-Solving Workshops in an Interconnected Context," *Paradigms: The Kent Journal of International Relations, 9,* 2, 150-67.

Kelman, Herbert C. 1992. "Informal Mediation by the Scholar/Practitioner," *in* Bercovitch and Rubin, op. cit., 64-95.

Kelman, Herbert C. 1994. "Promoting Joint Thinking in International Conflicts: An Israeli-Palestinian Continuing Workshop," *Journal of Social Issues,* 50, 1, 157-78.

Kelman, Herbert C. 1995. "Contributions of an Unofficial Conflict Resolution Effort to the Israeli-Palestinian Breakthrough," *Negotiation Journal*, January 1995, 19-27.

Kleiboer, Marieke 1996. "Understanding the Success and Failure of International Mediation," *Journal of Conflict Resolution,* 40, 2, 360-89.

Lederach, John Paul 1997. *Building Peace: Sustainable Reconciliation in Divided Societies,* Washington, DC: United States Institute for Peace.

Lund, Michael and Guenola Rasamoelina (eds.) 2000. *The Impact of Conflict Prevention Policy: Cases, Measures, Assessments,* Baden-Baden: Nomos.

McCartney, Clem 1986. "Human Rights Education," in *11th Annual Report. Standing Advisory Committee on Human Rights,* London: HMSO.

Miall, Hugh, Oliver Ramsbotham and Tom Woodhouse 1999. *Contemporary Conflict Resolution,* Cambridge: Polity.

Mitchell, Christopher 1993. "Problem-Solving Exercises and Theories of Conflict Resolution," *in* Sandole and van der Merwe, op. cit., 78-94.

Mitchell, Christopher & Michael Banks 1996. *Handbook of Conflict Resolution: The Analytical Problem-Solving Approach*, London: Pinter.

Otten, Hendrik & Werner Treuheit 1994. *Interkulturelles Lernen in Theorie und Praxis: Ein Handbuch für Jugendarbeit und Weiterbildung,* Opladen: Leske und Budrich.

Reychler, Luc & Thania Paffenholz (eds.) 2000. *Peacebuilding: A Field Manual,* Boulder, Co: Lynne Rienner.

Ross, Marc Howard & Jay Rothman (eds.) 1999. *Theory and Practice in Ethnic Conflict Management: Theorizing Success and Failure,* London: Macmillan.

Rothman, Jay 1998. "Dialogue in Conflict: Past and Future," *in* Eugene Weiner, op. cit., 216-235.

Sandole, Dennis J.D. & Hugo van der Merwe (eds.) 1993. *Conflict Resolution. Theory and Practice: Integration and Application,* Manchester: Manchester University Press.

Spencer, Tanya 1998. *A Synthesis of Evaluations of Peacebuilding Activities Undertaken by Humanitarian Agencies and Conflict Resolution Organisations,* London: Overseas Development Institute.

Weiner, Eugene (ed.) 1998. *The Handbook of Interethnic Coexistence,* New York, NY: Continuum.

Wimmer, Andreas, Richard Goldstone, Donald Horowitz, Ulrike Joas, and Conrad Schetter 2003. *Facing Ethnic Conflicts: Perspectives from Research and Policy-making* (forthcoming).

Wolleh, Oliver 2002. *Möglichkeiten und Grenzen interner Akteure bei der Friedensbildung in geteilten Gesellschaften. Die Conflict Resolution Trainer Group in Zypern (1993-1997)*, Berlin: LIT.

Zartman, I. William 1985. *Ripe for Resolution: Conflict and Intervention in Africa,* New York, NY: Oxford University Press.

Structural Reforms, Institutionbuilding and Violence Control

Günther Baechler 273
Conflict Transformation through State Reform

Wibke Hansen, Oliver Ramsbotham, Tom Woodhouse 295
Hawks and Doves: Peace Keeping and Conflict Resolution

Dusan Reljic 321
The News Media and the Transformation of Ethnopolitical Conflicts

Christine Bigdon, Benedikt Korf 341
The Role of Development Aid in Conflict Transformation:
Facilitating Empowerment Processes and Community Building

Conflict Transformation through State Reform

Günter Bächler

1. Introduction: Reform is more than just changing administration 274
2. Challenges in Crisis Regions 274
3. Participation and Democratisation 276
   - Participation of the rural population
   - Strengthening the civil society
   - Democratisation as a participatory process
   - Dialogue-oriented and intermediary institutions
4. Institutional Reform 280
   - Constitutional reform
   - Integration of minorities through power-sharing
   - Territorial divisions of power: federalism, devolution and autonomy
   - Accountability through decentralization
   - Protection of minorities
   - The rule of law
   - Human rights
5. Security Sector Reform 289
6. Summary and Outlook 290
7. Reference and Further Reading 292

Conflict Transformation through State Reform

Günter Bächler

1. Introduction: Reform is more than just changing administration

State reform and conflict are closely interrelated. While state reform can on the one hand be seen as a prerequisite for conflict transformation and sustainable peace, it can also easily become a source of conflict. The potential of state reform itself depends on the proper establishment of structures, values and attitudes that can enable the different groups within the society to handle their conflicts peacefully.

State reform must in any case encompass more than just a reorganisation of the administrative system or of the way in which resources are allocated. Rather, it must set the stage for the establishment of participatory and legitimised nation-building processes. By forging democratic development, the participation of the population and rule of law, it will also develop structures that can offer an effective means for the peaceful management of deep-rooted conflicts. As democracy takes root, it will itself have a pacifying effect since it is based on values such as pluralism, tolerance, inclusiveness and compromise, and because it helps to establish norms of behaviour such as negotiation, compromise and cooperation among the political actors.

Nevertheless, state reform can also have negative consequences. In situations of externally induced rapid change, it can well become a source of acute conflict, and provoke violent reactions on the part of the ruling regime. Poorly designed state reform can even lead to the deterioration of a conflict. In the case of Angola, for example, the resurgence of war after the peace accord of Bicesse was an unfortunate consequence of the prior establishment of a winner-takes-all system. State reform must therefore be seen as a 'tightrope walk', always seeking a fine line between conflict mitigation and crisis escalation.

This chapter will focus on the potential of state reform to prevent, to mitigate and to heal the effects of violent intrastate conflicts. Section II offers an overview of actual challenges in crisis regions, and describes some of the ways in which state reform can deal with these problems. In the following sections, these strategies will be discussed in more detail: section III addresses the possibilities of strengthening participatory processes; section IV deals with institutional reforms; and section V focuses on security sector reform. The article concludes with some open questions which deserve much more attention in the near future (section VI).

2. Challenges in Crisis Regions

While the number of armed conflicts between states has decreased in recent years, an increasing number of states are now torn by intrastate violent conflict. This development is linked closely to a new phenomenon that has emerged especially since the end of the Cold War:

the failure of nation-states, characterized by a general breakdown of government, economic privation, civil strife and overall human misery (Helman & Ratner 1993).

This failure of states can be traced to a lack of *vertical* as well as *horizontal* legitimacy in these societies (Holsti 1991; Heinrich 2000). In the case of a lack of vertical legitimacy the connection between the state and the society is severed. The common understanding and acceptance of the state elite's right to rule on the basis of a set of norms, rules and values is at least partially compromised. Horizontal legitimacy, on the other hand, refers to the membership and the definition of political communities. This kind of legitimacy is often lacking in war-torn societies characterized by ethnic struggle. In these countries, there is no positive notion of political community. The different ethnic groups share no national identity, so that they have no bond of loyalty or feeling of national unity (Soerensen 1998; Heinrich 2000).

In order to help these failed states to overcome civil struggle, to achieve economic development and to alleviate the human plight, it is necessary to enter into a process of reconstruction of the state. Traditional approaches for development assistance have proved to be woefully insufficient in these situations. Clearly, a more comprehensive approach is needed. A new political, economic and social environment must be established and society rebuilt.

One often cited catch-word in this context is 'good governance'. As defined by the Development Assistance Committee of the Organisation for Economic Cooperation and Development (OECD/DAC), the good governance of a country consists of four core elements:

- rule of law;
- management of the public sector;
- anti-corruption;
- reduction of excessive military expenditures;

as well as three further associated elements:

- participatory development;
- democratisation;
- respect for human rights.

Good governance alone is of course not sufficient to meet the pre-conditions for sustainable peace and development, since it only serves to re-establish vertical legitimacy and does not yet provide for the horizontal legitimacy that can enable a plural society to function on the basis of a wide consensus on fundamental values. Thus, whole groups within such a state can still feel estranged from it and lack a common identity, one that would bind these different groups together as a nation.

International actors – be they inter-governmental organisations (IGOs) or non-governmental organisations (NGOs) – focus in particular on the following aspects of state reform: participation and democratisation, federalisation and decentralization, constitution and justice reform, security sector reform, and dialogue-oriented or intermediary institutions. These activities can be brought together into three threads, that summarise the most important challenges to state reform, and which will be discussed in detail in the following sections:

- the need to foster participation and democratisation in order to enhance social and political stability;
- the need for institutional reform in order to create and maintain a more durable societal fabric;
- the need for comprehensive security sector reform.

3. Participation and Democratisation

War-torn societies are typically characterized by a significant gap between the rulers and the ruled. It seems that if and when rebel movements assume power, they tend to follow more or less the same patterns of bad governance as did their predecessors. Quite often, Track I diplomacy (as performed through direct talks between top leaders) is not feasible, because one or both sides refuse(s) to accept the other parties to a conflict as legitimate negotiation partners. Therefore, participation and democratisation are widely acknowledged to be essential to any serious effort at conflict transformation. This requires the successful resolution of various critical issues.

3.1 Participation of the rural population

If a transition process to peace and development is to be sustainable, it must enjoy the support of the entire population and not only of the political elite. Especially in societies in which 60% or more of the population are employed in the agricultural sector, it is critical to mobilize the people in rural areas, giving them the opportunity to participate in their own affairs at the lowest level possible (on the principle of subsidiarity). Rural citizens must be empowered to deal effectively with the socio-economic, environmental and communal issues that affect them, if they are to escape economic marginalisation, social decline, and, as a consequence, violence (for example cattle rustling in Kenya) or a general climate which encourages rebel mobilization

(as in the Democratic Republic of Congo). Social mobilization must seek to strengthen the self-help abilities of vulnerable groups (*empowerment*), to make these vulnerable groups the owners of a self-sustaining peace and development process (*sustainability*) and also to lay the foundation for effective reconciliation and conflict resolution at the village level (*mediation*) (SLE 1999).

Ensuring the participation of the rural population is a process-oriented task, and thus also the necessary complementary counterpart to the structure-oriented approach of decentralization/devolution. This participation can be enhanced through specific programmes initiated by governments and/or international donors. One particularly promising approach starts with a participatory baseline study designed to provide an inventory of all available human and environmental resources. Within the normative framework of sustainable development, this action oriented research can then help to support projects which aim at improving agricultural practices, changing attitudes towards resource use and distribution, revitalising local mechanisms of conflict resolution, upgrading local infrastructure and creating off-farm opportunities and related training programmes for young people (Ghebru and Kohler 1999).

3.2 Strengthening the civil society

When civil society is absent or inactive, it is a clear sign of the dominance of an oppressive regime, in a nation likely to be characterized by widespread insecurity, and in which aggravated exploitation of ethnic and cultural differences is also likely to create a climate of distrust and suspicion. In contrast, a strong civil society can serve as a guarantee for a sound societal fabric, one that can support civil conflict resolution. Civil society encompasses all elements of active citizenship, reaching from the local level (for example, councils of elders), across the mid-level (NGOs, intellectuals), to the top level. It combines various societal sectors, including the business world, trade unions, women's' associations, churches, peace and human rights activists, journalists and scientists.

Within the framework of multi-track diplomacy (Diamond & McDonald 1991) civil society may play a crucial role in building bridges between polarised groups, promoting dialogue and reconciliation across various societal levels, and fostering good governance at the official level. People-to-people talks, round tables, the creation of local capacities for peace, and cross-sector partnerships (such as The Prince of Wales Business Leaders Forum as described in Tennyson 1998) are some of the vehicles that have been effectively employed. In failed states or in areas out of governmental control, civil society can also help to mitigate grievances, to lessen ethnic hatred, to build peace across cultures and to establish stable peace constituencies. A good example of this can be found in the peace initiatives undertaken at the end of the 1990s by the Angolan churches which worked hard to organize the civil society in order to overcome the political stalemate between President Dos Santos and the rebel leader Savimbi.

International NGOs and donors providing assistance to these countries must be sensitive to the constraints that civil society faces if they want to have any chance of contributing to stable and long term peacebuilding from below. Throughout all these activities, civil society enhances or even creates a moral community among the different groups or nations within a state's territory. In this sense, it assists in the societal and moral construction of a state, complementary to parallel efforts at legal construction.

If actors, however, are insensitive or perceived as pushy then their efforts at promotion or even artificial creation of the institutions of civil societies can easily, in themselves, constitute a trigger factor for crises – especially if and when external actors become involved. In particular it is poorly developed civil societies in the context of a repressive or democratically inexperienced regime that can trigger violent reactions from above, lead to the manipulation or fragmentation of citizen participation movements and, as a consequence, to the overall destabilization of the society.

3.3 Democratisation as a participatory process

While presidential and parliamentary elections have now been held in most countries of the developing world, democratisation processes are still fragile and underdeveloped. Bad governance and poor state performance quite often coincide with a leadership that has reached power through a coup d'état, secession or civil war. Since democracy is now known to be a necessary factor for stable peace (*see*, among many others, Muravchik 1996, 573) the promotion of open and participatory democratic processes that are acceptable for both the state and the civil society is itself a valuable contribution to crisis prevention and conflict transformation.

Dialogue-oriented development cooperation efforts must integrate adapted democratisation into any long-term, coherent and coordinated development strategies. Democratisation is a complex and gradual process, and must be adapted to national conditions. It is notoriously difficult to induce such fundamentally value- and norm-challenging processes from outside the society. However, once these efforts get started, there are many entry points to be addressed: the empowerment of individuals and groups; the strengthening of communities; support for organisations that can influence public affairs and the sponsoring of existing intermediary institutions which have proven their ability to deal peacefully with conflicting interests of different stakeholders. Beyond all of this, democratic decision-making of governments can provide the means and mechanisms for power-sharing, for control of decision-making, for the proper balancing of political and economic power and for the establishment or consolidation of democratic institutions such as political parties or a court system. Finally, legitimate and strong institutions must be efficient in installing transparent and just procedures, in resisting corruption and in the performance of their core functions to the benefit of all citizens.

Box 1: Democracy Support as offered by the International Institute for Democracy and Electoral Assistance (IDEA)

A good example of professional assistance in the promotion of democracy is the Stockholm-based International Institute for Democracy and Electoral Assistance (IDEA). This international organisation, with members from both the North and the South, was created after the collapse of the former Soviet Union, as the wave of democracy swept over Eastern Europe. It has a global mandate to promote and advance sustainable democracy worldwide.While other international organisations have concentrated their efforts on helping to organize and monitor elections, IDEA focuses on providing a long-term strategy of democratic support beyond the first election. The Institute:

- helps countries to build the capacity to develop democratic institutions;
- develops and promotes norms, rules and guidelines that will apply to multi-party pluralism and democratic processes;
- promotes transparency, accountability, professionalism and efficiency in elections in the context of democratic development;
- provides a meeting-place for, and facilitates dialogue between, democracy practitioners around the world;
- increases knowledge about elections and election observation.

Source: IDEA Handbook (for further information see http://www.idea.int)

3.4 Dialogue-oriented and intermediary institutions

Political changes in former war-torn societies can be varied and far reaching, ranging from the decentralization of highly centralized or even authoritarian regimes to the fundamental rebuilding of weak or failed states with little or no central authority. What is common to all of these situations is that the civil society, because of the lack or breakdown of more established institutions, is forced to build on its own capacities.

Conflict resolution in this context must first of all deal adequately with dynamic changes of structures, also termed 'process-structures'. Within the framework of the transformation philosophy, conflicts are not to be regarded as isolated events to be addressed from a narrow managerial approach. Rather, they are a necessary and integral part of the transformation of the whole range of societal relationships. It is for this reason that the transformation of such process-structures is seen as the most appropriate method for intervention.

In short, a dialogue oriented approach is needed. A good way to achieve this might be found in the adoption of an *interactive problem-solving workshop* (IPSW), a specific type of third-party intervention which is particularly useful in situations of inter-group conflict. IPSW is an unofficial, academically derived third-party approach to the analysis and resolution of both international and domestic (inter-group) conflicts. It is anchored in social-psychological principles, and follows a scholar/practitioner model, focusing especially on the interaction between the parties. Such an approach aims to bring together politically influential members of conflicting parties in a private, confidential setting for direct, noncommittal communication. In the words of Herbert Kelman (2002, 62):

> *Workshops are designed to enable the parties to explore each other's perspective and, through a joint process of creative problem solving, to generate new ideas for mutually satisfactory solutions to their conflict. The ultimate goal is to transfer the insights and ideas gained from these interactions into the political debate and decision-making processes.*

As applied to the question of state reform, IPSW might well take the form of an interactive institution building workshop. Such a modified interactive institution building workshop geared towards state reform in crisis prone areas would be aimed first of all at changing perceptions and attitudes, at discovering shared interests underneath apparently contradictory positions, and at producing common ideas for the successful resolution of the problems of state reform and of the transformation of power structures.

A further challenge is the need to transfer these changes and ideas back into the political debate and decision-making processes within each constituency. This feeds into an adapted strategy, which aims to enhance both the vertical and horizontal legitimacy. The goal is to create an institutionalised 'culture of dispute' in the context of a generalized 'civic spirit', as expressed, for instance, in the following passage from the OECD/DAC report (1997, 37) report:

> *Broad acceptance throughout society of the legitimacy of the state and the credibility of the institutions of governance is a key aspect of forging such a civic spirit. When all people's human rights are respected, when society is governed by the rule of law, and when ordinary men and women are involved in the political process, resort to violence to effect political change is obviously less likely. Efforts to support participation, democratisation, and peacebuilding, through strengthened institutions of governance, are clearly interlinked.*

The workshop, or a series of them, can be linked with different approaches and expert dialogues at the local as well as the national level, including, in particular, constitutional dialogue among all stakeholders, human rights monitoring and reporting, discussions about the rule of law and its implementation at all levels of the state, suggestions for the development and establishment of new institutions (organisational development), redesign of the state's administration and market-oriented reforms to alleviate poverty and achieve social justice.

While I have so far dealt primarily with state reform from the perspective of societal approaches necessary in order to induce the transformation of conflict-prone structures, the following sections will be addressed to the question of the reform of state constitutions and institutions in a more technical sense.

4. Institutional Reform

Institutional reform is critical for the reconstruction and democratic development of failed states. If we are to solve the problems caused by the breakdown of government and ensuing civil strife, structures must be established in order to re-legitimise state power and make the peaceful management of conflicts possible.

Institutional reform should ideally address at least the following areas: constitutional reform; power-sharing arrangements; devolution of power and decentralization; protection of minorities; rule of law, and human rights. All of these objectives are, of course, closely interrelated. Constitutional reform in particular addresses many of them immediately: the question of whether to establish federal structures goes, for example, hand in hand with the design of the constitution of a state. But power-sharing arrangements, devolution of power via federalism or autonomy and decentralization should be looked at individually and in greater detail, as the nature of their design can be of utmost importance for the success or failure of any post-conflict arrangement.

4.1 Constitutional reform

In many post-war societies, the reform of a pre-war constitution is usually one big step forward towards national reconciliation, inter-group rehabilitation and the avoidance of the mistakes of the past. In post-apartheid South Africa, for instance, the all-inclusive process of developing the constitution proved to be of great value for confidence-building efforts between the black, white and other racial communities. The constitution is the cornerstone of the general rule of law. It determines the overall system for the living together of a people. It is thus also the starting point either for future turmoil or for societal stability and integration It is possible to indicate guidelines which may be of help to donors as they seek to support the constitution-building process from outside, without intervening in such a way that the new constitution becomes a (new) bone of contention. The constitution-making process:

- must be *sensitive to the past*, to historic and cultural values, and to national and group identities;
- must also *break with the past*, in the sense that it does not incorporate principles that have hindered national reconciliation and democratic development;
- should be *all-inclusive* and the product of commissions made up of representatives of all the major stakeholders;
- should be the *result of a national dialogue*, linked with the widest possible public consultation process, such as civic education seminars, public debates, town and village meetings (as in Eritrea after 1993);
- should *address all the sensitive issues* that have led and could therefore once again lead to further grievances, instability and conflict.

Nevertheless, even the best-written new constitutions will not solve all problems; this is a fact which is all too often underestimated both by the international community and by national authorities. If group grievances and historic traumas are not taken seriously, then even a well-meant process of drafting a constitution can, unfortunately, lead to the further deterioration of a political situation (as in the case of Ethiopia and the Oromo population). If the interim period between the designing of a constitution and its implementation lasts too long, the transition will get stuck automatically. If the implementation of the constitution is not embedded in socio-economic and institutional transformation at the local level (as well as in political transformation at the medium and the top levels), it will probably not be worth the paper it is written on.

A democratic and transparent constitution-making process, however, can always be of great help in efforts to foster national education, develop a civil society, and promote citizens' responsibility and tolerance for and among different societal and identity groups.

Some of these sensitive issues which must be clarified and directly addressed include: power-sharing agreements; the political control of security forces; the integration of ex-combatants; democratic control of the security sector; dealing properly with past crimes against humanity; the discrimination of societal groups; access to resources and corruption. This list must include tasks that are directly related to security sector reform, which will be discussed in section V below.

Constitutional commissions must carefully delineate the boundaries of the state to be created. Is it to be a federal system with some delegation of power to the regions, or rather an arrangement that provides greater autonomy for certain groups in specific areas of the country (*see* section IV.3)? Is it to have a unitary (presidential) system, or a parliamentary system with multiple parties? In any case, former colonial powers – which quite often provide expert input for these discussions – should refrain from exerting undue influence, or, at the very least, always be aware of the fact that their own constitution may not always be readily adaptable to the situation in a war-torn country of the South. Attitudes characterised by the phrases "Winner takes all" or "l'état c'est moi!" have contributed more to maintaining protracted violence than to mitigating it, as in the cases of Rwanda and of the Democratic Republic of Congo. (For a discussion of the relative advantages of power-sharing arrangements in contrast to majoritarian democracy, *see* section IV.2).

Constitution drafters must consider a number of factors as they move to choose an appropriate system of executive government. Both presidential and parliamentary systems have their advantages and disadvantages, and the important question is not which type is better but rather which is the most appropriate for a particular society with its particular social structure, political culture and history.

The principal difference between the presidential system and the parliamentary systems is the degree of relative independence that the executive branch of government enjoys. The former is characterized by a clear separation of the legislature and the executive, so that the latter is, by and large, independent. In parliamentary systems, in contrast, the legislative and executive branches are mutually dependent and inter-twined.

In the context of conflict transformation, however, another distinction is probably more important. Whereas in presidential systems authority is vested in a single person – the president – under a parliamentary system a broad range of parties and opinions can be represented within the executive. The obvious advantage of the latter is that it enables the inclusion of all groups within both the legislature and the executive. It is also true, however, that the inclusion of many groups and opinions also significantly increases the risk of deadlocks, as the different groups will find it increasingly difficult to agree on a coherent position on a variety of issues.

A presidential system can be quite favourable for conflict resolution, at least as long as the post of the president is held by a unifying national figure, who enjoys broad public support and thus becomes a "symbol of moderation of the 'middle ground' between rival political groupings" (Harris & Reilly 1998, 184). Such a unifying national figure might easily even be a monarch. On the other hand, the office of the president, with its single locus of authority, can also prove to be a disadvantage. This is especially the case when the presidency is in the hands of one political or ethnic group, ensuring them almost complete political power with only a limited proportion of the total vote. In these situations the president can become a symbol of ethnic domination, leading to an even deeper division in the society (*see* Harris & Reilly 1998, 179-190).

4.2 Integration of minorities through power-sharing

Many analysts have come to the conclusion that pure majoritarian democracy, under which the candidate with the highest number of votes is elected even if he or she does not have an overall majority, is ill-suited to deeply divided societies with ethnic tensions; they argue that specific arrangements which encourage power-sharing seem to be a more promising way to manage ethnic conflicts (*see* Sisk 1996). The reason for this is the very real danger of "majority dictatorship" that can evolve from majoritarian democracy (*see* Lijphart 1985, 102). In such an institutional setting, minorities can come to fear a permanent exclusion from power, and will equate democracy "not with freedom or participation, but with structured dominance of adversarial majority groups" (Sisk 1996, 31). Power-sharing, on the other hand, will ideally include in government all major ethnic groups, and assure them influence in policy on sensitive issues of legitimate concern to them, such as language use and education.

Practitioners distinguish between two fundamental approaches to power-sharing in a democracy: the *group building* approach and the *integrative* approach (*see* Harris & Reilly 1998, 140-146; also Sisk 1996, 34-45). The group-building approach (also referred to as *consociationalism*) views groups (usually ethnically homogenous political parties) as the basic building blocks of a common society, and therefore works first to secure the cooperation of ethnic group leaders. Elites form multiethnic coalitions after elections, with groups regarded as autonomous and minority rights guaranteed. Other key characteristics of this approach to power sharing are federalism and devolution of power to ethnic groups in the territories that they control, minority vetoes on sensitive issues and proportionality in all spheres of public life.

For several reasons, the group-building approach to power-sharing can also be criticized. First, it is dangerous because of its assumption that elites can effectively regulate conflict in divided societies; second, it brings with it a real further danger of reinforcing and entrenching ethnicity in the political system; and third, its design remains fundamentally anti-democratic (e.g. a grand coalition and the absence of an opposition).

The integrative approach is characterized first of all by its declared purpose of promoting social integration across group boundaries in order to overcome the ethnic divisions of a society. Parties are therefore encouraged, for example, to form coalitions across ethnic lines before standing for elections. Other characteristics of this approach are non-ethnic federalism that aims to diffuse points of power, promotion of intra-ethnic competition, electoral benefits as inducements for inter-ethnic cooperation and policies designed to encourage alternative social alignments. Potential weaknesses of this approach are the, perhaps, unchecked assumptions that politicians will always respond to incentives and that citizens will readily vote for parties from outside their own ethnic group.

There is, in the end, no single model for power-sharing democracy that is guaranteed to secure stability and peace. Different kinds of society require different types of institutional design. In addition to making use of the two ideal types of power-sharing discussed above (the group-building and the integrative approaches) practitioners should explore the whole range of power-sharing options, piecing them together in a way that best fits the conditions of a given conflict.

Unfortunately, even the best institutional design can fail when conditions are unfavourable: "For power-sharing democracy to work, there must be a sufficiently strong core of moderates – including both political elites and the broader civil society – that seeks pragmatic coexistence in a multi-ethnic society" (Harris & Reilly 1998, 143).

4.3 Territorial divisions of power: federalism, devolution and autonomy

Since many conflicts centre on the competition for state control, adjustments to the structure of the state can help to de-escalate these conflicts, especially those involving devolution of power. Federalism, devolution and the introduction of local and regional autonomy are all appropriate ways to devolve power. Federalism is an arrangement under which power is devolved equally to all regions, and in which each region maintains an identical relationship to the central government. An alternative construction is asymmetrical federalism. Here, one or more states of the federation are vested with special powers not granted to other provinces, to allow for preservation of the culture and language of its inhabitants. Autonomy is characterized by self-rule and administration by a regional entity, with some degree of independence granted by the central government in areas that do not question the status of the state as a whole (Harris & Reilly 1998, 156; Elazar 1994, xvi). Both federalism and autonomy grant to minorities at least some degree of state power and thus enhance their prospects for preserving their own culture. These arrangements are therefore well suited for the defusing of tension in conflicts involving minorities (*see* Harris & Reilly 1998, 161).

Federalism can serve consociational as well as integrative purposes. The distinctive question here is whether the territorial units also coincide with communal boundaries (*see* section IV.2). Despite the obvious advantages of federal structures and of allowances for autonomy, there is some resistance to these kinds of arrangements in states with ethnic conflict. This is primarily due to difficulties around the redistribution of resources. Majority leaders are first of all afraid of losing power and electoral support within their own community. Apart from that, they fear that autonomy might well lead to secession, or that other communities might feel encouraged to mobilize for autonomy as well (*see* Harris & Reilly 1998, 163).

As is the case with any political and social institution, federalism can easily degenerate: the case of Nigeria is perhaps the best example of this. Federalism has all too often been misinterpreted by leading political elites as some sort of order established from above – the central power – that everyone, at all levels and in all regions, is obliged to accept. For this reason, federalism now carries some fairly strong negative connotations for many of those subjected to it, and is described by them in terms of power struggle, asymmetric power distribution and the reinforcement of the significance of ethnic divisions.

To be instituted properly, federalism therefore needs of guidelines. The Charter of Basel, a document drawn up as a result of the international conference on *Federalism Against Ethnicity* held in 1995 (on the occasion of the 50th anniversary of the United Nations (UN) suggests, inter alia, two guiding principles (Baechler 1997, 319):

- Federations should guarantee the cooperation and independent self-determination of territorial groups in the framework of a pluralistic structure which functions from the bottom up, on the principle of subsidiarity (para 14).
- The members of a federation should have at their disposal the maximum amount of autonomy in the greatest variety of sectors. Furthermore, federal structures should distinguish themselves by allowing the greatest possible scope for the side by side existence of differing social values (para 15).

4.4 Accountability through decentralization

Decentralization is neither a panacea to achieve conflict transformation nor a guarantee for the protection of minority rights. If it is perceived by rigid elites as a threat to their central power (and especially to the allocation of resources), decentralization can well lead both to the mobilization of war-constituencies and to the rise of separatist movements. Thus, decentralization can provoke new conflicts at local levels, degrading social services and state performance, and opening the gap for the widespread corruption of local elites.

If this is not to occur, decentralization will need to be driven by a power-sensitive, process-oriented and balanced strategy, one thoroughly informed by national and local circumstances. That strategy must first of all generate a commitment to decentralization on the part of all the major actors, thereby stimulating broader participation in political decision-making. To the extent that it can improve the responsiveness of the central administration and effectively introduce the principle of subsidiarity, decentralization can then indeed enhance the accountability and legitimacy of a government, while at the same time strengthening local self-help capacities.

The OECD/DAC (1998, 58) lists four different channels for donor support for decentralization:

- provide specialized technical assistance in the field of planning, administration, resource allocation, etc.;
- clarify functional responsibility between central and local levels of government (including fiscal revenues and tax systems);
- strengthen organisational capacities of representative intermediary bodies such as regional Parliaments, local councils, etc.;
- enhance the representation of marginalized groups in civil service posts at all levels of the administration (including affirmative action).

In terms of peace promotion, decentralization only makes sense in the context of an overall qualitative change of structures and institutions. In many developing and transitional states, it is in fact less a process of decentralization (as evident, at least in part, in France during the last ten years) that can make a difference but rather a kind of reconstruction of state functions from below, one designed to prevent an autocratic re-centralization of power.

4.5 Protection of minorities

Since the end of the Cold War, we have increasingly come to question the common assumption that state territory must at least *prima facie* be preserved as it exists now. Consequently, we have, in many places, recognised a reassertion of alternative identities to national ones. The Minorities at Risk Project has, for instance, now identified 273 politically organized non-state identity groups that claim they have been subjected to discriminatory treatment by other (dominant) groups or stake-holders, or that have been mobilized for political action in order to defend their identity and to establish a platform for the expression of their group-interests (*see* Gurr 1997, 5). Certainly the protection of minorities – whether on the national or the international level – is essential if we are to prevent violent conflicts arising from the creation of separatist movements.

On the international level, international law unfortunately fails to provide comprehensive and adequate mechanisms for dealing properly with violations of minority rights. The UN Charter did not adopt the minority regime of the League of Nations and therefore it must now chiefly rely on a list of individual human rights, to which persons belonging to a violated or oppressed minority can appealed (*see* Heintze 1997, 444). The Organisation for Security and Cooperation in Europe (OSCE), on the other hand, has made more progress on this issue. This regional organisation has developed more detailed norms than those put forward by the UN, although these also only cover individual rights and are not legally binding. In particular, the Copenhagen Document: *The Human Dimension* of the Conference for Security and Cooperation in Europe (1990), emphasizes the need to protect ethnic, cultural and religious minorities, and proposes a comprehensive set of rights from the free use of the mother tongue language to the right to form cultural organisations and the right of organisational freedom (*see* Dicke 1995, 246).

A further milestone in the fight for the protection of minorities is the 1991 *Moscow Document*. Here, the signatories affirm that commitments entered into under the rubric of the "Human Dimension of the OSCE" remain matters of direct and legitimate concern to all participating states, and may therefore not be regarded as the exclusive internal affairs of individual states (*see* www.osce.org).

The OSCE has also established mechanisms for the review of the implementation of commitments (the mechanism on the human dimension), as well as practical instruments that allow for better protection of minorities. Especially the institution of the High Commissioner on National Minorities (HCNM) has evolved into a flexible and effective tool for early warning and preventative action in cases where minority conflicts could pose a threat to regional security. Max van der Stoel, who held the post of the HCNM from 1992 to 2001, engaged effectively in a number of potentially violent situations, working to facilitate talks between representatives of conflicting parties, and giving useful advice for the proper handling of minority-related problems (such as the promotion of native languages). Long-term missions are the other operational instrument of the OSCE. These are aimed, among other things, at the protection of minorities, and have often helped to de-escalate ethnopolitical conflicts.

On the national level, the protection of minorities should be examined in three areas of jurisdiction: first, the legal status of minorities; second the degree to which there are institutional arrangements such as the establishment of an office for minority questions or special participatory rights and, third, the extent of state sponsored activities designed to promote minorities (mainly in the field of education and culture) (*see* Dicke 1995, 243).

4.6 The rule of law

Ineffective justice systems unfortunately encourage people to take the law into their own hands. If this is to be prevented, justice systems must effectively protect, support and promote the rights of individuals within their societies, and be accessible to all. They must be impartial and politically independent. Governments have unfortunately all too often failed to acknowledge the value of the rule of law; neither have they been open to dialogue with external intervenors on this issue. In the course of socio-economic development, the advantages of the rule of law should become quite clear, at least to the liberal and globally oriented political and business elite that is thereby created in the society. The justice system is a basic responsibility of the state, and its proper functioning is crucial to the country's sovereignty.

A number of international standards have recently evolved to define the precise meaning of the rule of law (*see* Box 2). These offer an excellent road map for those involved in conflict transformation. Moreover, a growing body of UN Conventions and Reports has further elaborated these standards, dealing mainly with the questions of criminal procedures, free elections, the independence of judges and lawyers and compensation for victims of abuse.

Box 2: OSCE Catalogue of Political Standards

The OSCE has produced the most comprehensive catalogue of political standards to date, that provides useful guidance to its 53 member states. These criteria could easily be applied to other regions as well. They include:

- a representative government in which the executive is fully accountable to the elected legislature or to the electorate;
- the duty of the government to act in compliance with the constitution and the law;
- a clear separation between the state and the political parties;
- accountability of the military, the police, and other forces to political authorities;
- consideration and adoption of legislation by public procedure;
- publication of administrative regulations as a condition for their validity;
- effective means of redress administrative decisions, and provision of transparent information to the person(s) affected on the remedies available;
- an independent and easily accessible judiciary;
- protection of the independence of legal practitioners.

Abridged from Conference for Security and Cooperation in Europe (CSCE) 1990

Development cooperation can be effective in helping to develop and establish mechanisms that foster human rights, improve non-discriminatory access to legal and judicial services and promote civil conflict resolution. In many countries of the South, weak legal systems can be supported by still robust traditional codes of social conduct, upheld by village courts and councils of elders.

The OECD/DAC (1998, 61) has recommended that practitioners focus international assistance on four principal aspects of the rule of law:

- Formal law and justice institutions (courts, ombudsmen, law reform commissions, prison services);
- Communal and traditional law enforcement and dispute resolution;
- Other agencies which operate in areas of communal conflict (especially resource management);
- Facilitation of access to legal systems for individuals and groups.

There is a need for both great flexibility and great sensitivity when it comes to proposing and executing changes in a country's legal system. Project design, support for monitoring mechanisms and professional training must all be linked in ways that are appropriate to the context.

4.7 Human rights

At the core of both state reform and the rule of law must be the protection and further development of human rights. Experience has shown that in times of war and acute conflict within states, this is the area most affected and the least protected. It was the endemic abuse of human rights in many countries that led to the World Conference on Human Rights, held in Vienna in 1993. There, the participants emphasized the crucial role that national institutions could and should play in the promotion and protection of human rights. They defined these as also including the promotion and protection of minority rights (the individual rights of persons belonging to a group).

The responsibilities of these institutions are primarily to submit recommendations, proposals and reports on any matter relating to human rights (and their violation) to the government, parliament, and any other competent bodies including NGOs. They should urge conformity of national laws and practices with international human rights standards. They might further encourage parliamentary ratification and political implementation of these international standards. They should help to implement the reporting procedures required under international instruments. They might assist in formulating and executing human rights teaching and research programmes, working to increase public awareness of human rights through information and education. Finally, they will need to cooperate with the UN, regional institutions such as the African Union, and with the national institutions of the country (Center for Human Rights 1995).

These principles must be faithfully implemented if they are to be effective. The Vienna Conference therefore also proposed some specific functions and procedures which any national human rights system should have and follow:

- seeking amicable redress of alleged rights violations through conciliation, binding decision or other means;

- informing the complainant of his or her rights and of available means of redress and promoting access to such redress;
- hearing complaints or referring them to a competent authority;
- making recommendations to the competent authorities, including proposals for amending laws and regulations that obstruct the free exercise of human rights.

Box 3: Country-related Means and International Mechanisms for the Protection of Human Rights

Country-related means (a selection):

- high national standards for human rights legislation and practice (minorities);
- open bilateral political dialogue (standards, evaluations);
- specific (behind the scene) dialogue with difficult countries;
- political intervention (conditionality, sanctions, public declarations, reporting);
- specific mandates (human dimension in the Middle East peace process);
- experts for monitoring, fact-finding and truth missions;
- strengthening civil society & human rights activists;

International mechanisms (a selection):

- Universal Declaration of Human Rights;
- International Covenant on Economic, Social and Cultural Rights;
- International Covenant on Civil and Political Rights;
- Optional Protocol to the International Covenant on Civil and Political Rights;
- Second Optional Protocol to the International Covenant on Civil and Political Rights, aiming at the abolition of the death penalty;
- Declaration on the Rights and Responsibility of Individuals, Groups and Organs of Society to Promote and Protect Universally Recognized Human Rights and Fundamental Freedoms;
- Declaration on the Rights of Persons Belonging to National or Ethnic, Religious and Linguistic Minorities;
- Declaration on the Protection of Women and Children in Emergency and Armed Conflict;
- Convention against Torture and Other Cruel, Inhuman or Degrading Treatment or Punishment;
- Convention on the Prevention and Punishment of the Crime of Genocide;
- Geneva Convention relative to the Protection of Civilian Persons in Time of War.

(Additional Protocols I and II)

The principles and suggestions put forward by the Vienna Conference further include detailed guidelines on the proposed composition of national institutions, on guarantees of independence and on methods of operation – also in conjunction with ombudsmen and NGOs. Development agencies and donors can draw from this catalogue, but without ever losing sight of specific local and cultural conditions (especially with regard to both major constraints and windows of opportunities).

5. Security Sector Reform

The security sector plays an especially crucial role in the future development of post-war societies. In particular, the active support of the police and the military is crucial for the implementation of cease-fires and peace agreements, and hence for the consolidation of peace.

Nevertheless, the security sector can also pose a threat to a peace process. This is especially the case when security institutions (military and paramilitary forces, police forces and intelligence services) do not view themselves as subject to the rule of law, or when they are used by conflicting parties as instruments to advance their particular interests. It is security forces that are often responsible for the grossest violations of human rights, including torture, political crimes and the general oppression of the population.

Equally damaging to peace efforts can be a security sector that is simply ineffective. If the security of communities and individuals cannot be guaranteed by those charged with that task, both individuals and groups will increasingly take their protection into their own hands. The consequences are an increase of criminal violence, a proliferation of small arms and the emergence of private armies.

The reform of the security sector is thus often an indispensable task. While the main issue at stake is the (re-)establishment of the state's monopoly on power, supported by appropriate political and democratic controls, a number of further steps are also necessary. All together, the reform of the security sector should encompass activities on four levels (*see* GTZ 2000, 30-31):

- Reform activities on the *political level* aim to enhance the accountability of the security sector. Parliament and government must work together to control and monitor the armed forces. Civil society needs to be strengthened, with particular support for NGOs and the media in an effort at increasing overall transparency.
- The *economic level* of security sector reform includes measures such as disarmament, conversion and the reintegration of former soldiers.
- The *societal level* of the reform endeavour seeks to increase public security by controlling the spread of small arms and by combating the illegal trading of weapons.
- On the *institutional level*, security sector reform must work to 'professionalise' the security forces, redefining doctrine and missions and encouraging respect for the rule of law and for human rights within security sector organisations.

Obstacles to security sector reform in fragile democracies and weak states are many. Often, there is a tendency to view security in an authoritarian and militarist fashion, and there may well be resistance to reform from politicians and/or military officers. Military elites are sometimes subject to manipulation by foreign powers and neighbouring states. Quite often, there is a generalized culture of violence in countries vulnerable to endemic civil wars. 'Markets of violence' can emerge from war economies in countries with a history of civil wars, criminal violence, mercenaries and demobilized soldiers without income or land.

Other problems that can affect the success of security sector reform are the complexity of the reform, a lack of expertise and a lack of capacity. These factors mutually reinforce each other: the problem of complexity is compounded by a lack of organisational, managerial and financial expertise within a government. This is particularly the case if decision-makers are not familiar with international debates on security and defence and with the range of policy options from which they can choose. Even the best reform endeavour can fail if a state lacks the institutional capacity to implement it (*see* Nathan 1999, 7).

It goes without saying that international intervention in the security sector reform is a highly delicate endeavour. It needs to be combined with a general policy dialogue, with efforts at conflict transformation at all levels of the society, as well as with economic development aid. In addition to support for disarmament, demobilization and the reintegration of former combatants, security sector reform efforts must also include operational training of civilian security analysts in order to staff government posts and to fulfil monitoring functions.

A further necessary element of this reform centres on military and police education systems, with an emphasis on the goals of democratic education and societal organisation. Adherence to international security standards should also be furthered through the international exchange of security personnel (exchanges, courses and trainings with international academies such as the International Geneva Centre for Security Policy). A fourth element is the necessity to stop any extra-legal or criminal forms of recruitment to the security forces. Finally, the security sector management and budgeting must be made transparent.

6. Summary and Outlook

This chapter has offered an overview of the most important facets of state reform. There is, of course, still considerable scientific as well as political uncertainty about just what type of state structures and institutions are most likely to protect a society against violence and the outbreak of open conflict. More in-depth as well as comparative analyses of this question are certainly necessary.

There is widespread agreement among scholars that democracy is a necessary condition for stable peace. The debate centres on whether it is also a sufficient condition, and which factors must be combined in order to prepare the ground for a constitution that will insulate the society against violence.

Box 4 can only therefore serve as a summary, and cannot pretend to be the last word on this question. The table seeks to synthesize some of the measures addressed above, and thus to serve as a general model to guide practitioners seeking to set priorities as they move to make interventions in this important area.

Let us conclude on three open areas that involve the relationship between state reform, democracy and a stable peace that certainly merit further scientific and empirical work. In the author's view, future theoretical and applied research should pursue three tracks:

- Basic research on the indicators of a culture of dispute. This requires stocktaking of, and comparative research into, conflict transformation mechanisms and institutions in apparently peaceful societies, as contrasted with those in war-torn or war-prone societies;
- Evaluation of participatory approaches to dispute settlement which are specifically designed to mitigate poor state performance, to complement the rule of law and to overcome structural societal shortcomings that may induce conflict;

- Implementation of a culture of dispute as an element of a reformulated and enriched concept of good governance, one that could then be implemented by OECD/DAC and other (multilateral and bilateral) actors.

Some of the questions which still remain in this context are:

- Is there such thing as 'democratic peace'; if so, which factors are important to it?
- How can a culture of dispute be established or preserved in times of radical societal transition and/or rapid change?
- Which specific institutions, structures, or channels can be activated in order to strengthen a culture of dispute in multiethnic societies?
- In our quest for the right structure and dynamics of a peaceful dialogue in pluralistic societies, how can capacities for consensus be built up within the framework of an enriched concept of good governance?
- What are some adapted ways and means to strengthen anticipatory governance in the sense of crisis prevention and violence mitigation?

BOX 4: A Model of State Reform and Conflict Transformation

		Aspects of Crisis-Resistant and Less Violent-Prone Transition Processes		
Vertical Legitimacy	Credible Institutions	Strategic Approaches		
		Participation & Democratisation	Institutional Reform & Human Integrity	Security Sector Reform
		Participation of rural population	Inter- and trans-national protection of minorities	(Re)establishment of monopoly of power
		Strengthening civil society	Accountability through decentralisation	Objective & subjective civilian control
		Democratisation as participatory process	Integration of minorities through devolution & federal structures	Minimal resource use by the societal sector & professionalisation
		Dialogue oriented intermediary institutions	Constitutional & justice reform (human rights)	Physical security (for the population)
		Good Balance and Distribution of Social & Economic Resources		
		Membership to a Community of People & of Citizens		
		Horizontal Legitimacy		

291

7. Reference and Further Reading

Anderson, Mary B. 1999. *Do No Harm. How Aid Can Support Peace or War,* Boulder, Co.: Lynne Rienner Publishers Inc.

Baechler, Günther (ed.) 1997. *Federalism against Ethnicity?,* Chur/Zürich: Verlag Rüegger.

Baechler, Günther 1997. "Non-violent resolution of minority conflicts through federalism? The "Charter of Basel," *in* Baechler, op. cit., 313 – 321.

Baechler, Günther 1999. *Violence Through Environmental Discrimination,* Dordrecht: Kluwer.

Baechler, Günther 1999. *Transformation of Resource Conflicts: Approach and Instruments,* Basic Documents No. 3, Discussion Forum North-South, Bern: University of Bern, Centre for General Ecology.

Baechler, Günther and Truger, Arno 1999. *Krisenprävention: Friedensbericht 1999,* Chur/Zürich: Verlag Rüegger.

Ball, Nicole 1996. "The challenge of rebuilding war-torn societies," *in* Crocker et al., op. cit., 607-623.

Bernhardt, Rudolf 1981. "Federalism and autonomy," *in* Dinstein, op. cit., 23-47.

Brown, Michael E., Sean M. Lynn-Jones and Steven E. Miller (eds.) 1996. *Debating the Democratic Peace,* Cambridge Ma/London: MIT Press.

Brzoska, Michael 2000. "The concept of security sector reform," *in* Wulf op. cit., 6-13.

Center for Human Rights 1995. *National Human Rights Institutions: A Handbook on the Establishment and Strengthening of National Institutions for the Promotion and Protection of Human Rights,* Professional Training Series No. 4, Geneva: United Nations.

Chabal, Patrick 1998. "A few considerations on democracy in Africa," *International Affairs,* Vol. 74, No. 2, 289 – 303.

Chalmers, Malcolm 2000. *Security Sector Reform in Developing Countries: an EU Perspective,* Ebenhausen: Stiftung Wissenschaft und Politik.

Conference for Security and Cooperation in Europe (CSCE): *Second Conference on the Human Dimension of the CSCE – Document of the Copenhagen Meeting of the Conference on the Human Dimension of the CSCE,* Copenhagen 5 June-29 July, 1990.

Crocker, Chester A. and Fen Osler Hampson with Pamela Aall (eds.) 1996. *Managing Global Chaos: Sources of and Responses to International Conflict,* Washington, D.C.: United States Institute of Peace Press.

Diamond, Louise and John Mc Donald 1991. *Multi-track Diplomacy: A Systems Guide and Analysis,* Grinnell: Iowa Peace Institute.

Dicke, Klaus 1995. "Konfliktprävention durch Minderheitenschutz? Möglichkeiten und Grenzen multilateraler und innerstaatlicher Rechtsgarantien," *in* Ropers and Debiel, op. cit., 233-256.

Dinstein, Yoram (ed.) 1981. *Models of Autonomy,* New Brunswick, NJ: Transaction Books.

Elazar, Daniel J. 1994. *Federal Systems of the World: A Handbook of Federal, Confederal and Autonomy Arrangements,* Harlow: Longman Group UK.

Geller, Daniel S., David J. Singer 1998. *Nations at War: A Scientific Study of International Conflict,* Cambridge: Cambridge University Press.

Ghebru, Bissrat and Thomas Kohler 1999. *Soil and Water Conservation and Management in Eritrea: Current Status and Trends,* Proceedings of the AEAS/University of Bern, Bern: University of Bern, Centre for Development and Environment.

GTZ 2000. *Reform des Sicherheitssektors in Entwicklungsländern: Eine Analyse der internationalen Diskussion und Implementierungsmöglichkeiten der Reform mit Empfehlungen für die Technische Zusammenarbeit,* Eschborn: GTZ.

Gurr, Ted Robert 1997. "Why do minorities rebel? The worldwide geography of ethnopolitical conflicts and their challenge to global security," *in* Baechler, op. cit., 3-14.

Harris, Peter and Ben Reilly (eds.) 1998. *Democracy and Deep-Rooted Conflict: Options for Negotiators,* Stockholm: IDEA.

Hayner, Priscilla B. 1995. "Fifteen truth commissions – 1974 to 1994; a comprehensive study," *in* Kritz, op. cit., 235-237.

Heinrich, Wolfgang 2000. *Crisis Prevention in Practice. The Service Package of the GTZ, Module 2: Support For Local And Regional Institutions And Mechanisms For The Non-Violent Management of Conflicts (Draft Paper),* Eschborn: GTZ.

Heintze, Hans-Joachim 1994. *Selbstbestimmungsrecht und Minderheitenrechte im Völkerrecht,* Baden-Baden: Nomos.

Heintze, Hans-Joachim 1997. "Wege zur konstruktiven Konfliktbearbeitung: Autonomie und Föderation," *in* Senghaas, op. cit., 444-463.

Helman, Gerald B. and Steven R. Ratner 1993. "Saving Failed States," *Foreign Policy*, 89, 3-20.

Holsti, Kalevi J. 1991. *Peace and War: Armed Conflicts and International Order, 1648-1989,* New York, NY: Cambridge University Press.

Kelman, Herbert C. 2002. "Social-psychological contributions to peacemaking and peacebuilding in the Middle East," in Günther Baechler (ed.), *Promoting Peace The Role of Civilian Conflict Resolution,* Bern: Staempfli Publishers, 61-82.

Kritz, Neil J. (ed.) 1995. *Transitional Justice: How Emerging Democracies Reckon With Former Regimes,* Washington DC: Institute of Peace Press.

Kritz, Neil J. 1996. "The rule of law in the postconflict phase: building a stable peace," *in* Crocker et al., op. cit., 587-605.

Laubacher-Kubat, Erika 1999. *Einmischung für den Frieden: Prävention und Bearbeitung ethnopolitischer Konflikte in der Gesellschafts- und Staatenwelt,* Chur: Rüegger.

Leonhardt, Manuela 2000. *Conflict Impact Assessment of EU Development Cooperation with ACP Countries,* London: International Alert and Saferworld.

Lijphart, Arend 1985. *"Power-sharing in South Africa,"* Policy Papers in International Affairs No. 24., Berkeley, Ca.: University of California, Institute of International Studies.

Mansfield, Edward D. and Jack Snyder 1996. "Democratization and the danger of war," *in* Brown et al., op. cit., 301 – 335

Matlosa, Khabele 1998. "Democracy and conflict in post-apartheid southern Africa: dilemmas of social change in small states," *International Affairs*, Vol. 74, No. 2, 319-337.

Muravchik, Joshua 1996. "Promoting peace through democracy," *in* Crocker et al., op.cit., 573-585.

Nathan, Laurie 1999. *Security Sector Reform in New Democracies,* Paper presented at the International Conference on "The Contribution of Disarmament and Conversion to Conflict Prevention and its Relevance for Development Cooperation," Bonn, Bonn International Centre for Conversion and United Nations Office for Project Services, 30-31 August 1999.

OECD Development Assistance Committee 1998. *Conflict, Peace and Development Cooperation on the Threshold of the 21st Century,* Paris: OECD Publications.

Ropers, Norbert and Tobias Debiel 1995. *Friedliche Konfliktbearbeitung in der Staaten- und Gesellschaftswelt,* Bonn: Stiftung Entwicklung und Frieden.

Senghaas, Dieter 1997. *Frieden Machen,* Frankfurt am Main: Edition Suhrkamp.

Sisk, Timothy D. 1996. *Power-Sharing and International Mediation,* Washington DC: United States Institute of Peace Press.

SLE 1999. *Food Security and Conflict. A Participatory Development Concept for the Integrated Food Security Programme Trincomalee Sri Lanka,* Berlin: SLE (Seminar für Ländliche Entwicklung).

Soerensen, Georg 1998. *Democratization in the Third World: The Role of Western Politics and Research,* Paper presented at the Conference "Failed States and International Security: Causes, Prospects, and Consequences," Purdue University, West Lafayette, February 25-27.

Tennyson, Ros 1998. *Managing Partnerships: Tools for Mobilizing the Public Sector, Business and Civil Society as Partners in Development,* London: The Prince of Wales Business Leaders Forum.

Trujillo, Monica, Amado Ordonezand and Carlos Hernandez 2000. *Risk-Mapping and Local Capacities: Lessons from Mexico and Central America,* Oxfam Working Papers, Oxford: Oxfam Publishing.

World Bank 1998. *Conflict Prevention & Post-Conflict Reconstruction: Perspectives and Prospects,* Paris: The World Bank.

Wulf, Herbert (ed.) 2000. *Security Sector Reform*, Bonn: Bonn International Center for Conversion.

Hawks and Doves: Peacekeeping and Conflict Resolution

Wibke Hansen, Oliver Ramsbotham, Tom Woodhouse

1. Introduction 296
2. The Evolution and Development of Peacekeeping 297
   The Development of Peacekeeping: 1956-1988
   Post-Cold War Peacekeeping during the 1990s
3. New Challenges to Peacekeeping 300
4. New Developments in Peacekeeping 301
5. Conflict Research and Theory Building 303
   Conflict Analysis and Humanitarian Intervention
   Controlling Violence and Conflict Resolution
   Peacekeeping and Conflict Resolution Skills and Training
6. Lessons Learned and Applications 308
7. Future Priorities 311
   Improving Rapid Response Capability for Conflict Crises
   Co-ordinating, Balancing and Differentiating the Military, Policing and Civilian Roles of Peacekeeping
8. Future Options 316
9. Reference and Further Reading 318

Hawks and Doves: Peacekeeping and Conflict Resolution

Wibke Hansen, Oliver Ramsbotham and Tom Woodhouse

1. Introduction

Since the end of the Cold War both the concept and practice of United Nation (UN) peacekeeping have undergone substantial changes. While deployments during the Cold War generally operated under the principles of impartial, non-forcible intervention with the consent of the conflict parties and the precondition of an agreed peace, more recent peacekeeping missions have, increasingly, been undertaken in the context of internal wars. As a consequence, these principles have come under an ever-increasing strain and the UN's performance in recent missions has made it subject to severe criticism. It has variously been accused of doing too little, as in Bosnia, or too much, as in Somalia. In response to these criticisms, new thinking about peacekeeping has evolved on both the national and international (UN) levels. The caution about peacekeeping, which arose especially after the experience in Somalia, has been reviewed, favouring new doctrines that seek to combine a more robust approach with an increased capacity for peacebuilding.

The main theme of this chapter is to indicate where knowledge developed in conflict resolution research can be of relevance for peacekeepers as they seek to fulfil their responsibilities to manage conflict. It will further outline how peacekeeping doctrine is being developed in response to recent critiques and to comment on some preliminary lessons on the need for a closer relationship between peacekeeping and conflict resolution. Rather than engaging directly in the debate on whether force should be used in peacekeeping operations and, if so, to what degree, this paper will focus on the contribution that conflict resolution theory can make to evolving concepts of peacekeeping and to their application in practice.

Peacekeeping has long been treated as an instrument of conflict management, which is unfortunately flawed in that it usually fails to address the underlying causes of the conflict. However, we will focus on its capacity as a tool for conflict resolution, paying particular attention to the dual goal of containing violence on the one hand and furthering peacebuilding efforts on the other. While we recognise, of course, that peacekeeping has over the years been performed by various organisations, this chapter will centre on United Nations peacekeeping, reasoning that many of the aspects explored here are obviously relevant to the peacekeeping efforts of other organisations as well.

The first section outlines the parameters of contemporary peacekeeping. The second section elaborates on the significance of conflict research and theory building for peacekeeping practice. This will be further explored in three contexts:

- conflict analysis and its relevance for the establishment of intervention frameworks;
- differing time frames and the importance of distinguishing between these in managing violent conflict, especially in relation to the latest discussions on robust peacekeeping;

- specific skills and the training necessary for contemporary peacekeeping missions, focusing especially on the contribution of conflict resolution.

This section concludes with a discussion of perspectives on, and examples of, the application of conflict resolution theory in peacekeeping. The final section discusses future priorities and needs and concludes by commenting on the future of peacekeeping in the light of latest efforts to strengthen the UN's peacekeeping capacity.

2. The Evolution and Development of Peacekeeping

2.1 The Development of Peacekeeping: 1956-1988

The first mission explicitly labelled as 'peacekeeping' was the UN Emergency Force (UNEFI). It was dispatched to the Sinai Peninsula in response to the 1956 Suez Crisis to observe the cease-fire and withdrawal of the British, French and Israeli forces from Egyptian territory. As the first armed UN peacekeeping operation, UNEFI was an important precedent for other UN missions. It further served as a test case for the value that armed and neutral forces can play in restraining conflict. The mission was successful in the fulfilment of its mandate and thus established a set of principles that have since served as valuable guidelines for future missions. The principles were identified by Secretary General Dag Hammarskjold and General Assembly President Lester Pearson and are as follows:

- *consent by the parties* to the dispute for the establishment of the mission;
- *non-use of force* except in self defence;
- *voluntary contributions* of contingents from small, neutral countries to participate in the force;
- *impartiality;*
- *control of peacekeeping operations* by the Secretary General.

Of these principles, consent, impartiality and the non-use of force are often referred to as the three main principles of peacekeeping. Although a number of these principles have been contested and challenged, particularly in the debate concerning the application of peacekeeping in post-Cold War conflict, they still define the essence of peacekeeping today.

During the Cold War, a total of 13 peacekeeping operations were established. Missions during this time were mostly – with a few exceptions – deployed in inter-state conflicts. Their sole function was to monitor borders and establish buffer zones after the agreement of cease-fires. The missions were typically composed of lightly armed national troop contingents from small and neutral UN member states.

2.2 Post-Cold War Peacekeeping during the 1990s

From the late 1980s until 1994, the number of peacekeeping operations undertaken worldwide increased dramatically. At the beginning of 1988, as the Cold War was coming to an end, there were only five operations active in the field: three in the Middle East, a small observer mission in Kashmir, and UN Peacekeeping Force in Cyprus (UNFICYP). Between 1988 and

Box 1: The Growth Of UN Peacekeeping, 1988-2000				
	1988	1992	1994	2000
No. of Active Missions	5	11	17	14
Countries Contributing Troops	26	56	76	89
Military Personnel	9,570	11,495	73,393	30,350
Civilian Police Personnel	35	155	2,130	7,038
International Civilian Personnel	1,516	2,206	2,260	3,243
Annual UN Peacekeeping Budget	$ 230.4 million	$ 1,689,6 million	$ 3,610 million	$ 2,220 million

1996, 29 operations were created, compared to the establishment of only 13 operations undertaken between 1948 and 1987 and none in the decade between 1979 and 1988.

This significant increase in the number of peacekeeping operations has been accompanied by a fundamental change in their nature, or more specifically, in their *function* and *composition*. The single function associated with traditional operations has evolved into a multiplicity of tasks. At the same time, the composition of post-Cold War peacekeeping operations became more diverse and complex: peacekeepers were drawn from a wider variety of occupation (military, civilian police and diplomatic), nations and cultures. Contemporary peacekeeping can now be appropriately characterised as *multilateral*, *multidimensional*, *multinational* and *multicultural*.

Multilateral implies the involvement of several levels of actors in an operation; these could be the two or more conflicting parties, the peacekeepers themselves, as well as the UN and other international actors.

The terms multinational and multicultural suggest that both the military and the civilian components of the peacekeeping force are drawn from a diverse range of nations or agencies. Each of these will bring to the operation its own unique political and cultural background, its own varied understandings of the conflict situation and its own diverse approaches and techniques for conflict resolution. The first such multidimensional operation, established at the end of the Cold War (February 1989), was the United Nations Transition Assistance Group (UNTAG) in Namibia. It was followed, in 1992, by the launching of the large-scale operations in Cambodia, Somalia and in the former Yugoslavia.

The operations are multidimensional, incorporating military, civilian police and other civilian components, all of which fulfil their distinct functions (*see* Box 2). The military component, i.e. the land, naval and air forces contributed by UN member states, includes both armed and unarmed soldiers; the latter often referred to as military observers. Essentially the military component's function is to serve in a supporting role: to guarantee and maintain a secure environment in which the civilian components can conduct their work. Civilian police components have also become increasingly important players in peacekeeping operations, with a role that lies between the military and civilian actors. Operating under the authority of the UN Security Council, international police monitors assist in the creation of secure environments and in the maintenance of public order. Finally, there is a sizeable civilian component, which can sometimes outnumber the military. This component consists of two main groups. First, there are inter-governmental organisations (IGOs), or organisations which are mandated by agreements drawn up between two or more states. This includes all UN agencies, regional organisations such as the African Union (AU) or the Organisation for Security and Cooperation in Europe (OSCE), as well as the International Committee of the Red Cross/Red Crescent (ICRC). Secondly, there are non-governmental organisations (NGOs), national and international organisations that are constituted separately from the government of the country in which they are founded. In

Box 2: Functions of multidimensional peacekeeping operations

Component	Function
Military Component	• monitoring and verification of cease-fires • cantonment • disarmament and demobilisation of combatants • overseeing the withdrawal of foreign forces • mine-awareness education and mine-clearance • provision of security for UN and other international activities in support of the peace process
Civilian Police Component	• crowd control • establishment and maintenance of a judicial system • law enforcement • monitoring, training and advising local law enforce ment authorities on organisational, administrative and human rights issues
Civilian Component	*Political Element*: • political guidance of the overall peace process • assistance in the rehabilitation of existing political institutions • promotion of national reconciliation *Electoral Element*: • monitoring and verification of all aspects and stages of the electoral process; co-ordination of technical assistance • education of the public about electoral processes and provision of help in the development of grass-roots democratic institutions *Human Rights Element*: • monitoring of human rights • investigation of specific cases of alleged human rights violations • promotion of human rights *Humanitarian Element*: • delivery of humanitarian aid (food and other emergency relief supplies) • implementation of refugee repatriation programmes • resettlement of displaced persons • reintegration of ex-combatants

contrast to the military component, which draws its strength from the effective coercive influence it can exercise over belligerents, the civilian component's power base may be diplomatic, economic, ideological, scientific and technical, humanitarian, legal or a combination of them. With regard to the different functions and tasks performed, the civilian component can be further divided to include four sub-components or elements: political, electoral, human rights and humanitarian.

Deployments after 1988 were redefined under new forms of military doctrine that sought to elaborate the principles under which they should operate. These post-1988 missions are now variously referred to as 'multidimensional operations', 'second-generation peacekeeping operations', 'wider peacekeeping', or 'second-generation multinational forces'.

3. New Challenges to Peacekeeping

Two individuals credited with the launching of the initial peacekeeping operations have been separately awarded the Nobel Peace Prize: Lester Pearson in 1957 and, posthumously, Dag Hammarskjold in 1961. In 1988, the UN peacekeeping forces collectively were presented with the award. Nevertheless, during the 1990s, the image of the UN, and particularly its peacekeeping arm, has been seen in a less positive light.

While peacekeeping functions have diversified significantly in recent years as they strove to adapt to new tasks and challenges, the contexts and environments in which these missions are deployed have also become more complex. Although there have been exceptions,

such as ONUC in the Congo and UNIFIL in Lebanon, most peacekeeping operations set up before the 1990s generally operated in permissive environments where they had the consent and support of host governments for their presence. Increasingly during the 1990s, missions have also been deployed in the context of internal wars or in the shadow of complex political emergencies, also defined as situations of civil and international war. In these situations, the UN is all too often forced to work under conditions of lawlessness and violence, where militias and paramilitary groups act autonomously. Here, consent may be partial and UN agencies are all too often confronted and opposed.

These challenges posed by intra-state war in general, and by the impact of extremely violent civil conflicts, have variously called into question most of the received assumptions about the processes of peacekeeping. Conflicts in the post-Cold War period have tested the UN's capabilities to the limit, and the failures in Somalia, Rwanda, and Bosnia have led to widely damning assessments in the academic literature.

At the end of the decade, the UN organisation itself published the reports of inquiries into two events that marked the nadir of its experience with efforts to resolve conflicts (United Nations 1999a, United Nations 1999b). The genocide in Rwanda, where approximately 800,000 people were killed during April and July of 1994, was described as "one of the most abhorrent events of the twentieth century". A year later, in one of the worst war crimes committed in Europe since the end of the Second World War, the Bosnian Muslim town of Srebrenica, which had been designated the world's first-ever civilian safe area under Security Council Resolution 819 (16th April 1993), was besieged by Serb militias. During this siege, 8,000 Muslims were killed under the eyes of the UN peacekeeping contingent deployed there.

Both reports concluded that, faced with growing efforts to murder, expel or terrorise entire populations, the neutral, impartial and mediating role of the United Nations was proving to be woefully inadequate. In addition to this, there was also a call for: first, a process of reflection in order to better clarify and improve the capacity of the United Nations to respond to the various forms of conflict; and second, to "address the mistakes of peacekeeping at the end of this century and to meet the challenges of the next one" (United Nations 1999b, 81).

In short, it seems reasonable to argue that the major challenge for peacekeeping today remains in the development of a concept which clarifies the specific ways in which new peacekeeping efforts should properly function in the semi-permissive or non-consensual environment where they have increasingly been called to operate since 1988. This must include specific suggestions for the implementation of the concepts into practice.

4. New Developments in Peacekeeping

Disillusionment with the experience of UN peacekeeping has led to a marked reduction in the number of deployments since the peak of 1994 (*see* Box 1). Many observers have gone further and called for an abandonment of peacekeeping as a practice – except as undertaken in its limited and classical pre-1988 form – in favour of regional and 'great power' conflict management. Substantial critiques of peacekeeping have been presented by, for example, Richard Betts (1994), David Rieff (1994) and Edward Luttwak (1999).

On the other hand, there are still those who argue that the UN remains the only body capable of combining political, military and humanitarian functions in order to reduce and even eliminate the misery of conflict. These experts call for efforts to develop and reform the peacekeeping method of intervention in order to correct its operational and conceptual deficiencies. This is also, generally speaking, the course of action advocated in this chapter and selected new developments, innovative approaches and suggestions for reform will be explored in subsequent sections.

As can be seen in Box 1, the civilian and civilian police components of the more recent missions have grown significantly and now comprise over one third of the total number of military troops deployed. While the military contribution to recent peacekeeping missions has declined in absolute numbers, as well as in comparison to the number of civilians and civilian police deployed, peacekeeping doctrine has been developed in a way that will allow military peacekeeping a more robust role in the future.

The aim is to avoid any failure to protect civilians (as occurred in Bosnia and Rwanda) and also to ensure that there are adequate self-defence mechanisms for peacekeeping forces and UN staff (learning from situations such as in Sierra Leone and West Timor, where UN staff were kidnapped and murdered by mobs and militias). The shift in peacekeeping doctrine was principally initiated by the national defence academies of countries that had participated in the larger-scale deployments in the 1990s, and that would no longer agree to send their military forces into conflicts for which they are inadequately prepared and supported. This new way of thinking is best exemplified by the British peacekeeping doctrine.

The British military refers to this new form of peacekeeping as 'peace support operations' (PSO). The term is generally used to cover a wide range of potential operations, from conflict prevention to peacemaking, and to provide a doctrine that will be relevant to the post-Cold War geo-strategic environment. As expressed by Wilkinson (2000), one of its main theorists, the new doctrine starts from the premise, that in a world marked by civil wars, collapsed states and declining respect for international and humanitarian law, traditional notions of peacekeeping have become outmoded, so that the wider peacekeeping concepts developed in the 1990s are in need of updating.

In emerging doctrines of peacekeeping, peace enforcement is significantly redefined and assigned a larger place within the broader framework of intervention options. Consent and peacebuilding (not military victory) remain, however, the ultimate objectives. The crucial distinction lies between peace enforcement and war, with peacekeeping and peace enforcement operating on the 'correct' side of the impartiality line. Thus, peacekeepers will never lose sight of the objective of sustaining or restoring consent in the interests of the long-term demands of peacebuilding.

What defines the essence of peace support is the need to preserve not so much consent but impartiality. In PSO doctrine, consent of the belligerents for the deployment of an operation is not an unconditional requirement (Ministry of Defence, 1999). The aim of the new doctrine is to create peacekeeping operations that are sufficiently flexible, robust and combat-ready. These operations must be able to deal with a wide range of scenarios, including those in which 'spoilers' will attempt to undermine peace processes by means of violence and intimidation, or by threatening the local population and international staff serving the international community in the region (Wilkinson 2000). This concept has been embraced by an ever-increasing portion of the international military community, including North Atlantic Treaty Organisation (NATO), and has consequently become the doctrinal basis for the launching of modern peacekeeping operations.

It is arguable that the deployment of KFOR in Kosovo was an early example of the application of this strategy. Certainly, the use of Australian forces to lead the peace operation in East Timor in 1999 is a further example, as was the reinforcement of UN forces in Sierra Leone by British forces in the summer of 2000. PSO doctrine recognises that the military's role, while robust, must also be a limited one: its objective is to create and safeguard the secure space within which humanitarian and civilian organisations can work to re-establish peace.

These developments have unfolded not only on the national level but also within the United Nations itself. In the face of severe criticism, Kofi Annan has repeatedly emphasised the need for peacekeeping forces to develop new capabilities for what he refers to as "positive inducements", in order to gain increased support for peacekeeping mandates among populations in conflict zones. While he argues that peacekeeping forces are now in need of greater coercive capacity, he also recognises that reliance on coercion alone is insufficient. He reasons that not only will the effectiveness of coercion erode over time but also it is in principle always better to attempt to work to influence the behaviour of people in conflict situations by making use of the carrot rather than the stick.

While coercion can at least temporarily limit violence, Annan argues that it is unable to bring about a lasting peace. A durable peace and a lasting solution requires not only the cessation of violence but also "taking the next step". For Annan, this means offering positive incentives or inducements. Peacekeeping forces, in other words, must be empowered to make rewards available in the mission area. This concept of peacekeeping, seen as essential for the future effectiveness of peacekeeping operation, brings peacekeeping squarely into the realm of conflict resolution (Annan 1997, 27-28).

5. Conflict Research and Theory Building: Relevance for Peacekeeping

United Nations peacekeeping and conflict resolution as fields of academic research have much in common conceptually and both emerged as distinct topics at about the same time. Recently there has been an increase in cross-references between the two fields by both theoreticians and practitioners. It has become more common for conflict resolution theorists to refer to peacekeeping as an important instrument of positive conflict transformation, as practitioners have come to employ psychological and communication strategies as well as conventional military force. In the same way, one of the most striking features of recent analyses by practitioners of peacekeeping has been the frequency with which they have made reference to the relevance of the various aspects of conflict resolution.

Canadian General Clayton Beattie (1983, 209) has argued that training for peacekeeping must be considerably different in nature from conventional combat training, if only because peacekeeping:

> *involves the psychological change from an adversary to a pacific role; from confrontation to third party interposition. In peacekeeping there is no enemy: the objective is to avoid hostilities, to improve communications between the parties, and to advance the process of reconciliation. This necessitates a full understanding of the causes of the conflict – political, military, and economic – as well as the social and cultural environment. It demands a fair-minded and impartial approach while operating within an atmosphere of distrust and suspicion among the protagonists, often under difficult and provocative conditions.*

We would support this argument, although the objectives of peacekeeping are likely to be defined militarily (control and cessation of violence, securing the environment, etc.), politically (the restoration of legitimate government), and economically (assisting efforts for development). In the end on-the-ground peacekeeping operations are essentially a psychological process, requiring great sensitivity to and awareness of local perceptions and culture. This is because the original principles of peacekeeping (*see* section 2) can only be observed by a closer integration of the communication and problem solving strategies usually associated with conflict resolution with the doctrine and practice of peacekeeping.

It is noticeable just how much of the peacekeeping doctrine of the British Army, as elaborated in *Wider Peacekeeping*, is suffused with the language of conflict resolution (British Army 1994). The same approach is taken in the American doctrine covering PSO. Here the managing of consent is based on the principles of impartiality, legitimacy, mutual respect, use of minimum force, credibility and transparency and related to a wide variety of conflict resolution techniques. These include, for example, techniques of promoting good communication, negotiation and mediation, and of positive approaches to community relations through an active civil affairs programme that is sufficiently resourced to win 'hearts and minds'. These consent-promoting techniques constitute the soft skills and processes of peacekeeping as opposed to the hard or technical and military skills.

These activities are undertaken in order to provide an accurate base of information, so that peacekeepers will be able to counter rumour, uncertainty and prejudice, as well as to foster an atmosphere of trust and stability in conflict regions and bring about more positive perceptions of the role of peacekeepers and the nature of the peace process.

Elsewhere we have identified ten areas of academic research in conflict resolution which have particular relevance to the practice of peacekeeping (Ramsbotham and Woodhouse 1996). Here, we will elaborate on three of these, which seem especially germane to the latest developments in the practice of peacekeeping and humanitarian intervention.

5.1 Conflict Analysis and Humanitarian Intervention

Conflict resolution theory has provided the earliest and most relevant analysis of the roots and dynamics of ethnic and other communal conflict. This analytical contribution is best exemplified in the theoretical models of protracted social conflict (PSC) and international social conflict (ISC).

Following the work of Edward Azar (1990) and others, we have proposed a model that seeks to explain the emergence and persistence of the various kinds of conflicts in which peacekeepers have become involved since the end of the Cold War. Our model takes an approach not generally followed in international relations. We observe that protracted social conflict usually originates whenever communal groups (defined by shared ethnic, religious, linguistic or other cultural characteristics) are denied their distinct identity or the fulfilment of their collective developmental needs.

Azar's model lays out four specific indicators for the outbreak of protracted social conflict:

- *communal content*: Societies characterised by multi-communal social composition provide the starting point for PSCs.
- *human needs*: This implies that the denial of access needs (participation in the significant institutions of society), of acceptance needs (recognition of identity, as defined by shared cultural values and heritage) and of security needs (physical welfare), opens up the fault lines of a given society.
- *governance*: The provision or denial of collective goods depends primarily on the role and nature of the state. In general, states that experience or are prone to PSCs will have "incompetent, parochial, fragile and authoritarian governments that fail to satisfy basic human needs" of the entire community (Azar 1990, 19).
- *international linkage*: Once conflict is triggered in a multi-communal society, weak, rigid and sectarian states will seek to contain it, in part, by cutting off external support for the domestic conflict actors and by seeking external support for themselves. Resulting from this, the scope and intensity of the conflict will be enlarged and internationalised. Adapting Azar's term, we have referred to this level of conflict as international social conflict. An ISC is a crisis of the state, whether this takes the form of state-formation conflict (Bosnia),

struggle for state control (Rwanda), eventual state collapse (Somalia), or national identity secession conflict (Kosovo).

Azar's schema and other related approaches and models are important because they help us to better understand the roots and dynamics of these particular kinds of conflict. It is one of our main arguments that the nature of ISC needs to be understood in order to see why these conflicts so often invite third party intervention and to recognise the kinds of challenges that they will inevitably pose to UN peacekeepers.

Furthermore, the analysis of conflicts, as conducted from the perspective of conflict resolution theory, provides a useful framework for the international community. This framework can be informative in the formulation and development of appropriate policies for international intervention and the provision of humanitarian assistance to communities affected by civil wars. Jane Sharp (2000), reviewing the lessons learned from the intervention by NATO against Serbia in Kosovo in 1999, has noted that British Prime Minister Tony Blair sought to base the intervention on behalf of Kosovar Albanians on a new doctrine of humanitarian intervention adopted by NATO. However, when similar action was being considered to guarantee the protection of the people of East Timor, Britain, as a member of the Security Council, did not press for intervention.

If the world community is to be consistent in applying principles of humanitarian intervention, it is necessary both to clarify international law in relation to this question and to lobby member states to provide sufficient capacity for the UN to intervene (ibid, 78). It seems clear that the international community will need: first, to review carefully its role and capacity for humanitarian intervention; second, to clarify the principles and standards which guide this activity and finally, to assess realistically its capabilities to intervene. Particularly concerning the last issue, the role of peacekeeping is crucial and considerations regarding the relationship between peacekeeping and conflict resolution are of central importance.

5.2 Controlling Violence and Conflict Resolution

Conflict resolution theory has drawn attention to the importance of distinguishing carefully between different time frames in the management of violent conflict. The key implication for peacekeeping is that practitioners must always be conscious of the dual goal of short-term conflict settlement on one hand and long-term conflict resolution on the other. In this analysis, it is recognised that two fundamental problems must be addressed concurrently: first, the effective control of violence (primarily a military role in the short term) and, second, the rebuilding of co-operative relationships within and between communities to promote sustainable peacebuilding in the long-term. As outlined above, recent peacekeeping doctrine expressed by both individual states and the UN calls for a robust form of peacekeeping that is capable of responding to violence while working to promote political and civilian peacebuilding activities.

From the concept pursued in this new peacekeeping doctrine, it is evident that peacekeeping must engender two dimensions of activity. One brings it closer to a state of war (i.e. peacekeepers must always be prepared for combat and maintain an enforcement capability). At the same time, however, the impartiality principle prescribes that it must also be capable of building consent so as to limit the necessity for the enforcement of compliance. If this is not achieved, it becomes far more likely that peacekeepers will be drawn into a prolonged military enforcement role, thus increasing the danger of 'crossing the Mogadishu line', i.e. of taking sides and being drawn into the conflict directly. Unless practitioners engage seriously in the consent-promoting dimension of peacekeeping, by focusing on the goals of conflict resolution and post-conflict peace-building, they will, under this new doctrine, run the risk of becoming embroiled in full-scale warfare.

British and American peacekeeping doctrines explicitly recognise the importance of consent-promoting techniques in peacekeeping. These techniques are similar to Kofi Annan's stated objective of building and strengthening positive inducements in PSOs. The consent-promoting techniques in PSO doctrine are defined as follows: community information; media operations; civil affairs; negotiation and mediation. Negotiation and mediation are seen to be essential skills for all the different stages and levels of a PSO. They may involve service personnel, from senior commanders who meet with faction leaders to soldiers at isolated observation points who work to control an incident or even arbitrate a dispute.

Seen from a wider level and critically linking PSO objectives to the goals of conflict resolution, the doctrine also includes the objective of transforming the conflicting parties into 'stakeholders in the peace process' by providing opportunities for them to co-operate and the creation of incentives, rewards and sanctions. This broader concept of PSO will also potentially lead to the increased deployment of civilian staff in peacekeeping missions, including the use of 'white helmets' to balance and complement the use of military blue helmets. Subsequently, operations will become increasingly complex, requiring greater co-ordination of the civil and military components of peacekeeping. The implications of these developments for skills and training will be addressed in the next section.

5.3 Peacekeeping and Conflict Resolution Skills and Training

A central approach of conflict resolution analysis is that the traditional structural/political approach to peacemaking, which sees peace agreements as primarily concerned with the reform of national political institutions, must be complemented by a corresponding concern for conflict at cultural/communal levels. This is particularly relevant for peacekeepers, who are operating at the interface between concurrent efforts to broker mediated settlements on the structural/political level on the one hand and to implement them at the cultural/communal level on the other.

As can be seen in Box 2, many of the tasks performed by peacekeepers on the communal level require close interaction with the local population. It is, thus, essential that they develop some understanding of the impact of socio-psychological processes on behaviour in violent conflict and of the processes and skills that can enable divided communities to rebuild relationships. In brief, they will need to master a specific range of conflict resolution skills.

In addition the experience of recent missions has revealed that peacekeeping forces often encounter major difficulties in communication between themselves, because of their widely diverse multinational composition. They need to be aware of how to relate to each other within the force, just as they must become more conscious of the values of the communities in which they are placed.

The need for specific peacekeeping training that incorporates conflict resolution skills is further heightened when one considers the growing difference between the skills needed in combat and those needed in peacekeeping operations (*see* Box 3). In American military thinking, it is now recognised that, while combat operations will rarely involve any form of consistent interaction with civilians, in PSO, the military may well be required to control hostile crowds, distribute humanitarian relief to civilian populations and disarm local militias under the general terms of a peace agreement.

These tasks require a closer understanding of local realities as well as the development of good relationships with civilian populations. They further depend on the judicious use of negotiation skills at the tactical level (in the field) to secure objectives and to ensure the safety of one's troops. Such negotiations are likely to be conducted by company commanders or senior battalion staff officers. At the troop level, soldiers in the course of their routine duties may also be called upon to mediate or arbitrate in a whole range of local disputes. This shift towards the communicative aspects of peacekeeping usually does not come naturally to conventional military personnel, and will require considerable shifts in traditional military culture, moving it towards a culture or psychology more suitable for modern peacekeeping.

The contrast between cultures, and consequently between practises, is indeed dramatic. In conventional military thinking combat forces are not taught to negotiate with opposing armed elements, but rather to destroy them. A less extreme example of this is well illustrated in the context of the regular task of conducting a cordon and search operation, common in combat and in peacekeeping. In combat operations, the standard technique for opening a door of a building in such operations is simply to blow it open. Peacekeeping forces must now approach the same task using the far more difficult technique of persuading the occupants to open the door (Chayles and Raach 1995).

Box 3: Military operations and peacekeeping: Differences in behaviour displayed and skills required

Traditional Military Behaviour	Peacekeeping / Conflict Resolution
No contact with civilians	Intense interaction with civilians (control of hostile crowds, distribution of humanitarian relief to civilian population, disarmament of local militias, etc.); co-operation with civilian mission components
Basic military skills employed (non-contact skills)	Negotiation skills employed (contact skills)
Destruction of opposing armed elements	Negotiation with opposing armed elements
Adversary role	Pacific role
Identified enemy	No identified enemy; impartial role
End goal: military victory	End goal: resolving underlying conflict causes
Forcible	Consent based

Related to these needs, contemporary conflict resolution theory has identified and developed training programmes and techniques designed to help practitioners acquire the communication skills and concepts they will need for better interaction and for the negotiation of consent. Concurrently, many national training programmes are now being redesigned in an effort to equip peacekeepers with the skills necessary to address these new challenges. There is a wealth of relevant conflict resolution expertise, much of it already tried and tested, albeit in other contexts, which could further inform these programmes.

6. Lessons Learned and Applications

The integration of approaches from the field of conflict resolution into the practice of peacekeeping is as yet fairly unsystematic and rudimentary, although the importance of these insights is already quite widely recognised. The Lessons Learned Unit of the UN Department of Peacekeeping Operations (United Nations 2000b) has, for example, identified the support of the local population as an essential prerequisite for any successful peacekeeping operation. It has attempted to summarise the overall significance of the dimension of building good relations not only with politicians and leaders but also with the overall community in the area of conflict under the ten following points:

- The local population should perceive the mission and its staff as being impartial. When the parties to a conflict attempt to use the mission or some of its staff to their own advantage, as they often do, the mission and its information component must be able to maintain and project its image of impartiality and neutrality. The effort to maintain impartiality, however, must not promote inaction. On the contrary, peacekeepers must discharge their tasks firmly and objectively.
- The United Nations must also demonstrate a commitment to the principles of transparency and accountability in its activities. It must not be perceived as being above the law. Designating an ombudsman, or a focal point, to consider the grievances of the local population against the mission or its staff could be considered.
- Respect for the cultural traditions and social mores of the local population is an important part of maintaining good relations with the local population. Briefings on history, culture, and other aspects of life of the host country should be conducted for all staff.
- Efforts at peace-building – such as assistance in the restoration of basic civic services and support in rehabilitation and reconstruction of a devastated country – can be an effective way of winning over the local population and increasing grass-roots support for the operation.
- In its peacekeeping and peace-building efforts, the operation is best advised to work through existing local authorities and community elders and its peace initiatives must be closely tailored to indigenous practices of conflict management, provided these do not contradict accepted international standards of human rights and humanitarian law. However, in areas of recent and ongoing conflict, the operation must exercise great caution in identifying local community leaders, since it is often unclear as to who actually represents the community. Due to strife, population displacements and other extenuating circumstances, traditional societal patterns and roles may have become blurred or have submerged under new, often militaristic, hierarchies.

- As peacekeeping missions become more multi-faceted, peace-building is becoming an integral part of their activities. Emphasis should be placed on support of processes and institutions that reinforce reconciliation between warring parties and reconstruction of economic and social infrastructure, so that once the mission pulls out it does not leave behind a vacuum, but a foundation of peace and development that the country can build on.
- The United Nations must gear the composition of its peacekeeping forces to the new and changing role they are expected to play. The force could consist of mainly fighting troops when the imperative is maintenance of peace and security. This can be changed gradually, when the emphasis of the mission has changed to peace support and peace-building, to include more engineering or other units that could assist in the reconstruction of the country. Discretionary funds for peace-building should be made available to the SRSG [Special Representative of the Secretary-General] to enhance the SRSG's leverage with the local authorities and the humanitarian community. The mission could use these funds for quick-impact projects and infrastructure repairs, among other things.
- An integral part of United Nations peacekeeping should be the promotion of "indirect peace-building", i.e. the resurrection of a web of non-governmental civic, professional, business and other associations.
- During the liquidation of an operation, consideration should be given to what resources could be left behind in the country to assist in post-conflict peace-building.

In these recommendations it is recognised that solutions, if they are to be sustainable, need to be based on local realities and cultures. While these are useful guidelines, much will depend on how well they can be translated into action at an operational level.

There are a growing number of examples of good and bad practice in the application of conflict resolution approaches at local or tactical levels of operation. The following account of a particularly positive use of negotiation and liaison with local staff comes from Lt. Col. Bob Stewart, who commanded the British battalion serving with United Nations Protection Force in Bosnia (UNPROFOR) between August 1992 and May 1993. He says (Stewart 1993, 317):

> *.... we had no mandate for forcing a passage through, regardless. Negotiation was the way we always intended to achieve our aims. Launching a convoy towards a certain destination in the hope that it would get there eventually was not good enough. We had to create favourable conditions for our work with local contacts, which is why I established a comprehensive system of liaison officers who concentrated on improving relations in a particular area.*

Stewart claims that this network, effectively constituted by negotiators, produced a high level of knowledge about local people and conditions, and thus contributed greatly to the capability of the British battalion to deliver humanitarian aid throughout the area.

This is a good example of how conflict resolution can be successfully implemented at the operational level. Nevertheless, as David Last (1997, 129-130) has pointed out, soldiers, commanders and staff in the field "need more information about combat techniques, contact skills and the integration of these tactics at the operational level". To provide this kind of guidance, much practical research will need to be conducted, and experiences compared across a wider series of specific case studies. For example, how should peacekeepers behave when surrounded by a hostile crowd? How, in practice, can problem-solving, negotiation and mediation skills be employed effectively (in what situations in the field, to what purpose)?

At the more strategic levels, we can begin to discern the framework of an emerging post-1990s international conflict management system, one that has emerged primarily in response to the crisis in Kosovo. In June 1999, following an agreement between NATO and the Yugoslav army and a second one with the Yugoslav Government brokered by EU and Russian special envoys, NATO called off its air strikes. Concurrently, the Security Council (SC) announced its decision to deploy an international civil and security presence in Kosovo under UN auspices. This resolution to the conflict was to be based on the following principles, adopted on 6th May by the Foreign Ministers of the G8:

- an immediate and verifiable end to violence and repression;
- the withdrawal of all military, police and paramilitary forces of the Federal Republic of Yugoslavia (FRY);
- the deployment of an effective international and security presence, with substantial NATO participation and under a unified command;
- the safe return of all refugees;
- initiation of a political process to provide for self-government and for the demilitarisation of the Kosova Liberation Army (KLA);
- a comprehensive effort towards economic development of the crisis region.

The security force KFOR, authorised under Chapter 7 of the UN Charter and commanded by NATO's North Atlantic Council, entered Kosovo on 12th June. The SC furthermore authorised the Secretary General (SG) to establish an interim civilian administration in the region. By mid-July 1999, the SG presented a comprehensive framework for the work of what was to become known as UN Interim Administration Mission in Kosovo (UNMIK). UNMIK was given authority in Kosovo over all legislative and executive powers, as well as for the administration of the judiciary. Its work was to be integrated into five phases and encompasses: support for returning refugees; the restoration of public services (including health, education and social services); the deployment of civilian police (CIVPOL); the development of an economic recovery plan and the development of stable institutions for the promotion of democratic and autonomous self-government.

UNMIK was divided into four sections, each of them involved in the civilian aspects of restoring peace. These sections are known as the 'four pillars'. Pillar One consists of the civilian administration under UN direction; Pillar Two carries out humanitarian assistance as led by UNHCR; Pillar Three is concerned with democratisation and institution-building as led by the OSCE; and Pillar Four, led by the European Union, is charged with economic reconstruction.

This structure serves as a good example of just how a coalition of organisations is working to implement the broader goals of conflict resolution and peacebuilding. While it is still too early to comment on just how well this project in Kosovo has worked, it does seem clear that military interventions alone do not in themselves restore peace. We must therefore come to understand first how to effectively mobilise and utilise local and international resources for peacekeeping and peacebuilding under the auspices of the UN and/or other regional organisations working in partnership with the UN. Second, we must find more effective ways to improve and co-ordinate links with the control and containment of violence in war-torn regions (the security and policing function). This must run parallel to the development of processes whereby trust and co-operation can be sustained or restored and peacebuilding activities realistically supported (the civilian conflict resolution function). We look at these issues more closely in the concluding section.

7. Future Priorities

7.1 Improving Rapid Response Capability for Conflict Crises

Despite the difficulties encountered in former Yugoslavia and in Rwanda, most states continue to regard the UN as the body most appropriately charged with safeguarding international peace and security. This is because all states are represented in the General Assembly directly and in the Security Council, and because many have seen and become convinced of the value of UN peacekeeping missions. However, if effective peacekeeping is indeed to be practised by the UN and not left to the lead nations who are recognised military powers, or to military coalitions such as NATO, then the organisation will need to significantly expand its capability to operate decisively in potentially unstable conflict situations. While the peacekeeping missions of the future may become smaller, they must also be more professionally organised, more efficiently deployed and better prepared, trained and equipped than ever before.

Fortunately, there are clear indications that the UN, after a period of doubt, self-criticism and introspection, is beginning to develop its peacekeeping capability. Approximately 27 member states, collectively referred to as the Friends of Rapid Deployment, are building support for the establishment of a rapidly deployable mission headquarters (RDMHQ), and a UN Standby Arrangement System (UNSAS) was created in 1994 in an effort to improve the quality and range of peacekeeping resources available to the Department of Peacekeeping Operations (DPKO). More recently, the Danish government organised a multinational Standby High Readiness Brigade (SHIRBRIG), with a projected response time of 15-30 days and claiming a troop strength of 4,000-5,000. The Nordic countries, the Netherlands and Canada have been particularly supportive of efforts to improve the rapid deployment capability of UN forces through the creation of a variety of better stand-by arrangements of this kind (Langille 2000).

At the national level, many troop-contributing countries have made significant improvements in their peacekeeping capabilities during the 1990s. To raise standards, international training centres and programmes have been established, and they have proposed unified codes of conduct. In New York, a Situation Centre was established within DPKO in 1993, representing an important improvement over the previous situation, in which the UN headquarters was only accessible to peacekeepers in the field during office hours and on normal working days. This Situation Centre now functions on a 24-hour basis, with a staff of 24 that report on the major operations to the UN SG.

It is also clear, that current central resources remain insufficient for any adequate attempt to cope with the many challenges that the international peacekeeping effort must face. Within weeks of the arrival of the first UN Mission in Sierra Leone (UNAMSIL) troops, for instance, rebel groups took 500 captive, and the remainder were pinned down in the capital, Freetown. The evident weakness of that mission was largely due to the fact that, at that time,

UNAMSIL was a disparate group of over 30 national contingents, and lacked a common understanding as well as unified standards and training procedures. Operationally, UNAMSIL was supported by the DPKO in New York, but only manned with a capability which, at least according to an assessment by Wilkinson, most national defence ministries would consider inadequate (Wilkinson 2000).

There is some evidence that this lesson has been taken on board in the Brahimi Report (UN 2000a) concerning the future of peacekeeping. This report was produced by a panel convened by Kofi Annan and chaired by Lakhdar Brahimi, the former Foreign Minister of Algeria. The Panel published its findings in August 2000, laying out a wide-ranging set of recommendations for increasing the United Nations capacity for peace operations. The aim is to avoid the failures of the past by preparing forces in a more calculated way during the pre-deployment phase, and by more realistically appraising the level of forces and resources needed to achieve mandate objectives. The report recommends that forces must only be deployed if and when they have been given realistic and achievable mandates and only when it is clear that they will be provided with the resources necessary to achieve those mandate objectives.

Concerning rapid deployment, the report further recommends that the United Nations define 'rapid and effective deployment capacities' as the operational ability to deploy fully traditional peacekeeping operations within 30 days of the adoption of a Security Council Resolution, and within 90 days in the case of complex peacekeeping operations. To facilitate this objective, member states are encouraged to enter into partnerships within the context of the UN Standby Arrangement System (UNSAS) and to form several coherent brigade-size forces, ready for effective deployment within the prescribed response time.

However, the report does not only focus on improving military capacities: it also recognises the need to strengthen the civilian capacities of UN Peace Operations. Some of these recommendations will be considered below.

7.2 Co-ordinating, Balancing and Differentiating the Military, Policing and Civilian Roles of Peacekeeping

The ongoing effort to establish a more robust doctrine and practice of peacekeeping must be closely integrated with the long-term goals of conflict resolution and sustainable peacebuilding. It is essential to remember that even when conflicts have been effectively contained through the intervention of peacekeeping forces, the effects of violence on communities are usually long lasting. Societies that have once been exposed to the brutalising experience of civil war all too often come under the physical and psychological control of warlords. In the words of David Last, they become convinced that only hawks survive. In such situations, Last (2000, 82) suggests:

> *There are actually two gaps in our ability to help war-torn societies rebuild peace and co-operation. The first is a gap in our ability to control violence between the parties. This is required to put the hawks in a box. The second is a gap in our ability to rebuild the trust that permits co-operation between the parties. This lets the doves out of their boxes.*

Last further identifies a gap between the divergent objectives of containing violence and rebuilding relationships. As a Canadian military officer with practical peacekeeping experience, but also a leading academic who has pioneered efforts to bring the insights of conflict resolution analysis to the service of the operational needs of peacekeepers, David Last is especially well qualified to comment. His recent work in Bosnia is of particular relevance and interest here, and this section concludes with a review of his ideas on the experiences there (Last 2000, 80-96).

In order to close some of the gaps that Last has identified, it will be necessary in contemporary and future peacekeeping operations to make clear provision for an effective differentiation between the military, policing and civilian conflict resolution roles, and to continue to improve complementarity between these areas. The first level of such differentiation is that between military and policing functions: peacekeepers must provide security on different levels.

The traditional military role in peacekeeping has always been the effort to control violence by organised military force. The various tasks involved (*see* Box 2) deal with security at the level of military formations. Once these have been fully addressed, practitioners need to be concerned with another level of security: that of policing in communities. Experience has shown that while military forces can be quite effective in responding to military opposition, they are usually not so effective in dealing with riots, threats against individuals, intimidation and attacks on property. It is notoriously difficult for practitioners of post-conflict peacebuilding to overcome the criminal damage and violence that tends to flourish in conflict.

A recurring communal and personal security problem in recent deployments has been the question of the security and human rights of returned refugees and the policing of a secure environment in which people can establish business and democratic political projects, free from intimidation. To help address these problems, David Last and others have argued for the development of a broad spectrum approach to the control of violence and to the establishment of the rule of law. In most peacekeeping operations, international military forces are deployed in order to preserve order, after which civilian police forces are then gradually trained and introduced.

This necessary transition to effective local policing is, however, rarely straightforward. While it may take a long time for CIVPOL and international police trainers to train and legitimise an effective local police force, the need for confidence in police efforts to provide safety for people in communities is usually immediate. Last has proposed that paramilitary police forces and normal policing personnel should be fully integrated into the initial peacekeeping deployment.

The Auxiliary Transitory Police (PAT) developed within UN Observer Mission in El Salvador (ONUSAL) can serve as a particularly pertinent example of this. Here units were composed of cadets selected for a new civilian police academy and commanded by CIVPOL officers from ONUSAL, thus helping to effectively bridge the gap between the large-scale security provided by the military peacekeepers and the personal security at the community level.

It is plain that current peacekeeping operations suffer from a critical shortage of appropriately trained civilian police, as well as from the lack of a universally accepted rule of law. The UN is only slowly beginning to recognise the need for the development of:

- smaller back-up and gendarmerie police forces (trained not only in policing but also in military tactics, and capable of deploying in units as well as individuals or in small groups);
- indigenous policing and related judicial and penal institutions;

- experience in the managing of police academies, which should also include programmes in human rights, crime prevention and good community relations (Call and Barnett 2000 pp.43-68).

Box 4: Strategic Components, Tasks and Skills of Peacebuilding

Component	Tasks	Skills
Security	demobilisation disarmament de-mining protection of civilians police and security reform personal security (e.g. racial, cultural, gender-specific violence) human rights	non-violent civil defence witnessing accompaniment neighbourhood watch support and networking
Governance	institutional capacity building transparency/accountability electoral assistance	facilitation of meetings development of group leaders group decision-making techniques encouragement and support
Relief/Development	infrastructure development market reform economic institutions small business meeting basic needs social services	engineering/technical skills business acumen business development entrepreneurial skills leadership and teaching relationship building across boundaries
Reconciliation	psycho-social trauma refugee return peace education community initiatives	interpersonal communication group facilitation conflict resolution skills managing the psycho-social dynamics of conflict

(adapted from Last, 2000)

A second level of differentiation involves the necessary distinction between the military and police functions on the one hand, and broader civilian peacebuilding roles on the other. Last identifies four strategic components of peacebuilding. Each of these four components (security, governance, relief, development and reconciliation) involves a wide a range of tasks, and each task requires associated skills (*see* Box 4).

In practice, Last identifies a series of gaps between the range of skills needed to support peacebuilding and the skills embodied in typical international missions: "We have not been completely successful in deploying the skills necessary for each of the four major peacebuilding components identified" (ibid, 87). Thus, for example, while the military component of a mission can provide the necessary military stability, it usually lacks the skills necessary to rebuild cooperative relationships. One approach advocated by Last is to further the development of community-based civilian peacebuilding projects in order to better integrate civilian capacities into the mission, as well as to provide training in at least some of the skills vital for peacebuilding.

This approach was applied practically by the Lester B. Pearson International Peacekeeping Training Centre, in the form of a Neighbourhood Facilitators Project in the Bosnian town of Banja Luka. The project contained a team of 20 local (Bosnian Muslims, Serbs, and Croats) and 5 international facilitators provided the catalyst to stimulate community co-operation, enabling local people to draw on international skills and resources. A community centre with a mobile team was set up with the stated aim of helping to find peaceful solutions to local problems. Last summarises the work of the centre as follows:

> *A Community Centre and its teams can be the glue for all the other services and organisations that come to its area to help repair the damage of violent conflict. Because the teams are fundamentally local as well as international, they help to rebuild the country from the ground up, developing people who will stay there for the long haul.*

Last points out that these teams can serve as a valuable connection between the various components and actors in an intervention, such as the military force, international organisations, NGOs and the local population. Made up of specifically selected and trained individuals, the teams can further embody a wide array of different skills and thus manage to address many of the required tasks, as outlined in Box 4. This approach seems particularly promising, especially as it involves a balanced local/international composition, so that the wide range of peacebuilding skills are represented throughout the teams. As a result, they are equipped with a unique capacity to find local solutions to local problems.

The need to provide greater capacity for the integration of the different elements of what the UN is now terming 'complex peace operations' was also specifically recognised in the Brahimi Report. From the perspective of conflict resolution, there are several relevant structural changes that need to be made. The report recommends, for instance, that civilian police and human rights experts become better integrated into the peacekeeping mechanism. It also calls for more effective and integrated civilian roles in order to effectively augment and develop the military security function and, at the same time, to properly address the unique challenges of post-conflict peacebuilding.

More effective pre-deployment preparation is recommended for judicial, penal, human rights and other specialists, who, together with specialist civilian police, will then constitute collegial 'rule of law' teams. Most significantly in terms of the conflict resolution dimensions of peacekeeping, the Executive Committee on Peace and Security is enjoined to develop a plan to strengthen the permanent capacity of the United Nations to construct peace-building strategies, as well as to implement appropriate programmes in support of those strategies.

To further enable this process the report supported efforts to create a pilot Peace-building Unit within the Department for Political Affairs, and recommended that this unit should be fully funded, subject to a positive evaluation of the pilot programmes. This proposal marks a new and welcome recognition that the civilian elements of peacekeeping operations, which are vital to prospect of a long-term sustainability of the peace process, need to be adequately resourced, integrated and prepared (United Nations 2000a).

The majority of current UN peacekeeping missions interpret their roles in the traditional way: they seek to monitor cease-fires and disarmament agreements (in the Middle East, India and Pakistan, in Georgia, and in Ethiopia and Eritrea). Far more challenging objectives are those of strengthening policing and the rule of law, as is required in current peacekeeping operations in Bosnia, Kosovo and East Timor, where policing and civilian conflict resolution functions are in urgent need of enhancement. If the UN Organization Mission in the Democratic Republic of Congo (MONUC) is fully deployed, it is going to be essential for the full range of lessons identified in this report to be fully integrated into the mission.

8. Future Options

While peacekeeping and conflict resolution are beginning to speak the same language, there is still much to learn operationally about how the concepts in the two fields can best be applied in practice. The urgency of this will increase as the concepts of peace support, conflict prevention, and conflict resolution continue to gain currency not only in the UN but also in national and regional security organisations.

The events in Kosovo have been a stimulus to thinking about policy development in relation to conflict prevention and conflict resolution in the European Union, and there is emerging a new framework for a common European security policy that will have the same need for conflict resolution approaches. In Berlin (June 1996), the European Union launched the European Security and Defence Identity (ESDI), committed to the creation of a common foreign and security policy. By June 1999, following the EU summit in Cologne, this had evolved into the European Security and Defence Policy (ESDP). At the December summit in Helsinki, the stated objectives of developing an EU Rapid Reaction Force of 50,000-60,000 troops and a civilian resource for deployment in crisis situations, were also announced. At the European Council's meeting in Santa Maria in June 2000, the member states declared their willingness to provide a contingent of 5,000 civilian police by 2003 in order to strengthen the prevention and crisis management function of international missions. To ensure a timely response, 1,000 civilian police will be made available with a response time of 30 days. At the Istanbul Summit of November 1999, the Organisation for Security and Co-operation in Europe (OSCE) also committed itself to establishing Rapid Expert Assistance and Co-operation Teams (REACT) (Plesch and Symour 2000, 2).

Many commentators are now becoming increasingly concerned with efforts to strengthen the level of civilian capacity deployed in peace support and crisis management situations. They observe that, while military deployments are still amply resourced, funds made available to support civilian peacebuilding initiatives continue to be severely inadequate. The British American Security Information Council (BASIC) recently proposed the formation of a civilian Conflict Prevention Service for Europe, drawing on experience gained from the deployment of paramilitary policing units in the Balkans such as the Italian Carabinieri, which served as part of SFOR in Bosnia and KFOR in Kosovo (ibid).

This proposal puts forward a model under which well-protected teams of civilians can be mobilised in battalions or similar quasi-military force structures, with an aim to providing a full range of conflict prevention or peace-restoring services, thus complementing military security. The composition of battalions deployed in insecure and high-tension situations would necessarily contain a high proportion of paramilitary police; in low-tension situations, forces would be made up of a correspondingly high proportion of civilian experts to strengthen civil society with expertise for example in human rights, mediation, arms control and police and legal training.

In the more unstable situations, a strengthened battalion could be placed under the direct control of a military commander. An operational support company, modelled on the specialised police units deployed in Bosnia, would comprise platoon-sized units of criminal and war crimes investigators and intelligence experts, platoons for public security (riot control police) and groups of experts trained in mediation, human rights monitoring, arms control, police work and the collection and destruction of weaponry, as required. Such a battalion would also include a number of territorial police companies, equipped with light armoured combat vehicles for intelligence gathering, scouting or trouble-shooting.

Annual costs for such a force are roughly calculated in the BASIC plan at around $2 billion for a deployable force of 12,000, supported by Headquarters and training staff of a further 3,000. This compares with an annual conventional military budget of EU/NATO members of $156 billion, and is approximately the same as the current annual budget designated for UN peacekeeping operations.

While this particular proposal may be too heavily based on the structures of a quasi-military model, it does point to the urgent need to move towards reinforcing existing military peacekeeping capacities with civilian crisis management and conflict resolution/prevention expertise. In a similar vein, within the UN system, there have been repeated calls throughout the 1990s for the creation of specialised units of 'White Helmets', composed of civilian experts equipped to take on the political, human rights and civil society rebuilding tasks of peacekeeping, and leaving military security challenges firmly in the domain of the 'Blue Helmets'. In December 1995, the UN General Assembly passed resolution A-50-19, the White Helmet Initiative, proposed by Argentina, designed to strengthen the reserve capacity of developing countries in support of UN peacekeeping operations. This was closely followed by a Dutch proposal to form an international civilian volunteer brigade to be deployed in emergency and natural disaster situations.

Norway has also pioneered the development of non-military forms of peacekeeping. In the early 1990s, the Norwegian government supported the establishment of the Norwegian

Early Preparedness System (NOREPS), a network of NGOs that in turn provided a standby arrangement system (called NORSTAFF), allowing for the deployment of civilian specialists from a wide variety of fields within 72 hours. Since the 1980s, the Norwegian Resource Bank for Democracy and Human Rights has acted on the requests of UN agencies or parties to conflict, sending teams of relief workers, human rights monitors and mediators to areas of conflict.

There are now many precedents of this kind, even if the willingness and ability of member states in general to commit resources to the support of civilian conflict resolution capacity remains limited and disappointing. The lessons leaned from peacekeeping in the 1990s make clear that this is a problem that must be vigorously addressed if the international community in general and the United Nations in particular is to continue to play an effective role in the peaceful resolution of conflict in the future.

9. Reference and Further Reading

Annan, K. 1997. "Peace Operations and the United Nations: Preparing for the New Century," *Conflict Resolution Monitor,* Issue 1, (Centre for Conflict Resolution, Department of Peace Studies, University of Bradford).

Azar, E. 1990. *The Management of Protracted Social Conflict: Theory and Cases,* Darmouth: Aldershot.

Beattie, Clayton 1983 "Canadian Army," in H. Wiseman (ed.), *Peacekeeping: Appraisals and Proposals,* Oxford: Pergammon Press.

Betts, R.K. 1994. "The Delusion of Impartial Intervention," *Foreign Affairs,* 73, 6, 20-33.

British Army 1994. *Field Manual: Wider Peacekeeping*, Fourth Draft, London.

Call, Chuck and Michael Barnett 2000. "Looking for A Few Good Cops: Peacekeeping, Peacebuilding and CIVPOL," *in* Holm and Eide, op. cit., 43-68.

Chayles, A.H. and G.T. Raac 1995. *Peace Operations: Developing an American Strategy,* Washington DC: National Defense University Press.

Dobbie, C. 1994. "A Concept for Post Cold War Peacekeeping," *Survival,* 36, 121-148.

Holm, T. Tanke and E. Barth Eide (eds.) 2000. *Peacebuilding and Police Reform,* London: Frank Cass.

Langille, P. 2000. "Conflict Prevention: Options for Rapid Deployment and UN Standing Forces," *in* Ramsbotham and Woodhouse, op. cit., 219-253.

Last, D. 1997. *Theory, Doctrine and Practice of Conflict De-Escalation in Peacekeeping Operations,* Nova Scotia: Lester B. Pearson Canadian International Peacekeeping Training Centre.

Last, D. 2000. "Organising for Effective Peacebuilding," *in* Ramsbotham and Woodhouse, op. cit., 80-96.

Luttwak, Edward. 1999. "Give War a Chance," *Foreign Affairs*, 78, 4.

Miall, H., O. Ramsbotham and Tom Woodhouse 1999. *Contemporary Conflict Resolution*, Cambridge: Polity Press.

Ministry of Defence 1999. *Peace Support Operations: JWP 3-50,* London: Ministry of Defence.

OSCE 1999. "Report of the OSCE Mission in Kosovo," in *UNHCR/OSCE Overview of the Situation of Ethnic Minorities in Kosovo.*

Plesch, D. and J. Seymour 2000. *A Conflict Prevention Service for the European Union,* Washington, DC and London: BASIC.

Ramsbotham, Oliver and Tom Woodhouse 1996. *Peacekeeping: Terra Incognita – Here Be Dragons – Peacekeeping and Conflict Resolution in Contemporary Conflict: Some Relationships Considered,* Ulster: University of Ulster, INCORE/United Nations University.

Ramsbotham, Oliver and Tom Woodhouse 1996. *Humanitarian Intervention in Contemporary Conflict: A Reconceptualisation,* Cambridge: Politica Press.

Ramsbotham, Oliver and Tom Woodhouse (eds) 2000. *Peacekeeping and Conflict Resolution,* London: Frank Cass.

Rieff, D. 1994. "The Illusions of Peacekeeping," *World Policy Journal,* 11, 3, 1-18.

Sharp, Jane 2000. *Evidence to Foreign Affairs Committee. Fourth Report on Kosovo. Vol. II,* London: House of Commons.

Stewart, R. 1993. *Broken Lives: A Personal View of the Bosnian Conflict,* London: Harper Collins.

United Nations 1999a. *Report on the Fall of Srebrenica, A54/549,* New York, NY, United Nations.

United Nations 1999b. *Report Of The Independent Inquiry Into The Actions Of The United Nations During The 1994 Genocide In Rwanda,* New York: United Nations.

United Nations 2000a. *Comprehensive Review Of The Whole Question Of Peacekeeping Operations In All Their Aspects,* Doc A / 55 / 305; S / 2000 / 809, New York: United Nation.

United Nations 2000b. *Multidisciplinary Peacekeeping: Lessons From Recent Experience*, New York, NY: UN Department of Peacekeeping Operations *at http://www.un.org/depts/dpko/view.htm.*

Wilkinson, P. 2000. *Peace Support Under Fire: Lessons from Sierra Leone Briefing Series,* Brussels: International Security Information Service.

Woodhouse, T. 1999. *International Conflict Resolution: Some Critiques and a Response, Working Papers,* Bradford: Centre for Conflict Resolution, University of Bradford.

The News Media and the Transformation of Ethnopolitical Conflicts

Dusan Reljic

1. Introduction 322
2. Consensus (Consociation) Democracy and 'Constructive Journalism' 323
3. Determining Factors within the Media System 328
4. External Efforts to Transform Conflicts: Activities of International Organisations and NGOs 330
   The 'freedom of the media' versus the 'control of the media'
   What international law says
   NGOs activities for the protection of freedom of speech and journalists' rights
   The limits of coercive 'information intervention'
5. Conclusion 337
6. Reference and Further Reading 338

The News Media and the Transformation of Ethnopolitical Conflicts

Dusan Reljic

1. Introduction

For most journalists, reporting on conflict is not a special situation governed by a unique set of rules. The situation is, in fact, quite the reverse: reporting on political, economic and other collisions of interests within a society is very much a part of the journalist's everyday routine. Conflicts are, after all, part of daily life in a democracy. Subsequently, the absence of reports in the media on conflicts would suggest that democracy itself has been lost.

Ethnopolitical conflicts differ from other forms of political conflict in several crucial ways. The fundamental distinction is that the conflicting parties often resort to violence because they see this as the only means of resolving their grievances with other ethnic communities. In recent years, Europe has again experienced a significant number of ethnopolitical conflicts, especially following the disintegration of authoritarian regimes in Central and Eastern Europe.

Evidently, however, nationalism by no means seems to be restricted to eastern or south-eastern Europe. In western Europe as well, the media plays a significant part in whipping up nationalist feelings of xenophobia, racism or ethnic chauvinism. As immigration into Europe increases over the next few years, these ethnopolitical conflicts are likely to gain in significance. Nationalistic tensions, coupled with the creation and expansion of supranational institutions such as the European Union (EU), which are designed to serve as a counterweight and means to reduce or even eliminate nationalism, will continue to play a central role in European politics and thereby also in the media.

Most research into nationalism takes as its starting point the notion that centralised communications, social mobility and increased levels of economic contact can help surmount cultural differences between factions of the population and thus foster a more homogenous culture (Gellner 1983). However, there are also indications that increased communication can in fact produce the opposite effect, at least in areas where several equally developed cultures exist side by side. This occurs because improved communications and transport reinforce a sense of being different in those who belong to minority groups (Connor 1994). It is not surprising then that ethnic tensions and separatist demands are on the increase throughout the world.

In ethnically diverse communities, the media often serves to reinforce existing differences and thus accelerate a disintegrating effect on the homogeneity of the population. The key issue is, then, under which conditions, as Anthony Giddens (1997) suggests, do "negative spirals of communication" (mutual negative perceptions which degenerate into hate, feeding more hate) between ethnic communities develop and ultimately degenerate into violence?" Moreover, "Under which conditions can the media actively promote empathy, peace and political stability between differing community factions?"

This chapter explores the relationship between the political framework of conflict regulation and journalism. Second, it specifies what it sees as the determining factors within the media system. Third, it attempts to evaluate the efforts of external actors such as international and non-governmental organisations (NGOs) to support the transformation of conflicts. It indicates the limits of external intervention, including coercive measures. Finally, some conclusions on the potential role of the media are drawn and some recommendations proposed for improving the performance of the media in situations of tension and conflict.

2. Consensus (Consociation) Democracy and 'Constructive Journalism'

Throughout human history, there have been several commonly employed methods of resolving ethnic tensions and conflicts. Among these are a) genocide, b) enforced population exchange, c) partition of the state (secession/self-determination) or d) integration/ assimilation (McGarry and O'Leary 1993). Ethnic strife is generally regulated through four principal methods: a) hegemonistic control, b) third-party mediation, c) cantonisation or federalisation and d) establishing models of power-sharing or consensus democracy ('concordance democracy').

In reality, as intra-state conflicts are played out, these approaches tend to appear simultaneously and in varying combinations. Genocide and enforced population exchange are disapproved of from a moral perspective and are rejected by the international community. Secession too is generally considered unacceptable. The federalist model usually proves to be fragile if the population of the country in question is ethnically heterogeneous. Even the proponents of a federalist Europe have become noticeably quieter in the face of resurgent nationalism. The political *Zeitgeist* instead favours consensus democracy (power sharing between political subjects) as a means of transforming ethnic conflict.

It should be remembered that what we are witnessing is an experiment. Never before has a lasting solution to fundamental ethnopolitical conflict been brought about through consensus (consociation) democracy. Throughout the history of the formation of the nations in Western Europe, force has always been what defined political realities. Moreover, even established modern democracies such as Britain, France or Spain have failed notably in their efforts to end nationalist conflicts in places such as Northern Ireland, Corsica and the Basque Region.

The architects of the consensus democracy model for the resolution of ethnopolitical conflicts begin from the assumption that the usual democratic safeguards are insufficient to prevent the abuse of power in multicultural or ethnically divided societies. The principle of majority rule always harbours the danger that minorities will be overruled or disadvantaged. For this reason, political institutions have been proposed to ensure that all sections of society have their requisite share of power. The guiding principle is the proper balancing of interests on all levels of the political system.

The prerequisite for such a balance between ethnic groups in the state must be a corresponding compromise between the political elites that head the different ethnic groups. This must include a renunciation of violence such as the forced assimilation or persecution of weaker ethnic groups, as well as attempts at secession. The concept of consensus democracy in an ethnically heterogeneous state thus rests on the following four elements:

1. a grand coalition between the political elites of the various sections of the population;
2. a proportional representation system, with corresponding precautionary measures to ensure equal rights in important areas such as education, control of public expenditure, employment policy and public service broadcasting;
3. a right of veto for all those sharing power, enshrined in the constitution;
4. the guaranteed internal autonomy (self-determination) of all ethnic segments constituting the state.

Such a model of consensus democracy is admittedly idealistic, as it presupposes, on the part of the nationalistic centres of power, a conscious renunciation of the type of politics which seeks unilateral advantage. Therefore, consensus democracy must be viewed not so much as a state that can be realistically achieved in full, but rather as a goal or aspiration. One can concede, however, that even a mere process of conflict transformation which is based on such a model already incorporates a significant element of peaceful conflict transformation, to the extent that unilateral objectives and their achievement by pressure or force are ruled out from the outset.

In an ideal world, the media should at least attempt to orient its reporting style towards the creation of peace, instead of intensifying prejudices that in turn heighten conflict. Such ideal journalism is a critical part of the consensus democracy concept, and represents the proper role of the media in conflict prevention and resolution. Despite this, the media is often perceived as giving priority to negative aspects in its reporting of conflicts, with a suspicion that they do this consciously because it 'sells better'. Demands are often made upon the media to adopt a more constructive role in conflict prevention and experienced journalists are frequently accused of being innately sceptical. Nevertheless, it is too simplistic to expect the media as an entity to feel collectively obliged to actively promote the peace and development of civil societies.

Time and again, international state and non-state organisations, as well as other institutions, have issued statements expressing the view that the media could have an important role to play in constructively reporting about conflicts and combating the propaganda of hate. For example, in the closing declaration of the European Conference on Conflict Prevention (Amsterdam, 27-28 February 1997), the EU was called upon to examine how they might support the reporting efforts of independent local media in societies prone to conflict. In addition, special education was proposed for local and European journalists working in conflict regions. Journalists would be urged to convince the general public and politicians in power of the need to invest in conflict prevention. It was further suggested that this could begin with emphasis being drawn to the considerable humanitarian and material costs of conflict management.

The International Federation of Journalists (IFJ) remains convinced that the media can not only help to defuse conflicts, but also that it is uniquely positioned to encourage coexistence and co-operation between people of different origins. "By practising objective, fact-based reporting that avoids stereotypes or stirring up rumours, individual journalists and the media as a whole have a tremendous potential to contribute to understanding and bridge-building", was the view taken by IFJ in a manual addressing this topic (IFJ 1997). In the course of a debate about the reporting of ethnic conflicts in Africa, this organisation also drafted detailed and practical recommendations for more balanced and objective media reporting on such events. Neither is there any lack of sophisticated suggestions from other important players on the international stage as to the precise nature of positive or constructive journalism. Besides the classic five 'w's, (*why, what, who, where, and when*) which should be covered in news items, for instance, demands from the United States of America (USA) also call for an 's' (*solutions*) as well as a 'c' (*common ground*).

There are high expectations placed upon the journalist's role. These include the proposition that journalists reporting on conflicts should be trained in the techniques of resolving conflict, and should always aim at acquiring an impeccable reputation as promoters of peace. They are asked to enlighten the public, and tell the stories of the victims of conflict, rather than reinforcing the point of view of the perpetrators of violence.

It has even been suggested that the media may well be the most powerful means available for the resolution of future conflicts or even for the prevention of wars. Furthermore, journalists are well supplied with well-intended proposals to help them realise these expectations. Johan Galtung (1997) for instance suggests that journalists should:

- illuminate the story in detail from all sides;
- be careful to draw from diverse sources;
- restrict overuse of elites as sources, but should make use of different experts;
- avoid glorifying the technology of war;
- also use dramatic imagery to portray the horrors of war;
- offer sensible and well-written reports about ordinary people;
- supply more background reports;
- be aware that news makers (spin doctors) are out to manipulate them;
- avoid treating their work itself as a story;
- give ample coverage to and promote peace initiatives.

Box 1: Suggestions for Peace Journalism

Annabel McGoldrick and Jake Lynch (a correspondent for the British news media *Sky News* and *The Independent*) have developed a set of rules for the improved coverage of conflicts, which among others, include the following techniques:

1. AVOID portraying conflict as consisting of only two parties contesting one goal. The logical outcome of such a scenario is for one to win and the other to lose. INSTEAD, a peace journalist should DISAGGREGATE the two parties into many smaller groups pursuing many goals, thus opening up more creative potential for a range of outcomes.

2. AVOID drawing stark distinctions between the self and the other. These are often used to establish the impression that the other party is a threat or beyond the pale of civilised behaviour – both key justifications for violence. INSTEAD, seek the other in the self and vice versa.

3. AVOID treating a conflict as if it is only going on in the place and at the time that the violence is occurring. INSTEAD, try to trace the links and consequences for people in other places now and in the future.

4. AVOID concentrating on what divides the parties and the differences between what they say they want. INSTEAD, try asking questions that may reveal areas of common ground, and lead your report with answers that suggest that some goals may after all be shared or at least compatible.

5. AVOID reporting only the violent acts and describing the horror. If you exclude everything else, you suggest that the only explanation for violence is previous violence (revenge); the only remedy, more violence (coercion/punishment). INSTEAD, show how people have been blocked and frustrated or even deprived in their everyday life, as a way of explaining the violence.

6. AVOID blaming someone for starting it. INSTEAD, try looking at how shared problems and issues can lead to consequences that all the parties say they never intended.

7. AVOID focusing exclusively on the suffering, fears and grievances of only one party. This divides the parties into villains and victims, and suggests that coercing or punishing the villains might constitute a solution. INSTEAD, treat the suffering, fears and grievance of all sides as equally newsworthy.

8. AVOID victimising language such as 'destitute,' 'devastated,' 'defenceless,' 'pathetic' and 'tragedy,' which only tells us what has been done to and could be done for a group of people. This dis-empowers them and limits the options for change. INSTEAD, report on what *has* been done and could be done by the people. Don't just ask them how they feel, also ask them how they are coping and what they think. Can they suggest any solutions?

9. AVOID the imprecise use of emotive words to describe what has happened to people.

- 'Genocide' means the wiping out of an entire people.
- 'Massacre' is the deliberate killing of people known to be unarmed and defenceless. Are we sure? Or might these people have died in battle?
- 'Systematic' e.g. raping or forcing people from their homes. Has it really been organised in a deliberate pattern or is it a number of unrelated, albeit extremely nasty incidents?

INSTEAD, always be precise about what we know. Do not minimise suffering but reserve the strongest language for the gravest situations or you will beggar the language and help to justify disproportionate responses that escalate the violence.

10. AVOID demonising adjectives, for example, 'vicious,' 'cruel,' 'brutal' and 'barbaric.' These always describe one party's view of what another party has done. To use them puts the journalist on that side and helps to justify an escalation of violence. INSTEAD, report what you know about the wrongdoing and give as much information as you can about the reliability of other people's reports or descriptions of it.

11. AVOID demonising labels like 'terrorist,' 'extremist,' 'fanatic' and 'fundamentalist.' These are always given by us to them. No one ever uses them to describe himself or herself, and so, for a journalist to use them is always to take sides. They mean the person is unreasonable, so it seems to make less sense to reason (negotiate) with them. INSTEAD, try calling people by the names they give themselves. Or be more precise in your descriptions.

12. AVOID focusing exclusively on the human rights abuses, misdemeanours and wrongdoings of only one side. INSTEAD, try to name ALL wrongdoers and treat equally allegations made by all sides in a conflict.

13. AVOID making an opinion or claim seem like an established fact (e.g. "Eurico Guterres, said to be responsible for a massacre in East Timor.... "). INSTEAD, tell your readers or your audience who said what ("Eurico Guterres, accused by a top U.N. official of ordering a massacre in East Timor.... "). That way you avoid signing yourself and your news service up to the allegations made by one party in the conflict against another.

14. AVOID treating the signing of documents, which bring about military victory or cease fire, as necessarily creating peace. INSTEAD, try to report on the issues which remain and which may still lead people to commit further acts of violence in the future.

15. AVOID waiting for leaders on our side to suggest or offer solutions. INSTEAD, pick up and explore peace initiatives. Ask questions to ministers, for example, about ideas put forward by grassroots organisations. Assess peace perspectives against what you know about the issues the parties are really trying to address. Do not simply ignore them because they do not coincide with established positions.

McGoldrick and Lynch 2000

Reviewing these recommendations for good journalism in crisis situations, it is easy to fall into the false assumption that all that is needed is to report clearly, without prejudice, and ask probing questions in such a way as to enlighten readers/listeners/viewers about the 'real problems'. It is further implied that their audiences will only then begin to understand the 'real costs' and reassess their views accordingly. In a similar vein, many commentators simply believe that the new and better information technologies, such as the Internet, will almost automatically generate more peaceful means of overcoming conflict. A good example of this is the opinion of Jay Moore, a teacher of history at the University of Vermont and a specialist in conflict transformation. In his contribution to the debate on war and peace reporting (on *www.mediachannel.org*), he expressed his conviction that, in the age of the Internet, reporting on conflicts and wars will never again be the same. This has resulted from people now being able to communicate directly at a distance, across the front lines, as was clearly evident in the case during NATO's attack on Serbia in 1999!

Nevertheless, Moore cautions that the Internet is by no means a substitute for more traditional and established methods of reaching out, such as leaflets, vigils, sit-ins and various other forms of 'propaganda of the deed', i.e. forms of activism that have been employed by peace groups and other NGOs. He points out that access to the costly hardware and telecommunication facilities that make it possible to use the Internet for organising is skewed by race and class, as well as, to some degree, by gender. Although the Internet includes many kinds of people, it is also much more subdivided by interest and identity groups that may or may not communicate with one another. It seems best at linking those who already have some interest in communication and not as effective at reaching the unconverted.

But before we engage in a debate on how Internet and other new technologies might alter the ways in which conflicts and wars are perceived and opposed worldwide, we should first pose the question as to why humbler and simpler ideas have so far been unsuccessful. Any realistic evaluation of the degree to which the media can contribute to conflict prevention and resolution must be founded on an analysis of the general political, economic and social framework for media development in the country in question; only then can we hope to properly examine the specific opportunities for the individual members of that media. The following sections outline the basic elements of just such an analytical framework.

3. Determining Factors within the Media System

We can best assess the role of the media in the prevention and resolution of conflict and in the safeguarding of peace if we see that role as essentially a component and expression of overall social conditions. Any framework describing the most important influences on the media should therefore highlight four fundamental areas:

- *political context*: the rule of law versus despotic authority;
- *economic conditions*: the media as an autonomous economic organisation or one subject to governmental control (media as part of the state apparatus);
- *quality of journalism*: critical and analytic reporting or mere functioning as 'stenographers of power' using the 'language of hate';
- *public attitudes*: enlightened democratic traditions or authoritarian value systems.

Under this model, the media is seen as a vector, the direction of which is determined by the influence of each of the four individual elements. A weakness in one factor can only be partially compensated for by the strength of another. In short, no element can exert its full weight if the others are lacking or flawed.

This analytical framework allows for the exploration of the inter-relationships of the four elements under various scenarios. If, for example, journalistic training is seen as the best starting point to inculcate higher standards of reporting in the long term, it must be realised that any efforts in this direction will unfortunately remain unsuccessful, while authoritarian forms of rule do not allow for media autonomy or as long as economic necessity stymies any increase in media consumption.

On the other hand, media which has succumbed to the language of hate will find that their impact will be limited by the extent to which they are addressing an educated public raised in an enlightened, democratic tradition. Certainly, the evidence of established western democracies in times of economic prosperity supports this assumption. Moreover, in any state governed by the rule of law, media outputs that incite either ethnic hatred or illegal political action is usually dealt with in the courts.

There is, however, also some evidence that the long-term effects of the language of hate can be highly deleterious even in established democratic societies, and that legal counter-measures undertaken to combat it can themselves cause controversy. Different legal and political traditions also play a significant role here: whereas US courts will, in general, hesitate to impose limitations on the freedom of expression, most western European judges are notably apprehensive about Nazi propaganda or other similar remnants of an evil past.

Certainly, the propaganda of hate, even in marginal media, is capable of achieving a profound effect on the public if, under conditions of economic crisis, the fears and aggressive inclinations of the target audience are on the rise. In such situations, authoritarian political elites can come dangerously close to the levers of power, thus undermining the legitimate rule of law.

The analytical framework presented here points out at least three particular situations which can emerge whenever the media is forced to operate under conditions of increasingly violent tension and conflict. These can arise before, during and after such situations, although, in real life, these transitions are fluid.

If reports about tension and conflict are issued in a genuinely free and independent manner and presented in a fair and balanced way, they can indeed help to overcome conflict in that they will serve to educate the public, allowing their readers and listeners to form independent opinions. On the other hand, biased and manipulative reports can all too easily accelerate and intensify the crisis.

If the media is to be expected to function as a part of the consensus democracy approach to intra-state conflicts, other essential conditions and preconditions must also be fulfilled. These include: a clear commitment on the part of the political elites to resolve the conflict by peaceful means; a willingness to respect the rule of law; economic stability; high levels of education and a democratic awareness on the part of the target audience. Again, any strengthening of one of these fundamental elements will only bring about the desired result if progress has been achieved in the other areas as well.

Box 2: External Donations and the Impact of non-Nationalistic Journalism

In many transitional countries, especially under conditions governed by efforts at post-conflict rehabilitation, aid from the USA and western Europe has fuelled an NGO boom, with a correspondingly strong impact on the media. For instance, as part of various external attempts to establish long-term solutions for the conflict in the area, significant levels of foreign investment was channelled to non-government media in Bosnia and Hercegovina. At one stage this small republic had more media outlets than Berlin or Madrid, although less inhabitants! In this way, international institutions supported the growth of the media in this country. Western governments and NGOs caused, above all else, a significant increase in journalistic output, an increase that was unfortunately only rarely accompanied by a corresponding improvement in the quality of the journalistic product or of its political impact. The overall political situation, as illustrated by the uninterrupted dominance of nationalistic political parties in all elections after the Dayton peace accords in 1995, does not seem to have been significantly affected by the proliferation of new, anti-nationalistic media.Even the best-equipped media and the best-trained journalists will have little effect on their readers and listeners if economic recession persists in their country and as long as extremists call the political tune. Regardless of this, the better journalists are trained and the more technically equipped their media is, the better the prospects that they will be able to strengthen and reinforce key initiatives for politics, the economy and society.

Box 3: Aiding Democracy through the Media

A failed project: At the beginning of 1997, the US Government made $200,000 available to a group of liberal journalists in Croatia, thus enabling them to found the news magazine Tjednik. The Soros Open Society Institute and some other NGOs contributed considerable funding. Unfortunately, the magazine, although of high journalistic quality, had little impact and had to be closed a short time later under a burden of enormous debt. It seems that, at least at the time, the homogenised public of Croatia was unreceptive to a non-nationalistic discourse as offered by the magazine.

A successful project: There are fortunately more positive examples. One of these is the Belgrade-based Beta news agency, which was founded in the early Nineties by several journalists who opposed the prevailing nationalistic paradigm that was widespread among the Serbian public at that time. With the support from Western donors, the project has made a considerable impact by placing high emphasis on lean management and new information technologies. Over the past five years, this organisation has become the leading press agency in southeast Europe, supplying print and audio information to several hundred customers throughout the region, the rest of Europe and overseas.

The establishment of economically stable and a politically balanced media presupposes both an effective rule of law and a functioning market economy. Media that is well organised and functions democratically has a vested interest in ensuring that the public gains an insight into the workings of government and economic players. Only then, can it develop best practices and play a positive role in conflict transformation.

4. External Efforts to Transform Conflicts: Activities of International Organisations and NGOs

4.1 The 'freedom of the media' versus the 'control of the media'

There are certain conditions that contribute to the prevention of conflict. These can be summarised as: the rule of law, a tradition of tolerant and democratic political culture, and (financial) independence of the media. If in the course of conflict, it becomes clear that national justice is being perverted, international law provides some further measures that can be taken into consideration by international political committees. Nevertheless, there is not much evidence of effective measures undertaken to counter national authorities who fail to follow the media guidelines set out in internationally recognised documents such as those of the Council of Europe or of the Organisation for Security and Cooperation in Europe (OSCE), even though issues of this kind appear regularly on the agendas of international committees.

International agreements and authorities that can exercise political control serve as an important point for orientation. Thus ideal conditions, as set out in international agreements, can be invoked by democratic bodies in areas affected by conflict, as well as by the democratic media itself. Since the end of the Cold War, membership in the Council of Europe and observance of OSCE regulations have taken on a particular importance for former communist countries where there is believed to be a threat of intra-state conflict. For these countries, the incorporation of the political, legal and other principles of the Council of Europe is seen as an important prerequisite for subsequent entry into the EU, which is the most important means of integration into the European continent. The post-communist elites in these countries thus derive much legitimacy from their various promises to take their countries into the EU as a 'zone of permanent peace'. Effectively, they can always be taken at their word by comparing, particularly in times of crisis, the actual situation in their countries with the rules and standards implied by the international legal and political obligations their countries have agreed to.

A number of cases involving alleged infringement of press freedom in western European states have already been tried before the European Court of Human Rights. Most observers expect an increasing number of cases linked to intra-state conflicts to arise in other parts of Europe. However, it can take many years for infringements to be properly addressed in the international courts.

The international community, insofar as it seeks to emphasise its declared belief in the need for the timely prevention of conflict, must be constantly on the alert for problems affecting the media in crisis-ridden areas. The respect for freedom of speech and freedom of the press must become a primary component of international politics and not dealt with as something of secondary importance. A move in this direction was made at the end of 1997 with the appointment of Freimut Duve, a member of the German Social Democrat Party, as the first media ombudsman at the OSCE.

4.2 What international law says

In 1993, in direct response to the experiences of the civil war in Yugoslavia, the Council of Europe organised a seminar in Strasbourg dealing with issues faced by the media in situations of conflict and tension. The Deputy Chairman of the European Court of Human Rights, Rudolf Bernhardt, took this opportunity to analyse existing legal safeguards for media autonomy in the context of the state in crisis situations (*see* Reljic 1998, p. 102),

Article 10 of the *Convention on Human Rights*, in particular, protects freedom of speech and the press. It allows that "in the interests of national security, territorial integrity and public safety..." and other overriding interests, restrictions on this freedom are certainly possible. In fact, Article 15 states explicitly that in emergencies which "threaten the life of the nation", extensive restrictions to the freedoms guaranteed in Article 10 are permissible, as long as they are provided for under international law.

Bernhardt accentuated this crucial problem when he asked: "Where is the borderline to be drawn between media freedom and the permissible restrictions, especially in situations of conflict and tension?" And his answer was: "The extent of permissible intervention in the activities of the mass media is difficult to circumscribe". Thus, this senior judge held that advanced censorship is not permissible under any circumstances and that none of the available measures may be used without a legal basis. He added three further conditions that must be fulfilled before any restriction of media autonomy could be considered justified (ibid.):

- Restrictions and interventions that are imposed by public authorities must serve the purposes laid down in Article 10 of the Convention on Human Rights, such as "protection of national security, territorial integrity or public order."
- All restrictive measures must meet the test of being 'necessary' in a democratic society. The appropriate national authorities shall decide whether they are necessary, but their conduct must be reasonable. Furthermore, all national conduct shall come under international scrutiny, and must therefore be verifiable by the European Court of Human Rights.
- No measures taken by the authorities, even in situations of tension and conflict, may be outside the control of independent courts.

Bernhardt pointed out in particular that Article 15, which relates to the empowerment of the authorities in public emergencies and states of war, permits even more extreme restrictions than Article 10 that is intended for use in normal times. He writes, resignedly, "It is extremely difficult, and even impossible, to demonstrate clearly and convincingly the powers of public authorities as well as the limits of any measures taken in such emergency situations". His conclusion follows the same vein: "Any measures taken in such exceptional situations which are not designed to restore order, peace and democracy fall outside the proper function of public authority" (Reljic 1998, p103). On the occasion of International Press Freedom Day (3 May, 1996), the Council of Europe's Committee of Ministers issued a declaration and recommendations concerning the protection of journalists in situations of tension and conflict (Committee of Ministers of the Council of Europe 1996). These recommendations emphasised the importance of the role of journalists and the media in alerting the general public to infringements of national and international law and to human suffering in situations of conflict. In this way, they can help to prevent further infringements of human rights and human suffering. Principles for the physical protection of journalists and the guarantee of their rights and working conditions were also described in this document.

The recommendation was essentially an extension of Articles 10 and 15 of the *Convention on Human Rights*, augmented by a few practical tips stressing the need for adequate insurance cover for journalists reporting in war zones. National authorities were urged to make the work of journalists easier by removing restrictions on the use of telecommunications equipment and relaxing entry requirements. The recommendation also drew attention to the hotlines manned by the International Red Cross in Geneva and by other international organisations, to which journalists can turn for help whenever they feel their safety is threatened.

Box 4: Monitoring the Media Coverage in Potential Conflict Areas: The European Institute for the Media

Since 1992, the European Institute for the Media (an NGO located in Düsseldorf, Germany) has carried out more than 40 missions designed to monitor media coverage of parliamentary, presidential and other elections in countries of eastern and central Europe and in the former Soviet Union. The missions, mostly financed by the EU or OSCE, sought to evaluate whether the media provided impartial and balanced coverage of the issues to be addressed and the political choices facing the electorate in these situations. Especially in newly established democracies, the level of political communication during the election process is an important indicator of the overall state of the democracy.

EIM monitoring makes use of both qualitative and quantitative methods of analysis. The former is gleaned from the interviews that international experts conduct with media professionals, the candidates and their representatives, public authorities, researchers and others involved in political communication. Quantitative analysis measures the total amount of time and space devoted to political candidates as well as assessing the tone (positive, neutral, negative) of the reports.

The preliminary results of such monitoring are normally presented to both the local and international public in a press conference on the day following the elections. The final report, which essentially contains a detailed survey and analysis of the media situation in the country of mission, is then published several week later both in English and in the language of the country in which the elections took place (a list of publications can be found at *www.eim.org*).

Monitoring projects in this manner can affect events in several ways. The immediate influence arises from the presentation of the preliminary report to the local public, which thus receives impartial information as to how well it has been served by the media. Another outcome is that the international community also gains reliable information about the work of the media in newly established democracies. This information can prove useful for the subsequent planning of assistance policy and other actions from abroad.

EIM's media reports further serve as a type of early indicator for potential conflicts, especially those of an ethnopolitical nature. They describe the main substantive issues governing political communication, and also describe just how these are discussed. For instance, if public authorities suppress criticism, or if they tolerate hate speech and other forms of inflammatory public discourse, this is likely to lead to tensions and conflicts.

The EIM pointed out, for example, in its report on the Russian presidential elections, March 2000, that Vladimir Putin overwhelmingly dominated the media coverage during the campaign. The general reporting still did not live up to the standards and regulations set out in the laws of the Russian Federation or in the international agreements to which the Russian Federation is a signatory. Although there is still a long way to go, some improvements of reporting have been made in the 2000 election, which was less confrontational than the reporting about the State Duma campaign in the previous December or in the previous presidential elections in 1996. Large segments of the public, including many people working in the media, appeared to have accepted the outcome as a foregone conclusion, probably because of the popularity of the acting president and the overwhelming advantages enjoyed by him.

Nevertheless, during the final week of the campaign, the state-controlled TV channel ORT once again resorted to 'black PR', actively denigrating the opponents of the acting president. The methods contradicted fundamentally the ethical principles of the journalistic profession, as well as falling short of the international standards that Russia has endorsed. This reversal to past practices, coupled with disturbing signs that Vladimir Putin's administration intends to approach media-related questions in a more assertive way, indicate that freedom of expression and the autonomy of the media in

Russia is endangered. Subsequent developments, such as legal proceedings against and the imprisonment of several leading Russian media figures, seem to show that this warning was accurate.

4.3 NGOs activities for the protection of freedom of speech and journalists' rights

It is only relatively recently that NGOs have come to the fore in the fight to protect freedom of speech and the rights of journalists. Within the political framework established during the Cold War, governmental organisations such as the OSCE or UNESCO always functioned as the arena (among others) in which issues of journalistic freedom were discussed. Since the end of the Cold War, however, a growing number of NGOs have become increasingly involved in this process as well.

Among the best known of the organisations specialising in the field of media are: the International Federation of Journalists in Brussels (*www.ifj.org*), Reporters sans Frontières in Paris (*www.rfs.fr*), the Committee to Protect Journalists in New York (*www.cpj.org*), the Glasnost Defence Foundation (*www.gdf.ru*) in Moscow, the International Press Institute in Vienna (*www.freemedia.at*), Article 19 in London (*www.article19.org*), the International Freedom of Expression Exchange (*www.ifex.org*) in Toronto and many other NGO's and human rights groups.

All of these organisations collect and publish information about censorship and other forms of infringements on the freedom of expression and autonomy of journalists. Also acting as international pressure groups, they further demand that public authorities move to rectify such violations. Governments are, in general, sensitive to such exposure, as it tends to have a significant impact on their standing in the international community. Thus, criticism from international civil society, as personified by the NGO community, can sometimes produce highly adverse effects on uncivil governments, often making further external financial support conditional on demonstrated improvements to the country's human rights record, a record that must include respect for press freedom.

However, the debate surrounding legal and political protective measures designed to safeguard the freedom of the press and the safety of journalists in crisis situations has led most analysts to the disappointing conclusion that journalists and the media have only very limited direct means available in order to contribute significantly to the ending of conflict. As paradoxical as it may seem, the amount of media autonomy that can usually be achieved in violent situations is limited.

Nearly every intra-state conflict will attract the intervention of external powers. Whether it is through the will of major external powers acting alone or as a result of concerted action undertaken by the international community, the authorities of the country in question can almost always be induced to make concessions in the area of media autonomy in return for political, military and other forms of support. This was evident, for instance, in all parties' relative tolerance of pointed critical media attention in the course of the Yugoslav civil war. What remains unclear, however, is just how durable such media organisations can be, especially after international attention to their crisis region has dissipated.

4.4 The limits of coercive 'information intervention'

In the summer of 1997, the peace process in Bosnia had essentially ground to a halt. Diplomatic initiatives and threats of military action appeared to be having little effect on the situation, particularly on the actions of the extreme nationalist faction of the Bosnian Serb leadership. In fact, quite the opposite had occurred: the international peacekeeping troops were increasingly referred to as occupation forces in the television channels controlled by Serb nationalists. Thus images of NATO tanks were shown, interspersed with archive footage of Nazi occupation troops taken during the Second World War. Tension mounted (*see* Reljic 1998, p91).

Along with other Western politicians, the then German Foreign Minister Klaus Kinkel proposed that the international peacekeeping force should 'jam' such broadcasts in an effort to combat "one-sided, anti-Western, demonising reporting". Carl Levin, the Democratic Senator from the US state of Michigan, expanded on this suggestion a few days later. He pointed out the US military should make use of its capability to transmit radio and television programmes directly to the Bosnian-Serb population, using the EC-130E Commando Solo Aircraft, in order to suppress and drown out undesired propaganda. The US had already effectively employed similar methods in Grenada, Iraq and Haiti (ibid.).

A few weeks later, international peacekeeping troops in Bosnia moved to occupy important broadcasting centres, in a concerted effort to get some of the worst 'offenders' off the air. Even so, in the parliamentary elections held shortly afterwards in the Bosnian Serb Republic, the radical nationalist parties were able to maintain their position, despite the fact that the dissemination of their broadcasting propaganda had been significantly restricted by the actions of the international peacekeeping force. The strength of ethno-chauvinist political parties in elections in Bosnia and Hercegovina remained unbroken, even five years after the Dayton peace accords, and in spite of the massive amounts of foreign donations that had been invested into anti-nationalistic social and political programmes, including direct support for the media (ibid.).

At the same time, negative sanctions were exerted against the media, such as the closing of overt nationalistic outlets. The notion of this kind of forced intervention in the media during conflicts and wars is, of course, not new. More recently, the wide reach of modern electronic media and the accelerated development of information technology have lent credence to the idea that it may indeed be possible to develop highly complex news systems. These systems would be aimed at eliminating or at least transforming conflict through a combination of political and military means.

Such 'information intervention' was discussed at length in several issues of the influential US journal *Foreign Affairs in 1997* (Metzl 1997). Since the major powers are evidently becoming ever less willing to fight on a massive military scale the infringement of human rights, the author proposes the creation of an independent UN Information Intervention Unit, specifically geared for intra-state conflicts. The proposal envisages three principle duties for such a unit: the monitoring of information provided in crisis-torn regions; the broadcasting of peace promotion material – *peace broadcasting*, – and in extreme cases, the jamming of radio and television broadcasts in order to halt the flow of hate and war propaganda.

Earlier, two former high-ranking members of President Clinton's administration had voiced the opinion in the same US-journal that information campaigns "to spread the truth" early on in the Rwanda conflict might well have alleviated the tragedy. They also asserted that US air strikes in the summer of 1995 on communications equipment of the Bosnian Serb army could have produced the additional advantage of impeding Bosnian Serb propaganda. Their arguments rested on consideration of the many opportunities for effective intervention available to the United States by virtue of its technological advantage in the fields of data processing and communications, as well as in satellite monitoring and the direct broadcasting of programmes. It was felt that these methods, combined with military force, could well help the US to resolve successfully regional ethnic conflicts and effectively to expand its role as a world power by the successful resolution of regional ethnic conflicts.

I am convinced that methods such as those described above, which find their foundation in external information intervention, including coercive measures such as the jamming of transmitters or professional bans of outlawed journalists, are of very limited effect. Certainly, hate propaganda can be suppressed in part, but it is highly doubtful that the 'delicate plant of democracy' can be transplanted by force. Even the long-term effect of proactive measures such as the beaming-in of broadcasts from external transmitters is open to question. As media communication is always an expression of national culture, external broadcasts of programmes in the language of the recipient country can never achieve the authenticity and credibility of home-grown media material.

While it is true that in situations in which armed conflicts have broken out and the internal authorities have imposed open or covert censorship on the media, information from whatever source gains in importance, this is usually only the case for a relatively short period. Besides this, as the history of external broadcasting shows only too clearly, even neutral information prepared abroad is viewed by most of its recipients as merely an expression of the political strategy of the country from which it comes.

In principle, the optimal conditions for rapid and irreversible change come about only in the aftermath of larger crises and violent conflicts, as was the case after the unconditional surrender of Germany after the Second World War, or with the demise of most of the former socialist countries of Europe after the collapse of the Soviet Union. Under such conditions, the great majority of the population becomes receptive to change and there is little opposition on the part of those formerly in power.

But ethnopolitical intra-state conflicts, of the kind that have increasingly shaken Europe and the world in recent years, seldom end with a clear resolution – as the peace agreements in Bosnia and Chechnya have demonstrated all too clearly. It is far more likely that the crisis itself will create a lasting and determining influence on all aspects of life. The media will thus remain a perpetual victim of conflict, as the authorities maintain political and economic control over them and intensify conflict as they aggravate societal prejudices through biased and manipulative reporting.

The aim must be the safeguarding of peace by changing post-war society in such a way that future conflicts can be effectively resolved without resorting to violence. It seems clear that only concerted actions and initiatives on all fronts, involving politics, economy, media, society and, above all, education, can hope to have a lasting effect. Such actions are, unfortunately, rare.

It is, however, unfair to say that the West stood by passively while nationalist media reinforced conflicts in crisis areas. Many millions of Euros and US dollars have been invested in equipment, training and other forms of media aid. However, an integrated process has rarely been discernible; on the contrary, the EU increased its media aid to Serbia, for example, but prevented this country from participating in the PHARE democracy programme. In addition, Western willingness to provide outside support for securing long-term peace is all too often overshadowed by other, for the most part geo-strategic and power political, considerations. Chechnya and Bosnia are just two examples of this.

5. Conclusion

In most situations of tension and conflict, projects seeking to draw up ambitious guidelines and recommendations for the re-structuring of media communication usually remain in an ivory tower. However, one conclusion is certain: without proper co-ordination between the many media assistance and democracy programmes already established by the EU, NGOs and the other Western protagonists, as well as by the crisis-torn countries themselves, all initiatives run the risk that, at best, considerable financial resources will be wasted. This seems to be a lesson that still has not been learned, if the evidence of the plethora of media aid projects is any guide. They are meant to improve the situation in conflict-torn areas but often end up in competition and may prove redundant.

Box 5: Goals and Tasks of the European Media Agency

- promote transparency and rationality
- combat media concentration and encourage diversity of opinion
- act as clearing-house for the publicising of proposed international media projects
- evaluate project requests from countries in need
- develop the media in the target countries to become self-sufficient and autonomous
- organise, promote and award a 'quality mark' for the numerous training programmes
- increasing public awareness of the significance of journalism within the political process

If the international community indeed has the political will, a European Media Agency could well provide a remedy. Its primary task would be the promotion of transparency and rationality in this area. It could begin as a clearing-house for the publicising of proposed international media projects, as well as for the evaluation of project requests from countries in need. In this way, overlap, duplication and waste could be avoided.

The fundamental task of the European Media Agency in the long run, however, would be a concerted effort to put the development of the media in the target countries on a self-supporting footing. Rather than continuing to make charitable donations, the international community should instead stimulate economic growth in the media in countries threatened by conflict. Based on the recommendations of this new organisation, loans and credits from the World Bank, the European Bank for Reconstruction and Development (EBRD), the EU's Media programme for audio-visual media, or other funding sources, could provide the economic foundation for media autonomy in many regions. In established democracies, projects co-ordinated and supported by the European Media Agency could, for instance, help combat media concentration and encourage diversity of opinion.

Economic success depends essentially on appropriate expertise and product quality. Accordingly, such a new coordinating organisation, at the very least, could serve to organise, promote and finally award some kind of 'quality mark' for the numerous training programmes for journalists, media managers and other media professions.

In co-operation with media organisations and academic institutions, one important further activity of this organisation would be the continuous monitoring of media development on the Continent. The resulting database could serve as an informed starting point for action programmes and other activities of the organisation.

In addition to this, the European Media Organisation could contribute to increasing public awareness of the significance of journalism within the political process, especially in situations of conflict and crisis. It is very much in the public interest to understand just how centres of political power and journalists, as controllers and operators, handle the media, especially when the foundations of the state are shaken.

This need is particularly urgent when conflict becomes irreversible. After the bloodshed is over, it should not be the case, as it was in the former Yugoslavia, that commentators agree that one word led to another until it was all too late. Real violence, employed by those in power to impose their rule on all parts of the society and to diminish plurality, by restricting or even eliminating media autonomy for example, opens the floodgates for the language of hate in the media. This will incite further vicious circles of violence, until eventually the whole country goes up in flames. From beginning to end, the power driving the conflict is not the journalistic word, but rather the hand wielding the power in state and society.

6. Reference and Further Reading

Carothers, Thomas 1999. *Aiding Democracy Abroad: The Learning Curve,* Washington: Carnegie Endowment for International Peace.

Connor, Walker 1994. *Ethnonationalism: The Quest for Understanding,* Princeton, NJ: Princeton University Press.

Committee of Ministers of the Council of Europe 1996. *Recommendation No. (96) 4 of the Committee of Ministers to Member States on the Protection of Journalists in Situations of Conflict and Tension,* Strasbourg: Council of Europe.

Galtung, Johan 1997. "Peace Journalism: Why, What, Who, Where, When," *in* Projektgruppe Friedensforschung, op. cit.

Gellner, Ernest 1983. *Nations and Nationalism*, New Perspectives on the Past Series, Ithaca, NY: Cornell University Press.

Giddens, Anthony 1997. *Jenseits von Links und Rechts,* Frankfurt/Main: Suhrkamp

Hammond, Philip and Herman S. Edwards (eds.) 2000. *Degraded Capability. The Media and the Kosovo Crisis,* London: Pluto Press.

International Federation of Journalists and the Center for War, Peace and the News Media 1997. *Reporting Diversity. A Training and Resource Manual for Journalists on Covering Minorities, Inter-Ethnic-Relations and other Diversity Issues,* Brussels: IFJ.

McGoldrick, Annabel and Jake Lynch 2000. "Peace Journalism – how to do it?" *Activate*, 6-10.

McGarry, John and Brendan O'Leary (eds.) 1993. *The Politics of Ethnic Conflict Regulation,* London: Routledge.

Metzl, Jamie F. 1997. "Information Intervention. When Switching Channels Isn't Enough," *Foreign Affairs* (November/December 1997).

Projektgruppe Friedensforschung 1997. *War, Nationalism, Racism and the Media. Diskussionsbeiträge der Projektgruppe Friedensforschung,* Konstanz: Universität Konstanz.

Reljic, Dusan 1998. *Killing Screens. Medien in Zeiten von Konflikten,* Düsseldorf: Droste Verlag.

The Role of Development Aid in Conflict Transformation: Facilitating Empowerment Processes and Community Building

Christine Bigdon and Benedikt Korf

1. Introduction 342
2. Track III Strategies and the Role of Development Cooperation 343
3. The Logic of (Local) Empowerment and the Logic of Development Agencies 346
    The Logic of Management
    The Logic of (Local) Empowerment
    The Logic of Development Agencies
4. Empowerment in the Light of Different Discourses 351
5. Participation and Empowerment Approaches within the Context of Community Development 353
6. Spaces for Action 359
7. Conclusion: Development Agencies as Political Actors in Complex Emergencies 366
8. Reference and Further Reading 367

The Role of Development Aid in Conflict Transformation: Facilitating Empowerment Processes and Community Building

Christine Bigdon and Benedikt Korf

1. Introduction

This chapter will look into both the theoretical assumptions and expectations, as well as the practical experiences, of empowerment approaches within the field of development aid, with special regard to their potential for conflict transformation. The authors build upon the recent discourse in development policy that discusses the extent to which development cooperation can effectively contribute towards crisis prevention and conflict transformation.

The contemporary debate on the role of development aid as a contribution to conflict transformation focuses primarily on the relative strengths and weaknesses of three inter-related approaches:

- The *do-no-harm* approach developed by Anderson (1999), primarily aims to avoid doing more harm than good, and is vitally concerned with the unintended negative impacts of development aid, pointing out that these often tend to aggravate conflict rather than contribute to its resolution. This approach builds upon the experiences of a comprehensive field study conducted by the American NGO Collaborative for Development Action (CDA) in 13 conflict regions in Europe, Asia, Africa and Latin America.
- The *local capacities for peace* approach (Anderson 1999; Heinrich 1999) seeks to identify potential entry points for conflict transformation through development aid, and recommends that external donor agencies should focus on supporting local capacities for peace. This concept implies that peace cannot be imposed from outside but must be achieved from within a society.
- The *discourse on peace and conflict impact assessment* (PCIA) (*see* the contribution of Mark Hoffman in this volume; Bush 1998; Ross & Rothman 1999) stresses the need for a thorough analysis of the conflict context. From this it develops a methodology for the assessment and evaluation of peace and conflict impact that offers a framework for peacebuilding.

This chapter will focus on the practical experience of traditional relief and development projects working on complex emergencies in the field of community development. As the authors explore the nexus between conflict transformation on the one hand and participatory and empowerment approaches on the other, they will critically assess the potential of common empowerment approaches within community building not only to avoid doing harm but also to make a substantive contribution to conflict transformation at the local level. The empirical base of the chapter lies within participatory research and in the experiences of bilateral and multilateral development cooperation in the war-torn areas of Sri Lanka.

Sections II and III will explore recent aspects of the conflict transformation discourse, paying particular attention to conclusions that might be drawn concerning the role of development aid in complex emergencies. Sections IV and V introduce some common participatory and empowerment approaches within the field of community development, delineating their theoretical objectives as well as their practical implementation. Section VI critically discusses possible spaces of action, as well as constraints, dilemmas and ambivalences for the facilitation of empowerment processes through development aid within complex emergencies. The authors conclude with future prospects on the potentials, constraints and ambivalence of empowerment approaches and recommend a more political role for development aid in complex emergencies as it engages in more inclusive community building through processes of empowerment and recognition.

2. Track III Strategies and the Role of Development Cooperation

The current discussion of conflict interventions contains three principal discourses, each focusing on different levels and practices, building upon different theoretical discussions, understandings of conflict and each recommending different strategies for action (*see* the contribution of Cordula Reimann in this volume; Miall, Ramsbotham, Woodhouse 1999).

- The *conflict settlement* discourse deals with all strategies which are oriented to an outcome in the form of an agreement between the conflict parties which might enable them to end an armed conflict, but without necessarily addressing the underlying conflict causes. The typical area of practice here – Track I – is primarily reserved for the official and formal activities of diplomatic and governmental actors. It is thus not of particular relevance to this article on development aid.
- The *conflict resolution* discourse concerns itself with process-oriented activities that do aim to address the underlying causes of direct, cultural and structural violence. The area of practice – Track II – is typically represented by non-official and non-coercive activities by non-governmental parties. The instigators of such processes are usually either international and/or local conflict resolution NGOs, with special expertise in citizens diplomacy and civil mediation. They make use of vehicles such as problem-solving workshops, and are supported by academic institutions and civil society groups focused on conflict analysis.
- The *conflict transformation* discourse focuses on long-term peacebuilding efforts oriented to outcomes, processes and also structural changes. They aim at overcoming revealed forms of direct, cultural and structural violence, transforming unjust social relationships and promoting conditions that can help to create cooperative relationships. Here Track III actors, typically local grassroots organisations as well as local and international development agencies and NGOs, address themselves directly to those parties most affected by the effects of violent conflict. They engage in grassroots training, capacity building and empowerment, trauma therapy, human rights, development work and humanitarian assistance.

These three discourses and their intervention strategies are of course strongly interrelated. If they are to build domestic peace constituencies or strategic alliances between the different local, national and international actors, practitioners will need to link activities on all three levels, understanding the three strategies to be mutually integrative and complementary (*see* Reimann, ibid.).

It is the third discourse, on conflict transformation, that is most relevant for the context of development aid in complex emergencies. Further insight on the proper role that development aid should play in the context of proposed interventions designed to contribute to conflict transformation is provided by the Guidelines on Conflict, Peace and Development Cooperation of the Development Assistance Committee of the Organisation for Economic Cooperation and Development (OECD/DAC 1997). First, we must distinguish between the different phases and dynamics of conflict, each of which will necessitate different kind of interventions. DAC delineates four interrelated phases:

- situations of *submerged tensions*;
- situations of *rising tensions;*
- eruption phases of *open confrontation and violent conflict;*
- *fragile transitional and post-conflict* situations.

The situation on the ground, however, is usually far more complex (*see* Box 1). Often we experience abrupt shifts from one stage to the other and many countries are characterized by both peace and conflict simultaneously. It therefore seems more appropriate to refer to different conflict contexts or settings, rather than to stable situations which follow one another consecutively according to any sort of predictable logic. Under such conditions, donor agencies will need to be well equipped with appropriate instruments for observing indicators of increasing tension, so that they will be able to adjust flexibly to changing situations.

Box 1: Different conflict contexts or settings

In Sri Lanka, development intervention usually takes place in the war-torn areas in the Northeast, characterized by several different local scenarios. Here there are *uncleared* areas under the control of the Liberation Tigers of Tamil Elam (LTTE), *cleared* areas under the jurisdiction of the Sri Lankan army, and *semi-uncleared* areas (border areas) in which open conflict continues, especially at night. The situation can change abruptly, within a short time, from rising tension to violent conflict. In other parts of the country, development interventions are made in areas which can be defined as pre-conflict settings (situations of submerged tensions), such as the Estate Sector, with a potential escalation of the identity and labour conflict between Tamil estate workers and Singhalese plantation management. In the south of the country, development projects typically intervene in post-conflict areas. Here there has been no resolution of the root causes for the violent insurrections by the radical left wing party Janatha Vimukthi Peramuna (JVP), which were quashed by government forces.

As these conflict settings are inherently dynamic, the different types of interventions – emergency relief, rehabilitation and development operations – are often occurring simultaneously. It is precisely for this reason that many donor agencies have moved to introduce the concept of development-oriented emergency aid, linking relief with medium-term and long-term development efforts. Especially with a view to impacting on conflict transformation, these agencies now seek to take a more holistic approach towards mainstreaming peacebuilding within the traditional mandates of humanitarian assistance, poverty alleviation and sustainable development (*see* the contribution of Mark Hoffman in this volume).

In the DAC Guidelines (OECD/DAC 1997, p9), the role of development aid in complex emergencies is defined as follows:

> *Development cooperation efforts should strive for an environment of structural stability as a basis for sustainable development. An environment of structural stability is one in which there are dynamic and representative social and political structures capable of managing change and resolving disputes without resort of violence. (...) over the long term, it can contribute to alleviating the root causes of conflict and help to develop institutions capable of managing and resolving disputes in a peaceful manner.*

Development interventions should be focused on improving the general economic and social climate in partner countries, supporting measures to improve the legitimacy and effectiveness of the state, as well as aiding the emergence of a strong civil society. The promotion of democratic structural stability as a basis for sustainable development is thus facilitated through the introduction of participatory and empowerment approaches into project work. The overall aim is the integration of various societal groups – especially those that have been marginalized or who act as a firewall against violence, such as women and youth – into the decision-making processes of local development planning and negotiation. These development interventions also aim to develop institutions and mechanisms which are essential to the accommodation of competing interests within the society, as well as to the peaceful management of socio-political disputes (ibid., p18). The DAC guidelines go on to say "Promoting democratization is seen as a complex, gradual, and participatory process whereby citizens, civil society, and the state create a set of norms, values, and institutions to mediate their relationship in a predictable, representative and fair manner" (ibid., p38).

This means that development aid will need to be aimed at different levels, including the community level with its community-based organisations and the meso-level of local government institutions and NGOs, while at the same time also considering the macro dimension of the conflict context for the overall strategy of intervention. It must actively promote participation in mainstream society, but also work to support NGOs, community-based organisations (CBOs) and local government institutions, helping them to become more capable and responsive to their constituencies. Figure 1 shows the different conflict dimensions of development intervention, highlighting the interrelationship of the macro-conflict and village communities.

The DAC Guidelines (ibid., p52) stress the ongoing need for long-term support of peacebuilding and reconciliation at the community level, as well as simultaneous and continuing efforts to strengthen the peacebuilding elements of good governance on the regional institutional level.

Before looking more closely at participatory and empowerment approaches commonly used for community building, the theoretical underpinnings of conflict transformation should be discussed in more detail, especially exploring the extent to which the logic of (local) empowerment is consistent with the logic of development agencies.

Figure 1: The Interrelationship of the Macro-Conflict and Village Communities

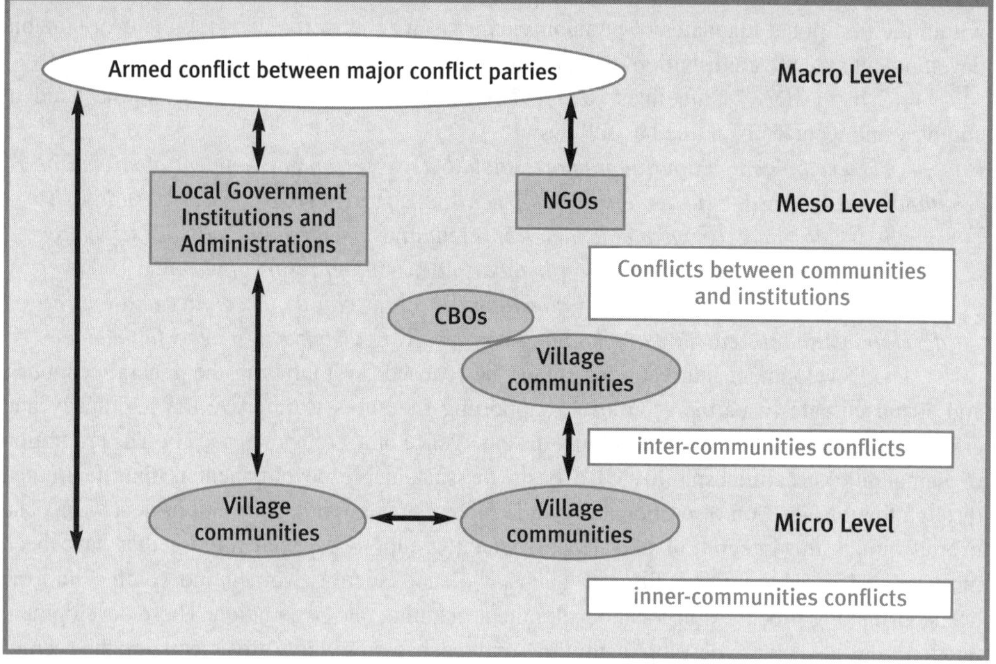

3. The Logic of (Local) Empowerment and the Logic of Development Agencies

The term conflict management is often used as an umbrella concept for all the outcome-oriented approaches, and the authors follow the same practice in this chapter. Conflict transformation, on the other hand, usually incorporates a shift from the logic of conflict management to a logic based on (local) empowerment. The theoretical assumptions of this shift have some implications for the role of development aid in complex emergencies. Particularly relevant is the question of the extent to which the assumed logic of (local) empowerment is consistent with the demonstrated logic of development agencies.

3.1 The Logic of Management

One useful framework for the analysis of conflict intervention is provided by Rothman and Friedman (2001). This approach distinguishes between different frames of conflict: resource conflicts, interest conflict and identity conflicts. The distinction follows the logic of the three different conflict discourses introduced above (conflict settlement, conflict resolution and conflict transformation). The point is not that there are three different types of conflicts, but rather that each conflict will evidence dimensions of all three frames. The most obvious dimensions in any conflict rather depends on how one understands and looks at them.

- The *frame of resource conflict* sees conflicts as a struggle over claims to scarce status, power and resources. Conflict is perceived to be a negative force, such as a threat or a disease. It is a natural consequence of competition among individuals and groups over material goods, economic benefits, property and power. Within this frame, the alternative to violence can only be the settling of the conflict through some sort of negotiation or bargaining process, which continues until the resources have been redistributed to the mutual satisfaction of all involved parties. The outcome is usually some sort of win/lose or compromise situation. It is problematic that, within this resource frame, underlying causes of the conflict remain and have not been dealt with, and deeper problems that are ignored may well later erupt.
- The *interest frame of conflict* rejects the notion of competitive resource framing. Although conflicts may be couched in terms of demands for resources, expressed bargaining positions are simply more or less concrete expressions of interests, which one can redefine as "needs, desires, and fears" (Fisher and Ury 1981). The *alternative dispute resolution* school of thought has developed a process of interest-based bargaining, which focuses upon articulating what each party is truly and legitimately seeking and then employs creative methods for working together with opponents to maximize the degree to which the interests of both sides can be satisfied.
- The *identity conflict frame* has emerged largely from longstanding efforts to deal with intractable ethnic conflict, and it appeals for alternative approaches to the static power-politics model of international diplomacy (Rothman and Friedman 2001, p590). Here conflict is recognized as a natural outgrowth of each party's needs, desires, concerns, and fears.

The interest frame provides a more optimistic view of conflict. Engaging in such a discussion will usually help the conflicting parties to clarify their own interests and perceptions, as well as to better understand those of the other side. The main criticism of this frame is, that, although it appears to be more successful in its efforts to find mutually satisfactory agreements, interest-based conflict resolution can often obscure the underlying nature of conflict. This kind of conflict resolution does focus on changing individual and collective action strategies, but leaves the underlying values and norms of each of the parties fundamentally unchanged.

Both the resource frame (conflict settlement discourse) and the interest frame (conflict resolution discourse) contain in them a certain logic of conflict management. In this analysis, we assume that any final resolution of the conflicts is unrealistic. The focus of the effort must therefore be on management and containment, and on trying to find constructive ways to bring opponents together, aiming to reach a compromise or win/win situation in which violence may then be laid aside (*see* the contribution of Hugh Miall in this volume). The more successful conflict resolution discourse focuses on re-framing positions and on identifying win/win situations, while still trying to manage the conflicts in this way. The logic of conflict management is a fundamentally pragmatic recipe for dealing with conflicts, not necessarily seeking out root causes of the conflict and the underlying values, norms and fears of the conflict parties.

3.2 The Logic of (Local) Empowerment

Rothman and Friedman's third frame, that of *identity* (critical for any conflict transformation discourse) involves a paradigm shift away from the logic of conflict management towards a logic of (local) empowerment. This model recognizes that the most intractable conflicts are really about the articulation and confrontation of individual and collective *identities*. Such conflicts find their source in threats to or the frustration of deeply rooted human needs such as dignity, recognition, safety, control, purpose, and efficacy (Azar 1990; Burton 1990). Analysts working within the identity frame do not see conflicts as problems to be resolved, or even managed. Rather, they argue that they offer opportunities for growth, adaptation and learning (Lederach 1995). Conflicts can lead all parties to clarify for themselves their needs and values, and can thus help them to better understand just what causes them dissatisfaction and satisfaction (Baruch Bush and Folger 1994).

Conflict engagement must therefore involve reflexive dialogue, in which parties to the conflict speak openly about their needs and values in the presence of their adversaries, well before any kind of negotiation can be expected to succeed. *Recognition* and *empowerment* are key processes. Through the recognition of others' articulation and assertion of self, conflict thus provides an opportunity for mutual transformation and empowerment (ibid.). From the perspective of the identity frame, the goal of intervention is not just to reach agreements or solutions. Rather, the process of engagement in conflict is seen as an opportunity for challenging the status quo (including the parties themselves), building on local capacities for peace in the process (Rothman & Friedman 2001, p592).

The logic of (local) empowerment puts the emphasis on bottom-up strategies which aim at nothing less than the support for or even generation of local struggles for social justice and hence for radical, structural change. Conflict transformation thus builds upon the theoretical framework of non-violent action, and sees conflict as a non-violent struggle for social justice. Non-violent struggle, expressed through demonstrations, strikes or non-cooperation is a concrete manifestation of peoples' power to bring about social and structural change.

Protracted violent conflicts in the conflict transformation discourse are therefore perceived as the natural consequence of unequal and repressive social and political structures. "Dealing effectively with it (violent conflict), therefore, will call for the *empowerment and recognition* of marginalized groups in the form of non-violent struggle. Only in this way will it be possible to deal with issues of immediate concern at the local level, or to put the appropriate pressure on Track I (and Track II) actors, to end the violence and enter into good-faith negotiations" (Reimann in this volume). Track III strategies put the civilian population, so far largely excluded from the discussion, and its potential for non-violent struggle at centre-stage. It thus becomes a key player in the local peace process.

What is convincing about the conflict transformation approach is its outcome, process and change orientation:

- The ultimate aim of conflict transformation is to achieve a settlement on substantive issues raised by the underlying needs and fears of the conflict parties (*outcome orientation*). This has two direct implications:
- First, *process orientation*, which means that the intervenors will need to materially change mutually negative conflict attitudes and values among the parties in order to enable cooperation and communication between them;
- Second, *change orientation*, which recognizes the political imperative to create a new infrastructure for empowerment and recognition of underprivileged groups, thus fostering

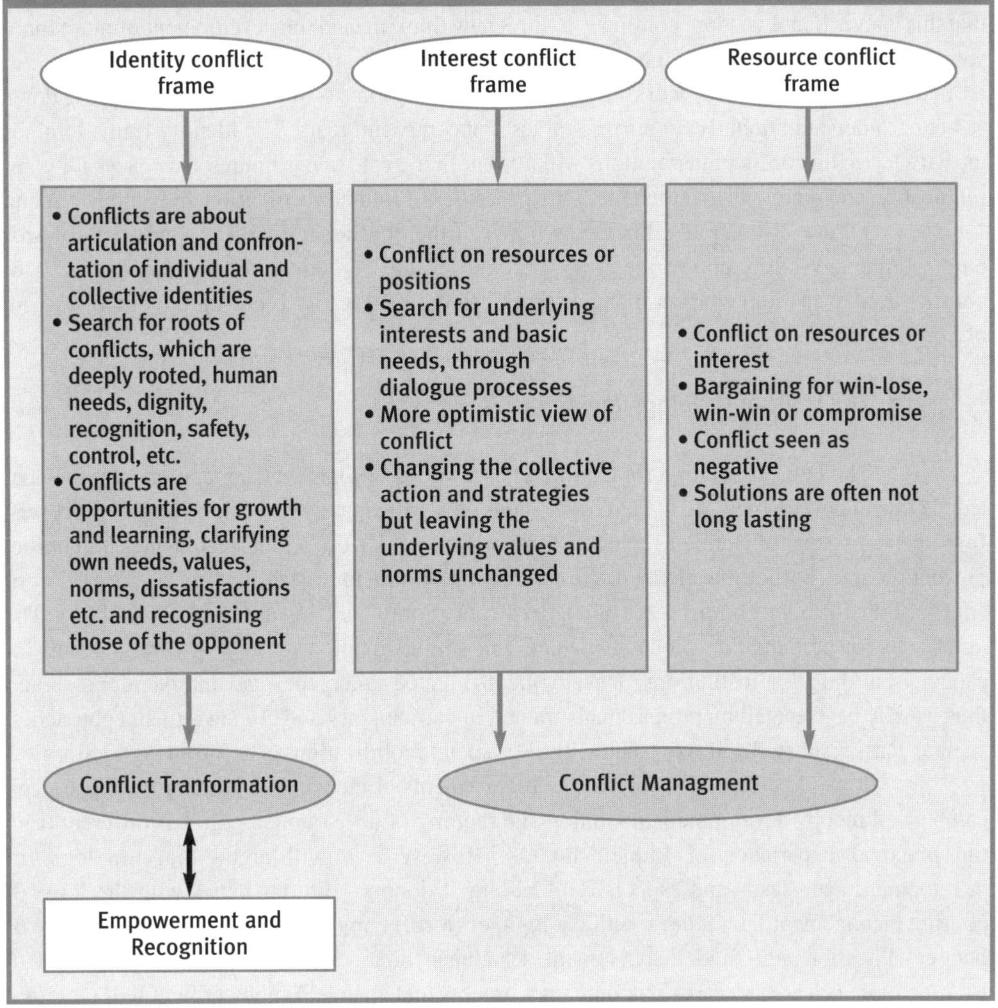

Figure 2: Empowerment and Recognition in the light of different Conflict Frames and Discourses

and enabling true social justice beyond the concerns of the parties directly involved in conflict (ibid.).

The conflict transformation approach, depending as it does on a logic of (local) empowerment, can be seen as an open-ended, long-term, multi-track and dynamic process, one which thereby significantly widens the scope of actors involved. Since they understand that the satisfaction of basic needs on the personal and relational levels will not be sufficient to truly transform the conflict, practitioners must also work on the larger goal of achieving equal access to resources and assembling the infrastructure that will make it possible to address larger structural inequalities, with the aim of longer-term social reconstruction and reconciliation (ibid.).

Rothman and Friedman (2001, p593) point out that the resource frame and interest frames of conflict continue to dominate the thinking of many practitioners and researchers, and that this conventional wisdom continues to limit new thinking and the development of more innovative approaches. In general, the experts continue to favour strategies of conflict avoidance or reduction, instead of actively working with the underlying causes of conflicts, and digging down to better understand underlying norms, values, concerns, and fears. The identity frame reminds us that successful conflict interventions will need to first create opportunities and spaces for communication and dialogue, and then facilitate processes of mutual recognition and empowerment.

Figure 2 illustrates this nexus between the conflict frames and strategies towards empowerment. While empowerment and recognition are of course both means and ends of conflict transformation, conflict management does not necessarily focus on the empowerment of conflict parties.

3.3 The Logic of Development Agencies

The DAC Guidelines for Conflict, Peace and Development Cooperation have delineated the role of development aid in facilitating more fully participatory and empowerment processes. In the concept paper of German Technical Cooperation (GTZ), the principal strategies for conflict prevention and conflict management are a) creation of structural stability and b) promotion of conflict-transforming competences of the relevant groups and institutions (GTZ 2001). The latter calls for participatory processes which will stimulate empowerment of certain groups or capacity-building for institutions. Development-oriented emergency aid interventions should thus usually be executed by professionals trained in participatory and empowerment approaches, such as Participatory Rural Appraisal (PRA) or social mobilization, (*see* following section).

It would certainly seem that the requirements of the conflict transformation strategy can be well met by development aid, unless the rhetoric of development policy is different from the practical experience of implementation. However we will argue that the logic of development agencies – and especially of bi-lateral donors – fits far better with the logic of conflict management than it does with the logic of (local) empowerment. Under the pressure of budget allocation and fund disbursement schedules, donor agencies will naturally tend to become more oriented towards outcome than process and change. Empowerment will therefore be often understood only instrumentally, causing project managers to integrate people into the implementation of projects, without granting them essential decision-making power in important questions such as budget allocation. Conflicts at the community or intra-community level which impede the implementation of projects will mainly be seen as obstacles or delaying factors, problems which need to be eliminated as quickly as possible.

Any effort to find an acceptable compromise between competing groups through conflict management is therefore much more likely to employ the logic of development agencies. They will fall short of the logic of a long-term facilitation of difficult empowerment and recognition processes, in that they fail to search for underlying roots of conflicts, which explore the values, norms and fears of the groups involved. As in-depth impact evaluation of projects is often neglected, donor agencies will all too often follow a simple implementation path, without giving particular emphasis to the question of the sustainable impact of the projects.

Project management and staff will often be caught in an endless process of analysing the local problems and immediately constructing short-term solutions, without spending much time talking to the local population and listening to their opinion. There is a very real danger that donor agencies will in the end impose solutions instead of creating spaces for local capacity building and decision-making.

In the worst cases, donor agencies will organize themselves internally in a very hierarchical and un-democratic manner, failing to integrate local field staff in important decision-making processes. With this kind of structure, it is rather questionable whether these agencies will be able to stimulate democratic processes and empowerment of groups, given that they have proved themselves unable to incorporate even basic democratic rules into their own internal procedures.

Let us look now at the theoretical conception and practical implementation of common participatory and empowerment approaches of development aid, so that we will then be able to assess critically their potential for contributing to conflict transformation.

4. Empowerment in the Light of Different Discourses

What exactly does *empowerment* mean in the context of the development-oriented discourse? What definitions are commonly in use and, more importantly, how can empowerment processes be successfully operationalised into practical action? Let us look once again at the ways in which empowerment is defined in the conflict transformation discourse, especially as compared with the development aid discussion. What can development cooperation learn from notions of empowerment as developed in the mediation discourse that might help further its own activities and actions in complex political emergencies?

In the *conflict transformation discourse*, the root causes of violent conflicts are seen to arise from unsatisfied human needs, as well as from unequal and repressive social and political structures which result in the deep dissatisfaction of marginalized groups. Empowerment must therefore first address unequal power relations, aiming to balance them with the intention to achieve greater social justice.

Barach Bush and Folger (1994, pp85-87) define empowerment within the transformative conflict mediation discourse as follows:

> *A party is empowered by gaining new awareness and understanding of (1) its goals (including underlying values, norms, fears), (2) its options, (3) its skills, (4) its resources, and (5) its decision-making, and is able to utilise these new insights in mediation and negotiation.*

Empowerment is first of all a process of supported self-reflection for improved action. It is not limited to the context of current mediation, but also enables the party to engage productively in future negotiations and conflict settlements. In transformative mediation, the complementary element to empowerment is recognition. In unmediated conflicts, parties are often primarily focused on self-protection and are therefore often on the defensive. They are thus largely unable to look beyond their own interests. Parties achieve recognition in mediation when they manage to expand their perspective to include an appreciation for another's situation.

This emphasis on the interrelatedness of empowerment and recognition implies a process of dialogue and active listening to what the opponent is saying. The recognition of interests, needs, fears and values of an opponent is a process, one which at the same time helps to clarify one's own interests, needs and values, leading to empowerment through recognition. For the other, being recognized contributes to a general feeling of being valued, and this is often the first step towards a tenable compromise. It is precisely this aspect of recognition that is all too often missing within the development-oriented empowerment discourse.

The *development-oriented* discourse assumes for its empowerment approaches that the major reason for poverty is the oppression or exploitation of the poorest by the more powerful. This implies that power relations must constitute an important part of the explanation of any lack of development in a society. The term empowerment in fact, originates from the social movements in the 1960s and 1970s, such as, for example, the black power movement in the United States and the emancipation movement in Latin America influenced by the work of Paulo Freire (1972).

At the third World Conference on Women in 1985 in Nairobi, the Womens' Network DAWN also introduced the term into their discourse on development and women's politics (Sen & Grown 1988). Dawn's definition of empowerment examines the relation between power and development within the existing development paradigm, and criticizes existing power relations between gender, race, class and nations, excoriating control and power which is based on discrimination and the repression of individuals and groups. Empowerment is understood to be a vision and a process of individual autonomy and transformation of a society towards more just and equal relations. As the empowerment process takes hold, the oppressed develop their own power to change the society. It is this individual process of awareness building, as well as the collective process of the empowerment of oppressed groups as a whole, which leads to overall social transformation.

It is clear that this definition of empowerment bears significant potential for revolution, as it refuses to accept existing power structures and calls for substantial change. It is natural that those NGOs which have their roots in social movements will operate from this understanding of empowerment processes in development. Their work is primarily political, and focuses on the raising of awareness in the most vulnerable groups, as well as on public demonstrations and campaigns for the rights of the oppressed. Today, although the term empowerment has become quite fashionable within the development discourse and is now a constituent part of the rhetoric of most bilateral and multilateral donor agencies, it has for the most part been denuded of its revolutionary content, and is used in a purely instrumental fashion, viz. as a means to improve the sustainability of project impacts and to reduce project costs.

All in all, however, the term empowerment remains vague. The key question is still the ways and the extent to which the empowerment approach is actually put into practice in the context of the provision of development aid. At first sight, it seems that empowerment is often understood as little more than some sort of process of building the capacities of marginalized groups. We would point instead to the need to distinguish clearly empowerment on the one hand and capacity building on the other.

Capacity building, under our definition, refers to the transfer of knowledge to individuals or groups with the intention of enabling them to carry out certain activities. It includes raising awareness, training and other forms of human resource development. Capacity building is a necessary but not a sufficient condition for empowerment. Empowerment, which always occurs in the context of the local social system, implies an increase in the relative power and ability of disadvantaged groups in their specific socio-political environment. Empowerment strategies must therefore address the needs of both the individuals and the groups that are to be empowered, as well as the larger strategic groups which dominate and determine the governance structure and institutional arrangements. Effective empowerment of vulnerable disadvantaged groups will thus be a natural outcome of both the capacity building of the disadvantaged, and the reform of oppressive rules and practices.

The concept of recognition, so familiar in mediation and alternative dispute resolution, is also essential to the success of empowerment strategies in community development. Intra-community and inter-community resource allocation and dispute resolution will always go beyond simply solving the issue, requiring that all parties involved be recognized as fully-fledged negotiating partners. This will often call for the services of a neutral and skilled person to facilitate the process. The development discourse has further emphasised that empowerment is always a process embedded in a larger and more complex societal system, so that it is not sufficient to strengthen individuals or groups without at the same time also encouraging the development of conducive institutional arrangements and governance structures.

In the following section, we assess some participatory development approaches that are currently being applied in development cooperation, especially with regard to their potential for empowering disadvantaged groups in less developed countries. Section 6 will then discuss implementation, examining the potential and constraints of participatory development approaches for any effort to contribute to meaningful conflict transformation.

5. Participation and Empowerment Approaches within the Context of Community Development

The terms participation and empowerment have now become orthodox in mainstream development cooperation; virtually all major bilateral and multilateral development agencies have adopted this rhetoric. The danger is, of course, that the term participation has by now been reduced to a slogan or label used only to attract donor funding. We must therefore define the terms carefully, looking especially at how they are best used in the context of community development.

Robert Chambers (1995, p30), one of the leading scholars advocating participatory approaches, has identified three ways in which participation can be used in the context of development cooperation:

- as a cosmetic label to embellish virtually any proposal, mainly to satisfy donor agencies;
- as a co-opting practice for mobilizing labour and reducing costs: communities contribute 'their' labour in 'our' project;
- to describe an empowerment process which enables local people to analyse their own situation, to take command, to gain confidence and to make their own decisions.

We distinguish between two different schools of thought. Some view participation principally as a means or instrument to improve project sustainability. The expectation is that, by encouraging involvement of the target groups in their own development activities and through their direct contribution to project costs, people will take ownership and thus themselves sustain the development process and maintain any assets which are created. Others argue that participation should be an end in itself: that the processes of participation should lead to an increase in decision-making power on the local level. Here empowerment, and not the physical project outcomes, becomes the major objective of participatory approaches.

Caroline Moser (1993, p101) also points to this difference between participation as a means for an increase of efficiency and cost sharing and participation as an end in itself towards empowerment:

> *Where participation is a means, it generally becomes a form of mobilization to get things done. This can equally be state-directed, top-down mobilization, sometimes enforced, to achieve specific objectives, or bottom-up "voluntary" community-based mobilization to obtain a large share of resources. Where participation is identified as an end in itself, the objective is not a fixed, quantified development goal, but a process, the outcome of which is an increasingly 'meaningful' participation in the development process.*

The critical question is how the approach is put into practice. Who participates in which activities, in which manner and why? Such participation can take various forms as is indicated in the following typology for the ranking of different levels of intensity of participation (adapted from Pretty et al. 1995):

- Passive participation as recipients (relief);
- Extractive participation through information giving (e.g. in surveys);

- Participation by consultation (getting informed about ongoing or planned activities);
- Participation for material incentives (providing resources in return for incentives);
- Functional participation (forming groups to meet predetermined objectives);
- Interactive participation (joint analysis with external support for collective action);
- Self-mobilization (initiatives are taken independent of external institutions).

Community development projects often seek to achieve empowerment through a well-balanced combination of input and process. On the one hand, the project provides incentives, material and funds for local collective action. On the other hand, local institutions and organisations are strengthened through the capacity building of staff. In practice, empowerment in community development is largely aimed at gaining the active participation of target groups in planning and implementing donor-funded village projects.

The facilitation of joint planning and decision-making and local management of project implementation also aim to stimulate a process of social learning. Community development makes use of a variety of instruments in this effort. We find two of *particular interest – participatory rural appraisal* (PRA) (*see* Box 2) and *social mobilization* (*see* Box 3) – both commonly propagated in the South Asian context and partly seen as complementary, partly as antagonistic to one another.

The advocates of the social mobilization approach often question the PRA approach on the grounds that it is social engineering which focuses on tools rather than on long-term processes. They suggest that true empowerment of disadvantaged groups demands a longer-term approach, one that goes beyond a one-week village workshop. PRA scholars emphasise, on the other hand, that a PRA village workshop can only be one small step in a long-term process of engagement involving negotiation, bargaining, dialogue and conflict resolution (Shah & Shah 1995). It is a necessary but not a sufficient instrument for the empowerment of vulnerable groups.

Box 2: Participatory Rural Appraisal (PRA)

Participatory Rural Appraisal (PRA) a term which commonly refers to a family of approaches, methods and behaviours that enables people to express and analyse the realities of their lives and conditions, to plan themselves what action to take, and to monitor and evaluate the results. The term is confusing and utilised under a variety of synonyms, such as Participatory Learning and Action (PLA), Participatory Needs Assessment (PNA) etc. The key elements of PRA are the methods used and the behaviour and attitudes of those who facilitate it.

Methods:

PRA employs methods to enable people to express and share information, and to stimulate discussion and analysis. Visual techniques enhance creativity, cross-checking information and encourage exchange of views. Using a combination of PRA tools enables the construction of a more comprehensive picture of the complexity and diversity of village life. Common tools are:

- mapping;
- flow diagrams;
- seasonal calendars;
- matrices and grids;
- village transect walk.

The tools are applied during group discussions and semi-structured interviews.

Facilitation:

Facilitators support the local population, helping them to do the analysis, investigation, and finally planning on their own. Information is shared between villagers and outsiders (planners, field workers) and among villagers themselves. PRA is often carried out in the form of village workshops: external facilitators join villagers for a few days to jointly carry out a PRA.

Behaviour and Attitudes:

The change in attitudes and roles of external facilitators and project planners is even more important than the methods. Chambers talks about 'handing over the stick' from outsiders to insiders, i.e. the villagers themselves. PRA facilitators should act as convenors and catalysts, but without dominating the process. They must show respect, take time, be open and self-critical. They need to gain confidence that local people are capable of carrying out their own analysis.

(Sources: Institute for Development Studies 1995; Chambers 1994a, 1995; Chambers & Guijt 1995)

Participatory Rural Appraisal (PRA) is best understood as a 'philosophy of development planning' or 'family of approaches', that enables people to express and analyse the realities of their lives and conditions, to plan for themselves what actions to take, and then to monitor and evaluate the results. Usually, the identification of development problems and basic needs in a given area and the subsequent planning of projects would start with a workshop at the specific location. In that exercise, a PRA team of several members and one moderator would facilitate a process of joint analysis and learning, using different tools such as flow diagrams and village transect walks in order to construct a comprehensive picture of the complexity and diversity of village life.

The local population must always take ownership of such a process, analysing their own reality and planning their own priority projects. PRA therefore will always make every effort to involve all the relevant social groups (women, youth, village leaders etc.), especially those that have been marginalized or neglected. The outcome of the PRA is not only the detailed development plan with its list of priority projects, but rather the process of joint learning itself, one which hopefully will also enable the local population to take on the responsibility for the development of their own village/environment.

Understood in this way, PRA indeed seems to be an eminently suitable way to stimulate an empowerment process at the local level. In reality, however, it is often implemented fairly mechanically, as PRA tools are used in the village purely in an effort to collect information, without much emphasis on the stimulation of any kind of process in which villagers actively take part in and are granted decision-making power for follow-up. All too often, researchers borrow PRA tools and use them only to collect data and information from the local level, without feeding back any results to the villagers. It is therefore not surprising that, in many rural areas, local residents become suspicious as soon as they see a PRA team entering their village. They are simply unwilling to spend any more time working with tools with no visible payback for them (Korf 2000a).

The term is also used to mean the strengthening of local organisational capacities, human resources and civic institutions, which then in turn reinforce the coping mechanisms of conflict-affected communities, leading the way towards participatory development (Sachithanandam 1996, p867). A social mobilizer, who can be either a person employed by the NGO or a selected village representative, acts as a facilitator (catalyst), stimulating group formation for collective action. In the South Asian context, social mobilization has become quite fashionable, and is now widely used by government institutions, bilateral donor agencies, as well as NGOs. It is understood differently by its various users, but often its employment is quite apolitical and practical. People are mobilized for group formation primarily in order to get projects implemented in a more efficient manner, without spending too much time on awareness creating and self-organisation.

Box 3: Social Mobilization

Social mobilization is a process of empowerment of vulnerable groups (e.g. the poorest, women, youth, lower castes, ethnic groups, war-affected, refugees etc.) and combines

- awareness creation;
- self-organisation; and
- action;

to improve the social and economic conditions of marginalized, poor people. Peopleform small groups and are made aware of their potential and of the resources available to them, e.g. existing governmental, non-governmental and private services.

Social mobilization therefore involves two dimensions:

- changing the individual, psychological self-perception of vulnerable groups;
- changing the social and economic conditions of the overall situation of exclusion and marginalisation.

Social mobilization is a long-term process:

Many NGO's in the South promote empowerment through the employment of trained village volunteers (change agents, or social mobilizers) who live and work in their village or area of origin. Other organisations have trained staff, who work as facilitators or social mobilizers on the community level. These volunteers or social mobilizers encourage poor villagers to form savings and credit groups as a primary cell for further development. Social mobilization focuses on a group-based approach. Over time, the small groups develop into larger ones with more formal structures (community-based organisations), thus strengthening local self-help capacities for collective action and for bargaining with service providers (government departments, NGOs, private businesses).

Social mobilization works through consciousness raising:

The poor are brought into a position where they become able to analyse just why they are poor and which conditions are triggering their poverty and to then identify possible solutions which can enable them to escape from the poverty trap by their own means.

In the discourse of conflict transformation in protracted conflicts, social mobilization brings in another dimension when it comes to human rights for minority groups. Marginalized groups (e.g. ethnic groups, women, low castes) are made aware of their rights to recognise and develop their identity, and consequently participate actively in the political process.

The context of development aid often makes use of both the PRA and social mobilization approaches. Here social mobilization is understood as the general project approach for getting people involved in planning and implementation and in assuming ownership of the development process of their village, using PRA tools for analysis and project identification. The social mobilizer, usually project staff, facilitate group discussion in order to identify priority projects, focusing on certain vulnerable groups and to identify group leaders who can then be trained by the social mobilizer in leadership or management skills in order to better carry out their duties.

The formulated objective is still the empowerment of the people. The difficulty in practical implementation of this objective is that, all too often, the social mobilizers themselves become 'heroes on the ground' by organising too much on their own, instead of leaving the ownership to the target groups and just supporting them in their efforts. While this might be more efficient in furthering the outcome of the project, we must also realize that it does undermine any meaningful larger process of local empowerment. As discussed above, the reasons for this bias towards a stronger outcome orientation rather than a process orientation are fundamentally to be found in the management logic of development agencies, although they are sometimes also a result of particular difficulties faced within the project context:

- Stringent fund disbursement schedules require projects to be executed under tight deadlines, and to present visible and quantifiable results within a short period. Such time pressure can be counterproductive for any effort to induce self-help processes on the local level. The impact of empowerment processes is difficult to measure in quantitative terms. How can we reasonably expect a project to demonstrate or prove its success along this dimension?
- Initiating processes of empowerment and societal learning within a community requires highly developed facilitation, communication and negotiation skills. Many development agencies find it difficult to recruit suitable personnel with the relevant knowledge and also the attitudes and behaviour which would be conducive to the encouragement of local initiative.
- Development agencies often put a lot of effort into participatory appraisals (in particular using PRA methods), but are much less clear about what should happen afterwards. When it comes to implementing projects, they then face administrative and capacity constraints, and often cannot follow up the processes they started in the communities. In many countries, villagers feel over-assessed by agencies, and are disappointed when few activities are actually implemented afterwards. Initial enthusiasm during intensive appraisal processes can then easily deteriorate into frustration, which is clearly detrimental to any effort at true empowerment.

Box 4: Project Example – The Integrated Food Security Programme Trincomalee (IFSP) of German Development Cooperation (GTZ)

The Integrated Food Security Programme Trincomalee (IFSP) is currently at work in the Eastern part of Sri Lanka, and pursues a dual project intervention strategy: while community projects generate assets which are useful for the whole community (and often benefit the middle-class and elite more than the vulnerable), the project also implements poverty projects especially geared for these vulnerable groups only (Bauer et al 1999). The project thus offers something to the leaders while at the same time creating bargaining space for specific support to the poorest or most disadvantaged households and individuals within the community.

The project seeks to be as transparent as possible, involving village leaders and the whole community in the identification of vulnerable groups. Since selection always implies that some will inevitably be left out, this is a very delicate task. The project's strategy is to involve village leaders in the whole process, and also to appeal to their sense of social responsibility for the poor. The project therefore cooperates on the one hand with existing community-based organisations, which are largely dominated by the village elite, as well as with informal action groups, where the vulnerable are better represented.

The project takes a pragmatic approach to empowerment. This "purposive social mobilization" approach (Bigdon & Engel 2000) regards community mobilization as the centrepiece of the project cycle of village activities, starting with the identification of needs and leading up to the planning and implementation of action. Communities are strengthened 'on the job', i.e. project implementation and community mobilization go hand in hand as an incremental local capacity building process (Korf 2000b). We must realize that this approach abandons any more ambitious concepts of empowering the disadvantaged *against* the existing establishment.

Another challenge for participatory development concepts in the context of development cooperation is achieving a mass impact. Many projects have reached significant results and successes in small 'project islands' of selected villages or communities, usually as a result of very intensive local interventions. The difficulty lies in expanding such an approach so that it can sensibly be applied to a larger number of villages, and possibly be integrated into the routine procedures of government departments. Here participatory development concepts usually face significant constraints (Bauer & Hoffmann 1997; Blackburn & Holland 1998; Chambers 1994c). Government procedures are rigid in budgeting and timing of projects. Participatory processes and empowerment are, however, unpredictable and sometimes very slow. They can hardly be pressed into formalised procedures without seriously harming the development of self-reliant processes of institution building and collective action.

Regardless of these constraints, it is still essential to keep up the effort for participatory approaches to stimulate local development, not only for efficiency and cost-cutting reasons, but also to overcome dependency and to stimulate self-help and empowerment processes among marginalized groups. Especially in situations of complex emergency, empowerment processes and recognition are the only way to bring about democratisation and to achieve a more inclusive, pluralistic and tolerant society, which is able to resolve its conflicts with non-violent means, as stressed by the DAC Guidelines (OECD/DAC 1997, p39):

> *Participation strengthens civil society and the economy by empowering individuals, communities, and organisations to negotiate with institutions and bureaucracies, thus allowing civil society to influence public policy and to provide a check on the power of government. Participation also aids in dealing with conflicting interests in a peaceful manner. It follows that the creation of a climate and the capacity for constructive interaction between civil society and government is a critical component for long-term peacebuilding.*

Section 6 will therefore look more closely at the spaces for action by development aid to facilitate empowerment processes in situations of complex emergency.

6. Spaces for Action

The major aim of this section is to examine just how far development agencies can intervene effectively in situations of complex emergency, contributing towards the empowerment of particular groups and the development of local communities and promoting inclusive citizenship. The question is the extent to which there are spaces for action within the context of situations of complex emergency?

Clearly, the objective of most development intervention is structural change: the transformation of unjust social relationships and the promotion of conditions that are most likely to create cooperative relationships. Within the more traditional mandates of most forms of humanitarian assistance, poverty alleviation and sustainable development, these considerations will mean that it is essential that any development interventions:

- Firstly, identify the unjust social relationships (who is marginalized or discriminated against in the local context, how, why and by whom?). In most situations of complex emergency, it is especially important to base these conclusions on a sound analysis of the conflict context, with special regard to its micro- and macro-dimensions as well as on a properly executed needs assessment of marginalized groups. As the ground situation can change very quickly, the local context must be monitored continuously.

- Secondly, formulate a strategy for effective transformation of unjust structures. Here intervenors need to make their own normative assumptions about justice very clear, so that they will be able to act in an accountable and transparent manner, providing a basis for cooperative relationships with local partners.
- Thirdly, develop a plan of action for the promotion of conditions that can create the necessary cooperative relationships, especially among the conflicting parties, but also more generally at any level of project intervention, e.g. the community.

Usually, violent macro-conflicts in a situation of complex emergency will exhibit specific dimensions on which development projects will have no, or at most very limited, influence. These can include the presence of armed personnel, battles on the ground or the general security situation. Project leaders simply have to work within the given circumstances, even if their activities are significantly inhibited by war.

But aid agencies can also affect the context of the intervention. Klem (2001) has introduced a framework for analysis from the perspective of do no harm, that distinguishes between the impact of donor agencies on the *agency component* and on the *structural component* of war. By *agency component*, Klem means the agents that can be held responsible for the war, such as insurgents, the Government, the Armed Forces etc. Without intending to, donor agencies might easily, by their interventions, find themselves strengthening the socio-cultural, economic or political position of one or other warring party.

But both the root and the dynamic causes of most wars also have a *structural component*, such as, for example, the relations between different ethnic communities on the local level, which often make the crucial difference between war and peace. Through their interventions and distribution of resources, donor agencies can have either a positive or negative impact on these structures, widening or narrowing the scope for peaceful relationships at the local level. Box 5 shows some possible negative impacts of project interventions on such structural relations.

Box 5: Negative Impacts of Project Interventions on Structural Relations – Examples from the Northeast of Sri Lanka

In the Northeast of Sri Lanka, development intervention at the community level might easily exacerbate conflicts between ethnic groups living in the same village (e.g. Tamils and Muslims), if only by selecting one group as a target for support.

Project interventions, by channelling resources mainly in Sinhalese areas, can incite attacks of the LTTE on Sinhalese farmer settlements.

Project interventions can create conflicts at the household level when they encourage groups of women to take up income-generating activities, projects which were until then predominantly the domain of men.

Project interventions must also often deal with community-based conflicts with roots in the particular security or war situation, such as, for example, conflicts that can arise between villagers and residents of nearby refugee camps. At first these social conflict are usually non-violent, but always with a potential for violent escalation. The project therefore needs to address them effectively, facilitating conditions that create spaces for dialogue, cooperative relationships and mechanisms for non-violent conflict management. It must recognize that often these conflicts are perceived as simple disagreements over resources, while the critical aspects of identity and recognition are usually neglected.

But what scope of action and spaces for manoeuvre do donor agencies have in facilitating empowerment processes within complex emergencies? What can they realistically do without creating a negative backlash from the agency and structural components of the violent conflict?

The key concern of development agencies is the delivery of support services and advice, as well as finding effective ways to interact with the actors in the local conflict arena without doing any harm (Anderson 1999) and perhaps even managing to contribute to conflict transformation on a local scale. But are empowerment processes within the context of community development conducive to conflict transformation and, thereby, to strengthen local capacities for peace? If the approach based on local capacities for peace is correct in claiming that the first task of a society in conflict is the re-learning of non-violent conflict mitigation mechanisms and the re-establishment of related institutional arrangements, then participatory approaches to community development might indeed be able to support such processes by rebuilding local groups and self-help institutions. In their efforts to facilitate participatory and empowerment processes at the community level in situations of complex emergency, relief and development oriented donor agencies will seek especially to:

- encourage the creation of platforms for discussions (e.g. during the PRA-workshop);
- initiate or strengthen community-based organisations;
- promote the creation of democratic procedures (e.g. through the forming of committees for CBO-management);
- promote the integration of particular interest groups within the village development process (e.g. through the encouragement of women's groups, youth groups etc.).

Considering the impact that the experience of protracted war has had on all affected, it is clear that the introduction of participatory and empowerment approaches to situations of conflict is never going to be easy. Actors in conflict areas have usually been long deprived of any kind of decision-making, even in trivial matters which directly affect their daily lives. In particular refugees and internally displaced persons will have long become dependent on relief and thus reduced to passive recipients of welfare.

Under this sort of dependency syndrome, people are increasingly unable to make any kind of decision concerning their own lives. They live in refugee camps which often set strict rules, and subsist on the basis of relief from humanitarian agencies which establish stringent conditions. Warlords and those who hold the monopoly of violence in the area impose their decisions and their regime on the population. Reintegrating people into development processes at the local level can thus provide an essential impetus for the reestablishment of institutional arrangements of civil society and popular participation at the community level.

Sachithanandam (1996, p206) describes a particular situation in which peoples' participation in such a process was encouraged by means of a micro-credit and savings project, in which democratic procedures were effectively integrated into newly-founded community-based savings organisations. Here an elected executive committee was made responsible for all major decisions concerning financial matters, projects and beneficiaries. Under the procedural rules of the committee, different democratic mechanisms, such as regular feed-back, structured supervision and rotating leadership were developed step by step, thus helping to overcome intra-organisational conflicts.

Women were particularly encouraged to participate actively in the committee. In general, the intervenors found that this building of a community-based saving organisation, with adequate checks and balances on power relations between the various functional bodies, and with the use of elected committees indeed ensured that the participation of the local population increased tremendously, bringing about a real sense of ownership amongst the members of the organisation.

Still, any such process of consciousness-raising will require enormous material and human resources over a long period of time, with outcomes that are often not sustainable, if only due to changing ground conditions, especially as regards security, which can force people to leave their homes from one day to the next. It is therefore more than questionable whether such efforts are worthwhile: all too often, they can rather seem like the futile building of sand castles. Some authors would argue, however, that such initiatives are still valuable, if only because they teach people how to build up their own community-based democratic institutions, together with a committed leadership, and also help them to acquire useful managerial skills and knowledge of community and governance structures. Even if they are destroyed, these institutions can usually be rebuilt after tense situations have been defused.

There are also other examples which clearly illustrate the unintentional impacts of local empowerment processes and institutional building at the community level. Klem (2001) describes a savings project of the Dutch NGO, ZOA, working in an uncleared (LTTE-controlled) area of Trincomalee District. While this project was initially intended to empower the most vulnerable war-affected poor by means of a savings and revolving fund mechanism, it later served to bring to light the considerable influence and power of the LTTE on the newly-founded village savings organisation. As time went on, funds were diverted to development projects other than those earmarked by the saving committees, decisions imposed retroactively by the LTTE and effectively superseding the participatory decision-making process of the saving groups. The facilitating donor agency, uncomfortable in the unintended role of indirectly strengthening the LTTE (agency component) when it had really sought to facilitate the empowerment of local groups and structures, faced a real dilemma. Its only alternative, aborting the savings arrangement, was not a reasonable solution, as that would have left the war-affected groups dis-empowered and vulnerable.

Another unintended consequence that Klem cites is the fact that the threats of armed groups, such as the Army or the LTTE, often have more influence on the social structures between communities than can any kind of project intervention. One example of this, from a refugee camp in Trincomalee, was a case in which camp inmates, supported by local communities, demonstrated at army headquarters in an effort to get the dead bodies of their relatives released, after they were shot by the army under suspicion of affiliation with the LTTE. The army reacted by threatening the local population, decreeing that any young man seen on the street after 6.00 p.m. would be shot. Intimidated by this threat, the local community withdrew its support for the refugee camp inmates. Social relations between these two groups deteriorated as a result, and open hostility erupted after the village community had trouble with the army, difficulties for which they blamed the refugee inmates. All of this does raise the question as to whether empowerment processes are even possible in threatening situations or in the context of hierarchical and authoritarian power structures. It would seem that, rather than becoming empowered, the local population will instead come to feel dis-empowered as their room for action is narrowed.

Indeed, in an environment of violence, attempted empowerment processes with local populations can amount to playing with fire. Goodhand & Lewer (1999) have observed in the context of the war-torn area of Sri Lanka that local leaders, and especially social entrepreneurs, are often intimidated by violence, and are very much afraid of being killed or injured. They will therefore be very careful not to expose themselves as local leaders and to become too noticeable, realising that such exposure can make them more vulnerable to militant groups. Thus conflict parties will always be carefully watching to see who initiates which processes in their particular sphere of influence.

The experience of war-torn Sri Lanka shows that development agencies must be very careful to balance the interests of the different parties to the conflict, while at the same time still pursuing their own objectives, such as poverty alleviation, food security or self-help promotion. This will often involve a bargaining process with those groups who possess the means of power and the monopoly of violence in particular areas.

Nevertheless, agencies should also be clear on their exit strategy: To what extent are they prepared to compromise? At what point must they face the fact that they are doing more harm than good, and in effect legitimising and stabilizing particular groups in power? Intervenors must always be conscious of which groups are supported by their efforts and which are left out. They may well find that, in the particular environment of complex political emergencies, it might be necessary to abandon a needs-oriented approach (supporting the poorest regardless of ethnicity) in favour of a more ethnically balanced strategy (Bauer, Bigdon & Korf 2000).

In consideration of the dilemmas that project interventions regularly face when working in situations of complex emergency, Klem (2001) recommends a strategy of "educated pragmatism". Basically, this means taking a feasible position on a case by case basis (pragmatic), while at the same time taking the relevance and complexity of the issues into account (educated). What is important here is that donor agencies must become aware of the dilemmas that they face and carefully decide where to accept compromises and where to stick to formulated core values.

Since conflict situations are invariably unpredictable in nature, projects must also take a flexible (Sachithanandam would call it "unstructured") approach, allowing them to respond to varying immediate needs of the target groups under changing conditions (Sachithanandam, 1996, p206). This can of course be difficult to combine with the management logic of donor agencies.

The ultimate aim of community development work should be the strengthening of institutional arrangements for bargaining, as well as negotiating appropriate and inclusive solutions for collective action, scenarios which also provide opportunities for vulnerable groups to voice their (legitimate) interests. It is also critical that intervenors correctly assess which institutions are strengthened by their actions at the expense of others. Building new structures of community-based organisation can, for instance, weaken other institutions at the village level, such as traditional authorities or official institutions of local governance. Intervenors must carefully consider the role of these bodies within the overall conflict situation. Do they offer potential capacities for peace? Could they be reformed to become more inclusive, e.g. offering space for disadvantaged groups as well?

Also important is the role of the facilitators or social mobilizers. In the ongoing effort to support empowerment processes, a facilitator will sometimes need to act as a mediator, carefully considering the different interest groups in the village. This will also mean that he or she will need to balance inequalities in capabilities of communicating and negotiating in public forums, and to support the efforts of vulnerable groups to defend their cause, always keeping a neutral stance and maintaining the support and confidence of all parties.

This element of trust and acceptance by all the different stakeholders is essential for community facilitators. Most national staff members will come to situations of complex political emergency with some sort of link to one side or the other in the conflict. This might be due to their affiliation with one ethnic group or social class, or to the membership in a particular political party. In nepotistic regimes and in many civil wars, conflict parties or powerful stakeholders will often interfere with community processes and establish their own representatives and interests at the local level. The power of facilitators will therefore be limited, as they will be afraid to challenge those actors in the bargaining process with specific contacts to political patrons or warlords. The conflict management skills required from facilitators are substantial. They dare not be underestimated, and must be strengthened through regular training and supervision.

Having discussed the key aspects of the nexus between participation, empowerment and conflict transformation, as well as exploring some of the conceptual and practical problems of participatory and empowerment approaches in the context of community development work, we should now attempt a preliminary assessment of the potentials and limitations of these approaches, with particular regard to their role in the context of conflict transformation and local peacebuilding. Such an assessment does not claim to be comprehensive, nor should it be regarded as a blueprint for fieldwork. The points considered in Box 6 are mainly based on experiences of development cooperation in the war zone of Sri Lanka and reflect the particular contextual factors of that complex political emergency.

Box 6: Participatory and Empowerment Approaches with Regard to their Impact on Local Conflict Transformation.

Potentials	Constraints
Participatory methods support transparency in decision-making at the community level.	Bargaining processes for project resources or recognition at the community level carry the inherent danger of stimulating new conflicts or of increasing conflict potentials (do harm).
Participatory village workshops (PRA) can provide platforms from which different strategic and social groups can voice their positions. Thus community development can support local bargaining and negotiation processes.	Local field staff and community facilitators can be part of the problem: as part of the societal system they are biased (or are perceived by others as being so) towards specific social, ethnic or political groups and movements.
Participation can contribute to the (re-) establishment of local institutional arrangements and social capital as an asset for building local capacities for peace.	Transparency in negotiation processes is not easy to promote in all cultural settings.
Participatory processes establish a culture of talking as opposed to a culture of violence or patronage.	Authoritarian or hierarchical systems can discourage communicative processes.
Empowerment processes can strengthen vulnerable groups and create a common identity as a basis for voicing own interests and needs (advocacy).	Interference in cultural traditions, on the other hand, can easily be perceived as a colonial imposition of westernised ideas.
Community development through participatory processes can create or (re-) establish links between different levels of the governance system (poor and rich, service providers and communities, different administrative levels).	In many countries, patronage systems provide social security to vulnerable people: the poor depend on support from the local leaders in times of distress. Empowerment might loosen these bonds without providing proper alternatives.
Social mobilizers, as agency staff, can act as external observers. This can help to stabilize ground conditions at the community level and reduce the incidence of human rights violations in situations of protracted conflict.	How do losers of the bargaining process react? Those who feel that they did not get their fair share can threaten to involve one of the conflict parties or political patrons.
	Vested interests of conflict entrepreneurs can counteract initiatives for collective action and empowerment. Conflict parties in a civil war might not be interested in having empowered villagers or may attempt to impose decisions on the village groups, thus undermining their autonomy.

Ambivalence

Empowerment of some can lead to disempowerment of others (gender, class, ethnicity, caste). Who is then the loser and who is the winner of donor interventions?

- Power asymmetries within donor agencies (expatriate versus local staff) are usually counter-productive to any joint effort to induce and sustain local empowerment processes.
- Participation can support conflict resolution, but can also induce new conflicts or exacerbate existing tension.
- Technical cooperation agencies often regard themselves as apolitical service institutions. They may well be wary of following a participatory approach, as this might involve them in local and regional power struggles, thus exceeding their mandate.
- Every actor in a socio-political system is, to some extent, partial. Development agencies often work through counterpart institutions: to which party in a conflict are they most closely affiliated? Do certain social or ethnic groups dominate an organisation? By choosing to work with some and neglecting others, they can easily be labelled good and bad among the local institutions (Schlichte 2000).

7. Conclusion: Development Agencies as Political Actors in Complex Emergencies

In this chapter, we have discussed the extent to which development agencies can reasonably function as political actors, intervening in situations of complex emergency and contributing towards the empowerment of certain groups and the development of local communities through promotion of inclusive citizenship.

We have reviewed the theoretical foundations of common participatory and empowerment approaches within the context of development projects, and also explored the problem of the fit between the traditional management logic of donor agencies and the requirements of (local) empowerment as stressed by the conflict transformation discourse. The practical implementation of the participatory and empowerment approaches – such as PRA or social mobilization – illustrate the instrumental understanding of these originally emancipatory approaches in many situations. Understood this way, empowerment is often reduced to the mere integration of people into the planning and implementation of donor projects.

Within situations of complex emergency, intervenors must carefully assess the scope for participatory and empowerment approaches. We illustrated potentials and constraints, success stories, stories of avoiding doing harm and common dilemmas of donor interventions within situations of complex emergency. Especially with these dilemmas in mind, we still want to stress how important it is for donor agencies focussing on conflict transformation to consciously promote empowerment processes and the rebuilding of local democratic institutions, primarily through a strategy of educated pragmatism.

"Democratisation enables the population to articulate its needs and interests and to protect the rights and interests of marginalized groups, and the most vulnerable" (OECD/DAC

1997, p30). "Donor assistance in this area should be used as part of a wider promotion of just and sustainable development, providing vulnerable and disadvantaged groups with knowledge about their human and legal rights, as well as the rights and responsibilities associated with citizenship" (ibid., p40).

Empowerment approaches of donor interventions should incorporate many more aspects of recognition to support the development of a truly inclusive citizenship. Such processes of recognition will need to be facilitated beyond the borders of the village community. Donor projects will need to find ways to link the project interventions at the local level with the meso-level of local government institutions and NGOs, always considering the significance of the conflict context for the overall strategy of intervention. Facilitating dialogue forums and promoting cooperative networks at the regional level can also help to stimulate processes of empowerment and recognition, which, in turn, can serve as an entry point for the transformation of some of the principal causes of the macro-conflict.

But a number of open issues remain and finding answers to these questions will require a more detailed analysis of best practices of donor policies within situations of complex emergency, focussing especially on the community as well as the regional and national perspectives of intervention:

- How can donor agencies transcend the limitations of their administrative procedures, achieving more flexibility in their efforts to adopt a logic of (local) empowerment?
- What are best practices for facilitating processes of empowerment and recognition at the community and regional levels in the context of development aid in situations of complex emergency?
- How can agencies then build up the capacities for an educated pragmatism, learning from donor experiences of dealing with the dilemmas faced in situations of complex emergency?

8. Reference and Further Reading

Azar, E. 1990. *The Management of Protracted Social Conflict: Theory and Cases,* Aldershot: Dartmouth Publishing.

Anderson, Mary B. 1999. *Do No Harm: How Aid Can Support Peace – or War,* Boulder, CO: Lynne Rienner Publishers.

Baruch Bush, Robert A. and J. P. Folger 1994. *The Promise of Mediation. Responding to Conflict Through Empowerment and Recognitio*n, San Francisco: Jossey-Bass Publishers.

Bastian, Sunil and Nicola Bastian (eds.) 1996. *Assessing Participation. A Debate from South Asia,* New Delhi: Konark Publishers.

Bauer, Eberhard et. al. 1999. *Food Security and Conflict. A Participatory Development Concept for the Integrated Food Security Programme,* Berlin: Seminar für Ländliche Entwicklung.

Bauer, Eberhard, Christine Bigdon and Benedikt Korf 2000. "Anspruch und Wirklichkeit in der Konfliktbearbeitung: Was kann Entwicklungszusammenarbeit wirklich leisten? Das Beispiel Sri Lanka," *Peripherie 79, 43-68.*

Bauer, Eberhard and Volker Hoffmann 1997. "Participatory Rural Appraisal (PRA): Challenges and Recommendations," *Quarterly Journal of International Agriculture,* XXXVI, 1, 81-99.

Berthoin, A., M. Dierkes, J. Child, and I. Nonaka, (eds.) 2001. *Handbook of Organisational Learning and Knowledge,* Oxford: Oxford University Press.

Blackburn, James and Jeremy Holland (eds.) 1998. *Who Changes? Institutionalizing Participation in Development,* London: Intermediate Technology Publications.

Bigdon, Christine and Antonia Engel 2000. *Social Mobilization Concept for IFS,* Working Paper 28, Trincomalee: Integrated Food Security Programme Trincomalee (IFSP).

Bush, K. 1998. *A Measure of Peace: Peace and Conflict Impact Assessment of Development Projects in Conflict Zones,* Working Paper No 1, The Peace Building and Reconstruction Programme Initiative and the Evaluation Unit, Ottawa: International Development Research Centre.

Burton, J. (ed.) 1990. *Conflict: Human Needs Theory,* New York: St. Martin's Press.

Chambers, Robert 1994a. "The Origins and Practice of Participatory Rural Appraisal," *World Development,* XXII, 7, 953-969.

Chambers, Robert 1994b. "Participatory Rural Appraisal (PRA): Analysis of Experience," *World Development,* XXII, 9, 1253-1268.

Chambers, Robert 1994c. "Participatory Rural Appraisal (PRA): Challenges, Potentials and Paradigm," *World Development,* XXII, 10, pp1437-1454.

Chambers, Robert 1995. "Paradigm Shifts and the Practice of Participatory Research and Development," *in* Nelson and Wright, op.cit., 30-42.

Chambers, Robert and Irene Guijt 1995. "PRA – Five Years Later. Where are We Now?" in *Forests, Trees and People Newsletter* 26/27, pp4-13.

Fahrenhorst, Brigitte (ed) 2000. *Die Rolle der Entwicklungszusammenarbeit in gewalttätigen Konflikten,* Berlin: SID.

Fisher, Roger and William Ury 1981. *Getting To Yes: Negotiating Agreement Without Giving In,* Boston: Houghton Mifflin.

Freire, P. 1972. *Pedagogy of the Oppressed,* London: Penguin.

Goodhand, J. and D. Hulme 1999. "From Wars to Complex Political Emergencies: Understanding Conflict and Peacebuilding in the New World Disorder," *Third World Quarterly*, XX, 1, 13-26.

Goodhand, J. and N. Lewer 1999. "Sri Lanka: NGOs and Peacebuilding in Complex Political Emergencies," *Third World Quarterly*, XX, 1, 69-87.

GTZ 2001. *Krisenprävention und Konfliktbearbeitung*, Eschborn: GTZ.

Heinrich, Wolfgang 1999. "Förderung von Friedensprozessen durch Entwicklung und Zusammenarbeit. Lokale Friedenspotentiale müssen genutzt werden," *Entwicklung und Zusammenarbeit*, XXXX, 4, 106-109.

Klem, B. 2001. *Coping with Chaos. Dilemmas of assistance in the war-torn areas of Sri Lanka,* Nijmegen: Centre for International Development Issues.

Korf, Benedikt 2000a. "Ökonomie der Zeit – Über Wege zu Wassermühlen, Partizipation und Gender," *Entwicklungsethnologie*, IX, 1, 28-42.

Korf, Benedikt 2000b. *Promoting Communication and Dialogue. Review of Community Mobilization,* Working Paper 32, Trincomalee: Integrated Food Security Programme Trincomalee (IFSP).

Lederach, J.P. 1995. *Preparing for Peace: Conflict Transformation Across Cultures,* Syracuse, NY: Syracuse University Press.

Miall, Hugh, Oliver Rambotham and Tom Woodhouse 1999. *Contemporary Conflict Resolution*, Cambridge: Polity Press.

Moser, Caroline 1993. *Gender Planning and Development. Theory, Practice and Training,* London: Routledge.

Nelson, Nici and Susan Wright (eds.) 1995. *Power and Participatory Development. Theory and Practice,* London: Intermediate Technology Publications.

OECD/DAC 1997. *Development Assistance Committee. Guidelines on Conflict, Peace and Development Cooperation,* Paris: OECD Publications.

Ross, M.H. and J. Rothman (eds.) 1999. *Theory and Practice in Ethnic Conflict Management: Theorizing Success and Failure,* London: Macmillan Press.

Rothman, J. and V.J. Friedman 2001. "Identity, Conflict, and Organisational Learning," *in* Berthoin et al., op. cit., 582-597.

Sachithanandam, S. 1996. "Participatory Approaches to Development under Civil War Conditions. The Experience in Batticaloa, Sri Lanka 1991-1995," *in* Bastian and Bastian, op. cit.

Schlichte, Klaus 2000. "Die Entwicklungszusammenarbeit und die Dynamik von gewaltsamen Konflikten," *in* Brigitte Fahrenhorst, op. cit., 45-54.

Sen, G. and C. Grown 1988. *Development, Crisis, and Alternative Visions: Third World Women's Perspectives,* London: Earthscan.

Shah, P. and M.K. Shah 1995. "Participatory Methods: Precipitating or Avoiding Conflict?" *PLA Notes*, 24, 48-51.

Selected Manuals for PRA:

Berg, Christian et al. 1997. *Introduction of a Participatory and Integrated Development Process (PIDEP) in Kalomo District, Zambia. Vol. II: Manual for Trainers and Users of PIDEP,* Berlin: Seminar für Ländliche Entwicklung.

Korf, Benedikt 2000c. *Field Guide to Participatory Needs Assessment,* Technical Paper 6, Trincomalee: Integrated Food Security Programme Trincomalee (IFSP).

Pretty, J., Irene Guijt, J. Thompson and Ian Scoones 1995. *A Trainer's Guide for Participatory Learning and Action*, London: International Institute for Environment and Development (IIED).

Schönhuth, Michael and Uwe Kievelitz 1993. *Participatory Learning Approaches. Rapid Rural Appraisal, Participatory Appraisal* (Schriftenreihe der GTZ 248) Eschborn:GTZ.

Schubert, Bernd et al. 1994. *Facilitating the Introduction of a Participatory and Integrated Development Approach (PIDA) in Kilifi District, Kenya. Vol. II: From Concept to Action: A Manual for Trainers and Users of PIDA,* Berlin: Seminar für Ländliche Entwicklung.

Various issues of the journal *PLA Notes* (earlier: RRA Notes), which publishes firsthand field experience with PLA. *PLA Notes* is edited by the International Institute for Environment and Development (IIED), London.

Berghof
Research Center
Forschungszentrum
for Constructive
für konstruktive
Conflict Management
Konfliktbearbeitung

Recovering from War: Reconstruction versus Just Peace

Martina Fischer 373
Recovering from Violent Conflict:
Regeneration and (Re-)Integration as Elements of Peacebuilding

David Becker, 403
Dealing with the Consequences of Organised Violence in Trauma Work

Gunnar Theissen 421
Supporting Justice, Co-existence and Reconciliation after Armed Conflict:
Strategies for Dealing with the Past

Kevin Clements 441
Towards Conflict Transformation and a Just Peace

Recovering from Violent Conflict: Regeneration and (Re-)Integration as Elements of Peacebuilding

Martina Fischer

1. Introduction 374
2. Terms and Concepts 374
3. Structural Preconditions for Successful Regeneration and Peacebuilding 379
4. The Challenge of Integration
5. Good Practice Design: Strengthening Local Capacities, Adressing the Needs of Woman and Gender-Sensitivity 388
6. Open Questions 391
7. Reference and Further Reading 398

Recovering from Violent Conflict: Regeneration and (Re-)Integration as Elements of Peacebuilding

Martina Fischer

1. Introduction

In the last decade of the 20th century 43 countries have been considered as countries emerging from violent conflicts. Most of them were affected by intra-state wars and civil wars, and most of these belong to the category of the poorest ("less developed countries" according to criteria of the Organisation for Economic Cooperation and Development (OECD). An extraordinary high percentage was located in the African continent. The international community pledged more than one hundred billion dollars in aid to war-torn societies (Forman, Patrick and Salomons 2000, p1). These were designed to build up infrastructure, to persuade formerly warring parties to resolve conflict in a non-violent way and to contribute to economic development and participatory governance.

Experts and political actors have stated that international agencies often used too narrow-minded a concept in the past, reducing their activities to technical reconstruction after the end of violent conflict. A broader conceptualisation is needed to support the difficult long-term process of transformation from war to peace. This chapter gives an overview of the variety of tasks required to make post-conflict recovery successful in the sense of preventing further conflict and some tensions and dilemmas are identified and discussed.

The second section deals with terms and concepts and points out general premises for post-conflict recovery activities in order to contribute to the transition from war to peace. In the third section structural preconditions for successful regeneration and sustainable peace are discussed. This includes co-ordination among the multiple approaches and strategies of actors engaged in the field. The fourth section highlights the importance of programs for (re-)integration of refugees, displaced persons and former combatants and is illustrated by examples mainly from experiences in Bosnia-Herzegovina (BiH). The fifth section discusses elements of best practice design for external intervention that includes sensitivity to the needs of the local population, the potential of women and the nature of gender roles in specific cultural contexts. The final section stresses dilemmas and open questions.

2. Terms and Concepts

Many terms are used to describe key tasks of humanitarian assistance and development work after violent conflict: reconstruction, recovery, rehabilitation, resettlement, repatriation, reintegration and so on. In the late 1990s international agencies started to link these terms with the adjective 'post-conflict' to emphasise that only after a sustainable truce could one move beyond relief towards some kind of normalisation on the one hand, and on the other hand to justify the return of refugees as early as possible. Following the definition of Forman and Salomons (2000, p2) post-conflict is usually defined as

> *(...) the period when hostilities have abated to the level where some reintegration and recovery activities can begin. In many cases this may be indicated when refugees or internally displaced persons have begun to return. As such, this definition encompasses a wide range of post-conflict scenarios ranging from continued low-intensity conflict to a fragile peace to a settled conflict.*

The militarisation of social life, politics and economy, as well as the deep traumatisation of individuals and communities, are the gravest legacies in post-war societies. This is why a position paper published by Caritas Suisse (2000, p83) criticises the use of the terms 'reconstruction' and 'rehabilitation' because they focus primarily on repairing physical damage and suggest that the primary objective is to restore pre-war conditions. Instead it would be necessary to deal with the causes of the conflict. Colleagues who participated actively in the peace process in Northern Ireland, like Mari Fitzduff, share these arguments. She suggests replacing both terms by 'post-agreement' or 'post-settlement peace work' (*see* box 1)

Box 1: View from Northern Ireland

We argue over the terms here in Northern Ireland. 'Reconstruction' is a 'no go' term – as it seems to echo the nostalgia of one side here for a time when there was no violence – but which to the other side was replete with structural violence. (…)

Re-construction implies that one reconstructs society to resemble what it was like before the conflict. (...) Most of today's conflicts are subnational, and caused by the inability or the unwillingness of governments to ensure that there is a recognition of equity, exemplified through structural, political and economic issues that serve all communities equally. To talk of reconstruction in a post-settlement stage implies going back to a past which exemplifies the very factors that created the conflict. 'Post-settlement conflict work' is probably best used, or 'post-agreement work'.

We also should not use the term 'post-conflict'. Conflicts in fact do not end – but they do change. The change most of us are looking for is from violence into politics, where the enmities get played out through more peaceful means, which eventually may lead to less violence, more cooperation and thus the development of more respect and trust building between the communities.

You can use the term 'post-violence' – but the problem is that violence often continues to dribble on – as I often say here conflicts do not end with a bang but usually with whimper after whimper after whimper ... Therefore the best term is probably 'post-agreement' or 'post-settlement work' – as in for example 'post-settlement political, economic and social work'.

Source: Interview, July 2003 with Mari Fitzduff (at that time director of the Incore, University of Ulster, Northern Ireland)

Nevertheless the experience in some conflict zones shows that reconstruction is not necessarily regarded as a 'no go' term but might also be understood as a moral attempt to correct past wrong and injustices done to the victims of violence, as Norbert Ropers concludes in relation to current development and peace activities in Sri Lanka (*see* Box 2).

Box 2: View from Sri Lanka

'Re-construction' and the other 'RRRs', in many crisis regions now called the 'triple R' (sometimes combined with reconciliation) have been criticised because they imply that it is possible to go back to the pre-war situation. The main point being that it has often been exactly the socio-political system which existed then that had lead to the conflict in the first place. This is undoubtedly true for many conflict regions. But the argument overlooks that the 'Re-' contains more than just a technical perspective, it also indicates a moral attempt to correct a wrong which was done to the victims of violence, destruction and expulsion. Giving up the perspective of re-construction might also be interpreted as giving up the right to re-turn, to re-settle and to re-build the homes and livelihoods for all those affected from the war. Because of this ethical dimension, it can be important to keep the term 'post-conflict reconstruction'. This is at least the view taken in many areas of territorially protracted conflicts.

Source: Interview, July 2003 with Norbert Ropers,
Director of the Resource Network for Conflict Studies and Transformation, Colombo.

Pugh proposes the term 'regeneration' or 'peaceful regeneration'. He argues that regeneration signifies a self-sustaining process, whereas rehabilitation tends to connote a power relationship, whereby so-called victims or offenders have things done to them because they are de-capacitated or deprived. He defines peaceful regeneration a "process of social, political and economic adjustment to, and underpinning of, conditions of relative peace in which the participants, not least those who have been disempowered and impoverished by violence, can begin to prioritise future goals beyond their immediate survival". Moreover he supports the concept of 'peacebuilding' which had been introduced by the peace researcher Johan Galtung (1976) and was revived by the former United Nations (UN) Secretary-General Boutros Ghali. In his Agenda for Peace, he pointed out that post-conflict recovery involves far more than simply repairing physical damage and shattered infrastructures. He called for collective actions to "to strengthen and solidify peace in order to avoid a relapse into conflict" and "to advance a sense of confidence and well-being among people" (Boutros Ghali 1992, p21). Following Pugh (2002, p2), peacebuilding thus can be defined as "activities intended to strengthen structures and processes with the aim of preventing a return to violent conflict". In this respect, peacebuilding and regeneration intersect with, and accompany, relief and development. This view has been widely accepted (*see* Matthies 2000, p105; Miall, Ramsbotham and Woodhouse 1999).

Even if very different points of view on the terms can be found among scholars and practitioners, there seems to exist a broad consent that a fundamental transformation of the war-torn society is needed. It is only by addressing the political, social, psychological and economic causes, as well as the effects of armed conflict that a recurrence of violence can be prevented and a viable peace established. This means that a variety of tasks has to be addressed and multidimensional approaches are needed.

1. Multidimensional Approaches

Many authors identify political renewal as the most important prerequisite in ensuring that the conflicts of interest that were partially responsible for the outbreak of war are resolved. To this end, it is necessary to create public and legal institutions that safeguard legal certainty and democratic participation (good governance), investigate human rights violations and reform and/or help to dismantle the apparatus of violence. If political structures are totally destroyed, they can and must be replaced by international organisations for a transitional period when necessary.

In addition to the physical construction of housing, infrastructure and health systems, social renewal primarily focuses on establishing civil society structures and promoting the social reintegration of former combatants as well as return of refugees and displaced persons.

In this context, the importance of the psychosocial or psychological dimension is emphasised (Miall, Ramsbotham and Wood-house 1999, p203), such as overcoming trauma and achieving reconciliation at individual and inter-group level as well as working on identity issues. The way in which the past is handled also plays a key role in this context. So that the victims of violence and expulsion can feel better in subjective terms, perpetrators must ultimately be brought to justice (see Gunnar Theissen's contribution to this volume).

In addition to infrastructure recovery (transport, communications, water and electricity) and agricultural rehabilitation, economic renewal must focus primarily on dismantling the war economy and "transforming the looting and pillaging economy into a peace economy" (Caritas 2000, p86). Macroeconomic development and job creation are prerequisites, not only to safeguard the supply of essential goods and services but also for psychosocial stability. As a rule, however, post-war societies continue to be dominated by structures or legacies of war economies (for example, black markets and mafia structures) long after hostilities end. A vicious circle emerges since these conditions can act as a genuine deterrent to serious investors. Many post-conflict regions, such as the Balkans or the Caucasus, face an additional problem: as well as the effects of war, the consequences of mismanagement under a socialist planned economy must also be addressed. A key objective of post-conflict recovery is therefore to dismantle not only the war economy but also "the legacy of industrial monocultures and centralised planning bureaucracy, as well as the lack of business know-how" (Caritas 2000, p87).

Another important question is how recovery initiatives can be designed in a way that contributes to overcoming cultures of violence. Even if formerly warring parties have signed a peace agreement, the issues of power, interest or identity, which spawn civil violence, do not disappear. In practice, violence may persist at lower levels within the society, continue unabated in certain regions, or flare sporadically. During prolonged violent conflict, persisting war alliances often create structures with an interest in perpetuating these conditions (Ropers 2000). They include sections of the armed forces and security services, arms dealers, owners of land, capital and political privileges and groups and individuals who are able to exploit the shattered structures in order to engage in illegal business (Berdal and Malone 2000). Cultures of violence and hostility between communities emerge. The goal of external assistance therefore should be to design "assistance packages that provide incentives for the non-violent expression, management and resolution of conflicts, even while attending to the pressing needs of their civilian victims" (Forman, Patrick and Salomons 2000, p14).

Box 3: Main tasks for War-to-Peace-Transition

- Transformation of cultures of violence;
- Establishment of tradition of good governance including respect for democracy, human rights and development of civil society;
- Healing of psychosocial wounds and long-term reconciliation;
- Integration into co-operative and equitable regional and global structures;
- Balancing of stable long-term macro-economic policies and economic management and locally sustainable community development.

Source: Miall, Ramsbotham and Woodhouse 1999, p203

Several scholars have pointed out that regeneration from violent conflict and gaining sustainable peace is a very long procedure and even more complicated and lengthy if the end of the war marks a period of nation-building and new risks (Perthes 2000, p452; Ferdowsi and Matthies 2003, p322). Based on case studies of different regeneration processes from five continents (Bosnia, Northern Ireland, Lebanon, Israel/Palestine, Vietnam, Cambodia, Bougainville, Solomon Islands, Somalia, Angola, Mozambique, Nicaragua, El Salvador, Guatemala), Ferdowsi and Matthies (2003) come to the conclusion that all these processes have something in common.

In most of these examples subordination of the military under the civil power and constitutional elements of democracy have been guaranteed, but the central questions of social justice remain unsolved. Obviously the question of overcoming social gaps has not been dealt with as an important issue in the process of designing and negotiating peace accords. Instead other problems were the immediate focus. Moreover the implementation of reforms such as improvement of the rule of the law and initiatives for constructive dealing with the past have not so far developed. In none of the cases was a functioning jurisdiction established which could control state administration and guarantee real division of power.

Despite these findings, four cases, the Lebanon, Somaliland, Bougainville and Mozambique are considered as examples of (relative) success. The development in the other cases investigated was either considered as failure, as in Somalia, Angola, Palestine and the Solomon Islands, or at least as highly problematic.

Based on lessons from these cases, Ferdowsi and Matthies (ibid.) summarise general premises for positive outcomes of recovery and peacebuilding processes:

- The principle of 'inclusivity' of all relevant stakeholders, especially of competing elites;
- The solution of the security dilemma (reducing and reforming the armed forces and police, guaranteeing their political control and establishing state monopoly of force and public security);
- Reconstruction or renewal of the political system and administration, establishment of a legitimised government and power sharing models;

- Mutual trust-building, capacity for dialogue and agreements and readiness for peace of the former warring parties;
- Extension of the 'top down' process to all levels of state and society in order to link it with a 'bottom up; strategy – support of civil society is an important prerequisite for fostering the peace process in the population;
- Creation of a social and economic basis for the peace process by reintegration of those who suffered from the war, guaranteeing access to nutrition, health and education, trust building in local community networks and transformation of war economies to peace economies by investments in the human capital of the war-torn society;
- Respect for the principles, norms and institutions that are linked with the history and culture of the war-torn society if they are useful for consent.

Efforts of external actors should take into account these principles. Moreover they have to be ready for long-term engagement, which should also aim to support structural changes.

3. Structural Preconditions for Successful Regeneration and Peacebuilding

Several elements and needs must be addressed very early in societies emerging from violent conflict in order to prepare the ground for sustainable peace and economic development. These include:

1. repatriation and resettlement;
2. public safety;
3. infrastructure recovery;
4. food security and agricultural rehabilitation;
5. health, education and social welfare needs;
6. governance and civil society and
7. macroeconomic stabilisation.

These activities can be applied in different phases of conflict. This is illustrated by a matrix, distinguishing four stages: crisis, post-crisis (before settlement), post-settlement and longer-term reconstruction (see figure 1).

According to this matrix most of the activities start in a post-crisis scenario, but human rights monitoring, distribution of food and water and essential health services for instance can take place already during a phase characterised as "hot" conflict. Some activities can be started before settlement (transport assistance for return, shelter, psychosocial counselling, family tracing, mine clearance and aware-ness, conflict resolution training, recovery of transport system, power generation, waste disposal, telecommunications, seeds and tools distribution, veterinary projects, medical facilities rehabilitation, employ-ment and skills training). For all the other activities a settlement is needed. Some of them are considered as longer-term projects such as the reform of the civil service, administration and judicial system, the monitoring of these sectors, and initiatives for the restoration of financial institutions. This requires a set of tasks for short-term activities to cover human needs (relief), but also initiatives for long-term social, economic and political renewal (development).

The transition period is complicated by a set of socio-economic, political and psychological challenges within an uncertain security environment. Current responses to these challenges are considered inadequate because of the different approaches, institutional arrangements and funding systems of different actors. A report published by the World Bank (Coletta and Cullen 2000, p120) points out:

> *Humanitarian assistance is often unsustainable, and donors often lack interest in the transition period. The arbitrary compartments of humanitarian activities and development do not transfer well to real-world societies, where the fragility of peace and the persistence of violence make it difficult to draw distinctions between the 'conflict' and 'postconflict' periods. Humanitarian operations focus on quick response and short-term planning, while development agencies are often slow and inflexible. Both tend to focus too much on mandates rather on the needs of those affected by war and neither seems to rely on the knowledge and expertise of the other that may help improve operations. To address this gap, multilateral and bilateral institutions must become more coherent in their strategies and operations.*

In the field of post-conflict recovery a variety of actors is engaged (see 'Useful links' in the reading list). The question remains how the strategies of different agencies can be linked and co-ordinated in order to fulfil these tasks.

3.1 Integration of Relief and Development as a Political Project

Until the early 1990s development and relief largely operated in separate conceptual and institutional fields. At most, there were attempts to link them in a chronological process, i.e. a relief – reconstruction – development continuum. According to this model, development ceases during conflict escalation and is replaced by relief and – once ceasefires are agreed – rehabilitation, before being resumed in the final phase. These activities are undertaken by different relief agencies, or by separate sectors within the individual organi-sations, during a conflict. A problem of these functional distinctions is that many international organisations operate independently in the conflict region during the relief and rehabilitation phases, whereas development focuses more strongly on partnership (Caritas 2000, p82).

In line with his comments on the requirements for peace consolidation, UN Secretary-General Boutros Ghali (1995) pointed out in his Agenda for Development that different development strategies are needed in post-crisis settings than in peacetime. These strategies, he argued, must be put in place before the end of hostilities, in the sense of "post conflict preparedness". Furthermore, relief and development should not be viewed as alternatives. The findings of the case studies undertaken by the Center for International Cooperation (CIC) at New York University point in a similar direction and illustrate that there is no simple 'continuum' linking relief, recovery and development aid – rather these spheres of activity overlap temporarily and spatially in crisis environments (Forman, Patrick and Salomons 2000, p23).

A number of international relief agencies and development organisations have come round to this view. They challenge the conceptual, chronological and sectorally defined functional distinctions between these fields and have concluded that in all phases of violent civil conflict, a multi-sectoral approach is essential. Throughout the 1990s, the continuum model was therefore steadily expanded to encompass the 'contiguum' approach: The chronological stages and separation of relief and development were abandoned in favour of a model in which the two elements are co-ordinated and integrated. Relief work is thus embedded from the outset in a long-term, development-oriented, holistic approach that remains in place throughout the conflict (see OECD/DAC 1998, p48).

Some development agencies have adopted this approach. At the end of the 1990s, the Deutsche Gesellschaft für Technische Zusammenarbeit (GTZ), for instance, elaborated the concept of 'development-oriented relief' which aims to support – through relief and rehabilitation – the establishment of social structures at local level and facilitate the transition from crisis to long-term development (GTZ 1998).

The World Bank, the United Nations High Commissioner for Refugees (UNHCR) and the United Nations Development Programme (UNDP) recently initiated a joint program in order to address the discontinuity between short-term humanitarian assistance and longer-term development and peacebuilding inter-ventions.

Figure 2 illustrates possible synergy and partnership between humanitarian and development agencies and shows that bonding social capital and related humanitarian assistance tends to address the legacy of conflict (problems like displacement, famine, disease and death), while social and economic development that supports bridging social capital addresses the underlying causes of conflict (inequity, exclusion, and indignity). According to this concept, a key task for humanitarian and development agencies is to build bridging and linking (horizontal and vertical) social capital within communities and between the state and civil society when providing relief and rehabilitation.

Meanwhile, a number of relief organisations have come to regard peacebuilding as a joint relief and development task and have begun to integrate conflict transformation and peacebuilding activities into their work. Caritas Suisse (2000, p79) has set up some 'Core Principles of a Development Strategy for Peace Consolidation' and notes that organisations and their local partners can become key agencies of multi-track diplomacy by integrating democratisation, human rights monitoring, encounter projects and elements of peace education in their work or helping to establish peace alliances. Apart from working on structural causes of conflict, development programmes must be geared to process oriented measures for renewing social relations, fostering dialogue and building confidence.

3.2 Coordinating Funding Procedures

Scholars from the CIC see an urgent need for an overarching framework to coordinate the efforts of multilateral organisations, bilateral actors, regional entities and NGOs (Forman, Patrick and Salomons 2000, p34). Moreover they demand a reform of the funding system, based on the observation that only part of the billions of dollars which have been pledged by the international community in aid to three dozen countries during the 1990s has contributed to recovery from conflict. A significant proportion of the pledged resources has never materialised or done so very slowly.

In order to improve co-ordination the Conflict Prevention and Post-Conflict Reconstruction Network (CPR) was established at a meeting of post-conflict/transition and emergency units of multilateral and bilateral organisations, convened by the World Bank in Paris in April 1998. This informal platform brings together 29 organisations that intend to improve operational effectiveness in conflict prevention and post-conflict reconstruction according to the DAC Guidelines.

Nevertheless, lack of co-ordination still seems to exist within the UN system, and budgetary, institutional and operational divisions limit cooperation between humanitarian and development actors in planning interventions, mobilising resources and implementing projects. Within many organisations relief and development activities are designed by different departments and funded through distinct budget lines. Moreover, as Forman, Patrick and Salomons (2000, p54) point out, within aid agencies incentive structures generally reward the ability to 'move money' rather than virtuosity in designing assistance appropriately. Consequently, societies emerging from conflict may receive aid that is redundant, harmful or squandered – too much of the wrong type of aid.

That is why the CIC scholars argue that a 'Strategic Post-Conflict Recovery Facility' (Forman, Patrick and Salomons 2000, p57) would be needed. They suggest a Trust Fund to 'bridge the gap', which should be seen as a mechanism to jump-start and synchronise the international community's response. It is to be used on a time-limited basis in each case, while a longer-term country plan is developed, dedicated country trust funds are established (possibly as sub-trust funds) and multilateral and bilateral aid agencies as well as NGOs become operational on the ground. The facility should be open for participation to the core organisations of the United Nations system (including the Bretton Woods institutions), to regional organisations, to governments who choose to contribute or pledge a set minimum and to NGO representatives. It would have dedicated funds available for its own analytical and preparatory tasks as well as a standing trust fund or a pre-negotiated stand-by funding arrangement to jump-start recovery activities. The World Bank would serve as fiduciary agent for any trust fund arrangement, while the UN Office for Project Services (UNOPS) could provide administrative and substantive support to the facility's secretariat.

4. The Challenge of Integration

Careful conflict analysis is needed in order to co-ordinate the activities of multiple actors but also to create realistic objectives for intervention projects. As Forman, Patrick and Salomons (2000, p14) state, the ambitious recon-struction schemes which accompanied many peace accords ending internal conflicts during the 1990s have been "addressing multiple and sometimes conflicting political social and economic objectives". Lessons from failure and unsolved dilemmas can be drawn from experiences with repatriation of refugees and internally displaced persons (IDPs) in Bosnia. One challenge is to meet the needs of the most vulnerable groups and to adapt programmes for reconstruction and regeneration according to the principles of social justice. At the same time it is necessary to identify groups who could be multipliers for social change and transformation. The following sections illustrate these challenges with concrete examples, especially taken from experiences in the Balkans.

4.1 (Re-)integration of Refugees and Displaced People

The question of repatriation and reintegration of refugees and IDPs has become one of the most important items on the international humanitarian agenda, attracting the attention not only of relief, development and human rights organisations, but also senior political and military decision makers. Starting with initiatives taken by the leaders of the Central American countries in the late eighties who called for a regional approach to this problem, almost every major peace agreement concluded around the world, whether in Bosnia, Cambodia, Mozambique or Namibia, has included specific provisions relating to the return of displaced populations. UNHCR plays an important part in this field. NGOs like Peace Brigades International have also rich experience in processes of repatriation, accompanying and giving assistance to people who returned in their homeland under insecure preconditions, as for instance in Haiti, Guatemala and Colombia (Mahony 1999; Mahony and Eguren 2003).

How can repatriation and reintegration contribute to the peacebuilding process in war-torn societies? This question has to be answered with reference to a number of interlocking issues:

1. There can be no hope of normalcy until the majority of displaced or expelled people are able to reintegrate themselves into their respective societies. Forced displacement or refugee movements are an aberration, symptomatic of a situation in which the state is unable to protect its citizens and in which different groups of citizens are unable to live in peace alongside each other. Because it represents a very tangible form of progress, the voluntary return of displaced people can have an important impact on public confidence in the peacebuilding process (UNHCR 1997, p9).
2. Repatriation plays an important part in validating the post-conflict political order. Providing refugees with the opportunity to go home and to express their political preference is inherent in the concept of a free, fair and democratic election.
3. The return and reintegration of an exiled population may be a precondition for peace in situations where refugees are politically and militarily active. The return of refugees and their separation from the military represented an important step in the transition from war to peace in Cambodia, Namibia, Nicaragua and Rwanda, for example.
4. The return of displaced populations can make an important contribution to the economic recovery of war-torn states, as a high percentage of displaced persons creates problems in the design of programmes for social services, agricultural systems and other basic programmes.

There are also examples, including from the Horn of Africa, and the Ogaden region of Ethiopia (UNHCR 1997), where former refugees and IDPs contribute to peace building processes after return by revitalising the local economy. Even if returnees do not bring a great deal of financial capital with them in many cases, they possess a considerable amount of human and social capital.

On the other hand, a large and sudden influx of returnees can impose a substantial burden on the area where they settle. This is the case when people are forced to go back by the country of asylum without having the chance to prepare for return and reintegration.

It has become apparent in the post-war regions, for instance in the Balkans, that various lines of conflict can overlap and reinforce each other: in addition to the conflicts between different religious or ethnic groups, the urban-rural conflict and its associated cultural differences often overlap with conflicts arising from the unequal distribution of resources. The return and reintegration of refugees and displaced persons in post-conflict regions may contain substantial conflict potential and result in renewed outbreaks of violence. This applies especially if they compete with local people for scarce housing and jobs, or if property claims remain unsolved. In particular the traditional urban/rural conflict gained additional importance through migration processes forced by the wars of the 1990s when great parts of the rural population settled in the cities and most of them remained for years, many until the present day.

Return of displaced people gained much attention in Bosnia, where 2 million out of a population of 4.4 million became refugees or IDPs. Nevertheless the process of return was marked by a series of failures. In particular, following the Dayton Agreement there were various problems raised by programs designed to motivate the return of members of minority communities or 'minority return'. Previously, the international priority was to press ahead with minority returns because the situation created by war – that is, expulsion and the division of Bosnia-Herzegovina into 'ethnically pure' territories – was unacceptable. Finally it proved to be impossible to motivate people to (re-)settle in regions and to a context were they were part of the ethnic minority. The experience showed that only elder people where ready to do so; younger and middle age persons stayed where they had migrated or went for different options. Years later, as a result of the obvious failure of the 'Year of Return' in 1998, the UN, the High Representative for Bosnia-Herzegovina (HR) and the EU started to review their political objectives for refugee return. The 'right to return' continues to be upheld, but the approach that is now followed is to provide legal and financial support for all persons wishing to return to their regions of origin while recognising their freedom of choice. UNHCR therefore decided to continue to support minority returns but also considered other solutions that facilitate integration in a new place of residence. This is a recognition of the fact that many refugees have put down roots in their new place of residence and have no wish to return to hostile territory. According to the former High Representative Wolfgang Petritsch, it is only gradually being recognised that the restoration of the old 'ethnic map', the "multiethnic and multicultural society in Bosnia which diplomats and artists rave about", is proving impossible because, as is stated by the former HR, "foreigners in pursuit of lofty political objectives cannot expect displaced persons to return to places where they do not feel safe and where they feel they have no prospects for the future" (Petritsch 2001, p313).

A further problem that was not taken into account when drafting the Dayton Agreement and implementing relief and return programmes is that war-related changes overlap with changes resulting from system transformation. For example, the process of urban-rural migration has speeded up tremendously due to the war, but might have happened anyway due to the economic processes associated with system transformation, for these migratory progresses are part of economic change (transition from an agricultural to an industrial society, etc.). In this respect, it is not only the over-emphasis on minority returns but also the forced return of large groups of people to depopulated (and economically bankrupt) rural regions – even when these were their homes before the war – which seems genuinely anachronistic.

Clarifying property rights and return of property to those who lost it during the war is an essential precondition for successful peacebuilding. In order to avoid unsolved property issues after forced migration leading to ongoing conflict, models of settlements and compensations should be integral elements of refugee policy. In Bosnia for instance, the European Union established a property commission. Experience shows that it takes much too long in post settlement situations for compensation to take place.

Forced migration processes driven by war have a tremendous impact for the distribution of resources between the stakeholders and also for the ecological balance in the areas of settlement. In this process there are winners and losers (Boschmann 2003, p37), and it would be too easy to assume that refugees are the losers in general and others the winners. The reality of war-torn societies is much more complicated.

Of course, refugees loose what they possessed. Nevertheless in those regions where they settle the local population outside the refugee camps also might be affected in serious manner and injustice might occurr. While the refugees are provided with food and goods for free, the refugees in addition use local resources such as water or land. If there is no compensation it may be that refugees live in better conditions than the local population.

One of the lessons is that (re-)integration activities should not focus too much on one special target group (with respect to the distribution of goods and services, such as, for example, seed material, tools, housing or education). Restricting support rigidly to just one target group (only refugees or only ex-combatants, for instance) carries a danger of implicit discrimination or exclusion of other groups who do not belong to this target group but whose living conditions are no better.

In repatriation assistance and reintegration initiatives, however, care must be taken to avoid the perception that the needs of the returnee population are being served to the exclusion of the current residents For reintegration to succeed, recovery efforts must include the entire community, with due regard for the rights of all.

It is important to determine if the project will impact on a conflict situation and how. Moreover there is a challenge to find out how conflict management initiatives and peacebuilding can be incorporated. In immediate post-war regions, antipathy is often so strong that initiating dialogue forums without careful preparation is counterproductive and can unleash dynamics that are hard to control. However, initiatives that encourage people to engage in joint action can be a basis for the shared process of designing pluralistic society for the future and dealing with the past, as an example from Bosnia-Herzegovina illustrates.

Box 4: "Youth building the future": Empowerment, Training and Income-Generation

In 2002 a joint initiative named Youth Building the Future was established by Bosnian activists from the NGO Ipak in Tuzla and German organisations – Schüler Helfen Leben and the Berghof Research Center. The project aims at constructing a youth centre and youth co-operative in Eastern Bosnia. The German-Bosnian NGO Ipak (Nonetheless) was set up in response to an attack on Tuzla on 'Youth Day' during the Bosnian war in 1995 that killed 71 young people and injured hundreds more. Ipak maintains a well-attended youth centre in Simin Han near Tuzla since 1997. The new project, 'Youth building the Future', is targeted at improvement of conditions for youth and aims at integrating Bosniak returnees and youth from Serb villages by offering space for gathering, international exchange, leisure, professional training and income-generating initiatives. Here, the objective is to integrate development approaches with peacebuilding and conflict management within the framework of community work oriented to training and employment.

Young people from different ethnic groups in rural communities will be encouraged to participate in joint activities involving construction of the youth centre, training in the skills needed in the wood-working industry and agricultural production. The intention is to move beyond the provision of training and also engage young people in income-generating production; funds generated should then flow back into the project. This will be accompanied by programs of psychological support (drug prevention and trauma work) and community work, by international youth exchange programmes and by seminars in non-violent action and conflict management. Some youngsters will also be involved in constructing the youth centre by joining a co-operative. Others will be involved in organising the centre's activities.

This idea was developed by young refugees/returnees due to the experience that international initiatives for reconstruction so far have mainly focused on the technical dimension of rebuilding houses and infrastructure but neglected the needs for community building.

In the first phase of the project the Ipak team focused on information within the local context, creating a network of young activists and involving parents, schools and especially teachers from different villages and ethnic backgrounds who support the project. One of the most exciting experiences of the project so far is that by implementing the project very slowly and carefully a network with special focus on youth, teachers and community workers could be created. The people engaged for these purposes have to put much emphasis on dialogue with representatives and local administration as local governments change frequently and political power structures in this region are still dominated by nationalist groups.

Underpinning peace and human rights work with income-generating initiatives involving young people is essential for several reasons. If young people generate revenue themselves, this improves their families' financial situation and enhances their self-esteem, as they thus gain a place in the community and a certain measure of respect. It may also improve opportunities for self-organisation; for example the youth centre or encounter activities can be co-financed with funds which the young people have generated themselves. This would help to reduce dependence on foreign donors and support the development of a viable local NGO sector, thus benefiting the emergent civil society.

Funding programmes for disadvantaged social groups are widely available in post-war regions, but very few initiatives are geared to supporting income-generating measures for young people. Micro-credit programmes are utilised to a disproportionate extent by young people, but do not focus specifically on their needs and are also of doubtful benefit. Micro-project funds that promote competition and individual initiative would be far more appropriate and should be introduced as a matter of urgency for this target group.

The ongoing brain-drain in particular demands initiatives to support youth in post-war regions: According to opinion polls, two thirds of young Bosnians say they would leave the country if they had any opportunity to do so and many of them do find ways to leave. And moreover there is the danger that youngsters otherwise get into illegal business or could be recruited by nationalist forces if they are left without viable prospects.

4.2 (Re-)integration of Former Combatants

Beneath refugee return, a special focus has been given to the reintegration of former combatants – men, women and child soldiers – as an important prerequisite for peace building in recent years (Boschmann 2003, p40, Kingma 2001, Steudtner 2001). Demobilisation and reintegration have to be considered as closely linked elements of post-conflict activity, because it is feared that ex-soldiers who are not adequately integrated into society could become a recruiting ground for criminal organisations or get involved in the black market. In Bosnia-Herzegovina, several waves of demobilisation took place after the war and they have been supported by international agencies. It took five years until it was realised that demobilisation and reintegration programmes should be embedded in a general concept of security sector reform (Heinemann-Grüder and Pietz 2003, p4). Major reintegration projects have been driven by the World Bank's International Development Association (IDA) and the International Organisation for Migration (IOM). These were primarily designed to assist economic reintegration and consisted of several components. The World Bank's Emergency Demobilisation and Reintegration Project (EDRP) for instance has set up mechanisms for labour market information, counselling and job finding services, education and retraining services and management assistance. Another World Bank programme, Pilot Emergency Labour Redeployment Project (PELRP) was focused on self-employment in agriculture and small-scale business, institutional education and on-the-job training. The IOM Transitional Assistance to Former Soldiers (TAFS) marketable skills.

An evaluation has been recently published by scholars from the Bonn International Center for Conversion, BICC (Heinemann-Grüder and Pietz 2003). The main findings are that the earlier World Bank activities (EDRP) suffered from a lack of cooperation with the ministries of the two entities and with the employment institutes at the regional or local levels. Moreover BiH's extremely high unemployment rate raised major difficulties, and the low level of education and passivity also contributed to the fact that only a small percentage of ex-soldiers could be integrated. The second project (PELRP) provided important feedback on the current labour market and stimulated institutional reforms among the employment institutes. IOM's activities were successful in that it managed to instil interest and trust in its services within the community of demobilised soldiers. Moreover it was possible to contact and inform soldiers while they were still in barracks. Employment activities proved to be effective and sustainable, instead of subsidising short-term jobs. There was close cooperation with ministries. IOM also introduced obligatory civic education seminars for applicants. These seminars focus on issues such as democracy, human rights and civil society. The BICC evaluation suggests that this component and some other elements of IOM's project were highly successful and should be transferred to other projects:

1 stimulation of self-employment and self-reliance;
2. individualised, needs-based approach to counselling;
3. financial assistance and
4. support of business start-ups.

One important result of the study is that international support should aim at creating sustainable national structures that can provide employment for ex-soldiers. Programs that are merely aimed at strategies for economic reintegration and offering job opportunities are too narrow. The individual and psychological situation of each soldier has to be considered as well. The Bosnia case has shown that the overwhelming majority of demobilised soldiers were not prepared for their post-military life while still in service– either by skills training education or psychological assistance. In particular the authoritarian patterns of thinking and ethnically-closed mindsets of many ex-soldiers should be recognised as well. Moreover many representatives of veterans' organisations stressed the vital importance of psychological assistance for war veterans, an aspect underrated in the major reintegration programs (Heinemann-Grüder and Pietz 2003, p31).

5. Good Practice Design: Strengthening Local Capacities, Addressing the Needs of Women and Gender-Sensitivity

Relief and development programmes which focus solely on providing for those affected by war and ignore the need for local ownership run the risk of creating long-term dependencies that undermine, rather than encourage, the process of building a lasting peace. In Bosnia-Herzegovina, for example, a dependency syndrome can be observed, as the former High Representative (HR), Wolfgang Petritsch (2001, p257), has stated: "every dollar in aid has led some people to assume that the international community will pay for everything – for ever." According to his experience, statutory measures of the HR frequently provided politicians in Bosnia-Herzegovina with "an excellent excuse ...not to do their work properly" and misled large sections of the population to expect the international community to assume exclusive responsibility for improving living conditions in Bosnia. In the period 1995–2000 Bosnia received four times the amount of money Europe received after the Second World War per capita.

To summarise the situation, one can state that the "paternalistic state was replaced by paternalistic humanitarian aid" (Stubbs 2001, p4). It seems that the dependency syndrome in Bosnia is caused partly by the scale of the international presence but also by dubious concepts of aid, as well as fundamental errors in the Dayton Agreement itself.

As Stubbs has illustrated, within the Constitution agreed under Dayton no supranational agency has social policy as its main focus in BiH and the efforts of the lead agencies have been much more oriented to merely technical frameworks of government, human rights, economic development, reconstruction and return. Thus social policies remains an under-developed theme. Relief interventions have tended to operate mainly through INGOs or local NGOs, often subcontracted to provide services. Local capacities and skills, established by Bosnian professionals in centres for social work before the war, have not been used. Thus, the welfare regime became "fragmented, and localised, residualised, category-based rather than needs-based, and depoli-ticised" (ibid., p5). The World Bank initiated several emergency funds to provide incomes in the poorest households but still this scheme lacked sustainability; it did not include any plans for how to continue the scheme once donations dried up (ibid., p11).

Despite the extraordinary attention which has been given to this post-war society by the donor community, in the view of most scholars the case of Bosnia is not considered as a positive example because the international aid had a couple of unintended side-effects (Schneckener 2003, p58):

1. The humanitarian aid industry replaced the public sector and was an obstacle for the development of a local labour market and economy. Qualified persons prefer working for international organisations or in the (artificially overblown) NGO sector and thus are not integrated into local labour structures.
2. It is estimated, that 1 billion dollars of international aid that has been spent for Bosnia-Herzegovina since the Dayton Peace Accord in 1995, have been misappropriated (which led to the establishment of an anti-corruption unit within the Office of the High Representative).
3. International finances stabilised local elites and power structures that are linked with corruption, the black market and organised crime. Those who already had benefited from the war, benefited again from the international engagement for peace.

Development policy institutions and relief organisations have often criticised the fact that peacebuilding measures have generally failed to view gender equality as a key element of social justice. Women are undoubtedly one of the most disadvantaged groups in crisis regions. In post-conflict regions in particular targeted employment and com-munity-oriented initiatives for women are therefore essential.

Margaret Vogt (2000, p85), Head of the United Nations Department for Political Affairs, has claimed in particular that programmes for (re-)integration should be developed and implemented with close involvement by local communities in order to prevent gross injustice. Very often male combatants or commanders who have committed human rights violations remain at liberty and so it seems that they are actually being rewarded after the event through their eligibility for support programmes; in other words, their crimes have paid. This type of distortion must be avoided at all costs. Furthermore, the situation of female fighters should not be overlooked: in many regions in Africa, Asia and Latin America, women fight side by side with men in guerrilla wars, thus gaining in apparent equality. After the end of hostilities, however, they are forced back into their traditional and generally subordinate roles. The social reintegration of women combatants receives far less attention, especially from foreign donor organisations. This has also been noted with respect to reintegration programmes in Bosnia-Herzegovina (Heinemann-Grüder and Pietz 2003, p19). Therefore women's organisations have called for measures relating to disarmament, demobilisation of combatants and reconstruction to be developed not only at the macro level but more importantly also within the local communities in order to ensure women's participation.

A fundamental problem is that normally women are only involved peripherally in decisions concerning reconstruction at the end of hostilities and in general aid programmes do not address their specific needs. Often, women also have little opportunity to express their views; for example, they have no access to the media. It is clear from the international debate that programmes to support physical and social reconstruction must develop a methodology for women's empowerment. There is also a need to focus on domestic violence, which is becoming an increasingly prevalent feature of post-war situations. For many women, the end of the public conflict and violence does not herald an end to all violence. As male ex-combatants return home, their trauma and frustration is often projected onto their wives and families. So the rape and assault of women increases. Often women are the likely targets of looting, attack and 'economic violence' perpetrated by ex-combatants (Anderlini 2001, p37).

Moreover in persistent war economies women are forced into oppression and prostitution or mafia-structures that gain from trafficking and enslavement of women. Reports on forced prostitution in Bosnia-Herzegovina have put this issue back on the agenda (Böhm 2000; Ludwig Boltzmann Institute for Human Rights 2001; Ulrich 2001). Consequently international women's organisations argue that debates about security problems should involve women as well as men, in order "to include gender perspectives into existing security agendas" (Anderlini 2001, p37).

The former United States ambassador, Swanee Hunt, founder of the initiative, Women Waging Peace, calls for a "concept of inclusive security", a "diverse, citizen-driven approach to global stability, which expands the array of tools available to police, military and diplomatic structures by adding collaboration with local efforts to achieve peace" (Hunt and Posa 2001). This concept emphasises women's agency, not their vulnerability. Moreover there is a claim for involving women to a greater extent in peace negotiations to make sure that they can participate in decisions on the future of their communities. This was one important argument of the campaign Women Building Peace: From the Village Council to the Negotiation Table, set up by the NGO International Alert (see the contribution of Diana Francis in this volume).

The task of supporting women in their efforts to secure equal opportunities for political participation and a role as stakeholders in society undoubtedly derives from the need for democratisation, equal opportunities and participation – principles which are also important elements of sustainable peace agreements. However, this does not mean that a higher proportion of women in political processes would necessarily lead to more intensive efforts for conflict transformation. It is important not to assume that women have natural attributes that endow them with better peacemaking skills for these tasks and they are no more inherently peaceable than men. After all, women are involved in countless civil and international wars, either supporting the combatants or serving as combatants themselves; elsewhere, women – like men – are actively involved in the dis-semination of nationalist and xenophobic ideologies. Nevertheless it turns out that in some conflict zones women proved to be important partners for peace constituencies or disarmament and demobilisation campaigns. In Mali the Mouvement National Femmes pour la Sauvegarde de la Paix et de l'Unité Nationale was leading a civil society movement that urged regional governments to adopt a 3-year moratorium on the import, export and manufacture of small arms. In Guatemala and Liberia women were engaged in campaigns to disarm combatants, using their traditional roles and acceptance in society for broader mobilisation (Anderlini 2000, p20).

External actors who intervene into conflict zones can address the potentials of women if they understand the social status and roles which women play in the society. In this context, attention has to be paid to the symbolic link between the dimensions of gender, power and culture (as has been highlighted by Diana Francis in this volume). A comparative case study that investigates the process of peace consolidation in the South Pacific (Böge 2002) argues that at least the inclusion of women's groups in grass roots activities and in the negotiation process (and also the inclusion of female peacekeepers who could function as connectors between internal and external efforts) has contributed to progress in Bougainville, because traditional forms of conflict management could be activated. In the Solomon Islands, on the contrary, the traditional role and significance of women (as owners of the land in a matrilineal society) was systematically neglected and the decision to send an exclusively male peacekeeping mission contributed to the failure of the peace process.

A real challenge for the organisations involved in post-conflict peacebuilding is therefore shaping peacebuilding approaches with special sensitivity for the situation of men and women in post war situations and their different realities and needs.

Female as well as male scholars and practitioners put emphasis on the special role of women as agents of change, which should be promoted in all reconstruction and economic development activities (Forman and Salomons 2000, p3). A policy study carried out for the German GTZ recommended that a gender impact assessment should be carried out when planning development and technical cooperation projects; this would critically analyse social processes in the target country and analyse to what extent women could be supported in their productive roles. The study also argued that development cooperation must "help to maintain the advantages which women have secured for themselves during a crisis; in some crisis situations, women take over jobs which they were previously barred from", and should be supported in preserving these new roles and ensuring that there is no retrograde development (Mehler and Ribeaux 2000, p136; this aspect has also been highlighted by Reimann 1999, 2001; Woroniuk 1999; Spearman 1999).

6. Open Questions

War-torn societies vary enormously in their ability to manage and absorb foreign assistance. Recipients often lack the human, technical and administrative capacities required to make use of large quantities of aid or to co-ordinate the multiple donors and NGOs that arrive to assist their recovery. Experiences such as those in Bosnia (and there are already similar signs in Kosovo) show that an abundance of external assistance, if it cannot be absorbed by local capacities, or if local capacities are simply not used for sustainable systems build upon local ownership, may result in an expectation that physical and social reconstruction must largely be undertaken by external agencies forever. Therefore one of the key challenges is to combine structural measures with process-oriented initiatives and to co-ordinate short- and long-term measures in a meaningful way. This includes overcoming the deficits and problems that arise from the practice of the international community in organising aid and assistance: a lack of coherence, co-ordination and effectiveness and a lack of realism concerning aims and means. This implies changes in the international donor community as well as in the UN system.

The argument for a 'strategic post-conflict recovery facility' in order to improve co-ordination of agencies and activities sounds convincing. The proposal to create a 'World Peace Foundation' or 'World Peace Security Council', which has been developed by other scholars and practitioners recently (Ferdowsi 2002, p19), points in the same direction. The question remains how to design such an agency in a way that it will be really effective and avoid additional bureaucracies that make things even more complicated and less transparent, especially for the recipients of aid.

If reconstruction and regeneration measures are to be effective, they must be based on the principle of justice. This means bringing perpetrators before the court and compensating

Figure 1: Matrix of Essential Activities

Sector/ Activities
1. Repatriation and Resettlement
1.1 Transport assistance for return
1.2 Shelter and reconstruction materials
1.3 Community reconciliation and psychosocial counseling
1.4 Family tracing and reunification
1.5 Property claims arbitration
2. Public Safety
2.1 Mine clearance and awareness
2.2 Demobilization: reintegration and alternate employment projects
2.3 Small arms control/buy-backs
2.4 Restructuring/retraining security forces (police, armed forces, paramilitary, intelligence)
2.5 Human rights monitoring
2.6 Conflict prevention and resolution training
3. Infrastructure Recovery
3.1 Water and sanitation
3.2 Transportation
3.3 Power generation
3.4 Housing
3.5 Solid waste disposal
3.6 Telecommunications
4. Food Security and Agricultural Rehabilitation
4.1 Targeted food distribution
4.2 Seeds and tools distribution
4.3 Livestock/veterinary projects
4.4 Land use planning
4.5 Land tenure issues
5. Health, Education and Social Welfare Needs
5.1 Essential health services
5.2 Medical facilities rehabilitation: reconstruction/material assistance
5.3 Public health sector capacity building and priority programming
5.4 Educational facilities rehabilitation (and reintegration)
5.5 Employment and skills training, incl. food-for-work rehab. projects
5.6 Microcredit
5.7 Microenterprise development
5.8 Essential production

for Recovery From Conflict

Point of Onset of Activities			
Crisis	Post-crisis (no settlement)	Post-settlement	Longer Term Reconstruction
	■		
	■		
	■		
	■		
		■	
	■		
		■	
		■	
		■	
■			
	■		
■			
	■		
	■		
		■	
	■		
	■		
■			
	■		
	■		
		■	
	■		
■			
	■		
		■	
		■	
	■		
		■	
		■	
		■	

Source: Forman, Patrick and Salomons (2000, p64/65)

Figure 1: Matrix of Essential Activities

Sector/ Activities
6. Governance and Civil Society
6.1 Public administration and recurrent cost
6.2 Civil service rehabilitation/reform
6.3 Non-governmental organizations capacity building
6.4 Electoral process and institutions
6.5 Voter education and participation
6.6 Elections monitoring
6.7 Free media training and legal advocacy
6.8 Judicial reform
6.9 Civilian oversight and monitoring of security forces
7. Macroeconomic Stabilization
7.1 National currency stabilization
7.2 Financial institutions restoration
7.3 Debt relief/arrears clearance

victims for the material losses they have sustained. Measures for regeneration must be effective in offering all members of the community opportunities for participation and viable economic prospects. Peace education and training efforts are unlikely to be effective if the overall conditions for conflict transformation are not in place (in other words if the social imbalances are too pronounced, if there are massive conflicts between war profiteers and war losers, or if there are no economic chances for some social groups). Conversely, long-term development strategies which focus on economic and social reconstruction can only play an effective role in peacebuilding if they involve different social groups, such as returnees, local population and refugees, as well as ex-combatants – or at least none of these groups should be neglected. Programmes for the integration of refugees, IDPs and ex-combatants have to be developed both on the local and on the national level, in order to avoid injustice as well as to address potential alliance partners for peace processes. In this context, youth should be considered as a special and important target group for two reasons. Neglecting youth means that their destructive potential could be activated, as young men who lack prospects might easily be recruited by warlords or join criminal structures. Secondly, involving youth means developing innovative social capital for renewal of society. The potential of women as alliance partners for peacebuilding is also important. With regard to social justice and human rights, it is an urgent task to focus on women's legal and social equality, their participation in the political process and their self-confident involvement in civil society.

According to the principle of justice the most vulnerable groups in post-conflict societies should be the priority for support by international aid. But any strategy for reconstruction and regeneration which is designed for post conflict peacebuilding has to cope for Recovery From Conflict

Point of Onset of Activities			
Crisis	Post-crisis (no settlement)	Post-settlement	Longer Term Reconstruction
		■	
			■
		■	
		■	
		■	
			■
			■
			■
			■
		■	
			■
		■	

Source: Forman, Patrick and Salomons (2000, p64/65)

with the dilemma that the most vulnerable groups are not automatically those who endanger peace nor are they automatically connectors or multipliers for peace processes. Strategies thus have to find a careful balance with respect to the principle of justice and, for instance, the need for reintegration of former combatants in order to reduce the risk of new outbreaks of violence.

It is a sign of progress that the reality of women's lives in post-conflict situations is increasingly becoming a focus of interest. Nevertheless there is a trend that agencies often reduce the gender concept to the special role and potential of women, regarding women either as a vulnerable group or as special agents of change. However, in order to overcome cultures of violence it is equally important to examine the psychosocial effects of war and post-war reality on men and masculine identity in order to analyse appropriately the significance of gender relations in the causes and dynamics of violence. This means also taking their trauma and loss of self-esteem seriously. Ex-soldiers for instance, as victims and perpetrators, need psychological counselling in order to be prepared for civilian life. This has not yet been addressed sufficiently in demobilisation and reintegration programmes, as the Bosnian examples have shown. Moreover the gender perspective must go beyond simple patterns of victims and perpetrators and has to address the questions of the extent to which social constructs of masculinity and femininity contribute to the dynamics of violent conflicts and how to change these constructs and symbolisms so that cultures of violence can be dismantled. If conflict impact assessment is extended to this view, there is no need for complicating things by establishing additional 'gender impact assessment' mechanisms. In order to incorporate gender aspects to the range of instruments for conflict analysis and impact assessment, criteria in relation to the influence of identity patterns have to be developed, such as militarised

Figure 2: Toward the integration of relief and development

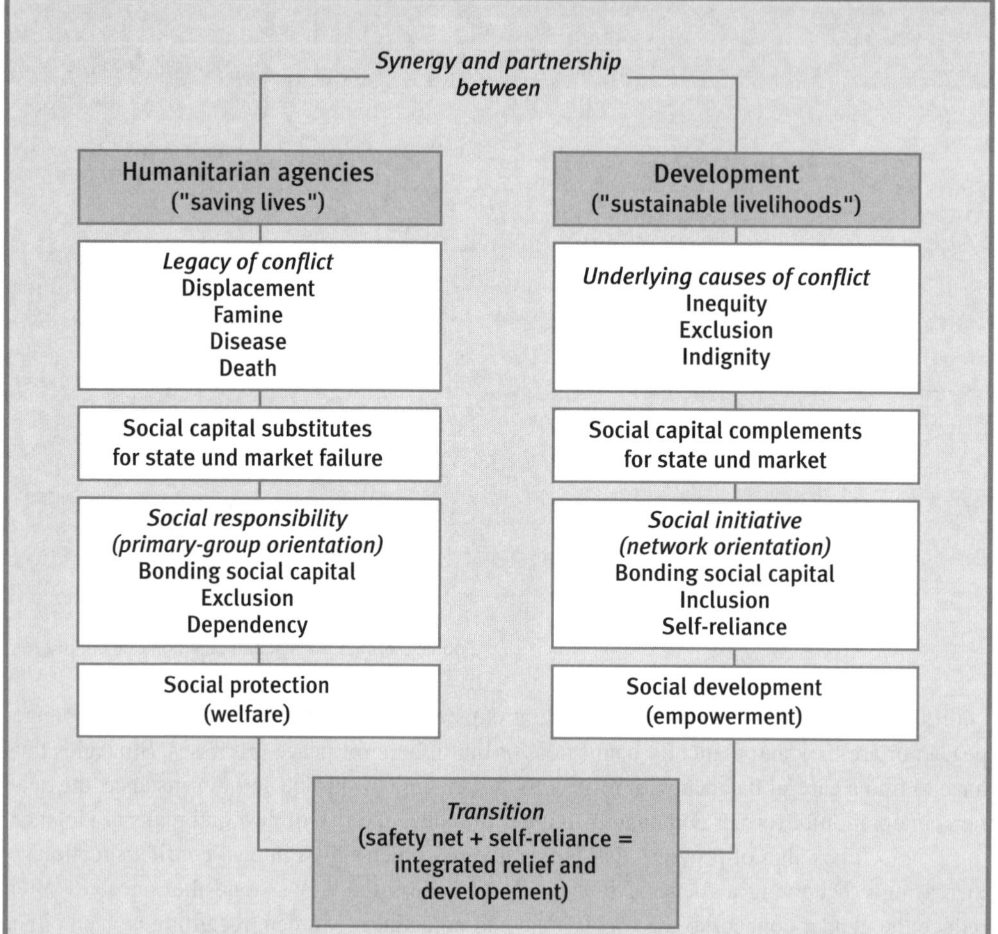

Source: Coletta and Cohen (2000, p119)

masculinity. Identifying approaches that overcome these patterns is a key element for strategies that aim at overcoming cultures of violence.

Approaches to conflict impact assessment must be developed further and applied within all the various agencies, i.e. IGO's and NGOs involved in relief, development, peace and human rights work. It proves difficult to apply "data-hungry models" in conflict-torn environments, where even baseline data may be lacking. Therefore benchmarks and indicators appropriate to war-torn settings are needed, taking into account the specific country context and situation. In this regard donors should shift their view and accept that earnest evaluations will be more likely if aid agencies adopt outcome-based program planning and hold management accountable less for the problems exposed than for the corrective actions taken in response to these appraisals (Forman, Patrick and Salomons 2000, p54). Agencies need to develop realistic benchmarks and criteria for success and to develop adequate methods of self-reflection and self-evaluation.

But even if external actors choose best practice design and self-reflective procedures for interventions they still have to face some dilemmas which result from the international context:

- Programmes of repatriation and reintegration of refugees and IDPs can play an important role in peacebuilding processes. But there is the dilemma that despite a well-established international principle that refugee repatriation should take place on a wholly voluntary basis and in conditions of safety and dignity, it is quite clear that a large proportion of the world's recent returnees have been repatriated under some form of duress, as has been admitted by many UNHCR reports in the past. Such duress has in many instances been deliberate, exercised by governments, host communities and other actors, with the specific intention of forcing refugees to go back to their homeland. Also the principle of non-refoulement, which prevents refugees from being returned to countries where their life or liberty would be at risk, has been flouted on a regular basis during the past few years (UNHCR 1997). This practice certainly obstructs well designed (re-)integration strategies in the field.
- The claim for better co-ordination of efforts for regeneration and reconstruction is confronted with a general problem. It is obvious that recovery of war-torn societies is an element of a competing international 'charity business', but it is also influenced by the conflicting business interests of private firms (and national governments who strive to represent the demands of those companies) engaged in crisis regions, at least as far as material (re-)construction is concerned. This was particularly debated in public in a very drastic way after the end of the US-led military intervention in Iraq in 2003. Before the fighting was over, governments and companies in several countries started to secure advantages for big business in rebuilding highways, houses and infrastructure, and to participate in the competition for phone rates and transmission frequencies and opportunities for rebuilding the banking system – and in this special case also restructuring the oil-market. The question that was discussed in the international media was who will gain the big business in the Bagdad Basar and who will pay for it (Pinzler and Vannahme 2003). The question of who will deliver what the Iraqi people really need was not so much discussed.
- It seems that UN-secretary Kofi Annan's (2001) proposal to establish a "culture of prevention of violent conflict" has been challenged at the beginning of the 21st century by doctrines such as unilateral preventive intervention (and aggression). An increasing tendency for military operations gained priority at least in the State Departments of some powerful Western nations, especially the United States. This tendency has been reinforced by the concept of "war against terrorism". Multilateral organisations such as the United Nations are not in a leading and decision-making role but more and more reduced to deal with the consequences of this policy: restoring and recovering of devastated societies, according to the slogan "US fights, EU funds, and UN feeds". Given this context, the following questions have to be raised: How does this international development affect third-party interventions for peacebuilding strategies? Can agencies that aim at conflict transformation and trust building work effectively in this scenario or will they loose their credibility? This dilemma had already been raised after the NATO-Intervention in Yugoslavia 1999. It is even more obvious in Afghanistan and Iraq.

7. Reference and Further Reading

Anderlini, Sanam N. 2000. *Women at the Peace Table. Making a Difference*, New York, NY: UNIFEM (*see also* http://www.unifem.undp.org/resour.htm).

Anderlini, Sanam N. 2001. *Women, Peace and Security: A Policy Audit. From the Beijing Platform for Action to UN Security Council Resolution 1325 and Beyond*, London: International Alert.

Annan, Kofi 2000. *We the Peoples. The Role of the United Nations in the 21st Century. Millennium Report of the Secretary-General*, New York: United Nations Department of Public Information. http://www.un.org/millennium/sg/report/full.htm.

Auswärtiges Amt (ed.) 2000. *Drittes Forum Globale Fragen. Gleichstellung in Politik, Gesellschaft und Wirtschaft*, Berlin: Auswärtiges Amt.

Berdal, Mats and David Malone (eds.) 2000. *Greed and Grievance. Economic Agendas in Civil Wars, A Project of the International Peace Academy*, Boulder, Co., London and Ottawa: Lynne Rienner Publishers.

Boschmann, Nina 2003. *Wiederaufbauprogramme und 'Complex Emergencies'. EZ-relevante Erfahrungen und Lessons learned*, Eschborn: GTZ.

Böge, Volker 2002. "Friedenskonsolidierung im Südpazifik: Bougainville und Salomonen im Vergleich," *in* Matthies, op. cit.

Böhm, Andrea 2000. "Freier für den Frieden. Die UNO kam einst nach Bosnien, um Mord und Vergewaltigung zu stoppen. Seit sie da ist, blüht die Zwangsprostitution," *Die Zeit*, January 13, 2002.

Boutros Ghali, Boutros 1992. *Agenda for Peace*, New York: United Nations Department of Public Information. http://www.un.org/Docs/SG/agpeace.html.

Boutros Ghali, Boutros 1995. *Agenda for Development*, New York: United Nations Department of Public Information. http://www.un.org/Docs/SG/agdev.html.

Ghali, Boutros 1995a. *Supplement To an Agenda for Peace*: Position Paper of the Secretary-General on the Occasion of the Fiftieth Anniversary of the United Nations, 3. January 1995. http://www.un.org/Docs/SG/agsupp.html.

Cahill, Kevin M. (ed.) 1993. *A Framework for Survival. Health, Human Rights, and Humanitarian Assistance in Conflicts and Disasters*, New York, NY: Basic Books and the Council on Foreign Relations.

Carbonnier, Gilles 1998. "Conflict, Postwar Rebuilding and the Economy. A Critical Review of the Literature, The Wartorn Societies Project," *UNRISD, Occasional Paper No. 2*, Geneva: UNRISD.

Caritas Schweiz 2000. "Allianzen für den Frieden," verfasst von Thomas Gass und Geert van Dok, *Positionspapier 8,* Luzern: Caritas-Verlag.

Cernea, Michael M. and Christopher McDowell (eds.) 2000. *Risks and Reconstruction. Experiences of Resettlers and Refugees*, Washington, DC: The World Bank.

Cohen, Roberta and Francis M. Deng (eds.) 1998. *The Forsaken People. Case Studies of the Internally Displaced*, Washington, DC: Brookings Institution Press.

Coletta, Nat J. and Michelle L. Cullen 2000. *Violent Conflict and the Transformation of Social Capital. Lessons from Cambodia, Rwanda, Guatemala, and Somalia*, Washington, DC: World Bank.

GTZ 1998. *Entwicklungsorientierte Nothilfe (EON). Arbeitskonzept der GTZ*, Eschborn: Deutsche Gesellschaft für Technische Zusammenarbeit (GTZ).

GTZ 2001. *Towards Gender Mainstreaming in Crisis Prevention and Conflict Management. Guidelines for the German Technical Co-operation*, Eschborn: Deutsche Gesellschaft für Technische Zusammenarbeit (GTZ).

Eberwein, Wolf-Dieter 2001. "Humanitäre Hilfe, Flüchtlinge und Konfliktbearbeitung" *in* Truger (ed.), op. cit.

Evers, Tilman (ed.) 2000. *Ziviler Friedensdienst*, Opladen: Leske & Budrich.

Ferdowsi, Mir. A. 2002. "Internationale Politik im 21. Jahrhundert, Introduction," *in* Mir. A. Ferdowsi (ed.). *Internationale Politik im 21. Jahrhundert*, UTB Wilhelm Fink Verlag, 9-29.

Ferdowsi, Mir A. and Volker Matthies (eds.) 2003. *Den Frieden gewinnen. Zur Konsolidierung von Friedensprozessen in Nachkriegsgesellschaften*, Reihe EINE Welt, Stiftung Entwicklung und Frieden, Bonn: Verlag J.H.W. Dietz.

Forman, Shepard and Stewart Patrick, 2000. *Good Intentions, Pledges of Aid for Postconflict Recovery*, Boulder, Co, London: Center on International Cooperation (CIC).

Forman, Shepard, Stewart Patrick and Dirk Salomons 2000. *Recovering from Conflict: Strategy for an International Response, Paying for Essentials*, Policy Paper Series, New York, NY: Center on International Cooperation, New York University.

Forman, Shepard and Dirk Salomons 2000. *Meeting Essential Needs in Societies Emerging from Conflict*, paper prepared by the Center on International Cooperation for the Brookings Roundtable on the Relief to Development Gap. http://www.nyu.edu/pages/cic/pubs/MeetingEssentialPrint.html.

Galtung, Johan 1976. "Three Approaches to Peace: Peacekeeping, Peacemaking, and Peacebuidling," *in* Galtung, op. cit., 282–304.

Galtung, Johan (ed.) 1976. *Peace, War, and Defence: Essays in Peace Research: Volume II.* Copenhagen.

Heinemann-Grüder and Tobias Pietz 2003. *Turning Soldiers into a Work Force. Demobilization and Reintegration in Post-Dayton Bosnia and Herzegovina*, BICC brief 27, Bonn: BICC.

Hunt, Swanee and Christina Posa 2001. "Women Waging Peace," *Foreign Policy*, May / June, 1-7. http://www.foreignpolicy.com/issue_mayjune_2001.

Kingma, Kees 2001. *Demobilisation and Reintegration of Ex-Combatants in Post-war and Transition Countries*, Eschborn: GTZ.

Kreimer, A., J. Eriksson, R. Muscat, M. Arnold and C. Scott (eds.) 1998. *The World Bank's Experience with Post-Conflict Reconstruction*, Washington, DC: World Bank Operations Evaluation Department.

Ludwig Boltzmann Institute for Human Rights (ed.) 2001. *Combat of Trafficking in Women for the Purpose of Prostitution. Bosnia and Herzegovina. Country Report*, Vienna: Ludwig Boltzmann Institute for Human Rights. http://www.univie.ac.at/bim.

Mahony, Liam 1999. *Risking Return. NGOs in the Guatemalan Refugee Repatriation*, Uppsala: Life & Peace Institute.

Mahony, Liam and Luis Enrique Eguren 2003. *Unarmed Bodyguards*, Connecticut, Kumarian Press.

Matthies, Volker (ed.) 1995. *Vom Krieg zum Frieden. Kriegsbeendigung und Friedenskonsolidierung*, Bremen: Edition Temmen.

Matthies, Volker 2000. *Krisenprävention. Vorbeugen ist besser als heilen*, Opladen: Leske & Budrich.

Matthies, Volker et al. 2002. *Friedenskonsolidierung*. Reihe EINE Welt, Stiftung Entwicklung und Frieden, Bonn: Verlag J.H.W. Dietz.

Mehler, Andreas and Claude Ribaux 2000. *Crisis Prevention and Conflict Management in Technical Cooperation. An overview of the National and International Debate*, Wiesbaden: Universum Verlagsanstalt.

Miall, Hugh, Oliver Ramsbotham and Tom Woodhouse 1999. *Contemporary Conflict Resolution: The Prevention, Management and Transformation of Deadly Conflicts*, Cambridge / Oxford: Polity Press.

OECD/DAC 1998. "Conflict, Peace and Development Co-operation on the Threshold of the 21st Century," *Development Co-operation Guidelines Series: 48*, Paris: OECD.

Perthes, Volker 2000. "Wege zum zivilen Frieden. Nachbürgerkriegsregionen im Vergleich," *Blätter f. Deutsche und Internationale Politik*, H.4, April, 445–455.

Pinzler, Petra and Joachim-Fritz Vannahme 2003. "Basar Bagdad," *Die Zeit*, Nr. 17, 16 April 2003, 19.

Petritsch, Wolfgang 2001. *Bosnien und Herzegowina 5 Jahre nach Dayton – Hat der Friede eine Chance?*, Klagenfurt u.a.: Wieser-Verlag.

Pugh, Michael (ed.) 2000. "Regeneration of war-torn societies," *Global Issues Series*, London: Macmillan Press, New York; St. Martin's Press.

Reimann, Cordula 1999. "The Field of Conflict Management: Why does Gender Matter?," *AFB-Texte No. 4*, Bonn: Arbeitsstelle Friedensforschung.

Reimann, Cordula 2001. "Engendering the Field of Conflict Management: Why Gender does Not Matter! Thoughts from a Theoretical Perspective," *Peace Studies Papers*, University of Bradford, Working Paper 2, January, 19–45.

Ropers, Norbert 2000. "Die internen Akteure stärken. Krisenprävention und Konflikttransformation durch Friedensallianzen," *in* Evers, op. cit.

Schloms, Michael 2001. "Humanitarianism and Peace. On the (im-)possible inclusion of humanitarian assistance into peacebuilding efforts," *Paper 01-306*, Berlin: Wissenschaftszentrum Berlin für Sozialforschung.

Schneckener, Ulrich 2003. "Bosnien-Hercegovina: Der aufgezwungene Frieden," *in* Ferdowsi and Matthies, op. cit., 42–69.

Soros Foundation (ed.) 2001. *International Support Policies to SEE-Countries – Lessons (not) learned in Bosnia-Herzegovina*. http:/www.soros.org.ba.

Spearman, Diane 1999. "Performance and Impact Indicators for Evaluating Projects and Progress towards meeting the Commitments to Women, 1999–2001," *Annex to WFP Commitments to Women: Mid-term Review of Implementation*, World Food Program.

Steudtner, Peter 2001. "Die soziale Eingliederung von Kindersoldaten. Konzepte und Erfahrungen aus Mosambik," *Berghof Report No. 6*, Berlin: Berghof Research Center for Constructive Conflict Management.

Stubbs, Paul 2001. "'Social Sector' or the Diminution of Social Policy? Regulating Welfare Regimes in Contemporary Bosnia-Herzegovina," *in* Soros Foundation, op. cit., Chapter 8.

Truger, Arno (ed.) 2001. *Zivile Konfliktbearbeitung*, Münster: Agenda-Verlag.

Ulrich, Stefan 2001. "Entfesselte Blauhelme. UN-Sonderberichterstatterin prangert sexuelle Gewalt von Friedenssoldaten an," *Süddeutsche Zeitung*, 11 April, 8.

United Nations High Commission for Refugees 1997. *State of the World Refugees*, http://www.unhcr.ch/cgi-bin/texis/vtx/publ

United Nations (eds.) 1996. *An Inventory of Post-Conflict Peacebuilding Activities*, Department for Economic and Social Information and Policy Analysis, UN, New York.

United Nations Development Programme (UNDP) Evaluation Office (eds.) 2000. *Sharing New Ground in Post-Conflict Situations. The Role of UNDP in Support of Reintegration Programmes*, New York.

Vogt, Margaret A. 2000. "Preventing and Managing Conflicts: What Role for Women? Statement, Berlin, 8–9.5.2000," *in* Auswärtiges Amt (ed.), op. cit., 82–86.

Wood, Adrian, Raymond Apthorpe and John Borton 2001. *Evaluating International Humanitarian Action*, New York, NY, London: ZED Books in cooperation with ALNAP.

Woroniuk, Beth 1999. *Gender Equality & Peace building: A Draft Operational Framework*, Ottawa: Canadian International Development Agency.

Useful links

Active Learning Network for Accountability and Performance in Humanitarian Action (ALNAP), *http://www.Alnap.org*

Bundesministerium für Wirtschaftliche Zusammenarbeit und Entwicklung, Germany (BMZ), *http://www.bmz.de/*

Bonn International Center for Conversion (BICC), *http://www.bicc.de*

Canadian International Development Agency (CIDA), *http://www.acdi-cida.gc.ca*

Caritas Suisse, *http://www.caritas.ch/*

Department for International Development (United Kingdom) DFID, *http://www.dfid.gov.uk*

Deutsche Gesellschaft für Technische Zusammenarbeit (GTZ), *http://www.gtz.de*

Direktion für Entwicklung und Zusammenarbeit, Schweiz (DEZA), *http://www.eda.admin.ch/*

European Community Humanitarian Office (ECHO), *http://europa.eu.int/comm/echo/*

European Commission General Directorate Development, *http://europa.eu.int/comm/development*

European Commission General Directorate External Relations (Relex), *http://europa.eu.int/comm/dgs/external_relations/*

International Organization for Migration (IOM), *http://www.iom.int*

Organization for Economic Co-Operation and Development (OEDC), *http://www.oecd.org*

OECD – Development Assistance Committee (DAC), *http://www.oecd.org/dac/*

Reflecting on Peace Project (Collaboration for Development Assistance CDA), *http://www.cdainc.com*

Relief Web, *http://www.reliefweb.int/w/rwb.nsf*

Swedish International Development Cooperation Agency (SIDA), *http://www.sida.se*

United Nations Commission for Human Rights (UNCHR), *http://www.unchr.ch*

United Nations Development Program (UNDP), *http://www.undp.org/erd*

United Nations High Commission for Refugees (UNHCR), *http://www.unhcr.ch*

United Nations Office for the Coordination of Humanitarian Affairs (OCHA), *http://www.reliefweb.int/ocha_ol/index.html*

United Nations Office for Project Services (UNOPS), *http://www.unops.org*

United Nations Research Institute for Social Development (UNRISD), *http://www.unrisd.org*

UNRISD – War-torn Societies Project http://www.wsp-international.org/, *http://www.unrisd.org/wsp*

United States Agency for International Development (USAID) – Office of Transition Initiatives, *http://www.usaid.gov*

Women Building Peace Campaign (International Alert) http://www.international. *alert.org/policy/women.htm*

Women, War and Peace, *http://www.unifem.org/index.php?f_page_pid=149"*

World Bank – Conflict Prevention and Reconstruction Unit (CPR), *http://www.worldbank.org/conflict, http://developmentgateway.org*

World Bank – Post Conflict Unit, *http://www.worldbank.org/postconflict*

Dealing with the Consequences of Organised Violence in Trauma Work

David Becker

1. Introduction 404
2. Trauma theorie 405
3. Potential and limits of psychotherapy 409
4. Beyond the framework of therapy: the importance of truth, justice, respect and empathy 412
   Respect
   Comprehension
   Relationship
   Psychosocial work as a method for dealing with individuals and their social context
5. The danger of traumatisation of the trauma worker: burn out prevention and supervision 417
6. Conclusions 417
7. Reference and Further Reading 418

Dealing with the Consequences of Organised Violence in Trauma Work

David Becker

1. Introduction

War and persecution cause not only material harm but also produce extreme psychological suffering for those who must both live and survive under such circumstances. This statement is self-evident to the point that one is always surprised by the fact that up until recently it was not an issue in humanitarian help and in development cooperation. Until recently help has always focused on material goods and general economic development. What people feel within the context of political and social destruction seemed to be of little interest: at best, it was an issue for religion; at worst, it was a luxury to be dealt with once the 'real' problems had been solved. Although this has changed somewhat in recent years (and nowadays we find trauma programs in most crisis regions of the world), the basic attitude of international agencies is still quite ambiguous. Professional opinions vary widely about both what trauma work is and what it should do.

This chapter does not pretend to offer a simple introduction to trauma therapy, nor is it a basic guideline on how to heal trauma throughout the world. Trauma can only be understood and addressed with reference to the specific contexts in which it occurs. Any attempt towards a 'globalized' presentation and discussion of trauma is therefore useless. The basic aim within this chapter is to offer information about the concepts currently under discussion in trauma work and to share a certain amount of practical experience as an invitation to the reader to reflect on his or her own experiences. I have worked for many years as part of the team of the Latin-American Institute for Mental Health and Human Rights (ILAS) in Santiago de Chile, which aims to help victims of political persecution. My opinion has been constituted by this experience, as well as by consultative work with similar institutions in Central America, Angola and the former Yugoslavia.

Section 2 will provide an overview, definitions and finally a review of existing trauma theories. Keilson's concept of sequential traumatisation is considered to be the most useful conceptual framework we have to date. One of the main events that drew light upon the limitations of both trauma concepts and terminology was the attempt to address the consequences of the Holocaust. In response to this inadequacy, the resulting concepts are outlined with reference to the 'extreme traumatisation' experienced by the victims. It will be argued that trauma concepts need to be continually reinvented and always contextualized within the specific social reality in which the traumatisation occurs. The third section will examine both the potentials and limitations of psychotherapy. These are explored through three questions: "How does it feel like to be traumatised and is it possible to understand these feelings?", "How do we relate to a traumatised person or group?" and "What is the basic aim of treatment with reference to trauma?" The fourth section focuses upon three central attitudes that can be employed in trauma work. After this, the wider application of trauma work, which lies beyond therapy, is illustrated through case studies. Special emphasis is given to an interdisciplinary approach that integrates aspects of psychology, economics and education. The penultimate section draws attention to the difficulties, needs and hazards that trauma workers themselves face and potential ways in dealing with this vulnerability.

2. Trauma theorie

The word 'trauma' originally comes from the Greek language where it means wound. Its analogous utilization in psychology and psychiatry began at the end of the nineteenth century as part of the effort to explain certain mental disorders. Trauma, thus, was the cause of these illnesses and understood as a psychological breakdown caused by external events that exceeded the capacity of the psychological structure to respond to them adequately.

By the end of World War I, the military had become interested in the problem when they realized that condition of 'shell-shock' needed to be addressed and explained, and could not be reduced to simple cowardice. It was during the Vietnam War that the United States finally established a set of identifiable symptoms, the so-called "Post Traumatic Stress Disorder" (PTSD) which was included in the *Diagnostical and Statistical Manual of Mental Disorders* (DSM) of the American Psychiatric Society. This resulted in the recognition of trauma by mainstream psychiatry. The negative impact, which occurred from the mainstreaming, was the categorisation of trauma as one more mental illness amongst many.

Box 1: Definitions of Trauma

In trauma theory, we need to distinguish between the traumatic situation, the trauma and the symptoms resulting from trauma. A traumatic situation is defined as an event or several events of extreme violence that occur within a social context: exemplified by war. Such a traumatic situation is a necessary but not a sufficient condition for trauma to occur. While trauma implies the destruction of individual and/or collective structures, it does not always follow that such destruction causes immediate symptoms. PTSD is the best known classification of symptoms that persist with the victim of a traumatic situation. This may cover accidental events such as natural disasters or instigated events such as combat, crime, rape, kidnapping and imprisonment.

Currently, trauma is conceptualised in three different ways:

- Trauma as a medical concept, e.g. PTSD, where the aim is to establish a more or less complete catalogue of symptoms.
- Trauma triggers highly complicated psychological processes (intra-psychic) that need to be analysed. This can be exemplified by the therapeutic work with victims of the Holocaust that was carried out primarily by psychoanalysts (*see* Bergmann and Jucovy 1982 and Bettelheim, 1943.
- Trauma as a social and political process: recent work in Latin America has established that

traumatisation is not only an individual process but also a social process that refers to the society as a whole. These studies have also shown that trauma can only be understood within a specific cultural and political context.

Concerning PTSD analysis, it is important to outline several important limitations. As mentioned above, PTSD diagnosis focuses on the symptoms without reference to the cause of these symptoms. The traumatic situation itself is either ignored or not addressed which allows the analysis to cluster what are in essence different situations in the same category ('stressor'), such as heart attacks, erupting volcanoes or human rights abuses. The shortcomings of PTSD diagnosis can be summarized as follows:

- Family diagnosis is impossible within PTSD categories. A torture victim, for example, can have PTSD but his wife and children can't, even if their symptoms can only be understood in the context of the destruction of the victim.
- PTSD provides a list of frequently occurring symptoms; however, it ignores many others. While one can say that if PTSD symptoms are present, then trauma has occurred, there is no guarantee that trauma has not happened if these symptoms do not appear. Somatic and psychosomatic symptoms in particular, as well as social behaviour indicative of trauma, are not included in the definitions provided by PTSD.
- PTSD works within a rigid definition of time. Consequently, this may lead to an incorrect diagnosis if symptoms do not occur within a certain time span (for example six months). This time limit contradicts everything we know about trauma symptoms with reference to man-made disasters. For example, the symptoms of Holocaust survivors can appear ten, twenty and up to fifty years after the original traumatic event. This same experience has been confirmed with survivors of political persecution in Latin America. There is considerable data to confirm that trauma can be transmitted trans-generationally from parents to their children. PTSD diagnosis does not deal with this phenomenon (for a more detailed critique of the PTSD concept, *see* Becker 1995).

In contrast to PTSD, a parallel and different development occurred with reference to trauma in psychoanalysis, especially amongst those working with survivors of the Holocaust. In 1943, Bruno Bettelheim wrote about his time in a concentration camp and justified the need for a new term to describe the experiences he and his fellow prisoners had suffered: "What characterized it most was its inescapability; its uncertain duration, but potentiality for life; the fact that nothing about it was predictable; that one's very life was in jeopardy at every moment and that one could do nothing about it" (Bettelheim 1943, 418). Thus Bettelheim suggested the term "extreme situation" to describe his experiences. He was the first to clearly illustrate that traumatisation resulting from a man-made disaster could not be categorized in the usual psychiatric or psychoanalytical language. New terminology was required to describe this type of trauma. In the years following the Holocaust (referred to as post-Shoah), the term "extreme traumatisation" was developed. The word 'extreme' conveyed the special nature of the trauma, which neither in its way of happening, nor in its short and long term consequences, nor in its symptomatology, nor in its socio-political implications could be compared to other traumatic events such as accidents, an earthquake or a heart attack.

Freud provided the idea that trauma can also be a product of several experiences (Laplanche and Pontalis 1977). This was further developed by Khan and led to his concept of "cumulative trauma" (Khan 1977), through which the dimensions of time and relationship are introduced into the discussion of trauma. According to Khan, trauma can be a product of a series of individually non-traumatic experiences, which develop and accumulate within an interactive framework and finally lead to a breakdown. These ideas are highly important because, although initially limited to the mother-child relationship, they transfer the emphasis from the trauma to the traumatic situation. This converts the event into a process and, without denying the intra-psychic wound, focuses on the importance of the interactive framework.

Both Bettelheim's and Khan's ideas were later developed by Hans Keilson in his concept of "sequential traumatization" (Keilson 1992, first published in German in 1977). In his important follow-up study of Jewish war orphans in the Netherlands, he identifies three traumatic sequences:

1. "Enemy occupation of the Netherlands and the beginning of terror" (Keilson 1992) against the Jewish minority. This implies attacks on the social and psychological integrity of Jewish families.
2. "The period of direct persecution" (Keilson 1992), which was the deportation of parents and children, the separation of mother and child, the hiding of children in foster families and the direct experience within the concentration camps.
3. "The postwar period during which the main issue was that of the appointment of guardians" (Keilson 1992). The alternatives were to leave the children with their Dutch foster families or return them to their original Jewish environment.

Keilson's concept implies a radical change in the understanding of trauma. Instead of an event that has consequences, we are now looking at a process in which the description of the changing traumatic situation is the framework that organizes our understanding of trauma. Keilson demonstrates, for example, that a severe second traumatic sequence and a 'good' third traumatic sequence implies better long-term health perspectives for the victim than a 'not-so-terrible' second traumatic sequence and a 'bad' third traumatic sequence. This is extremely important in explaining why trauma continues, even when the active persecution has stopped. We are thus able to understand not only why patients might develop symptoms immediately after the original traumatic event, but also why they might do so twenty, thirty or forty years later. Finally, Keilson's concept illustrates that, since there is no 'post' in trauma but only a continuing traumatic process, the helpers (the people who deal with the victims) are also always part of the traumatic situation and do not operate outside of it.

One of the advantages of Keilson's concept is that it can easily be used in different cultural and political settings. Unlike PTSD, it does not define a fixed set of symptoms or situations but actually only invites one to look closely at a specific historical process; it allows the quality and the quantity of the traumatic sequences to be very different in various contexts. One sequential change that seems to be relevant in most parts of the world is the change between active war and persecution and the period that follows. In many cases, this 'afterwards' needs to be divided into different sequences. For example, the war in Angola has continued for the last thirty years, being interrupted by small periods of supposed peace; in the former Yugoslavia there is now a condition that is different to war while not actually being peace.

Not being able to use PTSD with reference to our own patients and finding Bettelheim, Khan and Keilson extremely useful, we have adopted the term "extreme traumatization"

(Becker and Castillo 1990; Becker 1992) for the situation in Chile and defined it as follows:

> *Extreme traumatisation is an individual and collective process that refers to and is dependent on a given social context; a process that is marked by its intensity, its extremely long duration and the interdependency between the social and the psychological dimensions. It exceeds the capacity of the individual and of social structures to respond adequately to this process. Its aim is the destruction of the individual, of his sense of belonging to society and of his social activities. Extreme traumatisation is characterized by a structure of power within the society that is based on the elimination of some of its members by other members of the same society. The process of extreme traumatisation is not limited in time and develops sequentially.*

It is possible to see in our 'Chilean' definition that we incorporated many of the ideas described above, but placed greater emphasis on the collective aspect of trauma. This was an attempt to transcend the individual level (without denying it) and include the social reality. I am uncertain whether our definition is really better than the others I have described. Nevertheless, the definition at least acknowledges a basic difficulty, inherent to all trauma theories: on one hand, they must deal with individual intra-psychic processes; while on the other, they have to deal with society. Conceptually, it is very difficult to do justice to both at the same time. This results in either the individual or the collective aspect of trauma becoming overstated or understated. Nevertheless, I believe that our definition is contextually important. In Latin America, and especially in South America, the issue of the long fight against dictatorship was central. Many people know nothing about Chile, but nearly everybody has heard of its dictatorship and its central symbol, Augusto Pinochet. In this context, a very 'political' definition of trauma is therefore appropriate. In other regions of the world it might be different.

A good example of the relevance of contextualising our trauma definitions was an experience I had during a small workshop in a refugee camp in Bosnia. I asked my colleagues to forget everything they knew about psychological and psychiatric diagnosis, and to write down, in everyday language, what they thought constituted the refugees' trauma. This is what they wrote:

> *The destruction caused by the war, the grenades, the living in tents, the cold, the lack of food, the insecurity of when or whether they can return, the economic situation, the legal problems, the loss of family members, the memories of torture and concentration camps, the inexistence of privacy, the rejection by the local community...*

In fact, the list was a lot longer and included more details than can be written here. Although it was not a clinical definition, and did not fit into any standardised way of dealing with trauma, did not even differentiate well between the traumatic situation and the trauma, to my mind, it is one of the best definitions of trauma I have ever met. In terms of concrete information about the specific characteristics of the suffering of these refugees in Bosnia, it was excellent. It permitted us to start doing useful work because a good diagnosis is half the treatment. With this description in mind, it was possible to understand that 'treatment' in this case had little to do with typical 'therapy', but much more concerned with improving living conditions, initiating community work and facilitating collective grief processes.

In summary, I am suggesting that in each different social context people should create their own definitions of trauma within a framework, in which the basic focus is not so much on the symptoms of a person but on the sequential development of the traumatic situation.

Whereas it will always be important to register the specific symptoms of a patient (mainly because of the metaphoric message that symptoms convey about the illness), our primary approach must focus on the repressive experiences. Thus, we would differentiate between a person who has experienced torture in Chile, a Bosnian refugee or a Vietnam veteran much more than between depressive, hysteric or obsessive symptoms. We would not hold that psychosis is a typical consequence of torture, but if we treat a psychotic patient and learn that he was tortured, our treatment strategy and our way of understanding his psychosis would change. In general, our diagnosis must include the specific social context in which the illness appears. Respecting the fact that political traumatisation is always tied to the context obliges us to understand that a Turkish, a Chilean or a Vietnamese refugee might present similar symptoms, might even have some comparable experiences, like torture, but each one of them, in effect, suffers originally from a different illness. What might constitute their similarity is that they are all refugees coming from the same country and therefore undergoing the same traumatic sequence.

Box 2: Trauma and Organized Violence

The basic framework for trauma when dealing with the consequences of organized violence can be defined as follows:

1. Trauma implies a notion of tearing, of rupture, of structural breakdown.
2. Trauma can only be defined and understood with reference to a specific context, which must be described in detail.
3. Trauma is a process, which develops sequentially.
4. Trauma contains both an individual intra-psychic dimension and a collective, macro-social dimension that are interwoven.

3. Potential and limits of psychotherapy

The 'treatment' of extremely traumatised persons neither begins nor ends in a therapist's room. Nevertheless, therapy may become the first social space in which victims might begin to overcome their difficulties. The relative intimacy of therapy permits us to learn, in a more implicit way, about a number of key issues of trauma that are also always present in other contexts. These issues can be formulated as questions:

1. What does it feel like to be traumatized and is it possible to understand these feelings?
2. How do we relate to a traumatized person or group?
3. What is the basic aim of treatment with reference to trauma?

Sandor Ferenczi noted in his clinical diary on February 21, 1932 that fragmentation might be a useful defence in surviving a traumatic situation. Confronted with unbearable aggression, a child might 'give up his soul', mentally 'dying', while physically surviving death. Afterwards, the pre-traumatic personality structure will be partially re-established, but a part of the person will have ceased to exist, will go on being dead or lost in the agonies of fear. The task of analysis would be to overcome this process of splitting. It is at this point where the dilemma arises. If the traumatic experience is reconstructed through a cognitive process, then the splitting between the destroyed part and the part that is looking at the destruction is maintained, thereby denying any real access to the traumatic experience. However, if the patient makes a 'cathartic regression' to the stage of the traumatic experience, he feels, once again, his suffering, but cannot think anymore, and does not understand what happens to him. Once awake, the evidence immediately disappears and the trauma is again only perceived from the exterior, without the corresponding feelings (Ferenczi 1988). In short, it seems that neither approach can be successful.

Ferenczi here offers short and precise answers to some of the questions stated above. For him, trauma at its core would feel like extreme agonies of fear that lead to the psychological experience of death, which means that a basic split has to happen. This, Ferenczi shows, is helpful in order to survive trauma, although in the aftermath it implies sustained fragmentation; part of the person stays dead, while another part begins to function again. To overcome trauma, fragmentation would need to be overcome, but that is nearly impossible, because, 'within' the traumatic experience, there are only agonies, no words, and no capacity for reflexive thinking. 'Outside' of the trauma, thinking works and words exist, but without being totally connected to the traumatic experiences. So when dealing with traumatized persons, we always confront a double reality, on one side there is a person that can talk about, think about, and even tell us about what happened to them. On the other side, we have a person lost in the experience of death and of terror, for whom there are no words to explain their experience.

From Balint (1965), Winnicott (1965) and Bion (1990, first published 1962) amongst others, we have learned that the Ferenczi dilemma can only be solved through the ability of the therapist to connect with the 'agony of fear', to contain it and to offer an authentic but sufficiently secure space for the patient to begin the process of reintegration. The therapist needs to allow the appearance of his or her own potential for fragmentation while at the same time maintaining his or her disposition of containment. This aids the patient to recognize themselves in those fragmented parts, which implies the beginning of integration. This is more easily said than done. How does one connect to terror, how can one feel empathy towards something that is so unbearable, that the person who experienced it is, with good reason, dissociating? Can anybody wish to recognize themselves in images of destruction?

Clearly, nobody wishes to recognize themselves in images of destruction, but traumatized persons have no choice. They can try to forget, but this never works. The terror is part of them. So the question is not does the person want to look at the terror, but how will a person look at this terror? Will he or she do so alone? In nightmares? Or will there be a space of sharing, of interaction with others, where death can become part of a living relationship?

It is useful at this point to consider the ideas developed by the psychoanalysts Cohen and Kinston. Although they use a complex psychoanalytical language, they nevertheless have developed some crucial ideas:

> *We accepted Freud's view that meeting a need leads to mental representation in the form of a wish and argued that a failure in need mediation would result in a persistent absence of associated wishes (internal self/object relations) and thus a gap in emotional understanding (psychological structure). Such a failure was held to be the essence of trauma and the basis of mental illness; and the resultant absence was primal repression (Kinston and Cohen 1986, 337).*

They then go on to distinguish between being frustrated and being traumatised. They refer to Winnicott (1954; 1960) who argued with reference to treatment that 'id wishes' could and should be frustrated while 'ego needs' should be fulfilled. In accordance with him, they say "wishes often need to be frustrated and this is not traumatic; but frustration of needs, better termed failure of the environment to meet needs, is to be avoided. Such failure is traumatic and results, metaphorically, in a persistent wound or hole in the psyche" (Kinston and Cohen 1986, 337).

Box 4: Defining Primary Object and Primary Relatedness

The consequences that the task of frustrating wishes and containing (meeting) needs has for the therapeutic process can be understood more clearly by two additional concepts introduced by the authors: "primary object" and "primary relatedness". To broaden an original concept, Kingston and Cohen state:

Primary object: "The primary object originally includes the uterus-placenta, the childhood environment and later some amalgam of personal relationships, works, possessions, physical environment, social status and religious or secular faith. The primary object generates possessiveness and embodies hope; its alteration or loss, in whole or part, is resisted strenuously and may lead to illness and death. The analyst can and must become part of the analysand's primary object. However, for growth to occur, the analyst must make direct contact with the patient in a state of primal repression. This seems to be possible only in the presence of a specialized form of relationship, which we call primary relatedness."

Primary Relatedness: "Primary relatedness is the term we will use for the direct valuing, nurturing, confiding and reflecting relationship with others, which each person absolutely and objectively needs. It is characterized by intense mutual attachment and deep empathic communication. It is an environmental complement to the individual and so cannot be internalised. When no active form of primary relatedness exists, then the individual lives in a state of psychological death with the primary object."

Source: Kinston and Cohen 1986, 343

Kinston and Cohen help us to solve the dilemma described by Sandor Ferenczi. They apparently perceive psychological structure throughout life as the product of a mediating process with the environment. Primal repression, i.e. trauma, can happen at any point in life and although the defence mechanisms will vary, the final effect is always terrible: a hole in the psyche. The trauma begins to form part of the primary object of the person. Where there is no wish, there can be no representation and no symbolisation; there is only a hole. The therapeutic task thus consists of adequately selecting and differentiating the moments to interpret wishes from those to satisfy needs. The latter implies becoming part of the primary object of the patient and thus facilitating an environment, a space in which the patient can grow.

Years ago, while offering therapeutic help to victims during the dictatorship in Chile, we spoke about a "bond of commitment" ("vinculo comprometido", Becker and Castillo 1990), referring to something that seems closely connected to the concept of primary relatedness. We then wanted to express our conscious non-neutrality towards the victims, validate our own experience in the dictatorship and indicate our disposition to connect ourselves with a kind of suffering that, at that time, still did not receive any kind of public social recognition. I believe we learned then the importance of relating to our patients from an active position, breaking the silence and calling the atrocities the regime was committing by the name they deserved. We also learned then that the psychological death experienced by the people we were trying to help could only be integrated into a perspective of life if we, ourselves, were willing to recognize that death. We had to look at its causes and make it a part of a lively relationship, thus reconfirming the life of the patients. In this sense, to cure means not so much to repair destruction, rather it emphasizes a willingness to share it. Obviously, we also committed many errors. Doing the same work today we can appreciate the difficulties we have had in being able to recognize and frustrate wishes and we are conscious of our tendency to have only recognized and met the needs. This learning process has also permitted us to understand that primary relatedness, committed bond, containment and meeting needs does not only mean sharing the sense of destruction but also accepting and confronting the destruction within and between each other.

It is possible to summarise and formulate lessons from the original three questions we asked: what does it feel like to be traumatized and is it possible to understand these feelings?, how do we relate to a traumatized person or group? and, what is the basic aim of treatment with reference to trauma? The first lesson is that trauma implies the feeling of death, of extreme fear. Secondly the consequence of trauma is fragmentation. Thirdly an interpersonal space is needed to overcome trauma. This must consist of sufficient primary relatedness or (in our Chilean language) a good bond of commitment, in which some kind of symbolisation can slowly develop. Symbolisation implies that, instead of re-experiencing terror, a psychological level or space is found and created, which, because it is symbolic, loses its 'de-structuring' capacities and makes it possible for the past to really become the past and to establish a convincing difference between extra-psychological and intra-psychological reality.

4. Beyond the framework of therapy: the importance of truth, justice, respect and empathy

Although the psychological processes and dynamics described here appear to correlate with specific psychotherapeutic settings and theories, this does not mean that they only appear in psychotherapy. I strongly believe that the issues of primary relatedness, of the possibilities of symbolisation etc. are not limited to the psychotherapeutic setting. In fact, although it is much more difficult to find adequate words to describe it, I think that all of this also happens in the social and political space. Truth commissions and justice, for example, tend to re-establish some of the 'primary objects' of a society (*see* also the contribution of Gunnar Theissen in this Handbook). They also help symbolisation to occur and to find adequate words. This results in a good 'anti-traumatic' effect. Nevertheless, it would be wrong to expect only positive reactions to them, even in countries where these commissions act from a comfortable position of power, as in South Africa.

Quite the contrary, if they work, they have to produce contradictions, and discussions, and all types of feelings. They have to facilitate a process where a new and different confrontation can occur with reference to the terror that happened. In that sense, those who expect silence to emerge from these commissions will always be frustrated. But those who understand the basic issues involved in the healing of trauma will be able to celebrate the new difficulties and discussions that arise with and through these commissions. As we saw before, at the beginning of trauma work there are only needs. Wishes can only appear after some integration has occurred and fragmentation, albeit in part, has been overcome. Instead of the repetition of trauma, we will find feelings and relationships. Many of these will be of an aggressive nature that can be addressed in new and different ways within an emerging dialogue.

On a more individual level, we can deduce certain basic attitudes in trauma work from the ideas discussed above that should be valid for everybody working in the context of war and persecution. These basic attitudes can be summed as respect, comprehension and relationship. These three attitudes are something that should be present in every kind of relationship, but they are especially important in the context of trauma. In addition, there is a little more to it than may be obvious. Although other attitudes towards suffering seem very human, they actually may hinder rather than help the process of recovery. Victims, for example, hate compassion in so far as they often correctly fear that compassion is a disguised form of rejection. The receptor of compassion is further victimized while the giver reconfirms his or her own situation of not needing compassion. This does not mean that what victims long for is somebody who doesn't feel at all, but there can be no doubt that somebody openly un-empathetic is often experienced as less destructive than somebody who pretends feeling but in reality only insists on his or her status of not being a victim. The same can be applied to grief.

4.1 Respect

Most of us have learned early in our lives that when you see someone who is sad, you should help them to be happy again. In short, if someone cries you should try to make him or her stop. In the context of trauma and terrible loss, this can be exactly the wrong thing to do. If somebody has suffered a terrible loss, wouldn't it be more appropriate to cry rather than not to cry? In that sense, respect would mean letting a person express her or his distress and grief, without immediately insisting on calming her or him. Many years ago in Chile, I dealt with a family (a mother and her daughter) whose fourteen-year-old son had been killed during a public protest by the police. One of the difficulties of the case was that well-meaning friends of the family had said to the daughter that she shouldn't cry so much because that would wet the wings of her brother flying to heaven and thereby make his journey more difficult. Now this had meant for the little girl, alongside her terrible grief, accumulating feelings of guilt that evidently didn't help her much. In fact, she and her mother did not eat anything for days after the incident occurred. Only after we (the therapists) had confirmed two essential points could they slowly begin a more normal life, although their grieving obviously continued for a long time after. These points were: (a) the police, and not themselves, were responsible for the death of the son; and (b) crying was good and normal and, if anything, could only help the son's journey to heaven because it showed that his family loved him.

Thus, respect means a lot of things, of which the most important are not to further victimize the people with whom we are dealing, respecting their grief and destruction as well as their capacities for surviving and continuing through life. It means being interested in their history and respectful of their own way of expressing themselves without pretending to know everything about them. Respect means not running away once the people really start talking to us.

4.2 Comprehension

The second attitude, comprehension, is equally important. Comprehension of the dynamics of trauma is central when dealing with victims, although it does not necessarily mean that one should always act on what one understands. For example, certain issues like mistrust, insecurity, passivity and exaggerated fear can be understood in the context of trauma. Additionally, the fact that somebody is able to talk, communicate and even able to work, while at the same time feeling extreme inner terror, does not surprise us much, when we have a greater understanding of trauma. Clearly, comprehension is not something we can obtain a priori. It always depends on how well we know the context and how our concrete relationships develop. We can, at least, be willing to learn and thereby develop our comprehension, and, in a general way, we can have hunches about the best direction to take.

If, for example, trauma has all the destructive force we have postulated, and also develops sequentially, then we know that traumatized persons are involved in the very difficult struggle of reconstructing their personality. We would understand, for example, that an eleven-year old, ex-child-soldier in El Salvador, whose parents were killed at the beginning of the war, and who for years was a good and responsible soldier, would now, in a time of peace and back at school, begin to manifest serious problems. His parents are dead, the power and social importance he had as a soldier have disappeared, he is now only a schoolboy who does not read and write very well. We would understand that only now will he begin a grief process regarding the loss of his parents and his childhood, and also that, for him, it is possibly less fun being a 'stupid student' than a 'good soldier'. If we want to help him, we have to accept this specific part of his history. This would mean acknowledging both him and his past. It is necessary to take him seriously and to look for the possibility that his past can be valued, while at the same time making room for the needed educational process. This could happen, for example, by letting him also be a teacher, giving him the task of organizing and participating together with other young men in the educational work and teaching others to read and write.

4.3 Relationship

The third attitude, relationship, sums up the first two, but also goes beyond them. For psychotherapists it is quite obvious that they should never forget one of the basic laws of communication which states that communication always has two aspects: one referring to the relationship established between the persons communicating, and another referring to the content of the message that is being communicated. The relationship aspect is always more powerful and important than the aspect referring to the content. This implies, for example, that a teacher of mathematics, while teaching the subject to a group of students, might be talking about math on one side (content), but on the other side always establishes the specific teacher-student relationship, and that she and her students cannot communicate outside of this relationship. Moreover, the quantity of math that her students learn does not depend so much on the information she gives, but rather on the relationship she establishes with her students. One often wonders why the knowledge of this law should be limited to psychologists. Would it not make a lot more sense for everybody to know about this? This is especially true for teachers and technicians; that is, persons who hope to transmit information but who often forget that this implies a relationship, which in turn determines if the information they want to transmit really reaches the other person.

In the context of trauma work, this is a central issue. Finally, it should be understood that help, which is offered in crisis regions and in situations of catastrophe, is never only a question of what people need, but also a question of how the required help is put into effect. People might need food and shelter, but it makes an enormous difference if they participate actively in this or if they are just passive recipients of help. In the latter case it should not surprise anybody if these persons afterward stay passive and do not develop much energy to reconstruct an independent form of living. Building and developing relationships is thus a key activity in trauma work. The aim is always to respect and understand others and to build a framework in which change might occur. A relationship in this sense also implies trusting the traumatized persons; trusting that they have the energy and creativity of their own that they can use to help themselves. The ideology of 'help, in order to facilitate self-help' is not new in the cooperation for development. But not all actors seem to take it very seriously. In short, self-help can and will occur, even in the most terrible situations, if the helpers are willing to offer a kind of relationship that is committed and respectful; i.e. a framework of trust and protection in which new initiatives can develop.

4.4 Psychosocial work as a method for dealing with individuals and their social context

Everybody working in a crisis region should be aware that trauma work is not something that should be limited to specialists of psychology. There are a number of relevant psychological issues involved, but these should be shared in a clearly interdisciplinary approach to our work. It is quite sad to observe how in different places in the world the same error is repeated over and over again; trauma work is considered a mental health issue, absolutely independent of educational activities and economic reconstruction. Psychosocial work should never be an aim in itself. It should be understood as a method that obliges us to deal with individuals and their histories, as well as with their social context and the economic realities that are present. Thus, depending on the specific situation, trauma work can be therapy, but it can also be the reconstruction of houses in the community by the community itself, or even school work.

Case Study 1: Community Center, Bosnia

In Sanski Most, a small town in Bosnia, there exists a project in which women, who were traumatised during the war (most of them lost their husbands), take care of old people who live alone. Through this activity they are able to make a little money and, at the same time, they are offering a basic health and social service, one that is much cheaper than what the state could offer. In addition, through their work, they overcome their own isolation and form groups, in which they talk about the problems of the elderly people as well as themselves. They are being supervised by a group of local women activists that have organized this work as a kind of community centre with the help of Swiss development agencies. This project is a real self-help project. Despite the trauma of the participants, they still persist in inventing perspectives for change amongst themselves. In Bosnia, the relationship towards one's parents is culturally very deeply rooted and highly valued. Helping the old is also a way of not forgetting the past: the pre-war past. In short, we are looking at an integrated project that provides a social service, generates income, implies working through trauma and is being carried out by laypersons doing an excellent job.

Case Study 2: Grameen Bank, Bangladesh

A further example is the Grameen Bank in Bangladesh, the so-called bank for the poor. I don't think its founders ever thought about their work in terms of trauma. But when one reads about their work, how they build trust and relationships with the people, how they help them to organize themselves in groups, how they respect cultural traditions and how within this framework they develop economic perspectives, one cannot help feeling that what they are doing is excellent trauma therapy, although what they are known for is micro-credits, very small loans, that usually do not exceed U$ 200. So many economic projects have failed, simply because they are interested more in the money than in the people who deal with this money. The Grameen Bank works the other way around. Their first interest is the people, their histories and their needs. They then develop perspectives together with the people, while understanding that the problems people have and the possibility of autonomy and self-help are not a contradiction but a complementary function of the same issue. Furthermore, Grameen offers a group structure that facilitates containment in the most direct therapeutic sense. Thus, at the end they achieve a very respectable economic result, but they also achieve the result that the most exploited and traumatised persons begin to trust themselves and their capacities and begin to construct a more dignified life.

5. The danger of traumatisation of the trauma worker: burn out prevention and supervision

Finally, I would like to comment on the persons trying to help in the context of trauma. When one is trying to help others, one often tends to forget that nobody is invincible and that helpers also have needs. When dealing with extreme suffering, it appears to be a luxury to think about one's own well-being. Nevertheless, it is quite well known now that people working in extreme situations need to be very attentive to their own psychological processes. Quite frequently people overestimate their capacities to resist terrible situations and underestimate their need of receiving respect and validation through others. The consequence of not really dealing with oneself is known as 'burn-out'. What is meant by this is an absolute lack of distance towards one's work, a permanently exaggerated use of one's own capacities till the point of total fatigue is reached. At this point one works poorly, gets ill and begins to hate the people one previously wanted to help. The problem is recognized all over the world but is only very rarely dealt with in an adequate fashion. In fact agencies usually don't like to pay for supervision, training workshops and time-outs for trauma workers. Trauma workers themselves also tend to ignore the difficulties and frustrations in their work, and continue to the point where they fall ill.

If we really want to avoid these errors, we have to assume that working in a traumatic situation implies that the helpers, in one way or another, can become traumatised and that they need time to work through their own traumatisation. This must happen through regular external supervision. In this context, supervision is meant not as a further means of control, but rather as a space in which the trauma worker can talk about problems at work within a framework of trust and respect. If local supervision is not possible, then external supervisors from other countries need to be brought in, until a suitable local structure is in place. One should always encourage trauma workers to write and communicate about their work. This is a way of working through one's own experience and making sure that it does not convert itself into a private traumatic event, but becomes part of a public process again. Also vacations and trips to other places are necessary. Some of these can be official working trips, but it is also important to understand the legitimacy and importance of not working or taking a break.

Trauma teams all over the world have had severe crises because this issue was not addressed appropriately. In fact, most teams I have encountered, at some point in their development, have broken up because of these problems. Trauma always has to do with extreme aggression. If we do not learn to consciously deal with this aggression we will be condemned to repeat it amongst ourselves, at the least destroying our work, and, at worst, destroying ourselves through illnesses.

6. Conclusions

At first sight, it would seem a positive development that psychological dimensions are finally being considered with reference to the consequences of organized violence. However, this quickly becomes doubtful when trauma is understood and dealt with as a typical medical illness, like malaria or chicken pox. In this framework trauma work is just one more smoke screen of political propaganda that is used to give people the illusion of help. The basic issues of power and social conflict are not only ignored but, worse, are conceptually redefined as part of an individual psychological illness, thereby further hindering a person's capacity to act upon the situation. Exaggerating a little, one could say that first we have war and destruction, and then we offer individual therapy instead of social change.

When dealing with human suffering as a consequence of man-made disaster, we are confronting two problems. First, we have to try to understand the basic psychological dimensions involved and enhance the recognition of the importance of these dimensions. Second, we have to avoid a cheap psychologisation of political problems and make sure that the sociopolitical aspects are not ignored, but are actively recognized and integrated into our work. In other words, when confronting trauma arising out of man-made disasters, we have to deal with the individual and the society, with the material and the spiritual aspects of life, with politics and economics, justice and psychology.

Consequently, it is understandable why trauma is such a complex topic. However, this should not lead to the erroneous conclusion that only highly-trained professional therapists can do trauma work. We have recently seen not only a high number of trauma projects being set up in the crisis regions of the world, but also an army of trauma experts (usually from the rich industrialized nations) teaching the locals the techniques of trauma therapy. Most of these techniques fit well into the individualized culture of rich western countries and their corresponding structure of mental health care. Nevertheless, they are often quite beside the point in a crisis region, where trauma is a collective reality and the cultural context is different. Approximately 80% of trauma work in crisis regions is being carried out by lay persons. Some do therapy, but many conduct activities similar to community education, human rights work and economic reconstruction. Training in the field of trauma can only be worthwhile if it is understood that there cannot be either one model or one way of doing things. In different contexts, trauma work must be continually reinvented without being restricted to the activity of individual therapy.

Trauma work can be an important factor in helping individuals confront the consequences of organized violence throughout the world, if it is carried out in a responsible way and developed with reference to the specific cultural context. Trauma work needs to be part of an integrated approach that includes the dimensions of education and economics. Furthermore, it should always address both the individual and the collective aspects. To be carried out effectively support structures are needed on a national and international level. In that sense, we should try to avoid turning trauma work into an international business, but rather defend the possibility of international solidarity.

7. Reference and Further Reading

American Psychiatric Association 1994. *Diagnostic and statistical manual of mental disorders, 4th ed.; DSM-IV,* Washington, DC: American Psychiatric Association.

Balint, M. 1965. *Die Urformen der Liebe und die Technik der Psychoanalyse,* Bern and Stuttgart: Huber and Klett.

Becker, D. 1992. *Ohne Haß keine Versöhnung. Das Trauma der Verfolgten*, Freiburg: Kore Verlag.

Becker, D. 1995. "The Deficiency of the Concept of Posttraumatic Stress Disorder when dealing with Victims of Human Rights Violations," *in* Kleber et al., op. cit., 99-110.

Becker, D. and M. I. Castillo 1990. *Procesos de traumatización extrema y posibilidades de reparación,* Santiago, Chile: Instituto Latinoamericano de Salud Mental y Derechos Humanos (unpublished paper).

Becker, D. and E. Lira, (eds.) 1989. *Derechos Humanos: Todo es segun el dolor con que se mira,* Santiago, Chile: Instituto Latinoamericano de Salud Mental y Derechos Humanos.

Bergmann M. and M. Jucovy (eds.) 1982. *Generations of the Holocaust,* New York, NY: Basic Books.

Bettelheim, B. 1943. "Individual and mass behavior in extreme situations," *Journal of Abnormal and Social Psychology*, 38, 417-452.

Bion, W. 1990. *Lernen durch Erfahrung,* Frankfurt am Main: Suhrkamp.

Danieli, Y. (ed.) 1998. *International Handbook of Multigenerational Legacies of Trauma,* New York, NY: Plenum Press.

Ferenczi, S. 1988. *Ohne Sympathie keine Heilung. Das klinische Tagebuch von 1932,* Frankfurt am Main: S. Fischer Verlag.

Fischer, G. und P. Riedesser 1998. *Lehrbuch der Psychotraumatologie,* München: Reinhard Verlag.

Khan, M. 1977. "Das kumulative Trauma," *in* M. Khan, op. cit., München: Kindler Verlag.

Khan, M. 1977. *Selbsterfahrung in der Therapie,* München: Kindler Verlag.

Keilson, H. 1992. *Sequential Traumatization in Children,* Jerusalem: Magnes press, Hebrew University.

Kinston, W. and J. Cohen 1986. "Primal repression: Clinical and theoretical aspects," *International Journal of Psychoanalysis*, 27, 337-355.

Kleber, R, C. Figley and B. Gersons (eds.) 1995. *Beyond Trauma,* New York: Plenum Press.

Kritz, N. (ed.) 1995. *Transitional Justice, Vol. I, II and III,* Washington, DC: United States Institute of Peace.

Krystal, H. 1968. *Massive Psychological Trauma,* New York, NY: International University Press.

Laplanche, J. and J.-B. Pontails, 1977. *Das Vokabular der Psychoanalyse*, Frankfurt am Main: Suhrkamp Verlag.

Robben, A. and M. Suarez-Orozco (eds.) 2000. *Cultures under siege: Collective Violence and Trauma,* Cambridge: Cambridge University Press.

Stiftung für Kinder (ed.) 1995. *Children- War and Persecution. Proceeedings of the Congress of Hamburg*, Sep. 26 – 29, 1993, Osnabruck: Secolo Verlag.

Van der Kolk, B., A. Mc Farlane and L. Weisaeth (eds.) 1996. *Traumatic Stress: the effects of overwhelming experience on mind, body and society,* New York, NY: Guilford Press.

Winnicott, D. 1954. "Metapsychological and clinical aspects of regression within the psychoanalytical setup," *in* Collected Papers: Through Paediatrics to Psychoanalysis, London: Hogarth Press.

Winnicott, D. 1960. "Ego distortions *in* terms of true and false self," *in* The Maturational Process and the Facilitating Environment, London: Hogarth Press.

Winnicott, D. 1965. *The Maturational Process and the Facilitating Environment,* London: Hogarth Press.

Interesting Web Sites

www.amnesty.org
www.hri.ca
www.hrw.org
www.ncptsd.org
www.reconciliation.org.za
www.wits.ac.za/csvr/home

Supporting Justice, Co-existence and Reconciliation after Armed Conflict: Strategies for Dealing with the Past

Gunnar Theissen

1. Introduction 422
2. Instruments 422
International Criminal Tribunals, National Prosecutions and Community Courts
Amnesty Laws and Release of Political Prisoners
Disciplinary Measures
Truth Commissions
Land Commissions and Courts
Reparations
Grassroots Reconciliation Work
3. Principles and Strategies for Supporting Justice and Reconciliation 431
Ethical Standards and Official Guidelines
Local, Contextual and Combined Approaches
Proper Sequencing
Outsider Restraint
Possibilities for Third Parties
4. Open Questions and Perspectives 436
Resolvable Problems
Challenging Dilemmas
5. Reference and Further Reading 438

Supporting Justice, Co-existence and Reconciliation after Armed Conflict: Strategies for Dealing with the Past

Gunnar Theissen

1. Introduction

Civil wars and state repression have left many societies traumatised and shattered. Unsolved atrocities and injustices can easily provoke new cycles of violence. Impunity may undermine trust in the legal system, increasing the risk that vigilante justice will be resorted to and encourage further atrocities. Mistrust and hatred between former adversaries inhibits reconstruction, decision making and economic development. An amnesty deal may be required to end violence and enable a peace treaty. The call for compromise and national reconciliation may be necessary to ensure an end to hostilities, but past injustices that are never addressed can easily become a source of renewed violent conflict. Often victims can only make peace with their perpetrators if they know their own suffering and that of their loved ones is officially acknowledged. Furthermore, for the reintegration of perpetrators and victims into society they must be commonly accepted.

The first section of this chapter reviews various instruments and institutions that have been established to support peaceful coexistence and the restoration of law. It addresses the following questions: Under which conditions can criminal tribunals, truth commissions or amnesty laws be helpful in dealing with past atrocities? How can property issues be solved through mediation or in community courts? The chapter then outlines some general considerations as to the principles and strategies that should be followed by third parties who seek to support such institutions and instruments. Arguing for a long-term approach, the final section summarises some issues for further debate, pointing to some problematic assumptions and developments that have so far gone hand in hand with the current enthusiasm for international criminal law and truth commissions.

2. Instruments

2.1 International Criminal Tribunals, National Prosecutions and Community Courts

The criminal justice system may well serve an important function in efforts to regulate past injustices and transform potentially violent conflict into peaceful settlement. There is an increasing international consensus, supported by international law, that gross human rights violations, genocide, war crimes and crimes against humanity must be investigated and punished (*see* Box 3 for definitions). However, it may sometimes be impossible to pursue criminal prosecutions in the immediate aftermath of civil strife, or they may, if procedural standards cannot be maintained, provoke renewed violence or lead to new injustices. It must also be recognized that the impact of criminal prosecution on exposing truth, educating the public about past injustices and achieving conflict transformation is likely to be limited (Osiel 1997). The central arguments both against and in favour of criminal prosecutions are summarized in Box 1.

Since national criminal justice systems have often been either incapable or unwilling to bring genocide, war crimes and crimes against humanity to trial, the UN Security Council has recently established the International Criminal Tribunals for the Former Yugoslavia and Rwanda (Morris and Scharf 1995; 1997). Moreover, significant progress has been made in establishing a *permanent* International Criminal Court (ICC) to hear the most heinous crimes (Cassese 1999).

Box 1: Potentials, Shortcomings and Risks of Criminal Trials as Tools for Conflict Transformation

The key potentials of criminal trials lie in the fact that they...

- may break the culture of impunity, prevent future human rights abuses and increase awareness of human rights and humanitarian law;
- send a clear message that past atrocities are not legitimate (as is often claimed by the relevant parties to the conflict) but rather criminal acts;
- may provide victims with a certain satisfaction and prevent them from taking the law into their own hands;
- individualise accountability and guilt: Instead of portraying entire population groups as inhuman villains, those who were responsible for specific atrocities are made accountable for their actions. Suspected violations can thus be either substantiated or refuted and the reintegration of guiltless suspects accelerated.

However, there are limits and risks attached to criminal prosecutions – for example:

- The criminal justice system may be in shambles and lack critical resources.
- The accused may not be properly represented and procedural standards not maintained.
- Criminal trials may provoke violent resistance from former combatants or the potential accused and their supporters, and thus may contribute to increased support for presumed 'martyrs' who claim to be subjected to 'victors' justice'.
- Criminal prosecutions are often costly and time-consuming, and may thus fail to satisfy demands that some justice be done immediately.
- Suspects are only brought to trial selectively. Many crimes remain obscure, because perpetrators are not identified, have fled the country, have died or cannot be charged due to lack of evidence.
- Criminal prosecutions may be hampered, as victims may not trust the criminal justice system or be afraid to bring charges. The judiciary may also be viewed as partisan to one particular party to the conflict.
- Criminal prosecutions usually give more public attention to perpetrators than to victims.
- If well-known suspects are not found guilty because of lack of evidence, procedural errors or failure to call important witnesses, criminal trials may send a wrong signal that certain people remain above the law.

International criminal tribunals are usually able to establish high procedural standards and thus ensure a certain degree of neutrality. By serving as a yardstick for national tribunals, they may also encourage local efforts to prosecute past atrocities. However, their direct impact on local conflict transformation is likely to remain rather slim, since they are usually costly, only able to bring a small percentage of suspects to trial and often geographically and culturally removed from the communities that have suffered under past conflicts (Akhavan 1998; Alvarez 1999). Even the future permanent ICC is only constructed as an emergency tool, for the cases that national criminal systems fail. The court will only be able to hear a small percentage of atrocities that have taken place in conflict-ridden societies.

Sustainable conflict regulation and transformation in war-torn societies necessitate a (re-)construction of properly functioning local justice systems. Consider the International Criminal Tribunal for Rwanda: it has received international funding which was twice the amount of the total support given to the national criminal justice system in Rwanda. However in the five years since its establishment only about thirty cases have been heard compared to the daunting task which faces the national system of prosecuting around 120,000 suspects of genocide. This demonstrates that the effectiveness of international criminal courts is reduced when they are not accompanied by parallel efforts to build up local institutions.

Moreover, many developing countries are characterised by legal pluralism, that is, a rudimentary formal justice system exists along with traditional institutions to distribute justice and solve conflicts (Weilenmann 1999). Reactivating these communal courts by allowing them to handle less severe crimes or to arbitrate property and land issues may be one strategy to deal with past injustices: their procedures may better reflect culturally accepted practices or rituals and therefore local courts can more easily ensure strong community participation. They may thus be more capable of reintegrating wrongdoers into communal life (Pankhurst 1999). Instead of sending perpetrators to overcrowded jails, local institutions can order criminals to compensate their victims or to serve the community in some other appropriately reparatory way. One such example is the planned re-establishment of local community courts in Rwanda, known as *gacacas*, to deal with 'minor' crimes of the 1994 genocide.

There are, however, some major risks in such decentralised approaches with strong lay participation:

- After armed conflict, local justice systems are unlikely to be 'traditional'. Instead, they will probably reflect newly established power structures dominated by warlords or vigilante groups.
- Procedures and penalties may be incompatible with human rights standards and strengthen traditional patriarchal structures, instead of securing participation of women and young adults.
- Support for local, alternative justice systems may reinforce the dichotomy between customary legal systems and the formal legal sector, instead of increasing the linkage and co-operation between the two.
- State structures may prove to be incapable of supervising the work of local courts and thus fail to ensure due process.

2.2 Amnesty Laws and Release of Political Prisoners

Political prisoners detained in violation of fundamental rules of international law must be released immediately. Their release usually increases the ability of the society to regulate conflicts by means of civilian actors rather than armed forces. Often there is no agreement on who should be regarded as a political prisoner; however, the principles for the release of political prisoners in Namibia developed by the then-president of the European Court on Human Rights, Carl Age Nørgaard have established some precedent (Boraine and Levy 1995, pp. 156-60). More generally, international humanitarian law states that prisoners of war must be released after an internal armed conflict (*see* e.g., *Article 6 (5) of the 2nd Additional Protocol to the Geneva Conventions*). However, amnesty should be limited to combatants who have participated only in armed conflict, but not in genocide, war crimes, crimes against humanity or other gross violations of human rights such as torture or enforced disappearances. General amnesties, granting impunity for gross human-rights violations without investigation, such as the Argentine *Full Stop Law*, are thus incompatible with international law.

However, general amnesties for minor offences may be necessary to better enable the criminal justice system to prosecute more severe crimes. Amnesty for gross human rights violations should only – if at all – be an option after the individual perpetrator has appeared before an amnesty panel or a (community) court and made a full disclosure of his crimes. Victims should be allowed to participate in these amnesty procedures, as was done in the example of the amnesty proceedings of the South African Truth and Reconciliation Commission (*see* Box 2). Amnesty should, however, be limited to criminal liability, without automatically cancelling all obligations of the perpetrator to compensate the victim or his family. By passing legislation offering reduced or suspended sentences for those perpetrators confessing to their crimes, states may further speed up the investigation of past atrocities.

2.3 Disciplinary Measures

In order to restore public confidence in the criminal justice system, those responsible for war crimes or gross human-rights violations should be barred from public office in the police and military. Furthermore, the activities of informal networks responsible for fostering violence should be monitored and suppressed. In several East European countries, for example, high-ranking officials of the communist regimes were automatically disqualified from holding public office on the basis of so-called 'lustration laws' (Boed 1998). However, collective disqualification from public office, without the hearing of each individual case, violates the principle of due process and the right to a free choice of workplace. Moreover, lustration policies may lead to a complete breakdown of the public administration, or even provoke violent resistance by public officials and members of the security forces. In these situations, soft approaches, like transfers, early retirement or the appointment of new officials to strategic posts, are more suitable to ensure that unreliable officials are replaced. Rather than passing new legislation specifically aimed at members of the former regime, emphasis should be placed on the enforcement of ordinary disciplinary law.

2.4 Truth Commissions

In several Latin American and African countries, truth commissions have documented past human-rights abuses. Their mandate, powers and activities have varied from country to country (Hayner 1994). As a rule, truth commissions are based on a peace agreement, on governmental decrees or laws of parliament. Usually they are instructed to record human rights violations of a given period by collecting documents relating to these atrocities and by hearing victims as well as perpetrators. They usually have to provide the public with a detailed report about what has happened in the past and how such atrocities can be avoided in the future. In addition, churches and local human rights organisations often make similar efforts to document past human rights abuses, as, for example, in Brazil, Guatemala and Zimbabwe (Dassin 1986; REMHI 1998; Carver 1993).

The advantage of truth commissions supported by the government is that they can officially acknowledge and document past human rights violations. Furthermore, they can also be endowed with the powers of search and seizure and can subpoena suspects. On the other hand, if their mandate is too weak, and if they lack the necessary resources to work independently, official truth commissions may well risk becoming a mere exercise in governmental public relations.

Projects by non-governmental organisations (NGOs) to document past atrocities should be supported, particularly in situations where the executive will and capacity to do so is lacking. Profiting from closer links to victims, these projects can strengthen civil society and thus increase pressure on the government to launch its own investigations. More likely, however,

their findings will be ignored, or may even provoke government repression, including the assassination of human rights activists. NGOs are not necessarily more impartial than official enquiries by the government. NGOs may be perceived as allied to one particular party to the conflict as may be the case with official truth commissions supported by the government. The Guatemalan experience shows that both non-governmental and official attempts to document past atrocities have their advantages and can, ideally, mutually support each other's efforts (Salazar Volkmann 1999).

As an instrument for post-conflict rehabilitation, truth commissions are especially appropriate in situations in which:

- criminal prosecutions would inhibit an end to hostilities, prevent a peace agreement or even provoke new violence;
- most victims would not be able to successfully charge their offenders or secure reparations through criminal and civil proceedings;
- the criminal justice system fails to guarantee fair procedures, is overburdened or is mistrusted by the majority of victims;
- the judiciary is unwilling or lacks the necessary independence to investigate and prosecute past human-rights violations;
- judicial enquiries would be too slow or too costly;
- evidence is destroyed and is insufficient to ensure a reasonable chance to secure convictions.

Truth Commissions have the advantage that they:

- break the silence about past human-rights violations, and encourage people to speak out about past atrocities, since the risk of repression decreases as more people go public;

- leave space for informal communication between victims and perpetrators;
- expose past atrocities from a victim perspective, turn the public against the perpetrators and thus decrease their credibility and power in society;
- provide a comprehensive and well-written account of past human-rights abuses, and encourage public debate as to how peaceful co-existence can be secured in the future;
- identify victims and their needs for rehabilitation and reparation;
- increase empathy for victims and survivors of past human-rights violations. Public attention is focused on the needs and experiences of victims, without subjecting them to undignified cross-examination. Victims are no longer portrayed as legitimate targets and alleged terrorists, but personalised as human beings and innocent victims of arbitrary and inhumane cruelty.

Truth commissions may also:

- inquire into the causes of past injustices that cannot be fitted into the categories of criminal law, such as the failure by professional organisations to speak out against atrocities or their tacit support of human rights violations;
- investigate human rights abuses for which local courts lack jurisdiction, as the statute of limitations may apply, or the violations were not criminal under national law, or committed extra-territorially;
- record atrocities whose perpetrators remain unknown;
- provide the judiciary with well-documented evidence for follow-up prosecutions.

Past experience shows, however, that the recommendations of official and non-governmental truth commissions have all too often been ignored, and that their work has often failed to meet the expectations of victims. In many countries, well-known perpetrators of such offences remained in public office or were never even charged. In El Salvador, for example, the publication of a UN-sponsored truth commission report was used as an excuse to grant former perpetrators immunity by means of a general amnesty. Whereas Chile implemented a comprehensive reparation system for relatives of those who were murdered or who disappeared, and provided torture victims with health care, other governments never provided any substantial reparation to abused victims.

Box 2: The South African Truth and Reconciliation Commission

The most sophisticated truth commission to date has been the South African Truth and Reconciliation Commission (TRC), which was given the task of inquiring into gross human rights violations committed in that country between 1960 and 1994. The mandate of the TRC covered killings, acts of torture, abduction and severe ill-treatment, but excluded the legalised injustices of the apartheid system, such as prolonged arbitrary detention, systematic persecution on racial grounds and forced removals. In contrast to other truth commissions, the South African TRC held its hearings in public. The media, including national television, covered them extensively. To date, the South African TRC is the only truth commission that managed to combine the collection of statements by more than 23,000 victims with a unique amnesty process. Perpetrators could be granted amnesty provided that they made an application before 16 December 1997 to the Amnesty Committee of the TRC; but only on the basis that the applicant also offered a full disclosure of his deeds. Suspected perpetrators who failed to apply for amnesty or who were refused amnesty could then be prosecuted in court. The Amnesty Committee thus had the difficult task to decide on about 2500 applications related to politically motivated gross human rights violations. Whereas its amnesty provisions satisfied the state's obligation to investigate past human-rights violations, it is doubtful whether these provisions are in fact compatible with international law, as they allowed indemnity for unpunished acts amounting to crimes against humanity, such as widespread or systematic torture and murder. Compatibility with international law could have been increased by also granting partial amnesties, such as reduced or suspended criminal sentences. Although most black South Africans embraced and accepted the TRC's work, the promise of truth could not always be fulfilled. Instead, time pressure and the need to first investigate amnesty applications created a situation in which the Commission was able to do no more than corroborate most victims' statements, without investigating them in full detail. Whereas the Commission recommended a comprehensive reparation policy to Parliament, it was not itself empowered to provide any substantial level of financial support to victims. This led to the travesty that some perpetrators began to benefit from amnesty, while victims and survivors were left with little more than a public acknowledgement of their suffering.

Truth commissions should preferably be based on a parliamentary law that has been drafted with the participation of all relevant actors, including former adversaries, human rights groups and victims' organisations. Commissioners and staff should evidence integrity, be representative of all political organisations, religious communities and population groups, qualified in law, psychology or other relevant fields, and able to communicate in the languages of both victims and perpetrators. The mandate should be broad enough to include war crimes, gross violations of human rights and crimes against humanity, including human rights violations that were legalised under previous national laws. It should cover all important acts committed during the past conflict, and enable the commission to investigate abuses of all parties to the conflict. A specified time frame and sufficient financial resources should allow the commission to first establish itself (staff, offices, etc.) and then to conduct its work (Hayner 1996).

Although most truth commissions have made substantive recommendations to ensure that past atrocities are not repeated, more attention should be given to initiating an official review mechanism after the commission has published its report. Victim and perpetrator hearings should preferably be held in public, provided that the personal security of those testifying can be guaranteed. If their security is in danger, the commission should have the power to exclude the public. Truth commissions should open regional offices that are accessible to all victims and preferably hold hearings throughout the country. The final report, with its findings and recommendations, should be published and translated into all relevant languages. Truth commissions should also involve the local media and non-governmental organisations to report on and support its work.

If the commission is entitled to identify perpetrators, the implicated person should be given the opportunity to be heard (under the maxim *audi alterem parte*) and respond to the allegations before he or she is named in the report. The commission should have the power of search and seizure, to call witnesses and alleged perpetrators to a hearing, as well as to grant partial amnesties, such as reduced or suspended sentences. At the same time, if entitled to grant amnesty, a truth commission should also ensure that victims receive some compensation and psychological or medical support before perpetrators are granted amnesty or pardon.

2.5 Land Commissions and Courts

After civil strife, expulsion from land and housing is often a primary source of potential new conflict. Refugees may return to their old dwellings and find them occupied by new inhabitants, who may themselves have fled from other places or even been responsible for the eviction of the former owners. These problems may be further aggravated by a shortage of housing and shelter, so that sometimes many different parties, descendants or former owners, will have claims to the same property. The recent land occupations in Zimbabwe have demonstrated all too clearly how unresolved land issues can be politically utilised and threaten peace and stability even decades after the end of a liberation war.

One option to address this problem is the establishment of land or housing commissions that are empowered to mediate between old and new owners in order to find a compromise. If the return of property, payment of compensation or provision of alternative land or housing cannot be thus achieved, specialised courts should be established to make an appropriate ruling. The judgement or compromise thus reached should be officially documented, in order to defuse future conflicts about ownership. These efforts can only be successful with unequivocal and widely accepted regulations concerning how land and property issues are to be arbitrated. Compromise can be encouraged by the granting of housing subsidies, building materials or other support, but only on the condition that former owners be allowed to return to their property or be given adequate compensation.

2.6 Reparations

Reparations may contribute to the reintegration of victims and reduce the likelihood of renewed armed confrontation, by officially recognising the harm victims had to endure. They may even prove to be essential for many victims' survival. Besides restitution, special compensation laws should be implemented for those cases in which compensation can be achieved only very slowly or selectively by means of civil litigation. Compensation should be granted on an individual basis for physical, psychological and material damages, including medical and legal costs arising from gross human-rights violations (UN Secretary General 1997). According to established rules of state responsibility, states remain responsible for the damage caused by them or by their officials – even if a new government comes to power. In the case of whole communities that were victimised and torn apart by past violence, emphasis should also be placed on symbolic and communal forms of reparation.

After mass atrocities, states often have only limited capacity to compensate victims. Moreover, these restricted resources are very often spent unequally: former public officials and combatants are supported by costly pension schemes, while victims and survivors of human-rights violations receive very little or nothing at all. Third-parties should therefore insist that specific victim's groups are not excluded from official reparation policies and should further strengthen the self-organisation of marginalized victims. Compensation laws should be easy to understand and should not discriminate against any one group of victims. An efficient, transparent and fair administrative process with competent and trained staff, who respect the needs of victims, is as essential to this effort as are the actual amounts paid.

Occasionally, victims will refuse financial compensation if they feel that the government is attempting to buy their silence. Similarly, victims may also feel betrayed if instead their suffering or heroism is repeatedly acknowledged in official speeches and symbolic ceremonies, but hardly any material or financial effort is made to rectify the situation.

2.7 Grassroots Reconciliation Work

While most of the activities mentioned require the involvement of government and public administration, there is also ample room for non-governmental organisations to support processes of increasing mutual understanding and reconciliation. Besides lobbying governments or public administration to address past injustices and also assisting and complementing the work of official institutions, NGOs can run their own projects and programmes to increase trust and understanding between former adversaries. These programmes are often more successful if they are not aimed specifically at reconciling former enemies, but rather constitute practical steps supported by all parties: third parties, for instance, may provide neutral ground for former adversaries to meet. They may organise tours for representatives of former conflict parties to inspect specific problem zones that require attention. Ordinary citizens can be involved in programmes to rebuild destroyed buildings together, through youth exchanges and work camps and with the support of local community newspapers or radio stations. These activities should include people from all backgrounds and aim at enhancing co-operation. The attraction of such initiatives can be increased if they properly address the needs of all conflict parties and if they are built on identities that cross former conflict lines, such as gender or profession.

Local NGOs or churches can organise workshops to help deal with past trauma and to provide space to talk about past experiences in order to further mutual understanding and empathy across former conflict lines. Activities of this kind that use traditional frameworks and institutions are usually widely accepted by the community.

Sites of historical relevance, including atrocities or prisons, may be converted into places of remembrance, the importance of which can be explained by survivors to visitors and schoolchildren. Such projects should enlist community participation by encouraging those who were imprisoned or suffered violence there to contribute pictures or symbolic personal belongings.

Local initiatives to remember the victims of past conflicts in the form of common memorials, prayers or commemorations that are inclusive and pay respect to all victims may also help to demonstrate unity, or at least the end of hostilities. The way in which the past is remembered is essential, as such commemorations can unfortunately always be exploited for further hostility and resentment.

3. Principles and Strategies for Supporting Justice and Reconciliation

3.1 Ethical Standards and Official Guidelines

Neither states nor practitioners in the field of conflict resolution or development co-operation should support policies that fundamentally disregard international standards of human rights. Their work should always be guided by the basic assumption that states have a duty under international law to investigate, punish and compensate gross violations of human rights, war crimes and crimes against humanity. These duties are enshrined in the four Geneva Conventions, the *Genocide Convention*, the *International Convention on Civil and Political Rights* and the *Convention against Torture*, as well as in various regional human rights conventions (*see* e.g., Orentlicher 1991; Roht-Arriaza 1995; Randelzhofer and Tomuschat 1999).

The current state of international customary law is reflected in the *Rome Statute of the International Criminal Court*, which reiterated in its preamble the duty of nation-states to exercise appropriate criminal jurisdiction for international crimes (*see* Box 3).

Furthermore, the Sub-Commission for the Prevention of Discrimination and Protection of Minorities of the UN Commission on Human Rights developed the *Set of Principles for the Protection and Promotion of Human Rights through Action to Combat Impunity* (UN Commission on Human Rights 1997a) and *the Draft Basic Principles and Guidelines on the Right to Reparation of Victims of [Gross] Violations of Human Rights and International Humanitarian Law* (UN Commission on Human Rights 1997b 1997). Both documents are based on an international review of various attempts made by nation-states to deal with past injustices and give practitioners a basic orientation as to which principles should be maintained.

Box 3: Definitions

'International crimes': According to international law 'aggression', 'genocide', 'crimes against humanity' and 'war crimes' are regarded as international crimes since they pose a threat to international security and to the safety of mankind. They are breaches of fundamental norms of general international law, which cannot be modified by any treaty or national law (*see ICC-Statute 1998, Preamble, Article 5*).

'Crimes against humanity': Murder, extermination, enslavement, persecution, deportation, severe deprivation of physical liberty in violation of fundamental rules of international law, torture, rape, sex slavery and forced prostitution, sterilisation and forced pregnancy, enforced disappearance of persons, apartheid or other inhumane acts of a similar character, if they are committed as part of a widespread or systematic attack directed against any civilian population involving the multiple commission of the above-mentioned acts (*see ICC-Statute 1998, Article 7*).

'Genocide': Acts committed with the intent to destroy, in whole or in part, a national, ethnic, racial or religious group as such, by killing members of the group, causing serious bodily or mental harm to members of the group, deliberately inflicting on the group conditions of life calculated to bring about its physical destruction in whole or in part, imposing measures intended to prevent birth within the group or forcibly transferring children of the group to another (*see Genocide Convention 1948; ICC-Statute 1998, Article 6*).

'War crimes': Severe violations of humanitarian law committed during an international or internal armed conflict and directed against people not actively participating in combat, such as civilians, prisoners of war, the wounded or the sick. They include murder, mutilation, cruel treatment and torture, hostage-taking, outrages on personal dignity, in particular, humiliating and degrading treatment, and the passing of sentences and the carrying out of executions without previous judgement pronounced by a regularly constituted court, affording all the judicial guarantees which are recognised as indispensable by civilised peoples (*see IV. Geneva Convention 1949, Articles 3, 146 and 147; Additional Protocol I and II to the Geneva Conventions 1977; ICC-Statute 1998, Article 8*).

'Gross violations of human rights': Severe violations of human rights such as murder, torture, disappearances or prolonged arbitrary detention committed by state agencies (or non-state entities such as liberation movements). In comparison with 'crimes against humanity', this term is also often used for isolated acts that were not necessarily part of a widespread or systematic attack.

In the immediate aftermath of mass atrocities, practitioners should be aware that a state may be temporarily incapable of fulfilling its international obligations. In exceptional situations a state should abstain from criminal prosecutions. Such a policy is justified if the national courts are unable to uphold basic procedural standards, or if the prosecution and punishment of gross human rights violations seems likely to endanger the survival of a newly elected government or would result in the incarceration of large numbers of suspects and perpetrators in untenable prison conditions. An attempt to condemn past human rights violations should not lead to new human rights violations (Méndez 1997). Third parties and practitioners should insist, however, that the temporary inability of a state to fulfil its international obligations does not mean that it is entitled to act contrary to its obligations. Furthermore the inability of the state to punish perpetrators does not mean that the state is freed from the obligation to rebuild its criminal justice system or investigate past human rights violations. Third parties should, therefore, support local efforts to ensure that past atrocities are investigated and that the capacity to penalise human rights violations is regained. This can be done either in co-operation with governmental institutions, if there is enough political will to do so, or by supporting local human rights organisations in efforts to record past injustices or by enabling victims to bring charges against offenders.

3.2 Local, Contextual and Combined Approaches

Although ethical standards should be upheld, they should not be misunderstood as rigid recommendations; rather, they must take into account local needs and existing power relations:

1. The extent and type of past injustices often vary profoundly. A country might be confronted with mass atrocities, like genocide, or instead with more subtle injustices, such as those experienced in former communist countries. Large sections of the citizenry may have been subjected to persecution, imprisonment, torture or murder, or only a specific minority may have been victimised, have participated in acts of violence or gone through both experiences.
2. There are strong differences between countries emerging from a large-scale civil war, where much of the infrastructure has been destroyed, and countries in which an authoritarian regime has collapsed, but in which public institutions remain largely intact.
3. The balance of power between former adversaries will differ, depending on whether the armed conflict ended by negotiation, stalemate, defeat of one party or a process of democratisation largely controlled by the old elite of the former regime.
4. The degree of stability achieved in the country, the resources available, and the political will or power to support or implement specific instruments may also vary widely.

Only an approach that is appropriate to the specific country and context, that takes the existing options for action into account and is sensitive to local traditions and conflict resolution practices can hope to succeed.

Third parties can advise former adversaries, but usually have only limited influence on the policies pursued by local actors. In some situations, the international community may be strong enough to impose certain activities in the field of transitional justice, e.g., an international criminal tribunal. These institutions may well fail to be efficient tools of conflict transformation, however, if they are not supported by local actors and not supplemented by similar efforts to build up national institutions dealing effectively with the past. All instruments in the field of transitional justice exhibit their specific strengths and weaknesses. Therefore, a strategy should combine different approaches and ensure the participation of local actors from all levels.

3.3 Proper Sequencing

Important, too, is proper timing of instruments: institutions of transitional justice can easily fail or even abort an unconsolidated peace; activities can be implemented too early or too late to prevent the re-emergence of violent conflict.

In the immediate aftermath of armed conflict emphasis should first be placed on guaranteeing a minimum of physical security and preventing expulsion from housing or other shelter. Activities in the field of justice should first strive to investigate, prosecute and punish *current* injustices and human rights violations that could easily stir public emotions and set back the delicate peace process. Government, public administration and civil society should clearly indicate that violent means to solve conflict will not be tolerated. If local authorities are able to convince people that a long-term strategy to address past injustices will be implemented, they will then not expect overnight remedies. In cases in which most citizens have experienced arbitrary violence, even small improvements in the security situation will strengthen confidence in the peace process and legal system. Support in the field of justice should, therefore, first follow a minimalist approach and take into account the basic needs of people who have been locked in protracted conflict. Activities should then be increased and broadened step by step and, finally, be guided by a maximalist approach, directed towards the establishment of the rule of law, ensuring comprehensive protection of social and political rights (Pankhurst 1999).

Calls for national reconciliation have often been necessary to prevent further bloodshed in war-torn societies. But practitioners must be careful not to join the chorus of reconciliation too early; that is, as long as past injustices remain pending. Reconciliation is a legitimate long-term vision, but building capable institutions to deal with past injustices and peaceful co-existence – not reconciliation – should be the first aim. Third parties should avoid forcing their visions of mutual respect and friendship on former adversaries, as long as ongoing violence, structural injustices, hatred and disrespect do not allow people to reconcile.

Third parties should be aware that only a limited degree of understanding can be reached between former adversaries in the immediate aftermath of armed conflict. Usually, those who participated in armed conflict or torture will find it very difficult to acknowledge that their actions may have been useless, unjustified or even immoral. For some, they may have felt they had good reason for their actions because of the death of comrades, surviving life-threatening experiences or being interrogated for being a presumed terrorist. To admit to having engaged in these activities for a bad cause or for no purpose at all, to have been victimised by accident or in vain, or to have been personally responsible for actions commonly regarded as immoral or inhumane, any of these amounts to nothing less than a personal declaration of bankruptcy. Admitting guilt or acknowledging the futility of our experiences and actions is a fundamental threat to our self-esteem and personal integrity. Such self-realisation is contrary to many people's naturally delusional conviction that they are good and moral citizens.

As a rule, future generations are better equipped to reach a common understanding of what has happened. They do not have to confront themselves with negative and frightening thoughts about their own integrity. But even those born later cannot easily strip off their social identity. Usually second and third generations remain preoccupied with continuing feelings of victimisation or guilt, especially when past injustices have not been adequately addressed by their parents' generations and continue to shape social reality.

3.4 Outsider Restraint

Reconciliation cannot be imported into conflict-ridden societies. Development agencies and foreign NGOs can usually do no more than support institutional frameworks that may facilitate mutual understanding across former divisions. In the end, only local actors themselves can reconcile with one another.

Therefore, the ownership of initiatives for reconciliation or institutions dealing with past injustices should be in the hands of local activists. International or foreign institutions may have more resources at their disposal and their work may become crucial when local institutions have collapsed, but they risk becoming merely fleeting interventions. The impact of a truth commission dominated by international experts will diminish when staff and commissioners have left the country after the final report has been written. In contrast, local staff will continue to identify with their work and remain a pressure group within the country.

On the other hand, the participation of international experts in legal institutions dealing with past atrocities may well raise the national and international standing of an institution and protect its local members from repression. Furthermore, international experts can bring to newly established institutions knowledge gained in similar efforts and experiences in other countries. Also, the conflict parties will often explicitly request their participation, since they might not be able to agree on suitable candidates from their own ranks. If courts and commissions of inquiry are set up in such a way that they cannot be denounced as foreign interference in internal affairs, they are more likely to be accepted locally. Ideally, they should be regarded as genuine local or national efforts to bring about peace, justice and reconciliation.

Foreigners often lack the necessary language skills or have only limited knowledge of local traditions that could be useful in facilitating the reintegration of victims and perpetrators. Certain traditional ceremonies or rituals may indeed be compromised by excessive intervention from outsiders. This does not mean that outsiders and foreign experts should not play an important role in supporting or building up local initiatives and institutions, but they should work in the background, giving advice, training local staff, or functioning as neutral chairpersons to ensure fair proceedings.

3.5 Possibilities for Third Parties

Development agencies and human rights and conflict resolution NGOs can also support local attempts to deal with past injustices by lobbying decision-makers and by providing legal and organisational advice. They can, for instance, organise workshops and conferences with local experts from the former conflict parties, the legal sector, public administration, human rights and victims' organisations and other local non-governmental organisations, with the aim of drafting suitable legislation. Exchange programmes involving local and foreign experts can increase the incentives to find solutions appropriate to the given situation. Instruments and institutions that are developed locally with the participation of all conflict parties and actors from the governmental to the grass-roots levels are then more likely to be widely accepted.

Local and international human-rights organisations can have an important role in monitoring the rebuilding of the justice system. They can report unsolved atrocities, document cases of impunity, monitor truth commissions, judicial trials and prison conditions, call for the charge or release of detainees and support the work of local legal aid organisations and human rights and victims' organisations.

In situations in which local authorities prove unwilling to investigate, pay reparations or prosecute past atrocities, support should be concentrated on local NGOs. Official structures should only be supported when they meet basic criteria of procedural justice and evidence the necessary independence and power to carry out their work. As it is often difficult to assess how institutions that are only recently (re-) established are likely to work in the future, supporting the justice system after civil strife always involves a certain risk. Therefore, donors should concentrate on giving short-term financial support and remain flexible enough to increase or reallocate grants. Close networking between representatives of different funding agencies in the country can ensure that resources are spent efficiently and can increase the pressure on local institutions to adhere to internationally recognised standards. Official truth commissions should always receive a certain amount of funding from the authorities in the country, since the government is more likely to accept their work and recommendations when the state has contributed to its financial support. Third parties should be aware that local NGOs might also be aligned to one of the parties of the conflict. In these situations, they can support similar initiatives on both sides of the conflict, provide links and encourage co-operation between them.

Conflict resolution NGOs have shown that they can train members of communal courts or land commissions to mediate conflicts and provide opportunities for victim-offender mediation. But institutions of transitional justice can only work efficiently if they are understood and supported by civil society. Hence, special efforts should be made to inform local journalists about the work and procedures of tribunals, truth commissions or other similar local institutions. Third parties can support media reporting and assist in making information available in all local languages.

Non-governmental organisations are often essential for collecting statements or informing people about their rights. They can provide computer and database experts for data collection and analysis. Some organisations have also provided legal counsel for victims and perpetrators to ensure fair proceedings. Others have assisted criminal tribunals and truth commissions with the services of forensic experts to identify bodies in mass graves. Foreign governmental agencies have sent detectives, inspectors, criminologists and state attorneys to support the investigation of past human-rights violations. Foreign experts should be selected by local institutions and work closely with local colleagues to ensure that the independence of local institutions is always maintained and the necessary knowledge efficiently transferred.

4. Open Questions and Perspectives

The problem of justice after armed conflict and during the transition to democracy has received considerable attention in recent years. Nevertheless, many questions remain open. While some problems can be solved with the benefit of increased experience and knowledge, it may well be impossible to overcome certain irresolvable dilemmas facing post-conflict societies.

4.1 Resolvable Problems

To ensure that truth commission processes are high quality, existing international guidelines should be further refined. Recent developments in international criminal law have prompted the question of whether transitional societies may still lawfully grant amnesty in order to ensure peaceful settlements. As long as impunity remains widespread, this question may seem to be posed prematurely. Nevertheless, serious efforts should be made to develop international criteria for amnesty procedures that are compatible with the obligation to investigate and compensate gross human rights violations under international law. The UN principles against impunity developed by a sub-commission of the Human Rights Commission should be supplemented in this regard and receive official status as a declaration of the UN General Assembly.

So far the academic debate has mostly focused on the strengths and weaknesses of criminal prosecutions and truth commissions. Instead of presenting these as alternatives, it needs to be discussed further just how the different approaches can be combined and linked effectively. There is also no shortage of publications on the legalistic aspects of the emerging regime of international criminal law. However, the practical problems facing international and national criminal tribunals, truth commissions and land commissions, have unfortunately received far less attention. Additionally, practitioners need to gain more experience in integrating traditional courts and alternative dispute resolution approaches within the formal justice system, and with efficient methods of supervision of such institutions by state structures in order to ensure adherence to human rights standards.

The current enthusiasm for and interest in the international criminal tribunals may easily divert public interest and funding from rebuilding independent *local* justice systems in war-torn societies. The prominence that campaigns against impunity have achieved in human-rights circles may mean that current human-rights violations receive less attention. Although combating impunity and documenting past human-rights violations remains an important tool to prevent future abuses, this must not decrease the availability of funding for other activities in the domain of prevention.

4.2 Challenging Dilemmas

War-torn societies and countries that have experienced large-scale atrocities usually find themselves unable to deal adequately with all of the injustices that have been committed.
Often the physical and psychological damage caused by armed conflict or state repression cannot be repaired at all. Justice will therefore always be justice in only a limited sense, as it will be impossible to do justice comprehensively. Often, the political power structures that emerge after the end of open hostilities inhibit proper consideration of certain atrocities. As long as people who themselves have been responsible for past atrocities hold senior positions in, or are supported by, large sections of society, they will try to prevent any investigations into crimes for which they could be held accountable. Under these circumstances, it is very difficult to build up independent local judicial institutions, as necessary as these are for conflict transformation. Usually, third parties cannot fundamentally change structural constraints that are typical in many conflict-ridden societies, including the lack of financial resources and trained personnel, as well as a legal culture that was never based on an independent judiciary.

Practitioners should also be aware that legal institutions in and of themselves have only a limited ability to assist conflict-torn societies. Institutions like the South African TRC have often been described as positive examples of restorative justice, superior to retributive justice. But there is a danger of overemphasising what these institutions can in fact be reasonably expected to achieve. Some assumptions made about truth commissions are not realised as simply as it is often presented. Speaking out about past atrocities, for example, will not automatically lead to trauma recovery, healing or reconciliation within communities and entire nations.

It is also a myth that efficient institutions of transitional justice will enable societies to close the book on the past as soon as their findings or judgements are made public. More accurately, trials or truth commissions usually serve as a starting point for long-term reconciliation processes and should encourage – not stifle – public debate about past injustices. Legal institutions have an important function after the end of an armed conflict, as they have the potential to transform violent conflict into arbitrated settlements. Third parties can support the establishment of these institutions, or assist non-governmental organisations working to document or redress past injustices. Local initiatives can also re-establish social relationships across former conflict lines. External actors should nevertheless be aware that only former adversaries themselves can reconcile with one another and that the long-term aim of reconciliation may be reached neither quickly nor easily.

5. Reference and Further Reading

Akhavan, Payam 1998. "Justice in The Hague, Peace in the Former Yugoslavia? A Commentary on the United Nations War Crimes Tribunal," *Human Rights Quarterly,* 20, 737-816.

Alvarez, José E. 1999. "Crimes of States/Crimes of Hate: Lessons from Rwanda," *Yale Journal of International Law,* 24, 2, 365-483.

Boed, Roman 1998. "An Evaluation of the Legality and Efficacy of Lustration as a Tool of Transitional Justice," *Columbia Journal of Transnational Law,* 37, 2, 357-402.

Boraine, Alex and Janet Levy (eds.) 1995. *The Healing of a Nation?,* Cape Town: Justice in Transition.

Carver, Richard 1993. "Zimbabwe: Drawing a Line through the Past," *Journal of African Law,* 37, 1, 69-81.

Cassese, Antonio 1999. "The Statute of the International Criminal Court: Some Preliminary Reflections," *European Journal of International Law,* 10, 144-171.

Dassin, Joan (ed.) 1986. *Torture in Brazil: A Report by the Archdiocese of Sao Paulo,* New York: Vintage Books.

Hayner, Priscilla B. 1994. "15 Truth Commissions – 1974 to 1994: A Comparative Study," *Human Rights Quarterly,* 16, 4, 597-655.

Hayner, Priscilla B. 1996. "International Guidelines for the Creation and Operation of Truth Commissions: A Preliminary Proposal," *Law and Contemporary Problems*, 59, 4, 173-80.

Joinet, Louis 1997. "Set of principles for the protection and promotion of human rights through action to combat impunity," *in* UN Commission on Human Rights, op. cit.

Kritz, Neil J. (ed.) 1995. *Transitional Justice: How Emerging Democracies Reckon with Former Regimes*, 3 Volumes, Washington, DC: United States Institute for Peace Press.

Méndez, Juan E. 1997. "Accountability for Past Abuses," *Human Rights Quarterly,* 19, 255-82.

Minow, Martha 1998. *Between Vengeance and Forgiveness: Facing History after Genocide and Mass Violence,* Boston: Beacon Press.

Morris, Virginia and Michael P. Scharf 1995. *An Insider's Guide to the International Criminal Tribunal for the Former Yugoslavia,* Irvington on Hudson, NY: Transnational Publishers.

Morris, Virginia and Michael P. Scharf 1997. *The International Criminal Tribunal for Rwanda*, Irvington on Hudson, NY: Transnational Publishers.

Orentlicher, Diane F. 1991. "Settling Accounts: The Duty to Prosecute Human Rights Violations of a Prior Regime," *Yale Law Journal,* 100, 8, 2537-2615.

Osiel, Mark 1997. *Mass Atrocity, Collective Memory, and the Law,* New Brunswick, N.J.: Transaction Publishers.

Österreichisches Studienzentrum für Friedens und Konfliktforschung u.a. 1999. *Krisenprävention: Theorie und Praxis ziviler Konfliktbearbeitung,* Chur: Rüegger.

Pankhurst, Donna 1999. "Issues of Justice and Reconciliation in Complex Political Emergencies. Conceptualising Reconciliation, Justice and Peace," *Third World Quarterly,* 20, 1, 239-256.

Randelzhofer, Albrecht and Christian Tomuschat (eds.) 1999. *State Responsibility and the Individual: Reparation in Instances of Grave Violations of Human Rights,* The Hague: Martinus Nijhoff.

REMHI 1998. *Guatemala: Nie wieder – Nunca Mas,* Aachen: Misereor/Recuperación de la Memoria Histórica.

Roht-Arriaza, Naomi (ed.) 1995. *Impunity and Human Rights in International Law and Practice,* NewYork: Oxford University Press.

Salazar Volkmann, Christian 1999. "Erinnern oder vergessen? Auswirkungen der Menschenrechtsberichte in Guatemala," *Der Überblick,* 35, 3, 56-61.

Scharf, Michael P. 1997. "The Case for a Permanent International Truth Commission," *Duke Journal of Comparative and International Law,* 7, 2, 375-410.

UN Commission on Human Rights, 1997a. *Question of the impunity of perpetrators of human-rights violations (civil and political): Revised final report prepared by Mr. Joinet pursuant to Sub-Commission decision 1996/119,* New York, NY: UN Commission on Human Rights, E/CN.4/Sub.2/1997/20/Rev.1, 2 October 1997.

UN Commission on Human Rights 1997b. *Views and comments received from States on the note and revised draft basic principles and guidelines on the right to reparation for victims of [gross] violations of human rights and international humanitarian law,* New York, NY: UN Commission on Human Rights; E/CN.4/1998/34; 22 December 1977.

Weilenmann, Markus 1999. "Konfliktreglungsverfahren am Kreuzpunkt zwischen Mediation und Recht: Plädoyer für einen gesellschaftlich integrativen Ansatz der Konfliktbearbeitung," *in* Österreichisches Studienzentrum für Friedens und Konfliktforschung u.a., op. cit.

Internet sources:

Bibliographic information/Discussion Groups, *http://www.reconcilation.org.za*
International Criminal Tribunal for the Former Yugoslavia, *http://www.un.org/icty*
International Criminal Tribunal for Rwanda, *http://www.ictr.org*
International Criminal Court (ICC), *http://www.un.org/law/icc*
International NGO Coalition on the ICC, *http://www.igc.org/icc*
South African Truth and Reconciliation Commission, *http://www.truth.org.za*
United Nations Human Rights Home Page, *http://www.unhchr.ch*

United States Institute for Peace/Internet Library, *http://www.usip.org/library/truth.html*
Victim Organisations/Support for Victims
International Rehabilitation Council for Torture Victims, *http://www.irct.org*
Redress – Seeking Reparation for Torture Victims, *http://www.redress.org*
Project Disappeared/FEDEFAM, *http://www.desaparecidos.org*
Derechos Human Rights/Equipo Nizkor Impunity, *http://www.derechos.org*
Avocats Sans Frontières (Legal Representation), *http://www.asf.be*
Hirondelle Foundation (Media Work/Rwanda Tribunal), *http://www.hirondelle.org*
International Commission of Jurists, *http://www.icj.org*
HURIDOCS – Computer and Database support *http://homepage.iprolink.ch/~huridocs*
Physicians for Human Rights (forensic anthropology), *http://www.phrusa.org*
Argentine Forensic Team, *http://www.eaaf.org.ar*

Towards Conflict Transformation and a Just Peace

Kevin Clements

1. Introduction 442
2. Stable Peace 443
   The centrality and primacy of the political
   Critique of realpolitik
   Political sources of violence
   Criminalisation of politics
   Regional political impacts
   Economic greed as motivator
3. The Role of Peacebuilders in Transforming Violent Conflicts and Promoting Just Peace 453
4. Lessons Learned 458
5. Reference and Further Reading 461

Towards Conflict Transformation and a Just Peace

Kevin Clements

1. Introduction

Peace, justice, truth and compassion are central to most utopian and religious visions. For example, the concepts of Paradise and Nirvana both have strong connotations of justice, harmony, non-violence and union. These aspirations are religious ways of saying that most people in most communities and cultures, confronted with choices between order and chaos, peace and war, harmony and disharmony, structural stability and instability, equality and inequality, inclusion and exclusion, justice and injustice, tolerance and intolerance or abundance and poverty will wherever possible choose the former over the latter. There is a good justification for this as well. Stephen Jay Gould (2001), for example, states:

> *Good and kind people outnumber all others by thousands to one. The tragedy of human history lies in the enormous potential for destruction in rare acts of evil not in the high frequency of evil people. Complex systems can only be built step-by-step, whereas destruction requires but an instant. Thus in what I like to call the Great Asymmetry, every spectacular incident of evil will be balanced by 10,000 acts of kindness, too often unnoted and invisible as the "ordinary" efforts of a vast majority.*

The critical question, therefore, is how to ensure that these normal acts of kindness, altruism, reciprocity, justice and courtesy are translated into strong political commitments to justice, peace and conflict sensitive development. Why are these seemingly universal impulses so difficult to realise in political practice?

There are some factors, which occur with sufficient regularity to suggest a fairly universal correlation with violent conflict, and there are other factors (e.g. specific triggers or local means of mobilising group differences and discontent to violent ends) that are much more unique. The conceptual challenge is to identify the universal risk factors within potential or actual conflict situations while being sensitive to the cultural specifics.

In acknowledgement of the interdependent nature of these different dynamics, Nafziger, Stewart and Väyrynen (2000, Vol 2, 2), in *War, Hunger and Displacement*, state the following:

> *Economic, political and cultural sources [of complex humanitarian emergencies (CHE)] are intertwined; economic stagnation or collapse, especially when coupled with large disparities among groups (horizontal inequality) and individuals (vertical inequality), spur political discontent, which leaders use to mobilize people to support their struggles for power, thus deepening and exploiting perceived cultural differences. Group differences, based on differences in ethnicity, race, religion, caste or class, are reinforced, and sometimes created, by the conflict. While these differences are not the primary cause, they acquire an independent force that makes peacemaking difficult. Moreover, in war, collective action is the consequence of individual decisions. Individuals' political and economic aims may be served by war. Such motivation fuels and may even cause conflict.*

To ignore such dimensions and focus intervention processes on, for example, enhancing civil society capacity, attitudinal changes, relationship and confidence building may be useful at the level of community relationships, but it is unlikely to have any decisive impact on the underlying sources of structural or direct violence. On the contrary these community-based processes may generate a false consciousness of peaceful relations when the underlying processes are much more malign.

This chapter, therefore, is an attempt to do two things: first, to make sense of some of the economic, political and social origins and dynamics of organised violence; second, determine how conflict analysis and conflict resolution processes might enable diverse actors concerned with violent conflict at the official and unofficial levels to change the attitudes, behaviours and institutions which generate structural (indirect) and direct violence. It will begin with an acknowledgement of the centrality of structural transformation for stable peace and an analysis of some of the underlying political and economic dynamics that form the backdrop to modern conflict. It will then examine how and why conflict resolution practitioners should focus more attention on the political economy of conflict in the analysis, design and implementation of conflict intervention processes.

2. Stable Peace

Stable peace, by which is meant the persistence of non-violent cooperative relationships through time, cannot be delivered simply by addressing the presenting tensions, contradictions, disputes and manifestations of violence. There is a need for much deeper and shared analysis (between intervenors and intervened and all those with legitimate interests in the conflict) about the underlying structural sources of the conflict. It is particularly important to incorporate regional and global organisations in this analysis, especially where there is any indication that national state systems (responsible for order and human security) are the major sources of insecurity and humanitarian crises for their citizens.

This analysis should be undertaken prior to the design or development of assistance or intervention processes. It should focus on a radical contextualisation of the underlying problems, historical awareness of their origins and the development of a shared awareness of institutional impediments, obstructions, or deficiencies preventing the realisation of stable peaceful relationships. This initial analysis, which is so critical to the success of any subsequent intervention, may, for peacebuilders and others involved in conflict resolution, result in decisions not to intervene, or the development of interventions which look more political rather than procedural in order to address the underlying sources of the problems.

2.1 The centrality and primacy of the political

It is extremely difficult to tackle these deeper questions of structural violence and socio-economic injustice without paying attention to the institutions, mechanisms and processes that generate order and effective participatory governance. Kalevi Holsti (1996, 20-21), for example, asserts that:

Wars of the late twentieth century are not about foreign policy, security, honour or status; they are about statehood, governance and the role and status of nations and communities within states.

There is more and more evidence from the world's war zones for example, that many so called sovereign states and governments lack a monopoly of coercive capacity and are incapable of bringing order to territory under their control. Far from governing on behalf of and for the people (their citizens), they are either unable to extend legitimate authority and security to citizens or are intensely predatory and exploitative. International law confers sovereign equality on these states but the states, themselves, lack the basic means to confer the benefits of sovereignty and human security on their peoples.

In relation to these deficient sovereign entities, conflict resolution workers are caught in a terrible dilemma. If official and unofficial actors assume that failed or failing state systems are capable of delivering negotiated agreements when they are not, the negotiation process will be nullified in its implementation. If the opposite assumption is applied, namely that there is no point in negotiating with corrupt, ineffective or deficient states, there will be no negotiated solutions to violent problems. Somewhere between the Scylla of hypocrisy and the Charybdis of impotence lies the realm of the politically possible.

The major challenge facing all conflict resolution workers (official or unofficial) is identifying what that realm of possibility looks like and whether interventions are likely or unlikely to result in the achievement of just and sustainable relations between peoples.

There is a disposition on the part of Non-Governmental Organisations (NGOs), for example, to work with civil society actors to help them to deal with the problems that state systems are either causing, or are unwilling or incapable of addressing. This sometimes results in some segments of civil society having more organisational and professional capacity than key elements of the state system. In Burundi, for example, the Ministry of Human Rights has fewer resources available to it than many of the human rights NGOs working within the country.

This asymmetry raises two deeper issues. The first is how the civil society sector articulates its interests vis-à-vis the state and the second is whether this is useful or not in those situations where states are deficient, incapable of effective governance, predatory and/or corrupt. The second issue confronts governmental and intergovernmental actors. If official intervenors deal with failed, failing or predatory state systems as though they were capable of effective governance when they are not, then this may generate deep disillusionment for the excluded and exploited citizens. It will certainly result in bad faith negotiations and render effective implementation of any agreement extremely unlikely. Not dealing with putative authority, however, means no negotiations. Responding to violent conflict, therefore, at both civil society and governmental levels often generates as many problems as solutions.

2.2 Critique of realpolitik

The field of conflict resolution developed, to some extent, as a critique of and alternative to political realism and *realpolitik*. Conflict analysts acknowledge that power, although a major motivator, is not primary for most people. On the contrary, cooperative relations and a desire for the satisfaction of needs for identity, security, belonging and welfare are equally important sources of human motivation.

Conflict resolution workers, therefore, have always been somewhat ambivalent towards state and political systems. On the one hand there is a willingness to acknowledge the importance of the state, while on the other there is a critique of the state's monopoly of power and a rejection of threat and coercion as the primary means for generating order and stability. Because of this, there has been a strong inclination on the part of many conflict resolution workers to try and modify political behaviour by working with and through civil society groups.

One of the central arguments of this chapter is the necessity for conflict specialists to devote more time to specific analyses of the ways in which the state generates and sometimes escalates violent conflict. If this does not occur and there is no development of 'conflict sensitive politics' (in the same way as Peace and Conflict Impact Assessment (PCIA) methodology has contributed to 'conflict sensitive development') then the political agenda will continue to be set by the application of realpolitik, rather than by a less adversarial problem oriented politics. This is no easy task (witness the retreat of idealist politics in the face of the newly declared War against Terrorism) but it is one that should be undertaken in order to further test and develop non-violent alternatives to war and violence.

Another reason why realpolitik needs to be challenged is because State systems in the major conflict zones of the world are seriously deficient and more likely to be associated with the initiation and prolongation of violence than with its resolution. This poses very particular types of problems for conflict resolution workers seeking to devise processes for dealing with such violence.

2.3 Political sources of violence

In an analysis of 17 recent complex humanitarian emergencies (CHE), Kalevi Holsti (cited by Nafziger et al. 2000, Vol 2, 4) argues that the political factors likely to result in this type of emergency or large scale organised violence include the following:

> *The risk of an emergency is likely to increase with two or more distinct ethnic, language, or religious communities; among countries which acquired independence after 1945; where there is government exclusion and persecution of distinct social groups; where there is rule by kleptocrats or entrenched minorities; and where there is weak government legitimacy.*

These are all factors that generate structural disposition to violence and they are consistent with most of the political risk factors and indicators identified by those devising tools and methods for more conflict sensitive development strategies. Interestingly, Holsti concludes from his study of their application to 17 cases that it is not ethnic hatred or group divisions which generated violent behaviour, but the deliberate and intentional acts of politicians and government officials who organised violence against different groups within the communities under their control.

> *...organised politicides by governments have resulted in far greater casualties than other types of civil war, including rebellions. The presence of early warning indicators has not helped the international community to prevent such emergencies. (ibid.).*

This conclusion is made even more explicit by Väyrynen (*ibid., 437*) who states:

> *My key hypothesis is that humanitarian crises occur in societies in which the state is weak and elites greedy in pursuing their own interests. In the post-colonial neo-patrimonial state, a strong leader stands at the top of the power pyramid and supports a network of cronies in civilian and military bureaucracies. Beneficiaries of the political system are decided by coercion and clientalism, the key features of most peripheral states.*

He develops this hypothesis to elaborate the dynamics between the political and economic spheres through a theory of state predatory and rent seeking activities. The net result is state plunder, exploitation and anarchic, anaemic or failed state systems and increased reliance on force, coercion and the possibility of organised state sponsored violence against opposition forces.

If conflict resolution workers do not acknowledge these fundamental realities when devising intervention strategies, they may unwittingly generate peaceful illusions on unjust and untenable institutional bases. When the coercive power of the state and the exchange power of the market have been subverted by corrupt politicians and bureaucrats it makes the prospects for sustainable peace extremely unlikely. Trying to harness the integrative power of the community in such a situation by working in and through other civil society institutions, (families, religious, educational, health and others) may be helpful in terms of emergency relief and humanitarian assistance. However it will not yield sustainable peace in either the medium or long term. It may enhance the 'feel good factor' but generate even deeper despair at the incapacity of government and state systems to perform their social functions. These good initiatives will always be subverted by the actions of corrupt governments, and the increasing criminalisation of politics.

2.4 Criminalisation of politics

This is characterised by six core elements: subversion of the rule of law, impunity, organised crime, drugs, non-enforcement of law and corruption.

(i) Subversion of the rule of law: This has happened in most conflict zones around the world. First of all the police become corrupted; second there is a challenge to the independence of the judiciary and the court system breaks down. Anarchic states, for example Sierra Leone, Liberia, Somalia underwent a complete breakdown of central authority with no legal system that commands respect and no way of implementing the law. In short, this means that individual friendship and kin groups are the major providers of basic protection.

(ii) Impunity: When the rule of law is subverted cultures of impunity emerge. Impunity can lead to wide scale human rights abuses or even genocide, as happened in Rwanda and within Zimbabwe, where the Mugabe government has systematically undermined the rule of law. In situations where some have impunity and others do not, it is normally those with economic and political power who can rise above the law and those with no such power who become subject to arbitrary, corrupt and oppressive law. For example, the relatively weak and powerless are victims of petty corruption such as arbitrary police fines and also victims of high-level elite corruption such as expropriation of national revenues. They are also the ones most likely to be held to account for the petty corruption while those who are stealing millions utilise their authority to confer impunity on themselves.

(iii) Organised crime: In the United Kingdom (UK), the National Criminal Intelligence Service (NCIS) argued last year that organised crime was the major threat to British security (*see* NCIS 2000). Organised crime syndicates are a threat to democracy and stability in many parts of the developing world as well. In Colombia, drug syndicates directly confronted the state in an attempt to prevent an extradition treaty being made with the United States of America (USA). In the Caucasus, organised crime syndicates have at times threatened to undermine already fragile economies through smuggling of contraband, thus evading duties as well as using an extreme level of violence in their activities. In the Balkans, criminal groups became aligned with radical nationalist groups creating a criminal state as in Serbia under President Miloπevic. The Kosova Liberation Army (UÇK) in Kosovo has allegedly had strong links with Albanian criminal groups operating in the West. Organised crime groups such as the Chinese 'Snake Heads' are involved in smuggling people across the world. This is slavery by another name. The UN estimates that about 4 million people are illegally trafficked world-wide each year. The profits made from this trade are also significant, amounting to between $5 billion and $7 billion annually. Along side the human misery involved, the impact of the migrants can also cause conflicts in some recipient states.

(iv) Drugs: The United Nations (UN) estimates that the annual proceeds of illegal trafficking of narcotics amounts to about $500 billion. As long as the production of drugs (especially heroin and cocaine) remains economically attractive, the potential destabilising effects of drugs will continue in many countries. Addiction levels in the west are matched or exceeded in Iran, India and Pakistan. Problems associated with the impact of narcotics can also lead to international conflict. A key area of tension between the Taliban regime in Afghanistan and its neighbour Iran, for example, could be traced to the significant levels of heroin addiction inside Iran. About one million Iranians are thought to be addicts and over 3,000 Iranian police have been killed fighting gangs associated with the opiate trade. There is also recent evidence that smugglers are now choosing to direct heroin through the Former Soviet Union (FSU), especially Turkmenistan. This could well disrupt already unstable states. The profits from drug smuggling may also be used to help finance the activities of Islamic rebels in countries bordering Afghanistan.

(v) Non-enforcement of law: The contribution by the United State of America of up to $1.3 billion in military aid to Colombia in support of Plan Colombia is officially aimed at controlling the Colombian drug trade. There is evidence to suggest, however, that the Colombian army have diverted equipment intended for anti-drug use to the war against left wing guerrillas – thereby fuelling the dynamics of the civil war because the opposition forces become involved in an internal arms race. Similarly, in July 2001, the USA support to the Taliban of $34 million in support of an anti-drug trafficking campaign has undoubtedly been diverted towards fuelling the current conflict. Aside from the corrosive influence of crime, therefore, the interaction between crime and conflict – especially where ruling elites or subversive groups use organised crime to finance their activities – needs to be given more prominence in the design of conflict resolution processes.

(vi) Corruption: Corruption exists in virtually every country in the world. Normally it is an occasional aberration or alternatively an essential way of bypassing extensive bureaucracy. However, in cases of extreme corruption the very ethos of the state can be undermined. The

1999 coup in Pakistan was largely caused by military frustration at the levels of corruption practised by many democratic politicians. Similarly, the Estrada regime in the Philippines was overthrown in a demonstration of people's power, specifically roused by wholesale abuse of power by the politicians, as also happened in Serbia more recently. Corrupt regimes have stoked up ethnic hatreds as a way of gaining popularity, as in Serbia and arguably now in Indonesia. When corruption becomes institutionalised and cultures of theft become dominant and widespread, those who benefit most from them may resort to coercion and organised violence in order to defend their economic interests. The reality is that corruption subverts political processes everywhere and makes rational politics that much more difficult.

2.5 Regional political impacts

Failures of state systems, subversion of the rule of law, state depredation and the persistent political marginalisation of significant minorities are all potent internal sources of conflict. These dynamics are, however, exacerbated by the actions and decision of neighbouring states or powerful external powers. These regional dynamics very often shape and determine the major contours of national conflicts and can best be grasped in terms of sub-regional and regional conflict systems. In the South Caucasus, for example, there are two major bilateral disputes (Georgia and Abkhazia, and Armenia and Azerbaijan) neither of which can be resolved bilaterally; the Russian government is implicitly, if not explicitly, at every bilateral table. Any agreement that does not include the Russians will be subverted and spoiled by them. Similarly in Africa, regional hegemonic states (like Nigeria) and former colonial powers (UK, Belgium and France) influence the ways in which conflicts are defined, understood and dealt with in a variety of ways. Conflicts between them, as for example, between Belgium and France in relation to the Great Lakes often do not generate conditions conducive to negotiated settlement of disputes. Furthermore, the reasons outside actors get involved – like the US, the European Union (EU) and others in Macedonia or before that of the North Atlantic Treaty Organisation (NATO) in Kosovo – are very much determined by national and regional interest as much as a desire to see the conflicts managed and transformed. All of this suggests the importance of political analyses that capture complex internal and external realities and view them in systemic terms.

One of the deficiencies of many past interventions in conflict at the inter-governmental, governmental and NGO levels has been a reluctance to incorporate economic factors into the analytic or intervention phases. There has been a tendency in the past to assume that violent conflicts can be resolved at the political and civil society levels without paying much attention to the powerful economic motivators and sustainers of violence. This has sometimes resulted in an air of unreality around diverse dialogue and negotiation processes, which sometimes seem rather disconnected from their economic bases.

The local, national, regional and global economic systems underpin both the civil society and state sector levels of activity. These have their own dynamics, with key market (private and public sector) elements sometimes supporting, sometimes obscuring and sometimes subverting peace initiatives. The economic sphere of activity, has been relatively under-analysed by the conflict resolution community (official and unofficial), although recently it has been addressed specifically by organisations such as the World Bank, the United Nations (UN), the Development Assistance Committee of the Organisation for Economic Cooperation and Development (OECD/DAC) and key NGOs such as the Prince of Wales Business Leader's Forum, International Alert (IA) and the Council on Economic Priorities (*see* International Alert 2000). There are three general elements to this concern. The first has to do with relative and absolute deprivation and the role that this plays in the generation of conflict. The second concerns the breakdown of the social contract between state and citizen and unwillingness or inability on the part of the state to satisfy the public sector, developmental and welfare needs of citizens and the third has to do with the competition for and control over natural resources.

All these issues are beginning to be acknowledged within the field, and indeed there is now a specific area of specialization, that of Peace and Conflict Impact Assessment (PCIA), which has been stressing the necessity for more conflict sensitive approaches to development planning at macro and micro levels (*see* Gaigals and Leonhardt 2001; and the contribution of Mark Hoffman in this volume).

2.6 Economic greed as motivator

Economic factors have a major impact on conflict. Paul Collier, Mats Berdal, David Malone and others argue strongly that many conflicts can be explained in terms of a competition for control of the production and distribution of natural resources, including land (*see* Berdal & Malone 200). The econometric models that have been developed to test this demonstrate very interesting correlation between conflict and the ready availability of high value commodities such as diamonds, gold and coltan. These arguments suggest strongly that greed is arguably as important as *grievance* in generating conflict (*see* Collier & Hoeffler 1998). As with the political dynamics, these economic motivations need to be factored into conflict analysis. Much more attention needs to be paid to the development of adequate incentive mechanisms for motivating peaceful as opposed to warlike behaviour. 'Conflict diamonds' and the often illegal exploitation of other natural resources such as timber and oil in Sierra Leone, Angola, the Congo and Sudan point towards resource wars being a significant feature in future conflict transformation work.

These are perhaps the more visible examples of the political economy of war, which will become a key framework for helping to understand the causes of internal conflict. Such a framework should be understood in the context of globalisation which suggests that increased economic integration, though it is presenting new opportunities for growth for some, is also generating exclusion and hardship for many others and this may lead to violent conflict. The ways in which it does this are, however, extremely complex.

Wayne Nafziger and Juha Auvinen have advanced one of the more interesting arguments in this area (*see* Nafziger et al. 2000). They demonstrate that low per capita incomes, low or negative growth in incomes and stagnation in agricultural production are important factors leading to conflict. In addition, they note that high rates of inequality are also associated with a propensity to conflict "especially if it reflects or contributes to high inequality among regional, ethnic or class groups" (Nafziger et al. 2000, Vol 2,3). This idea of horizontal inequality between groups is an important development in thinking about economic sources of conflict because it suggests important new directions for targeting development or economic assistance programmes. The two non-economic factors that Nafziger and Auvinen identify as strongly correlated with violent conflict are levels of military spending and past history of conflicts.

It is a little surprising that the old literature on the political economy of war seemed to be ignored by conflict analysts for so many years, but reassuring that it has been rediscovered and is now being placed at the centre of new thinking about deep rooted and intractable internal conflicts. One author who has taken this idea further is Georg Elwert with his idea of "markets of violence" (*see* Box 1).

Box 1: Markets of Violence

Markets of violence are understood as economic fields dominated by civil wars, warlords or robbery, in which a self-perpetuating system emerges which links non-violent commodity markets with the violent acquisition of goods. It is the profit implied in the entwined violent and non-violent forms of appropriation and exchange that is the guiding principle of action. A self-perpetuating economic system emerges beneath the surface of moral, world-view and power conflicts – even in the absence of such attempts at legitimisation. It is possible that irrespective of the conscious motives of the actors (such as freedom, honour or revenge) only those actors who pursue economically profitable strategies – irrespective of their intentions – will survive.

Diamonds and gold smuggling in contemporary Congo/Zaire, trade of the drug qat in Somalia, emerald smuggling in Colombia and, last but not least, convoys carrying food aid in Sudan, Somalia, Liberia and Bosnia have made this "protection" the most important source of income during certain periods. An aid organisation paid $1,000 in 1994 to a Liberian warlord for each lorry with medical equipment which he allowed to pass through his territory.

Markets of violence will continue to emerge wherever there is a coincidence of areas open to violence, exploitable resources and corresponding markets, and where the economic environment remains neutral or favourable.

Source Elwert 1999

This renewed attention to the economic element will require shifts in the international community's development policies in order to make them more conflict sensitive and capable of providing economic disincentives to move warring parties away from war and incentives to move towards peace. In many of the conflicts that are afflicting the FSU, sub-Saharan Africa and elsewhere, these economic dimensions are the critical motivators and sustainers of conflict. To ignore them in favour of more 'epiphenomenal elements' will mean that there is a very slim chance of their resolution. Political economy factors that will continue to generate conflict in future include: unregulated transnational trade networks, fragile international financial system, the power of transnational corporation and the impact of aid and trade polices.

(i) Unregulated transnational trade networks: The unregulated and illicit trade in war commodities whether it be diamonds, timber, oil other natural resources, drugs, or guns are likely to continue to help explain the persistence of many conflicts (*see* Duffield 1994). The revenues made from these commodities by warring factions is increasingly seen as a key incentive for the perpetuation of war, and the international community will continue to seek ways to regulate the flow of these goods and restrict the funds from them that fuel conflict.

(ii) Fragile international financial system: The financial economic crisis in 1997/8 in Asia and the contagion that spread to many other developing economies drew attention to the fragility of the international financial system and the need to reform it in order to make international financial institutions (IFIs) and other relevant institutions more transparent and accountable to donors and recipients. Although not appreciated so much at the time, the link between neo-liberal economic reforms, political instability and, in turn, conflict is an issue that is of growing importance. There are, for example, arguable connections between the economic reforms embarked upon by Indonesia and growing violence in Aceh and other provinces. As Susan Woodward (1995) argues, it is also quite clear that economic reform processes certainly complicated the political transitions in the Balkans. However in a more recent study, Christian Morrison (cited in Nafziger et al. 2000, Vol 2, 4) suggests that International Monetary Fund (IMF) stabilisation programmes, while undoubtedly generating local discontent do not cause large scale complex humanitarian emergencies.

> *He [Morrison] distinguishes between 'soft repression' (involving, for example, strikes and demonstrations and moderate political instability which when repressed may lead to deaths) and 'hard repression' with major episodes of violence. The history of adjustment in Africa and Latin America in the 1980s and 1990s show that adjustment policies often involved social costs but not humanitarian emergencies.*

In this argument, the activities of the IMF and other financial institutions may generate limited, intense humanitarian emergencies for small segments of the population for short periods of time. Nevertheless, Morrison suggests that they are more likely to accelerate conflict rather than the primary or major causes.

(iii) The power of transnational corporation: Transnational corporations (TNCs) are key actors in many internal conflicts (such as Angola, Sudan, Colombia and Nigeria). The economic interests that they represent must be defended and there are numerous examples where these have resulted in conflict (e.g., the activities of Shell in Nigeria and BP in Colombia). In addition, the wealth and resources available to TNCs often remind other state and non-state actors of their relative powerlessness and inability to have a significant effect over economic affairs. There is growing recognition by corporations of their responsibility to be more attentive to the ways in which their investment, employment and other decisions generate violence, and there are growing opportunities for them to play a constructive role in helping resolve conflict in areas where they work (*see* International Alert 2000).

(iv) Impact of aid and trade polices: The link between development and conflict and how the assistance provided by the international community to war-affected countries might exacerbate rather than mitigate conflict will continue to be a controversial issue. The negative impact of humanitarian aid is seen by some as being relatively small in comparison to other drivers of conflict, but others (including many NGOs) consider it is a contributing factor. It gives governments political backing and allows them to offset social costs to donors, using money thus saved for military purposes (*see* Uvin 1998). The Congo war is a prime example of this. It is hoped that development aid will increasingly incorporate measures to encourage greater conflict sensitivity, but it may prove more difficult to secure effective implementation of this conflict sensitive approach to development on the part of national and multilateral donor agencies. It is likely, though, that in broader development debates there will be renewed focus on how trade relations affect poverty alleviation in developing countries as the World Trade Organisation (WTO) comes under increasing pressure to reform its polices and become more transparent. Although the EU has already focused on how its trade policies might impact upon conflict through the Cotonou Agreement with African, Caribbean and Pacific (ACP) countries, the WTO may well be forced to address these issues as well in the future.

There are other factors such as environmental issues, which are certain to have some impact upon future conflicts – whether these will be precipitated and driven by scarcity or abundance is a matter of debate. The predicted conflicts over access to safe and clean drinking water will clearly be fuelled by scarcity factors. The conflicts over wealth generating minerals are more likely to be spawned by concerns to protect and enhance existing wealth. Fairhead, for example, argues that environmental riches rather than poverty are the major precipitants of environmental conflict as groups struggle to gain control over wealth generating resources (*see* Fairhead in Nafziger et al. 2000, Vol 1, 147-179). He argues that societies become divided between those wealthy or politically connected groups who struggle for control of the resources and the destitute who become the foot soldiers of the struggles.

2.7 Long term conflict dynamics

There are several long-term global dynamics that will have a profound impact on violent conflict over the next 15 to 20 years. Most of these need specific national and international policies tailored for dealing with them. Three such elements are demography, refugees and internally displaced people (IDPs), and diasporas.

- **Demographic factors** need to be taken into account when considering the origins of future conflict since most recent civil wars are fought by young men who are either unemployed or under-employed. The world population is expected to grow from 6.1 billion in 2001 to 7.2 billion by 2015. Developing countries will account for 95 per cent of the increase, mostly in rapidly expanding urban areas. Given that many of these countries have fragile political systems, the combination of population growth and urbanisation will encourage instability by attracting resources from rural areas and by straining already stressed labour markets. Many states now have a disproportionate number of children under 15 (60 per cent in Algeria, for example). The increasing number of unemployed or under-employed youth in some of the potential conflict zones will provide a ready pool of people who see themselves as having nothing to lose by joining political (or pseudo-political) movements willing to use violence to realise their aims. Many of these people may feel better off in armed groups, able to loot and pillage for their survival, compared to a more peaceful way of making a living (*see* Jackson et. al. 2001, 1).
- The **world refugee situation** will continue to generate discontent and provide fertile recruiting grounds for soldiers and militia. In 1970 there were only two million refugees; by 2001 this number had leapt to over 21 million according to the United Nations High Commission for Refugees (UNHCR). With no solution in sight for Palestinian refugees,

conflict in that part of the Middle East is certain to continue. In West and Central Africa, Central Asia and the Caucasus, large refugee groups, if allowed to fester, will also continue to provide the basis for guerrilla bands to form. Recent refugee flows from Afghanistan, for example, are destabilising Pakistan and the region. These humanitarian catastrophes must be counted as major sources of future conflict. In addition, there are millions of internally displaced people in Africa and elsewhere, representing another potential source of conflict unless action is taken to resolve their plight.

- **Diaspora groups** of exiles or expatriates often fund guerrilla movements in their homelands. It is speculated, for example, that Tamils abroad send millions of dollars to the rebels in Sri Lanka every year. To try and resolve the Sri Lankan crisis without taking the interests of the Tamil and Singhalese diaspora into account will yield only partial solutions to that crisis.

3. The Role of Peacebuilders in Transforming Violent Conflicts and Promoting Just Peace

In the light of this analysis of some of the structural sources of organised violence, the challenges facing peacebuilders seem far greater than their current capacity to respond to them. This means that peacebuilders need to maximise their resources wherever possible, seeking higher levels of communication, cooperation and positive working relations with like-minded actors in the governmental, inter-governmental and non-governmental sectors.

For purposes of this discussion, primary consideration will be given to Track II initiatives and how they might catalyse Track I and Track I1/2 initiatives to address some of these harsh political and economic dynamics of conflict.

The NGO conflict resolution and peacebuilding sector, for example, is expanding, professionalising and acquiring more resources to engage in long term conflict transformation processes. However, it remains predominantly Northern, its resources are miniscule compared to those available to the world's military and armed non-state actors and it has limited capacity to challenge the political and economic dynamics of organised violence. It certainly has difficulty dealing with the criminalisation of politics, failed states, predatory states, institutionalised corruption and widespread subversion of the rule of law. The NGO sector cannot 'mediate with muscle' nor can it enforce solutions to problems. Its strength lies in other areas. It has flexibility, and an ability to respond to human suffering without being politically constrained.

In relation to the transformation of violence and the promotion of just peace it can forge partnerships with local people in conflict zones and respond to the immediate suffering. At the same time it can catalyse discussions and dialogues with those in conflict about ways in which they might resolve their differences, solve their problems and satisfy their human needs. It can and does use its micro-knowledge to try and influence the macro-policy decisions of donors and multilateral organisations in relation to economic development and the promotion of human security.

Sometimes the NGO role is catalytic, facilitating communications between conflicting parties. At other times its role is much more analytical and the processes much more deliberative (e.g., as in interactive problem solving workshops). In all of these activities the basic aim, however, is the same. Most conflict transformation NGOs and academics seek to build on the unifiers rather than the dividers in society on the assumption that strong and resilient communities are the fundamental prerequisites for human existence and security.

It is clear, however, from the preceding arguments, that resilient and tolerant communities are a necessary but not a sufficient condition for conflict transformation and just peace. Because of their dispersed and fragmented character, communities have difficulty mounting effective or sustained critiques of organised economic and political power. In those areas, however, where economic and political power is itself disorganised a little community organisation can be highly effective.

In order for humanitarian NGOs to realise their well intentioned and altruistic aspirations there is a much greater need to have clear and coherent strategies which are linked much more deliberately and explicitly to other official and unofficial Tracks. For all those seeking effective ways of dealing with violent conflicts and promoting just and sustainable peaceful relationships in conflict zones, the challenge is finding ways to share analyses, communicate these to all relevant actors and seek higher levels of synergy between all peacebuilding actors.

To develop better analytic and effective peacebuilding processes, it is absolutely essential that there is a process of radical and critical dialogue between the development and conflict transformation communities. Neither can deliver stable and lasting peace acting alone and neither can resolve the differences between themselves by subsuming the interests of one in the other. In other words, it is not just a question of adding a development or justice dimension to conflict transformation work or a conflict transformation perspective to development and justice work. Rather development and conflict transformation theorists need to sit down with each other in order to identify the comparative analytic and process advantages of both perspectives and ways in which the theoretical and practical contributions of each might be enhanced. This might produce contributions that are more informed and wiser, thereby aiding individuals, organisations and movements working for social and political change, structural stability and stable peace.

Conflict transformers and development specialists have set themselves a formidable task in trying to transform violent relationships, while helping catalyse processes aimed at challenging structural violence and injustice. The challenge is nothing less than that of devising ways and means of empowering citizens and societies so that they can transform violent relationships. At the same time it is necessary to ensure that economic, political and social institutions are developed (or changed when they are demonstrably incapable of achieving their purposes) so as to minimise the prospects of violence in future and guarantee these processes through time.

In order to do this effectively, it is essential that there are more hard headed discussions between development and conflict transformation specialists about ways in which negative economic processes such as neo-patrimonialism, or clientelist political networks (which benefit certain groups and disadvantage others) can be challenged and changed. These distorted economic processes generate malign social and political outcomes, which increase frustrations. As a result those in power are disposed to consolidate their increasingly untenable positions by violent means or force marginal groups to consider violent options. Too little attention is devoted to these issues in most conflict transformation activities.

To facilitate such discussions, however, requires higher levels of collaboration between development and conflict resolution experts. Instead of leaving such issues to the World Bank or bilateral donors, it is vital to incorporate civil society stakeholders as well, because this will help focus attention on who is included and who is excluded from the allocation of scarce national resources. How to place such issues on agendas so that they can be talked through and discussed is the central challenge facing those seeking not only to stop the violence but also to generate a just and lasting peace.

Although reducing fear, building trust and restoring confidence are all critical elements of any move towards a cessation of violence, they are not sufficient. This requires a much more active politicisation of the Track II conflict resolution process built on a different kind of politics. It demands a less adversarial, problem solving orientation to politics. Perhaps this is the major contribution that the conflict resolution community can make to transform corrupt deficient state systems. It can begin modelling political processes which are collaborative rather than competitive, unconditionally constructive rather than adversarial and where the interests of all are placed at the heart of the political process. This may sound rather utopian but it is essentially the direction in which most of the major development donors are moving.

Box 2: International Alert programme in Burundi: A case study

IA has developed programmes in a variety of violent conflict zones: the Caucasus, the Great Lakes, West Africa, Sri Lanka and Colombia. In all of these places, it has seen its role primarily in terms of catalysing and enabling locals to address their own conflicts and standing along side them as they devise their own solutions to these problems.

Burundi, for example, is an area of fairly extensive IA activity. Staff have worked with political and military leaders in a series of dialogue processes, which have been instrumental over the past few years in helping to lower the paranoia levels and to rebuild a measure of trust between key Hutu and Tutsi factional leaders. They have also developed confidence and trust building programmes between diverse women's groups and with the Catholic Church. There has been work with the Attorney General's department and the Ministry of Human Rights. Analyses of the Justice and Education systems in Burundi have highlighted some of the ways in which institutional arrangements are discriminatory and perpetuate grievances across the ethnic divide. All of these activities have been widely acknowledged as useful in terms of generating constructive bridges across a deeply divided community.

The trusting relationships that have been built up since 1995 have also enabled staff to start asking partners more probing and critical questions about some of the more sensitive political issues. Questions have been raised about the integration of the army and the gendarmerie and the lack of Hutu representation in both institutions; also about unequal access to jobs, schools and the benefits that flow from state power. By and large, however, there has not been a systematic effort to locate the dialogue processes or the development of civil society capacity in the context of what Patrick Gaffney (2000) calls, ". . . the economics of ethnicity and modernity and the diverse ways in which the different ethnic groups in Burundi are incorporated/excluded from the modern economy and world market system". This means that although there has been much effort dedicated to rebuilding working relationships across ethnic divides, the underlying economic gap and sources of division have been addressed much more obliquely.

There have been few discussions that have focussed specifically on issues such as, for example, the concentration of the labour force, economic dependence on coffee, budgetary allocations to the rural/urban sectors. Bujumbura and its immediate surrounds, for example, absorbs 50 per cent of the nation's total investment. When this is coupled with the 16 per cent allocated to Bururi – which is home to the political/military elite – this means that only one third of the nation's total investment is available for three quarters of the population (ibid.). This issue lies at the heart of who is included and excluded from Burundian society and yet because of its sensitivity there is often uncertainty about how to raise this and other issues effectively in conflict transformation processes. Dialogues about political economy would generate very different types of discussions than those that concentrate on bridging the Hutu/Tutsi ethnic divide or gaining understanding and agreements between the political groupings of UPRONA (Union for National Progress) or FRODEBU (Front for Democracy in Burundi). They are certainly very different from discussions about ways of incorporating rebels into peace negotiations. All of these have their place in the quest for peace but in terms of developing a just and sustainable peace some of these processes may, in the end, turn out to be more critical than others.

Track I actors (politicians, diplomats, representatives of regional and global organisations, and multilateral financial institutions) are all concerned to work out ways in which they can direct the bulk of their resources towards the prevention of violent conflict, rather than responding to it once it has occurred. There is a deepening reflection on the part of policy makers regarding the positive and negative impacts of different development interventions on violent conflict. This is coupled with a desire for more coherent conflict prevention and peacebuilding strategies and for methodological tools that will enable conflict sensitive development to take place (*see* Gaigals & Leonhardt 2001). Conflict prevention is truly at the heart of the political and development agendas.

What remains to be developed is more political commitment and greater recognition of how conflict sensitive development strategies might be mainstreamed and, most importantly, implemented in macro -policy and micro-programmes and project cycle frameworks. There are ongoing discussions at different levels about what constitutes the right programming needs and priority responses at all phases of violent conflicts and there are certainly many discussions about specific roles, responsibilities, burden sharing and basic operational co-ordination among development agencies. The fact that these discussions are taking place is in itself a positive sign and there is now general agreement that peace, stability and human security should be at the centre of bilateral, regional and multilateral development planning, funding, and implementation in violent conflict zones.

While many of the multilateral development initiatives place economic questions at the heart of their negotiations (e.g. in terms of stabilisation programmes and aid conditionality), these issues are normally missing from many conflict resolution initiatives by civil society. What remains more problematic for Track I actors (as it is for Track II and private sector actors) are appropriate ways and means of raising more difficult political questions.

The principle of non-interference in the domestic affairs of other states mean that official level negotiators often have to ignore many concerns they may have about whether *de facto* or *de* jure sovereign parties are able to exercise effective authority over the territory they control. They certainly have to stifle concerns about state challenges to human security and corruption and about anaemic or ineffective governance. They can discreetly ascertain, through diplomatic representation, whether national elites are promoting conflict or seeking to contain it and develop appropriate responses accordingly; they can also trigger concerns with the UN Department for Political Affairs (UNDPA) or raise humanitarian concerns with the Office for Co-ordination of Humanitarian Assistance (OCHA). They may, if the situation is sufficiently serious, ask the World Bank and the IMF to think about new conditionality in relation to corruption and illegal trade issues. The problem with this strategy, however, is that the Bank and the Fund are much more interested in efficiency than horizontal or vertical equity. If, as Nafziger et al. (2000) argue, these are the major sources of violent conflict in many war zones then it is up to other actors to put these items on the agenda.

The realities of international politics make it difficult for state actors to take unilateral initiatives in these areas and the opportunity costs of generating a wider coalition of like minded countries and then mobilising collective political will are often too high. This means that the questions that should be asked remain unasked and the actions that should be taken remain untaken. This is certainly so at the first signs of an impending conflict. The international community still has not figured out effective ways of responding to the acute crisis phases of conflict either. It is reasonably good at monitoring but not good at reacting. It is marginally better at mobilising itself for the post-conflict phases, especially in relation to peacekeeping, civilian policing, development of independent judiciaries, disarmament and demobilisation strategies. Even here, however, the difficult questions about who gets what, when, why and how from different political arrangements are more often than not left to locals to decide.

This may be an area within which the private sector can make an important contribution, since, by and large, business prefers to operate in stable zones rather than unstable; in corruption free rather than corrupt environments and with efficient state systems committed to public welfare rather than inefficient systems committed to greed. Certainly, it seems important that if governments cannot put the difficult political questions on the agenda that there should be Track I support for private sector, local and international NGO actors in trying to work out ways in which they can raise these issues at community and civil society levels. Donor and state support for free and courageous NGOs in war-torn societies is an important way of circumventing narrow interpretations of the sovereign inviolability of states.

The major problem with many of these war-torn societies is that deficient or failed states, by definition, neither have coherent or effective political leaders nor effective civil society actors to respond to bold acts by external intervenors. The international community through the United Nations cannot and does not want to assume 'trusteeship' over such societies in order to facilitate a return to viability. Thus political and community leaders in such environments develop vested interests in freezing the conflicts and deriving as much economic and social benefits as they can from rent, depredation, and exploitation of diminishing natural and political resources. This means that conflict transformers need to become much more aware of ways in which they can catalyse discussions about effective, democratic and incorrupt governance and the economic systems that are required to sustain such processes. This is the priority issue for effective conflict transformation and just peace. The prospects for stable and just peace seem very remote unless this issue is addressed and all that it means in terms of the political and economic inclusion of all key groups with a view to ensuring a dramatic reduction in horizontal inequality. Nafziger et al. (2000, Vol 2, 20) argue that

> *Preventive policies need to be applied to all countries vulnerable to conflict, which includes all countries exhibiting sharp horizontal inequalities, all low income countries, all countries with negative growth and countries which have had serious conflict over the past quarter of a century. Preventive action needs also to be concerned with countries in which the state is fragmenting and cannot govern the society in a legitimate manner.*

The agenda, for the future, therefore is very clear. There is a pressing need for all conflict resolution workers to become much more sensitive to the political economy of conflict and there is a much greater need for the development field to become much more aware of the conflict sensitive nature of development. This is going to require new perspectives, new ways of thinking about old problems and new processes for designing truly empowering and emancipatory partnerships between donors and recipients in war-torn societies. The fact that both the development and conflict resolution communities have realised this need is an optimistic sign. There is a reasonable expectation that in the very near future there will be an integration of both theoretical perspectives in the design of different sorts of intervention processes for war-torn societies.

4. Lessons Learned

Some of the lessons that IA and others have learned in relation to the development of these new perspectives are the following:

- First, it is important to *acknowledge the specificity and relative uniqueness of each conflict.* There are some universals – especially in relation to causes e.g. horizontal inequality and predatory states – but these are not as important as the specifics in relation to solutions. This means that the most important work conflict resolution experts can do is provide more than just an adequate analysis of the sources of the conflict, the parties to the conflict and impediments to its solution. They need to provide the best possible analyses of the conflict, viewing it from as many perspectives as possible; from the inside, the outside, the bottom, middle and top; from a socio-economic as well as the political perspective. This means a radical contextualisation of our analysis. Without this, all subsequent engagement is likely to be relatively flawed. Ed Garcia, from IA, is fond of saying "Text without context is pre-text!" To contextualise conflicts well requires a principled framework or Code of Conduct so that parties in conflict know where conflict resolution workers are coming from and whether their intentions are honourable. It also means that intervenors need to be learners first, second and third so that in their learning and listening they can be helpful to antagonists in understanding the issues, changing unhelpful attitudes and modifying negative behaviours and structures.

- Second, it is vital to *adopt a multi-disciplinary and multi-level analysis of the conflict.* It is fashionable to have a bias in favour of civil society organisations against state systems but the reality is that state systems are absolutely indispensable to the peacebuilding process and need to be analysed and engaged with in their own right. State systems alone cannot deliver peace; civil society organisations alone cannot deliver peace. We need to acknowledge the contributions of both spheres to the solutions of vexed intractable conflicts.
- Third, it is vital to *understand the linkages within and between different political complexes* and the networked nature of relations between the state, civil society, the formal and non-formal economic spheres, criminal and non-criminal groups, paramilitary, police and military elements. In particular, it is necessary to understand something of the relationship between the micro- and the macro-levels of activity and how these are connect to each other. There, is for example, no point making agreements at an elite macro-level which do not have any connections to what is happening at a grassroots micro-level of activity.
- Fourth, it is vital that we get a *more realistic analysis of the political economy of war and violence.* In particular, it is important to know much more about the incentive systems or motivations of those who wage war and the coping mechanisms of those who suffer from war. If we do not know what these are and who benefits and who loses from war we may be able to get a political agreement but we will never win a lasting and stable peace, especially when the economic incentives flowing from instability are greater than those flowing from stability. In West Africa, for example, what enticed Charles Taylor to abandon support of the RUF given that this support resulted in access to the Sierra Leonian multi-million-dollar diamond trade? To what extent did the UN's Security Council sanctions policy against Liberia increase the costs sufficiently to modify President Taylor's political and military behaviour?
- Fifth, it is important that more attention is focused on conflict dynamics rather than statics. Conflicts must be tracked through time, identifying patterns, trends and shifting coalitions. Tracking the dynamics of conflicts is also helpful to the parties since while one is immersed in conflict one is only dimly aware of the ways in which different actions contribute to escalatory or de-escalatory spirals. They are sometimes pleased to be shown how different conciliatory gestures might make a positive difference to the conflict.
- Sixth, in relation to responses to conflict, it is important to *acknowledge the roles and responsibilities of different actors.* Positive experiences will be unattainable until there is a clear sense of the division of labour in the field: who is specialising in what and how might they be incorporated into the work. At the least, higher levels of complementarity must be ensured; at maximum it is vital to know when to transfer different activities to other groups more specialised than our own. While it may be difficult to get high levels of co-ordination in the field, at the very least we need to avoid competition, and we need to make sure of the motivation for engagement.
- Seventh, *peacebuilding and conflict resolution work must not be dislocated from issues of justice and democratisation.* If a special sphere of activity known as peacebuilding is created that does not have a central focus on coercive agency, then peacebuilding becomes

depoliticised and loses its bite. Peacebuilding becomes impotent. Thus, it is paramount to be somewhat sceptical of work that focuses on civil society alone since civil society alone cannot deliver peace. Similarly, states, political systems and elites alone cannot deliver peace so there is a need to ensure that state systems value the role of civil society groups in relation to changing violent attitudes, behaviour and situations.

- Eighth, one of the most important lessons that IA has learned over the last few years is that *external organisations do not solve other people's problems* and, if they claim they do, they are engaged in a deception. All that external organisations can do is to provide a safe space, or some space, within which the local parties to conflict themselves might begin addressing the sources of their conflict and solving it for themselves. The most important principle in conflict transformation work is that it is the parties in conflict who must solve their own problems. Nor can the elite representatives of those groups deliver solutions alone. They have to bring their constituencies along with them and this requires more prior consultation and discussions than most ever undertake before reaching the negotiation tables. Richard Holbrooke, for example, knocked heads together at Dayton and reached a peace agreement for Bosnia that stopped ethnic cleansing, but it did not resolve the underlying sources of the conflict in the Balkans. Furthermore, it did not remove the animosities at civil society level. It did not address the underlying sources of the violence and, most importantly, it didn't address the historic grievances in the Balkans which continue to surface today.
- Ninth, there is a *need for proportionality* about what external parties (whether NGOs, IGOs or individual states) can bring to conflicts. The amount spent on non-violent conflict prevention and transformation is still pitiful. It is important to evaluate what is done in different locales in terms of the limited resources available. Nevertheless, it is clear that more could be achieved with better resource management: an area that should be further addressed. It is important, however, to ensure that peacebuilding and conflict resolution do not become the new vehicle for welfare dependency, as development was in the 1970s and 1980s.
- Tenth, much that has been said can be summed up in the dilemma of how individuals and organisations establish empowering and emancipatory partnerships. This is a difficult thing to do but it is vital to peacemaking. Who are effective intervenors? How do external intervenors work to build trust, cultural sensitivity, encourage accountability and promote autonomy? How do such intervenors accompany local partners so that they can ask the difficult questions and transform the problematic structures?
- Eleventh, it is critical that everything we do is aimed at *sustainability*. All of our work is process work and this only has an effect through time. This means that we have to commit to parties in conflict for the long haul, before, during and after conflict. There is no permanent peace, rather a series of negotiated agreements or understandings that enable us to think about the future hopefully and without the threat of violence.
- Twelfth and finally, all of this *work must be imbedded* in some theory of social and political change. What is our vision of a desirable future; what are the visions of parties to conflict; where do they intersect? How sensitive are we to visions that we have difficulty accepting but which might be very salient for others? How do we let go of our own visions so that we might enable the realisations of others and in that process discover some deeper meanings for ourselves.

5. Reference and Further Reading

Berdal, M. & D. M. Malone (eds.) 2000. *Greed and Governance: Economic Agendas in Civil Wars,* Boulder, CO: Lynne Rienner.

Collier, P. & A. Hoeffler 1998. "On Economic Causes of Civil War," *Oxford Economic Papers*, Vol. 50, 563-573.

Duffield, M. 1994. "The Political Economy of Internal War: Asset Transfer, Complex Emergencies and International Aid," *in* Macrae and Zwi, op. cit., 50-69.

Elwert, G. 1999. "Markets of Violence" *Sociologus: A Journal for Empirical Ethno-Sociology and Ethno-Psychology,* Supplement 1, Berlin: Duncker & Humblot, 85 – 102.

Fairhead, J. 2000, "The Conflict over Natural and Environmental Resources," *in* Nafziger et al., op. cit., Vol. 1, 147-178.

Gaffney, P. 2000. "Burundi," *in* Nafziger et al., op. cit., Vol. 2, 132-138.

Gaigals, C. and M. Leonhardt 2001. *Conflict Sensitive Approaches to Development,* London: Saferworld, International Alert and the International Development Research Centre.

Gould, S. 2001. *The Guardian,* 27th September.

Holsti, K. 1996. *The State, War and the State of War,* Cambridge: Cambridge University Press.

International Alert 2000. *The Business of Peace,* London: International Alert and Prince of Wales Business Leaders Forum.

Jackson, T., M. Page & D. Lilly 2001. *Conflict Trends and Dynamics to 2015*, Draft Paper, London: International Alert.

Macrae, J. and A. Zwi (eds.) 1994. *War and Hunger: Rethinking International Responses to Complex Emergencies,* London: Zed Books.

Miall, H., O. Ramsbotham & T. Woodhouse 2000. *Contemporary Conflict Resolution*, London: Polity Press.

Morrison, C. 2000. "Stabilization Programmes, Social Costs, Violence and Humanitarian Emergencies," *in* Nafziger et al., op. cit., Vol. 1, 207-239.

Nafziger, E W., F. Stewart and R. Väyrynen (eds.) 2000. *War, Hunger, and Displacement: The Origins of Humanitarian Emergencies,* Oxford University Press, Vols 1 and 2.

National Criminal Intelligence Service (NCIS) 2000. *2000 Annual Report*, London: Her Majesty's Stationary Office.

Uvin, P. 1998. *Aiding Violence. The Development Enterprise in Rwanda West,* Hartford, Conn: Kumarian Press.

Väyrynen, R. 2000. "Weak States and Humanitarian Emergencies: Failure, Predation and Rent-Seeking," *in* Nafziger et al., op. cit., Vol. 2, 437-480.

Woodward, S. 1995. *Balkan Tragedy: Chaos and Dissolution after the Cold War,* Washington, DC: Brookings Institution.

Glossary

Glossary

Writers in the field of conflict studies often use key terms in loose and contradictory ways, reflecting the reality that concepts have not been clearly defined. To encourage coherent usage of these terms the following definitions have been adopted for the purposes of the *Berghof Handbook* for Conflict Transformation. Nevertheless individual authors on occasion have used some terms in a specific way in relation to the particular argument in their chapter. In these circumstances the special use of the term is clearly explained and otherwise the following definitions are general usage in the *Handbook*.

Conflict Management

Activities undertaken to limit, mitigate and contain open conflict. In particular it refers to actions that aim to control and handle a conflict in order to limit its negative effects and bring it to an end and to prevent the vertical (i.e., intensification of violence) or horizontal (territorial spread) escalation of existing violent conflict. It applies to actions on all levels and Tracks (*see* below). One component is Crisis Management, which is active from the beginning of high tension to the cessation of violent conflict and crisis situations.

Conflict Prevention (or Crisis Prevention)

Activities undertaken in particularly vulnerable places and times over the short term to medium term that seek to identify situations that could produce violent conflict, to reduce manifest tensions, to prevent existing tensions from escalating into violence and to remove sources of danger before violence results. It may include Confidence-Building and Security-Building Measures, Early Warning, preventive Peace Keeping. Mainly used to refer to activities occurring before the outbreak of open violent conflict.

Conflict Resolution

Activities undertaken over the short term and medium term dealing with, and aiming at overcoming, the deep-rooted causes of conflict, including the structural, behavioural, or attitudinal aspects of the conflict. The process focuses more on the relationships between the parties than the content of a specific outcome.

Conflict Settlement

The achievement of an agreement between the conflict parties on a political level which enables them to end an armed conflict but which does not necessarily fundamentally alter the underlying causes of the conflict. It is usually content oriented and restricted to the Track 1 level.

Conflict Transformation

A generic, comprehensive term referring to actions and processes which seek to alter the various characteristics and manifestations of conflict by addressing the root causes of a particular conflict over the long term. It aims to transform negative destructive conflict into positive constructive conflict and deals with structural, behavioural and attitudinal aspects of conflict. The term refers to both the process and the completion of the process. As such it incorporates the activities of processes such as Conflict Prevention and Conflict Resolution and goes farther than conflict settlement or conflict management.

Peacebuilding

A generic term to cover all activities intended to encourage and promote peaceful relations and overcoming violence. A long term process that seeks to positively alter structural contradictions, improve relations between the conflict parties and encourage overall constructive changes in attitudes. It may also refer to activities connected with economic development, social justice, reconciliation, empowerment of disadvantaged/strategic groups and humanitarian support. It applies to all stages and levels of conflict, though mainly operates at Tracks II and III levels.

Peace Enforcement

Diplomatic and military measures to stop a violent conflict and/or enforce a peace agreement. They are usually carried out by a third party military force to bring an end to armed hostilities in a conflict situation (*see* the debate on Chapter 7 of the United Nations Charter).

Peacekeeping

The interposition of a third party military force to separate the armed forces of conflicting parties and reduce violence, normally at the request of the parties as part of a cease-fire agreement. It is now often associated with civil tasks such as monitoring and policing and supporting humanitarian intervention. It may involve restoring the status quo even if that preserves the underlying conflict and structural violence. It can occur preventively before the outbreak of open conflict as well as after the cessation of open conflict.

Peacemaking

Track I intervention consisting mainly of negotiation and mediation after the outbreak of open conflict aimed at moving towards the achievement of agreement on an end to the violent conflict. It is a process that is usually striving for a political settlement on the level of legitimate or de facto leaders. It is normally result oriented but may also seek to change the attitudes of the main protagonists.

Post-Conflict Rehabilitation

A generic term referring to the long term rebuilding of society in the aftermath of violent conflict. It may include structural, behavioural and attitude changes, e.g., by promoting trauma work, reintegration and repatriation, reconciliation, restorative justice and the reconstruction of the physical infrastructure and governmental institutions.

Track I

Activities on the stratum of high-level leaders, primarily in the form of conflict settlement.

Track II

Activities in parallel with the formal processes of communication and negotiation that are designed to open up dialogue and understanding between parties in conflict and encourage new thinking about future relationships after the conflict. As such they can inform and contribute to thinking and initiatives at the formal level. They do not normally involve the top leadership of the parties in conflict as they are not able to enter into the kind of open discussion implied by Track II process, but they often involve influential second level leaders and civil society actors who can interact more freely but at the same time have influence back in their own communities. As coined by Joe Montville it also refers to building co-operation and infrastructural connections between hostile parties so that they become more mutually dependent and can not revert to war in the future and he used the European Iron and Steel Community as a good example of this form of Track II activity.

Track III

Activities directed towards conflict transformation and peacebuilding normally at the grass roots level. It encourages interaction and understanding between formerly hostile local communities and involves awareness raising and empowerment within those communities and as such development cooperation, humanitarian assistance and post-conflict rehabilitation can play an important role at Track III level.

About the Contributors

Contributors

Mary Anderson

is President of the Collaborative for Development Action, Inc. She is an economist who specializes in promoting development strategies that originate in an assessment of existing local, national capacities. She has worked with many multi-lateral, bi-lateral and local development agencies in the areas of gender analysis, education and education policy, refugee programming, and disaster prevention, mitigation and development. Since 1995, she has launched and directed the Local Capacities for Peace Project to learn more about the relationships between humanitarian and development assistance and conflict. In 1999, she authored a book entitled *Do No Harm: How Aid can Support Peace or War* which sets out the lessons learned from the Local Capacities for Peace Project. She also organized the Reflecting on Peace Practices Project (RPP) and, in 2003, together with Lara Olson summarized the findings of RPP in the study *Confronting War: Critical Lessons for Peace Practitioners.*

Alexander Austin

received an MA in Peace Studies from Bradford University. His areas of interest are: early warning systems, monitoring, evaluation and various linkages between development cooperation, humanitarian assistance and conflict transformation.

Günter Bächler

studied art and history of art in Basel (1976 – 80) and political science at the Free University of Berlin (1980 – 85). From 1986 to 1988 he was a research fellow at the Institute for Peace Research and Security Studies at the University of Hamburg and completed his Ph.D. in political science in 1997 (University of Bremen). In 1988 he became the director of the Swiss Peace Foundation while working part-time as a researcher at the Center for Security Studies and Conflict Analysis at the ETH Zurich (1991-94). In 1996 he was a visiting research fellow at the Center for Science and International Affairs (CSIA) at the John F. Kennedy School of Government, Harvard University and also received training in mediation and negotiation at the Harvard Negotiation Program and at the Center for Dispute Settlement in Cambridge. Since 2001 he is the director of the conflict prevention and transformation unit at the Swiss Agency for Development and Cooperation (DEZA).

Rudi Ballreich

studied arts and pedagogic, worked as a teacher and in school management for 14 years. Since 1994 he has been an independent consultant and trainer in organisational and personnel development. As such he focuses on processes of change, strategy development and conflict resolution as well as training in group dynamics, team work and conflict management.

David Becker

Ph. D., psychologist, member of the Latinamerican Institute for Mental Health and Human Rights (ILAS), Santiago/Chile, member of the Chilean Institute for Family Therapy (ICHTF), Santiago/Chile, Professor for Clinical Psychology at the Universidad Diego Portales, Santiago/Chile, Wissenschaftlicher Mitarbeiter at the Institute for Intercultural Education at the Free University of Berlin, Geschäftsführer of the International Academy for Innovative Education, Psychology and Economy gGmbH (INA) at the Free University of Berlin, consultant for the Swiss Agency for Development and Cooperation (DEZA) for psychosocial projects in former Yugoslavia.

Christine Bigdon

is political scientist (MA), post-graduate in agricultural and rural development, and Ph.D. candidate at the Department of Political Sciences, South Asia Institute, University of Heidelberg, Germany. Her current research interest focuses on decentralization, local governance and conflict transformation with special reference to Sri Lanka. Between 2000 and 2003 she worked as Resident Representative of the Colombo Branch Office, South Asia Institute, University of Heidelberg.

Kevin Clements

was appointed Director of Australian Centre for Peace and Conflict Studies at University of Queensland in 2003, after being Secretary General of International Alert since January 1999. He is also the Vernon and Minnie Lynch Chair of Conflict Resolution at the Institute for Conflict Analysis and Resolution at George Mason University Fairfax, Virginia, USA. His career has been a combination of academic analysis and practice in the areas of peacebuilding and conflict transformation. He was formerly Director of the Quaker United Nations Office in Geneva and Head of the Peace Research Center at the Australian National University in Canberra. He has been a regular consultant to a variety of organizations on disarmament, arms control, conflict resolution, development and regional security issues. He has also written or edited 5 books and over 130 chapters/articles on conflict transformation, peacebuilding, preventive diplomacy and development.

Martina Fischer

Acting Director of the Berghof Research Center for Constructive Conflict Management. Her special fields of work are south-eastern Europe, European security policy within the framework of the European Union, civil-military relations and state-reform in transition periods, evaluation of peace building efforts in post war Bosnia-Herzegovina and evaluation of training schemes for preparation of specialist peace staff. Moreover, she is involved in initiatives that try to actively create linkages between state and non-state-agencies and to establish joint peace and development oriented activities in post-war regions, especially in the field of youth work and peacebuilding in Bosnia Herzegovina. Her publications include *Conflict Transformation by Training in Nonviolent Action. Activities of the Centre for Nonviolent Action (Sarajevo)* (Berghof Occasional Paper 18, October 2001) and (with Tobias Debiel) *Crisis Prevention and the European Union: Capacities, Concepts and Problems of Coherence* (Berghof Report 4, Berlin 2000).

Diana Francis

is a former President of the International Fellowship of Reconciliation and current Chair of the Committee for Conflict Transformation Support. As a freelance facilitator, trainer and consultant, she works mainly with people trying to address political/inter-ethnic conflict. While her greatest experience is in the post-communist world (especially the former Yugoslavia and the Caucasus region), she has also worked in the Middle East, Africa and Asia.

Friedrich Glasl

is a political scientist, economist, business consultant and lecturer for Organisational Development and Conflict Management at the University of Salzburg, Austria. He is the author of several books and articles on conflict management in organisations, public administration and international politics.

Wibke Hansen

received her Masters in Peace Studies from Bradford University and, at present, works for the Fern University, Hagen preparing a new course in Peace Studies and Democracy.

Mark Hoffman

is lecturer in International Relations at the London School of Economics. In addition to his teaching commitments, he is Director of the Conflict Analysis and Development Unit. His areas of expertise are: third party mediation and conflict resolution in protracted international and intranational conflicts; responses to complex political and humanitarian emergencies; contemporary international relations theory; Moldova; Sri Lanka; US domestic and foreign policy.

Benedikt Korf

is a researcher and doctorate candidate at the Department of Resource Economics, Humboldt-University of Berlin and at the Center for Development Research at the University of Bonn, Germany. A civil engineer and social geographer by training, he also works as a consultant and trainer for international co-operation agencies (Gesellschaft für Technische Zusammenarbeit, GTZ, and Asian Development Bank, ADB) with a focus on community development, social integration and participatory planning approaches in conflict situations. His current research interests focus on the institutional and political economy of resource management in complex emergencies.

Ron Kraybill

is an associate professor in the Conflict Transformation Program at Eastern Mennonite University. He formerly served as director of training at the Centre for Conflict Resolution in Cape Town, South Africa, and as director of the Mennonite Conciliation Service in North America. He holds a Ph.D. in religious studies from the University of Cape Town and has published numerous books, essays, and training manuals on mediation, facilitation and conflict transformation.

Hugh Miall

read history at Oxford and did his Ph.D. in peace and conflict research at Lancaster. He then worked for several years for Earth Resources Research and for the Oxford Research Group. Before coming to Lancaster he was a Research Fellow at the Royal Institute of International Affairs. He is Director of The Richardson Institute, and lectures in peace studies and conflict resolution. His books include *The Peacemakers: Peaceful Settlement of Disputes Since 1945; Nuclear Weapons: Who's In Charge?; Beyond Deterrence; Shaping the New Europe, (ed.); Redefining Europe: New Patterns of Conflict and Cooperation, (ed.); Minority Rights in Europe: The Scope for a Transnational Regime; Albania: Development and Conflict.* His research interests lie in conflict resolution and conflict prevention, especially in Europe.

Thania Paffenholz

was Director of the Center for Peacebuilding (KOFF) at the Swiss Peace Foundation (SPF) in Bern (2001-2002). She holds a BA in anthropology and economics and an MA in political science from the University of Munich (1990). She received her Ph.D. in international relations from the University of Frankfurt (1996), focusing on the theory and practice of mediation and peacebuilding in civil wars. After working as a research fellow at the Peace Research Institute, Frankfurt (1992-1996) she held a position as peacebuilding officer within the Somalia Unit of the Delegation of the European Commission in Kenya (1996-1999) and has worked as an independent advisor, consultant and researcher in the field of crisis prevention, peacebuilding and democratisation (1999-2000). Thania Paffenholz is a trained mediator with vast field research experience in the Horn of Africa and in Southern Africa. She has been lecturer in the International Peacekeeping and Peace Building Training Program in Schlaining (1994-1995) and at the Department of International Relations at the University of Frankfurt (1994-1996). She has participated in several UN missions in Africa and is member of the Board of the UN Lessons Learned Unit, Department of Peacekeeping Operations as well as Council Member of the International Peace Research Association (IPRA).

Oliver Ramsbotham

Oliver Ramsbotham is Professor of Peace and Conflict Studies and is currently Head of the Department of Peace Studies at the University of Bradford. He has published, together with Hugh Miall and Tom Woodhouse, a major study of the conflict resolution field, entitled *Contemporary Conflict Resolution: The Prevention, Management and Resolution of Deadly Conflict* (1999). He has also co-edited with Tom Woodhouse other studies on the relationship between conflict resolution and peacekeeping, including *The Encyclopaedia of International Peacekeeping Operations* (1999) *and Peacekeeping and Conflict Resolution* (2000).

Cordula Reimann

focuses in her research on the gender dimension of conflict and conflict management, particularly the gendered nature of conflict management/conflict resolution as theory and practice. She has worked in various peace research institutions. Recently, she conducted fieldwork and research on the gender discourse of different actors involved in conflict management/conflict resolution in Sri Lanka.

Dusan Reljic

has been the senior researcher in Berlin for the European Media Institute (EMI) since autumn 2000. Born in 1956 in Belgrade, Yugoslavia, he studied Communications Science, Political Science and Philosophy at the University of Vienna (1973-1978) and wrote his Ph.D. thesis on "Media policy of the non-aligned states". Reljic worked for more than a decade for the Yugoslav news agency Tanjug before becoming foreign editor of the Belgrade news magazine *Vreme* in 1991. He was one of the founders of the Belgrade press agency Beta (1993) and later became senior editor at Radio Free Europe in Munich before joining the EIM in 1996. In his numerous contributions to print and electronic media in Yugoslavia, Germany, Austria and Britain, Reljic concentrates on international relations and security, nationalism and ethnic strife, media performance in situations of tensions and conflict and media developments in Central and Eastern Europe.

Norbert Ropers

is the director of the Berghof Research Center and has worked as a facilitator, trainer, consultant and researcher. His work concentrates on the contributions by civil society actors and development agencies to peace building and on strategies to improve the inter-linkage of Track 1 and Track II approaches to conflict resolution. Dr. Ropers has dealt particularly with East West relations in Europe, security policy, the Organisation for Security and Cooperation in Europe (OSCE), the impact of transnational relations on political decisions and strategies and methods of conflict resolution. In 1992 he chaired the Young Leaders Conference from CSCE countries, which was organized by the German government. Since 1997 he has acted as one of the Co-Directors of the yearly Summer Academy on the OSCE in Schlaining (Austria).

Dieter Senghaas

is Professor of Peace, Conflict and Development Research at the Institute for Intercultural and International Studies, University of Bremen, Germany. His most recent publications include *The Clash Within Civilisations. Coming to Terms with Cultural Conflicts* (2001) and *Klänge des Friedens. Ein Hörbericht (Sounds of Peace. A Listener's Report)* (2001).

Dan Smith

has been Director of the International Peace Research Institute, Oslo (PRIO) since 1993. His most recent books are *The State of the World Atlas* (1999) and *The State of the World Atlas* (1997). He is author and co-author of five other books and over 70 articles and chapters in scholarly journals and anthologies. Current research interests focus on causes of armed conflicts and the ethics of humanitarian intervention. He is Chairperson of the Board of the Institute for War and Peace Reporting (London).

Gunnar Theissen

graduated in Political Science at the Free University of Berlin and holds a LL.M. degree in International and Human Rights Law from the University of the Western Cape, Cape Town. He is currently a doctoral candidate at the Transitional Justice Project at the Law Faculty of Humboldt University, Berlin.

Tom Woodhouse

Tom Woodhouse founded the Centre for Conflict Resolution at the University of Bradford's Department of Peace Studies in 1990 and was its first director. He is currently Professor of Conflict Resolution, holding the Adam Curle Chair. Together with Hugh Miall and Oliver Ramsbotham he has published a major study of the conflict resolution field, entitled *Contemporary Conflict Resolution: The Prevention, Management and Resolution of Deadly Conflict* (1999). He has also co-edited with Oliver Ramsbotham other studies on the relationship between conflict resolution and peacekeeping, including *The Encyclopaedia of International Peacekeeping Operations* (1999) and *Peacekeeping and Conflict Resolution* (2000).